SHEMITA

HALACHA MIMEKORAH

RABBI YOSEF ZVI RIMON

HALACHA EDUCATION CENTER IN
COOPERATION WITH MAGGID BOOKS

SHEMITA
HALACHA MIMEKORAH
Second Printing 2014

Maggid Books
A Division of Koren Publishers Jerusalem Ltd.

POB 8531, New Milford, CT 06776, USA
POB 4044, Jerusalem, 9104001, Israel
www.korenpub.com

Publication: Kehat Raanan, Shmuel Daniel
Project Manager: Yitzchak Bodner, Itay Levy
Translator: Rabbi David Strauss
Editor: Susan Wolf, Rabbi Dov Karoll
Associate Editors: Rabbi David Wolkenfeld, Yoni Teitz
Editorial Consultant, Content Review: Rabbi Yaakov Francus
Layout: Oranit Wreschner

Graphic Design: Eliahu Misgav

Halacha Education Center
POB 230 Alon Shevut, Israel 9043300
02-547-4542/7
Office@halachaed.org | www.halachaed.org

The photographs in this volume were taken by the author, with the exception of the following, for which special gratitude is offered:

Photographs of *gerama* devices – Zomet Institute
Photographs of detached bedding – Chasalat Company
Photographs of plowing and harvesting – Yael Rosenberg
Agricultural Illustrations – Yael Berger

Professional and scientific consultants:

Prof. Eliezer Goldschmidt – Hebrew University and *Machon le-Cheker ha-Chakla'ut al pi ha-Torah*
Moti Shomron, agronomist – *Machon ha-Torah ve-ha-Aretz*

ISBN: 978 159 264 257 1
Printed and bound in Israel

In loving memory

of our father, **Abraham Levovitz** z"l, whose sense of responsibility for Halachic education, both globally and in his own community was the inspiration for Birkat Avraham. Initiated in the Maimonides School in Brookline MA and now being disseminated all around the world, the objective of Birkat Avraham, in conjunction with the Halacha Education Center, is to promote dynamic and relevant Halachic education for both students and their parents.

With gratitude to Rav Yosef Zvi Rimon and his Halacha Education Center donors.

Reva and Harvey Gertel

"וה' ברך את אברהם בכל"

Best wishes for health and nachat ruach to

Mr. and Mrs. Chaim and Eydl Reznik

and their special family.

We all pray to Hashem for the zchut and siyata d'shmaya to raise our children with the fear of Heaven, Torah, derech eretz and the motivation to dedicate their lives to the physical and spiritual redemption of Am Yisrael in Eretz Yisrael.

May it be the will of Hashem, that in the merit of our thorough observance of Shemita, we should merit the continued rebirth and flowering of the Land of Israel, from which our sustenance and Torah will continue to spring forth.

With heartfelt gratitude and blessings of continued success to Rabbi Yosef Zvi Rimon, Rabbi Menachem Zupnik and Rabbi David Ebner.

Joe and Heather Gelb

ב"ה

MORDECHAI ELIAHU
FORMER CHIEF RABBI OF ISRAEL & RICHON LEZION

מ ר ד כ י   א ל י ה ו
הראשון לציון והרב הראשי לישראל לשעבר

בס"ד, י"ט תמוז תשס"ז
18-10061.07

הסכמה

ראה ראיתי את הספר "**הלכה ממקורה – הלכות שביעית**" אשר חיברו איש רב פעלים לתורה ולתעודה **הרה"ג יוסף צבי רימון שליט"א**, רבה של אלון שבות דרום.

ספר זה מבאר את ההלכות דרך המקורות, בתוספת סברות וטעמים והכל בצורה בהירה ומסודרת, דבר דבור על אופניו.

בטוחני שספר זה יועיל הן לתלמידי חכמים והן לציבור הרחב להיות מוכנים הלכה למעשה, לשנת השמיטה הבעל"ט.

הנני לברכו שחפץ ה' בידו יצלח, וימשיך הלאה להגדיל תורה ולהאדירה, ויתברך בכל מידי דמיטב, ברוחניות ובגשמיות , ויהי ה' עמו, אכי"ר.

מרדכי אליהו
הראשון לציון הרב הראשי לישראל לשעבר

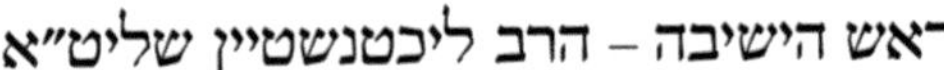
ראש הישיבה – הרב ליכטנשטיין שליט"א

ב"ה, חודש הרחמים והסליחות תש"ס[1]

בפתח שנת השמיטה תשס"א, אנו עדים לתופעה ברוכה ומרנינה. המודעות לעניין השמיטה ולהלכותיה בקרב ציבור שומרי המצוות הרחב גברה לאין ערוך לעומת הזכור משמיטות קודמות, והזהירות בהיבטים החקלאיים והצרכניים כאחד מקיפה רבים שבעבר בקושי נזקקו לתחום השמיטה.

התפתחות זו מגבירה את הצימאון להוראה בנידון, וזכה תלמידי היקר, ר' יוסף צבי רימון שליט"א, המכהן כר"מ בישיבת הר עציון, להיענות לדרישה לרוותו, על ידי פרסום והפצת קונטרס "שיעורי שביעית". הקונטרס מכיל סיכומי שיעורים שנאמרו בפני תלמידים בישיבה, ברם, מכיוון שיצא להם מוניטין, התעורר ביקוש להפיץ המעיינות חוצה ולהוציאם לאור עבור הציבור הרחב; ואשרי המחבר שזיכנו לכך.

בגין לחץ זמן, לא הספקתי להגיע לעיון מדוקדק בקונטרס, אך היות ואתמחי גברא, מובטחני שהלומדו יפיק תועלת רבה. משנתו של ר' יוסף צבי סדורה, הרצאתו ברורה ובהירה, ושיקול דעתו מרשים; ולתכונות אלו משמעות רבה במערך שמיועד לא רק לספק הנחיות אלא ללבן נושאים.

ובכן, יישר כוחו של ר' יוסף צבי - ושל כל העוסק בהכנת שיעורים אלו לדפוס - וחילו לאורייתא; ומי יתן וימשיך ללון באוהלה של תורה, להגדילה ולהאדירה.

בברכת התורה והמצווה
אהרן ליכטנשטיין

בעז"ה חודש התנחומים והרחמים, תשס"ז

את המכתב הרצ"ב, כתבתי, כמשתקף מתאריכו ותכנו, לקראת שנת השמיטה הקודמת. הנני בזה לפרסמו מחדש בליווי תוספת לעניין.

מני השמיטה הקודמת, שתי הנקודות המרכזיות שהודגשו במכתב הקודם, רק הלכו והתרחבו. התודעה הציבורית ביחס לנושא מצוות השמיטה התעמקה והתרחבה. מאידך, מיומנותו ושליטתו של הרב רימון שליט"א בתחום – התעצמה. אני מברך בפה מלא על שתי התופעות. אשמח להוסיף שורות אלה כנספח מעדכן לקודמו.

בברכת התורה והמצווה
אהרן ליכטנשטיין

1 ההסכמה ניתנה לספר "שיעורי שביעית" מאת הרב יוסף צבי רימון, תשס"א

CONTENTS

PREFACE

Whenever one engages in the study of Halacha, two contradictory objectives exist. On the one hand, one wishes to understand the sources of the law, its roots and reasons. One the other hand, one wants to learn as many laws as possible in order to know what to do in practice. If one dwells upon the sources of the law in order to understand its roots and reasons, he will master a narrower range of practical laws. Many who learn Halacha lack the time to achieve both objectives at the appropriate level. Which path should one choose?

It seems that the majority of those who study prefer to make use of halachic compendia that briefly summarize the relevant laws so that they will know what to do in practice. Clearly, such study is preferable to ignorance of basic laws.

There are, however, disadvantage with learning Halacha and arriving at halahic conclusions from such compendia. The Vilna Gaon in his commentary to the book of Mishlei (10:4) comments on the verse "A slack hand causes poverty: but the hand of the diligent becomes rich." He explains that the verse teaches that a person "Who does not study the roots of the laws but only brief compendia of the laws ... will be turned into a poor person because he does not properly understand each and every law and is liable to err, because in the end he will forget these laws as well, since he is not familiar with their roots. But the 'hand of the diligent' – he who studies the law together with its root and correctly understands each and every law will 'become rich,' because he knows everything about the topic." One can distill two problems with halachic compendia from the Vilna Gaon's comment:

1. Without knowing the roots of the law, one is liable to err (especially if circumstances have changed since the book was written).
2. When a person restricts himself to such compendia, he knows what to do, but does not understand the reasons for doing so. This being the case, he is more likely to forget the laws that he has learned.

Echoes of these difficulties may also be detected in the words of the Maharsha (Sota 22a): "But in these generations, those who issue rulings based on the Shulchan Aruch, without understanding the reasons for each matter – if they don't begin with a careful study of the Talmud … errors will fall into their rulings."

This work, *Shemita* – Halacha Mimekorah attempts to provide a solution to this difficulty. I have tried to record the sources of the laws, starting from the words of *Chazal* and the *Rishonim* and ending with the rulings of the *Acharonim* and contemporary halachic authorities. Moreover, the book has been arranged in such a manner that the student requires no prior knowledge of the material[1] and need not invest a great deal of time in order to understand what is written. I have tried to bring the main sources and arguments in clear formulation, so that the learner will be able to engage in a high-level study of the Halacha, its sources and its practical conclusions, without having to invest an excessive amount of time.

1. The core of this book is based on lectures that I delivered at Yeshivat Har Etzion in the summer of 5760. The book was expanded in the wake of lectures given at the yeshiva and at Herzog College in 5767, and also from lectures given in my wonderful Congregation of Alon Shevut South.

In addition, I have included a separate chapter, "A Summary of the Laws of *Shemita*," where the reader can determine what to do in practice, even when unable to delve into the sources that appear elsewhere in the book. Still, next to each law, I have noted where in the book the reader can find an expanded discussion of the issue (and he is advised to do so).

At the beginning of the chapter that summarizes the laws of *Shemita*, I have added a short unit entitled, "A Guide for the Perplexed Regarding *Shemita*," whose purpose is to provide an overview of all the issues relating to *Shemita*.

The halachic decision-making in the book is based on the rulings of the leading authorities of recent generations, and especially upon the rulings of the ***Pe'at ha-Shulchan*****, Rav Kook, the** ***Chazon Ish***, and contemporary *Posekim*.

Over the course of the book I have tried to cite most of the main sources. In order to make it easier for the reader, I have explained all the sources in such a way that the book can be understood even if one skips the citations. Thus, the citations allow for expanded study, on the one hand, and accelerated study, on the other.

In response to my Halacha column in the weekly pamphlet, "Shabbat be-Shabbato," I have received much feedback regarding the importance of the charts appearing in that column. I have tried, therefore, to conclude each unit with a chart that summarizes the material and provides an overview of the issue.

Understanding the principles of the laws of *Shemita* requires certain agricultural knowledge – a realm that we often overlook in the course of study. I have, therefore, added many photographs in order to illustrate the agricultural labors under discussion and to help demonstrate the proper way to observe the laws of *Shemita*. A tremendous amount of effort went into taking these pictures. Of the close to one thousand photographs that were taken, I selected only those photographs that, in my opinion, added the most to the written text. In the clarification of the professional and scientific aspects of the material, I was greatly assisted by Prof. Eliezer Goldschmidt and by the agronomist Moti Shomron, to whom I extend my deepest gratitude.

In cases of uncertainty regarding matters that were not adequately covered in the book, one should clarify the issue with a competent halachic authority. Other books dealing with the laws of *Shemita* might also provide answers to such questions.[2]

I pray that the study of this book lead to increased knowledge, love and observance of the laws of *Shemita*, and may no transgression occur through me.

❊ ❊ ❊

I wish to begin with words of tribute to Yeshivat Har Etzion and its Roshei Yeshiva, *shlita*. I have been privileged to be associated with the Yeshiva for over twenty years, and to absorb within its walls the study of Torah, the love of Torah and the fear of heaven. I would like to draw attention to the special blessing of the harmonious

2. Among other works, I wish to mention "*Katif Shevi'it*," published by *Machon ha-Torah ve-ha-Aretz*, and the book "*Mishpetei Aretz*," published by *Machon le-Cheker ha-Chakla'ut al Pi ha-Halacha*.

atmosphere that permeates through its educational staff and to the warm relationship with the highly supportive administration.

I wish to thank my revered father-in-law, Rav Eliyahu Blumenzweig, *shlita,* who, in addition to the many other things that he taught me, greatly enlightened me on matters pertaining to the *Shemita* year. His teachings have been integrated into the book with due attribution.

This is the third edition of the book.

The first edition of this book (5761) was based on lectures that I taught in Yeshivat Har Etzion, and was published in the merit of the students who took part in the classes, summarized the lectures and then promoted the publication of those lectures in book form: "I have been enlightened by all my teachers, but most of all by my students." Oriah Berkovitz, Amichai Schwartz, Harav Moshe Sheptar and Yitzchak Bart contributed to that edition. They worked diligently in learning the material, proofreading, editing and preparing the book for print amiably, and with such dedication and love. I would also like to thank Rav Zeev Weitman, *shlita,* the Rav of Tnuva and the author of the book "A National *Shemita* in the State of Israel," who went over the first edition in great detail and provided informative comments.

The second edition (5768) was in fact a brand new book, both in terms of the amount of material, as well as the diagrams, pictures and method of printing. This edition was edited by Shauli Bart, and many of the students in the Yeshiva assisted him. This book was written with significantly more familiarity of the field, and of the farmers and their needs, mainly due to my deep connection with those displaced from Gush Katif. In the last number of years, I was fortunate to spend significant time with the former residents of Gush Katif, as a result of the heavenly assistance I received in establishing the JobKatif organization which provides employment for the former residents of Gush Katif. Special gratitude must be extended to the staff and volunteers of JobKatif, who constantly labor with joy and love. Thank God we have succeeded in restoring many of the Gush Katif residents to suitable employment, and pray that the Holy One blessed be He will help us to assist even those that still remain without work.

We are now meriting the onset of another *Shemita* year. In principle, what was included in the *Shemita* book of 5768 remains accurate and nothing substantive has changed. However, with God's help from above, we have been fortunate to have this edition undergo revised and thorough editing.

Special thanks to my dear students, Rav Avraham Stav and Rav Daniel Fleishman – talmidei chachamim and outstanding Torah scholars who serve as Rabbis in the Halacha Education Center. They reviewed the Hebrew version of the *Shemita* book in great depth, edited it superbly, shared valuable input and brilliantly added to the final product. The book in its present format is much easier to study, and is more organized and refined.

Special thanks to Itay Levy and Yitzchak Bodner on their vital assistance in preparing this version in its current form. Thank you to Susan Wolf whose significant efforts in editing this book made a valuable contribution. An additional thank you to Oranit Vershner for all of the graphic work on this version. Thank you as well to Tamar Gutman, the graphic artist for the beautiful cover.

A special thanks to R' Kehat Raanan, the managing director of the Halacha Education Center, who operates with a high level of efficiency and an impressive pleasantness. He should be blessed with all that is good together with his wife Adina, *tichye,* and their dear children.

In the years since the previous *Shemita,* the Halacha Education Center has developed significantly. We merited the publication of many Halacha books, as well as books and curriculum in Israel and around the world. We also had the good fortune to train community and city rabbis and educators, and to learn *Choshen Mishpat* (the section of the *Shulchan Aruch* dealing with monetary issues). We merited a special group of rabbis and *talmidei chachamim* who study diligently and are deeply immersed in the depths of Halacha, stemming from scholarship, a connection to the posekim and devotion to the awe of Heaven. We were fortune to have been blessed with a wonderful staff on the educational and didactic side as well as on the administrative side.

Before the previous *Shemita,* my father and teacher R. David Rimon, of blessed memory, who together with my mother and teacher Rita, raised me to love God and to fear Him, to love Torah and to love humanity. At the time of the closing of this edition, it has been one year since the death of my mother, Sarah Rivka (Rita) Rimon, may her memory be for a blessing. My mother taught me to view the world positively, she taught me to love Torah and to love the Holy One blessed be He. It is my sincere hope that the learning in this book will contribute to the elevation of her pure soul, together with the soul of my father and teacher, who guided me into the world of Torah and values.

May God bless my wife, Sharon, *tichye,* without whose help I would never have been able to write this book, fulfill my responsibilities as Ram in the Yeshiva and Community Rabbi of Alon Shevut South, and continue my activities in the framework of JobKatif – an organization that finds employment for the former residents of Gush Katif. May God grant her a long and joyous life.

I am grateful to the creator of the world, who gave me the merit to study and to teach. I pray that he will continue to grant me and my wife Sharon, *tichye,* who is by my side at all times, the ability to continue to study and accomplish with joy, good health, and fear of Heaven, and that we will merit to raise our children in the way of the Torah, with moral values, and to raise a Jewish family with good deeds.

Until now Your mercy has helped us and Your kindness has not abandoned us, O Lord, our God; may You not forsake us, O Lord, our God, for evermore."

With God's assistance we hope that the current *Shemita* shall guide the Nation of Israel to become more sanctified, pure, moral, and ethical and will forge a stronger and more courageous connection to our Father in Heaven.

Yosef Zvi Rimon,
Alon Shevut, Iyar 5774

Unless indicated otherwise, all references to the Mishna, the *Talmud Yerushalmi*, the commentators to the Mishna and the commentators to the *Yerushalmi* relate to tractate *Shevi'it.*
Unless indicated otherwise, all references to the Rambam relate to *Hilchot Shemita ve-Yovel.*
References to the Rash relate to the Rash's commentary to the Mishna in tractate *Shevi'it.*
A detailed index may be found at the end of this volume.

INTRODUCTION TO *SHEMITA*

THE REASONS FOR *SHEMITA*

Then shall the land enjoy its Sabbaths (Vayikra 26:34)

In *Parashat* **Bechukotai**, in the context of the curses that will befall Israel should they stray from God's path, the Torah states: "Then shall the land enjoy her Sabbaths" (*Vayikra 26:34*). This means that Israel's failure to observe *Shemita* will lead the nation into exile. What underlies this central role of *Shemita*, and what is the rationale behind this *mitzva*?

There are two main passages in the Torah that deal with the *Shemita* year: one in *Parashat* **Behar** (*Vayikra 25:1–7*) and one in *Parashat* **Mishpatim** (*Shemot 23:10–11*).[1] In addition, in *Parashat* **Re'eh** (*Devarim 15:1–6*) cancellation of cash debts during *Shemita* is discussed. These passages have different emphases, in accordance with their respective contexts in the Torah: *Parashat* **Mishpatim** generally deals with social issues, placing the focus of *Shemita* on its social dimension. In *Parashat* **Behar**, on the other hand, the Torah focuses on the idea that "the land is Mine." Let us try to examine the various rationales for *Shemita.*

1. In addition, there may be a mention of the forbidden act of plowing during *shemita* in *Shemot* 34, but we will discuss that later b"eh when we get to the laws of plowing.

THE VIEW OF THE RAMBAM

The **Rambam** offers two reasons for the *mitzva* of *Shemita* in his ***Guide for the Perplexed***:

> With regard to all the commandments we have enumerated in *Hilchot Shemita ve-Yovel,* some of them are meant to lead to pity and promoting the well-being of all men, as the Torah states: "That the poor of your people may eat" (*Shemot 23:11*) ... and are meant to make the earth more fertile and stronger through letting it lie fallow. (*Guide for the Perplexed, III, 39*).

The second reason offered by the **Rambam** is an **agricultural reason:** If the land "rests" for a year, it will produce greater yields in the years that follow. The **Abravanel** rejects this understanding; the

Torah promises that the sixth year will produce a yield that will last **for three years.** If the land becomes progressively weaker from year to year, then surely by the sixth year it should be particularly weak. How then will the land produce a yield three times the size of an ordinary yield? This difficulty, however, appears to be reconcilable. The Torah states: "Then I will command My blessing upon you in the sixth year, and it shall bring forth fruit for three years" (*Vayikra 25:21*). In other words, if left to the forces of nature, the sixth year's yield would in fact be small, as argued by the **Rambam**, but owing to **God's blessing**, the crop will be triple its normal yield.

There is, however, another difficulty with the **Rambam's** rationale that was pointed out by R. Yitzchak Arama, author of the ***Sefer Akeda***. If the *Shemita* year is necessary for agricultural reasons, why is the Torah so insistent about keeping the *Shemita* year, to the point that failure to observe it is punishable by exile?

To answer this question, it is worth pointing out that the **Rambam's** rationale might have broader significance. If allowing the land to rest is important agriculturally, why doesn't the *mitzva* of *Shemita* apply outside of Eretz Yisrael? Doesn't all land require strengthening? The importance of observing *Shemita* in Eretz Yisrael might be that it raises our consciousness to the fact that it is a **holy land, therefore it must be protected, strengthened and nurtured.** According to this, the importance of preserving the quality of the soil flows from **the unique sanctity of the land.**[2]

At the beginning of the aforementioned passage, the **Rambam** offers another reason: *Shemita* stems from concern for the poor. The Torah does not advocate a communist doctrine nor does it call for property to be divided equally among all people. Rather, it allows a person to profit in accordance with the effort that he invests in his work. In order to protect the poor, the Torah commands that various gifts be given to those in need – charity, poor-man's tithe, gleanings (not gathering up all the grain), leaving behind the forgotten sheaves, leaving the corner of the field unharvested, and the like – and the observance of the *mitzva* of ***Shemita***. Every seventh year, all fruits and vegetables are declared ownerless so the poor may enjoy them.

2. The Rambam might disagree, as we find that he offers a similar explanation of the prohibited foods, namely, that they are harmful to the body. The Abravanel and others disagree with the Rambam on this point as well, and it is possible that the Rambam is consistent here with his own position. Elaboration on this point, however, is beyond the scope of this work.

If, however, this is the reason for *Shemita*, then it is difficult to understand why the Torah commands that working the land must stop. On the contrary, it should have commanded that work must continue in order to increase the yield for the benefit of the poor! Indeed, a careful reading of the various Scriptural texts dealing with *Shemita* teaches that *Parashat* ***Mishpatim***, which emphasizes the idea of helping the poor, does not forbid agricultural labor; it merely commands that the land be released (*"tishmetena u-netashtah"*; *Shemot 23:11*)[3] and declared ownerless.

The ***Mechilta***, however, interprets the verse as follows: "'You shall release it' (*tishmetena*) – from its work, 'and you shall leave it' (*u-netashtah*) – from eating it.' According to this interpretation, the prohibition of working the land appears in *Mishpatim* as well. While it might be argued that this prohibition stems from the other reasons for *Shemita*, my revered teacher, **Rav Aharon Lichtenstein *shlita***, understands this issue as follows: Working the land must cease, because the Torah is not only concerned with the poor man's **financial situation**, but also with removing the landowner's feeling of **superiority.** For this reason, the owner of the field does not work his property, and thus he does not **give** anything to the poor person. The fruit grows on its own, and the land is declared ownerless. The poor person is therefore entitled to take of the ownerless produce and is not dependent upon the landowner's kindness. (Thus, already the passage in *Mishpatim* alludes to the idea of equality that is explicit in the passage in *Behar*, verses 6–7).

3. One might be able to reconcile the differences between the two passages as reflecting two conflicting dimensions or aspects of *Shemita* (following the approach of Rav Mordechai Breuer z"l), but we have chosen to follow the integrative approach of *Chazal*, as will be explained below.

THE VIEW OF THE *SEFER HA-CHINUCH*

> There is another useful benefit to be gained from the observance of *Shemita*: to attain through it the quality of yielding and relinquishing (*mitzva no. 84*).

A third reason for the *mitzva* of *Shemita* is offered by the *Sefer Ha-Chinuch*.

Once every seven years, a person must declare his field ownerless, not only in order to assist the poor, but also to learn how to waive his property to protect himself from greed and avarice. When a person acquires this quality with respect to his land, it will presumably influence his conduct in other realms as well: his conduct with other people and his relationship with his family.

The *Chinuch* also cites another rationale for this *mitzva*:

> So that a man will remember that the land that grows produce for him ... produces not by its own power and ability, for there is a Master over it and over its owner ...

It is precisely with respect to a farmer, who tills his land and succeeds in producing something new that the concern arises that he will look upon his crop and say: "My power and the might of my hand have gotten me this wealth" (*Devarim 8:17*). Thus the Torah commands that a person must declare his property ownerless during the seventh year in order to show that the land is not really his: the land belongs to the Master of the universe. This commandment also highlights that the land does not produce its yield by itself, but by the grace of God. This teaches us a lesson about everything else in our world as well. Nothing comes into being on its own and nature does not operate independently but only by Divine decree. Thus, one of the main principles of *Shemita* is to emphasize that "the land is Mine" – it is not man, but God, who is the Lord of the land. This principle has various ramifications which will be discussed later in the book.

The *Sefer Ha-Chinuch* mentions one more reason for the *mitzva* of *Shemita* – intensifying man's trust in God:

> Yet another useful benefit to be found in this is that man increases trust in God ...

During the *Shemita* year, a person refrains from planting and working his land, and puts his trust in God. Moreover, a person declares all of his produce ownerless, without worrying about the consequences. This explanation is reminiscent of Israel's wanderings in the wilderness, when the people placed their trust in God that He would provide them with their daily portion of manna (see *Devarim* 8:2–5 regarding the desert and 8:6–20 about the proper attitude upon entering Israel).

The *Sefer Ha-Chinuch* brings one final reason for *Shemita* at the end of his description of this *mitzva*:

> At the root of the precept lies the establishment in our heart ... of the doctrine that the world was brought into being through creation, for in six days the Lord made heaven and earth ... and in order to remove, uproot and extirpate from our thinking any idea of the eternity [of the world], as believed by those who deny the Torah ...

The idea of *Shemita* is similar to the idea of *Shabbat*. Just as in the case of *Shabbat*, a person works for six days and on the seventh day he rests, so too in a *Shemita* year, a person works for six years, and in the seventh year he rests. One of the objectives of the *mitzva* of *Shabbat* is to serve as "a reminder of the creation" (as stated in the *Kiddush* on Friday night). By observing *Shabbat*, a person demonstrates that the world is not eternal, rather it was created by God. As a reminder of how the Creator rested on the seventh day, man also rests weekly. Similarly, ***Shemita*, the seventh year,** serves as a declaration that the world was created by God.

As an aside, the entire weekly cycle that is observed today points to the creation of the world. In nature, we are familiar with the daily cycle, following from the rising and the setting of the sun, and the monthly cycle, following from the waxing and the waning of the moon. The weekly cycle, however, has no foundation in nature. This cycle came into being in the wake of creation. The nations of the world followed the Jewish people and accepted the weekly cycle, and thus they too proclaim, at times unknowingly, the creation of the world.

THE VIEW OF IBN EZRA AND RAV KALISCHER

Rav Kalischer offers another understanding of *Shemita,* which is already alluded to by certain *Rishonim*:[4]

> Another reason is that people should not always be occupied in working the land for material purposes ... when a person is relieved of the yoke of work, he should occupy himself in Torah.

In ordinary years, a person is busy with his work and increasing his material wealth. The sabbatical year is meant to provide man with a break from preoccupation with material needs so that he might occupy himself in Torah study.

THE VIEW OF RAV KOOK

Rav Kook, in his introduction to *Shabbat ha-Aretz,* his comprehensive work on *Shemita,* follows the aforementioned approach but adds another element:

> The individual removes himself from mundane life on a regular basis every *Shabbat* ... The same effect that *Shabbat* has on the individual, the *Shemita* year has on the nation as a whole. It is a special need of this nation, because from time to time the Divine light within it reveals itself in its full glory, light that is not extinguished by mundane social life ... with all its ire and competition ... .

Shabbat is also a day of rest which is meant to serve as an opportunity for Torah study, but *Shemita* is a period of special rest. On *Shabbat* a person must not engage in creative work, and by rabbinic

4. See Ibn Ezra, *Devarim* 31:10–12.

decree he must even refrain from engaging in the sale or purchase of merchandise. During the *Shemita* there is no agricultural produce for sale.

Furthermore, on *Shabbat,* while a person must refrain from work, he retains possession of his property. During the *Shemita* year a person is commanded to declare his property ownerless for the benefit of **all people,** and to cancel all monetary debts owed to him. The entire economic system comes to a halt; debts are cancelled and personal property is declared ownerless.

All this leads to a fundamental distinction between *Shabbat* and *Shemita*: *Shabbat* involves the rest of each individual on his own, whereas *Shemita* involves the rest of the people of Israel as a whole.

Divine light lies concealed within the people of Israel at all times, but material occupation sometimes dulls the radiance of that light. Through the detachment from material affairs and the abandonment of the competition and struggle that characterizes mundane and commercial life, the soul becomes free to soar to spiritual heights. Then the previously hidden Divine light within the people reveals itself in all its intensity. The soul of the nation as a whole and the souls of every individual become purified and refined.

Upon examination of the biblical passages, it becomes evident that Scriptural support can be brought for each of the reasons for *Shemita* proposed above. The table at the end of this chapter shows the various reasons and the biblical source for each (the color of each reason corresponds to the color of the supporting passage).

THE RELATIONSHIP BETWEEN THE VARIOUS REASONS

What is the relationship between the various reasons? There might be room to embrace all reasons, as it is quite possible that many different rationales underlie the *mitzva* of *Shemita*.

One may suggest, however, that there is a single over-arching, all-inclusive reason for the observance of *Shemita*: "For the land is Mine" (*Vayikra* 25:23), the land belongs to God and not to man. This idea is expressed in the Gemara *Sanhedrin* 39a: "Plant for six years and release [the land] during the seventh, so that you shall know that it is Mine." All the other explanations can be shown to flow from this principle. During the *Shemita* year, a person must demonstrate that he is not the master; therefore his produce is declared ownerless.[5] For the same reason he must cease working in order that he not develop the sense that he is the creator of the produce.[6] This situation leads to the other **results** of *Shemita* mentioned above (**results,** rather than **objectives**); people refrain from proprietary disputes and competition (most of the strife in the world stems from mutually contradictory senses of possession). As a result of the lack of dispute and competition, the Divine spiritual spark that lies within each and every individual rouses to life, and each person is free to occupy him or herself with Torah study.

This approach also accounts for the prohibition to destroy *Shemita* produce. As will be explained below, it is forbidden to destroy *Shemita* produce, and therefore it is even forbidden to discard *Shemita* produce in the usual manner. The simple reason that destroying *Shemita* produce is forbidden is because it is endowed with special sanctity. There might, however, be another reason as well (as I heard from my revered father-in-law, Rav Blumenzweig, *shlita*); a person who borrows or rents an article is permitted to use it, but only the owner is permitted to destroy it. Any damage to property, other than that caused by the owner himself, incurs liability. Thus, it follows that nothing gives a person a greater sense of ownership than the right to destroy. During the *Shemita* year, it is forbidden to destroy produce, because we are not the owners of the produce.

5. For further discussion and practical ramifications (and for understanding the law of *hefker* with respect to *Shemita*), see pp. 142, 231, 264.

6. There are halachic ramifications that flow from this reason regarding reaping and gathering, see below, p. 149 Harvesting produce in an amount that will suffice for only a few days does not demonstrate ownership, and therefore this is permitted. Similarly, fruit growing at the beginning of the year (which lacks *Shemita* sanctity) does not have to be declared ownerless (in other words, its owner retains possession of it), and thus it is permitted to harvest the entire crop.

This idea also explains the concept of ***Otzar Bet Din***. As will be explained later in the book, a court is permitted to hire agents to harvest produce in the normal manner (and then distribute it among the entire community). Similarly, a court is permitted to hire agents to press grapes for wine. The *Rishonim* and the *Acharonim* (see Rash Sirillio, *Yerushalmi, Shemita 9:5; Chazon Ish 11:7*) ask: Why is this permitted even when performed in the ordinary manner? If we understand that the entire foundation of the prohibition is displaying ownership, the law makes perfect sense. The court is not acting as an owner; the fields do not belong to the court. The whole idea of ***Otzar Bet Din*** is that the ownerless produce should be distributed to the public by way of a body that has no proprietary rights in the produce. Therefore, even if the court harvests the produce or presses the grapes in the usual manner, there is no prohibition, because there is no sense of ownership.

The *Shemita* year teaches us that we do not truly own anything. This is also the underlying principle of the prohibition of "*bal tashchit*," the prohibition of destroying things of value. It is forbidden to wantonly destroy an article of value, absent just cause, because we do not really own it, just as it is forbidden to inflict injury to one's body.

SHEMITA IN OUR TIME

Today we do not live in an agricultural society and the *Shemita* year has lost much of its unique national flavor. Commerce continues as usual; people retain possession of their property. Serious consideration must be given to the question of how we can best develop the important ideas that characterize the *Shemita* year.

This question connects back to the various reasons for *Shemita* suggested above. In order to truly feel the idea that the land belongs to God, and to extend assistance to the poor, we must consider alternative ways of performing acts of kindness and charity that will be unique to the *Shemita* year.

In addition to performing the usual acts of kindness, it is possible to do things that will remind us of renouncing ownership of the land during the *Shemita* year. For example, professionals can provide their services to the needy free of charge or for a nominal fee (lawyers, doctors, teachers, plumbers, and the like). Of course, a person can give expression to the social aspect of *Shemita* by waiving a portion of the debts owed to him (and, perhaps, banks and other financial institutions can offer their customers better terms for repaying their loans and balancing their finances).

It is also possible to "declare as ownerless" a portion of our time. Both adults and children can dedicate time to special acts of giving and kindness during the *Shemita* year.

The special Torah study of the *Shemita* year can find expression in additional periods of study. For example, a person can dedicate time on Fridays for regular study, and perhaps additional frameworks should be established to encourage such study (Friday *kollels* and the like).

The rationale for *Shemita* that stems from the sanctity of the land and from the idea that God is its true owner is expressed in our increased efforts to purchase the produce of Eretz Israel, and especially *Shemita* produce, such as *Otzar Bet Din*. We should buy *Shemita* produce even if it costs a little more, and thus also merit becoming active partners in the *mitzva* of *Shemita*, and not allow it to fall solely on the shoulders of the 1.6% of Israel's population that works in agriculture.

We can appreciate the special sanctity of *Shemita* produce by eating such produce and giving special care to the uneaten portions and leftovers. This can be source of great joy, as every time we respect the special sanctity of the produce and do not discard it in the usual manner, we pay renewed attention to the unique sanctity that we are privileged to encounter during the *Shemita* year.

During the *Shemita* year we live on a higher level, in closer proximity to God. We discover new strengths and find ourselves capable of performing more acts of kindness and studying more Torah than in ordinary years.

A YEAR THAT IS ENTIRELY A SABBATH

There are surprising parallels between *Shabbat* and *Shemita*. The most obvious among them include: the seventh day and the seventh year; resting from work and resting from working the land; a Sabbath to God (*Shabbat*) and a Sabbath of the land to God (*Shemita*):

Shabbat [the sabbath of creation – *Shemot* 20]	*Shemita* [the sabbath of the land – *Vayikra* 25]
Six days shall you labor	Six years you shall plant your field
And do all your work	And gather in its fruits
But the seventh day is a Sabbath to the Lord your God	But in the seventh year shall be a Sabbath year of solemn rest in the land for the Lord
In it you shall not do any work	You shall neither plant your field, nor prune your vineyard
Neither you, nor your son, nor your daughter, your manservant, nor your maidservant	And the Sabbath produce of the land shall be food for you; for you, and for your servant, and for your maid
Nor your cattle, nor your stranger that is within your gates	And for your hired servant, and for your stranger that sojourns with you, and for your cattle, and for the beast in your land
For in six days the Lord made heaven and earth	For the land is mine

What is the significance of this correspondence?

Another interesting parallel might shed light on the matter. There seems to be a clear parallel between *Shemita* and the state of the world in the Garden of Eden, prior to Adam's sin:

Bereishit 1	*Vayikra* 25
(29) And God said, Behold I have given you every herb bearing seed, **which is upon the face of all the land**, and every tree, on which is the fruit yielding seed; **to you it shall be for food**. (30) **And to every beast of the land**, and to every bird of the air, and to everything that creeps on the earth, wherein there is life, **I have given every green herb for food**: and it was so.	(6) **And the Sabbath produce of the land shall be food for you**; for you, and for your servant, and for your maid, and for your hired servant, and for your stranger that sojourns with you. (7) And for your cattle, **and for the beast in your land, shall all its produce be food.**

The rest from work restores reality to its original state before Adam's sin: a world in which everything belongs to God, and all benefit equally. This is a world in which different groups of human beings, and even animals to a large extent (even though man rules over animals, he may not eat of their meat), coexist peacefully.

Shemita is, in a certain sense, even more exalted than that initial condition. As we have seen, there is a unique term that is common to both ***Shabbat*** and ***Shemita*****: "A Sabbath to the Lord."** What is the significance of this expression?

Shabbat is a reality that is beyond the ordinary reality of this world. God rested on the seventh day, but the world continued to function. Resting on the seventh day does not belong to the human reality of this world. The world and man should actually continue working on the seventh day, and not desist from their work. Resting belongs to exalted and lofty reality, the reality of the world-to-come. The people of Israel were privileged to receive on *Shabbat* the crown of kingship, a crown that belongs to the heavenly world: "Like the world-to-come is the sabbath of rest."

Resting on *Shabbat* likens us, as it were, to the Master of the universe. Shabbat provides us with special strength and supreme sanctity which impacts on the rest of the week. There is no comparison between a person whose entire week flows from the sanctity of *Shabbat,* and a person whose week stem from a reality devoid of sanctity, even if he has some physical rest.

The same is true of *Shemita*. The people of Israel were commanded to work the land – "to work it and to preserve it" (*Bereshit 2:15*). Resting from working the land is something that is found beyond ordinary reality. This teaches that the Land of Israel is unlike all other lands, and that the people of Israel are unlike all other peoples. Both of them have special God-like spiritual dimensions.

Resting from work during the *Shemita* year connects us to the world of the Garden of Eden (for there are also many parallels between the Garden of Eden and *Shemita*), the world of God. The people of Israel who reach their unique sanctity in the land of Israel elevate themselves to an even higher world – a world in which there is no competition or jealousy, a world of mutual assistance and fraternity, a world in which Torah study and connecting with God are natural and expected.[7]

With God's help, may we merit to enter in sanctity and purity to a year that is entirely *Shabbat*. May we merit experiencing the unique intensity and elevation of the *Shemita* year. And may we merit joining together to connect ourselves to God.

Come let us go out to greet the *Shabbat* queen!

7. See also Rav Kook's introduction to *Shabbat ha-Aretz*.

The Rambam (Guide, III, 39)	Some of these laws are meant to lead to pity and promoting the well-being of all men, as the Torah states: "That the poor of your people may eat" (*Shemot* 23:11) ... and are meant to make the earth more fertile and stronger by letting it lie fallow [periodically].
The *Chinuch* (mitzva 84)	There is another useful benefit to be gained: to attain the quality of yielding and relinquishing.
The *Chinuch* (ibid.)	So that a man will remember that the land that grows produce for him ... produces fruit not by its own power, for there is a Master over it and over its owner ...
The *Chinuch* (ibid.)	Yet another useful benefit to be found in this is that a man increases trust in God ...
The *Chinuch* (ibid.)	At the root of the precept lies the purpose of establishing in our heart ... the doctrine that the world was brought into being through creation, for in six days the Lord made heaven and earth ... and in order to remove and uproot from our thinking any idea of the eternity [of the world], as believed by those who deny the Torah ...
Ibn Ezra and Rav Kalischer	Another reason is that people should not always be occupied in working the land for material purposes ... when a person is relieved of the yoke of work, he will be able to occupy himself with Torah study ...
Rav Kook (introduction to *Shabbat ha-Aretz*)	The individual removes himself from mundane life on a regular basis every *Shabbat* ... The same effect that *Shabbat* has on the individual, the *Shemita* year has on the nation as a whole. It is a special need of this nation, because from time to time the Divine light within it reveals itself in its full glory, light that is not extinguished by mundane social life ... with all its ire and competition ...

Assisting the poor

Agricultural reason

The quality of relinquishing

The land belongs to God

Trust in God

Belief in the creation of the world

Break for Torah study

Interruption of the mundane life of society in order to allow the revelation of the Divine light that is concealed within it

1. And the Lord spoke to Moshe in Mount Sinai, saying:
2. Speak to the children of Israel, and say to them, When you come to the land which I give you, then shall the land keep a Sabbath to the Lord.
3. Six years you shall plant your field, and six years you shall prune your vineyard, and gather in its fruit.
4. But in the seventh year shall be a Sabbath of solemn rest for the land, a Sabbath for the Lord: you shall neither plant your field, nor prune your vineyard.
5. That which grows of its own accord of your harvest you shall not reap, nor gather the grapes of your undressed vine; for it shall be a year of rest for the land.
6. And the Sabbath produce of the land shall be food for you; for you, and for your servant, and for your maid, and for your hired servant, and for your stranger that sojourns with you.
7. And for your cattle, and for the beast in your land, shall all its increase be food.

(***Parashat Behar, Vayikra 25***)

18. And you shall perform My statutes, and keep My judgments, and do them; and you shall dwell in the land in safety.
19. And the land shall yield its fruit, and you shall eat your fill, and dwell therein in safety.
20. And if you shall say, "What shall we eat in the seventh year? Behold, we shall not sow, nor gather in our increase":
21. Then I will command My blessing upon you in the sixth year, and it shall bring forth fruit for three years.
22. And you shall plant the eighth year, and eat yet of old fruit until the ninth year; until her fruits come in, you shall eat of the old store.
23. The land shall not be sold for ever: for the land is Mine; for you are strangers and sojourners with Me.
24. And in all the land of your possession you shall grant a redemption for the land.

(***Parashat Behar, Vayikra 25***)

10. And six years you shall plant your land, and shall gather in its fruits.
11. But in the seventh year you shall let it rest and lie fallow; that the poor of your people may eat: and what they leave, the beasts of the field shall eat; in like manner you shall deal with your vineyard, and with your olive grove.
12. Six days you shall do your work, and on the seventh day you shall rest, that your ox and your donkey may rest; and the son of your handmaid, and the stranger, may be refreshed.

(***Parashat Mishpatim, Shemot 23***)

A GUIDE FOR THE PERPLEXED REGARDING *SHEMITA*

Studying the laws of *Shemita* appears to be a complicated, complex, and at times even threatening project. The truth, however, is just the opposite. Studying the laws of *Shemita* is fascinating and fulfilling; it involves the study of Scripture, Talmud and the halachic codes. It combines the study of ancient sources with practical law, the study of ancient sources with the real world, and the study of Halacha with the realms of Jewish thought and belief.

Let us try to briefly survey the main issues that arise during the *Shemita* year.

By Torah law: We find four prohibitions in the Torah: planting, pruning (removing branches from a tree in order to stimulate growth), reaping (annual crops) and gathering (perennial crops). Planting and pruning are forbidden in all situations. Reaping and gathering are permitted when performed in an altered manner (when a person picks only for his family in an amount that will last only a few days, and preferably in a manner different than usual – if the crop is usually harvested with a tool, he should harvest by hand, and the like).

There are also several positive commandments: a *mitzva* to declare *Shemita* produce ownerless, a *mitzva* to preserve the sanctity of *Shemita* produce, using it only for consumption, and a *mitzva* to remove *Shemita* produce from one's house (when there is no longer any of that species of produce left in the field).

By rabbinic decree: All other agricultural labors (watering, fertilizing, weeding, cutting, spraying pesticides and the like) are forbidden by rabbinic decree. The Sages, however, permitted these labors in cases of financial loss.

GARDENING AND POTTED INDOOR PLANTS

Since the Sages permitted labors that are forbidden by rabbinic decree in cases of financial loss, it is permitted to water one's garden when necessary (but less frequently than usual). So too it is permitted to mow one's lawn in the usual manner, inasmuch as this is done for aesthetic, rather than agricultural, reasons. Generally speaking, a private garden can be maintained even without performing any other labors, and therefore they are forbidden.

As for indoor potted plants, if the pot rests on a plate, or if the pot is both on the second floor (or higher) and under a roof, it is permitted to care for the plant in the usual manner.

BUYING FRUITS AND VEGETABLES

There are several sources of permitted fruits and vegetables during the *Shemita* year.

1. ***Heter mechira***: With the *heter mechira*, Israel's agricultural land is sold to a gentile (for two years). The halachic basis of the *heter mechira* is that when the land belongs to a gentile some of the labors that are otherwise forbidden are permitted. The *heter mechira* enjoys the support of some Torah authorities, though there are also authorities who do not accept it. For the consumer, the *heter mechira* is less problematic with respect to fruit than it is with respect to vegetables, because the trees on which the fruit grew were not planted during the *Shemita* year. (Vegetables during the first few months of *Shemita* share this advantage with fruit, as they too were not planted during the *Shemita* year). *Heter mechira* produce does not have *Shemita* sanctity (some authorities, however, are stringent on the matter).
2. ***Otzar Bet Din***: *Otzar Bet Din* is based on the rule that a court or its agents are permitted to harvest the produce growing in a field (but they may not plant). The produce may then be distributed free of charge, with a payment exacted solely to cover the labor costs. Since it is only permitted to perform those labors that are permitted during the *Shemita* year, the yield will usually be smaller than in ordinary years. In addition, sometimes the labor expenses are relatively high. Since this solution only allows harvesting, and not planting, it is only

useful for fruit (and vegetables in the first few months of the year which had already been planted during the sixth year).

This solution meets the highest halachic standards (it is based on the rulings of both Rav Kook and the *Chazon Ish*), and it is the only solution that allows for produce with full *Shemita* sanctity.

3. **Detached bedding:** This solution is based on the ruling that it is permissible to plant indoors (under a roof) in an *atzitz she-eino nakuv,* a container without holes in the bottom. This method is used today for growing tomatoes, peppers, leafy vegetables, and other products. This solution was initially developed with the approval of the *Chazon Ish,* and it has the approval of Rav Sh. Z. Auerbach and Rav Elyashiv (under certain conditions). Thus, this solution meets the highest halachic standards. Produce grown in this manner does not have *Shemita* sanctity.
4. **Sixth-year produce**: Certain vegetables can be stored for over a year, such as potatoes, carrots and onions. Clearly, such produce does not have *Shemita* sanctity.
5. **Southern Arava with the *heter mechira***: The rabbinic decree of *sefichim* (aftergrowth, that which grew on its own or was planted during the *Shemita* year) does not apply in this region, and therefore there is room for greater leniency. Such produce is not at all problematic, though solutions 2–4 are halachically superior.
6. **Vegetables grown by gentiles:** The *Bet Yosef* and the *Mabit* disagree whether such vegetables (and similarly fruits) have *Shemita* sanctity. According to the *Bet Yosef,* they do not have *Shemita* sanctity, whereas according to the *Mabit,* they do have *Shemita* sanctity. The common practice in Jerusalem and most of Eretz Yisrael is to treat such produce as lacking *Shemita* sanctity, whereas in Bnei Braq, the *Chazon Ish* instituted to treat such produce as having *Shemita* sanctity.

Order of priority: Priority should be given to buying *Otzar*

***Bet Din* produce, produce grown in hothouses on detached bedding, or sixth-year fruits and vegetables – all of which are Jewish produce meeting the highest halachic standards.** Next is produce grown in the Southern Arava (with the *heter mechira*), followed by *heter mechira* fruits (as there is no concern that the trees on which they grew were planted during the *Shemita* year).

Vegetables: Even with the *heter mechira*, Rav Kook only permitted the performance of labors forbidden by Torah law if they are performed by gentiles. In the past, however, such labors would often be performed by Jews. During the current *Shemita* year, almost all agricultural workers are gentile foreign workers. This being the case, *heter mechira* produce during the *Shemita* of 5775 is preferred over the produce of gentile farmers, even in the case of vegetables.

The times of *Shemita* sanctity: Fruit that comes to market at the beginning of the *Shemita* year does not have *Shemita* sanctity, and it can be purchased and used in the ordinary manner. Vegetables have *Shemita* sanctity if they were picked after *Rosh ha-Shana* of the *Shemita* year.

In practice: When there is no concern that the produce was planted during the *Shemita* year (all fruit; vegetables during the first few months of the year), one may purchase *heter mechira* produce, though it is preferable to purchase *Otzar Bet Din* produce, produce grown on detached bedding, or sixth-year produce.

As for vegetables the rest of the year (that were planted during the *Shemita* year, so that there is concern about the prohibition of *sefichim*), efforts should be made to purchase produce grown on detached bedding or sixth-year produce (such produce is available in *Otzar ha-Aretz* stores) or produce grown in the Southern Arava. If such produce is unavailable, buying *heter mechira* vegetables (certainly in the *Shemita* of 5775) is preferable to buying gentile produce (one should make sure that the store is certified as selling *heter mechira* produce), in order to avoid hurting Jewish agriculture in Eretz Yisrael (produce that is bought from gentiles even in ordinary years can be bought during the *Shemita* year as well).

SHEMITA SANCTITY IN THE KITCHEN

It is a privilege and perhaps even a *mitzva* to eat *Shemita* produce. Therefore, even if eating *Shemita* produces creates a certain difficulty, we should be grateful for the great privilege we have once every seven years.

It is not very difficult to manage a kitchen during the *Shemita* year. Here are the main rules:

1. Effort should be made to finish all the *Shemita* produce on one's plate, owing to its special sanctity.
2. **Leftovers:** Leftovers and remnants may be placed in a bag and thrown directly into an ordinary garbage can (or they can be collected in a bag and at the end of the day the bag can be tied and thrown into the garbage). There are those who are **more stringent** and instead set the bag aside for a few days until the *Shemita* leftovers begin to decay, and only then throw it into the garbage. This, however, is only a stringency, and one who wishes to be lenient can rely on the first solution. Even one who is stringent may rely on the more lenient solution when there is some special difficulty or when traveling. Institutions may be lenient without hesitation and throw the bags of leftovers immediately into the garbage.
3. It is recommended to label a container, such as a small waste-paper bin, "*kedushat shevi'it*," line it with a bag, and deposit all *Shemita* leftovers into that container. At the end of the day, the bag can be tied and thrown into the garbage (or kept for several days and then discarded).
4. It is not necessary to remove the *Shemita* leftovers from a salad that also contains non-*Shemita* produce. The entire salad may be deposited in the *Shemita* container (because the non-*Shemita* leftovers do not immediately cause the *Shemita* leftovers to spoil).
5. If *Shemita* produce was cooked together with non-*Shemita* produce, the entire mixture is treated as *Shemita* produce, (in such a case even the more stringent may throw the bag away

immediately because cooked food becomes unfit for human consumption very quickly). Therefore, vegetable soup or *cholent* that contains *Shemita* vegetables has *Shemita* sanctity and should be treated as described above.

6. It is permitted to cook *Shemita* produce that is regularly cooked. The *Posekim* disagree about squeezing *Shemita* produce for its juice. According to the *Chazon Ish*, it is permitted to squeeze any fruit that is ordinarily squeezed. It is therefore also permissible to mash *Shemita* produce, both for adults and for children. Simply preparing food in the ordinary manner should cause no special difficulty during the *Shemita* year.

To summarize: The role of the kitchen during Shemita consists of the privilege of eating Shemita produce, the attempt to eliminate all leftovers, and the placing of any leftovers in a bag before they are thrown into the garbage. It is permitted to cook or squeeze for juice any fruit or vegetable that is ordinarily prepared in that manner.

The reasons for *Shemita*: As we have seen, many reasons have been offered for the *mitzva* of *Shemita* (the land belongs to God, aiding the poor, equality, making time for Torah study, and others). Efforts should be made to apply these goals in the modern context (buying produce that has *Shemita* sanctity, increased activities involving acts of kindness, and perhaps even declaring a portion of our time as "ownerless" and dedicating it to others; increased Torah study, and the like).

With God's help, may we enjoy the special sanctity and spirituality of the *Shemita* year, connect ourselves more deeply to our Father in heaven, and fill ourselves with the love of God and the love of our fellow human beings.

A guide for the perplexed regarding the *Shemita*

Labors forbidden by Torah law

Planting and pruning are forbidden in all situations.
Reaping and gathering are permitted when performed in an altered manner (only for one's family in an amount that will last only a few days, and preferably with a tool that is not ordinarily used for picking).

Labors forbidden by rabbinic decree and maintaining a garden

All other agricultural labors are forbidden by rabbinic decree (watering, weeding, mowing, and fertilizing) and are only permitted when failure to perform them will cause the plants to die.
Therefore, it is permitted to water a garden, though one should increase the intervals between waterings. It is permitted, however, to extend the duration of each watering. (If the irrigation system is controlled by computer it can be programmed as usual before the *Shemita* year).
It is permitted to mow one's lawn in the usual manner, because this is done for aesthetic reasons.
Fertilizing: Slow-release fertilizers should be applied prior to the *Shemita* year.
During the sixth year, it is permitted to perform all types of labor until the beginning of the *Shemita* year, except for planting fruit trees (with exposed roots – until the 15th of *Av*; if the root stock is covered with soil – until the 29th of *Av*).
For other trees, flowers and vegetables – if the roots are covered with soil they may be planted until *Rosh ha-Shana*.

Purchasing fruits and vegetables during the *Shemita* year

Preference should be given to Jewish produce. The following possibilities exist:

a. *Otzar Bet Din* (the best solution, has *Shemita* sanctity)
b. Hothouses and detached bedding (recommended)
c. Sixth-year produce (recommended)
d. Southern *Arava* sold under *heter mechira* (a good solution, but the previous solutions are preferred)
e. *Heter mechira* fruit (permitted even for those who do not rely on the *heter*, because there is no problem of planting – Rav Sh. Z. Auerbach)
f. *Heter mechira* vegetables (provided that the planting was performed by a gentile – as is the situation in 5775). (This solution not as good as the previous solutions, but better than buying produce grown by gentiles or imported produce, unless it is produce that is bought from gentiles during regular years as well.)

* In the case of fruit, *Shemita* sanctity only begins during the last months of the *Shemita* year (during the first months, fruit may be purchased in the usual manner). In the case of vegetables, *Shemita* sanctity begins at the beginning of the year. The concern about planting and *sefichim* only begins several months later.

The kitchen during the *Shemita* year

It is a privilege to eat *Shemita* produce.
Leftovers: should be placed into a bag and then into the garbage (many are stringent and set the bag aside for several days until the leftovers begin to decay, and only then do they throw the bag away).
It is recommended to designate a certain container (preferably a nice one) for storing leftover food with *Shemita* sanctity.
It is permitted to wash dishes in the normal manner even if remnants of *Shemita* produce are found on the utensils.
If a cooked dish contains *Shemita* produce, *Shemita* sanctity applys to the entire dish (vegetable soup, cholent). Leftovers should be placed in a bag and then discarded.
It is permitted to cook, squeeze and mash *Shemita* produce that is ordinarily prepared in that manner.

A SUMMARY OF THE LAWS OF *SHEMITA*

The numbers in brackets refer to the page in this volume where the issue is discussed at greater length.

GARDENING DURING *SHEMITA*

LABORS THAT ARE FORBIDDEN BY TORAH LAW

1. The labors that are forbidden by Torah law are: planting, pruning (removing branches in order to stimulate growth), reaping (harvesting vegetables and other annual crops), and gathering (picking fruits and other perennial crops). [86]
2. The prohibition of planting applies even to plants that do not bear fruit. [89]
3. There is a fundamental disagreement whether the prohibitions apply exclusively to **the person**, or also to **the land** (belonging to the person). In other words, is it only that the person must refrain from planting himself, or must he see to it that his **land rests – "then shall the land keep a Sabbath"?** One possible ramification relates to indirect planting (by way of *gerama* – chain reaction or causation): If the prohibition relates to the land itself, then even indirect planting should be forbidden, but if the prohibition relates exclusively to the person, indirect planting might be permitted. While the *Acharonim* dispute this matter, in practice we are stringent. [94]
4. Planting a seedling or a tree is forbidden. The *Posekim* disagree whether this is forbidden by Torah law or only by rabbinic decree. [98]
5. Plowing is forbidden, but there is disagreement whether all plowing is forbidden by Torah law, or only plowing that accompanies the planting process. [122]
6. Pruning is forbidden by Torah law, but some authorities maintain that the Torah prohibition applies only to grapevines, whereas the pruning of other trees is forbidden by rabbinic

decree (because, in this view, the Torah only forbids pruning that stimulates the growth of fruit, as is the case with a grapevine).[115]

HARVESTING PRODUCE

1. By Torah law, it is forbidden to gather (the produce of perennial crops) or to reap (the produce of annual crops).
2. This prohibition stems from the fact that it is forbidden to demonstrate ownership over land, and therefore one is permitted to harvest a small, non-commercial quantity of produce that will suffice for his family for several days. Even in such a case, however, it is preferable that one harvest in an altered manner (such as harvesting by hand produce that is usually harvested with a tool).

The prohibition of harvesting produce only applies to produce that has *Shemita* sanctity. It is, therefore, permissible to pick fruit during the first few months of *Shemita* in the ordinary manner (since it does not have *Shemita* sanctity). On the other hand, fruit that has *Shemita* sanctity must be picked in an altered manner, even during the eighth year, despite the fact that planting is already permissible. The *Shemita* sanctity of vegetables is determined by the date on which they are picked, and therefore, from the very beginning of the *Shemita* year they may not be picked in the ordinary manner, but only in small quantities (as explained in the preceding paragraph). [132]

LABORS THAT ARE FORBIDDEN BY RABBINIC DECREE

In addition to the labors that are forbidden during the *Shemita* year by Torah law, it is forbidden by rabbinic decree to perform any action that enhances the growth of a plant. Therefore, it is forbidden to water, to remove weeds (with their roots), to cut weeds (without removing their roots), to fertilize, to remove stones (in order to prepare the land for planting), and to perform any other such activities. [166] [182]

One may perform labors that are generally forbidden by rabbinic decree during the *Shemita* year only when failure to do so will cause the plants to die. [169]

The *Acharonim* disagree about a case where failure to perform labors forbidden by rabbinic decree will not cause long-term damage to the tree, but will cause **damage to the *Shemita* fruit** (Rav Kook is stringent, whereas the *Chazon Ish* is lenient). There are grounds for leniency (since we are dealing with an uncertainty regarding a rabbinic prohibition), at least in the case of a public garden, or in a case of significant financial loss. Nevertheless, regarding a private garden, one should be stringent (but leniency may be practiced regarding irrigation, as will be explained below).[175]

REGULAR UPKEEP OF A GARDEN DURING *SHEMITA*

As we saw above, certain labors are forbidden by Torah law, while others are forbidden only by rabbinic decree. The labors of planting and pruning that are forbidden by Torah law may not be performed at all during the *Shemita* year, while the other Torah prohibitions of reaping and gathering may be performed only in small quantities, as explained above. Labors that are forbidden only by rabbinic decree (watering, fertilizing, weeding, mowing, spraying pesticides, and the like) are permitted during the *Shemita* year when performed in order to preserve that which already exists, so that it not die, but not when performed in order to strengthen and develop that which is growing in the field. Let us now examine the circumstances in which labors that are forbidden by rabbinic decree are permitted during the *Shemita* year:

Watering: One may water a garden during the *Shemita* year as is necessary to maintain the garden, but not more than that. According to many *posekim*, however, once a person turns his sprinklers on in order to maintain his garden, he may leave them on for as long as he wants. Therefore, during the *Shemita* year, sprinklers should be activated less frequently (as is minimally necessary), but may be allowed to operate for a longer duration.

As a rule, in most parts of Israel, sprinklers should be turned on once a week for half an hour to water grass (more sensitive plants, such as roses, may be watered every four or five days).

It is best if a person can program the computer that controls his irrigation system in advance of the *Shemita* year. In such a case, there is room to be lenient and program the computer as usual. (If he closes the main shut-off valve over the course of the year, there is room to be lenient and re-open it [indirect action in the case of watering which is only a rabbinic prohibition], but it is best that this be done by a gentile. In such a case, those who wish to be more stringent should reprogram the computer in accordance with the guidelines applying to the *Shemita* year, as explained above).[195]

Fertilizing: Today it is possible to apply slow-release fertilizer that will suffice for an entire year. Therefore, such fertilizer should be applied before the *Shemita* year begins. Only in special cases, when necessary to preserve that which is already growing, is it permitted to apply fertilizer during the *Shemita* year itself, and in such cases, it is preferable to apply the fertilizer through the irrigation system. [183]

Pruning: Pruning should not be performed during the *Shemita* year, unless there is a diseased branch which must be removed, or when it is clear that the pruning is being performed not for the sake of the tree, but for some other purpose (such as to clear a passageway). [190]

Hedges: Hedges that have not yet filled in should not be trimmed during the *Shemita* year, because trimming them will promote growth and cause them to fill in. Even if the hedges are full, it is preferable that they be trimmed prior to the *Shemita* year. If for some reason it is important that they be trimmed, and especially if they interfere with free passage, they may be trimmed (if they are full) in such a manner that it is clear that they are being trimmed for aesthetic, rather than agricultural, reasons. [209]

Pesticides: Spraying pesticides to protect fruit from damage is permitted, but it is preferable to spread a net over the tree instead. [186]

Weeding: In general, a garden can be maintained even without weeding. If, however, there is a strongly competitive weed, and there is concern that it will cause damage to another plant, removing the weed is permitted. Even in such a case, it is preferable to cut the weed without removing the roots or to kill the weed with a herbicide.

Cutting weeds for aesthetic purposes is permitted even during the *Shemita* year, but one should be careful to cut the weeds, and not remove them by their roots. Even in such a case, weeding is only permitted when it is clear to all that he is cutting the weeds for aesthetic purposes and not to promote growth. [205]

Mowing a lawn: Mowing a lawn is permitted during the *Shemita* year when performed for aesthetic purposes and not to stimulate enhanced growth. This may even be done in the usual manner. In practice, it is actually preferable to mow the lawn in the usual manner, because if the mowing is delayed and the grass is allowed to grow, mowing the lawn will then promote the growth of the grass (by allowing sunlight to reach the lower portion of the grass). In such a case, mowing the lawn might be forbidden, because it also serves an agricultural purpose. [205]

Picking flowers: Picking flowers for household use is permitted. This should be done in a non-professional manner so that it not promote additional growth. [535]

Uprooting a tree: Uprooting a tree (or chopping it down) is forbidden if it is done to prepare the ground for planting, and is permitted only for aesthetic purposes or for the wood (if the tree has fruit, the matter is more complicated, because of the destruction caused to *Shemita* produce). Cutting down a cluster of three or more trees is also more complicated (because of the problematic appearance of such an action – *Shevi'it* 4:4; Rambam, *Hilchot Shemita ve-Yovel* 1:18).

RULES FOR VARIOUS LABORS

In general, the aforementioned labors suffice for the upkeep of a private garden. In professional farming, such as in orchards, it is sometimes necessary to fertilize, spray pesticides and perform other labors for the upkeep of the orchard and to prevent the trees from dying. Leniency may only be practiced with regard to labors that are forbidden by rabbinic decree. Owners of a commercial orchard or field should consult with a competent halachic authority to receive the appropriate guidelines (professional guidelines are provided in the book "*Katif Shevi'it*," published by *Machon ha-Torah ve-ha-Aretz*).

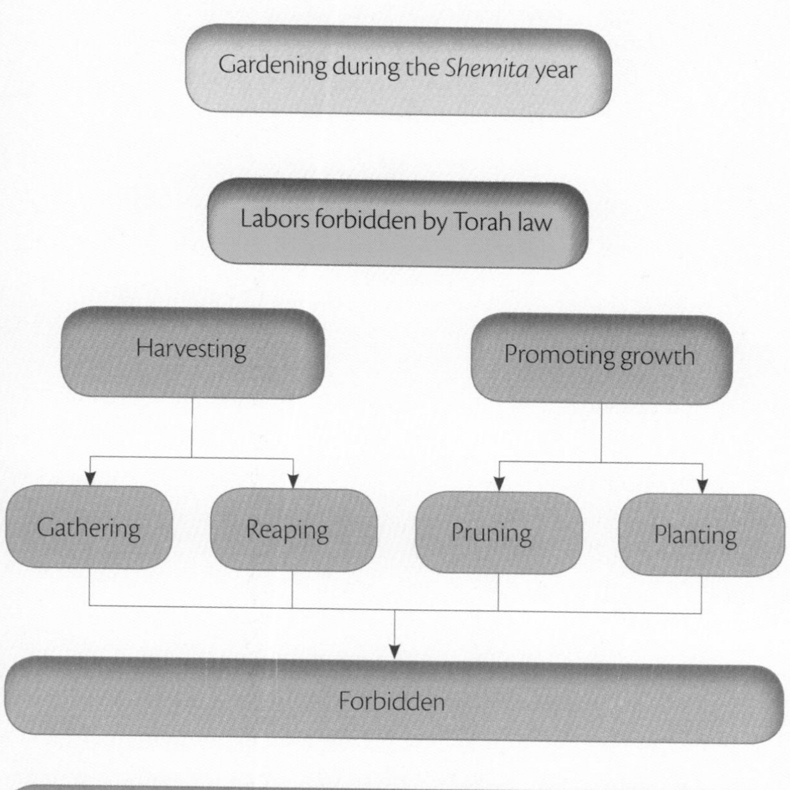

Labors forbidden by rabbinic decree

Watering, fertilizing, removing weeds (with their roots) cutting weeds (without removing their roots), spraying pesticides, and the like.

Permitted when performed to preserve that which is already growing.

- Fertilizing → **Before the *Shemita* year**: slow-release fertilizer. **During the *Shemita* year**: only in special cases.
- Watering → Water less frequently, but for longer duration.
- Weeding
  - Aesthetic → Permitted, when it is clearly being done for an aesthetic purpose, and should be limited as much as possible.
  - Agricultural → Forbidden (except for a case of financial loss). Preferable to cut without removing the roots or to kill with an herbicide.
- Mowing → Regular mowing is permitted. It is preferable not to delay mowing, so that the mowing not serve an agricultural purpose. Hedges: Trimming hedges should be avoided. Leniency is permitted in a case of special need, provided that the hedge is already full.

THE GARDEN OF AN APARTMENT BUILDING

A person living in an apartment building should try to arrange with his neighbors that only labors that are permitted during the *Shemita* year be performed in the building's garden. If his neighbors do not agree, he should tell them that his payment for joint expenses will only cover cleaning costs and the like, but not the gardening expenses, and that he will pay more than his neighbors for the cleaning costs. Such a statement, however, might not suffice, because each individual might be required by the Torah to see to it that his land rests, and in such a case, the land will not rest. It is, therefore, preferable, that prior to the *Shemita* year he declare in the presence of three people that he is renouncing ownership of his portion of the garden (according to Rav Sh. Z. Auerbach, his neighbors need not be informed about this).

POTTED PLANTS INSIDE THE HOUSE

Strictly speaking, **in an *atzitz she-eino nakuv* inside the house**, it is permitted to perform all labors in the usual manner, including planting. Nevertheless, in the absence of some special need, actual planting should be avoided. In a case of need, however, even planting is permitted, and this is the basis for the important solution of hothouses and detached bedding (as will be explained below).[108]

An *atzitz she-eino nakuv* is a pot that does not have a hole in its underside; a pot that has a hole, but rests on a non-earthenware plate; or a pot that has a hole, but rests on the second floor or higher of a building (not attached to the ground).

A house, for these purposes, is defined as any roofed structure. Ideally, the structure should have walls at least 80 centimeters (about 32 inches) high. [110]

Regular upkeep of potted plants inside the house: A pot that is inside the house (under a roof) and rests on a plate (or is not on the ground floor) **may be cared for in the usual manner** (watering, fertilizing, removal of leaves, and the like). **It is permissible to move plants around the house** from one place to another (strictly speaking, this is permitted even if the pot is perforated according to Rav Sh. Z. Auerbach; some practice stringency and only move the plant together with its plate). It is permissible to move a plant within the house to a sunnier area where it will grow better, and the like (Rav Sh. Z. Auerbach).

Moving pots in a garden: One should not move an *atzitz nakuv* from one place to another in a garden. An *atzitz she-eino nakuv* may be moved from place to place, even if it is in the garden, though one should make sure that all of the plant's foliage remains over the plate (or a plastic bag or the like). It is permissible to move an *atzitz she-eino nakuv* from the garden into the house (because fundamentally it is permitted to uproot a plant during the *Shemita* year, when one's intention is not to prepare the land for planting). According to Rav Sh. Z. Auerbach, it is even permissible to move an *atzitz she-eino nakuv* from the house into the garden, especially when the move is not meant to benefit the plant, but for some other purpose, such as to build a sukka (but some are stringent on this matter).

It is permissible to turn **an *atzitz nakuv* into an *atzitz she-eino nakuv*** by covering its base (because there is no prohibition to uproot a plant during the *Shemita* year). It is forbidden, however, to turn an *atzitz she-eino nakuv* into a *atzitz nakuv* by removing the plate upon which it rests (when it is outdoors, because that would be considered planting).

Buying potted plants in a store: It is permissible to buy potted plants from a nursery that observes the laws of *Shemita* and to bring them home in the usual manner (Rav Sh. Z. Auerbach; Rav Elyashiv is stringent and requires that they be wrapped in cellophane or the like during transport).

Window boxes: A pot that is not inside the house (such as a window box resting on an outside windowsill) should be handled in accordance with the guidelines for a garden outlined above. The same applies to a window box that sits under a roof, but is perforated and faces the ground. Only a window box that sits under a roof, and rests on a plate, is treated like a pot that is inside the house, and may be cared for in the usual manner (even in such a case, this only applies to a movable window box, but a window box that is attached to the building or is very large [40 *se'ah* = 650 liters, about 170 gallons] is regarded as if it were attached to the ground, and is subject to the laws governing a garden. [112]

DECLARING THE PRODUCE OWNERLESS

If fruits or vegetables that have *Shemita* sanctity are growing in a person's garden, one must allow anybody who so desires to enter and pick them. It is best to declare before three people that the produce is ownerless. If a person is concerned that strangers will enter his field, one may lock the field, but must then hang up a sign indicating when it will be possible to enter to pick the produce. Only produce that has *Shemita* sanctity is ownerless, and such produce is regarded as ownerless during the eighth year as well. [144]

One should ask the field's owner for permission to pick the *Shemita* fruits and vegetables growing in a garden (unless there is a sign expressly permitting this), so that one not become accustomed to entering another person's property without permission (Rav Kook, based on the Ra'avad). [151]

PREPARING THE GARDEN FOR *SHEMITA*

In the past, the law of *tosefet shevi'it* was in effect and certain labors were forbidden by Torah law even before the *Shemita* year began. Today *tosefet shevi'it* does not apply but there are still certain things that have become forbidden in the time leading up to the *Shemita* year. [158]

PLANTING BEFORE *SHEMITA*

Planting a fruit tree: A tree whose root stock is exposed (not covered with soil) may only be planted until the 15th of *Av* of the sixth year (it takes two weeks for a tree to take root, plus one month for the tree to be considered to have completed a year with respect to *orla).* The tree may not be planted after the 15th of *Av,* because then the *Shemita* year would count as the first year with respect to *orla,* and it would appear as if the tree had been planted during the *Shemita* year. [160]

If the count of *orla* years will start in the sixth year, however, one may plant the tree later in the year. If the root stock is covered with soil so that the tree can live for two weeks without being planted in the ground, the tree may be planted until the 29th of *Av*. Such a tree is regarded as already having taken root and the month that remains will count as the first year with respect to *orla.*

A tree whose root stock is packed in soil, in a container with has a two centimeter hole on the bottom that had been resting on the ground, may be planted until *Rosh ha-Shana,* The reason this is permitted is because it is unnecessary to start a new count of *orla* years.

Planting vegetables: It is permitted to plant vegetable seeds provided the seeds will begin to sprout (the first leaves emerging from the ground) before the *Shemita* year begins. Vegetables that were planted in a tray (where the seeds can live for three days) may be transplanted into the ground until *Rosh ha-Shana* of the *Shemita* year. [163]

Planting flowers: According to some authorities, flowers may only be planted if they will take root before the *Shemita* year begins (this is apparently Rav Kook's view); others, however, are lenient on the matter (*Chazon Ish*).

Unscented flowers, therefore, may be planted until *Rosh ha-Shana*. Ideally, however, they should be planted before the 26th of *Elul*, so that they will take root during the sixth year. [163]

Scented flowers should be planted before the 26th of *Elul* (according to some authorities, they are subject to the laws of *sefichim*, though other authorities are lenient on the matter). Flowers that were planted in a tray (even if they are scented) may be transplanted into the ground until *Rosh ha-Shana* of the *Shemita* year.

Perennials: It is suggested that one plant perennials in advance of the *Shemita* year so that one's garden will be in bloom during the *Shemita* year. [163]

Planting trees that do not bear fruit: Trees that do not bear fruit, and whose roots are exposed, should be planted before the 15th of *Elul*, so that they will take root before the *Shemita* year begins. If the root stock is covered with soil such that the tree can live for two weeks without being planted, the tree may be planted until *Rosh ha-Shana*, for in such a case it need not take root in the sixth year. [162]

Planting grass: During the first few months after grass is planted from seed, it must be mowed so that the grass will fill in (in the case of sod, mowing is necessary for the strips of grass to grow together). Therefore, grass should be planted early enough (from seed: three months before *Shemita*; from sod: a month before *Shemita*) to allow time for the lawn to be properly mown prior to the onset of *Shemita*, so that during the *Shemita* year the mowing will be performed solely for aesthetic purposes. **In a case of need** there is room to be lenient and plant grass from seed until several weeks before the *Shemita* year (and sod until two weeks before *Shemita*), provided that the following conditions are met: The grass should be planted three times more densely than usual, it should be fertilized and watered much more than usual, and it should be mowed at least once before the *Shemita* year begins. [163]

SUMMARY

Actions that should be taken in advance of the *Shemita* year:

1. **Planting:** Trees that bear fruit and whose root stock is exposed, until the 15th of *Av*, and whose root stock is covered with soil, until the 29th of *Av*; trees that do not bear fruit, and whose root stock is exposed, until the 15th of *Elul*, and whose root stock is covered with soil, until *Rosh ha-Shana*; flowers and vegetables, until several days before *Rosh ha-Shana*, so that they will begin to sprout during the sixth year; grass, from seed – three months before *Shemita*, from sod – a month before *Shemita* (in special cases, there is room for greater leniency – see the guidelines in this volume). **In general, most trees and seedlings come today in soil-filled containers;** therefore they may be planted until *Rosh ha-Shana*, with the exception of fruit trees that must be planted by the 29th of *Av*.

All of the following labors may be performed until *Rosh ha-Shana*:

2. **Watering:** It is suggested that a person program the computer that controls his irrigation system in advance of the *Shemita* year.
3. **Fertilizing:** It is suggested that slow-release fertilizer be applied before the *Shemita* year begins.
4. **Pruning:** Pruning should be performed wherever necessary. Trees should be staked and strengthened.
5. **Spraying herbicides:** Herbicides should be applied to prevent the growth of weeds and at the edges of lawns to prevent the unwanted spreading of grass.

During the *Shemita* year itself

1. **Watering:** Sprinklers should be activated less frequently than usual (when the grass is about to begin to turn yellow, and the like), but they may be allowed to operate for as long as is desired. In most parts of the country, it is recommended to water once a week for half an hour. If a person programs his

computer before the *Shemita* year begins, he may program it to water as usual.

2. **Pruning, weeding and cutting:** Pruning is only permitted for the sake of removing a diseased branch, or for clearing a passageway or the like, and only if it is clear that it is not being done for agricultural purposes. Weeding should be avoided, unless the weeds threaten to damage other plants (and even then cutting or spraying is preferable). Cutting weeds is only permitted when there is an important aesthetic need, and when it is clear that it is being done for an aesthetic purpose. **Mowing a lawn** should be performed as usual.
3. **Fertilizing:** One should not apply fertilizer during the *Shemita* year itself, unless failure to do so will lead to serious damage.

Upkeep of potted plants in the house

A potted plant that is inside a house (under a roof) and resting on a plate (or not on the ground floor) **may be cared for in the usual manner** (watering, fertilizing, removal of leaves and the like).

Window boxes: A potted plant, whether in an *atzitz nakuv* or an *atzitz she-eino nakuv*, that is not inside the house (such as a window box that is outside) should be treated in accordance with the guidelines for maintaining gardens as explained above.

Labors forbidden by rabbinic decree

- **Planting**
  - Fruit trees
    - With exposed roots → Until the 15th of ***Av***
    - With soil-covered roots → Until the 29th of ***Av***
  - Trees that do not bear fruit
    - With exposed roots → Until the 15th of ***Elul***
    - With soil-covered roots → Until *Rosh ha-Shana*
  - Flowers
    - Seeds → Until several days before *Rosh ha-Shana*
    - With soil → Until *Rosh ha-Shana*

Grass should be planted several months in advance, so that it will fill in before the *Shemita* year.

In general, most trees and flowers come with their roots packed in soil, and may therefore be planted until *Rosh ha-Shana*, except for fruit trees (with covered roots) which must be planted by the 29th of *Av*.

- **Care**
  - Anti-weed herbicides
  - Pruning
  - Slow-release fertilizer

All of these activities are permitted until *Rosh ha-Shana*.

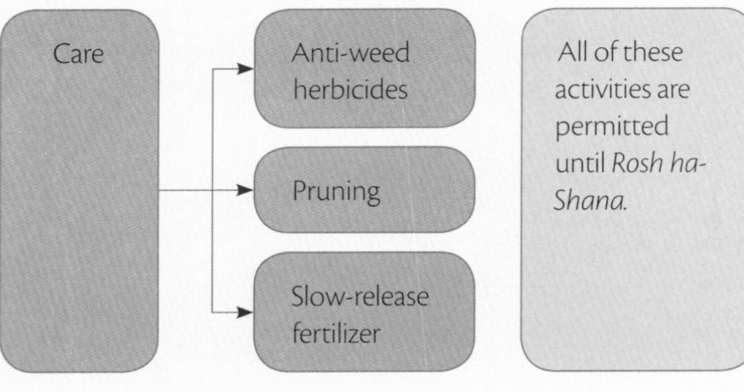

THE KITCHEN MANAGEMENT DURING *SHEMITA*

THE SANCTITY OF *SHEMITA* PRODUCE

Shemita produce has special sanctity. Some later authorities understand that according to the Ramban there is a *mitzva* to eat *Shemita* produce. While many authorities disagree, they certainly would agree that eating *Shemita* produce is both significant and commendable. This privilege imposes great responsibility: One must be careful not to destroy *Shemita* produce (even by using it in an inferior way, such as feeding animals with food that is fit for human consumption), or to use *Shemita* produce in unusual ways, as will be explained below. [226] [228] [236]

WHAT PRODUCE ATTAINS *SHEMITA* SANCTITY? [240] [252]

1. **Vegetables**: All vegetables that are picked during the *Shemita* year have *Shemita* sanctity. [242]
2. **Fruit:** All fruit that assumes form (*chanata*) during the *Shemita* year has *Shemita* sanctity. Accordingly, fruit coming to market during the first few months of the *Shemita* year has no sanctity, but fruit coming to market during the eighth year does have sanctity if it already began to assume form during *Shemita*. [243]
3. ***Etrog***: The commonly accepted view is that the critical stage for an *etrog* with respect to *Shemita* is *chanata*, as it is for other fruits. There are those, however, who take into consideration the view of the Rambam, who maintains that any *etrog* that is picked during the *Shemita* year has *Shemita* sanctity (there could be a practical difference between the two views regarding *etrogim* that come to market at the beginning of the *Shemita* year. It should be noted, however, that *etrogim* for *Sukkot* are generally picked before *Rosh ha-Shana*, and therefore all agree that they do not have *Shemita* sanctity during the seventh year). [248]
4. **Citrus fruit**: Despite their similarity to an *etrog*, the *Posekim*

(Rav Kook and the *Chazon Ish*) agree that they are treated like other fruits, so that their sanctity depends upon the year during which they reach the stage of *chanata.* [249]

5. **Grain, olives, legumes and grapes**: If these crops become a third grown during the *Shemita* year, they have *Shemita* sanctity. [240]

THE PROHIBITION OF *SEFICHIM*

By Torah law, one may eat vegetables and grains that grow on their own during the *Shemita* year. The Rabbis, however, decreed that such vegetables are forbidden because people would plant vegetables in secret and later claim that the vegetables grew on their own. This rabbinic decree is referred to as the prohibition of "*sefichim*" ("aftergrowth").

The prohibition of *sefichim* applies only to vegetables, because only regarding vegetables does concern arise that they might have been planted during the *Shemita* year in contravention of the law. The prohibition applies even to vegetables that were planted prior to the *Shemita* year, but only began to sprout during the *Shemita* year itself.

The prohibition of *sefichim* necessitates special care when purchasing vegetables that is not necessary with respect to fruit. We will explain below the various ways to buy fruits and vegetables during the *Shemita* year, as well as explain the order of preferences when deciding between the various alternatives. [303]

TIMETABLE FOR *SHEMITA* SANCTITY

Tables which indicate when one must be concerned about *Shemita* sanctity with respect to each different species of vegetable and fruit are included with this book. Here we present a general diagram for illustration purposes: [436]

Note that from the very beginning of the *Shemita* year, one must be

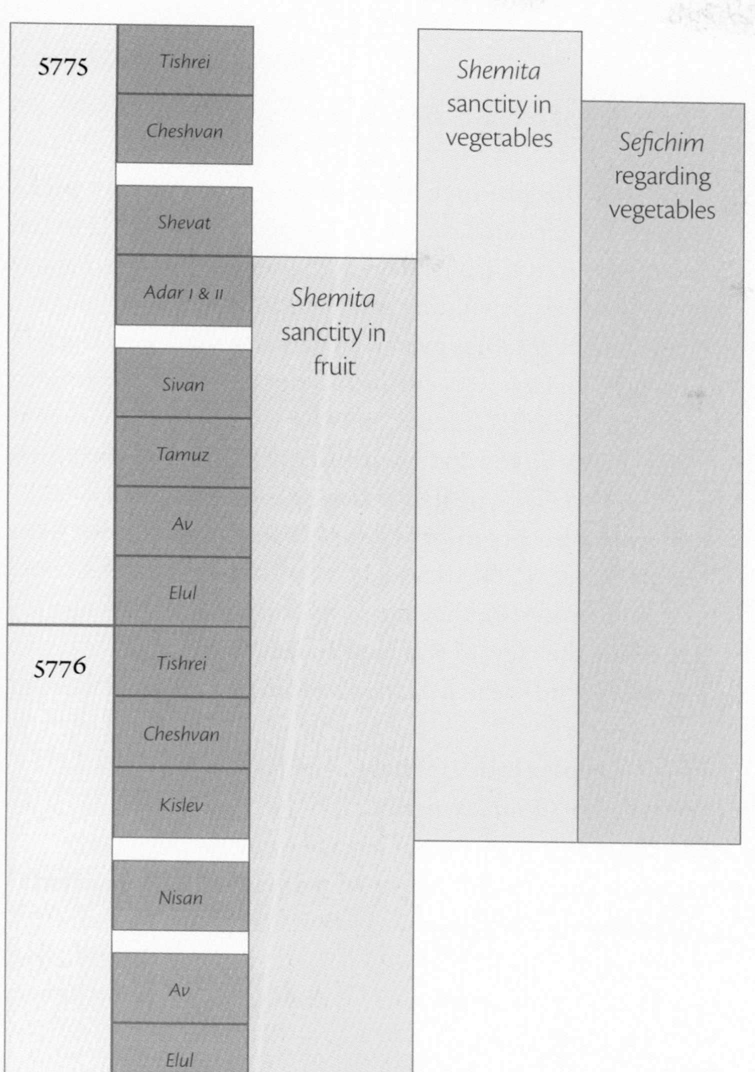

careful about vegetables, and that a few months later even greater care is necessary due to the prohibition of *sefichim*.

During the last few months of the *Shemita* year, one must also be careful about fruits (until close to the end of the eighth year).

CATEGORIES OF PRODUCE THAT HAVE *SHEMITA* SANCTITY

Which categories of produce have *Shemita* sanctity and which do not?

1. ***Otzar Bet Din* produce and produce that a person picks in his own garden** have *Shemita* sanctity (according to the criteria set above: fruits, depending on the time of *chanata*, and vegetables, depending on the time of picking). [261]
2. **Fruits and vegetables grown by gentiles** – in Jerusalem and most parts of Israel it is customary not to treat such produce as having *Shemita* sanctity, but the *Chazon Ish*, consistent with his view on the matter, instituted in Bnei Brak that such produce should be treated as having *Shemita* sanctity. [261]
3. ***Heter mechira* produce** – strictly speaking does not have *Shemita* sanctity (for those who rely on the *heter*), but some treat such produce as having *Shemita* sanctity as a stringency (following the view of Rav Kook). [261]
4. **Vegetables** grown on detached bedding do not have *Shemita* sanctity. [367]
5. **Medicinal plants** do not have *Shemita* sanctity. [255]
6. **Spices** have *Shemita* sanctity. [255]
7. **Unscented flowers** do not have *Shemita* sanctity. [255]
8. **Scented flowers that are used primarily for ornamental purposes** – according to Rav Sh. Z. Auerbach, do not have *Shemita* sanctity, while Rav Elyashiv disagrees. Both agree, however, that flowers grown for their scent do have *Shemita* sanctity. [258]
9. **Produce that is grown for animal feed** has *Shemita* sanctity, but some authorities maintain that this is only when the produce is grown specifically for animals. [254]
10. **Trees that do not bear fruit**, in general, do not have *Shemita* sanctity. [254]

Money that was used for the purchase of *Shemita* produce has *Shemita* sanctity. This money may only be used for the purchase of food, which must then be treated as having sanctity (it may not be thrown into the garbage, etc.). In general, one need not worry that any money encountered is *Shemita* money. If one knows with certainty that a cash register in a given store contains money that has *Shemita* sanctity, one must treat the change received there as having *Shemita* sanctity. We shall discuss below where one is likely today to encounter money having *Shemita* sanctity, and how one must conduct oneself in practice. [324]

WHAT SHOULD BE DONE WITH *SHEMITA* REMNANTS AND LEFTOVERS?

One should try to completely finish *Shemita* produce, minimizing leftovers to the greatest extent possible. [264]

Shemita remnants should not be thrown into an ordinary garbage can. There are two solutions to the problem of what to do with *Shemita* leftovers: [264]

1. A special receptacle should be designated for food remnants having *Shemita* sanctity, and at the end of each day the bag lining the receptacle should be replaced. The old bag should be set aside (for several days) until the food begins to decay, at which time the bag may be thrown into a regular garbage bin. [264]
2. The *Shemita* remnants are placed in a bag, and then the bag is tied up and thrown into a regular garbage bin. It is recommended when using this procedure that a separate receptacle be designated for the *Shemita* remnants, and at the end of the day the bag lining the receptacle be removed, tied up and thrown into the regular garbage bin.

It is preferable to use the first solution, but the second solution may also be used even *lechatchila* (certainly in institutions or when the first solution presents some special difficulty), because indirect destruction of *Shemita* produce is permitted in such a case, and also because garbage bags usually do not tear even when compressed in a large garbage bin.

It should also be emphasized that while the first solution is preferable, it is better to follow the second solution and purchase large quantities of *Shemita* produce than to follow the first solution and restrict one's purchase of *Shemita* produce.

Suggestion: In order to enhance a person's sense of the sanctity of *Shemita* produce, it is recommended that one set aside an attractive receptacle and write on it "*Shemita* sanctity" (and not "*Shemita* garbage"), and use this to deposit (in a bag) *Shemita* remnants. In this way, it will not seem as if there are two garbage pails, one for ordinary garbage and another for *Shemita* remnants. Rather, it will indicate **the great merit of eating produce that has *Shemita* sanctity** and the care taken for careful disposal of its remnants. (It is further suggested that this receptacle be placed on the counter in a dignified place, and not next to the ordinary garbage can.) [266]

Leftover salad: Whatever is left of a salad may be cast into the receptacle designated for *Shemita* produce. It is not necessary to separate out those portions that do not have *Shemita* sanctity (on *Shabbat* it is indeed forbidden to do this due to the prohibition of *borer* – sorting undesirable items away from desirable items in a mixture). [480]

Leftover soup: Even the broth of vegetable soup made with *Shemita* produce has *Shemita* sanctity, but the water used to boil potatoes does not have *Shemita* sanctity, because the water is not enhanced by the taste of the potatoes. There are those who are lenient and allow one to leave the leftover soup out of the refrigerator overnight, after which the soup is regarded as inedible, so that the soup may be thrown into an ordinary garbage can. A better solution, however, is to place the leftover soup into a sealed bag, and then throw the bag into the regular garbage. Similarly, if a *cholent is* made with potatoes or other vegetables that have *Shemita* sanctity, *Shemita* sanctity applies to the entire *cholent.* All of the leftovers may be placed in a sealed bag and thrown away into the regular garbage (in the cases of soup, *cholent* and the like, the bags may be thrown right away into the garbage, because in any event the leftovers will become spoiled within a few hours). In all cases, liquid leftovers should not be mixed with dry leftovers, to avoid directly causing the dry leftovers to spoil). [272]

Peels: It is permitted to throw peels that are not fit to be eaten, such as empty banana peels into a regular garbage can (once all the edible portions have been eaten).

Pits that still have bits of flesh of fruit attached to them: One should try to eat as much of the fruit as possible before discarding the pit. According to Rav Elyashiv, if bits of the flesh of the fruit remain attached to the pit, one may be lenient and discard the pit in the ordinary manner. Some are stringent and place such pits in the receptacle designated for *Shemita* produce. Accordingly, when such a receptacle is readily available, it is recommended that it be used, but when such a receptacle is not on hand, the pits may be thrown directly into the garbage. [274]

Leftovers that adhere to utensils: Pots and dishes with remnants of *Shemita* produce may be washed in the ordinary manner. [277]

Compost: *Shemita* remnants should not be thrown onto a compost heap if the top layer of compost has already begun to decompose. One may, however, cover the pile with a thin layer of sand or newspaper, and place the new *Shemita* remnants on top (so that it will be considered indirect destruction of the *Shemita* produce). Of course, the compost may only be used after the *Shemita* year, or during the *Shemita* year for preserving that which is already growing. The compost heap should not sit directly on the ground, but rather in the house or outside in a container. [544]

Feeding *Shemita* leftovers to animals: Leftovers that will not be eaten by people, especially several different leftovers that have already been mixed together, may be given to animals, especially if this is the common practice. One should not place such leftovers directly into the animal's mouth; rather they should be set down in front of the animal for the animal to eat on its own.

PREPARING *SHEMITA* PRODUCE IN AN IRREGULAR MANNER

In addition to the obligation to save *Shemita* remnants and leftovers, it is forbidden to divert *Shemita* produce from its ordinary manner of consumption. *Shemita* produce may be used, however, in any way that it is normally used by a large group of people. Therefore:

Cooking: It is permitted to cook any fruit or vegetable that is ordinarily cooked, but one may not cook something that people do not ordinarily cook (one may not cook watermelon that has *Shemita* sanctity). [280]

Squeezing: It is permitted to squeeze juice from fruit that is ordinarily used in that manner. Of course, even fruit that may be squeezed should be squeezed as thoroughly as possible, so as to minimize waste. [285]

Mashing: There is no problem with mashing *Shemita* produce with a fork or grating it with a grater. Pulverizing *Shemita* produce in a blender or creating a very liquid paste should be restricted to foods that are normally prepared in this manner. In any event, it is permitted to mash food for an infant, even if that food is not ordinarily mashed for an adult. [289]

RULES FOR EXCEPTIONAL USES FOR *SHEMITA* PRODUCE

In general, one should be careful not to use *Shemita* produce in an unusual manner. Therefore:

Medicine: It is forbidden to prepare medicines from *Shemita* produce; however medicines prepared from *Shemita* produce are not forbidden. *Shemita* produce may be used to prepare something that will be used both as a medicine for the ill and as food for the healthy. [292]

Laundry: *Shemita* produce may not be used for laundering. Accordingly, one should not remove stains with a lemon that has *Shemita* sanctity. [293]

***Havdala* wine**: When using *Shemita* wine, one should not fill the cup over the brim, so as not to waste the wine that spills out. This is only permitted if someone will drink the wine that spills onto the plate. In any event, one should not extinguish the *havdala* candle with *Shemita* wine, and at the *Pesach seder* one should not cast out drops of *Shemita* wine when enumerating the ten plagues. [278]

***Shemita* oil**: It is permitted to light *Shabbat* candles with oil that has *Shemita* sanctity. The *Posekim* disagree whether such oil may be used to light Chanuka candles. One should be stringent, but in a case of need (including financial need) one may be lenient. [521]

***Mishlo'ach manot* consisting of *Shemita* produce**: Leniency may be practiced; one who wishes to be stringent should make sure that his first set of *mishlo'ach manot* includes two items that do not have *Shemita* sanctity. [522]

The "four species" of *Sukkot* during the *Shemita* year:

According to most authorities, an *etrog* that is available for *Sukkot* of the *Shemita* year does not have *Shemita* sanctity. It is preferable, however, that the *etrog* be picked during the sixth year, in which case it certainly does not have *Shemita* sanctity.

An *etrog* that is available for *Sukkot* of the eighth year does have *Shemita* sanctity, even if it was picked in the eighth year (it is permitted to use such an *etrog*, but not to do business with it).

According to most authorities, the other species – *lulav, hadas* and *arava* – do not have *Shemita* sanctity. [517]

A person who uses *Shemita* produce in the ordinary manner and saves *Shemita* remnants and leftovers in the appropriate way fulfills the obligation to safeguard the *Shemita* sanctity of *Shemita* produce. While this demands special caution as well as familiarity with the available solutions, the effort is worthwhile and not as difficult as one might imagine. Moreover, such a person enjoys the great privilege of eating *Shemita* produce, strengthening Jewish agriculture in Eretz Yisrael and assisting in the observance of *Shemita* in the best possible manner.

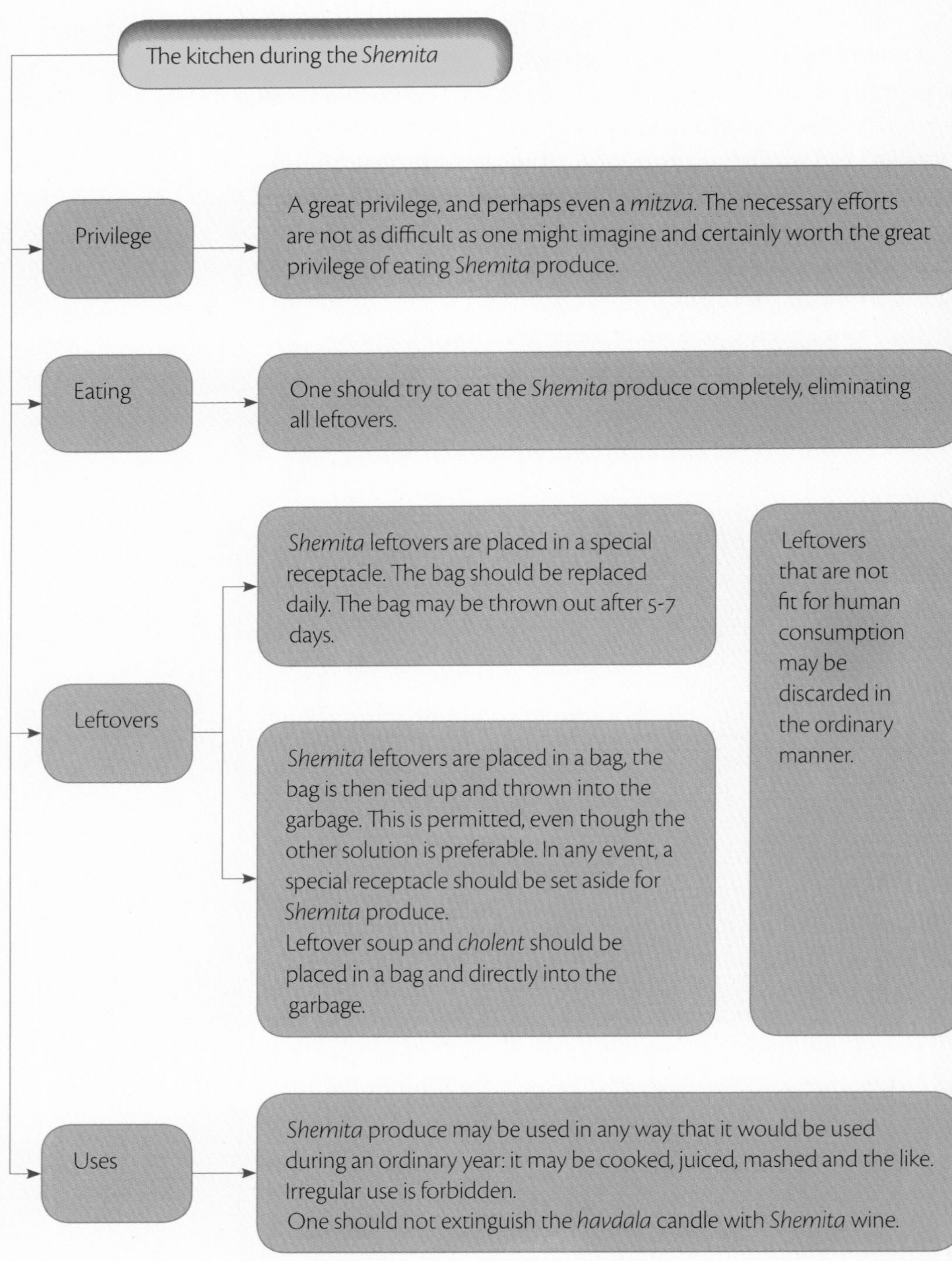
The kitchen during the *Shemita*
Privilege
A great privilege, and perhaps even a *mitzva*. The necessary efforts are not as difficult as one might imagine and certainly worth the great privilege of eating *Shemita* produce.
Eating
One should try to eat the *Shemita* produce completely, eliminating all leftovers.
Leftovers
Shemita leftovers are placed in a special receptacle. The bag should be replaced daily. The bag may be thrown out after 5-7 days.
Shemita leftovers are placed in a bag, the bag is then tied up and thrown into the garbage. This is permitted, even though the other solution is preferable. In any event, a special receptacle should be set aside for *Shemita* produce.
Leftover soup and *cholent* should be placed in a bag and directly into the garbage.
Leftovers that are not fit for human consumption may be discarded in the ordinary manner.
Uses
Shemita produce may be used in any way that it would be used during an ordinary year: it may be cooked, juiced, mashed and the like.
Irregular use is forbidden.
One should not extinguish the *havdala* candle with *Shemita* wine.

PURCHASING FRUITS AND VEGETABLES DURING *SHEMITA*

CHALLENGES AND POTENTIAL PROBLEMS INVOLVING THE PRODUCE ITSELF

1. ***Shamur*** ("guarded"): According to some authorities, if a field was not declared ownerless, the produce that grows there is forbidden. Rav Sh. Z. Auerbach wrote, however, that the common practice is to be lenient once the situation exists, though it should be avoided in the first place. [154]
2. ***Ne'evad*** ("worked"): According to some authorities, if forbidden labors were performed in a field in order to promote growth, the produce that grows there is forbidden. Rav Sh. Z. Auerbach wrote, however, that the common practice is to be lenient once the situation exists. [155]
3. ***Sefichim*** ("aftergrowth"): This problem applies solely to vegetables. The Rabbis prohibited vegetables that grow on their own during the *Shemita* year for fear that people would plant vegetables in secret and later claim that the vegetables had grown on their own. This prohibition does not apply during the first few weeks of the year when the available vegetables could not have been planted during the *Shemita* year. A table has been appended to this volume listing the time from which one must be concerned about the prohibition of *sefichim* for different species. The prohibition of *sefichim* does not apply to vegetables grown by a gentile, or in places that did not return to Israel's possession after the return from the Babylonian exile (even though they are part of Eretz Yisrael), such as in the Southern Arava. In addition, the prohibition does not apply to vegetables grown indoors in containers. [303]

CHALLENGES AND POTENTIAL PROBLEMS IN PURCHASES

1. **Handing over *Shemita* money to an *am ha-aretz*** (a person

who is not scrupulous in his observance of the commandments): When one purchases *Shemita* produce, *Shemita* sanctity applys to the purchase money. Therefore, in order to avoid violating the prohibition of "putting a stumbling block before the blind," (causing a fellow Jew to "stumble" into a sin), *Shemita* produce may only be purchased from someone who will safeguard the sanctity of the money received in payment for the produce. *Shemita* sanctity does not apply to the purchase money if payment is made on credit, with a check (preferably marked as non-negotiable or post-dated even for a day), with a credit card, or through *havla'a* (indirect payment for one thing by paying more for something else). In such cases the problem of handing over *Shemita* money to an *am ha-aretz* does not arise. [320] [324]

In certain cases *Shemita* sanctity does not apply to the money, even when paying directly and with cash. Such cases include: buying *Otzar Bet Din* produce (since the money is paid not for the produce itself, but for the labor), imported produce, sixth-year produce, or vegetables grown on detached bedding in hothouses (such produce does not have *Shemita* sanctity), buying produce grown by a gentile, (such produce does not have *Shemita* sanctity, except for in Bnei Brak, where it is customary to be stringent in accordance with the *Chazon Ish*) and strictly speaking, buying *heter mechira* produce (because *Shemita* sanctity does not apply to the money, though, as a stringency, some people treat the money as having sanctity, in accordance with Rav Kook). In general practice, when a person purchases produce during the *Shemita* year, *Shemita* sanctity does not apply to the money, except for those who are stringent and treat gentile produce or *heter mechira* produce as having *Shemita* sanctity.

2. **Trading in *Shemita* produce**: One must not purchase *Shemita* produce in order to resell it. If the seller bought the produce from another person and resells it, the seller violates the prohibition to trade in *Shemita* produce, and the buyer

violates the prohibition to "put a stumbling block before the blind." This is a problem today primarily for those who assign *Shemita* sanctity to produce grown by a gentile. [338]

3. **Measuring *Shemita* produce**: It is forbidden to weigh or measure *Shemita* produce (according to most opinions, the prohibition only applies when the produce is measured for commercial purposes). Instead, the produce must be sold through estimation. [341]

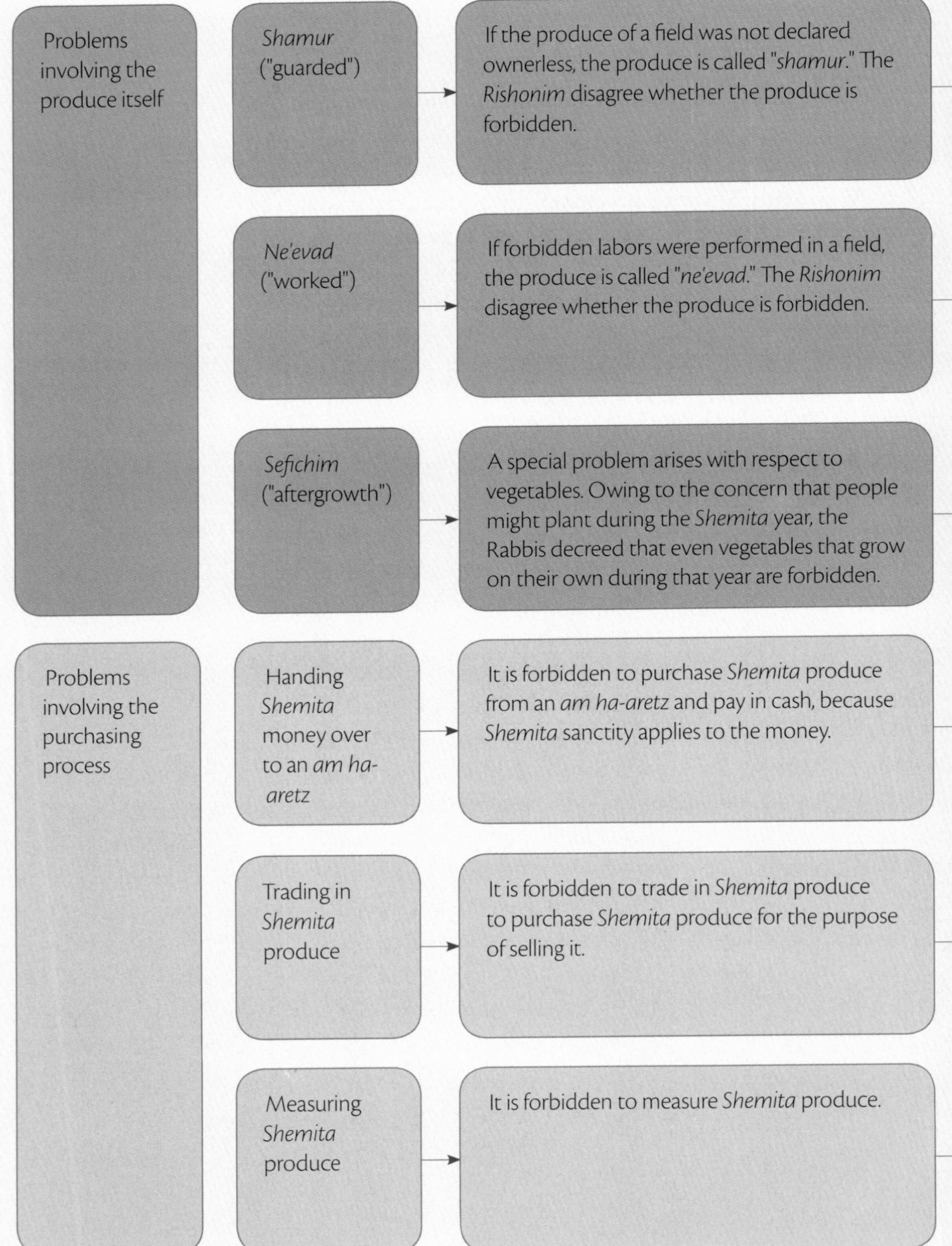
Problems involving the produce itself
Shamur ("guarded")
If the produce of a field was not declared ownerless, the produce is called "*shamur*." The *Rishonim* disagree whether the produce is forbidden.
Ne'evad ("worked")
If forbidden labors were performed in a field, the produce is called "*ne'evad*." The *Rishonim* disagree whether the produce is forbidden.
Sefichim ("aftergrowth")
A special problem arises with respect to vegetables. Owing to the concern that people might plant during the *Shemita* year, the Rabbis decreed that even vegetables that grow on their own during that year are forbidden.
Problems involving the purchasing process
Handing *Shemita* money over to an *am ha-aretz*
It is forbidden to purchase *Shemita* produce from an *am ha-aretz* and pay in cash, because *Shemita* sanctity applies to the money.
Trading in *Shemita* produce
It is forbidden to trade in *Shemita* produce to purchase *Shemita* produce for the purpose of selling it.
Measuring *Shemita* produce
It is forbidden to measure *Shemita* produce.

The custom is to be lenient.

The custom is to be lenient.

One must purchase from an alternative source during the period delineated in the table listing the dates of *sefichim*.

The problem does not arise when one buys on credit or pays with a check or charge card. Today, the problem rarely exists strictly speaking, but only for those practicing stringency..

There are various solutions to this problem, as will be seen below.

It is commonly accepted that the prohibition only applies when the produce is measured for commercial purposes.

SOLUTIONS FOR PURCHASING FRUITS AND VEGETABLES DURING *SHEMITA*

1. ***Otzar Bet Din***: A court has the authority to appoint agents to harvest produce on its behalf (usually it appoints the owner of the field himself), in which case the produce passes into the possession of the *Otzar Bet Din.* When following this procedure, it is permissible to harvest and market the produce in the ordinary manner. The money paid by the consumer is not for the produce itself, but rather for the **labor** invested by the workers. Accordingly, *Shemita* sanctity does not apply to the money, and there is no problem of trading in *Shemita* produce. It is customary practice to allow the regular weighing of such produce, though there are some who are stringent and sell the produce through estimation, so that it will be clear to all that the produce has *Shemita* sanctity. [346]

   This solution does not allow for planting, and therefore only works for fruit, and for vegetables during the first few months of the year (before the prohibition of *sefichim* goes into effect). *Otzar Bet Din* produce has *Shemita* sanctity.

2. ***Matza Menutak* (detached bedding)**: It was previously noted that strictly speaking it is permitted to plant in an *atitz she-eino nakuv* that is inside a house. Based on this, there are those who grow vegetables in bedding that is detached from the ground (in containers that rest on heavy polyethylene sheeting, or the like, that is spread out on the ground) inside a hothouse (defined as a "house" for these purposes). Rav Sh. Z. Auerbach accepted this solution, and, under certain conditions, Rav Elyashiv approved of it as well. This is an excellent solution and one should try to purchase vegetables grown in this manner. Such vegetables do not have *Shemita* sanctity. [104] [359]

   This solution places a heavy financial burden on the farmers (tens of thousands of shekels per acre); therefore, it is very important to purchase vegetables grown in this manner, both in order to encourage complete observance of *Shemita,* and in order to support Jewish agriculture in Eretz Yisrael.

3. ***Heter mechira***: The *heter mechira* is based on the assumption that the observance of *Shemita* in our time is only by rabbinic decree (because the majority of the Jewish people do not live in Eretz Yisrael, among other reasons) and is based on the assumption that land belonging to a gentile in Eretz Yisrael is not subject to *Shemita* sanctity, and a Jew is permitted to work such land. Some authorities have rejected this allowance, especially under current circumstances (Rav Kook only permitted planting when performed by gentiles; the sale might have no legal validity; it might be forbidden to sell land in Eretz Yisrael to a gentile even for this purpose). It should be noted that even according to those who reject the allowance, the main problem in using this solution relates to the farmers, while the problem is much less serious for the consumer who wishes to eat the produce. It should also be noted that the sale performed in anticipation of the current *Shemita* year of 5775 answers most of the objections raised against the *heter mechira* (planting performed by gentiles, legal force, sale performed directly by the Israel Lands Administration, consent established by way of a legal contract). [378] [408]

   Heter mechira produce does not have *Shemita* sanctity (for those who rely on the allowance), though it is proper to be stringent and treat such produce as if it has *Shemita* sanctity. [412]

   Even someone who does not accept the *heter mechira* may buy *heter mechira* fruits, or vegetables during the early months of *Shemita,* because they are not subject to the prohibition of *sefichim.* and it is customary to be lenient about *shamur* and *ne'evad.* There is also no problem of placing a stumbling block before the blind, or of assisting sinners, because the sellers who rely on the *heter mechira* operate on the basis of a halachic allowance issued by authoritative rabbis, even if the buyer does not rely on the *heter.* This was the ruling of both Rav Sh. Z. Auerbach and Rav M. Feinstein. [438]

4. **Produce grown by a gentile**: There is disagreement whether produce grown by a gentile has *Shemita* sanctity. The customary practice in Jerusalem and most of Eretz Yisrael is that such produce does not have *Shemita* sanctity. Accordingly, such produce can be purchased in the ordinary manner (it is not subject to the prohibition of trade and its remnants may be discarded as usual). According to the custom of Bnei Brak, produce grown by a gentile has *Shemita* sanctity, and therefore those who follow that custom must take care not to destroy such produce. The problem with this solution is that it strengthens gentile agriculture in Eretz Yisrael and it violates the spirit of the prohibition of "*lo techonem,*" not granting gentiles a stronghold in the land of Israel (one of the objections raised against the *heter mechira*) in its most profound sense. In addition, the gentile does not always own the field that is in his possession, and so the produce growing there is regarded as produce growing on Jewish land. Moreover, produce grown by Jews on Jewish land in contravention of the prohibitions of *Shemita* is sometimes marketed through gentiles. Vegetables that are purchased in ordinary years from gentiles may, however, be purchased from them during the *Shemita* year as well. [372]

WHICH SOLUTION SHOULD BE GIVEN PREFERENCE?

Rav Kook wrote that the *heter mechira* is certainly valid, but nevertheless we must continue to search for ways to observe the *mitzva* of *Shemita* without resorting to the *heter mechira*. Even today, the *heter mechira* is essential in many places, but there are other solutions that are halachically preferable. Therefore, if it is possible to purchase sixth year vegetables, *Otzar Bet Din* produce, produce grown on detached bedding in hothouses, or produce grown in the Southern Arava sold through the *heter mechira*, preference should be given to these alternatives. In any event, produce should not be purchased specially from gentiles if it is not bought in ordinary years, as this would strengthen the gentile hold on Eretz Yisrael. [421] [432]

Imported vegetables: When the planting of *heter mechira* fields is done by gentiles as Rav Kook demanded (today this is done routinely even in ordinary years), preference should be given to *heter mechira* produce over imported produce. [441]

Those who prefer not to eat *heter mechira* vegetables (once there is a problem of *sefichim*), but also do not want to weaken Jewish agriculture in Eretz Yisrael can often simply make slight changes in their eating habits (eating produce grown on detached bedding in hothouses, or vegetables that have a long growing season so that they are available through *Otzar Bet Din* or even *heter mechira* fruit) in order to solve these problems. In such a case, one may be lenient and buy a small amount of other vegetables grown by gentiles, making sure that the sum total of Jewish produce bought during the *Shemita* year is no less than the Jewish produce bought in regular years.

Of course, our goal should be that sufficient quantities of all kinds of vegetables grown by Jews, in accordance with the strictest halachic standards, be available. This goal is realizable today, but it requires the help and cooperation of world Jewry to finance hothouses, container farming, and other solutions. [443]

Eating in another person's house during the *Shemita* year: One may use the same *kashrut* standards as regular years. This is true even if the host eats *heter mechira* produce, while the guest does not, and even if the host only buys gentile produce, while the guest tries to buy nothing from gentiles. If the guest maintains that the *heter mechira* has no validity whatsoever (against our position), the host must explain to the guest that the produce served is *heter mechira*. In any event, the guest may use his host's dishes and does not have to *kasher* them. [546]

BUYING FLOWERS DURING *SHEMITA*

Annuals should be purchased with *kashrut* certification from the time that there is concern that the flowers may have been planted during *Shemita* (see the tables appended to this volume). [255] [318] [319]

Perennials (or annuals during the first few months of the year), such as roses and lilies, may be purchased in the usual manner, but it is preferable that they, too, be purchased with *kashrut* certification.

PURCHASING FRUITS AND VEGETABLES

[This table is for illustrative purposes only. For the precise times, see the tables for *Shemita* sanctity and the prohibition of *sefichim*.]

Fruit I – At the beginning of the *Shemita* year, fruits are not subject to the laws of *Shemita*. They may be purchased and handled in the usual way (the tables dealing with *Shemita* sanctity list the dates from which each type of fruit must be treated with *Shemita* sanctity).

Fruit II (beginning with the second half of the year) and **Vegetables II** (at the beginning of the year, as long as there is no problem of *sefichim*, based on the *sefichim* tables) – The order of preference is as follows: ***Otzar Bet Din*, sixth-year produce, produce grown on detached bedding, produce from the Southern Arava, produce from fields sold in the *heter mechira*** (even for one who does not rely on the *heter*).

Vegetables III – During the rest of the year (once there is a problem of *sefichim*) one should try to buy: ***Otzar Bet Din*, frozen or cold-stored sixth year produce, vegetables grown on detached bedding or in the Southern Arava.** When these alternatives are not available, preference should be given to *heter mechira* produce over produce grown by gentiles or imported produce, except for vegetables that are bought from gentiles even during ordinary years. [436]

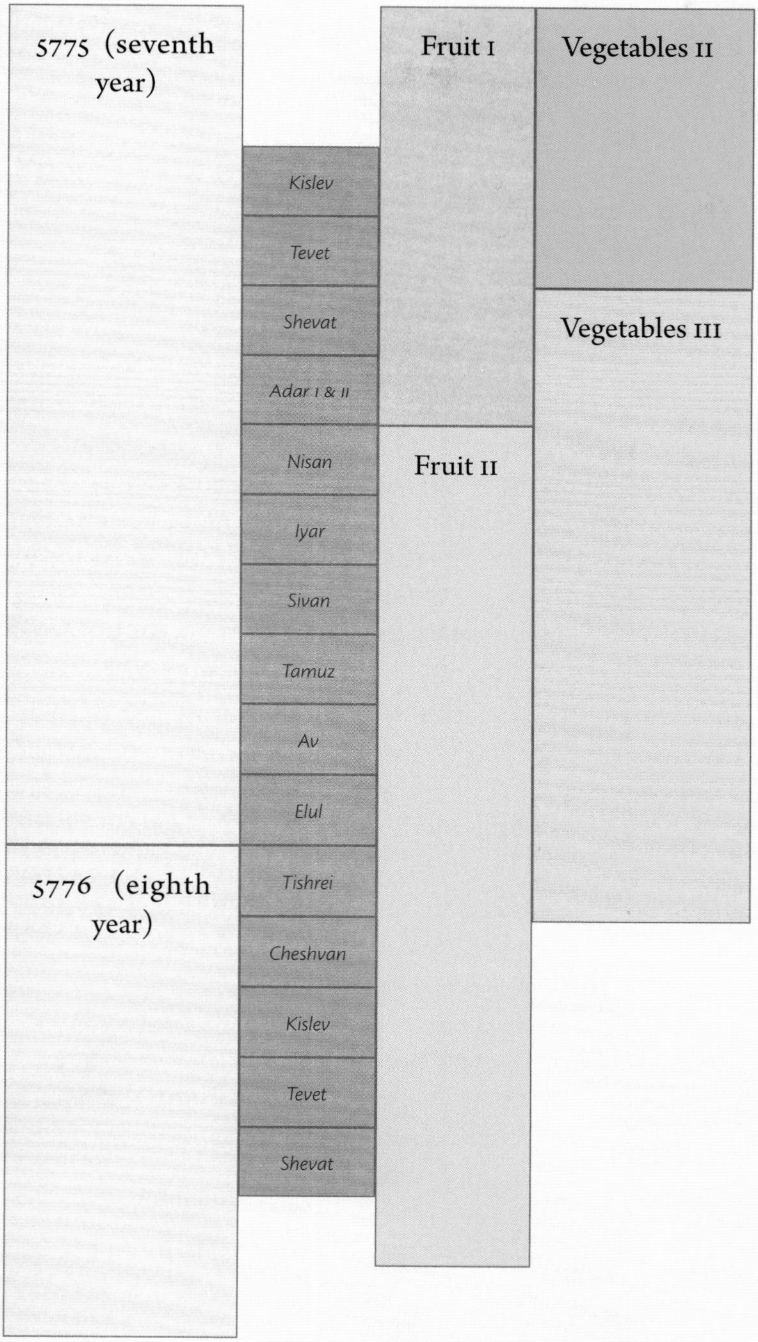

5775 (seventh year)

Kislev

Tevet

Shevat

Adar I & II

Nisan

Iyar

Sivan

Tamuz

Av

Elul

5776 (eighth year)

Tishrei

Cheshvan

Kislev

Tevet

Shevat

Fruit I

Fruit II

Vegetables II

Vegetables III

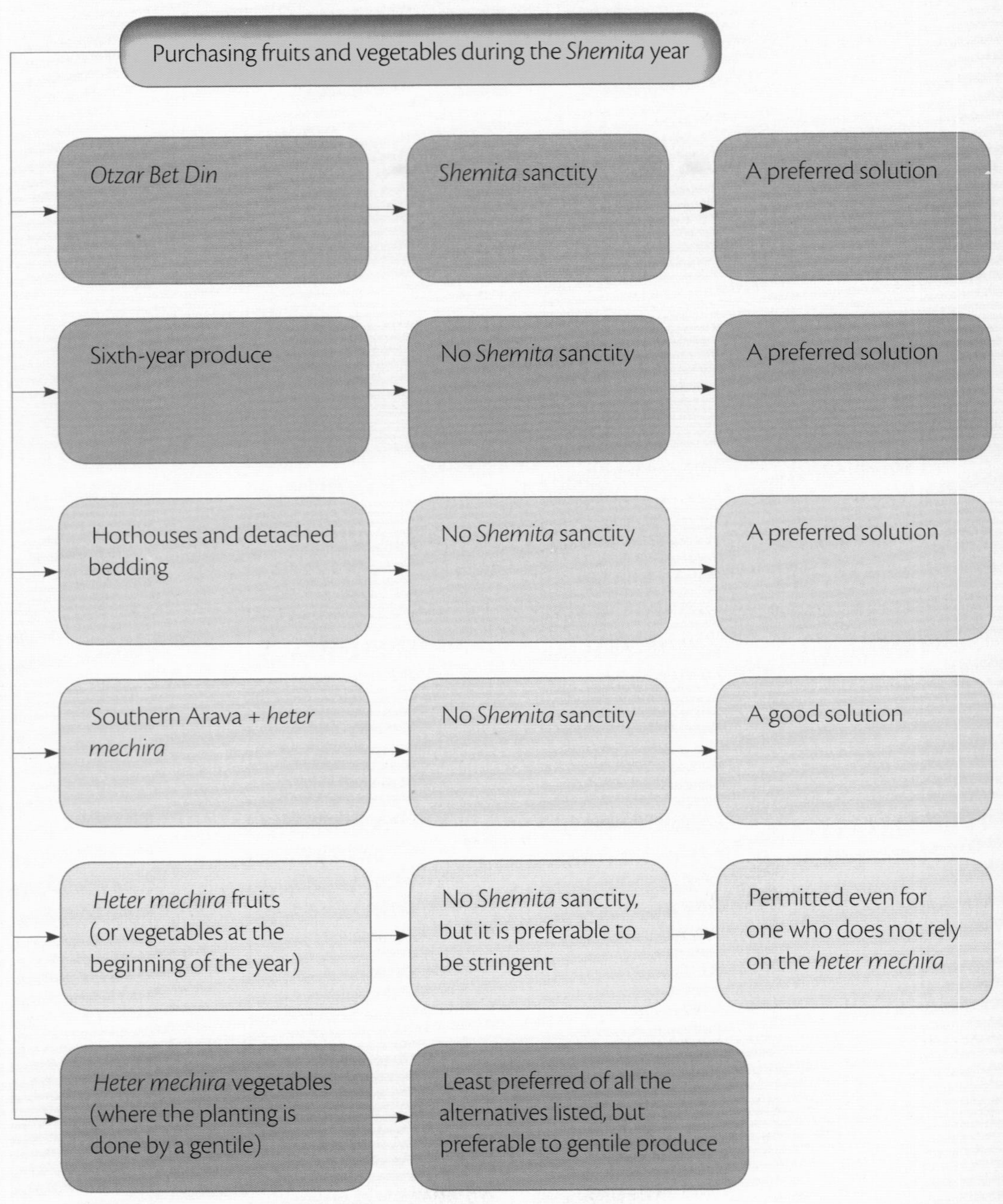
Purchasing fruits and vegetables during the *Shemita* year
Otzar Bet Din
Shemita sanctity
A preferred solution
Sixth-year produce
No *Shemita* sanctity
A preferred solution
Hothouses and detached bedding
No *Shemita* sanctity
A preferred solution
Southern Arava + *heter mechira*
No *Shemita* sanctity
A good solution
Heter mechira fruits (or vegetables at the beginning of the year)
No *Shemita* sanctity, but it is preferable to be stringent
Permitted even for one who does not rely on the *heter mechira*
Heter mechira vegetables (where the planting is done by a gentile)
Least preferred of all the alternatives listed, but preferable to gentile produce

BI'UR (REMOVAL) OF *SHEMITA* PRODUCE

Once produce of a particular species is no longer found in the field, the produce of that species in one's house is subject to the *mitzva* of *bi'ur*, "removal" (the *bi'ur* tables appended to this volume indicate when *bi'ur* must be performed with respect to each type of fruit and vegetable). Once the time of *bi'ur* arrives (toward the end of the *Shemita* year, or even in the eighth year), one must declare the produce that is in one's house ownerless in the presence of three people. It is preferable that one actually remove the produce from one's house, or at least outside one's front door. After declaring the produce ownerless, one may reacquire it.

If the time for *bi'ur* is in doubt, one should not reacquire the produce during the period in question. It is permissible, however, to bring the produce back inside one's house, and then reacquire the produce as needed. [552]

TERUMOT AND *MA'ASROT* DURING *SHEMITA*

Shemita produce is exempt from *terumot* and *ma'asrot*. Accordingly, *terumot* and *ma'asrot* are not set aside from *Otzar Bet Din* produce, or from produce that grows in one's own garden.

As for **produce grown by gentiles,** if the *gemar melacha* (completion of harvest and ingathering) was performed by a Jew, *terumot* and *ma'asrot* should be set aside without a blessing. This, however, is a rare phenomenon for the individual consumer, except for one who buys grapes from a gentile in order to make wine. If the *gemar melacha* was performed by a gentile, as is the case with most produce purchased from gentiles, there is no need to set aside *terumot* and *ma'asrot.*

As for ***heter mechira* produce,** *terumot* and *ma'asrot* should be set aside without a blessing. Strictly speaking, one should set aside *ma'aser sheni*, but it is preferable to set aside *ma'aser ani* as well. One should set aside *ma'aser sheni*, and then say: "If *ma'aser ani* must be set aside, then the portion set aside as *ma'aser sheni* should be *ma'aser ani*."

As for **produce grown on detached bedding,** *terumot* and *ma'asrot* should be set aside without a blessing.

As opposed to the laws of *terumot* and *ma'asrot,* the laws of *orla* and *reva'i* apply as usual to *Shemita* produce. [525]

SHEMITAT KESAFIM – RELEASE OF DEBTS

There is a *mitzva* to release all debts during the seventh year. According to most *Rishonim,* the negative precept of "he shall not exact," precluding collection of debts, goes into effect at the end of the *Shemita* year. The Rosh, however, maintains that the prohibition goes into effect already at the beginning of the *Shemita* year.

If the debtor wishes to repay his debt after the *Shemita* year, the creditor must say to him, "I remit it." If the debtor says, "All the same, take it," the Sages view this as commendable conduct.

Which debts are remitted?

Only debts that are subject to collection before the end of the *Shemita* year are cancelled by the *Shemita* year. A debt that will only become due after the *Shemita* year is not cancelled. [450]

Bank accounts: A term deposit that will only become due after the *Shemita* year is not subject to cancellation. If it becomes due before or during the *Shemita* year, it should be subject to cancellation. Many authorities, however, maintain that it is not subject to cancellation because, according to them, a debt that does not stem from a loan is not cancelled, and bank deposits from Jewish banks are received by way of the *"heter iska,"* recasting the loan as an investment, and an investment is not subject to this law. It is customary practice, however, to include bank deposits in one's *pruzbol* (see below). [456]

Wages and merchandise bought on credit: Strictly speaking, these debts are not subject to release because they do not stem from loans, but since there are those who maintain that they are cancelled, a *pruzbol* should be made for them.

Charity funds: Charity funds are not subject to the laws of release. [456]

Pruzbol: By writing a *pruzbol,* one hands over one's debts to a court, and thus they are not subject to the laws of release (it is preferable to write a *pruzbol* for bank deposits as well). After writing a *pruzbol,* some have the custom to grant a loan, even a small one, in order to fulfill the *mitzva* of release. The *pruzbol* should be drawn up before the end of the *Shemita* year (preferably toward the end of *Elul* in order to include all loans that will become due during the *Shemita* year). Some take into consideration the view of the Rosh and draw up a *pruzbol* before the beginning of the *Shemita* year as well. The text of the *pruzbol* may be found in the chapter dealing with *Shemitat kesafim.* [463]

A woman approached me with the question of what she should do at her daughter's Bat Mitzva celebration. Would it be better to use *Otzar Bet Din* produce that has *Shemita* sanctity, or would it be preferable to avoid such produce, so as not to become entangled in the problems of *Shemita* leftovers?

I told her that it would be better to buy *Otzar Bet Din* produce that has *Shemita* sanctity, and to instruct the waiters at the affair to bag all the leftover salads before disposing of them. Even if it they fail to fully comply with these instructions, there is good reason to say that no prohibition has been violated (see my article in *Techumin* 27, and below, p. 487).

I then added another point. Rather than worrying about *Shemita* sanctity, the entire event can be turned into a moving experience, in which all of the guests share in the special sanctity of the *Shemita* produce. A small bowl lined with a plastic bag is placed in the center of each table. An announcement is then made at the beginning of the meal that all those present will have the good fortune of enjoying food endowed with *Shemita* sanctity (and this is an opportunity that, unfortunately, many people are not afforded). This being the case, special steps must be taken to handle the produce in accordance with that special sanctity. The guests are therefore asked that at the end of the meal they place their leftover salads in the special bowl. In this way all will merit to eat of sanctified produce and preserve its sanctity in the required manner.

In the case of a Bat Mitzva celebration, the affair can open with a craft project for the girls, in which they decorate plastic bowls with the words "*Shemita* Sanctity." These bowls can then serve as centerpieces on the tables (or be taken home by each of the girls and used there).

We must not fear the *Shemita* year. On the contrary, we must rejoice in anticipation of its arrival. We must rejoice in the fact that we have merited to eat *Shemita* produce, that we have merited to preserve *Shemita* sanctity, and that we have merited to see this sanctity reaching ever wider sectors of the Jewish people and parts of Eretz Yisrael. By understanding the unique sanctity and privilege that we attain once every seven years, we will hopefully merit to draw closer to God and return to the fresh and natural dimensions of our inner selves.

THE AGRICULTURAL LAWS OF *SHEMITA*

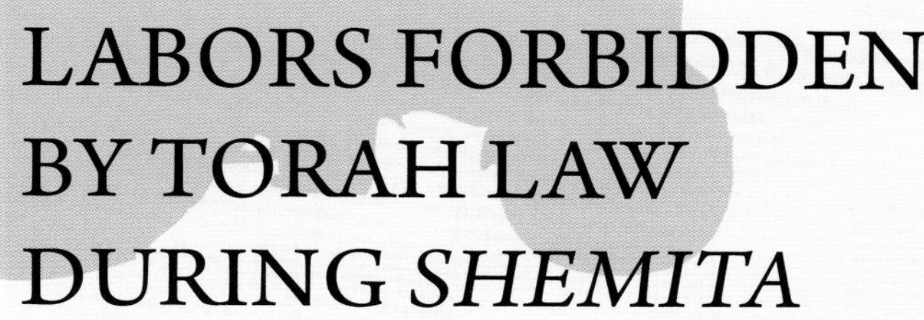

LABORS FORBIDDEN BY TORAH LAW DURING *SHEMITA*

A year of rest is essential for the nation and for the land! A year of peace and tranquility, free of oppression and domination ... No private property or exclusive privilege, Divine calm resting upon all filled with the breath of life ... Man returns to his invigorated nature ... a spirit of holiness and nobility is poured over all: "It shall be a year of rest for the land – a Sabbath for the Lord."

(Rav Avraham Yitzchak Kook, introduction to Shabbat ha-Aretz)

1. And the Lord spoke to Moshe on Mount Sinai, saying:
2. Speak to the children of Israel, and say to them, When you come to the land which I give you, then shall the land keep a Sabbath to the Lord.
3. Six years you shall plant your field, and six years you shall prune your vineyard, and gather in its fruit.
4. But in the seventh year shall be a Sabbath of solemn rest for the land, a Sabbath for the Lord: you shall neither plant your field, nor prune your vineyard.
5. That which grows of its own accord of your harvest you shall not harvest, nor gather the grapes of your undressed vine; for it shall be a year of rest for the land.
6. And the Sabbath produce of the land shall be food for you; for you, and for your servant, and for your maid, and for your hired servant, and for your stranger that sojourns with you.
7. And for your cattle, and for the beast in your land, shall all its increase be food.

(*Vayikra 25:1–7*)

But the seventh year you shall let it rest and lie fallow; that the poor of your people may eat: and what they leave, the beasts of the field shall eat; in like manner you shall deal with your vineyard, and with your olive grove.

(*Shemot 23:11*)

Six days you shall work, but on the seventh day you shall rest: in plowing and in harvest you shall rest.

(*Shemot 34:21*)

The Talmud derives the various prohibitions of the *Shemita* year from these verses. We will briefly outline these prohibitions:

1. "You shall not plant your field" – the prohibition of planting.
2. "You shall not prune your vineyard" – the prohibition of pruning (removal of branches so that the grapevine will produce more fruit).
3. "That which grows of its own accord of your harvest you shall not harvest" – the prohibition of harvesting.
4. "You shall not gather the grapes of your undressed vine" – the prohibition of gathering grapes.
5. "And the Sabbath produce of the land shall be food for you" – The Torah permits produce for purposes of eating, with three qualifications from the Talmud:
   A. To eat and not for trade (the prohibition to do business with *Shemita* produce).
   B. To eat and not to destroy (the sanctity of *Shemita* produce).
   C. To eat – allowance to harvest for the sake of eating (but not in the ordinary manner of reaping).
6. "But the seventh year you shall let it rest and lie fallow" – the obligation to declare the produce ownerless.
7. "In plowing and in harvest you shall rest" – the prohibition of plowing.
8. "And for your cattle, and for the beast in your land, shall all its increase be food" – the obligation of bi'ur, "removal" of *Shemita* produce.

The Torah prohibits two general categories of working the land. The first category, the prohibition of causing plant growth, includes *zeri'a*, growing a new plant, and *zemira*, pruning, or stimulating the growth of an existing plant. The second category, prohibitions relating to harvesting, includes *ketzira* (reaping), a general term for the harvest of annuals, meaning vegetables and grain, and *betzira* (gathering), a general term for the harvest of perennials, such as fruit.

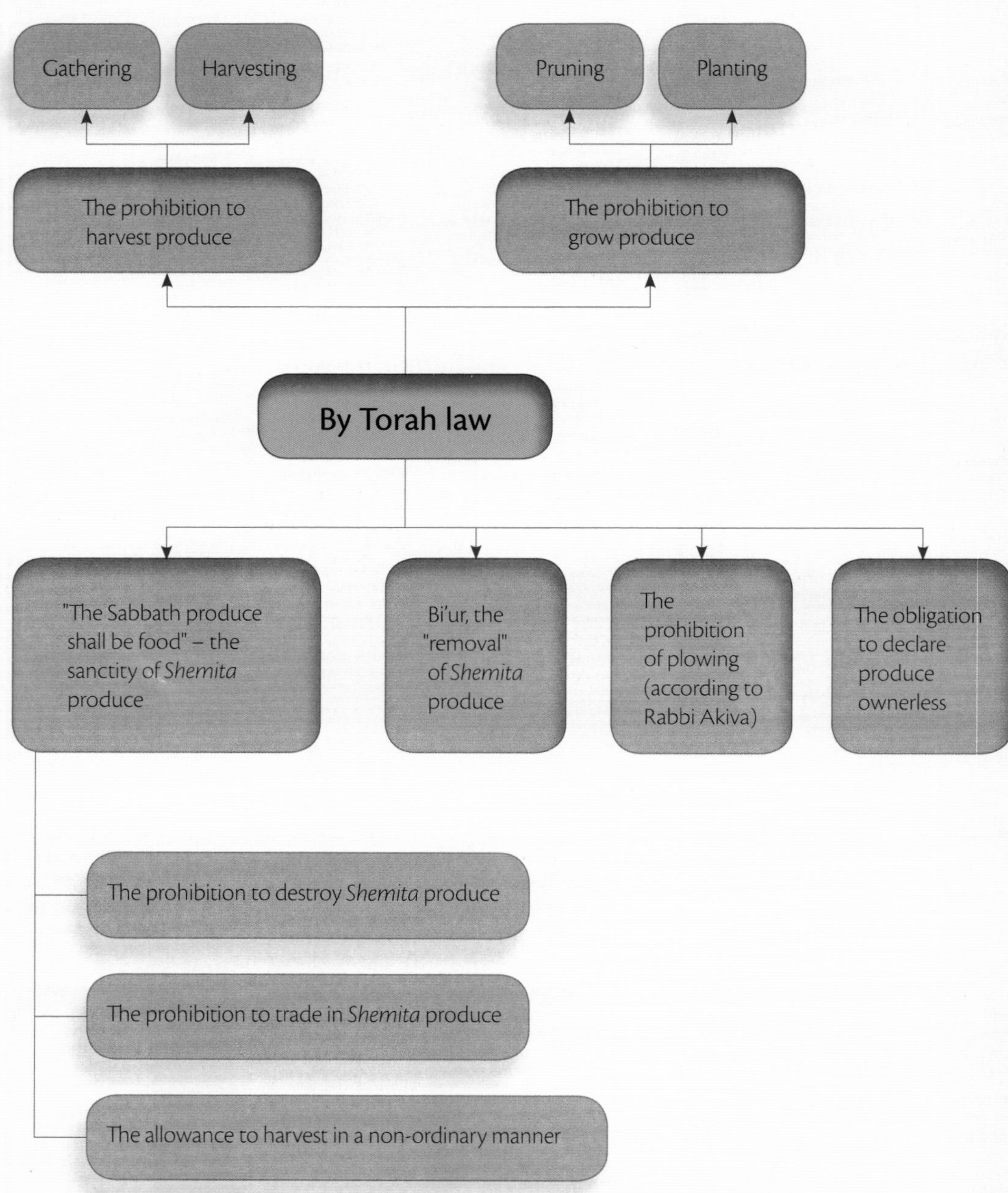
Gathering
Harvesting
Pruning
Planting
The prohibition to harvest produce
The prohibition to grow produce
By Torah law
"The Sabbath produce shall be food" – the sanctity of Shemita produce
Bi'ur, the "removal" of Shemita produce
The prohibition of plowing (according to Rabbi Akiva)
The obligation to declare produce ownerless
The prohibition to destroy Shemita produce
The prohibition to trade in Shemita produce
The allowance to harvest in a non-ordinary manner

THE PROHIBITION TO GROW PRODUCE

PLANTING VEGETATION

"But in the seventh year shall be a Sabbath of solemn rest for the land, a Sabbath for the Lord: **you shall not sow your field**."
(Vayikra 25:4)

Is one permitted to plant ornamental trees during the *Shemita* year?

The Torah clearly forbids the planting of seeds of edible plants during the *Shemita* year[1]. Does this prohibition extend to plants that are inedible? On the one hand, the Torah does not explicitly limit the prohibitions of *Shemita* to edible plants, but rather states generally "you shall not plant your field." On the other hand, the specific examples that the Torah offers are all of edible plants: "you shall not prune your vineyard;" "that which grows of its own accord of your harvest you shall not reap, nor gather the grapes of your undressed vine;" and the like.

A non-fruit bearing tree

The answer to this question depends upon the nature of the prohibition of planting during the *Shemita* year. If the prohibition of planting is a general prohibition against **working of the land itself during the *Shemita* year**, there should be no difference between fruit-bearing plants and non-fruit-bearing plants. On the other hand, if the prohibition of planting is based on a prohibition of **deriving benefit from the land** during the *Shemita* year, it is very possible that only eating is regarded as a forbidden "benefit" during the *Shemita* year. In that case, the prohibition of planting should be limited to edible plants.

The ***Talmud Yerushalmi*** (*Shevi'it 4:4*) records the view of Rabban Shimon ben Gamliel that the planting of trees that do not bear fruit is not forbidden during the *Shemita* year:

> Rabban Shimon ben Gamliel says: A tree that bears no fruit may be planted during the *Shemita* year.

1. What aspect of planting did the Torah forbid when it said that planting during the *Shemita* year is prohibited? Is the very act of planting forbidden, or does the prohibition lie in causing a seed to take root in the ground? This question has practical ramifications regarding seeds that are planted at the very end of the seventh year, but take root only in the eighth year. The same question arises with respect to seeds that are planted at the very end of the sixth year, but take root only in the seventh year, with, presumably, an opposite result. This question will be addressed more fully in the appendix.

Rav Shlomo Sirillo explains (*ad loc.*):

> The Torah forbids [planting] only in the case of fruit trees, which are similar to "you shall not plant your field," for "planting" refers to edible plants, similar to "you shall not prune," which is in the vineyard.

Clearly, according to Rabban Shimon ben Gamliel, the prohibition of planting applies only to edible plants.

The Rambam (*Hilchot Shemita ve-Yovel 1:5*), on the other hand, rules that the prohibition of planting applies even to plants that are not fit to be eaten:

> Even a tree that bears no fruit may not be planted during the *Shemita* year.

The Rambam's ruling is problematic, because it contradicts an explicit statement in the *Yerushalmi*. Apparently, because the *Yerushalmi* recorded the opinion that allows planting trees that bear no fruit only in the name of Rabban Shimon ben Gamliel, the Rambam understood the *Yerushalmi* to imply that the Sages disagree. According to the Sages, even the planting of trees that bear no fruit is forbidden, and the Rambam ruled in accordance with this view[2] (*Kesef Mishneh and Mahari Kurkus, ad loc.*). Since the Rambam

2. According to the Rambam, is this prohibited by Torah law or only by rabbinic decree? The *Aruch ha-Shulchan (he-Atid* 19:5) considers this to be merely a rabbinic decree, lest people come to plant trees that bear fruit (so too *Torat ha-Shemita, Tosefet Shevi'it*, no. 9, in the name of Rav Tzvi Pesach Frank). According to Rash Sirillo (*Shevi'it 4:4*), if planting trees is biblically forbidden (see below), then even planting trees that bear no fruit would be forbidden by Torah law. This is also the view of the *Chazon Ish* (*Shevi'it* 19:20, s.v. *u-ba-Tosafot*) and *Responsa Shevet ha-Levi* (III, 158, 5).

משנה תורה

הוא

היד החזקה

להנשר הגדול רבינו משה בן מיימון זצ"ל

עם שלשים וחמש הוספות כפי שנדפסו בדפוסי ווארשה־ווילנה

ועתה במהדורה ישראלית זו הוספנו עוד

שתים־עשרה הוספות חדשות וחשובות

מהן כמה ספרים גדולים מכתבי יד ודפוסים עתיקים כפי שמבואר בשער הבא

הוצאת ספרים פרדס, ישראל

ירושלים

THE RAMBAM

Rabbi Moshe ben Maimon was born in 1138, and lived in Spain and Egypt. He mastered all realms of Torah study and is regarded as one of the greatest medieval halachic authorities. His most important works include: *Mishneh Torah – Yad ha-Chazaka*; *Sefer ha-Mitzvot*; commentary to the Mishna; and *Guide for the Perplexed*. The Rambam had profound influence on the entire world of halacha.

rules that the prohibition of planting applies even to trees that bear no fruit. From this it seems that he understands the prohibitions of *Shemita* as stemming from a sweeping prohibition to work the land. Accordingly, the prohibition of planting applies even to plants that provide man with no material benefit whatsoever[3].

In practice, the halacha follows the position of the Rambam[4]. In line with this ruling, the prohibition of pruning, which is similar to planting in that it stimulates growth, also applies to trees that bear no fruit.

RABBI SHLOMO SIRILIO – RASH SIRILIO

Rabbi Shlomo Sirillo was born in Spain shortly before the expulsion from that country in 5252 (1492). He moved with his parents to Turkey, and later to Tzefat, finally settling in Jerusalem. His commentary on the *Talmud Yerushalmi* (on the order of *Zera'im* and tractate *Shekalim*) is considered one of the most important works on that Talmud. He also authored a book dealing with the *mitzvot* of *Shemita* and *bi'ur* (removal of *Shemita* produce).

SANCTITY OF *SHEMITA* IN TREES WHICH BEAR NO FRUIT

The Talmud (*Sukka 40a*) concludes that the special sanctity of *Shemita* does not apply to trees that bear no fruit (we shall expand upon this issue later):

> Wood does not have *Shemita* sanctity. As it has been taught: Leaves of reeds and leaves of the vine which have been piled up for storage in the field, if they were gathered for [animal] food, they have *Shemita* sanctity, but if they were gathered for firewood, they do not have *Shemita* sanctity.

According to the Talmud, while trees that bear no fruit are subject to the prohibitions of planting and pruning, they are not subject to the prohibitions of reaping and gathering since they do not have *Shemita* sanctity. Similarly, there is no obligation to declare them ownerless as one would have to do with normal *Shemita* produce. (The connection between the sanctity of *Shemita* produce, the

3. Even according to this understanding, we must deal with the issue of whether the *Shemita* prohibitions are directed to man or to the land (see below). Even if the *Shemita* prohibitions stem from the very working of the land, regardless of whether any benefit is derived from it, we must still examine whether the prohibition to work the land stems from **human actions** or from **the land's need to rest.**

4. In general, trees that bear no fruit are planted for one of two reasons: for lumber, or to serve as a natural fence. Planting trees that bear no fruit for lumber is certainly forbidden during the *Shemita* year. With respect to planting trees to serve as a fence, the ***Tosefta*** states (*Shevi'it 3:19*): "And similarly Rabban Shimon ben Gamliel said: A tree that bears no fruit may be planted during the *Shemita* year to serve as a fence." Do the Sages disagree with this ruling, and according to the Rambam should the law be decided in accordance with their view? ***Responsa Maharal Diskin*** (*27, 23*) allows such planting, but **Rav Kook** (*Shabbat ha-Aretz 1, 5; and Kuntrus Acharon*), the ***Sefer ha-Shemita*** (*p. 18*), and the *Chazon Ish* (*19, 20, s.v. be-Tosafot*) forbid it.

obligation to renounce ownership, and the prohibitions of reaping and gathering will be discussed in the chapter dealing with the sanctity of *Shemita* produce).

Rav Sh. Z. Auerbach (*Ma'adanei Aretz, 2*) rules accordingly that during the *Shemita* year one is permitted to cut branches for the *sekhakh* of a *sukka* and to cut willow branches for *aravot* of the *lulav* in the ordinary manner, for the prohibition of reaping during the *Shemita* year does not apply to trees that do not bear fruit. Rav Sh. Z. Auerbach adds (*Responsa Minchat Shlomo, 1, 51*) that even palm branches may be harvested in the ordinary manner for the *mitzva* of *lulav*, because they too have no *Shemita* sanctity. Though palm branches are fit for animal consumption, and as such should be bound by the *Shemita* prohibitions, Rav Sh. Z. Auerbach explains that since they are ordinarily discarded, they have no importance and are not regarded as food:

> The words, "shall be food for you," relate to things that are regularly eaten, and not to things that are ordinarily discarded. The words "shall be food for you" do not apply to things that in all the other years are regarded as dust of the earth ... And all the more so, a *lulav*, which is not food, in our time should be treated like wood, which from the very outset was never subject to any sanctity.

USING A MECHANICAL SEEDER

Is one permitted to use a mechanical seeder during the *Shemita* year? Is sowing by way of gerama, "causation" permitted?

Rav Tzvi Pesach Frank (*Responsa Har Tzvi, Orach Chayyim, I, 208*) writes that although planting during the *Shemita* year is forbidden, it may be permitted to plant using a machine. In his view, the Torah prohibition might be limited to planting by hand, which was the sole method of planting at the time that the Torah was given, and therefore planting via machine might be permitted (at least by Torah law). Accordingly, only hand planting is regarded as a "principal" category of forbidden labor (*av melakha*), whereas planting by machine is deemed a "derivative" category of labor (*tolada*), which is not forbidden during the *Shemita* year. (We shall discuss the relationship between *avot* and *toladot* with respect to *Shemita* in the chapter on the categories of labor that are forbidden rabbinically during the *Shemita* year):

Planting by hand

A planting machine

> For a long time I have wondered about the labor of planting as it has been practiced in recent times – planting by way of

RAV TZVI PESACH FRANK (HAR TZVI)

Rav Frank was born in 1873 in Kovno, Lithuania, and studied in the yeshivot of Telz and Slobodka. He was appointed as a member of Supreme Rabbinical Court in Jerusalem, and later served as the Chief Rabbi of that city for many years. Rav Frank was instrumental in the establishment of the rabbinate of Israel, and it he who brought Rav Kook to accept the position of Chief Rabbi. He was a prolific writer who dealt with many contemporary halachic issues, particularly those connected to the special commandments that apply only in Eretz Yisrael. His works include: *Responsa Har Tzvi*, *Mikra'ei Kodesh*, and *Mikdash Melech*.

an animal that pulls a perforated wagon filled with seed, and the field is sown while the animal crosses the field. Could one suggest that this is not an *av* of forbidden labor, but only a *tolada,* and with respect to the *Shemita* year, not be forbidden by Torah law?

In contrast to Rav Frank, the ***Chazon Ish*** (*27, 1; 36, 2*) concludes that even planting via machine is forbidden during the *Shemita* year. The *Chazon Ish* finds proof in a talmudic passage in *Makkot* (*21b*) that states that one who plows with an ox is liable even though it is the animal that actually performs the forbidden action. According to the *Chazon Ish,* the law regarding planting with a tractor is the same as the law governing plowing with an ox.[5]

This may be applied to the case of plowing with a tractor that is powered by steam or electricity, and a person guides it according to the furrows of the field. Even if no human force is exerted in the plowing itself, the machine is a facilitator of human labor. Setting the machine in the field and guiding its parts for the purpose of plowing is the labor of plowing, which if performed on Shabbat, renders one liable for a sin-offering [for a Shabbat violation].

5. The *Chazon Ish* (25, 38) adds that since a mechanical seeder does not change the manner of planting in any essential way, but only changes the planting process, the planting is regarded as planting that is forbidden by Torah law. Moreover, since the planting machine is operated by man, what it does is attributed to the person himself, and thus it is clearly subject to the Torah prohibition: "Something is only deemed a *tolada* of the labor when there is a change in the form of the labor ... But when there is no change in the form of the planting or in the form of the plowing, only that the person prepared a series of steps which separate his own action and the planting itself, we have only to discuss whether or not [the planting] is regarded as his action, and if it is regarded as his action, it is included in the *av* of planting.

PLANTING BY WAY OF *GERAMA* (INDIRECT CAUSATION)

We saw above that the *Acharonim* disagree about planting using a machine during the *Shemita* year. In practice, the leading contemporary *Poskim* tend to forbid this type of planting as well, in accordance

WHAT IS A *GERAMA* DEVICE?

A *gerama* switch (developed by the Zomet Institute for use in necessary situations on Shabbat) is equipped with a mechanism that automatically checks for changes in the system every minute. If such a switch is attached to a sowing machine, then when the operator presses the seeding button, nothing happens; a minute later, however, when the system checks itself, it discovers the change and executes the sowing.

with the view of the *Chazon Ish*. There may, however, be another way to permit planting during the *Shemita* year – namely, by way of a device that operates on the principle of *gerama*, indirect causation. Using this method, the person operating the machine does not plant the seeds directly, but rather pushes a button that causes a certain chain reaction that causes the actual planting. With respect to *Shabbat* law, performing a forbidden labor by way of *gerama* is not forbidden by the Torah ("You shall not perform any manner of work" – [direct] performance [of the work] is forbidden, but indirect causation is permitted) (*Shabbat* 120b). What is the law regarding *Shemita*?

Gerama outlet

As we saw in the beginning of the chapter, the Torah forbids certain labors during the *Shemita* year – "you shall not plant," and "you shall not prune," and the like – and also issues a general command that the land must rest: "then shall the land keep a Sabbath to the Lord" and "it shall be a year of rest for the land." **Why does the Torah add a positive requirement to rest in addition to the forbidden labors?** The simplest answer is that the Torah added this positive requirement so that a person who works his land during the *Shemita* year would transgress both a negative commandment and a positive commandment. But it is also possible to understand that the positive obligations to rest add another level of prohibitions to the *Shemita* year. It is possible that the negative commandments, "you shall not plant," and "you shall not prune," relate to **the person's work**, whereas the commandment that "then shall the land keep a Sabbath to the Lord" teaches that there is also an obligation that **the land itself must rest**! (This obligation that the land must rest would fall upon the person to whom the land belongs.)[6]

6. See the appendix at the end of this volume, where we expand on this issue.

One practical ramification of this analysis relates to **planting by way of *gerama***. If the *Shemita* prohibitions are all personal obligations, then work that is performed indirectly, by way of *gerama*, should be permitted. If, however, an additional prohibition exists during the *Shemita* year that mandates rest for the land, then it stands to reason that a person must ensure that his land is not worked, even indirectly. Even planting in an indirect manner would violate the prohibition of "then shall the land keep a Sabbath to the Lord."

In practice, the *Aruch ha-Shulchan* (*he-Atid, 19:6*) seems to rule leniently regarding indirect sowing. **Rav Frank** (*Har Tzvi, Zera'im, II, 32-34*) responds to the statement of the *Aruch ha-Shulchan* and links the issue of indirect sowing to the analysis presented above:

> Even if you say that *gerama* is not included in the negative commandment [of "you shall not plant"], because the Torah forbids [only] the act of planting, and here he is merely the indirect cause [of planting], one can still claim that it violates the positive commandment of "then shall the land keep a Sabbath," even though it is only the indirect cause [of planting] ... For one is required to ensure that his field rests, so that even if he is only the indirect cause of his land being worked ... he has not fulfilled the positive commandment of "then shall the land keep a Sabbath."

In practice, we are generally stringent about indirect planting,[7] though there are times when we accept the potential leniency in conjunction with other factors that permit leniency (see, for example, regarding the *heter mechira* [below, p. 411]).

7. Rav Frank appears to incline toward leniency: "And especially since we hold that *Shemita* today is only by rabbinic law, there is room to say that with respect to sowing by way of an animal that pulls a [perforated] wagon, it is an uncertainty regarding a rabbinic law, and therefore we are lenient." Nevertheless, the challenges raised by the *Chazon Ish* (cited above) regarding the method of planting by *gerama* still present difficulties. See also *Shemita Mamlakhtit* (ed. 2000, chap. 23).

Rav Goren checking *gerama* plowing in *Shemita*

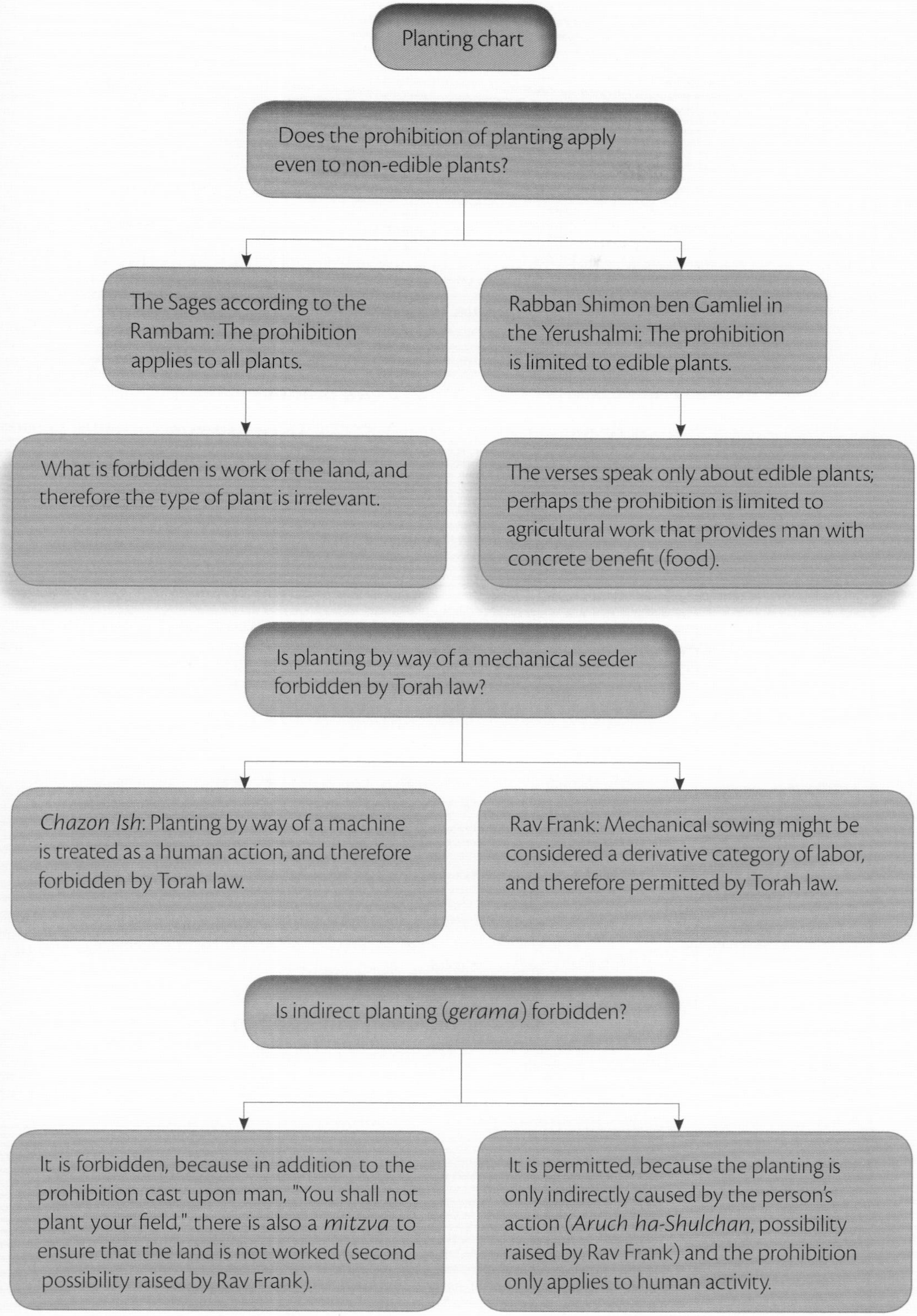

Planting chart

Does the prohibition of planting apply even to non-edible plants?

The Sages according to the Rambam: The prohibition applies to all plants.

What is forbidden is work of the land, and therefore the type of plant is irrelevant.

Rabban Shimon ben Gamliel in the Yerushalmi: The prohibition is limited to edible plants.

The verses speak only about edible plants; perhaps the prohibition is limited to agricultural work that provides man with concrete benefit (food).

Is planting by way of a mechanical seeder forbidden by Torah law?

Chazon Ish: Planting by way of a machine is treated as a human action, and therefore forbidden by Torah law.

Rav Frank: Mechanical sowing might be considered a derivative category of labor, and therefore permitted by Torah law.

Is indirect planting (*gerama*) forbidden?

It is forbidden, because in addition to the prohibition cast upon man, "You shall not plant your field," there is also a *mitzva* to ensure that the land is not worked (second possibility raised by Rav Frank).

It is permitted, because the planting is only indirectly caused by the person's action (*Aruch ha-Shulchan*, possibility raised by Rav Frank) and the prohibition only applies to human activity.

PLANTING TREES

Is planting of trees forbidden by Torah law? Is it possible that planting is not biblically proscribed, but pruning is?

The **Rash** (*Shevi'it 1:1, 2:6*) writes that *neti'a*, planting of a seedling or tree, is forbidden by Torah law during the *Shemita* year, and explains that this is derived from a logical comparison (*kal-va-chomer*) with pruning: If pruning is forbidden even though it merely enhances the tree's growth, certainly planting should be forbidden, for it causes the initial growth of the tree:

> The verse states: "You shall not prune your vineyard" – and planting all the more so, for that is a more fundamental labor.

The Rash's suggestion is supported by a Talmudic passage in *Gittin* (*53b*), which mentions that planting trees during the *Shemita* year is forbidden by Torah law.[8]

The **Rambam** (*1:4*), however, implies that the prohibition of planting trees is only by rabbinic law (this follows also from the words of Rabbenu Tam, cited by the Rash):

> And similarly, one who sinks a vine shoot into the ground, grafts, plants, or performs similar tasks relating to the tending of trees, is liable to lashes administered by rabbinic decree.

The ***Chazon Ish*** (*17, 20, s.v. dam heikhi dami*), however, explains that the Rambam agrees that planting trees is forbidden by Torah law. The lashes that are administered are only "by rabbinic decree" because **the prohibition is derived through a *kal va-chomer* argument**, and lashes are not administered by Torah law for prohibitions that are derived by way of a *kal va-chomer* argument ("We do not punish on the basis of *kal va-chomer* argumentation."):

> Perhaps this [ruling] is an application of the rule that we cannot use *kal va-chomer* reasoning to prove a punishment from Torah law. And therefore lashes are not administered for planting trees, even though it is forbidden by Torah law.

Most of the *Acharonim* (*Pe'at ha-Shulchan* (*20:4, 30*); *Minchat*

8. The context of the passage in *Gittin* 53b is an analysis of the position of Rabbi Meir, who maintains that when a person inadvertently transgresses a Torah prohibition regarding *Shabbat*, he is not penalized like a willful sinner, for there is no concern that he would willfully violate the prohibition, but if he inadvertently transgresses a rabbinic prohibition, the penalty of the willful sinner is imposed, to prevent willful violations. The Gemara raises an apparent contradiction from another statement by Rabbi Meir: "One who plants trees on *Shabbat* – if he planted inadvertently, he may leave it; if he planted willfully, he must uproot it. During the sabbatical year, whether inadvertently or willfully, he must uproot it; these are the words of Rabbi Meir .... Are not both by Torah law?" That is to say, planting on *Shabbat* and planting during the sabbatical year are both forbidden by Torah law. Why then does Rabbi Meir distinguish between *Shabbat* and the sabbatical year? The Gemara's question assumes that planting during the *Shemita* year is forbidden by Torah law.

Seeds (all agree that this is prohibited as planting vegetation).

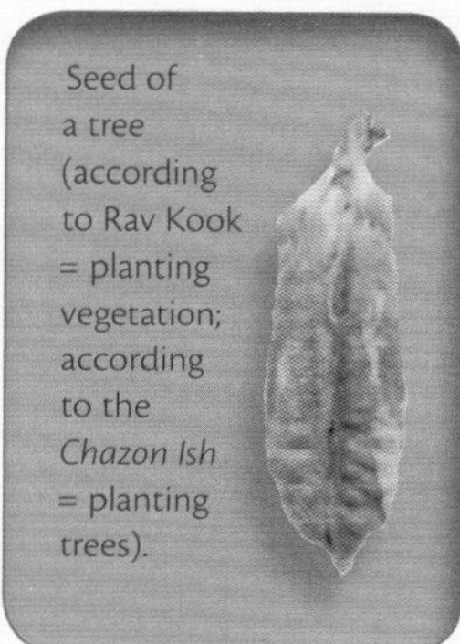
Seed of a tree (according to Rav Kook = planting vegetation; according to the *Chazon Ish* = planting trees).

A fruit tree seedling (all agree that this is planting trees).

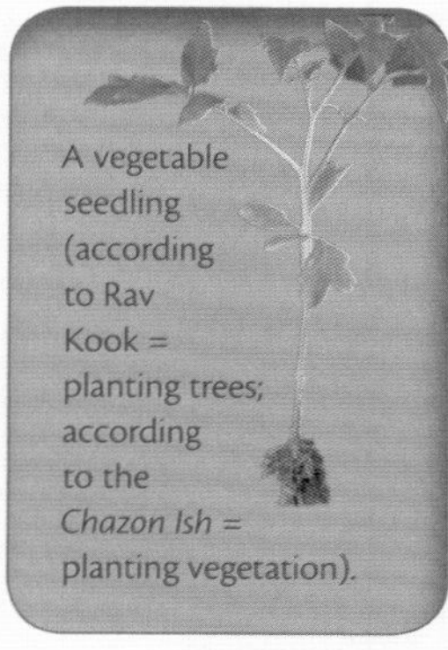
A vegetable seedling (according to Rav Kook = planting trees; according to the *Chazon Ish* = planting vegetation).

Chinukh, (*no.* 327); *Iglei Tal* [*Zore'a* 2:5; 5]); *Responsa Bet ha-Levi,* (*III, no.* 1;) and others) disagree with the *Chazon Ish,* and understand that the Rambam forbids planting trees only by rabbinic law.

In order to explain the Rambam's position, we must answer two questions:

1. How can the Rambam's ruling be reconciled with Gittin 53b, which mentions that planting trees during the *Shemita* year is forbidden by Torah law?
2. How does the Rambam account for the surprising outcome of his position that pruning trees is forbidden by Torah law, while planting them, which would appear to be much more significant, is forbidden only by rabbinic law?

The ***Minchat Chinukh*** (*mitzva* 327) answers the first question by explaining that the Talmudic passage in Gittin follows the view of Abaye (*Mo'ed Katan* 3a), who maintains that *toladot,* such as planting a tree, are forbidden by Torah law. The halacha, however, as quoted by the Rambam, is that *toladot,* such as trees planting, are forbidden only by rabbinic law (we will expand upon the issue of *avot* and *toladot* in the chapter dealing with the labors that are forbidden by rabbinic law).

Rav Kook (*Shabbat ha-Aretz, introduction, part 4, and Kuntrus Acharon, part 6*) provides a different answer to the contradiction between the Rambam and Gittin 53b. According to him, the term "planting" when used in relation to trees includes two distinct categories:

1. Planting a seedling, root, or tree.
2. Planting the seed of a tree (this usage appears in the Mishna, *Orla* (1:9): "One may not plant the nut of [a tree which is] orla").

Planting the seed of a tree (the second category) is included in the Torah prohibition of planting seeds, while **planting a seedling or a tree** (the first category) is not prohibited by Torah law. According to Rav Kook, the Gemara in *Gittin* refers to the second category and therefore it states that planting trees is a Torah prohibition,

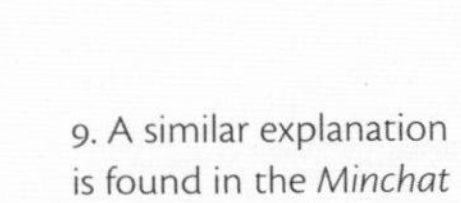

whereas the Rambam speaks of the first category of planting, which is forbidden only by rabbinic law:[9]

9. A similar explanation is found in the *Minchat Chinukh* (commandment 327) and in *Sefer ha-Shemita* (chap. 3, 1, par. 9).

> As to the objection to the Rambam's ruling that the prohibition to plant is only by rabbinic law from what is stated in *Gittin* (53b) … . I have already noted that the essential difference between planting trees and vegetation is with respect to the planting of a shoot, which is different in its form from planting seeds and grain. But if a person plants a tree by planting its seed in the ground, even though the term used for this is planting a tree (*neti'a*), given that it causes the growth of trees … nevertheless it is included in the category of planting seeds (*zeri'a*), as the Rambam states in *Hilchot Kil'ayim 1:6* … Therefore, regarding vegetables, the seeds of which are normally planted very close together in a bed, and when they grow, they are uprooted and replanted further apart – the first planting is forbidden by Torah law, whereas the second is forbidden [only] by rabbinic decree.

According to Rav Kook, the distinction between planting seeds and planting trees **is not that the former refers to annuals, whereas the latter refers to perennials**. Rather, the difference between them is that in the case of planting seeds, a person causes the plant that lies in potential within the seed to emerge, this being forbidden by Torah law, whereas in the case of planting trees, the plant had already emerged, and the person merely **causes the further development of the plant**, which is forbidden only by rabbinic decree.

As we saw above, the ***Chazon Ish*** (*17, 20*) understands that planting the seed of a fruit that grows on a tree is also regarded as "planting a tree" against the understanding of Rav Kook.

We now have two possible explanations as to how the Rambam could interpret *Gittin* 53b:

1. The passage in Gittin was not accepted as the halacha.
2. The passage in Gittin deals with the planting of the seed of a fruit that grows on a tree, which is indeed forbidden by Torah law, but the planting of a seedling, which does not create a new plant, is forbidden only by rabbinic decree.

We now come to the second question posed above: What is the reason for ruling that planting trees is forbidden only rabbinically? How do we deal with the Rash's argument that if pruning is prohibited biblically, then all the more so planting should be forbidden?!

One possible answer is that the Torah forbids only those labors that can result in produce that can be eaten during the *Shemita* year. If the labor will not result in produce that can be eaten during the *Shemita* year, then it is forbidden only rabbinically. Therefore, since a person will derive benefit from planting vegetation and pruning in the *Shemita* year itself, these actions are forbidden by Torah law. Planting trees, on the other hand, will only provide benefit several years down the line, after the tree has grown and the years of *orla* will have been completed, and is therefore only forbidden by rabbinic enactment.[10]

10. I heard this explanation from my revered teacher and father-in-law, Rav E. Blumenzweig. *See Responsa Maharitatz ha-Chadashot* (176) who offers a similar explanation, that the Torah only forbids labors that will give rise to produce having *Shemita* sanctity. According to this approach, however, the planting of a vegetable seedling is forbidden by Torah law, against the explanation offered by Rav Kook cited above, according to which the planting of a vegetable seedling is forbidden only by rabbinic decree.

RAV AVRAHAM YITZCHAK HAKOHEN KOOK

Rav Kook was born in Latvia in 1865. At a young age he married the daughter of the noted Torah sage, the Aderet. After studying in the Volozhin yeshiva, he served as rabbi in several communities, until he moved to *Eretz Yisrael,* where he served as the Chief Rabbi of Yaffo, the Chief Rabbi of Jerusalem (where he established Yeshivat Merkaz ha-Rav), and later the Chief Rabbi of *Eretz Yisrael.* Rav Kook was a tremendous scholar in Gemara, Halacha, Jewish thought and Kabbala, and he greatly influenced the development of religious thought in the developing State of Israel. Rav Kook's special love for *Eretz Yisrael* and its agricultural pioneers brought him to intensive occupation with the *mitzvot* that apply only in Eretz Yisrael and the *mitzva* of *Shemita* in particular, to which he dedicated an entire book: "*Shabbat ha-Aretz.*" In this book, he explains the laws of *Shemita* as well as the foundations for the *heter mechira.* His halachic works include: *Orach Mishpat; Mishpat Kohen; Shabbat ha-Aretz; Da'at Kohen; Halacha Berura*; and *Ezrat Kohen.* His philosophical texts include: *Orot; Orot ha-Kodesh; Orot ha-Teshuva* and others.

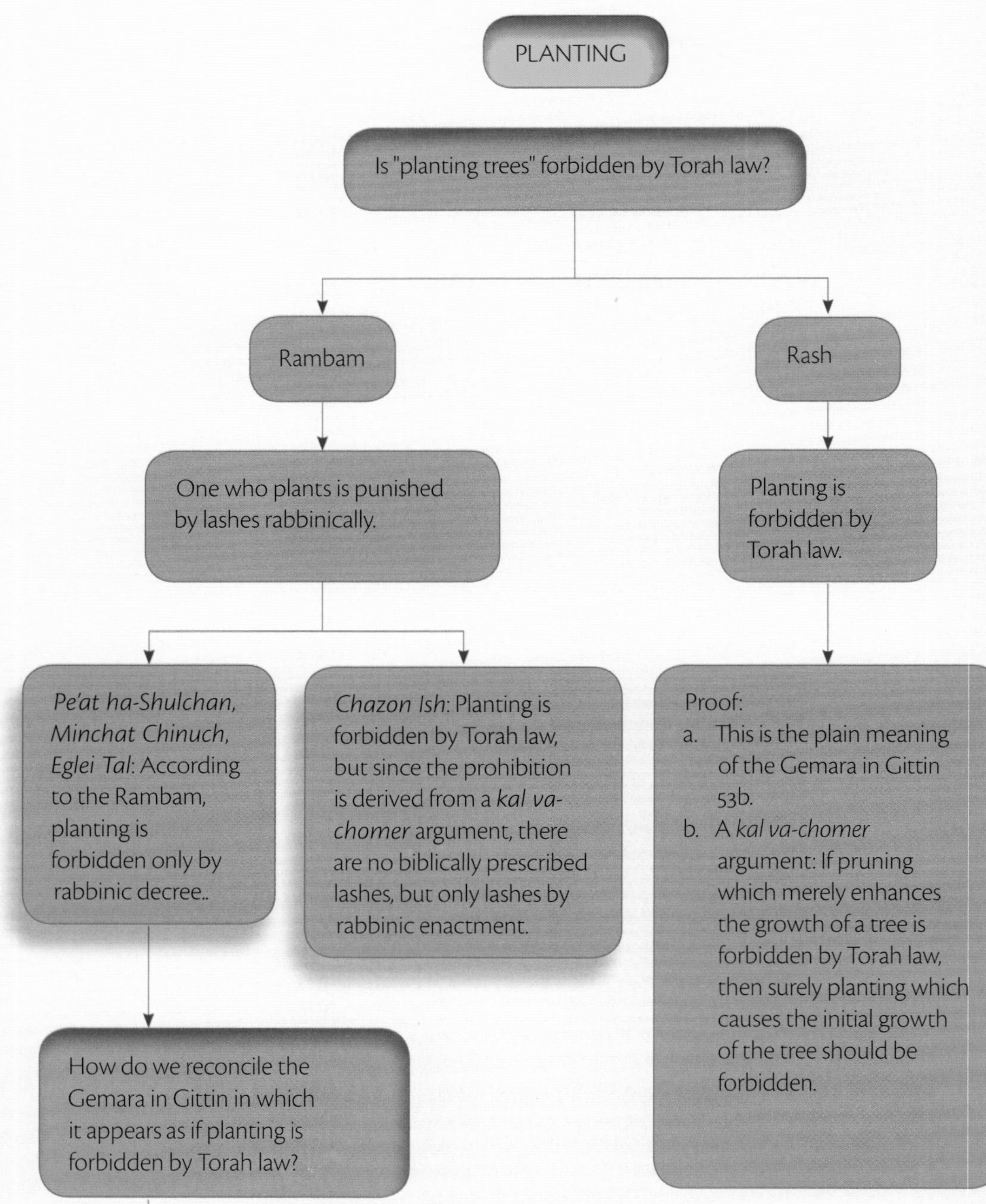
PLANTING
Is "planting trees" forbidden by Torah law?
Rambam
Rash
One who plants is punished by lashes rabbinically.
Planting is forbidden by Torah law.
Pe'at ha-Shulchan, Minchat Chinuch, Eglei Tal: According to the Rambam, planting is forbidden only by rabbinic decree..
Chazon Ish: Planting is forbidden by Torah law, but since the prohibition is derived from a *kal va-chomer* argument, there are no biblically prescribed lashes, but only lashes by rabbinic enactment.
Proof:
a. This is the plain meaning of the Gemara in Gittin 53b.
b. A *kal va-chomer* argument: If pruning which merely enhances the growth of a tree is forbidden by Torah law, then surely planting which causes the initial growth of the tree should be forbidden.
How do we reconcile the Gemara in Gittin in which it appears as if planting is forbidden by Torah law?

Minchat Chinuch:
There are other talmudic passages that disagree with the Gemara in Gittin.

Rav Kook: The Gemara in Gittin refers to the seed of a fruit, the planting of which involves a biblical prohibition. The Rambam refers to a seedling, the planting of which is forbidden only by rabbinic decree, because the plant had already emerged from its seed. Planting by way of a machine is treated as a human action, and therefore forbidden by Torah law.

What is the logic in the position that planting is forbidden only by rabbinic enactment, despite the fact that pruning is forbidden by Torah law?

The prohibition may be limited to sowing which results in produce during the *Shemita* year itself, to the exclusion of planting, from which it will be possible to derive benefit only after the *Shemita* year.

PLANTING INSIDE THE HOUSE

Is it permissible to plant in a pot inside a house? What is the source for leniency regarding planting in greenhouses and hydroponics?

The **Yerushalmi** (*Orla 1:2*) discusses the status of plants grown indoors (as will be clarified below, "indoors" means inside a roofed structure, even if the plants are growing in the ground itself). It is clear to the Yerushalmi that planting indoors does not obligate the setting aside of *terumot* and *ma'asrot* (at least not by Torah law). The Torah states, "You shall surely tithe all the produce of your seed, that the field brings forth" (*Devarim 14:22*), implying that the obligation of *terumot* and *ma'asrot* applies only to produce growing in the field. On the other hand, it is equally clear to the Yerushalmi that the laws of *orla* apply even to produce grown indoors, since the biblical passage dealing with *orla* does not mention a "field."

"Indoor" greenhouse (of Lev Ran – former Gush Katif residents) with plants growing on the ground itself

The Yerushalmi does not come to a conclusion regarding the prohibitions of *Shemita*: On the one hand, the Torah states: "You shall not plant *your field*," implying that there is no prohibition indoors; on the other hand, the Torah states: "Then shall the land keep a Sabbath," and even that which grows indoors can be regarded as growing out of "the land"[11]:

> Rabbi Yochanan said in the name of Rabbi Yannai: A tree that was planted inside a house is subject to *orla*, but exempt from tithes. As it is written: "You shall surely tithe all the increase of your seed, that which the field brings forth." With respect to the seventh year, it must be asked, for it is written: "Then shall the land keep a Sabbath for the Lord," and it is written: "You shall neither sow your field, nor prune your vineyard."

As for the halacha, **Rav Israel of Shklov, the author of Pe'at**

11. According to the explanation that we have offered, the Yerushalmi is in doubt about which verse should be assigned priority. However, a difficulty arises regarding the doubt raised by the Yerushalmi: why not accept both verses, and say that produce grown in the field is subject to both a negative commandment and a positive commandment, whereas produce grown indoors is subject only to the positive commandment?! **Rav Kook** (*Shabbat ha-Aretz, Kuntres Acharon, 3*) explains the matter more fully and thereby resolves the difficulty. According to him, the Yerushalmi is in doubt regarding whether the positive commandment and the negative commandments are conceptually independent of one another, in which case we should learn from the verse, "Then shall the land keep a Sabbath," that a positive commandment governs planting indoors; or else the positive commandment imposes an obligation to rest only with respect to that which is governed by the negative commandments,

ha-Shulchan (*20:52*), rules leniently, because in our time the laws of *Shemita* are in effect only by rabbinic decree[12] (we will deal with this assumption below).

> A doubt arises with respect to a tree that was planted inside a house, whether it is subject to all the laws of *Shemita* ... Below I will clarify that the Vilna Gaon and the *Acharonim* have ruled that *Shemita* in our time is [only] by rabbinic law, and therefore one can be lenient in cases of uncertainty.

The ***Chazon Ish*** (*22, 1; 26, 4*), however, inclines toward stringency:

> In my opinion, the *Pe'at ha-Shulchan's* principle of being lenient in cases of uncertainty has not been decisively demonstrated. For it can be argued that since the root of the uncertainty relates to a Torah law, about which we must be stringent, we should follow the more stringent position. Moreover, it can be argued that one ... should be stringent, for perhaps ... it involves a [certain] rabbinic prohibition.

It seems clear that two factors brought the *Chazon Ish* to rule stringently:

1. Fundamentally speaking, the Yerushalmi's uncertainty stems from a doubt regarding a Torah law, (although practically speaking, it is an uncertainty regarding a rabbinic law, because today all the laws of *Shemita* are rabbinic). Since it is an uncertainty regarding a Torah law, we rule stringently even in our day when *Shemita* is rabbinic.
2. It is possible that the Yerushalmi was only in doubt as to whether there is a Torah prohibition, but is not in doubt as to whether there is a rabbinic prohibition. (This argument was also raised against the *Pe'at ha-Shulchan's* ruling by *Minchat Shlomo* [21, 7].)

in which case the positive commandment does not apply to that which does not fall into the category of "your field" or "your vineyard." (In other words, does the positive commandment add only that, in addition to the negative commandments, there is also a prohibition inferred from a positive commandment [a new level of prohibition], or does it add a prohibition of resting even with respect to that which is not a field [wider scope of prohibition])? Thus, according to one side of the uncertainty, there is no prohibition whatsoever with respect to produce that grows indoors.

12. Rav Ovadya Yosef is also lenient on this issue (*Ha-Shevi'it ve-Hilchoteha, p. 22, note 5*).

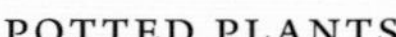

POTTED PLANTS

A plant that grows in an *atzitz nakuv,* a planter with holes in the bottom, is considered as if it is growing in the ground, as is stated in a Mishna regarding detaching a plant on Shabbat (*Demai 5:10; Shabbat 95a*):[13]

> One who detaches [a plant] from an *atzitz nakuv* [on *Shabbat*] is liable.

There is no explicit discussion in the Gemara, nor in the literature of the *Rishonim,* regarding the *Shemita* status of a plant in a pot without holes (*atzitz she-eino nakuv*). In other areas, such as *terumot* and *ma'asrot* (*Rambam, Hilchot Terumot 5:16*) and *kil'ayim* (prohibited plant mixtures), (*Rambam, Hilchot Kil'ayim 1:1*), an *atzitz she-eino nakuv* is considered like an *atitiz nakuv* on a rabbinic level.

Rav Sh. Z. Auerbach (*Minchat Shlomo 41, 4*) suggests a rationale for leniency regarding an *atzitz she-eino nakuv* with respect to the *Shemita* laws. He suggests that since the prohibition to plant in an *atzitz she-eino nakuv* is generally because of a rabbinic decree lest one come to plant in an *atzitz nakuv,* (regarding *Shabbat, kil'ayim, terumot* and *ma'asrot*), it is possible that no such decree was enacted regarding *Shemita.* This is because we are dealing with a phenomenon that occurs only once in seven years, and the Sages may have limited their decrees to phenomena that occur annually[14] (a similar suggestion could be made regarding *orla*). However, Rav Sh. Z. Auerbach does not accept this suggestion in practice, because the *Rishonim* on *Gittin* 7b imply that one should be stringent on the matter:

Planting in a pot without holes standing on the ground (in general, forbidden by rabbinic law; regarding *Shemita* – possibly governed by a rabbinic prohibition

13. Rav Sh. Z. Auerbach (*Minchat Shlomo, no. 40*) is in doubt whether an atzitz nakuv is always considered like the ground or only after the plant contained therein begins to grow and draw sustenance from the ground. If the latter, then it might follow that as long as the plant is not being sustained by the ground, the plant is not considered planted in the ground, and planting in it is permitted by Torah law. Rav Sh. Z. Auerbach leaves this question unresolved, but the *Chazon Ish* (20, 5) makes no distinction, and rules as a matter of course that planting in an *atzitz nakuv* is forbidden by Torah law.

14. This argument requires further examination, for while it is true that *Chazal* do not issue decrees about uncommon phenomena, the case under discussion, namely, *Shemita,* is indeed common, for it effects all of Israel (living in Eretz Yisrael), even if it is only once every seven years. Since this is a situation that everyone will encounter in the [ultimate] future, there is good reason for a decree, precisely because it takes place only once every seven years, and people are liable to forget and become confused about the laws of *Shemita.*

Responsa Nechpa be-Kesef (*vol. I, Yoreh De'a, no. 5*) and *Sedei ha-Aretz* (*vol. III, Yoreh De'a, no. 28*) write that planting in an *atzitz she-eino nakuv* pot during the seventh year is forbidden. Their main reason is that they compare *Shemita* to *teruma* and *ma'asrot*. In truth, we find that with respect to *kil'ayim* as well, [the Sages] forbade an *atzitz she-eino nakuv* on account of an *atzitz nakuv* … [15]

In any event, it would appear that these rabbinic decrees must not be compared one to the other, for the Sages did not universally prohibit an *atzitz she-eino nakuv* lest one come to use an *atzitz nakuv*. See also *Or Zaru'a* (*Hilchot Orla, 313*), who rules that one who plants in an *atzitz she-eino nakuv* is exempt from the laws of *orla*.

We must, therefore, say that it is only with respect to *terumot, ma'asrot* and *kil'ayim*, which apply every year, that the rabbis issued a decree about an *atzitz she-eino nakuv*. Therefore, there is no prohibition regarding *Shemita*, which occurs only once in seven years.

However, all the *Rishonim* on *Gittin* 7b, who explain the *Tosefta* describing one who puts the *lof* plant (an edible bulb) in the ground for preservation during the *Shemita* year as referring to an *atzitz she-eino nakuv*, imply that only preserving is permitted, but planting is forbidden.[16]

Other *Acharonim* write that in practice, one should be stringent about an *atzitz she-eino nakuv* and treat it as the ground itself (*Chazon Ish 20:5; 22:1; this is also implied by the Radbaz on the Rambam, Hilchot Shemita ve-Yovel 1:6*).

An *atzitz nakuv* (perforated pot) standing on the ground (planting in this would be forbidden by Torah law).

15. What he means to say is that *Responsa Nichpa be-Kesef* and *Sefer Sedei ha-Aretz* maintain that it is forbidden to plant in an *atzitz she-eino nakuv* during the *Shemita* year, just as the Sages decreed about an *atzitz she-eino nakuv* with respect to *teruma, ma'aser* and *kil'ayim*. Rav Sh. Z. Auerbach argues that there may be a difference between the various realms, as he explains in the next paragraph, for it is possible that the Sages did not issue a decree about *orla* or *Shemita*, because they do not apply every year.

16. Regarding the matter of putting *lof* into the ground during the *Shemita* year (not for planting, but for the purpose of preservation), the *Rishonim* explain (*Gittin 7a*) that this is only permitted in an *atzitz she-eino nakuv*. From this it follows that the Sages only permitted preservation, but not planting, in an *atzitz she-eino nakuv*, against what Rav Sh. Z. Auerbach said above.

A POTTED PLANT INSIDE THE HOUSE

The Chazon Ish (*22:1; 26:4*) writes that there is adequate support to permit planting indoors in an *atzitz she-eino nakuv*, because in such a situation, it is possible to combine two reasons for leniency: first, the view of the ***Pe'at ha-Shulchan***, who is lenient about planting indoors even in a perforated pot; and second, the fact that there is no explicit source stating that one is forbidden to plant in a *atzitz she-eino nakuv*, even outdoors:

> When the pot is indoors, even if you say that planting indoors is forbidden by rabbinic law, it can be argued that with respect to an *atzitz she-eino nakuv* [the Sages] did not issue a decree. For even planting it [outdoors] is forbidden only *rabbinically*. And given that the author of the *Pe'at ha-Shulchan* has already ruled leniently even with respect to planting indoors [in a perforated pot], one who is lenient about an *atzitz she-eino nakuv* indoors, has what to rely on.

The *Chazon Ish's* halachic considerations are clear, but his rationale still requires explanation: As we have explained, we are stringent both about planting indoors and about planting in an *atzitz she-eino nakuv*. Why should we be lenient when we combine these two factors? Several explanations can be offered:

1. The *Chazon Ish* is lenient because we are dealing with a case of *sfek safeka*, a double uncertainty as to a prohibition, leading to a permit: it is uncertain whether planting indoors is permitted, but even if we say that this is forbidden, it is uncertain whether or not the Sages decreed against planting in an *atzitz she-eino nakuv* during the *Shemita* year.
2. The *Chazon Ish* is lenient here because it is a case of uncertainty regarding a rabbinic law. As we saw earlier, we rule stringently with respect to indoor planting because it is an uncertainty regarding a Torah law. In the case of an *atzitz she-eino nakuv* outdoors, however, we are stringent only because of the rabbinic decree, lest one come to plant in a perforated pot. Accordingly, when a doubt arises about an *atzitz she-eino*

nakuv indoors, **this is an uncertainty about a rabbinic law** – whether the Sages decreed about an *atzitz she-eino nakuv* even when it is found indoors – and so we invoke the rule that "in cases of doubt regarding a rabbinic law, we rule in favor of leniency."[17]

3. My revered teacher, **Rav Aharon Lichtenstein**, suggested that there is additional room to be lenient about indoor pots based upon the Biblical verses about *Shemita*. As stated above, the Yerushalmi raises a doubt about planting indoors, because a house is certainly not included in a "field," but it is included in the "land," for the earth upon which the house is constructed is part of the land. A pot, on the other hand, might be considered a field, when it is found on the ground in an open area, but it is certainly not governed by the verse, "the land shall keep a Sabbath," for it is detached from the land (see *Sefer ha-Shemita, p. 15*), and cannot be regarded as an integral part of the earth on which it rests. Thus, it should

17. It is also possible that the Sages themselves were in doubt about the law applying to indoor planting (as we see from the Yerushalmi), and so they issued a decree concerning an *atzitz she-eino nakuv* only in a case of certainty (outdoors), and not in a case of uncertainty (inside).

ספר
פאת השלחן
הלכות שביעית
שני בתים ושתי שלחנות
פאת השולחן ובית ישראל
שו"ע לשבת ובית רידב"ז
הפנים
ירושלם

RAV ISRAEL OF SHKLOV

(*Pe'at ha-Shulchan*)

Rav Israel of Shklov was born in 1770. He is counted among the disciples of the Vilna Gaon, even though he studied with him for only one year, the last year of the Gaon's life. He moved to Eretz Yisrael in 1809, heading a group of the Gaon's disciples. His book, *Pe'at ha-Shulchan*, on the special mitzvot applying only in the land of Israel is regarded as one of the most important works dealing with these issues. Particular attention is given to the laws of *Shemita* which are thoroughly explained in the book.

be permissible to plant in a perforated pot indoors by Torah law on both counts: it avoids the problem of, "you shall not plant your field," for this prohibition does not apply inside a house. It also avoids the prohibition of, "the land shall keep a Sabbath," for, while a house may be included in "the land," a pot is not.[18]

18. Rav Lichtenstein did not propose this understanding in the context of a practical ruling.

In practice, as mentioned above, there is adequate basis to allow one to plant in an *atzitz she-eino nakuv* inside a home. It is reasonable that there is more weight to this leniency when the planting is necessary, such as whenever the planting is done for the purpose of eating. Therefore, farmers whose livelihoods are at stake can certainly be lenient about planting indoors. This is **the halachic basis for planting in a detached, soil-less, hydroponic bedding and in greenhouses** (we will discuss this at length in the chapter dealing with buying fruits and vegetables during the *Shemita* year).

A potted plant standing indoors – the entire plant is contained within the pot

Once we have defined planting indoor potted plants as being only a rabbinic prohibition, there is room to be lenient and permit watering in the ordinary manner. Indoor potted plants may be cared for during the *Shemita* year in an almost regular manner, and fertilizing[19] and weeding[20] are also permitted. These labors will be discussed below at greater length.

19. Generally speaking, however, houseplants can flourish without fertilizers. Slow release fertilizers are also now available that can be applied before the *Shemita* year begins and remain effective for the entire year.

20. In addition to what was said above about indoor potted plants, it should be added that even outdoors, irrigation, weeding and fertilizing are forbidden only by rabbinic law, and there are those who permit unlimited irrigation when the plants are in need of water (see below, p. 195).

WHAT IS A "HOUSE" AND A "POT"?

Thus far we have explained the various laws governing plants grown indoors or in pots. We must now define more precisely what is regarded as a "pot" and what is regarded as a "house." The *Chazon Ish (21:1)* argues that in this context the term "house" refers to a roofed area (at least 80 cm. high [*Rav y. efrati, Halichot Sadeh 86, p. 14*]), but according to some opinions there must also be walls 10 handbreadths (80 or 96 cm.) high.[21]

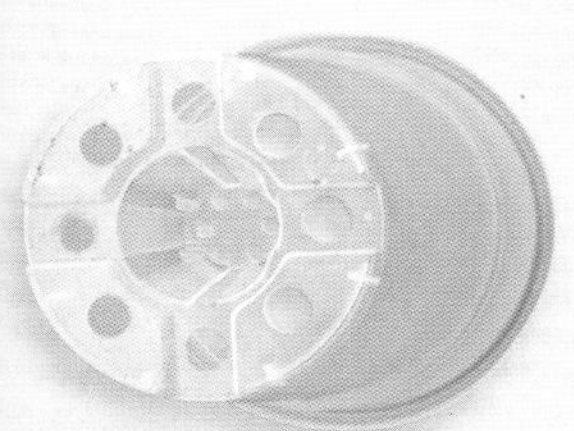
atzitz nakuv
(perforated pot)

What is an *atzitz nakuv*? The Mishna in *Uktzin* (*2:10*) states that a container that has a hole large enough to allow a small root to pass through is *nakuv*. The Mishna does not, however, clarify the precise size of the hole. The Rambam (*Hilchot Terumot 5:15*, based on *Shabbat* 95b) writes that even a hole that is less than the size of an olive renders the container *nakuv*, whereas the *Chazon Ish* (*32, 1*) writes that we do not know the precise measurement, implying that even a smaller hole suffices.[22]

A pot that sits on a plate (as is often the case with potted plants) is treated as an *atzitz she-eino nakuv* (unless the plate is made of clay, in which case the plant can absorb water through the clay [see *Rashi, Gittin 7b*, s.v. afar; *Tosafot*, ad loc., s.v. *atzitz; Shulchan Aruch, Choshen Mishpat 202:12*, in *Rema; Chazon Ish, Dinei Orla, 32*]).

As for a pot that sits on the floor, Rav Sh. Z. Auerbach writes (*Responsa Minchat Shlomo, 41, 2*) that if the plant lies directly on the ground floor, the pot is regarded as nakuv, (unless it sits on a plate). But if the pot sits on the second floor, so that there is a space between the floor and the ground,[23] it is regarded as *eino nakuv*.[24]

21. The *Chazon Ish* is uncertain whether walls are required. Rav Wosner writes that walls are necessary, whereas Rav Frank rules that a roofed structure is treated as a house even if it lacks walls (*Har Tzvi, Zera'im, II, no. 34*).

22. "The hole may be no larger than a hole large enough to allow liquids easily to escape." The reference here is to a hole large enough to allow water to drip out drop after drop (*Mishna Berura 159:7; see Responsa Minchat Yitzchak, VIII, no. 92; and Chiddushim u-Bei'urim Shevi'it, no. 11*). Owing to the uncertainty, any container with a hole (the diameter of which is more than a millimeter) should be treated as an *atzitz nakuv* with respect to the laws of *Shemita*.
It should be noted that the law of an *atzitz nakuv* has practical ramifications regarding the laws of **orla**: If a tree is being transplanted (from a nursery or the like), and it is moved together with root stock and soil that would suffice to maintain the tree for at least two weeks, and the container or plastic wrapping holding the root ball has a hole (turning it into an *atzitz nakuv*), there is no need to restart the count of *orla* years. For this purpose, we generally require a hole having a diameter of at least two centimeters.

23. The space suffices to turn the pot into a pot that is totally detached from the ground. In such a case we can also take into account the view of the ***Ritva*** that whenever a space of ten handbreadths separates the pot from the ground, even if there is no physical barrier between them, the pot is not treated as *an atzitz nakuv*, because there can be no absorption through a space of ten handbreadths.

24. *Responsa Shevet ha-Levi* (*VI, no. 167*) is stringent regarding both cases. On the other hand, the *Chiddushim u-Bei'urim* (*Zera'im, II, no. 11, letter 8*) implies that he is lenient even with respect to a pot resting on a stone that is lying on the ground.

THE PLANT INSIDE THE POT

The leaves and flowers of a potted plant often extend beyond the plate on which the pot is resting, in which case part of the plant is found directly above the floor. In such a case, the question arises whether the plant is regarded as resting on the plate or connected to the ground. The *Rishonim* disagree on this point. Most *Rishonim* understand that in such a case the pot is treated like an *atitz nakuv* (*Mishna, Uktzin 2:6,* as interpreted by most *Rishonim*). The Rambam (commentary to the Mishna, ad loc., and *Hilchot Tum'at Okhelin 2:9*), however, seems to say that the leaves and flowers extending beyond the plate do not cause the plant to be considered connected to the ground.

In practice, when there is flooring, one may be lenient, at least with respect to the leaves and flowers, and treat the pot as *eino nakuv* and thus perform all types of labor that are forbidden by rabbinic law.[25]

To summarize, with respect to houseplants: On the ground floor, a (non-clay) plate should be placed under the pot, and thus the pot is regarded as detached from the ground (even if the leaves and branches extend beyond the plate) and the plant can be cared for in the ordinary manner.[26] On upper stories, the plant can be cared for in the usual manner, even if it is not sitting on a plate.[27]

25. The reasons for the leniency are as follows: First of all, common sense dictates leniency in the case of a potted plant resting on household flooring. Today, flooring is laid on a layer of concrete, and there is total separation between the floor and the ground. As for those who are stringent about potted plants resting on the floor, it must be asked whether their stringency is based on a concern about absorption from the ground (in which case it stands to reason that with today's flooring there is no absorption whatsoever), or perhaps they view the flooring and the ground as a single unit (in which case there could sometimes be room for stringency even today, at least on the ground floor). There is room for disagreement on this issue in light of the **Rosh's** comments on the matter (*Responsa ha-Rosh, rule 2, 4*), but according to the simplest understanding, today's flooring should be regarded as a total barrier, thus turning the pot into an *atzitz she-eino nakuv.* Second, we are not talking about planting in these pots, but rather about caring for potted plants through the performance of labors that are prohibited during the *Shemita* year by rabbinic law. Thus, we are dealing with an uncertainty regarding a matter of rabbinic law. Third, since by definition, potted plants require care for their upkeep, labors forbidden by rabbinic law are permitted, however the *Acharonim* disagree about the precise parameters of this allowance (as will be discussed below). In our case, therefore, we can apply a sweeping allowance regarding all labors forbidden by rabbinic law, something that is very close to the allowance issued by the lenient authorities even with respect to plants growing outdoors. Furthermore, the situation when the pot is resting on a plate, and only the leaves and flowers extend beyond the plate, is subject to disagreement among the *Rishonim.* To this we may also add that today the entire observance of *Shemita* is by rabbinic law.

26. Watering, fertilizing, weeding, and the like (see the list of labors that are forbidden by rabbinic law on p. 165) are permitted. Planting in one's home should be avoided, unless it is necessary for the sake of eating.

27. Planters: Planters that are structurally part of the building are treated like the building itself (provided that they are under a roof), and not like pots. We therefore rule stringently, and one must not plant in them during the *Shemita* year (as for watering, there is room for leniency, but it is better to water only in the amount that is necessary for the survival of the plants. If the planters are not under a roof, they are subject to all the laws of a field.

"House" (uncertainty of the *Yerushalmi*; in practice we are stringent). In the picture: produce growing in a hothouse out of the ground itself (is a hothouse treated like a house? We shall deal with this issue below.)

Perforated pot outdoors (prohibited by Torah law).

Unperforated pot outdoors (prohibited by rabbinic law).

"House" + an unperforated pot (*Chazon Ish*: there are reliable grounds for leniency). If the pot is unperforated, but the flowers and leaves extend beyond the pot – inside the house, there is room for leniency and normal care of the plant.

"House" + an unperforated pot, where the flowers and leaves do not extend beyond the plate on which the pot is resting.

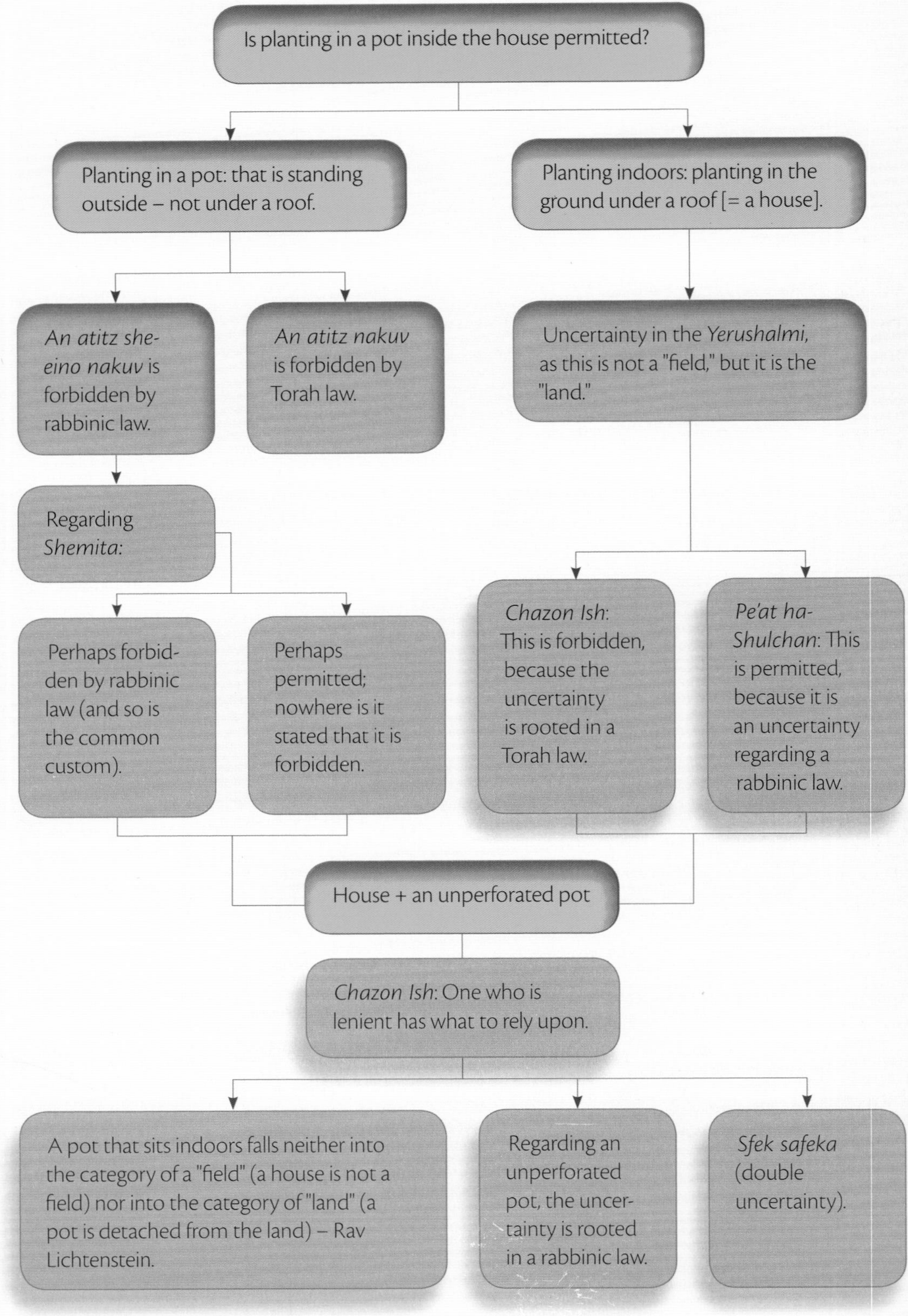
Is planting in a pot inside the house permitted?
Planting in a pot: that is standing outside – not under a roof.
Planting indoors: planting in the ground under a roof [= a house].
An atitz she-eino nakuv is forbidden by rabbinic law.
An atitz nakuv is forbidden by Torah law.
Uncertainty in the *Yerushalmi*, as this is not a "field," but it is the "land."
Regarding *Shemita*:
Perhaps forbidden by rabbinic law (and so is the common custom).
Perhaps permitted; nowhere is it stated that it is forbidden.
Chazon Ish: This is forbidden, because the uncertainty is rooted in a Torah law.
Pe'at ha-Shulchan: This is permitted, because it is an uncertainty regarding a rabbinic law.
House + an unperforated pot
Chazon Ish: One who is lenient has what to rely upon.
A pot that sits indoors falls neither into the category of a "field" (a house is not a field) nor into the category of "land" (a pot is detached from the land) – Rav Lichtenstein.
Regarding an unperforated pot, the uncertainty is rooted in a rabbinic law.
Sfek safeka (double uncertainty).

PRUNING

> "But in the seventh year shall be a Sabbath of solemn rest for the land ... you shall neither plant your field, **nor prune your vineyard**."

What is the similarity between planting and pruning?
Is there a difference between pruning a grapevine and pruning other trees?

Pruning refers to the removal of branches in order to promote superior growth of the tree. The Torah refers to "pruning" in connection with the grapevine – "nor prune your grapevine"[28] – as opposed to "planting" which is mentioned in connection with a field – "you shall neither plant your field." This seems to imply that the prohibition of pruning is restricted to the grapevine, to the exclusion of other trees. Nevertheless, the **Rambam** (*Hilchot Shemita ve-Yovel 1:2*) ruled differently:

> According to the Torah, one is punished with lashes only for planting or pruning, and for reaping or gathering the harvest. **This rule applies equally to a vineyard and to other trees.**

The simple understanding of the Rambam is that the prohibition of pruning applies to other trees as well. This is also the understanding of the *Tosafot Yom Tov* (*Shevi'it 4:4*) and the *Eglei Tal* (*zore'a, 2*). The ***Tosafot Yom Tov*** writes as follows:

> Both pruning and cutting down a tree are [forbidden] by Torah law, both for a vine and for other trees, as the Rambam writes.

In contrast, the ***Chazon Ish*** understands that the biblical prohibition of pruning applies only to the grapevine (*21:15, 26:1*), and as proof he cites the Gemara in *Mo'ed Katan* (*3a*):

> From where do we know not to cut back shoots [*kirsum*], or thin twigs, or put up props for supporting [fruit trees]? From the verse which states: "Your field you shall not ... Your vineyard you shall not ... " – [which means] no manner of

28. Actually, the Torah uses the term *"kerem"* both in reference to the grapevine and in reference to the olive tree.

> work in your field, no manner of work in your vineyard … . [That is only] by rabbinic law, and the verses are cited merely as a support.

That is to say, when the Gemara wishes to clarify the source for the prohibition of "*kirsum*" and the like, it first tries to provide a biblical source, but in the end it concludes that the prohibition is only of rabbinic origin, and the verses are merely supports. What is "*kirsum*"? Rashi (ad loc.) says:

> This is the same as pruning, only that *kirsum* applies to other trees.

As we saw, the Gemara argues that the prohibition of *kirsum* is rabbinic in origin. We see then that the pruning of trees other than a grapevine is forbidden only by rabbinic law. The *Chazon Ish* understands that this is also the view of the Rambam, and he is therefore forced to give an alternative explanation of the Rambam's statement that seems to state that one is liable for lashes by Torah law for pruning, "whether a grapevine or other trees." The *Chazon Ish* explains that the Rambam's words "whether a grapevine or other trees" refer not to pruning, but to gathering. The Rambam found it necessary to mention that harvesting is prohibited because one might have thought that gathering the fruit of other trees is not forbidden by Torah law, for the verse speaks exclusively of the grapevine: "You shall not gather the grapes of your undressed vine." Thus, the Rambam concludes that gathering is forbidden by Torah law, both with respect to the grapevine and with respect to other trees. Pruning, however, is forbidden by Torah law only in the case of a grapevine.[29]

> [The Rambam] seems to be saying that one is liable for lashes for pruning other trees. This is difficult! … It seems, however, that our master's intention here is to prevent one from mistakenly saying that the law of *Shemita* with respect to trees applies only to the grapevine, as the verse states:

29. One could also explain the Rambam in accordance with the simple understanding of his words, that prohibition of pruning exists with regard to all trees, and explain the Gemara in *Mo'ed Katan* regarding cutting shoots differently. And, indeed, in his commentary on the Mishna, the Rambam writes (*Shevi'it* 2:3, *Pe'ah* 2:7): "*Mekarsemin* is to cut the stalk by hand and to leave the grain, which is similar to *mekharsemin*, cutting in harvest." Thus the Rambam's view is that *kirsum* is synonymous with cutting for harvest, and it seems that he is dealing with stalks or vegetables. This labor is therefore unrelated to pruning, which is removing branches so the tree grows better (see also the Rambam's commentary to *Shabbat* 12:2, and the *Chazon Ish* 26:1).

"You shall not prune your vineyard ... nor gather the grapes of your undressed vine." If one would say this, one would be permitted to pick [the fruit of] other trees in the ordinary manner ... Therefore our master said that even though the verse refers to a "grapevine," both the grapevine and other trees are subject to the prohibition of tending trees [and therefore all labors are forbidden even with respect to other trees, although pruning is in fact forbidden only in the case of a grapevine].

What is the rationale behind making a distinction between pruning a grapevine and pruning other trees? The ***Chazon Ish*** explains that there is an essential difference between pruning a grapevine and pruning other trees (*Chazon Ish, Shevi'it 21, 15*):

The pruning of other trees is different than the pruning of the grapevine in the very nature of the work.

In the case of a grapevine, pruning promotes the growth of the grapes themselves – pruning stimulates the growth of new branches on which the coming year's crop of grapes will grow. In the case of other trees, pruning merely strengthens the tree, and sometimes even improves it, but it is not essential for the growth of the fruit during the coming year as is the case with grapevines.

This principle also appears in the writings of **Rav Kook**, who wanted to suggest that, even with respect to the grapevine itself, pruning is sometimes permitted and sometimes forbidden:[30]

According to experts in the matter, the pruning that is practiced in our time, the cutting back of all the branches, comes not **to increase the fruit production or enhance the tree,** but rather **to extend the life of the tree** [and this is not forbidden by Torah law, but only by rabbinic decree].

In light of this distinction, it can be suggested that the Torah only forbids **pruning** that is **similar to planting** (as we have seen, both planting and pruning are labors that cause the plant to grow). The pruning of the grapevine, which is similar to planting in that

30. Rav Kook, in a novel ruling, asserted that the way that grapevines are commonly pruned today is not forbidden by Torah law, because the Torah only prohibits the removal of part of a branch, but not the removal of an entire branch: "From the words of the Ramban (*Milchamot, chap. Lulav ha-Gazul*) ... The large branches that grape producers commonly prune and whose ends they cut each year so that they will produce more fruit are called *daliyot*. And the whole branches are called *badim* ... *Zemora* is a branch whose end was cut off ... It seems clear that *zemira*, (pruning), refers to cutting off the end of the branch, so that the grapevine will produce more fruit. And this indeed is the old method of pruning practiced by the Arabs to this very day. But as for cutting off the entire branch, and leaving only a small portion of it, this cutting is intended primarily to preserve the health and extend the life of the tree. It might be argued that this is not subject to the stringency of pruning by Torah law." In practice, however, Rav Kook did not rely on this argument by itself but only in conjunction with other factors (see, for example, *Iggerot Ra'aya, 555*). It also must be clarified whether grapevines are pruned today in the manner described by Rav Kook decades ago. Regarding pruning today, see *Halikhot Sadeh, 47, p. 15*.

it promotes the growth of new fruit which would not have grown were it not for the pruning, is therefore forbidden.

According to this line of thought, it is possible that if other trees are comparable to grapes in this way (such as the kiwi), the pruning of such trees should also be forbidden by Torah law, even according to the *Chazon Ish* (see *Mishpetei Torah, chap. 2, note 9;* and in *Shemita Mamlakhtit*).

The *Chazon Ish* proposed other novel leniencies regarding pruning, the most important of which relates to pruning performed in an **imprecise** manner. According to the *Chazon Ish* (*19:14*), only precise pruning is forbidden, but imprecise pruning is permitted:

> All pruning requires precision and skill. Many things can hinder the growth of a tree or its fruit. Careless pruning can impair the fruit. Regarding *Shabbat,* it falls into the category of pruning nonetheless, because the pruning is beneficial even when performed imprecisely. But regarding *Shemita,* since that is not the ordinary manner [of pruning] and he has in mind to gain the wood [rather than improve the tree], it is permitted.[31]

According to the *Chazon Ish,* imprecise pruning is not beneficial and therefore permitted. For example, it is exceedingly important to prune a grapevine in a professional

31. The ***Chazon Ish*** based this ruling on what the Rambam writes (*Hilchot Shemita ve-Yovel 1:20*): "He who trims grapevines and cuts reeds may do so in the ordinary manner with a spade, sickle, saw or whatever he desires." The *Chazon Ish* (19:14-15) understands that the Rambam is not discussing pruning that is forbidden by Torah law, because the person does not intend to promote growth, but only to use the wood. He understands that here there is not even a prohibition of *mar'it ayin* (an act that is prohibited because it looks like a problematic one) because the cutting is not performed in the usual manner of pruning. In this way, the *Chazon Ish* also explains a strange story related in *Sanhedrin* (*26a*). The Gemara tells that Rabbi Chiyya bar Zarnuki and Rabbi Shimon ben Yehotzadak once went to Assia to intercalate the year, and Resh Lakish joined them to see if they did so properly. Shockingly, along the way, they saw a man pruning his vineyard during *Shemita,* and the two elders did not rebuke him. Resh Lakish got upset, asking, "Why do you not rebuke him for pruning during *Shemita*?" They replied: "He could say that he needs the twigs to make a bale [*akkel*] for the winepress, [a legitimate purpose, and not to promote growth of the grapevines]." Resh Lakish answered: 'The heart knows whether it is for *'akkel'* or *'akalkalot'* [perverseness]." Meaning, I can tell that his intention is to prune and not to use the wood. [The topic of judging others favorably that arises here is worthy of discussion, but this is not its place.] The *Tosafot* (ad loc.) ask: Even if he does not intend to prune, his action clearly involves pruning and promoting the growth of the tree! They answer: "He did it in a manner that was certainly hard on the tree," meaning, the pruning was performed in such a manner that it caused the grapevine harm. The *Chazon Ish* asks: If the *Tosafot* are correct, why did Resh Lakish say, "The heart knows, etc."? According to the *Tosafot,* pruning that is damaging to the tree is a difference that is clearly visible (and Resh Lakish should have said that one can *see* that the person is committing a transgression, and there should be no need to consider what he was thinking). Therefore, the *Chazon Ish* concludes that the episode concerned pruning that is beneficial to the grapevine, but that was not the person's intention. If the person's goal was pruning, his action involved a Torah prohibition, and Resh Lakish understood that this indeed was his goal. But if his intention was really to use the twigs (as the other sages understood), his action was permitted, even though the grapevine benefited from the pruning.

manner: the pruning must always be performed immediately past a joint, and generally after leaving two joints on the branch. Pruning the grapevine in a non-professional manner is far less beneficial.

In practice, one must not prune a grapevine or any other tree growing in a home garden.[32] It is nevertheless sometimes possible to permit certain kinds of pruning for farmers in order to avoid economic loss. This is especially true for trees other than grapevines.[33]

Professional pruning

Non-professional pruning

32. The *Chazon Ish* writes that if a person is not trained in pruning, he may cut off branches should he need them, and need not be concerned that he is thereby improving the tree: "If he is a layman, and lacks precise knowledge of pruning, it would appear that he is permitted to cut off [branches], because most such actions of a layman are not performed in the manner of proper pruning, and even if he happens to prune it in the proper way, since this was not his intention, it might not be regarded as pruning … ."

33. See *Halikhot Sade* 47 (*p. 10ff*), for suggested methods of pruning that should be permissible in a case of economic loss, according to the *Chazon Ish*.

ZEMIRA (PRUNING) – PROFESSIONAL AND SCIENTIFIC BACKGROUND

What is *zemira*? Pruning a vine or tree, and removing its outer branches, generally encourages the growth of lateral branches from dormant buds. Since pruning stimulates the growth of an existing vine or tree, it is regarded as a derivative category of labor (*tolada*) under the principle category of labor (*av*) of *zeri'a* (planting).

The word *zemira* is related to the word *zemora*, the branch of a grapevine. All along the branch of a grapevine there are joints, and at each joint there is a bud.

Pruning a grapevine involves two steps. Most of the branches are entirely removed (those branches will yield no produce in the following year). A small number of branches are cut back leaving two buds (or sometimes more).

Pruning requires professional skill and judgment. Which branches should remain? (Generally the stronger branches are allowed to remain, but this varies in accordance with the positioning of the vine and other factors.) How many buds are to remain? In which direction should the remaining branches be encouraged to grow? Due to the professional nature of this act, the *Chazon Ish* considered the possibility that non-professional pruning is permitted.

Grape pruning is considered an essential act of maintenance, performed during the winter, when the vine is dormant.

What is the goal of pruning? In the case of a grapevine, pruning is understood today as a means of limiting the number of grape clusters that the vine will produce in the following season. If the vine is not pruned, new shoots will issue forth all along the main branches and produce more grape clusters than the vine can successfully bear. Many of the grapes will not ripen properly and the fruit will have reduced value (they will be watery, sugar-deficient, and small).

Proper pruning leaves an appropriate number of buds and thus regulates the yield for the following year.

PRUNING

Is pruning forbidden by Torah law only with respect to the grapevine or also in the case of other trees?

The simple understanding of Rashi and the *Chazon Ish*'s understanding of the Rambam:

The pruning of a grapevine is forbidden by Torah law.
The pruning of other trees is forbidden by rabbinic decree (called *kirsum*).
(*Chazon Ish*: When the Rambam says: "Whether a grapevine or other trees," he refers not to pruning, but to picking fruit.)

Rav Kook: Pruning a grapevine differs from other trees because it promotes the growth of new fruit on the pruned branches.

According to this, it is possible that pruning a kiwi tree is forbidden by Torah law according to all authorities, because it too promotes the growth of new fruit on the pruned branches.

Simple understanding of the Rambam: "Whether a grapevine or other trees."

The pruning of all trees is forbidden by Torah law.

PLOWING

In *Parashat Mishpatim* (*Shemot 34:21*) the Torah forbids plowing and harvesting:

> Six days you shall work, but on the seventh day you shall rest: in plowing and in harvest you shall rest.

There is a dispute regarding the interpretation of this verse. The anonymous Tanna of the mishna in *Shevi'it* (*1:4*) and Rabbi Akiva (cited in a Baraita in *Rosh ha-Shana 9a* and in *Mo'ed Katan 3b*) maintain that this verse refers to the law of *tosefet shevi'it*, a law that applied during the time of the Temple, according to which some of the laws of *Shemita* would be practiced for a month before the beginning of the *Shemita* year. (The law of *tosefet shevi'it* will be discussed at length below). According to this view, plowing the field at the end of the sixth year is forbidden. If plowing is forbidden by Torah law during the end of the sixth year the prohibition to plow during the seventh year is certainly biblical.

Rabbi Yishmael disagrees with Rabbi Akiva, arguing that the verse is not addressing the laws of *Shemita*, but rather it teaches that harvesting the *omer* overrides *Shabbat*:[34]

> "In plowing and in harvest you shall rest" (*Shemot 34:21*) – Rabbi Akiva says: There is no need to be told to desist from plowing or reaping in the seventh year, for it is already stated [elsewhere]: "You shall not sow your field, etc." (*Vayikra 25:4-5*). [It can be taken] only [to prohibit] plowing in the pre-sabbatical year [which may cause agricultural benefits] extending into the seventh year and [likewise] to the harvest of the seventh year's crops which mature in the post-sabbatical year. Rabbi Yishmael says: [It is purely a *Shabbat* law]; as the plowing [forbidden on *Shabbat*] is optional plowing, so is the harvest [mentioned here] optional harvesting. This comes to exclude the harvesting [of the new barley] for the *omer*, which is a religious duty, a *mitzva*.

At first glance, Rabbi Akiva's position appears very difficult to understand: How can he argue that the latter part of the verse refers

34. The simple understanding of Rabbi Yishmael's position is that plowing during the *Shemita* year is permitted by Torah law, as explained by Rashi and the Rash. The *Pe'at ha-Shulchan* (20:1), however, writes, that Rabbi Yishmael agrees that plowing during the *Shemita* year is forbidden by Torah law, and that he only disagrees with Rabbi Akiva about *tosefet shevi'it*. This is also the way the *Pe'at ha-Shulchan* understands the Rambam, who, on the one hand, learns from "in plowing and in harvest" that plowing is forbidden by Torah law, but, on the other hand, writes that the law of *tosefet shevi'it* falls into the category of *Halacha le-Moshe me-Sinai*, laws given by tradition to Moshe at Sinai but not recorded in the Torah (as argued by Rabbi Yishmael [*Mo'ed Katan 4a*])

to the *Shemita* year, when even he agrees that the first part of the verse deals with *Shabbat*? **Rashi** (*Rosh ha-Shana 9a,* s.v. *ein tzarikh lomar*) resolves this difficulty:

> There is no need to be told to desist from plowing or reaping in the seventh year – even though the first part of the verse refers to *Shabbat,* as it is written: "Six days you shall work," the latter part of the verse refers to *Shemita,* for if it refers to *Shabbat,* are plowing and harvesting forbidden, while other labors permitted?!

In other words, the second half of the verse cannot be referring to *Shabbat,* because many types of labor are forbidden on *Shabbat.*[35]

So far we have assumed that the first part of the verse, "Six days you shall work," undoubtedly refers to *Shabbat* and that the Gemara's discussion relates solely to the final clause. The *Ritva* (*Makkot 8b*), however, cites the view of Rabbi Meir Halevi Abulafiya (the *Ramah*) who argues that according to Rabbi Akiva both clauses refer to *Shemita*:

> Rabbi Meir Halevi interpreted the entire verse as referring to *Shemita,* and the "days" mentioned here are years. In my opinion, this is incorrect, despite the fact that the Torah uses the word "days" to mean "year," as in the verse: "Within days [i.e., a full year] he may redeem it" (*Vayikra 25:29*), and "Days [i.e., a year] or ten" (*Bereishit 27:44*). Yet, when there is a count of a certain number of days or of a certain date, a year is not called days. The Torah will not state a given day meaning that given year … The correct explanation is, rather, that of Rashi.

We see that the *Ritva* himself disagrees with the *Ramah,* but we must still understand the *Ramah's* novel suggestion that the words, "six days you shall work," relate to the first six years of the sabbatical cycle, and not to the six days of the week. An analysis of the entire biblical passage seems to strengthen the *Ramah's* position. Such an analysis also shows that Rabbi Akiva's understanding that the first part of the verse refers to *Shabbat,* whereas the second part refers

35. The *Penei Yehoshua* (ad loc.) raises an objection: Granted that we cannot say that the verse comes to teach us that plowing and harvesting are forbidden on *Shabbat,* but why not say that it comes to teach us about *tosefet Shabbat,* sanctifying additional time at the beginning and end of Shabbat? Just as with respect to *Shemita* we do not say that the verse teaches that only plowing and harvesting are forbidden, but rather it teaches a general law regarding *tosefet shevi'it,* so too we can say the same thing with respect to *Shabbat.* What advantage is there to learn the law of *tosefet shevi'it,* and not *tosefet Shabbat*?
The *Penei Yehoshua* answers that if the verse had only listed one prohibition, one could claim that it is addressing *tosefet Shabbat,* citing one category of work as an example. But given that the verse lists two prohibitions, one cannot derive the notion of *tosefet Shabbat* regarding all work categories. Thus, we cannot learn *tosefet Shabbat* from this verse.
However, this suggestion of the *Penei Yehoshua* is itself difficult, for, even regarding *Shemita,* plowing and harvesting are not the only prohibited labors! One could answer the *Penei Yehoshua's* question differently, and explain that since the Gemara learned out the law of *tosefet Shabbat* from another source, "On the ninth of the month in the evening" (see

to the sabbatical year, accords a deeper understanding of the plain sense of the text.[36]

Chapters 23 and 34 of the book of *Shemot* parallel each other in an astonishing manner. We present here the two chapters, one alongside the other, highlighting the parallelisms that are pertinent to our discussion:

RABBI MEIR HALEVI ABULAFIA (*Ramah*)

ספר
יד רמה
חידושי רבינו מאיר הלוי אבולעפיה זצ״ל
על
מסכת בבא בתרא
דפים ב א — עג א
מוגה ומתוקן ע״פ דפוס ראשון ועוד מקורות
ובתוספת מראי מקומות הערות והארות

Rabbi Meir Halevi was born in 4930 (1170) in Burgos, Spain. He wrote a commentary to the Talmud, called *Yad Ramah*, only parts of which have endured. He also wrote many responsa and tracts on Jewish thought and tradition. Rabbi Meir Halevi was among those who opposed the Rambam's philosophical outlook. He died in 5004 (1244).

Yoma 83b), it was forced to say that our verse addresses *tosefet shevi'it*.

36. The idea presented here is briefly mentioned by Rav Kalman Kahana (*Cheker ve-Iyyun*, I, p. 108; and also in *Masekhet Shevi'it, Cheker ve-Iyyun*, I, p. 277). We, however, have expanded upon this idea, and applied it to the entire biblical passage.

RAV AVRAHAM YESHAYAHU KARELITZ (*the Chazon Ish*)

ספר

חזון איש

זרעים

דמאי, כלאים, שביעית, מעשרות, ערלה

(ובסופו ליקוטים שונים בעניני זרעים)

בני־ברק

ערב שנת השמיטה התשל״ג

Rav Avraham Karelitz was born in 5639 (1878) in Lithuania. From an early age he studied on his own and with great diligence. Rav Karelitz was exceedingly modest; his first book was published anonymously under the title *Chazon Ish* and was very favorably received in the Torah world. Over the course of his life he wrote twenty-two volumes under that title, and he himself became known as the *Chazon Ish*. Rav Karelitz moved to Eretz Yisrael and settled in Bnei Brak. He dealt extensively with the commandments that apply only in Eretz Yisrael. Already during the first week following his arrival in the country, he sent a query to Rav Kook concerning *terumot* and *ma'asrot*.

The *Chazon Ish* devoted great attention to *Shemita*-related issues. He did not accept the *heter mechira*, but he was exceedingly responsive to the needs of the Jewish farmers, and developed solutions that allowed them to raise certain crops during the *Shemita* year. His rulings on the laws of *Shemita* are of fundamental importance. They include many novel positions and critical leniencies, which were made possible by his unique erudition and authority.

The *Chazon Ish* dealt with many issues in all areas of Torah study. He is famous for his disagreement with Rav Chayim Naeh on the matter of halachic measurements. He argued that these measurements are substantially larger than what is commonly accepted (following the view of the *Noda Bi-Yehuda*).

Even though he never held any official position, the *Chazon Ish* was one of the most important charedi rabbinical leaders in Eretz Yisrael. His books are imposing in their scholarship and profound in their depth, and constitute an important basis for halachic decision-making. The *Chazon Ish* died in 5714 (1953).

Shemot 23	*Shemot* 34
(10) And six years you shall sow your land and gather in its fruits. (11) But the seventh year you shall let it rest and lie fallow; that the poor of your people may eat: and what they leave, the beasts of the field shall eat. So shall you do with your vineyard, and with your olive grove.	(14) For you shall worship no other god: for the Lord is a jealous God. (17) You shall make yourself no molten gods.
(12) Six days you shall do your work, and on the seventh day you shall rest: that your ox and your donkey may rest; and the son of your handmaid and the stranger may be refreshed.	(18) The feast of unleavened bread shall you keep; seven says you shall eat unleavened bread, as I commanded you, in the time of the spring month: (for in the spring month you came out from Egypt).
(13) And all the things that I have said to you be mindful of: and make no mention of the name of other gods, neither let it be heard out of your mouth.	(21) Six days you shall work, but on the seventh day you shall rest:
(14) Three times you shall keep a feast to Me in the year. (15) You shall keep the feast of unleavened bread: you shall eat unleavened bread seven days, as I commanded you, in the appointed time of the spring month; for in it you did come out from Egypt; and none shall appear before Me empty.	... you shall rest from plowing and in harvest.
(16) And the feast of harvest, the first fruits of your labors, which you have sown in the field, and the feast of ingathering, which is at the end of the year, when you have gathered in your labors out of the field.	(22) And you shall observe the feast of weeks, of the first fruits of wheat harvest, and the feast of ingathering at the year's end.
(17) Three times in the year all your males shall appear before the Lord God.	(23) Three times in the year shall all your males appear before the Lord God, the God of Israel.
(18) You shall not offer the blood of My sacrifice with leavened bread; neither shall the fat of My sacrifice remain until the morning.	(25) You shall not offer the blood of My sacrifice with leaven; neither shall the sacrifice of the Feast of the Passover be left to the morning.
(19) The first of the fruits of your land you shall bring to the house of the Lord your God;	(26) The first of the fruits of your land you shall bring to the house of the Lord your God;
You shall not boil a kid in its mother's milk.	You shall not boil a kid in its mother's milk.

As is evident, the chapters repeat themselves, both stylistically and with respect to their contents.

There is only **one** *mitzva* that appears in chap. 23, but is missing in chap. 34: the *mitzva* of *Shemita*. It seems that the solution of the problem of the "disappearance" of the *mitzva* of *Shemita* is found in the position of Rabbi Akiva, who maintains that the words, "in plowing and in harvest you shall rest," refer to the sabbatical year. According to Rabbi Akiva's understanding, the parallelism between the two chapters is complete; both chapters contain all the same *mitzvot*. It might be added that according to Rabbi Akiva the Torah chose to write the *mitzva* of *Shabbat* and the *mitzva* of *Shemita* in a single verse, in order to allude to the essential connection between them: the day of rest and the year of rest (for more on this topic, see above regarding the reasons for *Shemita*).

CONTRADICTION IN THE RAMBAM?

The **Rambam** (*Hilchot Shemita ve-Yovel 1:1*) rules in accordance with the view of Rabbi Akiva:

> There is a positive commandment to desist from working the land or tending the trees in the seventh year. As it is stated: "Then shall the land keep a Sabbath unto the Lord" and "In plowing time and in reaping time you shall rest."

This implies that the prohibition of plowing during the *Shemita* year is by Torah law. Later in the same chapter, however, he writes (*1:4*):

> He who digs or plows for the benefit of the soil … is punished with lashes by rabbinic decree.

This implies that the prohibition to plow is by rabbinic decree! The **Radbaz** (*Responsa ha-Radbaz, II, no. 196 [1560],* as well as in the Mahari Kurkus on the Rambam) explains that there are three different types of plowing: plowing for the sake of the land, which takes place prior to planting; plowing after planting, in order to cover the seeds; and plowing around a tree in order to promote its growth:[37]

37. As opposed to digging a cavity around a tree to be filled up with water which is permitted.

> You asked for my opinion regarding what the Rambam writes … . The correct understanding of the words of the master is that there are three types of plowing:
>
> 1. Plowing to improve the land is not forbidden by Torah law whatsoever. This is what the Rambam writes in the same chapter: "How so one who digs or plows for the benefit of the soil, [receives lashes by rabbinic decree] etc."
> 2. Plowing to cover the seeds is equivalent to planting. Planting and harvesting are subject to a positive commandment and a negative commandment. The positive commandment is: "In plowing time and in reaping time you shall rest." And the negative commandment is: "You shall neither sow your field … that which

> grows of its own accord of your harvest you shall not reap."
>
> 3. There is also a third type of plowing, to promote the growth of trees, which is included under the category of planting. Just as pruning is a *tolada* of planting, for it is to promote the growth of a tree, so too plowing for the sake of trees is included under planting, for on account of this type of plowing, the tree will grow better, just as by way of plowing, a seed grows.
>
> Thus plowing around trees during the seventh year is forbidden by Torah law. Therefore the master was precise in his formulation: "He who digs or plows for the benefit of the soil." Only when [the plowing] is for the benefit of the soil is it prohibited by rabbinic law. But when it is for the benefit of the seeds or for the benefit of trees, it is prohibited by Torah law.

According to the *Radbaz*, the Rambam maintains that the second and third types of plowing are forbidden by Torah law (the second as planting and the third as pruning), whereas the first type of plowing is forbidden only by rabbinic law (see also *Shabbat ha-Aretz 1, 2:2*).

The *Chazon Ish* (*18:3*) disagrees with the *Radbaz*. He raises an objection from the fact that the source of the prohibition during the *Shemita* year is the verse that forbids plowing during *tosefet shevi'it*, prior to the sabbatical year itself. Thus, it is impossible to argue that the plowing that takes place prior to planting is forbidden only by rabbinic law. Accordingly, the *Chazon Ish* explains that all types of plowing are forbidden during the *Shemita* year, but nevertheless the lashes for plowing during the sabbatical year are only "rabbinic" because it is a prohibition derived from a positive commandment (*issur asei*):

> Plowing is forbidden by Torah law both according to Rabbi Yishmael and according to Rabbi Akiva, for [plowing] is forbidden by Torah law even thirty days before [the *Shemita* year], yet there are no biblically mandated lashes, for it is a violation of a positive commandment.

HOEING AND DIGGING

In principle, hoeing during the *Shemita* year is forbidden only by rabbinic decree (Rambam 3:9; see also *Tosafot Yom Tov, Shevi'it* 2:2). However, hoeing and plowing are similar activities and often it is difficult to distinguish between them. *Sefer ha-Shemita* (chap. 5) deals with this issue, and defines "hoeing" as plowing performed by hand (with a hoe, of course), whereas "plowing" is performed by an animal or a machine (see also *Shabbat ha-Aretz* 1, 7:2–3; 3, 9:1).

Plowing before planting

Plowing to cover the seeds

RABBI DAVID BEN ZIMRA (the *Radbaz*)

Rabbi David ben Zimra was born in Spain in 5239 (1479). When he was thirteen, the Jews were expelled from Spain, and he moved with his family to Morocco. He later reached Tzefat and Jerusalem. Owing to the attacks on the Jews and the difficult economic situation, he moved to Egypt. He served there for forty years as head of the court and head of the yeshiva. He later returned to Jerusalem and from there back to Tzefat. In Tzefat he was close to Rabbi Yosef Karo and the *Mabit*, both of whom held him in high regard. He died in Tzefat in 5333 (1573) at the age of ninety-five.

The *Radbaz* wrote several works that are relatively unknown (such as *Kelalei ha-Gemara; Metzudot David* – a commentary to the 613 *mitzvot*). He is best known for his commentary to the Rambam's *Mishneh Torah* and for his magnum opus – *Responsa ha-Radbaz*.

The *Responsa ha-Radbaz* is comprised of over two thousand responsa, and we know that thousands of other responsa were lost. From a quantitative perspective, the *Radbaz* was one of the greatest rabbinic responders in Jewish history.

Another labor that is similar to plowing is digging. *Torat Kohanim* (*Behar, parasha 1, halacha 4*) relates to digging:

> "Then shall the land keep a Sabbath to the Lord" – You might think that one may not dig wells, ditches and caves or repair ritual baths. Therefore the verse states: "You shall neither sow your field, nor prune your vineyard."

In other words, only actions connected to planting are forbidden, but digging alone is permitted (this is also the implication of the Rambam *10:14*, and this understanding is corroborated by the *Pe'at ha-Shulchan 21:23*). The Rambam qualifies this allowance, ruling explicitly that even digging without the intention of planting is forbidden, if the resulting hole is likely to be used for planting. The Rambam adds that spreading earth over the field without passing a plow over it is also regarded as plowing, and therefore, during the *Shemita* year one must pile the earth in mounds (end of chap. 2, and thus it follows from *Shevi'it 2:3*).

ספרא דבי רב
הוא ספר
תורת כהנים
כולל
מדרשי התנאים הקדושים זכרונם לברכה לספר ויקרא
עם
פירוש החסיד אור ישראל וקדושו הרב רבינו אברהם בן דוד
מפשקירו בעל ההשגות על הרמב"ם זכרו לחיי עד
יצא עתה בפעם הראשון בדפוס בשלמות על פי כתב יד אשר באוצר הספרים שבאקספארד
מסורת התלמוד
יעקב הכהן שלאסבערג
ווין

TORAT KOHANIM

Chazal refer to the book of *Vayikra* as *"Torat Kohanim,"* "The Laws of the Kohanim" (*Shir ha-Shirim Rabba* 5, 20). The halachic midrash on the book of *Vayikra* is sometimes referred to by this name, "*Torat Kohanim*" (*Kiddushin* 33a), or as the "*Sifra*" (*Berakhot* 11b). The work is an early halachic midrash, mainly attributed to Rabbi Yehuda bar Ila'i, a disciple of Rabbi Akiva. Thus, the Gemara (*Sanhedrin* 86a) states a general rule that, "Anonymous statements in *Sifra* are presumed to be from Rabbi Yehuda."

HARVESTING *SHEMITA* PRODUCE

> "Nor shall you gather the grapes of your protected vine" (*Vayikra 25:5*) – From that which has been guarded you shall not gather, but you may gather from that which has been declared ownerless.
>
> "Nor shall you gather" – you shall not gather in the usual manner. (*Torat Kohanim, Sifra Behar, parasha 1*)

Torat Kohanim relates here to what appears to be a contradiction in the Torah itself. On the one hand, as we have already seen, reaping and gathering are forbidden during the *Shemita* year. On the other hand, the Torah explicitly states: "And the Sabbath produce of the land shall be food for you" (*Vayikra 25:6*). How can the produce be eaten if it is not harvested? ***Torat Kohanim*** comes to teach us what types of reaping and gathering are permitted.

The *Rishonim* disagree about how to understand the relationship between the two parts of the passage from ***Torat Kohanim***, namely between the first part which allows gathering of produce that had been declared ownerless and the second part which allows gathering produce in an unusual matter.

1. ***Tosafot* cite Rabbenu Tam's** view as follows (*Rosh ha-Shana 9a,* s.v. *ve-katzir; Sukka 39b,* s.v. *bameh devarim amurim,* and elsewhere):

   > Rabbenu Tam says that produce that has been guarded is forbidden, as we have learned in *Torat Kohanim*: " 'Nor shall you gather the grapes of your protected vine (*nezirecha*)' – from that which has been declared ownerless you may gather, but you shall not gather from that which had been guarded." For the word "*nezirecha*" implies that people are set apart (*nazar*) from it.
   >
   > Even produce that was declared ownerless is forbidden if gathered in the usual manner of gathering. But when gathered with a change (*shinuy*), not in the usual manner of gathering, it is permitted. But that

which had been guarded is forbidden even if gathered in an unusual manner.

According to *Tosafot*, eating and harvesting produce that had been guarded (*shamur*, produce whose owner had guarded it for himself and failed to declare it ownerless) is forbidden, while produce that had been declared ownerless may be harvested with a *shinuy*.[38] The two parts of the passage in *Torat Kohanim* teach us each of these laws. The first teaches that produce that had not been declared ownerless is absolutely forbidden, and that produce that had been declared ownerless is permitted. The second teaches that even produce that had been declared ownerless may only be harvested in an altered manner.

2. **The position of the Rash** (*Mishna Shevi'it 8:6*):

The entire prohibition here relates to produce that had been guarded. But produce that had been declared ownerless is permitted, even when harvested in the usual manner, as is proven in the *Yerushalmi* …

According to the Rash, a *shinuy* in the manner of harvesting is only necessary to permit produce that had been guarded,[39] but **produce that had been declared ownerless may be harvested in the usual manner!** How does the Rash understand *Torat Kohanim*? He apparently understands that the second part of the passage ("You shall not gather in the usual manner") relates back to the first part, and it explains how one is to gather produce that had been guarded: Do not gather guarded produce in the usual manner (the first part), but rather gather it with a *shinuy* (second part). If, however, the vineyard had been declared ownerless, the produce may be gathered in the usual manner.

Thus far we have seen two positions:

Rabbenu Tam: *Shamur* may not be harvested at all. Produce

38. Rabbenu Tam explains the verse, "Nor shall you gather the grapes of your protected vine (*nezirecha*)," as drawing on the concept of a Nazirite, one who separates himself from wine. That is to say, an owner who separates others (*nazar* = *hinzir*) from eating his grapes – is forbidden to consume them himself.

39. The Rash permits *shamur*, as will be discussed below. The Radbaz (*Hilchot Shemita ve-Yovel* 4:22) raises an objection: "I have a difficulty with his position. Surely all fields are ownerless during the *Shemita* year. Do we need a verse that teaches that one may not gather produce in the usual manner for one who transgressed and guarded his vineyard rather than declare it ownerless?" That is to say, according to the Rash it turns out that the *shinuy* required by the Torah is only necessary in a guarded vineyard, but guarding the vineyard is forbidden by the Torah! The Rambam also permits *shamur* (as will be explained below), and he too maintains that the harvesting of such produce must be performed with a *shinuy*, but in his opinion the Torah requires that all produce gathered during the *Shemita* year be gathered in an unusual manner, whether the produce is *shamur* or it had been declared ownerless.

that had been declared ownerless may only be harvested in an altered manner.

Rash: *Shamur* may be harvested in an altered manner. Produce that had been declared ownerless is permitted even when harvested in the usual manner.

3. **The view of the Ramban** (*commentary to Vayikra 25:5*):

> He is not to guard them for himself, but he is to gather them with the poor as if they were ownerless ...When the Rabbis have said that seventh-year figs may not be cut with a special fig-knife, and grapes may not be pressed in a wine-press, they are creating laws to be a rabbinic fence in order that people should not come to guard and gather their crops and thereby rob them from the poor.

The Ramban agrees with the **Rash's** interpretation of the verses, that by Torah law it is permitted to harvest produce that had been declared ownerless in the usual manner – "he is to gather them with the poor as if they were ownerless." He, however, maintains that by **rabbinic decree** the produce **must be gathered with a *shinuy*.** In other words, the Ramban's understanding of the biblical passage is identical to that of the Rash (who permits the gathering of ownerless produce without a *shinuy*). But on the practical level he rules like Rabbenu Tam[40] (who requires a *shinuy*). Rabbenu Tam, however, maintains that the *shinuy* is required by Torah law, whereas Ramban maintains that the *shinuy* is required only by rabbinic decree.[41]

4. The **Rambam** (*Hilchot Shemita ve-Yovel 4:22*) maintains that a *shinuy* is necessary whether the produce is *shamur* or it had been declared ownerless.[42] A *shinuy* is always necessary, but a *shinuy* is also always effective (even with respect to produce that is *shamur*); namely, all produce harvested in an unusual manner is permitted:

40. There is another difference between the Ramban and Rabbenu Tam regarding produce that had been guarded. According to Rabbenu Tam, such produce is forbidden, whereas according to the Ramban, it is forbidden only as long as it remains guarded, but if it is later declared ownerless it is permitted. Elsewhere (*Yevamot 122a*) the Ramban writes that *shamur* is not forbidden.

41. This is also the way that the *Chazon Ish* (*Shevi'it* 12, 5, s.v. *da'at ha-Ramban*) understood the Ramban.

42. This is the simple understanding of the Rambam, and this is the way his words were understood by *Mishnat R. Natan* (*Shevi'it* 6:2); Mahari Kurkus (on the Rambam, *Hilchot Shemita ve-Yovel 4:22*); and the *Chazon Ish* (*Shevi'it* 12, 5, s.v. ***ve-da'at ha-Ramban***; 12, 8, s.v. *8:6*). Rash Sirillo (*Yerushalmi, Shevi'it 8:6, s.v. ve-nir'eh li*), however, understands that the Rambam forbids *shamur* (like Rabbenu Tam). On the other hand, the *Minchat Chinuch* (*mitzva 328*) writes that the Rambam might maintain that only produce that had been guarded must be harvested in an altered manner, but produce that had been declared ownerless may be harvested in the usual manner (like the Rash). In any event, most *Acharonim* understand that the Rambam does not forbid *shamur* (see

> Fruit yielded by a tree during the *Shemita* year may not be gathered in the same manner as in other years, as it is said: "And the grapes of your protected vine you shall not gather." If he gathers it as part of the regular cultivation of the tree, or in the usual manner of grape gatherers, he is subject to lashes.

According to the Rambam, the second part of the *Torat Kohanim* passage (regarding a *shinuy*) is an independent clause, and it relates to all the cases mentioned in the first part of the passage (both produce that is *shamur* and produce that had been declared ownerless).[43]

A Short Summary:

	Produce that is *shamur*	Produce that had been declared ownerless
Rabbenu Tam	Forbidden	Permitted with a *shinuy*
Rash	Permitted with a *shinuy*	Permitted even without a *shinuy*
Ramban	Permitted with a *shinuy*	Permitted, but by rabbinic decree a *shinuy* is necessary
Rambam	Permitted with a *shinuy*	Permitted with a *shinuy*

The *Rishonim* disagree about how produce is to be gathered during the *Shemita* year:

In practice, even produce that had been declared ownerless must be harvested in an altered manner (whether by Torah law or by rabbinic decree), in contradiction to the Rash (though in certain situations his position may be counted as an auxiliary factor to allow leniency, such as regarding *Otzar Bet Din*).

Kappot Temarim [*Sukka* 39b, s.v. *katvu ha-Tosafot*] and ***Pe'at ha-Shulchan*** [22:1]. Rambam does not distinguish between *shamur* and *ne'evad*, see ***Ma'adanei Aretz***, no. 2 and ***Chazon Ish***, 12, 5.

43. See below, that according to Rambam the *shinuy* is in **the quantity of produce being harvested and not in the manner of harvest.** According to this approach, another possible understanding of the *Torat Kohanim* passage may be suggested. It is possible that the second part of the *Torat Kohanim* that speaks of a *shinuy* in the harvest relates back to the first part and means the same thing: You, the owner of the field, must declare your field ownerless (the first part of the *Torat Kohanim*), for the field is not really yours. Thus, you must not harvest a large measure of produce in the manner of an owner, but only a small amount in the manner of a guest.

Torat Kohanim	First part: **One may not gather produce that had been guarded, only produce that had been declared ownerless**	Second part: One may not gather produce in the usual manner, only with a *shinuy*
Rabbenu Tam	**One may not gather produce that had been guarded, only produce that had been declared ownerless**	The requirement of a *shinuy* applies to produce that had been declared ownerless [but *shamur* is forbidden]
Rash	One may not gather, in the regular manner, produce that has been guarded. Only produce that has been declared ownerless may be gathered in the regular manner.	The requirement of a *shinuy* applies to produce that is *shamur* [but produce that had been declared ownerless is permitted even without a *shinuy*]
Rambam	**One may not gather produce that had been guarded, only produce that had been declared ownerless**	The requirement of a *shinuy* applies to both parts [both *shamur* and produce that had been declared ownerless are permitted with a *shinuy*]

WHAT TYPE OF *SHINUY*?

> Seventh-year figs may not be cut with a *muktzeh*, but they may be cut with a *charba*. (*Shevi'it 8:6*)

The *Rishonim* disagree about how to understand this Mishna. The **Rosh** (ad loc.), **Bartenura** (ad loc.) and ***Tosafot*** (*Rosh ha-Shana 9a; Sukka 39b*) write that the **act of harvest itself** must be performed in an altered manner, that is to say, one must perform the harvest with a tool that is not designed for harvesting. As **Bartenura** states:

> Seventh-year figs may not be cut with a *muktzeh* – *a* tool especially intended for cutting figs.
>
> But they may be cut with a *charba* – a knife, from the word *cherev*, sword.

The **Rambam** (*Hilchot Shemita ve-Yovel 4:1;* and similarly, *Sefer ha-Mitzvot,* negative *mitzva 222*), on the other hand, writes that the *shinuy* is in the **quantity of produce being harvested**, and makes no mention of a *shinuy* **in the act of harvest**:

> As for the Torah prohibition, "That which grows of its own accord of your harvest you shall not reap" (*Vayikra 25:5*) – it means only that one may not harvest in the same manner as he does every year. If he does harvest in the customary manner, he is subject to lashes. How so? For example, if he harvests the whole field ... rather, he harvests a little at a time, processes it and eats of it.

How does the **Rambam** explain the Mishna, which seems to imply that the act of harvest itself must be performed in an altered manner – "Seventh-year figs may not be cut with a *muktzeh*, but they may be cut with a *charba*?" It would appear from his commentary to the Mishna (as well as the language of *Hilchot Shemita ve-Yovel 4:23*), that **Rambam** understands that the Mishna is dealing with the processing of produce **that had already been harvested**. In other words, according to the Rambam, the harvest itself need not be performed in an unusual manner, but once the produce is harvested, it may not be processed (by rabbinic decree) in the usual manner. For example, figs may not be dried in the shed where figs are usually spread for drying; grapes may not be pressed in a wine-press, but only in a large vat; and the like (Rambam understands that the word *"kotzin"* used in the Mishna means to dry, rather than to cut):

> *Muktzeh* – the name of the place where fruits, such as figs and grapes, are spread out to dry … .

What quantity of produce may be harvested?

We saw above that the **Rambam** writes that a person is forbidden to harvest his entire field at the same time, but he is permitted to harvest a little at a time.

How much is "a little at a time"? The ***Chazon Ish*** explains that "one may gather the amount that a person requires for household use for a few days" (*26, 6*), and after he has eaten or sold that amount, he may go back and harvest the same amount once again.

In practice, it is best to make both *shinuyim* – a *shinuy* both in the **manner of harvesting** and **the quantity of the harvest.** The ***Chazon Ish*** (*12, 8,* s.v. *shevi'it*), however, writes that when it is impossible to perform the harvest in an altered manner, one may be lenient in this regard:

> Since, according to the Rambam, there is never a requirement of a *shinuy* in the reaping or gathering itself, but rather the *shinuy* is that he doesn't harvest a large quantity in the manner of an owner – one who relies on this leniency and picks or gathers a small amount of produce that had been declared ownerless without a *shinuy*, where it is impossible to make such a *shinuy*, loses nothing [meaning he acts appropriately].

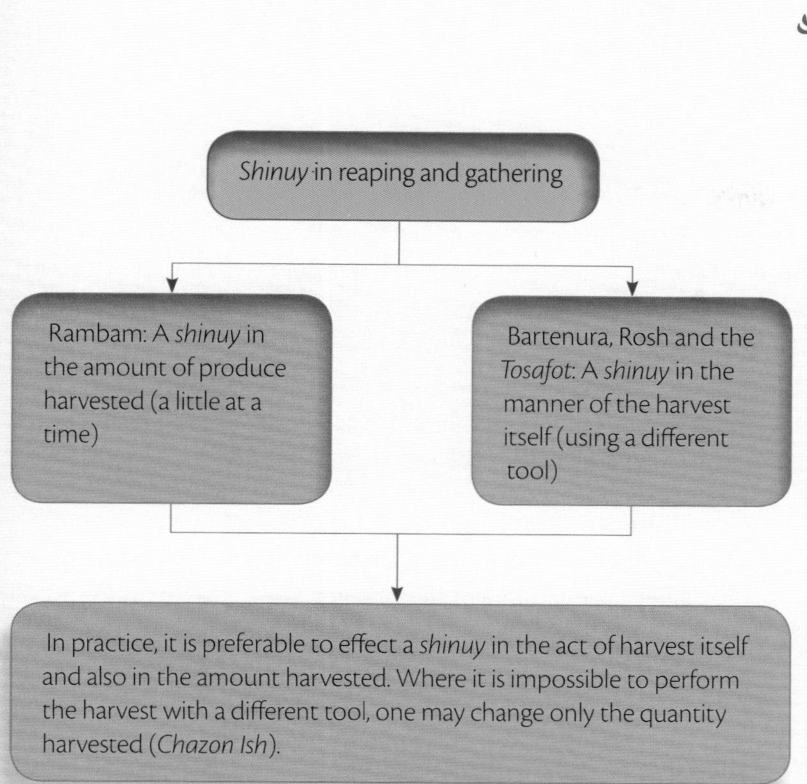

HOW DOES A SHINUY HELP?

According to the Bartenura, harvesting is only permitted when performed **in an altered manner**. Perhaps the Torah did not forbid the action when performed in an unusual manner, as we find with respect to the prohibitions of *Shabbat*. According to Rambam, however, it is permitted to harvest in the usual manner, **provided the harvesting is done in smaller quantities**. Why should one be permitted to harvest "a little at a time?" May one likewise plant in limited quantities? Certainly not.

In light of the aforementioned words of the ***Chazon Ish*** – "he doesn't harvest a large quantity **in the manner of an owner**," it may be possible to understand how the *shinuy* in quantity can permit reaping and gathering. Reaping and gathering are not problematic in and of themselves, for they are permitted when limited to a quantity that will suffice for several days of eating. However *Shemita* produce is ownerless, and a person must not demonstrate ownership over the produce. Therefore, a *shinuy* involving a reduction in the quantity of produce harvested demonstrates that the harvesting is not an act of ownership, but merely taking ownerless produce for one's household consumption, which is permitted to all, owner and stranger alike. (Planting, on the other hand, is forbidden in and of itself, and not just because it demonstrates ownership).

This principle is also implied by the language of the Rambam in his *Sefer ha-Mitzvot* (negative *mitzva 222*):

> God does not desire that the produce that grows during *Shemita* not be harvested at all, since He says, "The Sabbath produce of the land shall be food for you." The meaning is that the manner of reaping must be different from that of ordinary years: One must reap the produce as one would reap ownerless growth.

The Rambam implies that it is forbidden to harvest in the manner that an owner harvests his crop. Therefore, according to the Rambam, harvesting is permitted when performed in a manner that does not express ownership.[44]

Another ramification of this principle follows from the words of the *Chazon Ish*. The ***Chazon Ish*** (*12, 6,* s.v. *ve-nir'eh*) writes that if a person did not harvest the entire field, he has not violated a prohibition (even if he harvested a substantial amount). It is rabbinic decree only, that one must harvest just a small amount, so that it will not appear as if he were doing business with *Shemita* produce. The Torah prohibits giving the appearance that he owns the produce. If he does not harvest the entire field in the manner of an owner, he does not violate the Torah prohibition. The Sages extended this prohibition to limit harvest to a small amount (enough to satisfy his household needs for several days).

Another important ramification of this principle is found in the continuation of the *Chazon Ish's* words (*12, 8,* s.v. *Shevi'it 8:6*):

> If the produce is picked on behalf of *Otzar Bet Din* for all the residents of the town, it is unnecessary to [pick the produce] in an altered manner.

44. It is possible, however, that this principle is only valid according to the Rambam who maintains that the *shinuy* is in the quantity of produce harvested. According to those who say that the *shinuy* is in the manner of the harvest itself, reaping and gathering might be forbidden in and of themselves. The Torah permitted only non-professional manners of harvest, which are not included in the category of forbidden harvesting, just as the Torah only forbade planting and pruning, and not other forms of working the land. It is also possible that harvesting in an altered and non-professional manner is permitted because it does not demonstrate ownership.

Since *Otzar Bet Din* is based on the understanding that the individual landholders waive their proprietary rights and authorize the court to administer their fields during the *Shemita* year, there is no need for a *shinuy* in the manner of the harvest in order to express the absence of ownership.[45]

45. The ***Chazon Ish* himself was inclined to say that in an ownerless field** (or in a field belonging to another person), one may harvest in the usual manner, because harvesting there is not a demonstration of ownership.

WHY ARE REAPING AND GATHERING DIFFERENT THAN THE OTHER LABORS?

All of the labors that are forbidden because of *Shemita* are forbidden during **the seventh year** – from the first of Tishrei to the end of Elul. [46]

46. Fruit trees must be planted before the fifteenth of Av of the sixth year, but this is for a different reason. See below, pp. 158–164 (and see there regarding trees that do not bear fruit).

Reaping and gathering are exceptions, for as we saw above in ***Torat Kohanim***, there is a connection between the prohibitions of reaping and gathering and the obligation **to declare the produce ownerless**. **Rambam** also writes in this vein (*Sefer ha-Mitzvot,* negative *mitzva* 222): "The manner of reaping must be different from that of ordinary years: one must reap the produce as one would reap **ownerless** growth." As was explained above, the reason is that reaping and gathering are not problematic in and of themselves, as can be seen by the fact that they are permitted when limited to a quantity that will suffice for only several days of eating. However, **it is forbidden to demonstrate ownership over *Shemita* produce**.

This has significance for **the time that reaping and gathering are prohibited**. As stated, the prohibitions of reaping and gathering only apply to produce that must be declared ownerless, which is produce that has *Shemita* sanctity. It is, therefore, permitted to pick fruit in the usual manner during the first few months of the *Shemita* year, for *Shemita* sanctity only applies to fruit that took shape during the seventh year, and the fruit that grows during the first few months of the *Shemita* year already took shape in the sixth year.[47] On the other hand, during the eighth year, when all other agricultural labors are permitted, it is still forbidden to reap and gather produce that has *Shemita* sanctity (such as fruit that took shape during the seventh year) in the usual manner. These labors

47. See below, pp. 243–248.

must, therefore, be performed in an altered manner, because the produce is ownerless and it is forbidden to demonstrate ownership over it (see *Ma'adanei Aretz, 2–5; Chazon Ish 3:23,* s.v. *sham im; 9, 12;* and elsewhere).

SUMMARY:

Reaping and gathering are forbidden when performed in a manner that demonstrates ownership. This has several important ramifications:

1. It is permitted to harvest produce in an **altered manner**: **Harvesting is not forbidden in and of itself**, but only because it demonstrates ownership. By performing the harvest in an altered manner, one shows that he is not acting as an owner. According to the **Bartenura,** the *shinuy* must be made **in the act of harvest itself**, whereas according to the **Rambam**, the *shinuy* must be in the **quantity** of produce being harvested. Strictly speaking, the law follows the position of the Rambam, that it is permitted to harvest an amount that will suffice for several days, even without a *shinuy*, but preferably one should also perform the harvest itself in an unusual manner. (Generally speaking, in private, non-commercial gardens, produce is always picked in a non-professional manner, and thus the only thing that can be changed is the amount of produce being harvested.)
2. The prohibition of harvesting applies **only to produce that has *Shemita* sanctity**, for only with respect to such produce is it forbidden to demonstrate ownership. It is therefore permissible to pick fruit as usual at the beginning of the *Shemita* year (for the produce does not have *Shemita* sanctity), but *Shemita* produce must be picked in an altered manner even if the picking is only performed in the eighth year. As for vegetables, the prohibition applies from the first of Tishrei of the *Shemita* year to the end of the *Shemita* year.
3. If a person did not harvest the entire field, he has not violated the Torah prohibition (because he did not act as an owner), though by rabbinic decree one may only harvest a small amount that will suffice for several days.

4. Through *Otzar Bet Din*, it is permissible to harvest everything in the usual manner, because *Otzar Bet Din* is not a private entity, and this harvest is not regarded as showing ownership.

RENOUNCING OWNERSHIP OF *SHEMITA* PRODUCE

"But the seventh year you shall let it rest and lie fallow" (*Shemot 23:11*).

The Torah commands: "But the seventh year you shall let it rest and lie fallow" (*Shemot 23:11*). The Gemara derives from this verse that one is obligated to declare his *Shemita* produce ownerless. This obligation can be understood in two ways. The Torah might be saying that an obligation falls upon each person **to actively declare his *Shemita* produce ownerless**, in the same way that ordinary objects can be declared ownerless. Alternatively, the Torah might be saying that the produce is automatically ownerless – **"a dispensation of the King"** – in which case there is no obligation to actively repudiate ownership of the produce.

The logic underlying the first approach is that when a person willingly declares his produce ownerless he internalizes the message that the land and the produce growing on it do not belong to him. On the other hand, the very act of repudiating title to produce can infuse a person with the sense that he is the owner, because only an owner can declare his produce ownerless. Thus, according to the second approach, it is precisely the Torah's insistence that all produce is automatically regarded as ownerless during the *Shemita* year that will bring a person to internalize the message that "the land is Mine; for you are strangers and sojourners with Me" (*Vayikra 25:23*).

Theoretically, all produce having *Shemita* sanctity is regarded as ownerless.[48] Such produce remains ownerless in the eighth year as well (*Chazon Ish 3, 23*).[49] On the other hand, fruit at the beginning of the *Shemita* year is not regarded as ownerless, for it does not have *Shemita* sanctity.

The **Rambam** (*Hilchot Matenot Aniyim 6:5*) asserts that *terumot* and *ma'asrot* are not set aside during the *Shemita* year:

> The produce of the *Shemita* year is all ownerless, and neither *terumot* nor *ma'asrot* are separated from it.

The *Bet Yosef* and the *Mabit* disagree about the rationale

48. Is it necessary to declare *Otzar Bet Din* produce ownerless? The Rashbash (*Responsa ha-Rashbash*, no. 258, s.v. *od sha'alta*, and s.v. *u-le-inyan*) implies that *Otzar Bet Din* produce does not have to be declared ownerless. This is particularly reasonable if we understand that the obligation to renounce ownership of the produce is based on the need to internalize that we do not truly own the land, and therefore, the *bet din*, which is not a private entity, is not bound by this obligation. However, according to the *Chazon Ish*, even a court may not assert ownership over a field and bar people from taking the produce (see *Halichot Sadeh 50*).

49. The *Chazon Ish* raises a doubt about this law, but he concludes that ownership status follows the sanctity of the produce. In contrast, the *Kehilot Ya'akov* (*Zera'im*, end of section 3) writes that it is possible that the obligation to renounce ownership over produce stems from the sanctity of the land, and not from the sanctity of the produce, in which case *Shemita* produce which continues to grow during the eighth year is not ownerless.

underlying this law, and in light of this dispute they also disagree about whether the produce of a gentile is subject to *terumot* and *ma'asrot* during the *Shemita* year. The ***Bet Yosef*** (*Responsa Avkat Rochel,* section 24) writes:

> *Shemita* produce is exempt from *ma'asrot* because it is declared ownerless, but anything that is not declared ownerless is not exempt from *ma'asrot.*

That is to say, the exemption from setting aside *terumot* and *ma'asrot* during the *Shemita* year is because all *Shemita* produce is declared ownerless. Since a gentile is under no obligation to renounce ownership of his produce, it is subject to *terumot* and *ma'asrot,* even during the *Shemita* year (provided, of course, that the completion of processing of the harvest and ingathering, *miru'ach,* is performed by a Jew, as otherwise there is no *teruma* or *ma'aser* obligation on gentile produce even in other years).

The ***Mabit***[50] (*Responsa ha-Mabit, vol. 1,* no. *11*) proposed a different explanation for Rambam's position:

> A Jew who fenced in his vineyard and failed to declare it ownerless during the *Shemita* year ... the Torah declared his land ownerless with respect to both the poor and the rich, and therefore there is no obligation of *ma'aser.*

That is to say, the land is automatically regarded as ownerless during the *Shemita* year, and produce that has no owner is not subject to *terumot* and *ma'asrot.* According to this understanding, even the produce of a gentile is exempt from *terumot* and *ma'asrot,* for it is also automatically regarded as ownerless.

We see that the *Mabit* and the *Bet Yosef* disagree precisely on the point raised above. According to the *Bet Yosef,* an obligation falls upon each and every Jew to renounce ownership of his produce during the *Shemita* year. Therefore, if a gentile does not declare his produce ownerless, it is not ownerless, and the produce is subject to *terumot* and *ma'asrot* (provided that the completion of the processing is performed by a Jew.) According to the *Mabit,* produce growing during the *Shemita* year is automatically ownerless, and thus even

50. This is also the position of his son, the Maharit (vol. *1,* section 43).

the produce of a gentile is ownerless, and therefore exempt from *terumot* and *ma'asrot.*

The ***Minchat Chinuch*** (*mitzva* no. 84, s.v. *ve-ani mistapek*) suggests that this disagreement has various ramifications. Let us examine one of them:

> I am in doubt whether this *mitzva* is upon the person, that is to say the Torah commanded him to declare his produce ownerless during the *Shemita* year and he is obligated to fulfill this obligation; if he declares it ownerless, it is regarded as ownerless, but if he does not declare it ownerless, it is not regarded as ownerless [even though he violates a positive *mitzva*] ... If this is so, nobody else may take it, and it would be regarded as stolen property in the hands of another person, as long as the owner does not declare it ownerless ... Or perhaps there is no need for the owner to declare the produce ownerless, it being a "dispensation of the King" which automatically makes the produce ownerless ... and if another person acquired the produce against the owner's wishes, it is his, for he acquired it from an ownerless state even if the owner did not declare it ownerless ... The view of the *Bet Yosef* is that it is a commandment that is upon the owner, whereas the opinion of the *Maharit* is that it is a "dispensation of the King."

If a person fails to renounce ownership of the produce, is the produce automatically regarded as ownerless? May another person eat of that produce without the owner's permission? If a person is obligated to declare his produce ownerless, then if he fails to do so, the produce is not ownerless, and thus it would be forbidden for another person to eat it. If, however, the produce is automatically regarded as ownerless, then the produce is ownerless whether or not the owner agrees, and anybody may take of the produce even without the owner's permission.[51]

It should be noted that the *Bet Yosef* himself maintains that *Shemita* sanctity does not apply to the produce of a gentile, and thus such produce can become subject to *terumot* and *ma'asrot.*

51. The *Minchat Chinuch* suggests additional practical ramifications. For example, why are women bound by the obligation to renounce ownership of their *Shemita* produce? If *Shemita* produce is automatically regarded as ownerless, this clearly applies to a woman's produce as well. But if an obligation falls upon each individual to declare his produce ownerless, this should be regarded as a time-bound positive commandment, from which women are generally exempt. See the end of this chapter as to why, according to the *Minchat Chinuch*, women are indeed obligated to declare their produce ownerless.

According to the *Mabit,* on the other hand, the produce of a gentile has *Shemita* sanctity. But the *Bet Yosef* argues that even according to the *Mabit's* view, the produce of a gentile can become liable to *terumot* and *ma'asrot,* because it is never declared ownerless.[52]

Another possible ramification of the disagreement between the *Bet Yosef* and the *Mabit* relates to the question whether or not a person must verbally renounce ownership of his produce at the beginning of the *Shemita* year. According to the *Mabit,* this would appear to be unnecessary,[53] for the produce is automatically regarded as ownerless, and all that a person must do is allow access to his field to those who wish to take of its produce. According to the *Bet Yosef,* on the other hand, it is quite possible that a person must verbally renounce ownership.

The ***Iggerot Moshe*** implies that a person should verbally declare his produce ownerless, and this is also the recommendation brought in the name of **Rav Sh. Z. Auerbach** (cited in *Dinei Shevi'it, Degel Yerushalayim, 14, 3*). According to other authorities, however, this is unnecessary, and the only demand placed upon field owners is to leave the gates to their property open in order to allow access to those who wish to enter. In practice, it is preferable to verbally renounce ownership of one's produce.[54] An intermediate position regarding the fundamental question posed above may be implicit in the words of the **Rambam** (*Sefer ha-Mitzvot, 134*):

> He commanded us to **renounce ownership** of all produce of the land during the *Shemita* year, and the Torah **declared ownerless** whatever grows in our fields so that it is permitted to everybody.

According to Rambam, every individual is bound by the *mitzva* to renounce ownership of his produce – "He commanded us to renounce ownership." On the other hand, the Torah also declared the produce to be ownerless – "and declared ownerless." It would seem from here that while a person is bound to renounce ownership of his produce, if he fails to do so, the Torah declares his produce ownerless in any case. Indeed, this is precisely the explanation of

52. All this assumes the position of the Rambam that *Shemita* produce is exempt from *terumot* and *ma'asrot* because it is ownerless. The *Tosafot* (*Rosh ha-Shana 15a,* s.v. *yad ha-kol*) understand that the very fact that the produce is *Shemita* produce exempts it from *terumot* and *ma'asrot.* See the chapter dealing with *terumot* and *ma'asrot* during the *Shemita* year at the end of this volume.

53. This indeed is the way that the *Mabit* was understood in *Torat ha-Aretz* (vol. *I, 8, 6,* s.v. *ve-nir'eh*). In contrast, the Ridbaz (*Bet Ridbaz, 4,* section *8,* s.v. *ve-hineh*; and section *13,* s.v. *lefi aniyut da'ati pashut*; and so too in *Responsa Maharsham,* vol. *VI,* section *127*), writes that "the *Bet Yosef* and the *Maharit* disagree ... whether there is a 'dispensation of the King' or if one is obligated to renounce ownership, but all agree that there is a *mitzva* to verbally renounce ownership."

54. According to this position, when must a person renounce ownership of his produce – at the beginning of the *Shemita* year, or whenever there is produce? I have not found any discussion of this issue, but it stands to reason that it is not necessary to renounce ownership each time that new produce grows.

Rav Moshe Feinstein (*Responsa Iggerot Moshe, Yoreh De'a,* vol. *III*, section *90*):

> The owner of a field is obligated to verbally renounce ownership. Even without his statement that he is renouncing ownership, the produce is nevertheless regarded as ownerless. This is the implication of the wording of the Rambam, *Hilchot Shemita* 4:24[55]: "It is a positive commandment to leave ownerless all that the land produces in the *Shemita* year, as it is stated: 'But the seventh year you shall let it rest and lie fallow' *(Shemot 23:11)*," which implies that he must verbally declare it ownerless.[56]

55. Rav Feinstein learns this from a different passage in the Rambam, but it seems that the passage that we have cited (from *Sefer ha-Mitzvot*) expresses this position more clearly.

56. This is also the view of the *Mirkevet ha-Mishneh* on the *Mechilta* (*Mishpatim, parasha 20*, no. 19, based on the Rambam and Rashi, *Rosh ha-Shana 15*).

The ***Chazon Ish*** (*20, 7,* s.v. *u-mihu*) ruled in accordance with the *Mabit* that *Shemita* sanctity applies to the produce of a gentile. He writes, however, that it is possible that such produce is not regarded as ownerless, because the Torah only declared the produce of a Jew to be ownerless. The *Chazon Ish* explains the distinction by arguing that since a gentile is not bound by the *mitzva* of *Shemita*, *Shemita* may not influence the relationship between him and his produce, and therefore the produce is not regarded as ownerless. *Shemita* does, however, impact the relationship between a Jew and his produce, and therefore that produce is automatically ownerless.

In practice, the ***Pe'at ha-Shulchan*** (*23:12*) and the ***Chazon Ish*** (*9, 20, 17*) write that *terumot* and *ma'asrot* should be separated from the produce of a gentile because of legal uncertainty (see below, p. *525*, regarding *terumot* and *ma'asrot* during the *Shemita* year, and below, p. *387*, regarding the *heter mechira*).

As for *Shemita* sanctity in the produce of a gentile, the ***Pe'at ha-Shulchan*** (*23:29*) rules in accordance with the *Bet Yosef*, while the ***Chazon Ish*** (*19, 24; 20, 7,* s.v. *u-mihu*), as we have seen, follows the *Mabit*. In general, the accepted practice in Israel is that the produce of a gentile does not have *Shemita* sanctity in accordance with the *Bet Yosef*, but in Bnei Brak many follow the view of the *Chazon Ish* and the *Mabit* (for additional discussion on this see the section in the chapter dealing with the *heter mechira*, "Does Gentile Ownership Cancel the Sanctity of Eretz Yisrael?" – p. *386*).

To summarize, the *Acharonim* disagree whether *Shemita* produce automatically becomes ownerless or whether each person must declare ownerless the produce in his possession. This question has several practical ramifications: Is produce regarded as ownerless, even if its owner did not declare it so; is verbal renunciation of ownership necessary; and others.

In practice, the generally accepted ruling is that *Shemita* sanctity does not apply to a gentile's produce (though the *Chazon Ish* rules in accordance with the *Mabit* that gentile produce does have *Shemita* sanctity). So too it would appear that, strictly speaking, a person is not required to verbally renounce ownership of his produce, though it is good and proper to do so. *Terumot* and *ma'asrot* should be set aside from gentile produce without reciting the blessing normally recited for their separation. As for the disagreement regarding a person who failed to declare his produce ownerless (whether indeed the produce is treated as ownerless), we shall see below that, in light of the view of Rav Kook, this disagreement has little practical significance, for in any event, permission must be obtained before taking any produce.

MAY ONE FREELY ENTER INTO ANOTHER PERSON'S FIELD?

Does it suffice to declare one's produce ownerless, or is it necessary to renounce ownership over one's fields as well?

The **Mishna** in ***Nedarim*** (*42a*) states:

> He who is forbidden by a vow to benefit from his neighbor … If the vow was imposed in the seventh year, he may not enter his field, but he may eat of the overhanging branches from outside the field.

The mishna deals with someone who is forbidden by a vow to derive benefit from another person The mishna teaches that it is permitted for such a person to derive benefit from the other person's *Shemita* produce provided that he eat only from the produce that overhangs over the street. At first glance, this stipulation is difficult, for surely the field is ownerless during the *Shemita* year, and therefore the person who is forbidden by the vow should be permitted to enter the field to take of its produce? Indeed, the Gemara raises this very question (ibid. *42b*):

> Why may he eat of the overhanging fruits? Because they are now ownerless. But the land too is ownerless!

The Gemara objects that just as the produce is ownerless, so too the field is ownerless, and therefore the person who is forbidden to derive benefit from his fellow should be permitted to enter his field, for during the *Shemita* year, the field does not belong to that individual, and therefore no benefit is derived from him. The Gemara proposes two solutions to this difficulty:

> Ulla said: This refers to trees standing on the border. Rav Shimon ben Elyakim said: It is forbidden lest he stand and linger there.

According to Ulla, the mishna describes a situation where trees straddle a property border. Therefore, the person who made a vow against deriving benefit may not enter the other person's field, since he can reach the produce from the street outside. According to Rav Shimon ben Elyakim, the mishna is concerned that the person will remain in his neighbor's field longer than necessary. Therefore, they restricted the allowance to a case where he takes the produce while standing outside the property.

At first glance, both answers are difficult, for if the field is ownerless, the person should be allowed to eat all of its produce, not only that which overhangs the street, and he should not be barred from lingering on the other person's property. The ***Tosafot*** and the **Rosh** explain that the field is not exactly ownerless; it is only regarded as ownerless for the purpose of taking its produce. Accordingly, if a person can take of the produce without entering the field, he may not enter.

We see from here that a person's field is not itself ownerless during the *Shemita* year, but nevertheless a person must allow others free access to his produce.

The **Mechilta** (*Mishpatim 20*) adds that, strictly speaking, a person should be required to crate gaps in the fences surrounding his field in order to demonstrate that free access has been granted. The Sages, however, relaxed this requirement for the benefit of the landowners, to prevent free entry to animals (*Chazon Ish 14, 4*). But there must still be an opening through which people can enter the field and take of its produce. This is codified by the Rambam (*Hilchot Shemita ve-Yovel 4:24*):

> Whoever locks his vineyard or fences in his field in the seventh year has thereby nullified a positive commandment.

A person who is concerned about leaving his gate open for fear that his field or garden will suffer damages may lock the gate, provided that he posts a sign declaring that the produce is ownerless, and where the key can be obtained and that it may be taken without his permission (*Derech Emuna* in the name of the *Chazon Ish, Hilchot Shemita ve-Yovel, 4:34,* no. *297;* ibid. *7:18,* s.v. *ve-ad; Mishpetei Aretz, Shevi'it, 10,* note *9*):

> We heard in the name of our master [the *Chazon Ish*], that when necessary, it is permitted to lock the door and post a sign that whoever wishes to take [of the produce] may obtain a key in the house, even though this causes extra work.

IS IT PERMITTED TO TAKE *SHEMITA* PRODUCE WITHOUT THE OWNER'S PERMISSION?

The **Mishna** in ***Shevi'it*** (*4:2,* and *Eduyot 5:1*) states:

> Bet Shammai say: *Shemita* produce may not be eaten as a favor. But Bet Hillel say: It may be eaten, whether they are regarded as a favor or otherwise.

According to Bet Shammai, someone who enters another person's field in order to take *Shemita* produce must not regard the field's owner as having done him a favor, and therefore he may not thank him (Rambam, commentary to the Mishna, and Rash, ad loc.). Bet Hillel, on the other hand, maintain that it is permitted to acknowledge the owner and even do the owner a favor in return for the produce.

The law follows the view of Bet Hillel (Rambam,[57] *Hilchot Shemita ve-Yovel 6:15*), and therefore, it is permitted to thank the owner of the field and even return the kindness (but not with money, so that it does not appear as if he bought the produce [*Chazon Ish 13, 23*]).

The **Ra'avad** and the **Rash**, however, had a different text of that mishna, according to which Bet Hillel's view should be read as follows: "Bet Hillel say: *Shemita* produce must be eaten as a favor." According to this reading, Bet Hillel maintain that a person must express his gratitude to the produce's owner or return a favor in exchange for the produce that he took. The Ra'avad understood that according to Bet Hillel, whose view is accepted as law, it is forbidden to enter another person's field during the *Shemita* year without permission, so that he not become accustomed to entering other people's property without permission in ordinary years as well.

As for the law, the ***Chazon Ish*** seems to be of the opinion that there is no need to ask for permission to go into another's person's field to take *Shemita* produce.[58] On the contrary, he implies (*15, 11*) that if a person locks the gates to his field in order to prevent others from taking his produce, it is even permitted to break the lock in order to gain entry. In such a case, the person who breaks the lock is not even liable to compensate the owner of the field for having broken the lock. (This is all according to the *Mabit*, but according to the *Bet Yosef*, following the *Minchat Chinuch*, the produce in such a case is not ownerless and may not be taken.) **Rav Kook** (*Shabbat ha-Aretz 6, 15*), on the other hand, ruled in accordance with the Ra'avad, that **one must obtain the owner's permission** to eat of his produce.[59]

In practice, one should follow the ruling of Rav Kook,[60] especially today, when entering the fields of religiously non-observant people without permission **is liable to lead to a severe desecration of God's name.** Moreover, in the case of a private garden, entering without permission is liable to infringe upon the privacy of the

57. Rambam interpreted the mishna in a different manner. According to Rambam the mishna refers to the owner of the produce. He may return a favor to another person by providing him with *Shemita* produce.

58. He may have had a different understanding of Ra'avad's position. See also what he writes in *Hilchot Shevi'it* (13, 23; and *Derech Emuna* 6, 122). And similarly, see *Chazon Ish* (19, 18), where he explains an incident recorded in the *Yerushalmi*, where it is related that Rabbi Tarfon was beaten when he did not ask permission to enter a field (it was in fact his field, but the workers were not aware of this), and it is possible that he too agrees that one should seek permission before entering another person's field.

59. Rav Kook adds, however, that the owner of the field is obligated to grant permission to enter his field, and that he may not prevent anybody from eating his produce. *Hilchot Shevi'it* (7, 15, and *Kisei David* there, no. 110) disagrees and says that it is unnecessary to obtain permission, though in practice one should follow the view of Rav Kook.

60. Rav Sh. Z. Auerbach (cited in *Dinei Shevi'it ha-Shalem*, 14, 7) also maintains that this is the proper way to conduct oneself.

residents, and in the case of agricultural land, it is possible that the land was sold in accordance with the *heter mechira,* in which case the produce is not ownerless. Therefore, in the absence of a sign that explicitly permits picking, permission must always be obtained from the owner of the property.

The ***Minchat Chinuch*** (*mitzva 84*) asks: Why are women obligated in the *mitzva* of "But the seventh year you shall let it rest and lie fallow?" Surely it is a **time-bound positive commandment**, from which women are generally exempt! He answers that inasmuch as *Shemita* sanctity continues to apply to the produce even after the *Shemita* year, the *mitzva* is regarded as a positive commandment that is not time-bound, and such a commandment is binding upon women as well.[61]

61. The *Minchat Chinuch* notes that according to the **Rosh**, who maintains that a garment that is ordinarily worn during the day requires *tzitzit* even at night, but nevertheless the *mitzva* of *tzitzit* is regarded as a time-bound positive precept, even if *Shemita* produce continues to have sanctity during the eighth year, the *mitzva* of renouncing ownership of produce during the *Shemita* year should still be regarded as a time-bound positive precept.

SUMMARY:

The gates to one's field should be left open during the *Shemita* year in order to allow all people free access to the field and its produce. Alternatively, a sign may be posted at the gate indicating where a key may be found. In the absence of a sign that permits picking, permission must be obtained from the owner of the field before entering, so that one not become accustomed to enter other people's fields in ordinary years as well.

The obligation to declare one's produce ownerless applies to all *Shemita* produce, and therefore it applies all year long with respect to vegetables, and starting in the middle of the year with respect to fruits (until the middle of the eighth year).

SHAMUR (PRODUCE FROM A FIELD THAT WAS GUARDED)

As we saw (p. *144*), it is forbidden to guard one's field and prevent others from taking its produce for themselves, and whoever does so nullifies a positive commandment.

What is the law governing produce that had not been declared ownerless? We saw above (p. *132*) the words of *Torat Kohanim*: "'Nor shall you gather the grapes of your protected vine' (*Vayikra 25:5*) – from that which had been guarded in the land you shall not gather, but you may gather from that which had been declared ownerless." **Rabbenu Tam** (*Yevamot 122a,* s.v. *shel azeka; Sukka 39b,* s.v. *bameh devarim amurim*) argues based upon this midrash that it is forbidden to eat *Shemita* produce that had not been declared ownerless (*"invei **nezirecha**"* – grapes that had not been declared ownerless and from which he had set people apart (*nazar*), are forbidden to be eaten). On the other hand, **Rashi** (*Yevamot* ibid.), the **Ramban** (*Vayikra 25:5*), and the ***Chinuch*** (*mitzva 329*) all write that guarded produce may be eaten.[62] How do these *Rishonim* understand *Torat Kohanim*? Two explanations may be suggested:

1. We saw earlier that the **Rash** understands that *Torat Kohanim* means to say that produce that had been guarded must be harvested in an altered manner.
2. The **Ramban** (ad loc.) suggests that according to Rashi *Torat Kohanim* means to say that one must not harvest the produce before he has declared it ownerless, but one may renounce ownership and then harvest it. In any event, according to this explanation, *Torat Kohanim* does not say that guarded produce is forbidden.

The ***Aruch ha-Shulchan*** (*21:8*) rules that if a person wishes to rely on the more lenient position, he may do so and we do not raise objections against him. The ***Chazon Ish*** appears to contradict himself on this issue. In some places, he implies that he is stringent (*10, 5*), but elsewhere it appears that he rules leniently (*3, 25; Seder Shevi'it; Kovetz Iggerot,* vol. *II,* no. *162*). It is generally accepted that the *Chazon Ish* was lenient on the matter (see, for example, *Ma'adanei Aretz,* notes, no. *7; Dinei Shevi'it 22, 1*). See also below, regarding *ne'evad* (produce that had been worked during *Shemita*).

62. Logic dictates that if *Shemita* produce is automatically regarded as ownerless, then even if a person guards his field, another person should be permitted to enter the field and pick of the produce.

NE'EVAD (PRODUCE FROM A FIELD THAT WAS WORKED)

The ***Mishna*** in ***Terumot*** teaches that one who plants vegetation or trees, sinks a vine shoot, or grafts during the *Shemita* year, must uproot the plant, since he violated the prohibition of "You shall not sow your field" (*Terumot 2:3; Gittin* 53b; Rambam, *Hilchot Shemita ve-Yovel 1:12*[63]). Based on this, **Ramban** writes (*Yevamot 122a*) that any *Shemita* produce that grew as a result of a violation of the prohibitions of *Shemita* may not be eaten (the Rashba and Ritva, ad loc., cite this in the name of the Ramban; Ra'avad, *hasagot* on Rif, *Sukka* 40a, also takes this view). In contrast, the **Rambam** (*Responsa Pe'er ha-Dor,* no. 15) writes that produce that grew as a result of a violation of the prohibitions of *Shemita* is permitted. According to the Rambam, even produce that had been planted during the *Shemita* year is not forbidden, and the Mishna is dealing exclusively with the prohibition of *sefichim.*[64]

Some authorities write that produce that had been sown during

RAV MOSHE FEINSTEIN

ספר
אגרות משה
חושן משפט
והם מה שחנני השי"ת להשיב לשואלים אותי מתלמידי וחברי דבר
ה' זו הלכה, וגם מה שבאתי בכתובים לגדולי תורה
להשתעשע בדברי תורה
מאת
משה פיינשטיין
ר"מ מתיבתא תפארת ירושלים בנוא יארק
ולפנים אבד"ק לובאן, פלך מינסק
בן אאמו"ר הגאון הצדיק חסיד ועניו מרן ר' דוד זצ"ל
שהיה אבד"ק אוזדא וסטראבין ברוסיא
נוא יארק
שנת תשכ"ד לפ"ק

Rav Moshe Feinstein was born in Russia in 5655 (1895), and later immigrated to the United States. Rav Feinstein was regarded as one of the greatest halachic decisors of his generation. His responsa span the entire spectrum of halachic topics, including matters that relate to science and medicine. His work, *Responsa Iggerot Moshe,* is regarded as one of the most important collections of responsa of our the twentieth century. Rav Feinstein combines impressive Torah scholarship with broad mastery of halachic decision-making. Rav Feinstein died in 5746 (1986).

63. See also the Mishna in *Shevi'it* (4:2) which implies that Bet Hillel permit produce that grew in a field in which forbidden labors were performed during the *Shemita* year. This proof is not absolute for various reasons: 1) The *Chazon Ish* (*Shevi'it* 19:18) argues that the Mishna might not be dealing with planting, but only with labors performed in maintenance of trees and the like. 2) The *Derech Emuna* (chap. 4, 26, *be'ur halacha* s.v. *ha-sefichin*) suggests that the Mishna might be dealing with labors performed prior to planting, but labors performed following the planting do indeed cause the produce to be forbidden.

64. In his commentary to the Mishna (6:1), however, the Rambam writes that produce that had been planted during the *Shemita* year is forbidden to be eaten.

the *Shemita* year is indeed forbidden, but produce that had been sown prior to the seventh year and was only worked during the *Shemita* year is not forbidden (*Chazon Ish 10, 6,* s.v. *perek dalet*).

The **Chazon Ish** (*10, 6,* s.v. *ve-etrogav*) rules that it is permitted to purchase an *etrog* that had been guarded and worked. This implies that he rules leniently with respect to *shamur* and *ne'evad.* Elsewhere (*9, 17,* s.v. *tevu'a u-peirot*), however, he writes that it is forbidden to purchase produce from one who is suspect about *shamur* and *ne'evad,* and in his summary of the laws in *Seder Shevi'it* he rules that it is forbidden to purchase produce that had grown in a guarded vineyard, and that guarded produce is forbidden (end of section 21). One might suggest that the *Chazon Ish* was only lenient about an *etrog* purchased for the sake of a *mitzva* (see *Responsa Mishnat Yosef,* vol. *IV,* p. *149*), but in his letters (*Iggerot,* vol. *II,* no. *162*) the *Chazon Ish* writes that one may be lenient about eating guarded produce.[65] In practice, it is generally accepted that the *Chazon Ish* is lenient regarding both *shamur* and *ne'evad.*[66]

The *Acharonim* appear to be lenient about *shamur* and *ne'evad,* especially today when *Shemita* observance is only by rabbinic law. **Rav Sh. Z. Auerbach** writes: (*Ma'adanei Aretz,* notes, no. *7*):

> According to the common practice in accordance with the ruling of the *Acharonim* to be lenient today about the prohibitions of *shamur* and *ne'evad,* and the ruling of the *Chazon Ish* to this effect in 10, 6 – once the forbidden action has been performed, the produce is not forbidden and it may be eaten by others.

This practice may be explained as follows: Since the produce belongs to all of Israel, and not to the individual "owner," it is not in his power to cause the produce to become forbidden through his actions.

Nevertheless, one should not buy produce that had been guarded or worked, so as not to support sinners. The allowance is restricted to produce that was received as a gift (see *Sukka 39b,* and *Chazon Ish, Shevi'it 10, 5*). (See also the chapter on the *heter mechira,* regard-

65. It is forbidden, however, to buy such produce (though this problem can be overcome; see below, p. 438–439). In the continuation, the *Chazon Ish* writes regarding the bananas marketed by Tenuva [in his time], that there was concern about *ne'evad.* It seems, however, that he meant only to say that one should not buy them, but eating them is permitted, as is the case with *shamur.*

66. In his discussion regarding buying an *etrog,* the *Chazon Ish* speaks explicitly about *ne'evad.* The author of the book *Derech Emuna* (chap. 4, nos. 317–318) reports that the *Chazon Ish* told him that he had intentionally contradicted himself, because on the one hand, he maintains that strictly speaking there is room to be lenient, but on the other hand, he wanted to show that there is also room to be stringent (similarly in *Kerayna de-Igreta,* 147. See also *Kuntres Dinei Shevi'it,* page 33, Rav Greineman's letter, and *Responsa Tzitz Eli'ezer,* vol. VI, no. 39).

ing buying *heter mechira* produce, for one who does not rely on the allowance).

To summarize, there is room to be lenient and permit the eating of produce that had been guarded or worked.[67] While one should not buy produce from a person who violated the prohibitions of *Shemita* and guarded or worked his field, there are ways to overcome the problem of buying such produce, and then one may practice leniency and eat the produce.[68]

RABBI YOSEF BABAD – THE *Minchat Chinuch*

ספר

מנחת חינוך

חלק ראשון

ירושלים

Rabbi Yosef Babad was born in 5561 (1801) and served as a *dayan* in many communities. His major work, the *Minchat Chinuch*, is a commentary to the *Sefer ha-Chinuch*, which explains the fundamental principles of all 613 biblical commandments. The *Minchat Chinuch* analyzes each *mitzva* based on the Talmud, the *Rishonim* and the *Posekim*. The *Minchat Chinuch* is very popular in the yeshiva world, owing to its insightful analyses and its presentation of interesting practical ramifications of the many halachic disputes that it addresses.

For many years the available edition of the *Minchat Chinuch* was difficult to read and filled with many abbreviations. The new Machon Yerushalayim edition has made the study of this important work much easier and more enjoyable. Rabbi Babad died in 5634 (1874).

67. This ruling is of great significance with respect to the question that will be discussed below: When buying produce during the *Shemita* year, should one give preference to *heter mechira* fruit or to the fruit of a gentile? Since there is room for leniency regarding *shamur* and *ne'evad*, it is certainly preferable to buy *heter mechira* produce rather than the produce of a gentile, even if one does not rely on the *heter mechira*. In addition, it should be noted that some authorities maintain that if a person works his land during the *Shemita* year relying on an allowance that permits him to do so, the produce that grows there is certainly not forbidden (*Kerem Tziyon* 19:3; *Responsa Iggerot Moshe, Orach Chayyim*, no. 186. See also below, in the chapter on the *heter mechira*, the view of Rav Sh. Z. Auerbach).

68. It is possible to be lenient when payment for the produce is made indirectly (*havla'a*) (see *Responsa Yeshu'at Moshe*, vol. 1, end of section 13). One may also be lenient and eat of produce that had been worked in a field that had been sold in the framework of the *heter mechira*, even if one does not rely on the *heter mechira*, as was mentioned at the end of the previous note.

TOSEFET SHEVI'IT – PROHIBITION OF LABORS AT THE END OF THE SIXTH YEAR

Even though the laws of *Shemita* only begin to apply from *Rosh ha-Shana* of the seventh year, the Gemara (*Rosh ha-Shana 9a*) teaches that there is a law of ***tosefet shevi'it***, "addition to the *Shemita* year," which means that there is a Torah prohibition to plow a field starting thirty days before the *Shemita* year.

Though the Torah law of *tosefet shevi'it* goes into effect thirty days before the *Shemita* year, the Sages forbade plowing from an even earlier date, as soon as the plowing is not performed for the benefit of the sixth year's crop, but as preparation for planting in the seventh year. We learn in the first two chapters of tractate *Shevi'it* that in a grain field the prohibition begins on *Pesach* of the sixth year, whereas in an orchard it begins only from the festival of *Shavu'ot*.

What is the source of this law? According to **Rabbi Akiva** (*Shevi'it 1:4*), this law is learned from the verse, "in plowing and in harvest you shall rest" (*Shemot 34:21*). He understands that this verse is superfluous as a source for the laws of *Shemita* itself (because the laws of *Shemita* are taught again in *Parashat Behar*), and thus they come to teach the law of *tosefet shevi'it*:

> It is stated: "In plowing and in harvest you shall rest" (*Shemot 34:21*) – it is unnecessary to teach about plowing and harvesting during the seventh year, but rather it teaches about plowing in the sixth year going into the seventh year, and about harvesting of the seventh year going into the eighth year. Rabbi Yishmael says: This verse teaches that just as only discretionary plowing is prohibited, so too only discretionary harvesting is prohibited, to the exclusion of the harvesting of the *omer* offering.

Rabbi Yishmael disagrees with Rabbi Akiva and maintains that this verse refers to *Shabbat* (see a fuller treatment of this dispute in the chapter on plowing). The *Rishonim* disagree whether or not plowing during the seventh year is forbidden according to Rabbi Yishmael. *Rosh ha-Shana* 9a states, however, that Rabbi Yishmael agrees that there is a law of ***tosefet shevi'it***, only that he learns that it is a law that was transmitted by an oral tradition that traces back to Moshe at Sinai (*halacha le-Moshe mi-Sinai*), not from any textual source.

Rabbi Yishmael further teaches that this prohibition of *tosefet shevi'it* is in force only when the Temple stands, but following the destruction of the Temple, the law of *tosefet shevi'it* no longer applies (*Rosh ha-Shana 9a*).

Following the destruction of the second Temple, the law of *tosefet shevi'it* was still observed (rabbinically), until **Rabban Gamliel** and his court abolished the law (*Mo'ed Katan 4a*). This ruling of Rabban Gamliel is codified by the **Rambam** (*Hilchot Shemita ve-Yovel 3:9*):

> And all these laws [of *tosefet shevi'it* apply] during the time of the Temple, as we have stated. But nowadays working the land is permitted until *Rosh ha-Shana* [of the *Shemita* year].

It is, therefore, permitted to work the land until *Rosh ha-Shana*. This includes all labors: plowing, fertilizing, weeding and the like are all permitted until *Rosh ha-Shana*.

There are, however, cases in which planting is forbidden even before the *Shemita* year begins for other reasons. The **Mishna** in ***Shevi'it*** (*6:5*) states:

> One may not plant, sink or graft [trees] on the eve of the seventh year less than thirty days before *Rosh ha-Shana*. If one planted, sank or grafted, it must be uprooted. Rabbi Yehuda says: Any grafting that does not take root within three days will never do so. Rabbi Yossi and Rabbi Shimon say: Two weeks.

That is to say, in addition to the prohibitions of plowing and preparing the field, which are in force even before the *Shemita* year begins, **planting, sinking and grafting are also forbidden**. Let us explain the mishna in general terms: according to the anonymous first tanna of the mishna, planting and the like must be completed a month before the beginning of the *Shemita* year. Rabbi Yehuda maintains that three days before *Rosh ha-Shana* suffices (for grafting). Rabbi Shimon either adopts an intermediate position and requires two weeks (according to Rabbenu Tam, cited in *Tosafot, Rosh ha-Shana 10b*), or he is adding a stringency to the position of the anonymous first tanna, requiring thirty days plus two weeks before *Rosh ha-Shana* (Rashi, *Rosh ha-Shana 10b;* Rambam, see below). Why is planting forbidden before *Rosh ha-Shana?*

The *Rishonim* offer three different explanations:

1. According to the **Rash** (ad loc.), the prohibition is based on the law of ***tosefet shevi'it***. According to this, today, when the law of *tosefet shevi'it* is no longer in force, it is permissible to plant trees until the beginning of the *Shemita* year.
2. According to **Rabbenu Tam** (*Tosafot, Rosh ha-Shana 10b,* s.v. *sheloshim*; so too *Rashi, ad loc.,* s.v. *tzarich sheloshim*), the prohibition is not related to the law of *tosefet shevi'it*. Rather it is based on the prohibition to cause a plant to take root during the *Shemita* year. Therefore, one must not plant shortly before the *Shemita* year, as in such a case the plant will only take root during the *Shemita* year.[69] Since the law is in accordance with Rabbi Shimon (*Bartenura,* ad loc.), today, one may only plant until **two weeks** before *Rosh ha-Shana*.[70]
3. The **Rambam** (commentary to the Mishna, ad loc.; *Hilchot Shemita ve-Yovel 3:11*) suggests an entirely different explanation: According to him, the prohibition is not due to either ***tosefet shevi'it*** or taking root during the *Shemita* year. Rather the problem is the **appearance** of a prohibition:

> Even nowadays, one may not plant a tree, sink or graft on the eve of the seventh year, unless the planting will take root thirty days before *Rosh ha-Shana* of the seventh year, and taking root generally requires two weeks. This is always forbidden due to the problem of giving the appearance of a forbidden act, lest an observer say that it was planted during the seventh year.

According to this ruling, trees may only be planted until the 15th of Av. This date is calculated based on a law regarding *orla* – the prohibition applying to fruit that grows in the first three years after

69. See *Minchat Chinuch* (*mitzva 326*); *Eglei Tal* (*zore'a 8, 2*); *Minchat Shlomo* (I, no. 48, no. 51, 4), that a tree taking root during the *Shemita* year is problematic because of the law that "the land must keep a Sabbath." The *Chazon Ish*, (17, 25; 22, 5) however, understands that there is no problem with a tree taking root during the *Shemita* year, and that the prohibition according to Rabbenu Tam is one of *tosefet shevi'it*.

70. There is no difference between fruit-bearing trees and trees that do not bear fruit.

a tree has been planted. In order for the sixth year to count as the first of the three years of *orla*, 14 days are required for the sapling to take root, plus an additional 30 days for the tree to be considered as if it has grown for a year (based on the principle that thirty days out of a year can be considered a year for certain purposes). In other words, if the sapling is planted before the 15th of Av, the sixth year can be counted as the first of the three years of *orla*. If, however, it is only planted after the 15th of Av, the count of *orla* years can only begin from the seventh year. If the count only begins from the seventh year, observers are liable to mistakenly think that the tree was planted during the *Shemita* year. For this reason, the Sages forbade planting a tree during the sixth year **after the 15th of Av** (on the 15th itself, planting is permitted).

According to the Rambam, then, the prohibition is in force today as well (since it is not connected to the law of *tosefet shevi'it*), though it only applies to fruit-bearing trees.

Is it possible to plant after the 15th of Av? We have seen that the required 44 days include 14 days for the sapling to take root. Therefore, if a person plants a tree whose root stock is covered with soil (such that the tree can live for two weeks), he may plant it until Rosh Chodesh Elul (until sunset of the 29th of Av), because the tree is regarded as having already taken root. Today, almost all trees are purchased from nurseries with their root stock covered with soil, and therefore they may be planted until the 29th of Av. If a person transplants a tree (from a nursery or the like), and it is moved together with root stock and soil that would suffice to maintain the tree for at least two weeks, and the container holding the root has a 2 centimeter hole (and in the nursery it had rested on the ground and not on plastic), it may be replanted until *Rosh ha-Shana*, because in such a case there is no need to restart the count of *orla* years (so writes *Mishpetei Aretz 1, 6, 8*).

In order to plant a tree after the 29th of Av: If a person wishes to plant a tree after the 29th of Av, but cannot find a tree in the nursery in a container that has a 2 centimeter hole, there is an easy solution. One can buy a regular tree with covered root stock, and before the 29th of Av remove it from the container or bore a 2 centimeter hole in the bottom, and rest it on the ground. The count of *orla* years begins immediately (even though the tree is still in the pot and not in the ground, because it is resting on the ground and the container has a 2 centimeter hole), and thus one can plant it until *Rosh ha-Shana.*

Trees that do not bear fruit and non-fragrant ornamental plants: According to the Rambam, there is no problem to plant a tree that does not bear fruit until *Rosh ha-Shana,* since there is no problem of *orla.*[71] As we saw, however, according to Rabbenu Tam, a tree must be planted 14 days before *Rosh ha-Shana,* because it is forbidden for the tree to take root during the *Shemita* year, since that would interfere with the land's rest. According to Rabbenu Tam, then, even a tree that does not bear fruit must be planted at least 14 days before the *Shemita* year (no later than the 15th of Elul).

This is the way many *Acharonim* understood Rabbenu Tam's position (*Minchat Chinuch, Eglei Tal, Shabbat ha-Aretz* – see above in note). The *Chazon Ish* (*17, 25; 22, 5; 25, 13*), however, understands that even according to Rabbenu Tam there is no prohibition for the tree to take root during the *Shemita* year (see note above, where he explains that even Rabbenu Tam understands the mishna's rule as stemming from the law of *tosefet shevi'it,* and is therefore no longer in force today).

These *Acharonim* seem to disagree about the fundamental question regarding *Shemita,* whether the *Shemita* prohibitions apply only to the **person** ("You shall not plant," etc.), or also to the **land** (a person must make sure that his land rests). It is possible, however, that the *Chazon Ish* is only lenient about an action that causes the land to work during the *Shemita* year when a person performs that action before the *Shemita* year.[72]

According to the *Chazon Ish,* then, a tree that does not bear fruit may be planted until *Rosh ha-Shana,* whereas according to Rav Kook (*Shabbat ha-Aretz 3, 11*), Rav Sh. Z. Auerbach (*Minchat Shlomo 48; 51, 4*) and others, a tree that does not bear fruit may only be planted until the 15th of Elul.

All agree that a tree that does not bear fruit may be planted until *Rosh ha-Shana* if its root stock was covered with soil that would

71. See, however, Ri Kurkus on the aforementioned Rambam, who understands that the requirement of 44 days before *Rosh ha-Shana* does not stem from the laws of *orla*. Instead, he maintains that the issue is that an observer will see a young tree during the *Shemita* year, and conclude that it was planted during the *Shemita* year. According to this, the concern exists even with respect to trees that do not bear fruit. This, however, is not the accepted ruling (especially today, when the common practice is to plant more mature saplings).

72. That is to say, even the *Chazon Ish* agrees that sometimes there is a problem stemming from the obligation for the land to rest, but only when labors are performed during the seventh year itself (such as when a non-Jew works the land).

suffice to maintain the tree for at least two weeks (*Mishpetei Aretz* 1, 17). In contemporary circumstances, therefore, there are generally no ramifications to the disagreement between Rav Kook and the *Chazon Ish,* because almost all the trees that we plant come with their root stock covered with soil.

Vegetables must begin to sprout during the sixth year (and therefore they must be planted by the 26th of Elul), so that they are not subject to the prohibition of *sefichim* (see below, p. 305).

Flowers that do not have a fragrance – according to the *Chazon Ish,* may be planted until the beginning of the *Shemita* year, but according to those who maintain that they must take root before *Shemita,* they should be planted by the 26th of Elul.

As for **flowers that have a fragrance** – the halachic authorities disagree whether or not they have *Shemita* sanctity (since they are not grown for their fragrance – see the chapter dealing with *Shemita* sanctity). Those who are lenient on this issue will therefore permit planting them until *Rosh ha-Shana.* Those who adopt the more stringent position will only permit planting them until the 26th of Elul, owing to the prohibition of *sefichim.*

If **seedlings of flowers or vegetables** are planted together with their soil – they may be planted until *Rosh ha-Shana,* as they are already considered as having taken root (see above). Of course, the soil must be firm enough to maintain them for two weeks without crumbling.

It is recommended that one plant perennial flowers before the *Shemita* year, in order for one's garden to remain attractive during the *Shemita* year as well.[73]

Planting grass: (See the chapter on maintaining a garden during the *Shemita* year.) Grass should be planted early (carpet grass should be laid at least a month before *Shemita*; grass from seed should be planted even earlier), primarily because the first few times that a lawn is moved, the mowing stimulates the grass to fill in, which is an agricultural need. The subsequent mowing of the lawn is considered maintenance, like a "haircut," and is thus permitted.

All other labors – fertilizing, spraying pesticides, pruning and the like – are permitted until ***Rosh ha-Shana.*** As will be explained

73. Another advantage is that the work performed on perennials has ramifications beyond the *Shemita* year, and therefore falls into the category of "preserving the tree," which is permitted according to all opinions (see the chapter on labors that are forbidden during the *Shemita* year by rabbinic decree).

in the chapter on maintaining a garden during the *Shemita* year, it is recommended that one apply slow-release fertilizer that will suffice for the entire year, spray herbicides that will prevent the growth of weeds, prune everything that requires pruning and prepare the garden as much as possible for the *Shemita* year (it is preferable that even labors that are permitted during the *Shemita* year be performed prior to the *Shemita* year – *Chazon Ish* 21, 17).[74]

SUMMARY:

The law of *tosefet shevi'it* is no longer in force today, and therefore it is permitted to tend a garden in the usual manner until *Rosh ha-Shana.* It is recommended that one apply slow-release fertilizer, spray weed-killer and prune before the *Shemita* year (it is also recommended that one program the sprinkler system before *Shemita* – see the chapter on maintaining a garden).

Planting: Fruit trees – without a soil-covered root stock – until the 15th of Av; with a soil-covered root stock (that can maintain the tree for two weeks) until the 29th of Av.

Trees that do not bear fruit – without a soil-covered root stock – best until the 15th of Elul (in consideration of those who forbid allowing trees to take root during the *Shemita* year); when necessary – until *Rosh ha-Shana* (the 29th of Elul); with a soil-covered root stock – until *Rosh ha-Shana.*

Vegetables and flowers – without soil – until the 26th of Elul (regarding flowers there is room for leniency when necessary until *Rosh ha-Shana,* especially if the flowers lack a fragrance); with soil – until *Rosh ha-Shana.*

It is recommended that one plant **perennial flowers** in anticipation of the *Shemita* year.

74. It seems that this depends on how we understand the allowance to perform a labor that is meant "to preserve the tree" – is the labor not at all a forbidden labor, or is it a forbidden labor, but permitted in the case of financial loss (and therefore it would be preferable that one do whatever can be done prior to the *Shemita* year). See the discussion of this question in the chapter on labors that are forbidden during the *Shemita* year by rabbinic decree. It is also possible that this depends on the status of the *Shemita* year relative to *Chol ha-Mo'ed* (there are similarities between the laws of the *Shemita* year and *Chol ha-Mo'ed* that are mentioned at the beginning of tractate *Mo'ed Katan*), as it is possible that labors involving a loss were never forbidden on *Chol ha-Mo'ed* (see *Chazon Ish*, 18, 4). It is also possible that even though strictly speaking there may be room for leniency, especially according to the *Chazon Ish* who maintains that labors performed in order to preserve a tree were never forbidden (see the discussion in the chapter on labors that are forbidden by rabbinic decree), the *Chazon Ish* preferred to take into consideration the position of the *Nimukei Yosef* at the beginning of *Mo'ed Katan*, that only watering is permitted during the *Shemita* year, but not any other labors.

LABORS FORBIDDEN BY RABBINIC DECREE DURING *SHEMITA*

LABORS FORBIDDEN BY RABBINIC DECREE DURING *SHEMITA*

> But in the seventh year there shall be a Sabbath of solemn rest for the land, a Sabbath for the Lord: you shall neither plant your field, nor prune your vineyard. That which grows of its own accord of your harvest you shall not reap, nor gather the grapes of your undressed vine; for it shall be a year of rest for the land. (*Vayikra 25:4-5*)

The Gemara in *Mo'ed Katan* (*3a*) asks why the Torah specifies four labors: planting, pruning, reaping and gathering; surely it could have written only planting and reaping, and we would have deduced that pruning and gathering are forbidden as well, learning pruning from planting, as both simulate growth, and learning gathering (of perennial produce) from reaping (of annual produce).

> Now since pruning comes within the general process of planting, and grape-gathering within the general process of reaping, what law did the Torah wish to teach by including these derivative processes (*toladot*) in the verse? It is to indicate that only for these [specified] *toladot* one is liable, and for [any] other [*toladot*] one is not liable.

The Gemara's answer is that the Torah's expansion teaches us that it is only for these *toladot* (pruning and gathering) that one violates Torah law, whereas for other *toladot* one violates only a rabbinic decree (unlike *Shabbat,* where *toladot* are prohibited by Torah law).[1]

The labors that are forbidden during the *Shemita* year by rabbinic law include: watering, weeding (by the root), cutting (without the root), fertilizing (the ground with manure), removing stones (in order to prepare the ground for planting), plowing (according to those who maintain that plowing is not forbidden by Torah law, or that some types of plowing are forbidden only by rabbinic law, see above, p. *128*), and others[2] (see *Shevi'it,* chap. *2; Mo'ed Katan 3a; Yerushalmi, Shevi'it* chap. *7;* Rambam, *Hilchot Shemita ve-Yovel 1:4* and on).

1. This is based on Rashi's explanation. The Ritva understands that the verse teaches us that pruning and gathering, which are *toladot* on *Shabbat*, are regarded as principal labors (*avot*) with respect to *Shemita*. According to him, the *toladot* of *Shemita* are always permitted by Torah law, and are forbidden only by rabbinic decree. In any event, both according to Rashi and the Ritva, these four labors are forbidden by Torah law and everything else is forbidden by rabbinic decree.

2. According to the *Chazon Ish*, this list should also include the pruning of all trees other than the grapevine which is forbidden by Torah law.

Rav Kook (*Shabbat ha-Aretz 1, 4,* section 10; *Kuntres Acharon 7,* based on the Ramban, *Vayikra 23:24*) adds that, in certain situations, these and other labors are forbidden by Torah law:

> One who works his land during the seventh year in the ordinary manner as in all years, even if he does not plant, or prune, or reap, or gather ... it would appear that he transgresses a positive Torah commandment.

According to Rav Kook, there is a general requirement for the land to rest, beyond the labors that are specifically prohibited during the *Shemita* year, specified by the verse: "But the seventh year shall be a Sabbath of solemn rest for the land" (*Vayikra 25:5*). The Sages forbade certain labors by rabbinic decree, beyond the scope of the Torah's prohibited labors, so that a person would fulfill the command to let the land itself rest. Thus if a person consistently performs labors that are forbidden by rabbinic decree, he will violate the Torah law that the seventh year "shall be a year of rest for the land:"

> The overall obligation of rest is by Torah law ... one who violates it by consistently performing labors that are forbidden by rabbinic decree violates a Torah law.

There are similar situations in which the Sages applied their understanding of the Torah's underlying intentions and added prohibitions in order to preserve the overall character of a particular law. For example, the prohibition of *muktzeh* governing the movement of certain items on *Shabbat* is a rabbinic institution, but it is based on the understanding that the Torah itself demands that Shabbat not be treated like an ordinary weekday.

This principle of *Shabbat* law is explained by the **Ramban** (*Vayikra 23:24*).[3] The prohibition of muktzeh is rabbinic, as are the prohibitions of measuring, weighing, buying and selling. According to the Ramban, however, if a person were to engage in all these activities he would negate Shabbat rest, thereby violating a Torah law.

> It appears to me that this interpretation comes to teach that we are commanded by Torah law to rest on a festival day even from activities which are not in the category of *melacha,*

3. Rav Kook himself noted the connection between this statement of the Ramban and his principle regarding *Shemita* in *Kuntres Acharon* section 7.

(work). Thus we are not to be engaged the whole day in wearisome tasks, such as measuring out crops of the field, weighing fruits and gifts, filling barrels with wine, clearing away vessels, and moving stones from house to house and from place to place … with the marketplace filled with business transactions, the shops standing open and the shopkeepers giving credit, and the money-changers sitting before their tables with the golden coins before them, and the workers rising early to go to their work and hiring themselves out for such works – [as described above] just as on weekdays. And since all these matters do not entail *melacha*, they would be permissible on a festival day and even on *Shabbat* itself. Therefore the Torah said that [the festival should be a day of] *shabbaton* (solemn rest), meaning that it should be a day of rest and ease, not a day of labor [and weariness].

PRESERVING A TREE AS OPPOSED TO STRENGTHENING A TREE

Why did the Sages permit rabbinic labors during the *Shemita* year? What is the significance of this permission?

The Gemara in *Avoda Zara* (*50b*) asks:

> What is the underlying difference between *zihum* which is permitted and *gizum* [both terms are defined below] which is prohibited? *Zihum* is done for the preservation of the tree and is therefore permitted, whereas *gizum* is done to strengthen the tree and is therefore prohibited.

According to the Gemara, *zihum* (treating a tree to drive away worms[4]) is permitted during the *Shemita* year, whereas *gizum* (pruning a tree's dry branches in order to stimulate growth) is forbidden, because *zihum* is essential for the preservation of the tree, whereas *gizum* is performed only to strengthen the tree.

Why are labors that are needed for the preservation of a tree permitted? **Rashi** (*Mo'ed Katan 3a,* regarding closing up fissures) implies that the reason for this permission is to prevent financial loss:

> This is permitted – because not engaging in this activity would lead to a financial loss.

The **Ritva**, however, understands differently:

> It is simply an act of preservation ... and is not considered work.

That is to say, a labor that is defined as "preservation" is not considered a forbidden labor.[5] According to **Rashi**, preservation work is work **that was permitted to prevent financial loss.** According to the **Ritva, it was never prohibited.**

At first glance, the Ritva's position is astonishing. Why should work that is performed in order to save a tree from dying not fall into the category of work? The ***Chazon Ish*** (*17, 27*) explains:

4. This is based on the Rambam's understanding that *zihum* involves smearing a tree with foul-smelling oil in order to drive away pests. The Rash explains that *zihum* involves applying manure to portions of a tree where the bark has peeled off.

5. In fact, Rashi himself (*Avoda Zara 50a*) follows the Ritva's explanation cited above that labors performed for preservation are not considered forbidden labors: "... the Torah forbids labors that involve working the land, **but these do not involve working the land, for it is merely to preserve the tree** that it not die, and it does not enhance the tree, but retains it as it is."

It seems that work that involves the preservation of a tree is only permitted with respect to *Shemita*, where the objective of the prohibition is [not to bring about] growth. But with respect to *Shabbat*, where the objective of the prohibition is [to prevent] a person from exerting himself in work, even the preservation of a tree falls into the category of planting.

In other words, when the Sages expanded the list of labors that are forbidden during the *Shemita* year, they added labors that are not forbidden by Torah law, but nevertheless stimulate the growth of a tree.[6] With this we can understand the position of the Ritva: Labors performed to preserve a tree are indeed labors, but they are not labors that stimulate growth,[7] and thus they were never forbidden.[8]

6. According to **Rashi**, labors performed for the purpose of preservation are permitted in order to prevent financial loss, whereas according to the **Ritva**, they are permitted because they are not regarded as forbidden labors, because only labors that **stimulate growth** are forbidden. According to the Ritva, the logic may be the reverse of Rashi, namely, that labors that are performed to prevent financial loss are permitted because they are defined as labors to preserve the tree (this was pointed out to me by my revered father-in-law, Rav Blumenzweig). In other words, according to **Rashi**, "loss" is the **reason for the allowance**, whereas according to the **Ritva,** "loss" is just a **sign** that a given labor does not stimulate growth, but the reason for the allowance is **the fact that the person does not perform a labor that stimulates growth.**

7. If we assume that a labor of preservation is not considered forbidden labor, one could claim that labor that is clearly for preservation, performed only to prevent damage and not to enhance the tree, **is permitted even for labors forbidden by Torah law**. The Gemara in ***Avoda Zara* 50b** states that *gizum* is forbidden because it is performed to strengthen the tree. According to this, were *gizum* to be done to prevent damage, it would be permitted (unless one claims that *gizum* by its very nature strengthens the tree). The simple understanding of *gizum* is that it refers to the pruning of trees other than a grapevine (see below). Thus, according to those who maintain that the pruning of all trees is forbidden by Torah law, the permit of labor to prevent damage would apply even to labors that are prohibited by Torah law. According to the simple understanding of the **Rambam**, the pruning of all trees is forbidden by Torah law (though the *Chazon Ish* maintains that even according to Rambam, this is forbidden only by rabbinic decree; see the chapter on pruning). Thus, it is possible that a labor to prevent damage is permitted even if it is a labor that is forbidden by Torah law (unless we say that all agree that pruning that does not stimulate growth, but merely preserves that which already exists, is not considered pruning, and is thus not forbidden by Torah law).
Indeed, **Rav Sh. Z. Auerbach** (*Minchat Shlomo, 51, 8*) permits preservation labor even in the case of pruning that is forbidden by Torah law.
We must, however, distinguish between "preservation" and "loss." The Gemara in *Mo'ed* Katan 3a permits watering during the *Shemita* year. The *Rishonim* ad loc. (Rashi and Rabbenu Chananel) imply that the allowance is based on financial loss, and not on preservation (It appears that the Rambam (*Hilchot Shemita ve-Yovel 1:8-10*) did not make this distinction. Rashi also mentions the idea of loss with respect to preservation, so the distinction is not absolute.) In other words, there are labors that do not merely maintain the tree but clearly promote growth, such as watering, yet the Sages permitted them in order to prevent financial loss. Accordingly, there are two principles:

A) Labors meant for preservation which do not promote growth (such as pruning that is not done to promote the development of fruit, but rather to extend the life of the grapevine) might be permitted even if the labor itself is forbidden by Torah law. They should also be permitted in the case of labors that are forbidden only by rabbinic decree, even if there is no financial loss, and even at the end of the seventh year, even though they can be delayed until the eighth year (see *Chazon Ish, Shevi'it, 17*, sections *19, 20* and *27*).

B) An allowance based on **financial loss**. This allowance is restricted to labors forbidden only by **rabbinic law** (and the allowance applies even to labors that promote growth, such as watering). These matters are, however, very complex and require careful examination by halachic authorities in each case (see also *Chut ha-Shani*, Rav Karelitz, *5, 5*, p. *78; Shemita Mamlachtit*, part *1*, chap. *4*; and Rav Sh. David, *Mishnat ha-Shemita 1*, p. *186* and on, regarding pruning peach trees).

8. There are many practical ramifications to this disagreement. For example, according to the Ritva, it is possible that an action that does not stimulate growth was never forbidden,

such that it may be performed during the *Shemita* year itself, even if abstaining from such work would not cause a financial loss. This follows from the words of the *Chazon Ish* (17, 20; 27). *Shabbat ha-Aretz* (1, 5), however, implies that we may be lenient only in a case where abstaining would lead to loss.

Let us try to formulate a practical difference between these two positions. Does one need to try to complete all of his gardening work before the *Shemita* year begins, or can one wait to perform tasks that are only prohibited by rabbinic law until the *Shemita* year itself?

The answer to this question should depend on the disagreement mentioned above. If labors of preservation are permitted only to prevent financial loss, one must try to prevent the loss before the *Shemita* year begins, and thus reduce the performance of rabbinic labors during the *Shemita* year. But if rabbinic labors that are performed in order to preserve a tree **were never forbidden**, it is possible that it is permitted to intentionally push them off to the *Shemita* year itself.

A similar question can be raised regarding the opposite case: Is it permitted to perform preservation work **toward the end of the *Shemita* year** if it can be pushed off to the eighth year? If the allowance is based on financial loss, here it should be forbidden, since the person can wait until the eighth year with no loss. But if the allowance is based on the fact that the task does not stimulate any growth, it should be permitted, as there is no forbidden labor whatsoever (see *Chazon Ish, Shevi'it, 17,* sections *19, 20,* and *27*).

On this matter, the **Chazon Ish** writes (*21:17*):

> One must fertilize and weed prior to *Rosh ha-Shana* 5712 [the Sabbatical year in question], so that it will not be necessary to fertilize and weed during the seventh year. And even if it will not suffice for the entire year, one is obligated to reduce [performing these labors during the *Shemita* year] as much as possible. Similarly, whatever can be delayed until after *Rosh ha-Shana* 5713, must be put off and is forbidden during the *Shemita* year.

That is to say, all the requisite work **must be performed prior to the *Shemita* year,** in order to reduce the work that will be performed during the seventh year, even if it involves labors that are performed in order to preserve that which already exists. Similarly, one must push off to the eighth year any work that can be pushed off to that time. This ruling might stem from the understanding that labors forbidden by rabbinic decree were only permitted in order to prevent financial loss, or perhaps it is simply a public policy guideline to educate people that they must prepare for the *Shemita* year, and not exert themselves with permitted labors that could have been performed before the *Shemita* year.[9]

Are all labors that are forbidden by rabbinic decree permitted in a case of financial loss? The Mishna in *Mo'ed Katan* (*2a*) states: "An irrigated field may be watered in the seventh year." The Gemara there cites a disagreement: According to Abaye, the allowance stems from the fact that today the observance of *Shemita* is only by rabbinic decree, and the Rabbis did not include the case of potential loss in the decree. According to Rava, on the other hand, watering itself is a task that is forbidden by rabbinic decree, and therefore even when *Shemita* applies by Torah law there is no decree in a case of financial loss.

We rule in accordance with the position of Rava, and therefore most *Rishonim* (Rashi, Rambam) conclude that all rabbinic labors are permitted during the *Shemita* year in a case of financial loss.[10] The *Nimukei Yosef* (ad loc.) explains, however, that the allowance owing to a financial loss was only stated with respect to rabbinic labors that are trivial. According to him, labors that are performed on a regular basis, such as watering, do not fall into the category of "important work," and only labors of this sort are permitted in order to prevent a financial loss.

As for the halacha, the *posekim* generally rule that all labors that are forbidden by rabbinic decree are permitted in a case of financial loss, as asserted by most *Rishonim*. The *Chazon Ish* adds that there is another reason that one may be lenient today, since we are dealing with a matter that is a two-fold rabbinic decree ("*trei de-rabbanan*"): the labor is forbidden by rabbinic decree, and our entire observance of *Shemita* today is by rabbinic decree (*21, 17–18*).[11]

Is it possible today (when the observance of *Shemita* is by rabbinic decree) to permit labors that are forbidden by Torah law on account of financial loss, as argued by Abaye? In order to answer this question, we must clarify whether Rava agrees that labors that are forbidden by Torah law are permitted when the entire observance of

9. **Another practical ramification**: Is it permitted to spray the ground with an herbicide that prevents weeds from growing in a situation that does not involve financial loss? On the one hand, there is no loss; on the other hand, no labor is performed that promotes growth. All that happens is that an action is performed that maintains the present situation and ensures that no weeds will grow (*mavri'ach ari*, like "chasing away a lion" from someone else's field, which is not defined as objective benefit for it simply prevented a potential loss). If the allowance regarding labors that are forbidden by rabbinic decree is based on **loss**, then this is forbidden. But if the allowance applies to **labors that do not promote growth**, there is room to allow the practice. The ***Chazon Ish*** (*17, 20, 27*) implies that he is lenient in such a case, whereas ***Shabbat ha-Aretz*** (*1, 5*) implies that there is room for leniency only in a case of loss.

10. We have cited the position of Rashi. As we have seen, the Ritva maintains that labors that are performed in order to preserve a tree are permitted because they do not stimulate growth. There is much to discuss regarding the relationship between "preserving a tree" and financial loss, but that is beyond the scope of this chapter.

11. We will discuss the observance of *Shemita* in our time below, p. 378.

Shemita is only by rabbinic decree.[12] *Responsa Maharit* (11, 52) rules that when *Shemita* is observed only by rabbinic decree, even labors that are forbidden by Torah law are permitted in cases of financial loss. Rav Kook (*Shabbat ha-Aretz, Kuntres Acharon 2, 2*) and the *Chazon Ish* (21, 17), however, are stringent on the matter.[13]

ספר

חדושי

הריטב"א

על מסכת

שבת

ספרי הריטב"א ז"ל כבר נדפסו פעמים רבות בדפוסים שונים. וכולם מלאים טעותים וקמשונים. והמביאים לביהד לא שמו עיניהם ולבם לתקנם. ועי"ז כמה מהלומדים נמנעו מלקנותם. ע"כ קמתי אנכי בעזה"י והבאתי מחדש ספרי הריטב"א על מכבש הדפוס ועשיתי כל השתדלותי לנקותם ולבררם מכמה טעותים אשר נפלו בדפוסים הראשונים. ועל כי קשה עלי המעשה לבצע מחשבת, לבדי נלוה אלי הנגיד מוה"ר מרדכי קאלינבערג מחו"ק סקלאר ספרים פה ווארשא ונקוה כי בזמן לא כביר בעה"י נברך על המוגמר להשלים הדפסת כל ספרי הריטב"א הנמצאים אצלינו:

בהוצאת

תלת

תנועה להפצת תורה

RABBI YOM TOV BEN AVRAHAM ASHBILI (*the Ritva*)

Rabbi Yom Tov ben Avraham Ashbili was born in 5010 (1250) in Saragosa, Spain. The *Ritva* was a disciple of the Rashba and the Re'a, who, in turn, were disciples of the Ramban. The *Ritva* composed novellae on the Talmud, which draw upon the teachings of the Ramban and the Spanish tradition generally, and also incorporate the teachings of the Tosafists and the *Rishonim* from Ashkenaz. The *Ritva*'s works stand out in their clarity and readability.

The *Ritva* held the Rambam's philosophical writings in very high regard, and authored *Sefer Zikaron*, in which he defends the Rambam's *Guide of the Perplexed* against the Ramban's criticism. The *Ritva* died in 5090 (1330).

12. This depends on how we understand the disagreement in the Gemara: Does Rava disagree with Abaye? Or perhaps he means only to explain the Mishna as applying even when *Shemita* is mandated by Torah law, but he agrees with Abaye that all labors are permitted in the case of financial loss when *Shemita* is only mandated by rabbinic decree.

13. The *Chazon Ish* only permits labors that are forbidden by rabbinic decree, in deference to the position of the *Nimukei Yosef*. The Rambam (*Hilchot Shemita ve-Yovel* 1:10) also implies that labors that are forbidden by Torah law are forbidden even when the whole observance of *Shemita* is only by rabbinic decree.

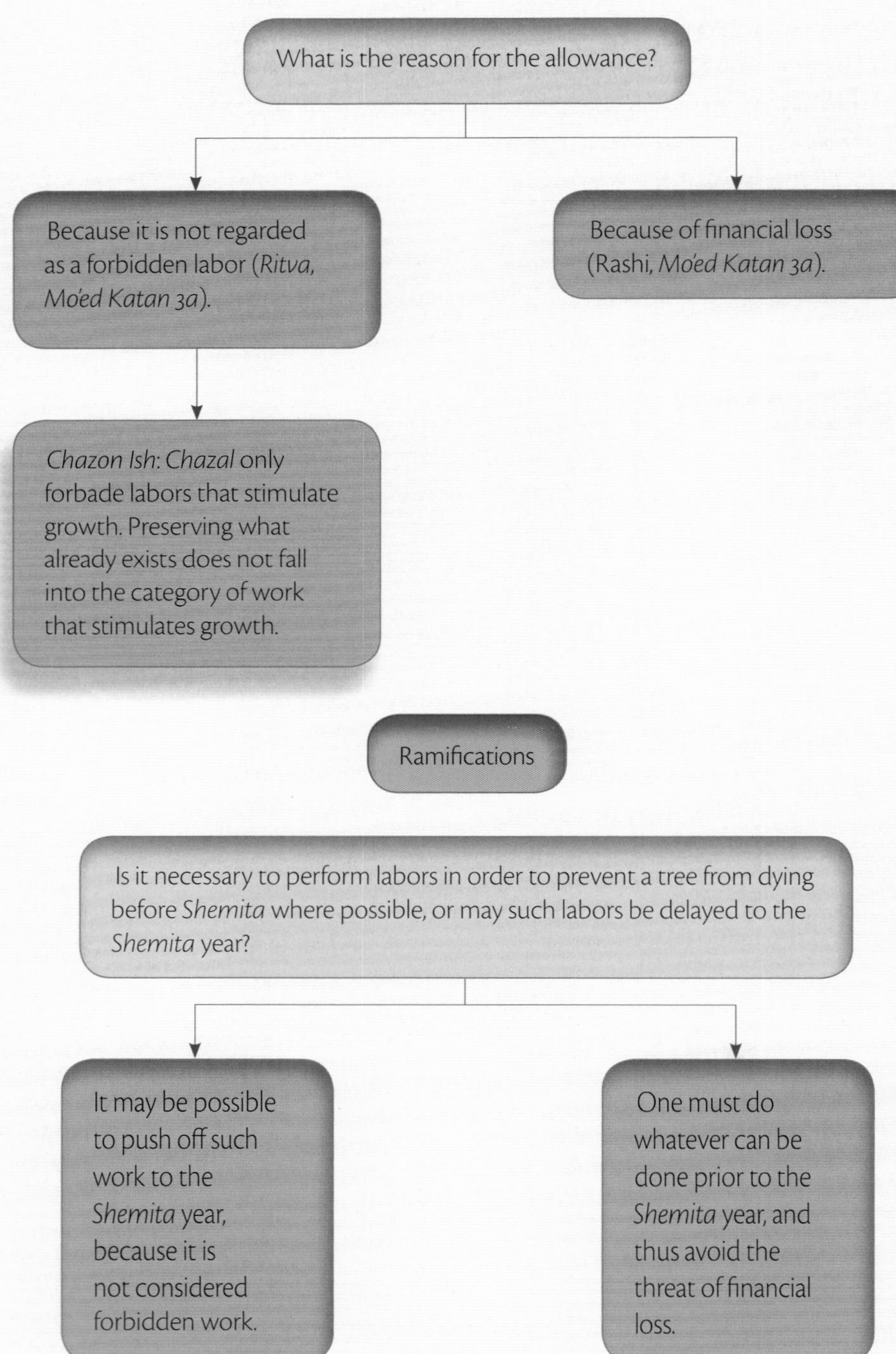
Labors that are forbidden by rabbinic decree are permitted when they are performed in order to prevent a tree from dying
What is the reason for the allowance?
Because it is not regarded as a forbidden labor (*Ritva, Mo'ed Katan 3a*).
Because of financial loss (Rashi, *Mo'ed Katan 3a*).
Chazon Ish: *Chazal* only forbade labors that stimulate growth. Preserving what already exists does not fall into the category of work that stimulates growth.
Ramifications
Is it necessary to perform labors in order to prevent a tree from dying before *Shemita* where possible, or may such labors be delayed to the *Shemita* year?
It may be possible to push off such work to the *Shemita* year, because it is not considered forbidden work.
One must do whatever can be done prior to the *Shemita* year, and thus avoid the threat of financial loss.

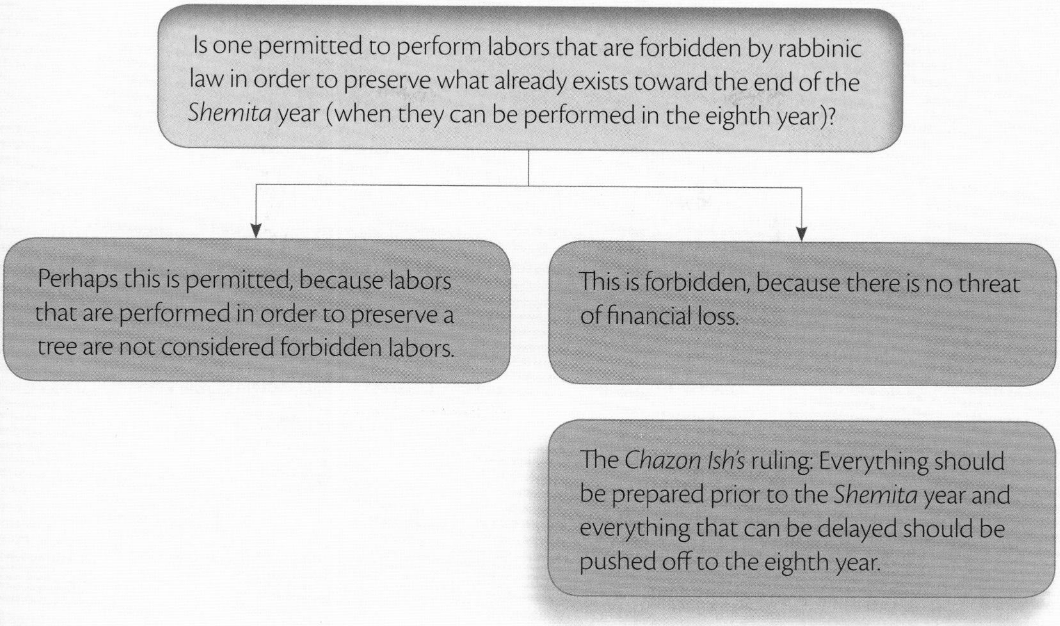

Is one permitted to perform labors that are forbidden by rabbinic law in order to preserve what already exists toward the end of the *Shemita* year (when they can be performed in the eighth year)?

Perhaps this is permitted, because labors that are performed in order to preserve a tree are not considered forbidden labors.

This is forbidden, because there is no threat of financial loss.

The *Chazon Ish's* ruling: Everything should be prepared prior to the *Shemita* year and everything that can be delayed should be pushed off to the eighth year.

TO PRESERVE THE FRUIT OR TO PRESERVE THE TREE?

When the **Rambam** (*Hilchot Shemita ve-Yovel 1:10*) explains why the Sages permitted labors for the purpose of preservation of the tree, he writes:

> Why did the Sages permit all these things? Because if one fails to water the soil, the land would become salty, and every tree on it would die.

The Rambam implies that the Sages only permitted labors whose purpose is to prevent a tree from dying. From this it follows that in a case where the tree will continue to live even without any tending, one may not perform any forbidden labors even if refraining from such work will result in damage to the fruit growing on the tree. This indeed was the understanding of Rav Kook (*Shabbat ha-Aretz 1, 5*):

> Removing thorns that protrude from a tree and damage the fruit is forbidden according to all opinions. Even those who

> say that it is permitted to perform work that is necessary for the preservation of a tree, even to the tree itself – that is only to preserve the tree so that it will be fit after the *Shemita* year. But work that is needed for the fruit was cancelled by the Torah, **which declared the produce of the seventh year as ownerless and removed it from the hands of the owner.** Even if the fruit will [otherwise] be lost, work performed for their sake is forbidden.

Rav Kook explains his position as follows: given that *Shemita* produce is ownerless, its ruin does not cause a financial loss to the owner of the field, and thus the Sages did not permit labors for the purpose of preservation of the fruit (see *Shabbat ha-Aretz 1, 8; 15*).

The ***Chazon Ish*** disagrees with Rav Kook. According to him, not only labors whose purpose is to preserve the tree are permitted, but so too are labors whose purpose is to preserve the fruit.[14]

The *Chazon Ish* reconciles his position with the words of the Rambam as follows:

> He does not mean that the tree will dry up and never again produce fruit, but rather that it will die this year and not cause its fruit to ripen. His words, "it will become salty,"constitute the cause of what follows, "and every tree on it would die,"but he is not referring to loss of the land for the following year.

In other words, when the Rambam allows a person to work the land during the *Shemita* year, so that "every tree on it"should not die, he is referring to the tree's fruit, for a fruitless tree is regarded as dead (the essence of the tree being its fruit). This being the case, the land is considered salty because there is no fruit this year (even though the trees are still alive).

But how does the ***Chazon Ish*** contend with **Rav Kook**'s objection, that, given that *Shemita* produce is ownerless, its ruin should not be regarded as a financial loss for the owner of the field? **Rav Sh. Z. Auerbach** (*Ma'adanei Aretz,* beginning of section 7) answers this question, based on the position of **Maharil Diskin** (*Kuntres Acharon* no. 259):

14. The *Chazon Ish* (*21, 14*) proves his position from the Gemara at the beginning of *Mo'ed Katan*, which records opinions that derivative labors are forbidden by Torah law: "Surely Rav Yosef and Abaye maintain that derivative labors are forbidden by Torah law, and thus they are only permitted in our time because all of *Shemita* observance is rabbinic. This being the case, [by Torah law] all the trees growing in an irrigated field [the *Mishna's* case] will die during the *Shemita* year! We are, therefore, forced to say that watering is permitted for the sake of the fruit." In other words, if we assume that the Sages did not permit labors that are performed for the purpose of preserving *Shemita* produce, it turns out that according to those opinions in the Gemara that maintain that the allowance of "a financial loss"only applies when *Shemita* is observed by rabbinic degree – when *Shemita* was observed as Torah law, all produce that required irrigation would die! The *Chazon Ish* regards such a conclusion as untenable. It is, therefore, necessary to say that derivative labors are permitted during the *Shemita* year even to save ownerless *Shemita* produce from ruin. He also notes that the same allowance applies to *Chol ha-Mo'ed*, as the Rambam writes (*Hilchot Yom Tov 7:2*): "One may water irrigated fields on *Chol ha-Mo'ed* ... for if he does not water ... all the trees

Even though, generally speaking, when we permit a prohibition because of financial loss we do not apply the allowance to that which is ownerless, nevertheless, with respect to *Shemita,* we permit working the land because of loss of the produce, even though it is ownerless. This is because *Shemita* produce is different; since the verse states: "that the poor of your people may eat" (*Shemot 23:11*) – this produce is regarded as **jointly owned by all of Israel.**

That is to say, *Shemita* produce is indeed ownerless, but this does not mean that they do not belong to anybody. The ownerless produce is meant to be eaten by all of Israel, and therefore out of concern for all of Israel, it is permitted to perform labors that are forbidden by rabbinic decree in order to preserve the produce.

It might be added that according to the *Chazon Ish, Chazal* permitted labors forbidden by rabbinic decree in order to preserve the produce, not because of a **financial loss** suffered by any particular person, but because of **the loss of the produce.** *Chazal* expanded the prohibitions of *Shemita,* but it was not their intention that the added prohibitions would cause *Shemita* produce to become ruined or for them to cause property to be damaged (whether or not it contains *Shemita* produce), and therefore they permitted labors to preserve the tree or its produce.

Did Rav Kook disagree with these arguments? Why was he not concerned about the financial loss to all of Israel? Rav Kook, apparently, believed that *Chazal* did not want us to concern ourselves with ***Shemita* produce**. This produce **grows on its own, and people must completely refrain from agricultural work** – as it is God's produce. People are not partners in its growth. *Chazal* permitted labors forbidden by rabbinic decree **only in the case of long-term damage for the coming years.** *Chazal* did not want there to be the need to plant trees anew in the wake of the *Shemita* year and thereby be without produce for years. **Therefore, *Chazal's* allowance applies exclusively to things that will have an effect on the coming years.**

It may be possible to offer another explanation for the

will be ruined."In the case of *Chol ha-Mo'ed,* we are certainly not dealing with long-term damage to the tree (for we are talking about a week), but rather with damage to the fruit, and nevertheless the Rambam permits watering, saying that otherwise, "the trees will be ruined."We see then that when the Rambam talks about "trees,"he is not talking only about the trees themselves, but also about the fruit.

disagreement. We saw above that the allowance of labors for the purpose of preservation can be understood in two ways:

1. Because of the financial loss
2. They are not defined as forbidden labors.

Thus, according to the *Chazon Ish*, labors generally forbidden by rabbinic decree, when performed for the purpose of preservation, are not defined as forbidden labors. He therefore permits work whose purpose is preservation, even when it is aimed at protecting ownerless produce (for no forbidden labors are performed). In contrast, Rav Kook maintains that labors whose purpose is preservation are indeed regarded as forbidden labors, but they are permitted on account of the financial loss. Thus, in his view, forbidden labors are only permitted when the life of a tree is in jeopardy. When produce alone is liable to be ruined, but there is no loss to the tree's owners because the fruit itself is already ownerless, forbidden labors are not permitted.

What is the level of loss that permits labors forbidden by rabbinic decree? The *Chazon Ish* mentions in one place the loss of all the produce (*21, 17*). It is, however, reported in the *Chazon Ish's* name (*Hilchot Shevi'it le-Chakla'im,* chap. *7,* note *6,* pp. *24-25*) that he permitted such labors whenever there is concern that more than a sixth of the produce will suffer damage.

To summarize: According to Rav Kook, forbidden labors may not be performed for the sake of any **plants that have *Shemita***

RABBI YEHOSHUA LEIB DISKIN (*Maharil Diskin*)

Rabbi Yehoshua Leib Diskin was born in 5577 (1817) in Grodno, Lithuania. After having served as the rabbi of various communities, including the important community of Brisk, he moved to Eretz Yisrael and settled in Jerusalem.

Maharil Diskin served as the Rabbi of Jerusalem together with Rabbi Shmuel Salant. He was one of the major opponents of the *heter mechira* as it was formulated in 5649 (1889), but by the time of the next *Shemita*, he supported the *heter* under certain conditions. His writings include *Responsa Maharil Diskin* and *Torat Ohel Mosheh*.

sanctity because those plants are ownerless. Accordingly, forbidden labors may not be performed for ***Shemita* fruit**, and certainly not for **annual vegetables**, where all work performed is solely for the vegetables themselves and no long-term damage is involved (see *Shabbat ha-Aretz 1, 8; 15*). Labors for the purpose of preservation that are forbidden by rabbinic decree may only be performed in order to prevent damage to the tree in coming years, damage to sixth-year produce, and damage to plants that do not have *Shemita* sanctity.[15] According to the ***Chazon Ish***, agricultural labors otherwise forbidden by rabbinic decree are permissible **in all cases**, whenever there is risk of damage to the tree, to its fruit, or even to vegetables.

THE HALACHA

Since we are dealing with an uncertainty regarding a rabbinic law (labors forbidden by rabbinic decree), and since the observance of *Shemita* today is only by rabbinic decree, farmers for whom agriculture is their livelihood, or others who have large tracts of agricultural land and are subject to substantial financial loss, may be lenient in accordance with the *Chazon Ish's* allowance and perform labors forbidden by rabbinic decree, even when the purpose is preservation of the fruit (even when there will be no damage to the tree itself).[16]

Thus, there is room to permit the performance of labors forbidden by rabbinic decree even for the sake of vegetables, even if they have *Shemita* sanctity.

15. Such as flowers that lack a scent. According to Rav Sh. Z. Auerbach, even flowers that have a scent do not have *Shemita* sanctity, unless they are grown for their scent. Thus, Rav Kook would permit labors performed for them as well (see the chapter dealing with *Shemita* sanctity).

16. According to this opinion, it is clearly permissible to perform labors forbidden by rabbinic decree for the sake of fruit growing on the tree, even if the fruit is still small. Is one permitted to perform forbidden labors, not in order to prevent damage to these immature fruit, but in order to prevent a significant decrease in the quantity of fruit? **Rav Yisraeli** (*Ha-Torah ve-ha-Medina 9-10, pp. 346-355*) is strict regarding this matter, but it is related in the name of the *Chazon Ish* that he was lenient about it when the damage was substantial, for a tree without fruit is regarded as dead for that year. According to him, it is permitted to perform labors forbidden by rabbinic decree (in the manner described above) even **in order to ensure that the tree bear fruit. In *Dapei Halacha le-Chakla'im* published by *Po'alei Agudat Yisra'el*** (*p. 24*), it is related in the name of the ***Chazon Ish*** that the "substantial damage"that permits the performance of labors for the sake of future produce is a sixth of the usual crop (see also. *Chazon Ish, 21, 14; Ha-Torah ve-ha-Medina 9-10, pp. 348-354; Mishpetei Aretz 3*, note 5). Today, the tendency is to be lenient on this matter, though an attempt is made to combine this with other grounds for leniency, such as watering and fertilizing by automatic computer control.

In a private garden, one should be stringent and refrain from work that is not essential for the tree that is intended only for the fruit. But as stated above, even Rav Kook was only stringent with respect to plants that have *Shemita* sanctity (because they are ownerless), and even according to him, it is permitted to water trees at the beginning of the year in order to prevent damage to the fruit since they are not ownerless (because they did not blossom in the seventh year).[17] It would also appear that one may be lenient with respect to garden plants and tend to them (even if they are annuals) so that they not die, based upon those authorities who maintain that flowers do not have *Shemita* sanctity (see the chapter dealing with *Shemita* sanctity, where we discuss the opinion of Rav Sh. Z. Auerbach, who argues that since they are not grown for their fragrance, they do not have *Shemita* sanctity).[18] Today, then, Rav Kook's stringency finds expression primarily with respect to vegetables and with fruit that blossoms during the *Shemita* year. As stated above, one should be stringent with respect to such produce growing in a private garden[19] but farmers or others who are liable to suffer substantial financial loss may follow the lenient position of the *Chazon Ish*.

17. It is certainly permitted to water trees for the sake of the fruit during the eighth year, even though the fruit is *Shemita* produce, because agricultural labors are not forbidden after the *Shemita* year is finished (with the exception of harvesting and gathering fruit, where the prohibition is to display ownership).

18. It is, however, preferable to plant perennial flowers, because then the watering and other labors are performed not only in order to maintain them during the *Shemita* year, but for future years as well.

19. It would seem to be permissible to program a computerized watering system before the *Shemita* year to operate during the *Shemita* year even in the case of a private garden – see the section dealing with tending gardens.

RABBI OVADYA OF BARTENURA

Rabbi Ovadya of Bartenura was born circa 5200 (1440) in Italy. He later moved to Egypt and from there to Jerusalem and Hebron, both of which he found exceedingly desolate.

The Bartenura authored several books (a supercommentary to Rashi's commentary on the Torah, novellae on the Rambam's *Mishneh Torah*, and others), but his most famous work is his commentary to the Mishna, a clear and comprehensive commentary based on the works of the earlier *Rishonim*. The Bartenura died in 5290 (1530).

Are labors forbidden by rabbinic decree permitted when performed for the purpose of preserving fruit?

Rav Kook (and the simple understanding of the Rambam): Such labors are only permitted for the purpose of preserving the tree.

The fruit is ownerless, and thus there is no financial loss, and so the labors are forbidden.

Chazal did not want us to concern ourselves with *Shemita* produce, because it is not man's produce but rather God's produce. Therefore, the Sages permitted such labors only with respect to produce that does not have *Shemita* sanctity and in cases where the work is **necessary for coming years**, so that the *Shemita* not cause long-term damage.

Chazon Ish: Such labors are permitted even for the purpose of preserving the fruit.

Maharil Diskin: The fruit belongs to the poor and to all of Israel, and thus a financial loss is suffered by the collective, and so the labors are permitted.

Additional explanation: Perhaps the allowance is based not on the financial loss, but on the loss and destruction of the fruit.

Another explanation of the disagreement between Rav Kook and the *Chazon Ish*

Labors performed for the purpose of preservation are permitted because of the financial loss, and here there is no such loss.

Labors whose purpose is preservation are permitted because they are not regarded as forbidden labors, and thus it makes no difference whether the objective is preservation of the tree or preservation of the produce.

WHAT LABORS ARE FORBIDDEN BY RABBINIC DECREE DURING *SHEMITA*?

There is no single passage in the Gemara that provides a complete list of the agricultural labors that are forbidden by rabbinic decree during the *Shemita* year. These labors are discussed primarily in the second chapter of *Shevi'it* and in two additional passages, one in *Mo'ed Katan* (3a) and the other in *Avoda Zara* (50b).

Generally speaking, all agricultural labors are forbidden by rabbinic decree, except for the four labors mentioned in the Torah (planting, pruning, reaping and gathering, and perhaps also plowing).[20] These include labors that stimulate the growth of trees as well as labors that make it possible to prepare the ground for planting (such as removing stones).

The **Chazon Ish** (*Shevi'it 17, 19*) compiled a list of twenty-two labors that are forbidden by rabbinic decree:

> We find in the *Mishna* and the *Gemara* twenty-two derivative categories of labor that are forbidden during the *Shemita* year, seventeen of them in our chapter [chapter two of *Shevi'it*]: 1. fertilizing; 2. hoeing; 3. excising blemishes on trees; 4. removing leaves; 5. applying dust; 6. fumigating; 7. removing stones; 8. pruning (trees other than a grapevine); 9. removing green branches; 10. removing all side branches; 11. applying manure or a foul-smelling oil; 12. wrapping or tying; 13. covering roots with ashes; 14. building shelters for saplings; 15. watering; 16. smearing unripe figs with oil; 17. piercing unripe figs. In *Mo'ed Katan* (3a): 18. removing weeds with their roots; 19. cutting weeds without removing their roots; 20. supporting a tree; 21. hoeing under an olive tree. In *Avoda Zara* (59b): 22. removing the branches of a tree.

A few more labors may be added to this list, as indicated below.[21] As we have already seen, labors that are forbidden by rabbinic decree are permitted when performed in order to prevent a financial loss.

20. See the chapter on planting (p. 89). The *Acharonim* discuss whether a labor that is slightly different from the biblical labor is automatically defined as a rabbinic labor (Rav Frank, *Har Tzvi, Zera'im, II, 35*), in which case it is possible that planting by machine is a derivative labor that is forbidden only by rabbinic decree; or perhaps only a change in the form of the labor itself (such as watering, which is regarded as a derivative labor under the category of plowing or planting) turns it into a rabbinic prohibition, but a labor that only involves a slight change in the way it is performed is still forbidden by Torah law (*Chazon Ish, 25, 38*).

21. Such as sinking or grafting, which may be related to other listed labors.

It is therefore exceedingly important to know which labors are forbidden by Torah law (and therefore forbidden in all situations) and which are forbidden by rabbinic decree.

We shall now examine the sources and try to explain each forbidden labor. The *mishnayot* in the second chapter of tractate *Shevi'it* describe the labors that must be performed during the **sixth year**[22] in advance of the *Shemita* year.

The implication of this list is that all these seventeen labors are forbidden during the *Shemita* year itself. We shall examine the main *mishnayot*, and through them try to understand the rabbinic prohibitions regarding *Shemita*.

The *Mishna* in *Shevi'it* states (2:2):

> One may fertilize and hoe among the melons and gourds until *Rosh ha-Shana*; and so too in irrigated fields. One may excise blemishes, remove [leaves], apply dust, [and] fumigate [trees] until *Rosh ha-Shana.*

The *Mishna* implies that all the labors listed above are forbidden during the *Shemita* year by rabbinic decree.

How is one to prepare for fertilizing one's garden during the *Shemita* year?

***Mezablin* – Fertilizing:** During the *Shemita* year, it is forbidden to fertilize a field in order to enrich its soil. Today, there are three main ways to fertilize a field:

1. Regular fertilizers that are applied every few weeks.

Regular fertilizers (permitted in special circumstances)

Fertilizers that break down slowly – should be applied prior to the *Shemita* year

22. The *mishnayot* relate to the period of "*tosefet shevi'it.*" Certain labors are permitted during *tosefet shevi'it*, while others are forbidden. Today, the law of *tosefet shevi'it* no longer applies, as we shall see in the chapter devoted to *tosefet shevi'it.*

Liquid fertilizers that are applied through the irrigation system (permitted in special circumstances)

2. Fertilizers that break down slowly and are applied every few months.
3. Fertilizers that are applied through the irrigation system.

Since it is possible to use fertilizers that break down slowly, such fertilizers should be applied at the end of the sixth year in an amount that will suffice for the entire year of *Shemita*. As we shall see below, in certain cases it is permitted to apply fertilizers even during the *Shemita* year itself. In such case it is preferable to fertilize the field by way of the irrigation system which is a more indirect manner of application.

***Me'adrin* – Hoeing**: *Iddur* refers to digging in the ground. *Iddur* is forbidden only by rabbinic decree, as opposed to the similar labor *charisha*, plowing, where there is a disagreement about whether or not it is forbidden by Torah law (the custom is to be stringent). The Rash (*Shevi'it* 2:2) explains that *iddur* refers to digging by hand with the help of some implement (and so too Rambam, *Shevi'it* 1:7): "This refers to digging by hand using an iron tool."

Hoeing by hand

Generally speaking, one should not hoe during the *Shemita* year except for exceptional circumstances where there is a risk of damage and economic loss.

Removing an abnormal growth appearing on a tree

***Meyablin* – Excising blemishes from trees:** During the *Shemita* year, it is forbidden to remove abnormal growths from a tree. As the Bartenura explains: "*Meyablin* – excising blemishes that appear on a tree."In certain cases, however, when there is concern about possible damage to the tree, these abnormal growths may be removed.

***Mefarkin* – Removing leaves:** During the *Shemita* year, one may not remove the leaves of a tree for an agricultural purpose. What is the

Removing leaves from a tree (forbidden by rabbinic decree)

agricultural benefit of removing a tree's leaves? The Rash and the Bartenura (ibid.) explain that the leaves are removed in order that the tree will not be too heavy: "One removes leaves from a tree in order to lighten its load." The *Tosafot ha-Rosh* (*Mo'ed Katan 3a*) explains, however, that the goal of removing the leaves is to allow sunlight to reach the fruit: "One removes leaves so that they not shade the fruit and the fruit will be able to ripen in the sun."[23]

AGRICULTURAL EXPLANATION – REMOVING LEAVES

Leaves are sometimes removed from a tree in order to lighten the weight that the tree must bear. They may also be removed in order to allow light to reach the fruit. Today citrus trees may be pruned for a similar purpose. Sometimes the foliage is so thick that light cannot penetrate to the inner branches. In such a situation, fruit will grow only on the outer, exposed branches, while the inner branches will be empty of fruit. Therefore, the tree is pruned so that light will penetrate and fruit will grow on the inner branches as well.

***Me'avkin* – Applying dust:** The Bartenura explains: "*Me'avkin*

Dusting – dusting roots (forbidden by rabbinic decree)

For an agricultural explanation of the significance of covering the roots, see below with respect to the labor of *kotemin* – covering the roots with ashes.

23. The *mishna* concludes: "Rabbi Shimon says: He may remove the leaf from the cluster during the seventh year." This implies that the leaves are being removed for the sake of the fruit, for Rabbi Shimon speaks of a "cluster." Why then does Rabbi Shimon permit this during the *Shemita* year? The Rash explains that Rabbi Shimon permits this because the procedure is necessary for the preservation of the tree. According to this, however, it is difficult to understand why the dissenting Tanna forbids the practice. It might be suggested that, according to the first Tanna, rabbinic labors are permitted only for the preservation of the tree but not for the preservation of the fruit, as argued by Rav Kook above. In practice, we rule in accordance with the first Tanna, so that according to the explanation that we have suggested, it is forbidden to perform labors for the purpose of preservation of the produce. How can we understand the first Tanna according to the *Chazon Ish*, who says that rabbinic labors are permitted for the preservation of the produce? The *Chazon Ish* (21, 17) understands that the first Tanna forbids the practice because there is only a minor loss to the produce, but all agree that if failure to remove the leaves will cause damage to most of the produce, removing them is permitted.

– exposed roots are covered with dust." In contrast, the Rambam (*1:5*) explains that *ibbuk* refers to spreading dust on the tree-top. Rash Sirillo cites a third explanation, according to which the term *ibbuk* is connected to "And there wrestled (*va-ye'avek*) a man with him" (*Bereishit 32:25*). According to this understanding, *ibbuk* means binding a tree in a place where there is a crack in the branch in order to close the gap.

Is it permitted to fumigate a tree during the *Shemita* year? Is it permitted to spray a tree with pesticides?

***Me'ashnin* – Fumigating:** In the past, it was common to create smoke under a tree in order to kill worms and other pests. As the Rash explains: "*Me'ashnin* – smoke is created under a tree, in order to cause the worms to fall from it or die." Why is this forbidden during the *Shemita* year, as surely this action is needed to save the tree from being harmed by worms? This is a highly relevant issue in our time, for the modern equivalent of "fumigating" is spraying pesticides.

Fumigating a tree – forbidden by rabbinic decree

The **Rambam** (commentary to the Mishna, ad loc.) writes: "*Me'ashnin* – one creates smoke under [the trees] in order to kill the worms that eat the fruit and cling to it." In other words, we are dealing with worms that damage the fruit. In light of this, we can explain the mishna in accordance with the view of **Rav Kook**, who forbids the performance of labors that are forbidden by rabbinic decree in order to prevent damage to the fruit. Indeed, Rav Kook (*Shabbat ha-Aretz, Kuntres Acharon, 10;* and so too *Responsa*

AGRICULTURAL EXPLANATION – FUMIGATION

Fumigating a tree is a familiar agricultural procedure. Similar procedures are followed today as well. Sulfur is sometimes placed beneath a tree in order to kill pests.

Spraying pesticides – forbidden by rabbinic decree (but permitted when withholding pesticides will lead to financial loss). Picture of fumigation at the Atzmona gard

Maharil Diskin, 27, 25) writes that the mishna is dealing with a case where the worms merely hinder the development of the tree but do not cause it damage. According to this, if the worms threaten to damage the tree, fumigation is permitted.

As we saw above, however, the ***Chazon Ish*** maintains that labors that are forbidden by rabbinic decree are permitted even for the purpose of preserving the fruit. How, then, does he explain the mishna? The *Chazon Ish* (*17, 19*) writes that while strictly speaking, fumigating a tree is permitted, the Sages forbade certain labors because they give the appearance of promoting growth of the tree, even if in fact their objective is to save the tree from dying.[24]

The ***Pe'at ha-Shulchan*** (*20, 11*) suggests another answer: Labors may not be performed on the tree itself even if they are only forbidden by rabbinic decree and they are performed for the purpose of preservation. Rav Kook (*Shabbat ha-Aretz, 1, 5,* and *Kuntres Acharon,* section *10*), however, rules against the *Pe'at ha-Shulchan* (and this is also the view of the *Chazon Ish, 17, 19;* and *Rav Elyashiv, Mishpetei Aretz, 4,* note *24;* we shall deal with this idea below in connection with the labor of *mezahamin*).

The *Chazon Ish's* position can also be explained based on the explanation of the ***Tosafot ha-Rosh*** (*Mo'ed Katan 3b*; as well as the Meiri, ad loc., and the Ra'avad, *Torat Kohanim, Behar*), who understands that the fumigation discussed in the mishna is not meant to kill worms, but rather to fatten the fruit. According to this, spraying pesticide to kill worms and other pests would be permitted.

As for the halacha, Rav Elyashiv (*Mishpetei Aretz, 4,* note *24*) rules that pesticides may be applied in order to kill worms and other pests, and according to the *Chazon Ish,* this application is permitted even to prevent damage to the fruit itself.[25]

Let us now move on to the next mishna (*Shevi'it 2:3*) which

24. In Rav Kafah's edition of the Rambam's commentary to the *mishna* we find: "*Me'ashnin* – one raises smoke under [the trees] in order to kill the worms that eat the *tree* and cling to it." According to this version, the Rambam writes of damage to the *tree,* and this should be permitted according to all opinions! And yet the *mishna* permits this only before *Rosh ha-Shana* of the *Shemita* year. According to this reading, we must find an answer, for the opinion of Rav Kook, based on one of the answers brought below. See also *Sefer ha-Shemita,* p. 24, note 5.

25. One can also argue that spraying pesticides does not constitute a forbidden labor, inasmuch as it does not enhance the tree whatsoever, but merely removes an external source of damage (see Rashi, *Avoda Zara 52b,* s.v. *kan ve-kan*; Ritva, *Mo'ed Katan 3a,* cited above).

relates to additional labors that are forbidden by rabbinic decree during the *Shemita* year:

> One may clear stones [from a field] until *Rosh ha-Shana*. One may prune [trees], remove green branches, and remove the side branches until *Rosh ha-Shana.*

***Mesaklin* – Removing stones:** Removing stones from a field is a derivative labor under the category of plowing, because the removal of stones prepares the ground for plowing.[26]

Several *mishnayot* state, however, that removing stones is permitted for the purpose of preparing ground for construction or the like, rather than for plowing. For example, we read in *Shevi'it* 3:7:

> Someone clearing stones from his field may remove the upper [ones] but must leave those which touch the ground.

Removing stones from a field – forbidden by rabbinic decree

The mishna permits a person to remove stones (that he needs for building purposes or the like), provided that he leaves those that touch the ground, because in that way it is clear that his objective is not to prepare the ground for plowing.[27]

In light of this allowance, one can ask whether it is permitted to clean a garden of stones, branches, or other undesired objects. In small home gardens this is generally done solely for aesthetic purposes, and not to prepare the ground for plowing. Indeed, Rav Sh. Z. Auerbach (*Minchat Shlomo 51, 10*) writes that it stands to reason that this is permitted:

> Clearing debris in a garden adjacent to a house – the *Yerushalmi* states that if a person's animal or oven is there [in the courtyard], it is permitted to gather branches and give them to his animal or put them in his stove, and it does not give the appearance that he is removing [debris in preparation for plowing], because his animal and his oven demonstrate

26. According to *Tosafot ha-Rosh* (*Mo'ed Katan 3a*), *Tiferet Yisra'el* (section 18) and *Melechet Shlomo* (on the Mishna), the prohibition to remove stones only applies to stones that are connected to the ground, the removal of which causes the movement of soil, which is considered plowing. According to them, removing stones that lie on the ground is forbidden only on account of appearances (*mar'it ayin*). This distinction, however, is not mentioned by the other commentators on the mishna, and the *Chazon Ish* (17, 26) rules that there is no difference between the two cases (this is also implied by a later mishna (3:7); see *Tosafot Yom Tov*, ad loc.).

27. This also explains the end of *Mishna Shevi'it 3:8*.

his intentions. And I am in doubt, for it is also possible that in a small garden adjacent to a person's house, it might be permitted to remove stones and branches. For just as his animal and his oven justify an allowance, so too here **since it is adjacent to his house, everybody knows that it is common practice to clean up the entire area around his house for the purpose of cleanliness,** and not for the sake of planting. The matter requires further study.

Removal of debris that clearly has no agricultural objective – permitted

While Rav Sh. Z. Auerbach concludes by saying that the matter requires further study and does not rule that it is permitted, the ***Sefer ha-Shemita*** (5, 4) explicitly permits such behavior.[28] In practice, there is room to permit the removal of stones when it is clearly being done solely for the purpose of cleanliness. Therefore, if one wishes to clear one's garden of stones during the *Shemita* year, it is preferable to do so by hand and without any special equipment. In addition, one should not remove stones that are not ordinarily removed for cleanliness that are removed only to prepare the lawn for mowing or the like.

Just as there is no prohibition to remove stones when it is not done for the purpose of plowing, so too there is no prohibition of plowing when it is clear that one's objective is not to prepare the ground for planting,[29] as it is stated in the *Sifra* (*parashat Behar*):

> "Then shall the land keep a Sabbath to the Lord"– You might think that one may not dig wells, ditches and caves or repair ritual baths. Therefore the verse states: "You shall neither plant your field, nor prune your vineyard."

Leveling land for construction with a tractor – permitted (when the objective is clear)

28. Rav Karelitz also allowed this (*Mishpetei Aretz* 5, note 15). Rav Elyashiv (cited there), however, forbids the practice. It would appear, however, that he too would permit the practice when performed in accordance with our guidelines, for then it is clear that the debris is being removed solely for the purpose of cleanliness.

29. As is stated in the third chapter of tractate *Shevi'it* regarding the removal of stones, one must be careful about performing a permitted action if it might be mistaken for prohibited conduct.

The three additional labors mentioned in the Mishna – *kirsum*, *zirud*, and *pisul* – all involve the removal of branches from a tree for various purposes.

Why was the *Chazon Ish* lenient about pruning citrus trees?

Mekarsemin **– Pruning:** Rashi (*Mo'ed Katan 3a*) explains: "*Mekarsemin* – this is like pruning a grapevine, only that *kirsum* applies to other trees." That is to say, *kirsum* refers to the removal of branches in order to promote the growth of a tree, and it parallels pruning – *zemira* – of a grapevine (see also Rash, *Shevi'it 2:3*).[30]

According to this understanding, the pruning of trees other than a grapevine – *kirsum* – is forbidden only by rabbinic decree. This is the position of the ***Chazon Ish*** (*21, 15*, and *Eglei Tal's* understanding of Rashi and the Rash *[Zore'a 1, 4]*). We have already seen, however, that most *posekim* understand that according to the Rambam, even the pruning of other trees is forbidden by Torah law (as opposed to the *Chazon Ish*, who understands that even according to the Rambam, the pruning of other trees is forbidden only by rabbinic decree).[31]

Pruning trees other than a grapevine: According to the *Chazon Ish*, this is forbidden only by rabbinic decree, and permitted in a situation of financial loss. Others maintain that this is forbidden by Torah law, and therefore forbidden even in a situation of financial loss. For an agricultural explanation of pruning with respect to a grapevine and other trees, see the end of the chapter dealing with pruning.

The **Rambam** (in his commentary to the Mishna, ad loc. and in *Shabbat 12:2*) explains *kirsum* differently. According to him, *kirsum* refers to the pruning of vegetables, namely, the removal of the leaves of a vegetable in order to improve the vegetable itself.[32] The Rambam's opinion may be that pruning all trees is forbidden by Torah law, whereas pruning vegetables is forbidden only by rabbinic decree.[33] Indeed, the *Chazon Ish* (*26, 1*) writes that, even those who understand

30. Y. Felix (*Mishna, Shevi'it 2:3, p. 35*) explains that *kirsum* refers to the removal of shoots that grow from the roots of a tree and compete with the branches for nutrition.

31. The *Eglei Tal* (*Zore'a 4*) explains that *kirsum* does not refer to regular pruning, but specifically to the removal of dead branches. According to this explanation, it is only *kirsum* that is forbidden merely by rabbinic decree, but regular pruning might be forbidden by Torah law.

32. This is the way Rambam understands *kirsum* in his *Commentary to the Mishna, Shabbat 12:2*. He offers a similar explanation in his commentary to our mishna, namely, *kirsum* refers to the removal of ears of grain, leaving the straw uncut and attached to the ground.

33. This is found in the writings of the *Netziv* (*Ha'amek She'ela, Behar, 61, 1*). The *Or Same'ach* (*Hilchot Shemita 1:15*), however, writes that even the pruning of vegetables is forbidden by Torah law. This is also the position of Rav Kook (*Shabbat ha-Aretz 2, 15*), following the Rambam (and the mishna in *Shevi'it 2:10*) that "one may stir the ground of a rice field with water, but one may not cut [the rice leaves]." According to Rav Kook, "*kisu'ach* is the *zimur* mentioned in the Torah."

that the Rambam considers pruning other trees to be forbidden by Torah law, will agree that according to the Rambam pruning vegetables is forbidden only by rabbinic decree.[34] This position might have practical ramifications with respect to mowing a lawn, as we shall see below.

In any event, the *Chazon Ish* (21, 17) maintains that the pruning of other trees is forbidden only by rabbinic decree. Therefore, he permits pruning during the *Shemita* year (except for a grapevine) if refraining from pruning will lead to a financial loss:

> Regarding pruning, weeding, fertilizing, and hoeing with respect to an orange tree which is very delicate and prone to drying out ... in a case of financial loss where the whole tree will die (or all the fruit will be ruined), one may be lenient regarding all these labors. One must consider with each procedure separately whether there is concern that the tree will die, and whatever is done for extra gain is forbidden.

Removing the lateral branches of a tree

***Mezardin* – Removing green branches:** The Rash and the Bartenura understand *zirud* as the removal of unnecessary new branches, so that the remaining branches will have more room to grow: "*Mezardin* – when a tree has too many new branches, one removes some and leaves some." The difference between *kirsum* and *zirud* is that *kirsum* involves the removal of dry branches from the previous year so that the tree will grow better, whereas *zirud* involves the removal of new branches in order to allow the other branches more room to grow.[35]

34. According to those who maintain that pruning other trees, and not only grapevines, is forbidden by Torah law, it may be suggested that the *kirsum* mentioned in this mishna refers to the removal of branches in order to prevent disease or the like, rather than to promote the growth of the tree.

35. The Rambam (in his *Commentary to the Mishna*) implies that *zirud* is the same thing as *zemira*. The *Chazon Ish* (26) understands that the Rambam forbids the pruning of other trees by rabbinic decree, and thus he has no problem understanding that *zirud* is *zemira*, even though it is only forbidden by rabbinic decree. The *Chazon Ish* (21, 15) adds that according to the other *Rishonim* it is possible that in the case of a grapevine both the removal of dry branches and the removal of green branches (*kirsum* and *zirud*) are forbidden by Torah law, and it is only in the case of other trees that a distinction is made between these two tasks.

***Mefaslin* – Removing all side branches:** The Rash and the Bartenura understand that *pisul* involves the removal of a tree's branches in order to promote the thickening of the tree's trunk, so that it can later be used for the production of beams. For this reason it is called *pisul*, "sculpting," for in essence it involves shaping the tree.[36]

Removal of new branches

It is possible that the prohibited action is the very shaping of the tree.[37] It is more likely, however, that the problem lies not in shaping, but in the fact that the removal of the lateral branches causes the trunk to thicken.

> THE WOOD INDUSTRY
>
> Even today, the lateral branches of trees grown for wood are regularly removed. In this way, the central trunk thickens, and over the course of several years a trunk develops that is suitable for commercial use.

The next mishna in *Shevi'it* (2:4) discusses several additional labors:

One may fumigate saplings, and one may wrap them, put ash on them, make shelters for them, and water them, until *Rosh ha-Shana*.

May labors done to preserve the tree be performed on the tree itself?

***Mezahamin* – Fumigating, applying manure or a foul-smelling oil:** The Rash explains that *zihum* refers to the application of manure to those portions of a tree where the bark peeled off: "When bark of a tree is removed – manure is applied to the spot."[38] The Rambam (commentary to the Mishna, ad loc., and *Hilchot Shemita ve-Yovel*

36. Compare this with the cutting of an untrimmed sycamore tree (*Shevi'it* 4:5). There too the trunk of the sycamore is used for the production of beams, and there too the trunk is sometimes thickened by removing the lateral branches. See also the mishna dealing with the trimming of grapevines (*Shevi'it* 4:6). The *Chazon Ish* (19, 14-15) understands that trimming grapevines is permitted, because the person's intention is not to promote growth, but to use the branches (see above, the *Chazon Ish's* position that *zemira* that is not performed for the sake of promoting growth should be permitted).

37. This is how Y. Felix (*Mishna, Shevi'it*, 2:3, p. 37) explains it.

38. The Gemara in *Avoda Zara* (50b) states that there is a permitted type of *zihum* which is performed to preserve a tree, and a type of *zihum* which is done to strengthen a tree, and is thus prohibited. The Rash explains that our mishna refers to *zihum* to strengthen a tree, and therefore it is forbidden by rabbinic decree. In contrast, the Rambam writes that *zihum* is forbidden here even when performed to preserve a tree. He apparently follows the *Yerushalmi* (the *Lechem Mishne* explains that the Rambam understands that the *Bavli* does not issue a decisive ruling on this issue).

See further on, regarding how the *Acharonim* understand the Rambam's stringency.

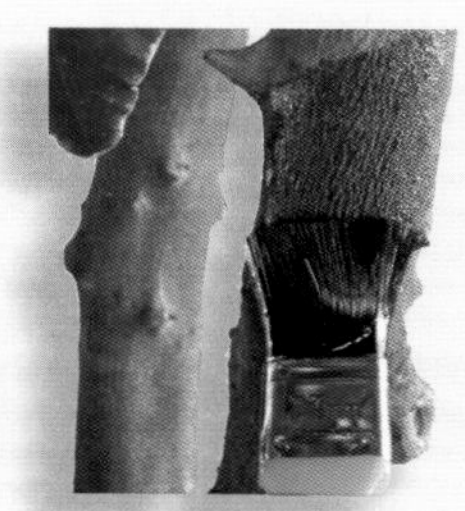

Zihum – rubbing the tree with foul-smelling oil to drive away pests (according to the Rambam).
Based on this law, the *Pe'at ha-Shulchan* forbids all labors that are performed on the tree itself (even to prevent a financial loss). Rav Kook and the *Chazon Ish*, however, permit labors to prevent a financial loss, even when performed on the tree itself.

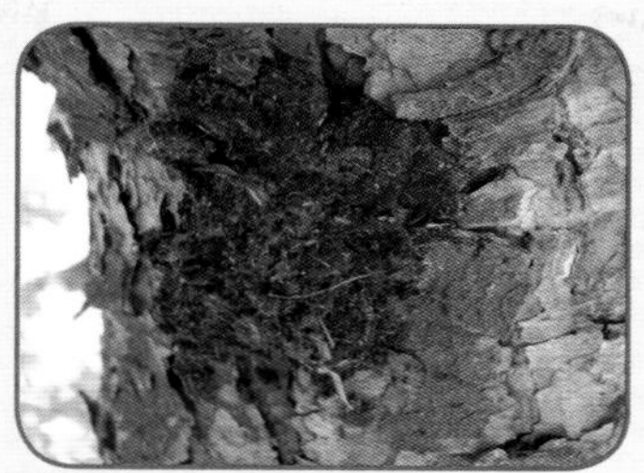

Zihum – patching with manure (according to the Rash)

1:5) explains differently: "One must not rub foul-smelling oils on the saplings to prevent birds from eating them while they are tender." That is to say, *zihum* refers to the application of foul-smelling oil to a tree in order to drive away pests. It is not clear why the Rambam forbids such a procedure, since its purpose seems to be the preservation of the tree.

The *Pe'at ha-Shulchan* (*20:11*) explains that the Sages did not permit labors that are performed on the tree itself, even to prevent financial loss, but only those labors that are performed on the ground. It should be noted that for contemporary agriculture this ruling is a major stringency. The *Chazon Ish* (*17, 19*) explains this stringency differently, claiming that since *zihum* is generally performed to promote the tree's growth, the Sages forbade it even when performed to prevent a loss, lest one come to perform the procedure in order to promote growth. According to him, in general one may perform labors forbidden by rabbinic law when the purpose is to prevent a financial loss, even when those labors are performed on the tree itself. This is also the ruling of Rav Kook (*Shabbat ha-Aretz 1, 5, 8, Kuntres Acharon. 10-11,* and *Iggerot, II,* no. *555,* p. *192*),[39] and it is generally accepted as halacha.

***Korechin* – Wrapping or tying:** According to the Rash, *kericha* refers to wrapping fabric around a tree in order to protect it from the cold or from the sun: "*Korechin* – wrapping to protect from

39. See references to this position in *Shabbat ha-Aretz* (letter 8, note 44).

the cold and the sun."The Rambam (*Commentary to the Mishna*) disagrees, arguing that *kericha* refers to tying together the upper branches of a tree.

Picture of tying the upper branches of a tree (Rambam)

Picture of covering a tree with fabric (Rash)

Kotemin **– Covering roots with ashes:** The Rash, based on the *Aruch*, explains that *ketima* involves covering a tree's roots with ashes: "*Ve-kotemin* – the *Aruch* explains: with ashes."The Rash cites another understanding according to which *kotemin* involves breaking off the ends of a tree's branches (this is also the explanation of the Rosh and the Bartenura).

Covering roots with ashes

AGRICULTURAL EXPLANATION

We have come across two labors that involve covering the roots, *ibbuk* (with dust) and *ketima* (with ashes). The Rosh had difficulty accepting that there are two similar labors (and therefore explained *ketima* as cutting off the ends of a tree's branches). Covering the roots is an essential procedure for the tree, because exposed roots are liable to dry out and suffer great damage.

Apparently, this concern led to the development of different ways to protect roots, sometimes by covering them with dust or ashes (see also Ribmatz on the Mishna, ad loc.).

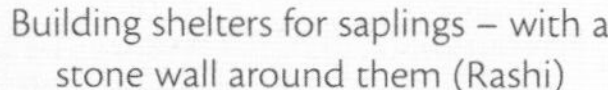

Building shelters for saplings – with a stone wall around them (Rashi)

Building shelters for saplings – with a covering (Rambam)

Osin lahen batin **– Building shelters for saplings:** According to the Rambam (*Commentary to the Mishna*) and the *Yerushalmi* quoted by the Rash, this refers to covering saplings in order to protect them. In contrast, Rashi (*Avoda Zara 50b*), the Rash and the Bartenura understand that this refers to the building of a cubit high fence around a sapling and filling it in with earth (for an expanded discussion, see appendix, p. 370.)

How should one water plants during the *Shemita* year? Must one wait until the grass has turned yellow? May one water generously?

Mashkin **– Watering:** As we have seen, the Mishna counts watering among the labors that are forbidden during the *Shemita* year. However, in the tenth mishna of this chapter the *tannaim* disagree regarding whether one may "water white soil" (a field of grain or vegetables), and according to Rabbi Shimon this is permitted during the *Shemita* year:

> One may water white soil; these are the words of Rabbi Shimon. Rabbi Eliezer ben Ya'akov forbids this.

Harbatza is a form of watering, and the *posekim* disagree about the type of watering that Rabbi Shimon permits during the *Shemita*

40. According to them, Rabbi Shimon speaks of *"harbatza"*(which implies minimal watering), because he is dealing with a field that does not require significant watering, and therefore watering in that manner is regarded as full watering. In truth, however, one can water in a generous manner in all situations, even when additional watering is not essential.
It should be noted that according to this opinion, it is permitted to water in the regular manner in all situations, except for vegetables that grew during the *Shemita* year and will be picked in that year. The problem here does not appear to be a prohibition of watering, but rather the prohibition of *sefichim*. Accordingly, if the vegetables started to grow in the sixth year, they may be watered in the regular fashion (see *Chazon Ish* 16, 4; some authorities explain this differently).

41. The *Chazon Ish* (16, 3, 13) disagrees, arguing that according to this explanation, the law does not follow Rabbi Shimon. It should be noted that the *Chazon Ish* maintains that the law in fact follows Rabbi Shimon, but only according to the explanation to be brought below.

year. The Rash and the Bartenura explain (*2:10*) that according to Rabbi Shimon watering is permitted even in situations where it is not absolutely necessary, as the laws governing watering are more lenient than the laws governing other labors forbidden by the Sages during the *Shemita* year.[40] The Bartenura even rules in accordance with this position (see also his commentary to *Mo'ed Katan 1:1*).[41] The Rambam (*Commentary to the Mishna,* and *Hilchot Shemita ve-Yovel 1:8*) understands *harbatza* as watering among trees. Rabbi Shimon permits such watering only when necessary to prevent a financial loss (according to the Rambam, Rabbi Eliezer ben Ya'akov forbids even such watering).

The *Chazon Ish* presents an intermediate position (*16, 13,* based on Rashi, *Tosafot* and *Meiri* in *Mo'ed Katan 6b*). He understands that the mishna refers to a *sadeh lavan* – a field that relies on rainfall and requires little irrigation. Therefore, Rabbi Shimon permits only *harbatza,* watering with a smaller amount of water than usual. This applies only to a *sadeh lavan* where irrigation is not absolutely necessary. But a *bet ha-shelachin,* a field that depends on irrigation, may be watered in ample fashion. The *Chazon Ish* rules in accordance with this position.

According to the *Chazon Ish,* a field that relies on rainfall may be watered minimally, whereas a field that relies on irrigation – as is the case with our gardens today – may be watered amply. This also seems to follow from the unqualified language of the *Mishna* in *Mo'ed Katan* 1:1:

> An irrigated field may be watered during the festival [week] and in the seventh year.

When is it permissible to water a garden during the *Shemita* year? Is there a difference between watering with sprinklers and watering with a hose?

How should a person water his garden during the *Shemita* year: As we have seen, labors that are forbidden by rabbinic law are permitted for the purpose of preservation, that is, to preserve that which is already growing. According to this, when watering one's garden, one should water minimally, in a manner that will merely prevent the grass and flowers from shriveling and drying out.[42]

However, in light of the principles that emerge from the *Mishna*, it is possible that **watering is different** than other labors.

When watering a field or garden that requires irrigation in addition to rainfall, some authorities permit watering in ample fashion that suffices not only to preserve, but even to strengthen that which is growing there. According to these authorities, the allowance is sweeping regarding an irrigated field and permits even generous watering.[43] Other authorities imply, however, that the factors governing watering must be considered for each case in terms of its own merits.[44]

It seems that, in a case of need, one may adopt a middle position: to expand the intervals between waterings, but at the same time increase the duration of each watering.[45] Let us explain.

The *Chazon Ish* (21, 17) writes the following with respect to labors that are forbidden during the *Shemita* year by rabbinic law:

> Therefore, in a case of financial loss where the whole tree will die (or all the fruit will be ruined), one may be lenient regarding all these labors. One must consider with each procedure separately whether there is a concern that the tree will die, and whatever is done for extra gain is

42. *Responsa ha-Mabit* (II, section 64) permits labors performed for the sake of preservation even in the case of plants grown for aesthetic purposes. For an expanded discussion, see *Shabbat ha-Aretz* (*Kuntres Acharon*, section 12; *Minchat Shlomo* 51, 8; *Ma'adanei Aretz* 8, 8). The book *Katif Shevi'it*, published by *Machon ha-Torah ve-ha-Aretz*, 2007, includes tables that indicate how much water is required for each type of plant. Simple guidelines for private gardens will be provided below.

43. Rabbi Akiva Eiger (*Orach Chayyim*, 537) permits extra watering in a field that requires irrigation on *Chol ha-Mo'ed*. According to him, if one began to water in a permitted manner he may water as much as he wants. If such extra watering is permitted on *Chol ha-Mo'ed*, it should certainly be permitted during the *Shemita* year when the law regarding watering is more lenient (see *Responsa ha-Mabit II*, section 64, and *Kerem Tziyon, Halachot Pesukot* 88, note 1). Rav Binyamin Zilber also writes that one may be lenient about this matter during the *Shemita* year (*Hilchot Shevi'it* 1b). The *Chazon Ish* (18, 4), however, implies that one should be stringent, because according to him, watering a *bet ha-shelachin* on *Chol ha-Mo'ed* is not at all forbidden, whereas during the *Shemita* year it is generally forbidden, and permitted only when performed for the purpose of preservation. See, however, below, in the name of Rav Karelitz, that one may be lenient even according to those who follow the stringency of the *Chazon Ish* (see also Rashi, *Mo'ed Katan* 6b, s.v. *kedei she-yatz'u*)

44. See, for example, *Responsa Mishnat Yosef* (I, section 1).

45. It should be emphasized that even with respect to a field that requires irrigation, watering is not permitted when there is no need for such watering, for at those times it is not defined as a field that requires irrigation. Watering is only permitted when it is necessary. See *Shemirat Shabbat ke-Hilchatah* (II, 67, 63).

> forbidden. If it is possible to suffice with doing something once, it is forbidden to do it twice. Likewise, one must fertilize and weed prior to *Rosh ha-Shana* 5712 [a Sabbatical year], so that it will not be necessary to fertilize and weed during the seventh year. And even if it will not suffice for the entire year, any way in which one can reduce [performing these labors during the *Shemita* year], one is obligated to do so. Similarly, whatever one can delay doing until after *Rosh ha-Shana* 5713, he is obligated to put off and it is forbidden during the *Shemita* year.

In other words, even though labors that are forbidden by rabbinic labor are permitted when performed for the purpose of preservation, one is obligated to do whatever can possibly be done before or after the *Shemita* year, and one must consider the necessity of each labor separately. If it is possible to suffice with doing something once, there is no allowance to do it twice (see also *Chazon Ish 14, 9,* s.v. *R"M*).

Garden sprinklers

Rav Karelitz, however, argues (*Chut ha-Shani 1, 10, p. 101*) that the *Chazon Ish*'s rule about limiting *Shemita* labor does not apply to watering:

> It seems that strictly speaking, a *bet ha-shelachin* may be watered as needed without restriction ... Since *Chazal* established that a *bet ha-shelachin* is a case of financial loss and now the field is in need of water, it is permitted to water it even if refraining from this watering will not cause a serious loss ... for it is unnecessary to consider each watering ...
>
> As for what the *Chazon Ish* writes that one must consider each procedure separately, whether [without it] there is concern that the tree will die, and that one is obligated to fertilize and weed before the *Shemita* year, so that it not be necessary to fertilize and weed during the *Shemita* year ...

Garden irrigation

> it may be argued that this applies only to other *toladot*, but as for watering ... wherever *Chazal* established that it is a case of financial loss, there are no restrictions, so that whenever the field is in need of water, it is permissible to water it. But regarding other labors where *Chazal* did not establish that there is a situation of financial loss, for those cases one must consider each procedure separately, to see whether the field is a situation of financial loss ...
>
> It seems that grass that is grown for aesthetic reasons is regarded as a *bet ha-shelachin* that one may water if it is in need of water.

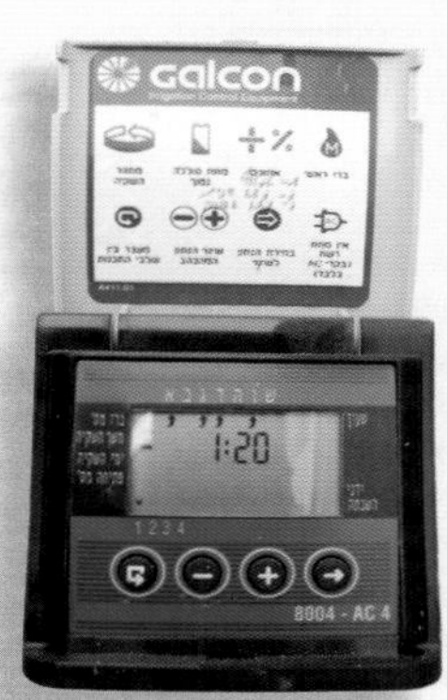

Irrigation Computer

Rav Karelitz argues that with respect to watering, as opposed to all other labors that the Sages permitted only in a case of financial loss, the Sages defined a *bet ha-shelachin* as a case of financial loss, and therefore did not forbid watering at all.

According to this, a field that requires watering is not subject to the prohibition of watering whatsoever, and therefore it is permitted to water it freely. Rav Karelitz, however, adds an important condition:

> However, at times when the *bet ha-shelachin* does not require watering, there is no allowance, for at that time it does not have the status of *bet ha-shelachin.*

In other words, when a garden doesn't need water, it is not governed by the law of a *bet ha-shelachin,* and watering it is forbidden.

Rav Karelitz adds that while there are *posekim* who disagree with him and argue that even watering must be done in a restrictive manner, they too would agree that when watering with sprinklers, if the sprinklers were put on when the garden was in need of water, they may be left on for as long as one wants:

> In any event, one who waters with sprinklers (rather than with a hose) is not required to turn them off as soon as they have watered what is minimally necessary, for all the watering relates to an action that was permitted. It seems however that strictly speaking, a *bet ha-shelachin* may be watered without restriction, as was stated above, even if one waters by hand or with a hose.

It may be concluded from this that sprinklers should be turned on less frequently (such as once a week, rather than every two days), but for longer duration. Computerized sprinklers may be subject to even greater leniency, as we will explain below (where practical guidelines will also be offered).

The next mishna (2:5) continues the discussion of labors that are forbidden during the *Shemita* year by rabbinic decree:

> One may smear oil on unripe figs and pierce them until *Rosh ha-Shana.*

***Sachin* and *Menakvin* – Smearing unripe figs with oil and piercing unripe figs:** *Pagim* are unripe figs, which bear that designation from the time that the fruit first appear. The Bartenura explains that *sicha* involves rubbing the fruit with oil or the like in order to

Rubbing unripe figs with olive oil

Piercing unripe figs with a twig dabbed with a little oil

hasten its ripening: "One may smear unripe figs – fruit that has not fully ripened may be smeared with oil while still attached to the tree in order to hasten their ripening."

This procedure was not always sufficient, and, in order to hasten the fruit's ripening, the figs would be pierced with a twig dabbed with a little oil.[46] The Rambam notes (Commentary to Mishna, ad loc.) that this practice was still common in his time: "And one may pierce – they would pierce figs. Even today there are places where figs do not ripen unless they are individually smeared with oil and pierced."

***Havracha* and *harkava*:** Let us move on to the next mishna:

> One may not plant, sink, or graft on the eve of the seventh year less than thirty days before *Rosh ha-Shana*.

The mishna mentions three labors: *neti'a* – planting (a sapling);[47] *havracha* – sinking; and *harkava* – grafting. As for planting, we saw above, p. 98, that the *Rishonim* disagree whether planting a sapling is forbidden by Torah law or only by rabbinic decree: According to the Rash (2:7), this is forbidden by Torah law (by way of a *kal va-chomer* argument from the prohibition of pruning), whereas according to Rabbenu Tam and the majority understanding of the Rambam (to the exclusion of the *Chazon Ish*), it is forbidden only by rabbinic decree.

AGRICULTURAL EXPLANATION – *Havracha* – SINKING:
In the sources, *havracha*, or sinking, is always mentioned together with planting and grafting. The term *havracha* is derived from the word *berech*, "knee." A long branch, like that of a grapevine, is drawn into the ground, and the end of the branch is allowed to emerge from the ground some distance away. Over the course of time, the part that is in the ground will send out roots, so that now the plant has two root systems – the original roots and the new ones. The new plant is regarded as part of the original plant with respect to the laws of *orla*, unless the connection between the two is severed.

46. This is also the understanding of the Rash and Rosh. The Rash brings another explanation, according to which the purpose of piercing the figs is to allow rainwater to penetrate the unripe figs and thus hasten their ripening.

47. See the chapter dealing with planting, where we noted the position of Rav Kook that the planting of a sapling of a tree or a seedling of a vegetable is regarded as the separate category of *neti'ah*, or "tree planting,"whereas the planting of a seed of a vegetable or a pit of a fruit is treated as *zeri'ah*, or "vegetable planting."This stands in contrast to the position of the *Chazon Ish*, who maintains that the planting of a sapling of a tree or a pit of a fruit is regarded as "tree planting,"while the planting of a seed or a seedling of a vegetable is regarded as regular vegetable planting.

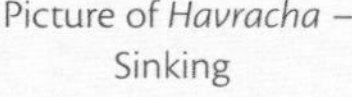

Picture of *Havracha* – Sinking

Sketch of Havracha – Sinking

Havracha and *harkava,* on the other hand, are *toladot* of planting, and according to all authorities are forbidden only by rabbinic decree.[48] This is accepted even by those who maintain that planting a sapling is forbidden by Torah law, as is explained by the *Derech Emuna* (Rav Chayim Kanievski, *1:4,* no. 27):

> On *Shabbat,* they [*havracha* and *harkava*] fall into the category of planting ... but here [regarding *Shemita*], even if planting trees is [forbidden] by Torah law, these are [forbidden] only by rabbinic decree.

48. According to those *Rishonim* (on the Mishna, *Shevi'it 2:6*) who forbid planting trees, sinking and grafting even before the *Shemita* year begins, based on the law of *"tosefet shevi'it"*(when the law of *tosefet shevi'it* was in effect), it would appear that all of these labors are forbidden by Torah law (as they write explicitly with respect to planting trees), because, according to them, *tosefet shevi'it* only applies to labors that are forbidden by Torah law. See *Eglei Tal* (*zore'a,* 3), who indeed maintains that sinking and grafting are equivalent to planting trees.

These labors are forbidden during the *Shemita* year because they are creative, rather than preservative labors. Let us briefly explain each procedure:

***Mavrichin* – Sinking:** *Havracha,* or sinking, involves taking the shoot of a plant, directing it toward the ground, and completely covering it with soil except for the end. The portion in the ground will send out roots, and grow as an independent plant exactly like the original plant. After the shoot has sent out roots and taken, the new plant can be cut off from its parent at the point where they are connected, and both plants will continue to grow on their own.

As long as the offshoot is connected to the parent plant it is considered an extension of it, and therefore if the parent plant is no longer subject to the laws of *orla,* then the fruit growing on the new

AGRICULTURAL EXPLANATION – *Havracha* – GRAFTING: Plants are propagated in various ways. Some plants are propagated through seeds that are planted and develop into new plants. This is most common among field crops and vegetables. In the case of fruit trees and ornamental trees, the most common methods of propagation are rooting and grafting. For fruit trees, a branch is inserted into the trunk or branch of another (related variety, so that the prohibition of *kil'ayim*, prohibited plant mixtures, does not apply). For many ornamental trees the practice is to graft directly on the branches.

Rooting involves taking a cutting of the parent plant and sticking it into the soil. Roots grow from the buried section, and it becomes a complete plant. Grafting involves taking a cutting from the parent plant, and inserting it into the trunk or branch of another plant that is attached to the ground instead of sticking it into the soil. In time the two grow together.

In the case of fruit trees, rooting and grafting is preferable to propagating trees from seeds because rooting and grafting guarantees the stability of the variety, whereas seeds may be the product of cross-pollination between different varieties.

Why is grafting the favored method? Because there are certain varieties of fruit that are more resistant to pests and disease when grown on the rootstock of other varieties. For example, the vineyards of Baron Rothschild were decimated by an insect, called *Phylloxera*, until the desired varieties of grapes were grafted on rootstock of more resistant varieties.

Picture of the branch and tree before being grafted

Picture of completed grafting

Sketch of grafting

Sketch of branch and tree before grafting

plant may also be eaten. However, the moment that the connection between the two plants is severed, a new count of *orla* years begins with respect to the new plant.

***Markivin* – Grafting:** *Harkava*, or grafting, involves taking the shoot of one tree, inserting it in the trunk of another, and binding the two together. Over the course of time, the two become one and a new branch is created.

Additional labors that are forbidden during the *Shemita* year by rabbinic decree are learned from the talmudic passage in *Mo'ed Katan* (*3a*):

> From where do we know that weeding, hoeing and the trimming of wilted parts [is forbidden]? From the verse that states: "Your field you shall not,""Your vineyard you shall not."
>
> From where do we know not to cut back shoots, or thin twigs, or put up props for supporting trees? From the verse that states: "Your field you shall not,""Your vineyard you shall not"– [which means] no manner of work in your field, no manner of work in your vineyard shall you do … . Shall I say that one may not hoe under an olive tree? … That is by rabbinic law, and the Biblical verse is brought merely as a support. But is it permitted to hoe [under an olive tree]? … Rav Ukva bar Chama said: There are two sorts of hoeing, one for strengthening the olive tree, and another to close up fissures; hoeing for strengthening the tree is forbidden, whereas for closing up fissures is permitted.

Several labors are mentioned in this passage that do not appear in the *mishnayot*: *nikush, kisu'ach, pisug* and *kishkush*. Initially, the Gemara understands that these are all forbidden by Torah law, but it concludes that *nikush, kisu'ach* and *pisug* are forbidden only by rabbinic decree. As for *kishkush*, the Gemara differentiates between permitted *kishkush* and forbidden *kishkush*. We shall now explain each of these labors.

Nikush* – Weeding:** *Nikush* refers to removing weeds by their roots. As stated, this is forbidden during the *Shemita* year only by rabbinic law. In the previous passage (*2b*), we find a disagreement whether *nikush* is a derivative labor of *zore'a,* planting (because it promotes the growth of the plants growing near the weeds), or of *choresh,* plowing (because it prepares the ground for plowing). The **Rambam** (*Hilchot Shabbat 8:1*) rules that it is forbidden because of planting, while the ***Or Zaru'a rules that it is forbidden because of plowing. The *Mishna Berura* (*336, 26*) writes that one should be concerned about both planting and plowing.

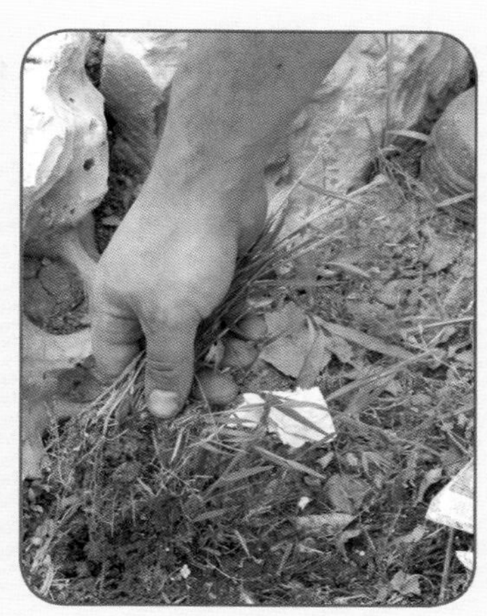

Picture of weeding (without cutting roots) – should be avoided when possible

Generally speaking, there is no basis to permit weeding, because abstaining from weeding does not cause plants serious damage (see *Responsa Meshiv Davar 56, Kuntres ha-Shemita,* s.v. *ve-afilu.*[49]) If indeed weeds are causing considerable damage, they should be removed by way of *kisu'ach,* rather than *nikush,* that is, without removing the roots. *Kisu'ach* is preferred over *nikush,* because it does not involve an action performed on the ground itself.

If *kisu'ach* does not suffice, and plants are liable to suffer significant damage, the weeds may be removed even by way of *nikush*. As the *Chazon Ish* writes (*21, 17*):

According to some authorities, the *baraita* that forbids weeding and other labors applies only to a field sufficiently watered by rain ... but regarding a field that will suffer damage if these labors are not performed, they are permitted ... Since it is twice removed from Torah law by rabbinic decree, it seems that we may be lenient.

What is the best way to mow a lawn during the *Shemita* year?

***Kisu'ach* – Cutting weeds:**

49. According to him, however, weeding is forbidden even when performed for the purpose of preservation, in contrast to positions that will be cited below.

Picture of weeding (cutting roots) – permitted only to prevent significant loss

Kisu'ach refers to cutting weeds without removing them by their roots. Like *nikush, kisu'ach* is also permitted in order to prevent significant damage.

Is there room to permit *kisu'ach* when it serves no agricultural purpose, but only gives the plant a more attractive appearance? This question has practical ramifications with respect to mowing a lawn during the *Shemita* year. Rav Sh. Z. Auerbach (*Responsa Minchat Shlomo, 51, 8*) was in doubt about this very issue:

> I have my doubts about ornamental flowers whose primary purpose is their beauty, regarding which cutting and pruning in order to maintain their shape might be regarded like "preserving a tree," and [therefore] permitted. The matter requires further study.

In practice, there seems to be grounds for leniency with respect to mowing a lawn as a "haircut." It stands to reason that mowing a lawn does not constitute pruning, and certainly not pruning prohibited by Torah law. First of all, grass is not a tree, but rather similar to a vegetable, and the *Chazon Ish* (*26, 1*) writes that pruning vegetables is undoubtedly forbidden only by rabbinic decree.[50] Furthermore, according to the *Chazon Ish*, the pruning of trees (other than a grapevine) is not forbidden by Torah law (see above, regarding *kirsum* and the law of pruning). Beyond that, the *Chazon Ish* writes (*19, 14–15*) that pruning whose purpose is not to promote growth is not regarded as pruning (see above, p. *115*):

> Regarding trees that do not bear fruit and that most people do not prune, a question may be raised whether the removal of branches for firewood or other uses falls into the category of pruning ... It is certainly permitted provided that it is not done with precision in the normal manner of pruning.

50. See above, however, regarding *kirsum* and notes ad loc., that Rav Kook maintains that pruning vegetables is forbidden by Torah law. This applies however only when the purpose of the pruning is to promote growth, as we shall see below (see also our discussion of the labor of pruning).

When a person mows his lawn, not only is his objective not to promote the growth of the grass, but on the contrary, he wants **his grass not to grow any further** and to remain at its current height. Indeed, the *Sefer Shemita Ke-hilchatah* (Rav Sternbuch; *1*, note *11*) writes that lawn-mowing is permitted:

> Experts say that mowing a lawn does not strengthen the grass at all, unlike pruning, and therefore as long as a person's objective is aesthetics, mowing a lawn does not fall into the category of pruning ...
>
> It seems, however, that if possible, it is preferable to mow a lawn in an altered manner, and only when necessary.
>
> Some authorities, however, forbid this because mowing grass causes it to renew itself, and it prevents it from turning yellow, retaining its attractive appearance. According to them, it will not be ruined [if it is not mowed] until after the *Shemita* year. An expert, God-fearing gardener must be consulted to clarify this issue; if the grass will suffer damage [if not mowed] until after the *Shemita* year, [mowing] is permitted as necessary, and with a change, as stated above.

Rav Sternbuch cites authorities who forbid lawn-mowing because it promotes the growth of the grass, and a similar approach is presented by Rav Tykoczinski (*Sefer ha-Shemita 3, 2, 4 – pg. 19*). However, Rav Sternbuch himself writes that in general mowing does not promote growth of the grass. In any event, he writes that one should consult with a professional gardener.

Mowing a lawn

According to the professionals that we have consulted, mowing does indeed promote growth when an extended period of time lapses between one mowing and the next.[51] **According to this, it would seem preferable to be stringent and mow one's lawn over the course**

51. Even timely mowing benefits the lawn in that it prevents it from reaching the state that it lacks light and turns yellow. But since the mowing is done solely for aesthetic purposes and the prevention of yellowing is only an indirect result, it is of no concern, according to the *Chazon Ish*. It should be noted that the unintended benefit of mowing a lawn is not the same as the unintended benefit of pruning. Pruning promotes growth, whereas mowing provides only indirect benefit, as reducing the height of the grass allows light to penetrate to the lower portions of the grass. This is similar to *mavri'ach ari*, "causing a lion to run away"(where one has prevented damage rather than provided benefit; here the person causes the upper portions of the grass to "run away"whereby the light can reach the lower portions). The *posekim* disagree about the ruling in a case of *mavri'ach ari*. The *Chazon Ish* (*17, 20*, s.v. *ve-nir'eh*; *27*, s.v. *ve-yesh*) permits actions that benefit in the manner of *mavri'ach ari*, whereas Rav Kook (*Shabbat ha-Aretz, 1, 5, 27*) inclines toward stringency in such cases. In our case, however, there is more room for leniency, because when a person mows a lawn, his objective is solely to give the grass "a haircut,"and he does not think at all about the indirect benefit of allowing the sun to penetrate to the lower portions of the grass. Thus, it seems that all would agree that mowing a lawn is permitted.

of the *Shemita* year as usual, rather than wait until the grass turns yellow, at which point mowing the lawn is necessary in order to revive it.

Cutting weeds for aesthetic purposes: This is permitted only when it is clear that it is being done for aesthetic purposes. Therefore, it is generally preferable to keep weeding to a minimum and to cut the weeds at the same time that one mows the lawn, or in some other manner that demonstrates that the weeding is being done for aesthetic purposes.

A lawn that has not yet filled in: Generally speaking, there is a problem with mowing a lawn that has not yet filled in, because the mowing causes the grass to fill in and thicken. One should therefore plant grass from seed at least three months before *Rosh ha-Shana* and not immediately prior to the *Shemita* year. As for carpet grass, there is no problem with the grass filling in, but the grass must take root prior to the *Shemita* year, and therefore it should be laid down at least a month before *Shemita* (in exceptional cases, there

AGRICULTURAL EXPLANATION – GRASS

There are many different types of grass; we will address the most common:

"Layered"grass – In most cases, the grass does not come as a complete cover. In addition, the grass needs to spread and grow, growing such that these layers merge. As it takes several days for the grass itself to take root, layered grass should be planted at least a month before *Shemita* (in exceptional cases one may be able to exercise greater leniency – see note 52).

"Seed grass"– In many cases there are no outgrowths, but the mowing of the grass causes a lowering of the tops of the grass, which causes the grass to be hunched over. Since this grass is generally quite thin, there should be three layers of grass that grow before *Shemita*, therefore one should plant this several months before *Shemita* (The author heard this from agronomist Moti Shomron. In exceptional cases one may be more lenient – see note 52).

is room for leniency in certain circumstances).[52]

Trimming for aesthetic purposes

Hedges: The principles governing hedges are similar to those governing a lawn. Here too, trimming for aesthetic purposes should be permitted. However, hedges may be different from lawns because trimming a hedge may be more similar to pruning (for we are usually talking about a tree), and because it is generally not as necessary as mowing a lawn. Moreover, everybody knows that mowing a lawn is performed for aesthetic purposes (certainly when the lawn is green), whereas hedges are often trimmed in order to promote growth and fill in the hedge. Thus, it is not always evident that one is trimming a hedge solely for aesthetic purposes.

Therefore, if a person wishes to trim his hedge for aesthetic purposes, he may do so, but it is preferable that he only do so when it is truly necessary. In other words, as opposed to grass, there is no reason to trim the hedge on a regular basis. Furthermore, if the hedge is not full, it may not be trimmed, because trimming it causes it to fill in. Rav Sternbuch writes to this effect in *Sefer Shemita ke-Hilchatah* (1, note 11):

> Regarding hedges grown alongside houses, when the trimming is not performed to promote growth, but rather to prevent its growth and preserve it as is – since he trims solely for aesthetic purposes, it would seem that this is not called pruning, and [therefore] it is permitted during the *Shemita* year. Some authorities are stringent and require that the trimming be done in a manner that is clearly not for the purpose of pruning, and therefore it should be done in an altered fashion … A hedge that has not yet fully grown in, however,

52. **Planting grass after these dates:** Planting grass from seed should be done several months before the beginning of the *Shemita* year in order that there be time for several mowings, which will allow the grass to fill in. If this was not done, one should plant three times as much seed as usual, so that the grass will be very thick from the outset. In such a case, one may be lenient and plant the grass up to several weeks before the beginning of the *Shemita* year. As stated, however, it is preferable to plant grass several months before *Shemita*. As for carpet grass, if the grass is full and thick, and it is planted professionally so that the seams are quickly invisible, the grass may be planted up to two weeks before *Rosh ha-Shana* (based on what the author was told by the agronomist Moti Shomron).

AGRICULTURAL EXPLANATION – THE INFLUENCE OF APICAL DOMINANCE ON PRUNING HEDGES

Plants contain a hormone called auxin (also called plant hormone) which forms at the head of the growing branches, and spreads down to the roots. Auxin causes the central stem to grow while preventing the side stems or branches from growing and competing with the central stem. **Thus, cutting the head of the branch reduces the auxin supply, which leads to the increased growth of the side stems or branches. This phenomenon is called apical dominance.**

Pruning an incomplete hedge causes the hedge to fill in. Pruning from the top reduces the apical dominance, thus the side branches will thicken the hedge. This same phenomenon occurs when cutting an incomplete bed of grass. Since this leads to increased growth it falls into the category of planting (similar to pruning), and is thus prohibited during *Shemita*. For the same reason one may only cut the grass when the bed is full, and cut the hedge only when the hedge is full.

Auxin in roses: in the past, wheat was inserted under roses, and this caused them to grow quickly. The Chatam Sofer deliberated as to whether this activity is defined as a case of *harkava*, grafting. Today we know that the purpose of this is to extract auxin from the wheat to induce the roses' growth, thus it is a growth-related activity.

should not be trimmed, as experts say that trimming promotes its thickening, which is like pruning.

***Mefasgin* – Supporting:** Rashi understands that *pisug* involves supporting a tree with a stick or the like: "*Mefasgin* – supporting a tree that is overly weak." However, since we permit labors for the purpose of preservation, if the tree will be ruined without support, or the support will prevent a branch from breaking off with its fruit, adding a support is permitted. Rav Kook states this as follows (*Shabbat ha-Aretz, 1, 5, 13*):

> The prohibition of *pisug* involves supporting a tree that is overly weak. According to those who permit all labors for preservation, this prohibition only applies when the tree

can stand without support, but will not continue to grow. But if it is liable to suffer damage if it is not supported, it is permitted to support it for the purpose of preservation.

Picture of supporting a tree

In contrast, the *Chazon Ish* (*17, 19, s.v. sham mi-derabbanan*) maintains that the Sages forbade *pisug* even when performed for preservation, because it looks like working the land.

***Kishkush* – Hoeing under an olive tree:** We saw earlier the Gemara in *Mo'ed Katan* 3a which distinguishes between permitted *kishkush* and forbidden *kishkush*. What is *kishkush*? Rashi (ad loc.) explains:

Picture of hoeing under an olive tree

"*Yekashkesh* – This is the same thing as *iddur*, hoeing, only that *iddur* applies to grapevines and *kishkush* to olive trees."

In other words, *kishkush* is identical to *iddur* performed on a grapevine.[53] This procedure is forbidden when performed in order to promote growth of the tree, but it is permitted when performed in order to protect it from being ruined. The Meiri implies that ordinary hoeing under an olive tree is forbidden, but hoeing performed in order to cover the roots so that they will not be exposed to the wind is permitted (see above about the importance of protecting roots).

***Gizum* – Removing branches:** The Gemara in *Avoda Zara* 50b states:

> Why is *zihum* permitted while *gizum* is prohibited? Are they really comparable? The purpose of *zihum* is the preservation

53. This is the understanding of most *Rishonim:* Rabbenu Gershom, ad loc.; *Tosafot ha-Rosh*, ad loc.; Meiri, ad loc.; Mahari Kurkus, *Hilchot Shemita ve-Yovel* 1:7. Rabbenu Chananel (ad loc.), however, understands that *kishkush* refers to the removal of the dried up portions of the tree, and in *Avoda Zara* 50b, he writes that it refers to watering and fertilizing the tree (cited by *Shabbat ha-Aretz*, 1, 7, section 4). The first explanation is the accepted one, and this is also cited by the *Chazon Ish, Shevi'it*, 17, 19, s.v. *m"k*).

of the tree and is thus permitted, while the purpose of *gizum* is to strengthen the tree and is thus prohibited.

The Gemara asks why *zihum* (according to the Rambam – rubbing foul-smelling oil on a tree in order to drive away pests) is permitted, whereas *gizum* is forbidden. The Gemara explains that the purpose of *gizum* is to strengthen the tree. This implies that removing branches in order to promote a tree's growth is regarded as *gizum*. According to the plain meaning of the Gemara, *gizum* is forbidden only by rabbinic decree. This being the case, removing branches in order to promote a tree's growth is forbidden only by rabbinic decree. This understanding fits with the position of the *Chazon Ish* that the Torah prohibition of pruning is limited to the grapevine. It is possible, however, that removing a tree's branches in order to promote growth is forbidden by Torah law (see *Yalkut Yosef, Shemita*, p. 25), in which case the Gemara is referring to a different type of *gizum* that is beneficial to a tree but does not promote growth.

In practice, one should avoid pruning, because there is no consensus about what is considered permitted pruning. There is, however, room to permit pruning in order to allow for a passageway (see above, regarding hedges), as well as pruning in cases where refraining from pruning is liable to hurt the tree (such as where a branch is sick).[54]

Thinning out fruit or blossoms: It is sometimes necessary to thin out or remove some of the fruit growing on a tree for agricultural reasons in order to allow the remaining fruit to grow sweeter and larger. This procedure is not explicitly discussed in the early sources, but certain inferences about it may be drawn from the words of the *Rishonim*.

Thinning out the fruit may involve the following halachic problems:

1. The procedure may be similar to pruning branches or removing leaves which are forbidden when the purpose is the improvement of the tree.[55]
2. It may be included in the prohibition of harvesting fruit for

54. See the practical guidelines brought in *Katif Shevi'it*, chap. 10.

55. See above: *mefarkin, mekarsemin, mezardin*. According to the *Chazon Ish*, however, pruning in the case of trees other than a grapevine is only forbidden by rabbinic decree.

the benefit of the tree (Rambam, *Hilchot Shemita ve-Yovel* 4:22).[56] The *Aruch ha-Shulchan* (21:2) defines this labor as follows: "To remove some of the fruit in order that the remaining fruit should grow bigger."

3. Destroying *Shemita* produce, because the fruit that is removed is discarded.
4. According to Rav Kook, one may not engage in labors forbidden by rabbinic decree for the benefit of the **fruit**. As we have seen, however, especially with respect to farmers, one may rely on the position of the *Chazon* Ish regarding labors performed for the benefit of the fruit, and especially today, when the entire observance of *Shemita* is only by rabbinic decree.

In practice, one should avoid thinning out fruit[57] unless some special need necessitates it. Farmers and others who would otherwise suffer a substantial loss may, however, practice leniency if the removal is **at the blossoming stage** (before the fruit appears). In this case, there is no destruction of *Shemita* fruit, and it is not considered harvesting for the benefit of the tree because harvesting applies only

56. *Pe'at ha-Shulchan*, 23, 12; *Shabbat ha-Aretz*, 4, 22, 5-6; *Chazon Ish*, 12, 7, s.v. *omnam*; 21, 15, s.v. *omnam*. Harvesting fruit for the benefit of the tree is forbidden by Torah law (see sources cited above).

57. Thinning out the fruit so that the branches won't crack under the weight of the fruit is a preferable solution.

AGRICULTURAL EXPLANATION – *Dillul* – THINNING OUT THE FRUIT:

Why is it important to thin out the fruit growing on a tree? If too much fruit grows on a tree, the individual fruits will be small, because the tree cannot provide sufficient nutrients for such a large quantity of fruit. If the fruit is too small, people will not buy it, even if it is of good quality.

An attempt is therefore made to change the ratio between the area of leaves and the quantity of fruit, so that the leaves will be able to provide the fruit with what they need. The green color in the leaves absorbs the sun's rays, and thus provides the necessary nutrients for the fruit through photosynthesis.

The proper time to thin out fruit: From a halachic perspective, it is best to thin out the fruit during **the blossoming stage**, or even earlier, during **the budding stage**. Farmers should follow this procedure whenever thinning out is necessary.

Sometimes, however, farmers find it necessary to thin out at a later stage, after the fruit has begun to take shape or even later. While early thinning is better, farmers sometimes prefer a later thinning, because then it is clear which fruits are not good and can be removed, while the good fruits can be saved. From a halachic perspective, this is less desirable, and therefore a competent halachic authority should be consulted in each case.

58. For practical guidelines for farmers, see *Katif Shevi'it*, chaps. 13 and 34. See also *Shemitat Karka'ot*, 5, 48, and note 120.
A few brief remarks: According to **Rav Sh. Z. Auerbach,** the prohibition of harvesting fruit for the benefit of the tree stems from the fact that it constitutes a **display of ownership.** Thus, according to him, this should be permitted in the case of *Otzar Bet Din* (cited in *Shemita Mamlachtit*, 4, note 2. This is also the position of Rav Elyashiv – ibid. and in *Shemitat 5747 bi-Kefar Etzyon*, p. 49, note 44. See also *Ma'adanei Eretz*, 3, 2, 5-11). According to **Rav Sh. Z. Auerbach,** there is room to permit **the destruction of *Shemita* produce for the benefit of other *Shemita* produce** (based on *Tosafot*, *Pesachim 66b*, s.v. *ve-ha*). I heard this also from my revered father-in-law **Rav Blumenzweig**, *shelita*, who heard this from Rav Sh. Z. Auerbach (this is also brought in his name in *Peri ha-Aretz, Shevi'it*, p. 9. See also *Shemita Mamlachtit*, 4, 3). According to this, there is room to permit thinning out the fruit even after the stage of blossoming. We are still left with the prohibition of harvesting fruit for the benefit of the tree, but as stated above, according to Rav Sh. Z. Auerbach, this difficulty can be resolved through *Otzar Bet Din*. This is a very important issue for farmers. (See the agricultural explanation.)

to fruit and there is no fruit yet (Rav Karelitz – cited in *Shemitat Karka'ot* 5, note 120). Alternative procedures exist that are halachically preferable, such as spraying the blossoms. Farmers should, therefore, consult competent halachic authorities regarding the matter.[58]

A tree with a cracked branch

The Mishna in the fourth chapter of *Shevi'it* (4:6) records another labor forbidden by rabbinic law during the *Shemita* year:

> A tree which has cracked may be tied during the seventh [year], not so that it will heal, but so that it will not deteriorate further.

Ilan she-nifshach – a tree that has a crack: When a tree has a crack, the broken branch is bound up. This binding serves two purposes:

1. To prevent further damage to the branch.
2. To promote the healing of the branch through tight binding (over the course of time the branch will grow back together again). According to the Mishna, it is only permitted to bind the tree to prevent further damage. Such a procedure is apparently regarded as preservation of the tree.

Short summary of labors that are forbidden during the *Shemita* Year by Rabbinic law

1. *Mezablin* – Fertilizing.

AGRICULTURAL EXPLANATION – *Ilan she-nifshach* – A TREE THAT IS CRACKED

Even today, the lateral branches of trees grown for wood are regularly removed. In this way, the central trunk thickens, and over the course of years a trunk develops that is suitable for commercial use.

RABBI SHIMSON BEN AVRAHAM OF SENS ("*the Rash Mishantz*")

Rabbi Shimshon ben Avraham of Sens was among the greatest of the French Tosafists. He was a prominent disciple of Rabbi Yitzchak of Dampierre, "the elder Ri,"and also studied under Rabbenu Tam. During a period of intensive persecution of the Jewish community in France, he moved to Eretz Yisrael with several hundred other rabbis from France and England, eventually settling in Jerusalem. The Rash died in 4990 (1230) and was buried in Akko.

His most important works are the *Tosafot Shantz* – a collection of his teachings on the Talmud – and a commentary on the Mishnaic orders of *Zera'im* and *Taharot*.

2. *Me'adrin* – Hoeing (under a grapevine).
3. *Meyablin* – Excising blemishes on trees.
4. *Mefarkin* – Removing leaves:
    a. Bartenura – Removing leaves so that they do not weigh down on the tree.
    b. Rash – Removing leaves so that sunlight will reach the fruit and promote ripening.
5. *Me'avkin* – Dusting exposed roots.
6. *Me'ashnin* – Fumigating a tree in order to kill pests.
7. *Mesaklin* – Removing stones from a field. This is permitted provided that it is evident that the purpose is not agricultural. It is therefore permitted to level land with a tractor.
8. *Mekarsemin* – Pruning trees other than a grapevine (removing their dead branches).
9. *Mezardin* – Removing green branches.
10. *Mefaslin* – Removing all branches in order to thicken the trunk.
11. *Mezahamin:*
    a. According to the Rash: applying manure to the injured area of the bark of a tree.
    b. According to the Rambam: rubbing a tree with a foul-smelling substance in order to drive away pests.

12. *Korchin:*
    a. According to the Rash: Wrapping fabric around a tree in order to protect it from the heat or from the cold.
    b. According to the Rambam: Tying up the branches on the upper part of the tree.
13. *Kotemin* – Putting ashes on the roots of a tree.
14. *Osin batin* – Building shelters for saplings:
    a. According to Rashi: Building a fence around saplings.
    b. According to Rambam: Covering saplings.
15. *Mashkin* – Watering (details below).
16. *Sachin* – Rubbing unripe figs with oil in order to hasten the ripening process.
17. *Menakvin* – Piercing unripe figs and dabbing the inside with oil in order to hasten ripening.
18. *Nikush* – Removing weeds with their roots.
19. *Kisu'ach* – Cutting weeds without removing their roots.
20. *Mefasgin* – Supporting a tree with a stick.
21. *Kishkush* – Hoeing under an olive tree (parallels *iddur* under a grapevine).
22. *Gizum* – Removing the branches (perhaps in order to promote growth of the tree; perhaps for other purposes).
23. *Havracha* – Sinking a branch into the ground so that it will take root and give rise to a new tree.
24. *Harkava* – Grafting the shoot of a tree onto a branch or trunk of another tree.
25. *Dillul peirot* – Thinning out the fruit or blossoms of a tree in order that the remaining fruit will be larger and sweeter.
26. *Ilan she-nifshach* – Healing a broken branch.

PRACTICAL GARDENING GUIDELINES

In light of all the principles discussed above, let us present several practical guidelines for caring for a garden during the *Shemita* year.[59]

Watering: We saw above that it is preferable to extend the interval between waterings, watering only when truly necessary (one need not wait until the grass has already turned yellow, but rather one should water when it is necessary to prevent yellowing). Once the watering has begun, it may be done freely and the sprinklers may continue to operate continuously.

Generally speaking, in most parts of the country, an ordinary lawn should be watered once a week for about an hour and a half.[60] Other plants (such as roses) can be watered up to twice a week.

Computerized watering: In many gardens today, the watering system is controlled by a computer. Is it permissible to program the computer **before the *Shemita* year** so that it will water during the *Shemita* year as usual? While it would seem that this should be permissible, as no human action is performed during the *Shemita* year (this is not even indirect action [*gerama*]), some authorities forbid it. As we saw in previous chapters, the *Acharonim* disagree about whether or not there is a *mitzva* for the land to rest in addition to the *mitzva* that people must rest. Some authorities forbid programming a computer in advance because of the requirement that the land rest during the *Shemita* year (Rav Sh. Z. Auerbach, cited in *Dinei Shevi'it ha-Shalem, 10, 5;* see above.[61] Even the *posekim* who are not concerned about this factor raise the concern of *mar'it ayin,* "the appearance of problematic behavior,"and therefore allow the practice only when no such concern exists (*Rav Elyashiv, ibid.*).[62]

There is, however, another reason for leniency. It is possible that even according to those who require the land to rest, that requirement is only with respect to labors forbidden by Torah law, while there may be no such concern whatsoever for labors that are forbidden only by rabbinic law (*Or le-Tziyyon* on the Rambam, 1:3).

In practice, since there are those who permit watering a *bet*

59. The principles and applications included here relate to home gardens. As for farmers and professional gardeners, see at length the professional guidelines for the *Shemita* year found in *Katif Shevi'it, Machon ha-Torah ve-ha-Aretz, 2007.*

60. Based on what the author was told by the agronomist Moti Shomron.

61. Even if the rest of the land is significant, it is still unclear that a person is required to concern himself about the land's rest prior to the *Shemita* year. It would appear that Rav Kook (*Shabbat ha-Aretz, 3, 11, 2*) and the *Chazon Ish* (22, 5) disagree on this point, with Rav Kook ruling stringently and the *Chazon Ish* ruling leniently. Regarding watering, which is forbidden only by rabbinic decree, there may be room for leniency even according to Rav Kook, as will be explained below.

62. Today, when watering is commonly regulated by computer, it would appear that in most situations there is no problem of *mar'it ayin.*

ha-shelachin (an irrigated field) even with large quantities of water, if a person programs his irrigation computer prior to the *Shemita* year he may follow the more lenient authorities and **program his computer as usual.**[63]

Watering by way of sprinklers: We saw above that it is permitted to operate sprinklers less frequently than usual and then leave them on for as long as one wants. While this procedure may be followed even if one turns the sprinklers on by hand, it is preferable to do this by computer (even if one programs the computer during the *Shemita* year itself).[64]

Weeding: Generally speaking, one can do without weeding the entire *Shemita* year, because refraining from weeding will not kill the plants. Nevertheless, if weeding is necessary in order to prevent plants from dying, one may cut the weeds back without removing them by the roots. If cutting them back will not suffice to save the plants, one may remove the weeds even by their roots (this also applies when weeding is necessary to prevent a snake problem or for some other clearly non-agricultural purpose).

It is preferable, however, to instead use sprays that prevent weeds from growing[65] or that kill them once they have grown. This spraying should be done before the *Shemita* year begins, because generally speaking, a single year without regular weeding is not sufficient time for a serious weed problem to develop.[66]

63. If the computer was turned off during the *Shemita* year, it should be reset in accordance with the laws of *Shemita*. (If only the faucet was closed there is room to allow for reopening it [preferably via a *shinuy*, a diversion from the usual manner, or by having a gentile open it], although, even then, it is best to reset the computer according to the laws of *Shemita*.)

64. This may be regarded as *gerama*, (though this is debatable, inasmuch as it is the usual manner of watering). If it becomes necessary to increase the watering, and the sprinklers had not been adjusted before the *Shemita* year, it may be possible to allow a gentile to reprogram the computer, and to rely on those opinions who allow watering freely in the case of a *bet ha-shelachin*.

65. According to the *Chazon Ish* (17, 20), this does not fall into the category of forbidden labor. According to Rav Kook (*Shabbat ha-Aretz*, 1, 5, 27) it is defined as a forbidden labor, though in this case he would agree that it is permitted because it is being performed for the purpose of preservation.

66. During the *Shemita* year itself, it is certainly preferable to apply herbicides that prevent weeds from growing, rather than herbicides that kill them after they have already grown, both because the former might not be defined as a forbidden labor (as explained in the previous note), and because there are those who maintain that weeds that are fit for animal consumption have *Shemita* sanctity, even if they are not intended for that purpose. The reason is as follows: If a person plants a specific plant, and it has no scent, it has no *Shemita* sanctity, because it is not intended for animal consumption even if an animal could eat it. A weed that grows on its own, however, is not connected to man any more than it is to animals, and since everything is regarded as ownerless, a person's intention not to feed the weed to an animal is irrelevant (see *Responsa Mishnat Yosef*, III, p. 111, and see *Mishpetei Aretz*, 4, 13, and note 20, in the name of Rav Elyashiv and Rav Karelitz.)

Fertilizing: In general, fertilizer that breaks down slowly can be applied before the *Shemita* year begins, and that should suffice for the entire year. In large gardens, there are occasionally plants that require fertilizer over the course of the year, and if there is concern that without the fertilizer the plant will suffer damage, a minimal amount of fertilizer may be applied. The need for fertilizer, however, must be carefully established, and even when necessary, it is preferable that the fertilizer be applied through the watering system.

Pesticides: Spraying pesticides to protect fruit from damage is permitted. Nonetheless, where covering the tree with netting or the like will solve the problem, this is preferable.

Pruning: Picking fruit for consumption or flowers for enjoyment is permitted (with the limitations mentioned above,). When cutting roses, one should do so in such a way that it is evident that the flowers are not being picked in order to prepare the bush for new flowering.

Pruning trees in order to promote a tree's growth is forbidden during the *Shemita* year. Pruning a tree in order to remove a portion that is diseased is permitted. Any other situation in which the pruning is done for the sake of the tree must be examined on its own merits. In general, pruning is a problematic labor, and it occasionally involves the biblical prohibition of *zemira.*

Both pruning and mowing a lawn for aesthetic purposes are permitted, provided that these labors have no agricultural objective, are clearly being performed solely for aesthetic purposes, and bring no agricultural benefit (even if that is not the purpose). It must be emphasized that pruning for aesthetic purposes does not refer to pruning that will cause the plant to grow differently and become more aesthetically pleasing in the future, but rather to pruning which immediately accomplishes the aesthetic objective: for example, mowing a lawn so that it be more comfortable to walk on or more attractive to look at (and, certainly, trimming a bush so that it acquire a particular shape).

Mowing a lawn during the *Shemita* year is, therefore, permitted. It is preferable to mow the lawn frequently, because, according to experts it is precisely mowing of this sort that serves solely an aesthetic purpose. If mowing is delayed and the grass grows tall, mowing the lawn serves also an agricultural purpose because it allows sunlight to reach the lower portion of the grass. A newly laid lawn should be mowed at least once before the *Shemita* year begins because mowing the lawn causes the grass to fill in (a mature lawn generally does not need to be filled in. A lawn grown from seed should be mowed several times before the *Shemita* year).

Cutting weeds: Cutting weeds for aesthetic purposes is permitted only when it is clear that it is being done for aesthetic purposes. It is therefore preferable to cut weeds at the same time that one mows the lawn, so that it will be evident that the activity as a whole is being performed for aesthetic purposes.

Apartment buildings: A person living in an apartment building should try to arrange with his neighbors that only labors that are permitted during the *Shemita* year be performed in the building's garden. If his neighbors do not agree, he should declare that his payment for joint expenses will not cover the gardening costs (and that he will pay a larger sum for the cleaning costs or the like). It is also proper for him to declare, in the presence of three people, that he is renouncing ownership of his portion of the garden (*hefker*).[67]

Regarding gardening work that should be performed before the *Shemita* year begins, see the chapter on "*Tosefet Shevi'it*" (p. 158). See also the diagrams that summarize the laws of *Shemita* found at the beginning of this book.

67. In general, the *heter mechira* is not applied to gardens.

TO SUMMARIZE IN BRIEF:

Watering should be done less frequently than usual, but the sprinklers may be left on for as long as one wants. **If one programs a computer before the *Shemita* year,** it may be programmed in the usual manner.

Mowing a lawn may be done in the usual manner. Other labors should be avoided **in a home garden,** but may be performed in order to prevent a plant from dying, such as spraying pesticides

Picture of trimming hedges for aesthetic purposes

(farmers generally will need to fertilize, apply pesticides and the like).

Regarding work that should be performed in the home garden before the *Shemita* year – see the chapter on "*Tosefet Shevi'it*." It should, however, be noted briefly that fruit trees may be planted until the fifteenth of Av of the sixth year (in certain circumstances there is room for leniency even after that date), and other plants can be planted until just before *Rosh ha-Shana* of the *Shemita* year or **reak down slowly** should be applied (which will last for the entire year). It is preferable to spray a weed killer before the *Shemita* year. **It is also recommended to plant perennial flowers.**[68]

68. The advantage of perennial flowers is twofold: a) If a person plants perennial flowers in the sixth year, his garden will look nice during the seventh year. b) Since they are meant to grow in future years as well, one may be lenient and water them even according to Rav Kook, who forbids labors for the purpose of preservation of fruit. Perennial flowers are watered not only for the sake of the *Shemita* year, but also in order that they continue to flower in the following years as well. In any event, it is permitted to water flowers (even annuals), even according to **Rav Kook**, for the following reasons: a) According to Rav Sh. Z. Auerbach, ornamental flowers have no *Shemita* sanctity, even if they have a scent, because they are not grown for their scent, and if so, even according to Rav Kook, it should be permitted to care for them (with respect to rabbinic labors in order to prevent a loss) because they are not ownerless. b) Even if we are stringent and refrain from labors for the purpose of preservation of fruit, watering should be permitted (see above, section on watering). Rav Kook himself, however, was more stringent regarding watering than with regard to other labors because watering promotes growth (see *Kuntres Acharon* 2, 2). As stated above, however, it is still preferable to plant perennial flowers.

WHEN SHOULD I COME TO ISRAEL?

An American Jew was planning to come to Eretz Yisrael. He had arranged to take a year off from work, and decided to spend the time in Eretz Yisrael.

Suddenly, however, he began to worry that perhaps he had made a mistake, and called me in a panic: "I had completely forgotten that this year is *Shemita.* What should I do now? Would it be better to cancel my trip or push it off for a year, so as not to become involved in all the problems presented by *Shemita*?"

"If you have one year to come to Eretz Yisrael," I told him, "choose the year of *Shemita*. The *Shemita* year is a year endowed with special sanctity, a year during which *Shemita* sanctity is added to the sanctity of the land, a year during which the words, 'a Sabbath for the Lord,' echo throughout the land. Do you really want to miss out on a year like this?"

KITCHEN MANAGEMENT DURING *SHEMITA*

THE SANCTITY OF *SHEMITA* PRODUCE

THE SANCTITY OF *SHEMITA* PRODUCE

ASPIRATION OR OBSTACLE?

We have discussed the various prohibitions concerning agricultural work during the *Shemita* year. In addition to these prohibitions, there are many laws that govern the way we must treat the produce that grows during the seventh year.

One of the fundamental questions for the consumer during the *Shemita* year is whether to purchase produce that has *Shemita* sanctity (such as *Otzar Bet Din* produce), and then treat it with the appropriate sanctity, or whether, perhaps, it is preferable to purchase produce that does not have *Shemita* sanctity (such as stored sixth year produce, or imported produce), so as to "avoid all the trouble."

The difficulties involved in safeguarding the sanctity of *Shemita* produce are described poignantly by *Tosafot* (*Sukka 39a,* at the end of s.v. *she-ein*):

> There are countless laws and prohibitions that govern the produce of the seventh year which must be treated with *Shemita* sanctity!

At first glance, *Tosafot*'s comments are cause for much concern: Will we be able to meet the challenge of preserving the sanctity of *Shemita* produce? If we choose to purchase *Shemita* produce and safeguard their sanctity, are we not liable to fail in our attempts to adequately preserve their sacred character?

In the humble opinion of this author, the answer is clear: **dealing with the sanctity of *Shemita* produce is a unique privilege, and therefore we must yearn for the opportunity to eat the sacred produce of the seventh year!** Indeed, it is easier and more convenient to buy produce that does not have *Shemita* sanctity, but, without a doubt, the difficulties arising from the use of sacred *Shemita* produce are manageable. Generally speaking, a person who eats in a normal manner, in the way that most people eat, does not have to make significant changes to his eating style. The major differences, for such a person, will be in the way that he treats leftovers of *Shemita* produce.[1]

1. It should be noted that even the aforementioned *Tosafot* does not relate to normal domestic use of sacred *Shemita* produce, but to safeguarding the sanctity of *demei shevi'it,* money that had been involved in the purchase of *Shemita* produce, which is indeed complicated and problematic. In practice, the laws that govern the household use of *Shemita* produce are not so numerous or complex.

Moreover, even if some of the laws relating to the sanctity of *Shemita* produce require extra effort on our part, the great privilege of eating *Shemita* produce – which, according to the Ramban, might even involve the fulfillment of a *mitzva* (see below) – outweighs all the challenges involved. This can be compared to a person who owns diamonds and goes to great lengths to safeguard them. Of course he is willing to exert himself for the privilege of having precious jewels in his possession. We, too, should gladly exert ourselves to safeguard the sanctity of *Shemita* produce and rejoice in the privilege granted to us to eat the sacred produce of the *Shemita* year.

It is worth nothing that eating ***Otzar Bet Din* produce** (explained below) is **especially meritorious**. God-fearing farmers who seek to meticulously observe the *Shemita* laws encounter overwhelming difficulties, including a drop in income, and they need to invest great effort to finding an appropriate solution. One of the best solutions available to them from a halachic perspective – one that was accepted both by Rav Kook and by the *Chazon Ish* – is to utilize *Otzar Bet Din*. Today, when less than two percent of the Israeli population bears the burden of preserving the sanctity of *Shemita* by refraining from forbidden agricultural labors, it is our responsibility to share in this *mitzva* and to offer all possible help to those working so hard to observe the *Shemita* restrictions. Even if using this produce entails some difficulty for us, it is a trivial challenge relative to the difficulties faced by these farmers. In order to become partners with "the mighty ones who do His bidding" (*Tehillim 103:20*), we too must exert ourselves and do everything to ensure their success, and thus fulfill the *mitzva* of "that your brother may live [comfortably] with you!" (*Vayikra 25:36*)

In summary, **our aspiration is not to run away from the produce of Eretz Yisrael that is sanctified with *Shemita* sanctity.** On the contrary, **we strive to fulfill the command that "the Sabbath produce of the land shall be for your consumption"** (*Vayikra 25:6*). Eating the produce of Eretz Yisrael, and especially eating *Shemita* produce, is a great privilege, and we ought to rejoice in the effort involved in preserving its sanctity!

WHAT IS THE SANCTITY OF *SHEMITA* PRODUCE?

THE NATURE OF THE SANCTITY OF *SHEMITA* PRODUCE

The gemara in *Megila* (*26b*) quotes a *baraita* that categorizes sacred objects and notes a difference between *tashmishei mitzva* – "accessories to a *mitzva*," which are items used to perform a *mitzva*, such as a *shofar* or a *lulav*, and *tashmishei kedusha* – "accessories to sanctity"– items that are related to sacred objects, such as the cover of a Torah scroll or *tefillin*:

> Our Rabbis taught [in a *baraita*]: *tashmishei mitzva, mitzva* accessories, may be disposed of in a normal way, whereas *tashmishei kedusha,* sanctified objects, must be buried. The following are *tashmishei mitzva*: a *sukka,* a *lulav,* a *shofar, tzitzit.* The following are *tashmishei kedusha*: the storage place for the Torah, *tefillin* and *mezuzot,* the case for a Torah scroll, *tefillin,* and the straps of *tefillin.*

According to this *baraita, tashmishei kedusha* are sanctified with *kedushat ha-guf,* "intrinsic sanctity," whereas *tashmishei mitzva* lack such sanctity.

Nevertheless, the Rema rules that even *tashmishei mitzva* must not be treated in an undignified manner since they had been used in the performance of a *mitzva* (*Orach Chayim 21:1*):

> According to some authorities, even if they [*tzitzit* threads] are torn, one should not treat them in an undignified manner by casting them in a disgraceful place; but they do not require burial.

Another type of sanctity is the sanctity of consecrated property, *hekdesh*. Like *tashmishei kedusha,* consecrated objects are also sanctified with *kedushat ha-guf*. Unlike sacred objects, however, consecrated objects are also subject to the prohibition of *me'ila* – "abuse of sanctity."

RABBI MOSHE BEN ISRAEL ISSERLIS (*the Rema*)

Rabbi Moshe ben Israel Isserlis was born in 1525 in Krakow, Poland. His major work comes in the form of "notes" or "comments" on the *Shulchan Aruch* that comprise rulings that were accepted by Ashkenazic Jewry as authoritative. Among his other compositions are the *Darkei Moshe* commentary on the Tur, and the *Torat Chatat,* a work on the laws of *Kashrut*. He had already begun to write his own original work on halacha when he learned of the composition of the *Shulchan Aruch*. Rather than write a complete halachic work, the Rema decided to unite all of Israel in a single work. Toward that end he wrote his notes on the *Shulchan Aruch,* in accordance with Ashkenazi rulings, thus enabling nearly all of Israel to study the same text to learn halacha. The Rema generally opens with comments with the word, "הגה" which means a note or comment.

Yet another type of sanctity is the sanctity of *teruma,* the portion of agricultural produce that must be set aside and given to a *Kohen*. In addition to the sanctity of *teruma,* there is also an obligation to safeguard it, as is explained in the *Yerushalmi* (*Challa 3:2*):

> "Behold, I also have given them the guarding of my *teruma* – *mishmeret terumotai*" (*Bemidbar 18:8*) – this phrase teaches that *teruma* requires safeguarding.

Rashi (*Sukka 35b*) adds that the safeguarding referred to by the verse is safeguarding from ritual impurity:

> One is forbidden to cause *teruma* to become ritually impure, as it is written: "The guarding of my *teruma*" – The Torah said: Provide it with safeguarding.

As for *Shemita* produce, the *Talmud Yerushalmi* (*4:7*) learns that the produce of the seventh year has sanctity from the verse: "For it is the jubilee; it shall be holy to you" (*Vayikra 25:11*):

> "For it is the jubilee; it shall be holy to you" ... – just as it is holy, so, too, its produce is holy.

Which is stricter – the sanctity of *Shemita* or *hekdesh*?

The question arises: What is the nature of the sanctity of *Shemita* produce? On the one hand, *Shemita* produce, as opposed to *teruma,* may be eaten even in a state of ritual impurity and even by a non-*Kohen.* On the other hand, certain laws of sanctity governing *Shemita* produce are even more severe than those that apply to *hekdesh,* consecrated property. With regard to consecrated property, redeeming the object with money removes the sanctity from the original object, transferring the sanctity to the money, whereas when *Shemita* produce is purchased with money, the *Shemita* produce retains its sanctity even as sanctity is transferred to the money, as is stated in *Sukka* (*40b*):

> A *baraita* supports the view of Rabbi Elazar: *Shemita* sanctity is transferred to money used to purchase the produce, as the verse states, "For it is the jubilee, it shall be holy to you" – just as for *hekdesh,* that which is holy, the sanctity is transferred to the money that redeems it and it becomes prohibited for ordinary use, so, too, *Shemita* produce transfers its sanctity to money that purchases it, and it becomes prohibited for ordinary use, while the produce itself remains holy.

It seems that the added sanctity of *Shemita* produce stems from the fact that, unlike *teruma, Shemita* produce is holy from its inception. The sanctity of *teruma* (and *hekdesh*) applies to produce (or other objects) through human action when a person sets aside *teruma,* with the caveat that one can also redeem the produce and transfer the sanctity to the money. The sanctity of *Shemita* produce, on the other hand, is natural and innate, and therefore the owner cannot remove the sanctity even if he tries to redeem the produce.[2] Yet, despite the stringency stemming from this innate sanctity, given that the consumption of *Shemita* produce is available to every Jew, the Torah did not require that it be safeguarded from ritual impurity.

While the suggestion that the stringency of *Shemita* sanctity stems from its innateness seems plausible, it does not seem to be a universal principle. For *neta revai* produce (the fruit of a tree during

2. This is also the reason that the prohibitions of *orla* (produce from the first three years of a tree's growth which is prohibited) and *kil'ei ha-kerem* (prohibited produce from a grapevine that was cross-bred with other crops) cannot be terminated by way of redemption with money. As opposed to *Shemita* sanctity, however, in the case of *orla* and *kil'ei ha-kerem,* by Torah law only the produce itself is forbidden, but not the money. On the Rabbinic level, at least, there is a similarity in this regard between *Shemita* sanctity and the sanctity of *orla* and *kil'ei ha-kerem* (see *Kiddushin 58a; Chullin 4b* – Rashi and *Tosafot,* ad loc.).

the fourth year after it was planted) also has innate sanctity, but nevertheless it may be redeemed and its sanctity removed![3]

This difference between *neta reva'i* and *Shemita* produce may result from the fact that *neta revai*, unlike *Shemita* produce, must be eaten in Jerusalem.[4] Since *neta reva'i* must be brought to Jerusalem, the Torah made it possible to remove the sanctity from the fruit, so that the owner would be able to go to Jerusalem, carrying only the money, and buy new produce once he gets there. However, given that *Shemita* produce may be eaten throughout Israel, there is no compelling reason to allow redemption.

This explanation highlights the unique importance of *Shemita* produce. One of the special characteristics of *Shemita* sanctity is that it extends to every member of the Jewish people (as opposed to *teruma*, which is consumed only by *Kohanim* and their families) and to every corner of the Land of Israel (as opposed to *neta revai, ma'aser sheni, shelamim* offerings, firstborn animals and the like, which may only be eaten in Jerusalem). The ubiquity of *Shemita* sanctity teaches us how extensively this *mitzva* is supposed to influence Jewish life in the Land of Israel. *Shemita* is not a localized obligation, but rather a comprehensive and far-reaching *mitzva* that impacts upon the entire people even when they are in a state of ritual impurity!

This idea might also explain the prohibition against wasting *Shemita* produce, which we will deal with below. The simple understanding is that one is forbidden to destroy *Shemita* produce because of its sanctity. It is possible, however, to propose an alternative explanation: when a person rents or borrows an article, he may use the property but he may not destroy it. The right to destroy the object belongs solely to its owner. Nothing provides a greater sense of ownership than the right to destroy one's property. During the sabbatical year, the produce growing on a person's property does not belong to him, and thus he also lacks the authority to waste or ruin any part of it.[5]

In this context, another point may be added. It may be that the sanctity of *Shemita* produce does not terminate when it is sold because **there is no human owner who has the authority to sell this produce**. One of the underlying notions of *Shemita* is that it

3. This objection was raised by Rav Mordechai Immanuel. [According to him, *neta revai* is an exceptional case, and the removal of the produce's sanctity through redemption is possible owing to the analogy to *ma'aser sheni*.] It should also be noted that there are other instances of innate sanctity where redemption is possible, such as the firstling of a donkey, and sanctified animals that have been disqualified. This, however, is beyond the scope of discussion here.

4. *Shemita* produce may be eaten anywhere within Eretz Yisrael. We will not discuss the prohibition to remove *Shemita* produce from Eretz Yisrael here, but merely note that, even if such a prohibition exists, according to most *Posekim* it is merely a Rabbinic decree (see *Chazon Ish, Shevi'it* 13, 3; see also *Bet Ridbaz* on *Pe'at ha-Shulchan* 5, 18), and, even according to the views that it is prohibited by Torah law, after being exported, the produce may be eaten.

5. I heard this explanation from my revered teacher and father-in-law, Rav Blumenzweig, *shlita*.

highlights the fact we do not own the land, as God asserts, "The land is mine; for you are strangers and sojourners with me" (*Vayikra* 25:23). Thus, a person lacks the authority to sell the produce of God's land. During the *Shemita* year, a person does not control the fruit of the earth and therefore he cannot assert himself as owner to remove their sanctity![6]

6. It may be possible to combine the two proposed explanations: *Shemita* sanctity is innate sanctity which teaches the so-called "owner" that in fact he lacks true mastery of his land.

These notions may stem from another unique conceptual element of *Shemita*. *Shemita*, as we have seen, is parallel to Shabbat. Shabbat is *me'en olam ha-ba* – it gives us a taste of life in the world to come – thus it stands to reason that ***Shemita* also gives us a taste of life in the world to come**. Meaning, in the *Shemita* year, the land of Israel is elevated to a level of reality that rises above the natural existence which normally governs it. In this year, sanctity descends upon the land from above, such that even the fruit that grows from the land in this year is sanctified, in its very essence. **It is due to the unique sanctity of this year, which is beyond human reality, that a person cannot attain ownership of the fruit.**

According to this approach, once in seven years we have the opportunity to eat from the **fruit of the Garden of Eden.**[7] On the one hand, this fruit has a heavenly sanctity and no human ownership can attach to it; on the other hand, this fruit was given by God to the people of Israel, "And the Sabbath of the earth shall be for your consumption." God granted us the opportunity to eat this fruit in order to elevate us above our normal spiritual level, thereby enabling us to arrive at spiritual heights that are normally unattainable to us. If we are able to internalize this idea, when the *Shemita* year is complete we will be able to resume the normal reality of "and you shall harvest your grain, wine [grapes] and oil [olives]," with a new fervor, inspired by the sanctified world from which we were sustained during the *Shemita* year.

7. See the introduction for the parallels between *Shemita* and Shabbat, as well as the parallels between the *Shemita* year and the creation of the world.

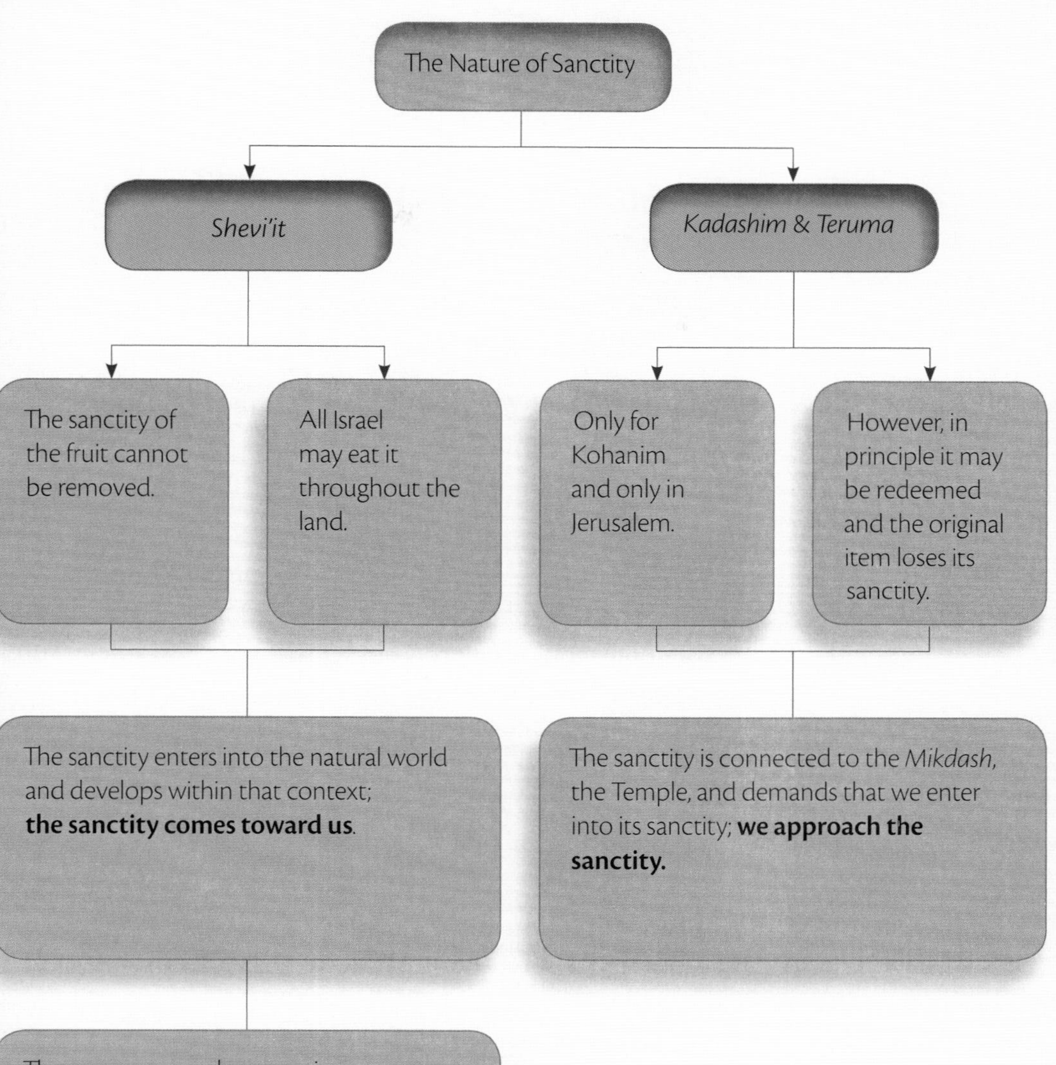

There are apparently two unique aspects to *shevi'it*:

A. Innate sanctity (as opposed to teruma and most kadashim)

B. "For the land in Mine" – we are not, and have never been, the owners of this produce [for the sanctity stems from the "birth" of this produce], so we have no right to remove that sanctity.

Thus, it is impossible to remove *kedushat shevi'it*, yet the sanctity impacts the entirety of the Jewish people throughout the land, so they can eat it there as well.

MUST ONE WASH ONE'S HANDS BEFORE EATING *SHEMITA* PRODUCE?

The *Tosefta* (*Shevi'it 7:6*) forbids the use of *Shemita* produce in a state of ritual impurity:

> One must not rub oil of the seventh year [on the body] with impure hands.

Rav Kook (*Shabbat ha-Aretz 5, 7*) rules that this law is not applicable today, because the rules of purity and impurity for food are not in practice. Rav Kook adds (*Kuntres Acharon, 25*) that even today the special status of *Shemita* produce should be emphasized, and therefore one should only rub oneself with *Shemita* oil after first washing one's hands:[8]

> Even though we no longer observe the rules of ritual cleanness for food, one should nevertheless, out of respect for *Shemita* sanctity, wash one's hands before rubbing with *Shemita* oil, just as hand washing was enacted for a meal… and all the more so is this fitting with respect to *Shemita* oil, which is called holy. He who sanctifies himself to observe this law is worthy of a blessing.

Rav Kook further adds that while the Gemara is generally opposed to washing hands for dry fruit ("A person who washes his hands for fruit is of those that are haughty in spirit;" *Chullin 106a*), one is permitted to wash one's hands before eating *Shemita* produce, owing to the sanctity attached to it. The *Chayei Adam* also writes that it is proper to wash one's hand before eating *Shemita* produce (*Sha'arei Tzedek 17, 17*; and similarly *Mishnat Yosef, Shevi'it* chap. *8, p. 118*).

Even though the *Posekim* (authorities) have generally refrained from citing this ruling, it is nevertheless instructive about the unique sanctity of *Shemita* produce. In the humble opinion of this author, despite the lofty idea underlying the requirement to wash one's hands prior to using *Shemita* produce, in actual practice it is preferable to follow the majority of *Posekim* and not be stringent

8. It should be pointed out that this *tosefta* is not necessarily speaking about washing one's hands, and it could be explained otherwise. For instance, the Or Sameach (*Hilchot She'ar Avot Ha-tumot 8:8*) claims that it is only regarding *teruma* that we considered one's hands to be automatically "*sheniyot*," containing second-degree *tuma* such that they need to be washed, whereas regarding *shevi'it*, there is only a problem if one has certainly come in contact with *tuma*. In light of this distinction, the Or Sameach also explains a discrepancy between the language of the Rambam in the laws of *teruma* and the laws of *shevi'it*. Regarding *teruma*, the Rambam writes (*Hilchot Terumot 11:7*) that one may not anoint one's soiled hands with *teruma* oil, whereas regarding *shevi'it* he writes (*Hilchot Shemita ve-*

in this regard. Stringency in this matter will bring people to avoid eating *Shemita* produce and thus the losses will outweigh the gains. It should be emphasized that it is only with respect to washing one's hand prior to eating that one may practice leniency. Without a doubt, however, one must meticulously observe the prohibition to waste or sell *Shemita* produce, or to remove such produce from Eretz Yisrael.

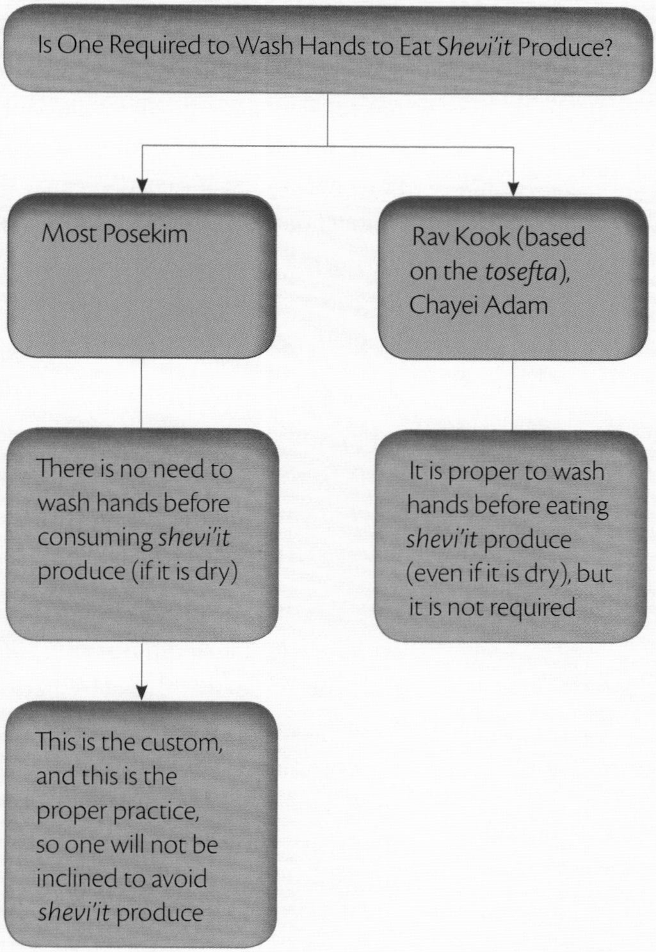

Is One Required to Wash Hands to Eat *Shevi'it* Produce?

- Most Posekim
  - There is no need to wash hands before consuming *shevi'it* produce (if it is dry)
  - This is the custom, and this is the proper practice, so one will not be inclined to avoid *shevi'it* produce
- Rav Kook (based on the *tosefta*), Chayei Adam
  - It is proper to wash hands before eating *shevi'it* produce (even if it is dry), but it is not required

yovel 5:7) that one may not anoint one's impure hands with *shevi'it* oil. (See also the *Derech Emuna, Hilchot Shemita Ve-Yovel* 5:7, note 43.) According to the Or Sameach, the *tosefta* teaches a requirement to wash one's hands only if one has come in contact with an object that is definitely *tamei*. Another way to explain the *tosefta* is that there is no fundamental problem of touching *shevi'it* produce with impure hands other than the fact that this contact renders the produce itself impure, and thus they can no longer be consumed in a state of purity. Thus, the obligation to wash does not stem from the sanctity of the produce, rather from the requirement to preserve them. (See the *Chazon Yechezkel* and the *Minchat Bikkurim* on the *tosefta*.)

IS THERE A *MITZVA* TO EAT *SHEMITA* PRODUCE?

The Ramban in his addendum to the Rambam's *Sefer ha-Mitzvot* (*positive mitzva* 3) writes:

> That which the Torah stated, regarding *shevi'it* produce, "And the Sabbath of the land shall be for your consumption," regarding which the Rabbis taught, "For consumption and not for commerce..." And this *mitzva* was repeated through the expression, "And the poor of your nation shall eat [the produce," but it does not say, "Leave it for the poor of your nation," as it says regarding the *mitzvot* of *leket* (the grains forgotten during the harvest) and *shich'cha* (the forgotten sheaves), but, rather, the language is one of consumption.

According to the *Megilat Esther's* (ad loc.) understanding of the Ramban, the verse, "And the Sabbath produce of the land shall be for your consumption," teaches that there is a *mitzva* to eat *Shemita* produce:[9]

> It seems that the reason that the master [the Rambam] did not count it is that [he understood that] what the Sages said "for consumption and not for commerce," does not mean that there is a *mitzva* to eat it, but rather that it is permitted to you "for consumption," but not for trade.

The *Megilat Esther* disagrees with

9. The fact that *there is a mitzva to eat Shemita produce* is also found in the words of the Maharit Algazi in his explanation of the Ramban. (*Hilchot Challa* of the *Ramban*, 26b). Support for this approach can be found in the *tosefta*: "There is no obligation to eat moldy bread or cooked foods that have rotted." The Rash Mi-Shantz (chapter 8, mishna 2) explains that there is no obligation to eat moldy bread or rotten food because people do not generally consume food when it is in this condition, such that there is no loss of produce by eliminating it. The implication of the Rash's statement is that there is an obligation to eat produce that has not spoiled to prevent it from coming to loss, or, in other words, there is a *mitzva* to eat *Shemita* produce. [See Rav Kook's notes on *Kuntres Acharon*, note 21; *Sefer ha-Shemita* 7, note 2.] However, it is possible that the *tosefta* is teaching that it is permissible to ruin moldy bread, which is what it means by the phrase "there is no obligation to eat it." This is the explanation of the *Torat Ha-aretz*, 8:26. The Megilat Esther (cited above) explains that one might have thought that there is an obligation to eat the produce because of the prohibition, not because of a positive commandment. The *tosefta* teaches us that there is no such obligation in this case. Responsa *Shevet Ha-levi* (4:232) derives from here that there is no positive *mitzva* to eat *shevi'it* produce, but rather that there is a *mitzva* to eat produce which will be wasted if it is not eaten. He writes that there are two *mitzvot* in the consumption of sanctified food: one *mitzva* to eat a proper amount (*ke-zayit*), and a second *mitzva* to prevent the food from coming to waste, in violation of the principle of *notar*, (maintaining sanctified food past its proper time). He writes that this latter *mitzva* exists regarding *shevi'it* produce.

Ramban and explains that Rambam did not count the command, "And the Sabbath produce of the land shall be for your consumption" as a *mitzva*, because he understood that the verse does not come to obligate the eating of *Shemita* produce, but rather to permit it. The corollary of this permission is the prohibition to allow the produce to wasted.

If we understand that according to the Ramban there is a positive precept to eat *Shemita* produce, then every time a person eats produce of the seventh year he would fulfill a positive *mitzva*.[10] It stands to reason that even according to the Ramban there is no obligatory *mitzva* to eat *Shemita* produce, *mitzva* "*chiyuvit*," but rather the fulfillment of a voluntary *mitzva* "*kiyumit*." That is to say, the Ramban does not mean to say that one who fails to eat *Shemita* produce nullifies a positive precept, but only that one who eats *Shemita* produce fulfills a *mitzva*.

10. If indeed we follow the Ramban's logic, we might come to the conclusion that to fulfil the commandment one may need to eat ***Shemita*** produce in the amount of an olive, as is the case with all *mitzvot* involving eating (Maharit Algazi, *Hilchot Challa* of the Ramban, 2; *Minchat Chinuch* 329, 13; *Responsa Har Tzvi, Orach Chayim*, vol. II, 111, and *Har Tzvi, Zera'im*, vol. II, 54)

RABBI YITZCHAK LEON BEN ELAZAR (*Megilat Esther*)

Rabbi Yitzchak was an Italian sage who lived in the sixteenth century. He was a descendant of Spanish exiles who had settled in the city of Ankona, where he served in the Rabbinate.

His work, Megilat Esther, explains the *Sefer Ha-mitzvot* of the Rambam, and seeks to resolve the questions Ramban raised against the Rambam.

Authors often hint at their own name or their topic in the name of their work. The author of the Megilat Esther chose to memorialize his mother, Esther, by naming his work for her.

In contrast to these explanations, the *Seridei Eish* (vol. *II, 116, 1*; new edition, vol. *II, 90*) and the *Chazon Ish* (*14:1*) understand that even according to the Ramban, one who eats *Shemita* produce does not fulfill a positive precept.[11] According to them, the *mitzva* that the Ramban refers to is not actually a positive *mitzva*, but rather a "prohibition derived from a positive *mitzva*." In other words, the Torah commands us neither to trade *Shemita* produce nor to waste it, formulating these prohibitions in positive terms – "it shall be for consumption." The Ramban counts this commandment as a

11. The *Derech Emuna* (*Shemita ve-Yovel 5:1, be'ur halacha*, s.v. *peirot*) proves that there is no *mitzva* to eat *Shemita* produce from the absence of any special blessing over such eating (unlike *teruma* and *ma'aser sheni*, regarding which there is a *mitzva* to eat and accordingly a special blessing as well). He adds that this also follows from the Torah's language. The Torah does not say, "And you shall eat it," but rather, "the Sabbath produce of the land shall be available for your consumption" – that is to say, an obligation exists to renounce ownership of the produce so that everyone can partake of it but there is no separate *mitzva* to eat it. He notes that if there is a *mitzva* to eat the produce, it is only at the time of *bi'ur*, when the eating is part of the *mitzva* of *bi'ur*.

positive *mitzva*, but the *mitzva* instructs us what **not to do** with *Shemita* produce.

It should be emphasized that even if there is no positive commandment to eat *Shemita* produce, there is still significance in eating it, as *Shemita* produce bestows additional sanctity on those who eat it.[12]

12. See, however, *Kalkalat Shabbat* (*p. 476*), who writes that *Shemita* sanctity is only expressed in the prohibitions associated with it (such as the prohibitions to waste or sell *Shemita* produce), but has no positive sanctity. The other *Posekim* do not appear to have adopted this approach, but rather they maintain that *Shemita* produce has positive sanctity (see *Mikdash David*, 59, no. 5; *Aruch ha-Shulchan he-Atid* 24:15).

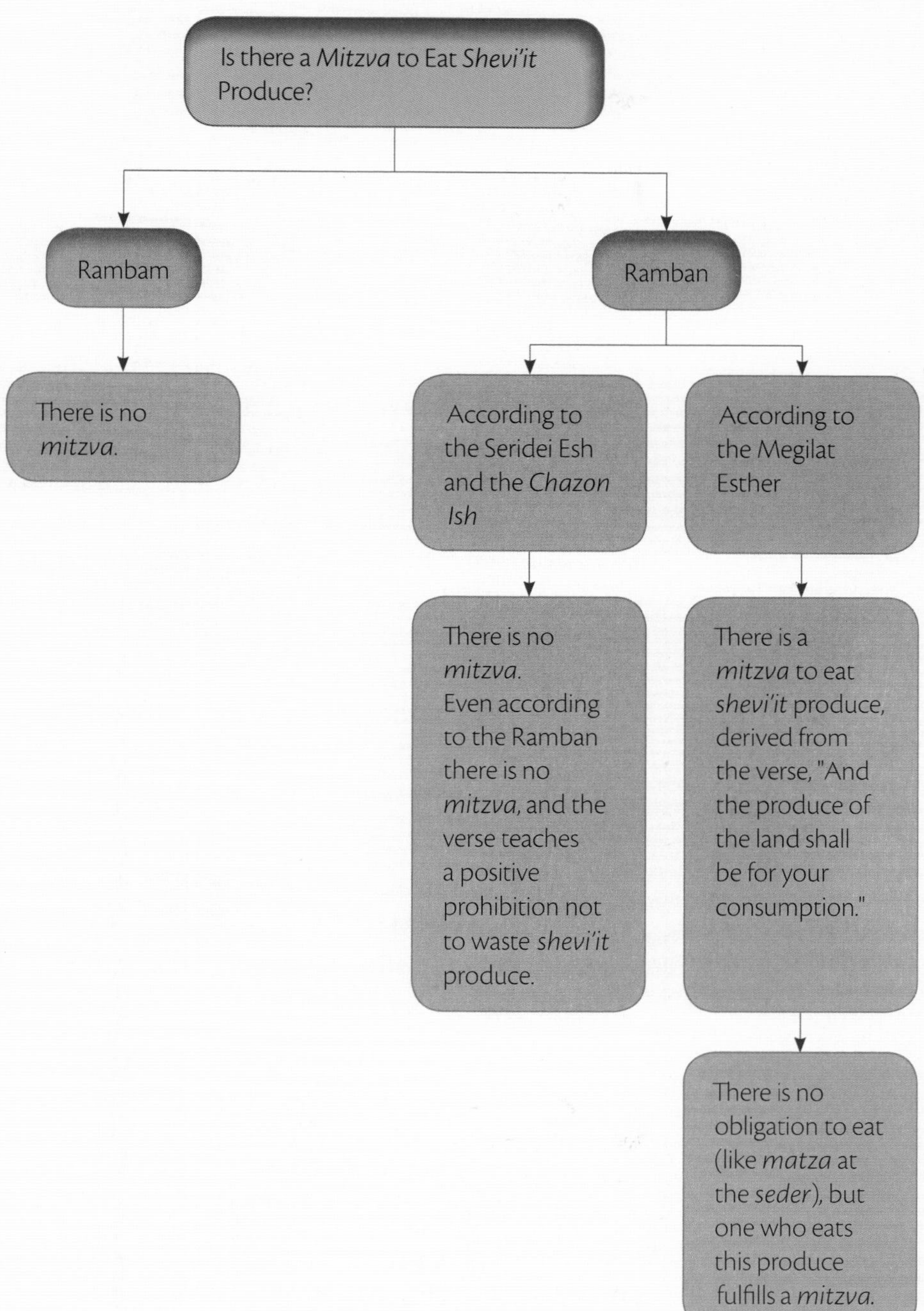

The bottom line is that, according to most Posekim, there is no *mitzva* to eat *Shemita* produce, but there is special significance to this produce, owing to its sanctity.

TO WHAT DOES *SHEMITA* SANCTITY APPLY?

What is the difference between fruit and vegetables?

The Mishna at the beginning of *Rosh ha-Shana* notes that the first day of *Tishrei* marks the New Year with respect to *Shemita*. The Gemara (*Rosh ha-Shana 8a*) explains that this is derived from a *gezera shava*, a comparison based on an identical phrase, between two instances of the word "year": regarding the *Shemita* year, the Torah states in *Sefer Vayikra*: "But in the seventh ***year***..." (*Vayikra 25:4*), and in *Sefer Devarim* the Torah states: "The eyes of the Lord your God are always upon it [the land of Israel], from the beginning of the ***year***" (*Devarim 11:14*). From here we see that that the word "year" denotes the "beginning" of the year, namely the first of *Tishrei*.[13]

One might have thought that if the sabbatical year begins on the first of *Tishrei*, then the sanctity of the year should begin from that date as well. The Gemara (*13b*), however, distinguishes between various types of produce:

> Rabba said: The Rabbis have said that [the tithe year of] a tree is determined by the [time of the] emergence [of fruit], that of grain and olives by one third of their ripening, that of vegetables by their picking.

That is to say, fruit is regarded as *Shemita* produce if the fruit emerged after the first of *Tishrei* of the seventh year; grains and olives are considered *Shemita* produce if they became a third ripe during the seventh year;[14] and vegetables are classified as *Shemita* produce if they were picked during the seventh year. The principle that arises from this passage is that **each crop is regarded as *Shemita* produce if the most crucial formative stage of its growth took place during the seventh year.** We shall now expand upon the details of each type of produce.

GRAIN, LEGUMES, OLIVES AND GRAPES:

The Gemara in Rosh ha-Shana (*13a*) derives from the Torah that the

13. The Gemara there explains why this verse cannot be referring to the first of Nisan – see there.

14. There is much discussion about the definition of a "third" ripe: does this mean a third of its ultimate weight (*Haskamot ha-Ra'aya*, no. 6) or a third of its ultimate size (*Chazon Ish* 19, 23; Rav Sh. Z. Auerbach, *Kerem Tziyon, Terumot*, 4, *Giddulei Tziyon*, no. 1)? According to the prevailing view, we follow a third of its ultimate size, but the way that this is calculated still requires clarification. (Do we follow one-third of its physical size, or one-third of its ripeness? According to the *Chazon Ish* (19, 23), for grain and olives we follow one-third ripeness, similar to the status of "cooked to the level of *ben derusay*," food cooked to one-third of its normal degree, which is a definition of cooking in *Hilchot Shabbat*, though this still requires clarification). Some explain that "one-third grown" takes place at the time when the seed of grain has been filled, and has the complete amount of dry mass it will contain (*Halichot Sadeh*, 4, page 6; Rav Shmuel David, *Emunat Itecha* 41.)

tithe year of grain and olives is determined by when they become a third grown:

> "And it shall bring forth produce for the three years" (*Vayikra 25:21*) – do not read *li'shlosh* [for three], but *li'shlish* [to a third].

Grapes grown to a third

On the previous page (*12b*), the Gemara records an alternative derivation:

> Grain and olives are determined by the time that they are a third grown. From where do we know this? Rav Asi said in the name of Rabbi Yochanan, and some say in the name of Rabbi Yose the Galilean: "The verse says: 'At the end of every seven years, in the set time of the year of *Shemita*, in the feast of *Sukkot*' (*Devarim 31:10*). Now why is the year of *Shemita* mentioned here? The feast of *Sukkot* is in the eighth year! Rather it is to teach you that if the produce has grown a third in the seventh year before *Rosh ha-Shana*, the rules of the seventh year are applied to it in the eighth year."

That is to say, the Torah refers to the festival of *Sukkot* in the eighth year as "the time of the year of *Shemita*," because the produce that is gathered into the house at that time had reached a third of its growth during the seventh year, and all produce that reaches a third of its growth during the seventh year is sanctified with *Shemita* sanctity.

The Rambam maintains that for this purpose "produce" includes not only wheat and barley, but legumes as well. Rashi (*Rosh ha-Shana 12b*) disagrees and says that legumes are treated like rice. According to Rashi, legumes are regarded as *Shemita* produce if they reach their full growth during the seventh year.[15] Rashi adds that grapes are also regarded as *Shemita* produce if they reach a third of their growth during the seventh year. [The *Chazon Ish* rules in accordance with this position (*7, 16; 9, 17*).] In practice, **grain, legumes,**

15. The term "legumes" (*kitniyot*) refers to annual crops whose seeds are eaten (Rambam, *Hilchot Kil'ayim 1:8*; *Chazon Ish 27:7*, s.v. *ve-im ken*), such as corn and sunflower seeds.

olives and grapes have sanctity if one third of their growth took place during *Shemita*.

VEGETABLES:

The Gemara in *Rosh ha-Shana* (14a) derives from the Torah that the tithe year of vegetables is determined by the time that they are picked or harvested:

> Rabbi Akiva said: "After you have gathered in from your threshing-floor and wine press" (*Devarim 16:13*) – just as [the products brought to the] threshing-floor and wine press are unique in that they are nurtured by rainwater and [consequently] are tithed as produce of the preceding year, so to all products that are nurtured by rain water are tithed as produce of the preceding year. This excludes vegetables, which are nurtured by all kinds of water [including irrigation] and are consequently tithed as produce of the following year.

Tomato picking.

That is to say, since grain and grapes grow on rainwater, the critical point in their development is the time that they reach a third of their growth (as explained above). Vegetables that require irrigation throughout their time of growth are tithed for the following year – namely, according to the year in which they are picked. Rashi explains that grain and grapes can be harvested, if need be, once they have reached a third of their growth, and that is why this is regarded as the crucial point in their growth process. Thus, this is also the stage that determines to which year they are assigned.[16] Vegetables, on the other hand, can only survive if they are continuously watered. Therefore, they cannot be assigned

16. It might be added that while it is true that grain and grapes continue to grow even after they reach a third of their growth, that is merely a quantitative improvement, as opposed to the stage when they reach a third of their growth, which marks a qualitative jump in their growth process (from that point they are fit for human consumption if necessary). However, it is difficult to make this agricultural determination in practice.

to the previous year unless they were also picked in that year, for until they are harvested they must be watered and without such watering they will die.[17]

FRUIT:

As we saw earlier, the Gemara in *Rosh ha-Shana* learns that the stage that determines the tithe year of fruit is the point when the fruit first emerges ("*chanata*"). Rashi (*Rosh ha-Shana* 14a, s.v. *af kol*) explains that when the fruit first emerges, the sap rises in the tree, and it is only on account of this sap that the tree continues to survive. It is for this reason that the time when the fruit first emerges is regarded as the most crucial formative stage in the fruit's growth, and therefore the stage that determines the year to which the fruit is assigned:[18]

> Therefore regarding a tree they went after emergence [of the fruit], for its fruit grows entirely from the sap stored in the tree prior to the emergence [of the fruit].

What precisely is "*chanata*"? The *Tosafot* (*Rosh ha-Shana 12b,* s.v. *ha-tevu'a*) and the Rash (2:7) understand that *chanata* is reached when the blossom falls away and the fruit begins to emerge.[19] In contrast, the Rambam (*Hilchot Shemita ve-Yovel 4:9*) maintains that *chanata* is reached only much later, when the fruit has already grown and is slightly fit for eating, the stage that is elsewhere referred to as "the time of tith-

17. While this law appears to be obvious, the Mishna in *Shevi'it* (5:3) seems to imply otherwise. The Mishna states: "*Lof*, an onion-like plant, that grew past the end of the *Shemita* year – Rabbi Eliezer says, if the poor picked its leaves, this is well. If not, the owner must make an accounting with the poor." The discussion here is regarding a case where some of the leaves grew during the *Shemita* year and others grew in the eighth year, and, according to Rabbi Eliezer, the part that grew during *Shemita* has *Shemita* status, thus the poor are entitled to it. The implication of Rabbi Eliezer's teaching is that a vegetable that grew during *Shemita* has sanctity even though it was picked in the eighth year! The Rash (there) objects to this explanation, explaining that the *mishna* speaks of a case where some of the leaves were picked during *Shemita* but they were replanted in their original place, and the leaves grew further in the eighth year. Thus the vegetable is considered to be *Shemita* produce, and even the leaves that actually grew in the eighth year have *Shemita* sanctity.
The Rash Sirilio explains the Mishna otherwise. According to him, the *lof* is not considered like a vegetable but rather like a legume, thus the determining time is not the harvest. However, even according to him, the defining moment for vegetables is the harvest, and this is the determination of the *Chazon Ish* (15:3), that a vegetable that grew during *Shemita* but was harvested afterward lacks *Shemita* sanctity. (See, however, Tosafot [*Rosh ha-Shana 13b*, s.v. *achar* and *14b*, s.v. *ve-la-shevi'it*], who speak of the completion of growth, but this is beyond the scope of our discussion.)

18. The Rash (2:7) explains the significance of this stage differently. According to him, the fruit of most trees emerges at the same time before the fifteenth of **Shevat**, and therefore this is the critical stage in their regard.

19. This definition also appears in Rashi (*Pesachim 52b*, s.v. *de'amar*) in another context: "When the grape blossom falls away and the form of the grape appears, which is *semadar*."

ing." This disagreement is explained by the *Chazon Ish* (*Shevi'it 7, 11-12*):

> The words of our master [the Rash] teach that the *chanata* about which they speak is *semadar* [the budding stage], which immediately follows the end of *chanata* [the falling of the blossom] ... However, the view of the Rambam ... that the *chanata* that is mentioned refers to the time of tithing [a third of the growth] ... which is the beginning of the fruit [when it is already fit for eating if need be] some time after *chanata*.

Before chanata – the "flower" (of an apple)

Right after the flower fell

The *Shulchan Aruch* (*Yoreh De'ah 331:125*) rules in accordance with the Rambam, but the position of the *Chazon Ish* is unclear; in one place (*7, 12*) he writes that the *Shulchan Aruch* already decided in favor of the Rambam, but elsewhere (*21, 16*) he writes that fruit, the blossoms of which fell away during the sixth year, do not have *Shemita* sanctity, even if they reached the time of tithing only during the seventh year, in accordance with the Rash.

The disagreement between the Rash and the Rambam has practical ramifications regarding **winter fruit**, including some strains of avocado and kiwi. The blossom of this fruit falls away in the sixth year, but the fruit itself reaches a third of its growth only after *Rosh ha-Shana.*[20] According to the Rash, such fruit does not have *Shemita* sanctity, whereas according to the Rambam it does. In practice, we generally follow the stringency of each position (Rav Sh. Z. Auerbach, Rav Yisraeli, and Rav Eliyahu; cited in *Katif Shevi'it,* chap. *6,* note *7*).

20. This factor varies with different strains of avocado, as some strains reach the budding stage and a third of growth in the same year.

Third of growth (of an apple)

We explained above that since the sabbatical year begins on the first of *Tishrei*, this is also the date that determines which produce is regarded as *Shemita* produce. The Mishna at the beginning of *Rosh ha-Shana*, however, implies that the law governing fruit is different:

> There are four new years. On the first of *Nisan* is the new year for kings and for festivals. On the first of *Elul* is the new year for the tithe of cattle. Rabbi Elazar and Rabbi Shimon say: On the first of *Tishrei*. On the first of *Tishrei* is the new year for calendar years, for *Shemita* and for jubilee years. On the first of *Shevat* is the new year for trees, according to the ruling of Bet Shammai. Bet Hillel say: On the fifteenth of the month.

Though the Mishna establishes that the first of Tishrei marks the new year with respect to *Shemita*, regarding fruit it says that the new year is on the fifteenth of *Shevat*. Thus the question arises; is the decisive date regarding fruit the first of *Tishrei* or the fifteenth of *Shevat*?

The Rambam (*Hilchot Shemita ve-Yovel 4:9*) implies that the first of *Tishrei* is the determining date with respect to all the laws of *Shemita*:[21]

> The first of *Tishrei* is the beginning of the year in regard to the sabbatical year and the jubilee year. If the produce of the sixth year is left over into the seventh year… if it reached the stage of tithing before *Rosh ha-Shana*, it is permitted.

The Torat Kohanim (*Behar 1, 4*), however, explicitly states that the critical time is the fifteenth of *Shevat*:

> "A Sabbath of solemn rest for the land" (*Vayikra 25:4*) – as soon as the seventh year is finished, even though its fruit is

21. This is the way the Rambam was understood by the Radbaz (ad loc.), the *Minchat Chinuch* (329, 4), and most *Acharonim*. The *Shela* (*Sha'ar ha-Otiyot*, end of section ***kof***) understood him differently, thus the qualification that this halachic decision is merely "implied" by the Rambam. According to the *Shela*, when the Rambam writes: "The fruit of the tree… before the new year," he is not referring to the first of Tishrei, but rather to the **new year of fruit**, namely, the ***fifteenth of Shevat***: "This 'new year' does not refer to the first of *Tishrei*, but to the new year of fruit, which is on the fifteenth of *Shevat*."

Shemita produce, you are permitted to do work on the tree itself. But its fruit is forbidden until the fifteenth of Shevat.[22]

22. That is to say, fruit that reaches *chanata* until the fifteenth of *Shevat* of the eighth year is *Shemita* produce.

Rabbenu Chananel (*Rosh ha-Shana 15b,* s.v. *eitivei*) rules in accordance with the *Torat Kohanim*:

> We apply the laws of *Shemita* to that which reached *chanata* during the seventh year, after the fifteenth of *Shevat.*[23]

23. How would the Rambam explain the *Torat Kohanim*? The Vilna Gaon emends the text of the *Torat Kohanim*, eliminating the phrase, "but its fruit is forbidden until the fifteenth of *Shevat*." This might also have been the Rambam's version of the text. This is a plausible reading, for the midrash is addressing the verse, "a Sabbath of solemn rest for the land," which is unrelated to the status of the fruit. (On the other hand, one could claim that since the midrash speaks of the permissibility to work a tree in the eighth year with *Shemita* fruit, the status of that fruit must also be defined.) See, however, the *Chafetz Chayim's* commentary to *Torat Kohanim*, where he writes that even according to the Vilna Gaon's reading the decisive date for *Shemita* regarding fruit is the fifteenth of *Shevat*.

RABBENU CHANANEL

Rabbenu Chananel ben Chushiel (died 965), was born in Keruan in North Africa.

Rabbenu Chananel lived in a transitional stage between the Geonim and *Rishonim*. He was the teacher of Rabbenu Gershom, Me'or Ha-gola, as well as the Rif and Rabbi Natan, author of the *Aruch*.

Rabbenu Chananel wrote a commentary of the Talmud which is printed on the daf in our editions. In his commentary he resolves difficulties that arise in understanding the meaning of the Gemara. He also often adds the perspective of the *Talmud Yerushalmi*, as well as the halachic ruling.

The disagreement between the Rambam and Rabbenu Chananel seems to be tied to the discussion of the rationale for the establishment of the fifteenth of *Shevat* as the new year regarding trees. The *Yerushalmi* (*Rosh ha-Shana 1:2*) brings two explanations:

1. By the fifteenth of *Shevat* most of the year's rain has already fallen and the sap has already been stored in the trees. Accordingly, this date constitutes the **natural beginning of the agricultural year** with respect to trees.
2. Fruit that appears prior to the fifteenth of *Shevat* grows from the sap that was stored in the tree before *Tishrei*, and therefore **it is regarded as having appeared before *Tishrei*.**[24]

According to the first explanation, the fifteenth of *Shevat* marks the beginning of the agricultural season with respect to trees, with

24. The **Rash** in his commentary of *Torat Kohanim* (*Behar, 1:4*) addresses this connection, and this issue is also discussed by the **Turei Even** (*Rosh ha-Shana 14a*) and the **Mikdash David** (section *60*).

this date signifying the start of the "fruit year." According to the second explanation, the fifteenth of *Shevat* is merely an indicator as to whether the fruit formed before or after the first of *Tishrei*. Thus, according to the second explanation, only fruit that appears after the fifteenth of *Shevat* of the seventh year is sanctified with *Shemita* sanctity, for all the fruit that appears prior to that date was already formed in the sixth year. In contrast, according to the first explanation, there is room to say that while the natural, agricultural year of a tree generally begins only on the fifteenth of *Shevat*, the year of *Shemita* is determined by the rest imposed upon the land, and the date that marks the beginning of the year for that purpose is different.

The Rash (5:5) maintains a third position, incorporating the stringencies of both previous positions, namely that fruit has *Shemita* sanctity from the first of *Tishrei* of the seventh year until the fifteenth of *Shevat* of the eighth year. A similar approach is adopted by the Ra'avad in his commentary to *Torat Kohanim* (*ibid*).

In practice, Rav Y.M. Tykoczinski (*Sefer ha-Shemita*, chap. 1, note 3) in the name of Rav Chayim Berlin rules stringently, following the Ra'avad and the Rash. On the other hand, the *Minchat Chinuch* (*mitzva* 328, 4) and the *Pe'at ha-Shulchan* (22:9) rule in accordance with the Rambam, that the laws of *Shemita* apply to fruit that reaches the stage of ***chanata* between the first of *Tishrei* of the seventh year and the first of *Tishrei* of the eighth year**. Both Rav Kook (*Shabbat ha-Aretz* 4, 9) and the *Chazon Ish* (7, 13) decided the law in accordance with the *Minchat Chinuch*. The *Chazon Ish* formulated this as follows:

> It seems that with respect to *Shemita*, the year regarding trees is determined by *Rosh ha-Shana* [the 1st of *Tishrei*] and not by the fifteenth of *Shevat*... Just as the prohibitions of plowing and planting apply from *Rosh ha-Shana* to *Rosh ha-Shana*, so too all *Shemita* sanctity depends on the seventh year. Therefore, **fruit that reached *chanata* on the first of *Tishrei* of the seventh year is governed by the laws of *Shemita*, whereas fruit that reached *chanata* on the first of *Tishrei* of the eighth year is permitted**.

According to this, the requirement of **special care** in the handling of fruit that is imbued with ***Shemita* sanctity** only begins in the **second half of the *Shemita* year**, when the fruit that had reached *chanata* after the first of *Tishrei* of the seventh year first comes to market, and **continues into the eighth year**, until all the fruit that reached *chanata* before the first of *Tishrei* of the eighth year disappears from the market.[25]

25. See the appendix to this volume which provides a detailed list of the dates when *Shemita* sanctity applies to each type of fruit.

ETROG AND CITRUS FRUIT:

The Gemara in *Kiddushin* (*3a*) states that, owing to the fact that an *etrog* tree requires constant watering just like vegetables, its tithing year is determined in the same manner as vegetables, namely, according to picking:

> An *etrog* is like a vegetable – just as vegetables grow by all waters [irrigation], and its tithing is determined by the time when it is picked, so too an *etrog* grows by all waters, and [therefore] its tithing is determined by when it is picked.

The *Tosefta* (*Shevi'it,* end of chap. 3) cites the view of "our Rabbis in Usha," who maintain that an *etrog* is treated like a vegetable with respect to *Shemita* as well. Accordingly, an *etrog* that was picked after the first of *Tishrei* of the seventh year has *Shemita* sanctity. The Rambam codified this ruling as follows (*Hilchot Ma'aser Sheni 1:5*):

> Only the *etrog,* of all fruit, has the same rule as a vegetable, and is subject to the time of its picking, in regard to both tithes and the *Shemita* year.[26]

26. For further study see *Kesef Mishne* (*4:12*), Radvaz (*1:5*) and *Chazon Ish* (*7:10*).

On the other hand, the Mishna in *Bikkurim* (*2:6*) states that the critical stage for the *etrog* with respect to *Shemita* is *chanata,* as it is for all other fruit. This is also the conclusion of the *Bavli* (*Rosh ha-Shana 15b*) and most of the *Rishonim,* as is brought by Rav Kook (*Shabbat ha-Aretz 5:12*):[27]

27. It should be noted that the *Chazon Ish's* ruling on this matter is unclear; in one place (*7, 10*) he writes that the custom is to be stringent in accordance with the Rambam. Elsewhere (*21, 16*), however, he rules that one can rely on those *Rishonim* who disagree with the Rambam. Presumably the resolution, as presented below, is that fundamentally the law follows the majority view of *Rishonim* that the determining date is *chanata,* but the preferred practice is to follow the Rambam where his position is more stringent.

> Some authorities say that with respect to an *etrog,* we never follow the picking. Thus, if it reached *chanata* during the

sixth year, it is governed by the laws of sixth year fruit for all purposes, even if it was picked in the seventh year.

It seems that the defining moment for the *etrog* is that of *chanata*, as this seems to be the simple understanding of the conclusion of the Gemara and the majority view among the *Rishonim*. However, this is not entirely clear, and the practice is to be stringent in accordance with the view of the Rambam, observing *Shemita* sanctity for an *etrog* that was picked during *Shemita*.

What is the law governing **other citrus fruit** (oranges, tangerines, lemons, and the like)? Given that these fruits also require great amounts of water, one would think that they should be treated like an *etrog*. However, **both Rav Kook** and the ***Chazon Ish*** ruled leniently, that the determining date for **other citrus fruits** is the time of ***chanata***.

The rationale for this ruling, as implied by the *Chazon Ish* (*21:16, Kuntres Seder Ha-shevi'it, 3*), is based on a combination of factors. First, in principle, even for an *etrog*, we rule that *chanata* is the determining date, despite the fact that we are stringent regarding the *etrog* itself. Given that there is a **doubt** as to whether other citrus fruits should be considered like an *etrog*, this stringency need not apply to other citrus, and they are to be considered like other fruits. (This is similar to the halachic principle of *sfek safeka*, a "double uncertainty" where three of four options lead to leniency.)

Rav Kook also rules leniently, not out of doubt, but rather by a **definitive determination** that other citrus fruits are unlike the *etrog*. Rav Kook investigated and researched the nature of the fruit, and discovered that the *etrog* differs from all other citrus fruit in several ways. One difference is that the *etrog* continues to grow as long as it remains on the tree, as opposed to other citrus fruits, which reach a maximal size and stop growing. Moreover, the *etrog* can reach *chanata* at any time of the year, as opposed to other citrus fruits which reach *chanata* at a particular time of the year (the lemon is also exceptional and similar to an *etrog* in this way).[28] Rav Kook's conclusion is that the growth of other citrus fruits is not a result of the constant water that they receive, but rather due to the sap that

28. Another difference is that other citrus fruits rot when left out excessively after harvest, whereas the ***etrog*** (and lemon) dry out, shrink and harden instead.

rises within them at the time of *chanata*. Accordingly, *chanata* is the determining stage in their growth.

Rav Kook's view on the matter is cited by Rav Tykoczinski, author of *Sefer ha-Shemita,* based on a communication between the two (*p. 11, note 5*):

> The Gaon, Rav Avraham Yitzchak Kook, ztz"l, wrote to me while he was the Rabbi of Yafo and the surrounding farms, that at first he too was in doubt about this matter. But after carefully examining the growth processes of the etrog, the orange and similar species, he came to the understanding that, while with respect to watering the latter are like the etrog, [nevertheless] they are very different from each other: The *etrog* "lives [on the tree] from year to year" and continues to grow as long as it is on the tree... unlike the orange... which, when it reaches its full size, does not continue to grow. With respect to *chanata* as well, the *etrog* is different in that it can reach *chanata* at any time during the year... unlike the orange... and even the lemon, which reaches *chanata* during much of the year, is unlike the *etrog* in this regard. It seems then that the orange and similar species, like other fruits, grow from the sap of the year of *chanata*. Accordingly, he agreed to be lenient about the orange and similar species, and to follow *chanata* exclusively.

Thus, **the halacha is that other citrus fruits are considered like regular fruit, and their status follows the time of *chanata*.**[29]

SUMMARY

1. **Vegetables** – we follow the time of picking. Accordingly, there is *Shemita* sanctity from the very beginning of the seventh year.
2. **Fruit** (including citrus fruit) – we follow *chanata*, and therefore during the first few months of the seventh year, there is no *Shemita* sanctity. The time when the *Shemita* produce begins to reach maturity depends on the type of fruit: some fruits

29. **The law regarding a lemon** is as follows: Based on the agricultural conditions described by Rav Kook, one should be **stringent** regarding a lemon, as it shares many characteristics with an *etrog* (*chanata* throughout the year, drying up and shrinking rather than rotting). And, indeed, the **Rash Sirilio** (*Shevi'it 9:4*, s.v. *Chazor u-zechi bah*) writes that the lemon has the **same law as the etrog**. It would seem that practically one should follow the stringencies of both *chanata* and harvest (at least as much as for an *etrog*), which is the view of **Rav Mordechai Eliyahu** (cited in *Katif Shevi'it, 6:11*). On the other hand, the ***Minchat Shlomo*** (51:22) wrote that one can be lenient and that a lemon should be considered like other citrus fruit, explaining that since the lemon was known in the time of the Rambam, and the Rambam nonetheless wrote that the ***etrog*** is the only exceptional fruit, it is clear that the lemon is to be considered like other citrus fruit: Since this fruit [lemon] was known and available in the time of the Rambam, for he cites it in his medical writings repeatedly (as well as in his introduction to [the

reach *chanata* around the time of *Tu be-Shevat,* and reach the market several months later (for example almonds, loquats, and apples) and therefore they are considered *Shemita* fruit from the middle of the seventh year until the middle of the eighth year. There are other fruits where almost a year passes between *chanata* and harvesting (such as citrus fruit), and therefore these will be *Shemita* fruit only in the eighth year.

3. **Grain and legumes** – we follow the time that they reach a third of their growth. Accordingly, *Shemita* sanctity begins several months into the seventh year.

mishna of] *Seder Taharot,* s.v. *U-ve-tum'at mashkin*), nonetheless he wrote in [his commentary to the mishna of] the first chapter of *Ma'aser sheni* (Mishna 5) that the only fruit that follows harvest is the *etrog,* adding the word "only," which is absent in the Gemara. It seems [clear] that, regarding the lemon, we follow the time of the *chanata* rather than the time of harvest like the *etrog.*

RAV TYKOCZINSKI [*Sefer ha-Shemita*]

Rav Yechiel Michel Tykoczinski (died 1956) was a master halachist who was also a great codifier of the customs practiced in Eretz Yisrael, in a book titled "*Sefer Eretz Yisrael*". He also published a calendar in which he clarified the various laws and practices for each time of the year (this calendar is still reissued annually by his son). He also authored a work titled "*Gesher Ha-Chayim*" which is central to the laws of mourning. Rav Tykoczinski dealt extensively with determining the halachic times of the day, and wrote a book on the topic titled "*Bein ha-Shemashot*". He also dealt with matters pertaining to Jerusalem and the Temple, writing a series of books titled, "*Ir ha-Kodesh ve-ha-Mikdash.*" Rav Tykoczinski also wrote a book on Shemita titled "*Sefer ha-Shemita,*" in which he details the practical halacha for Shemita, including an extensive treatment of the *heter mechira.* He wrote of Rav Kook with great respect, citing his rulings numerous times in his own works.

Rav Tykoczinski was the *rosh yeshiva* of Yeshivat Etz Chayim in Jerusalem.

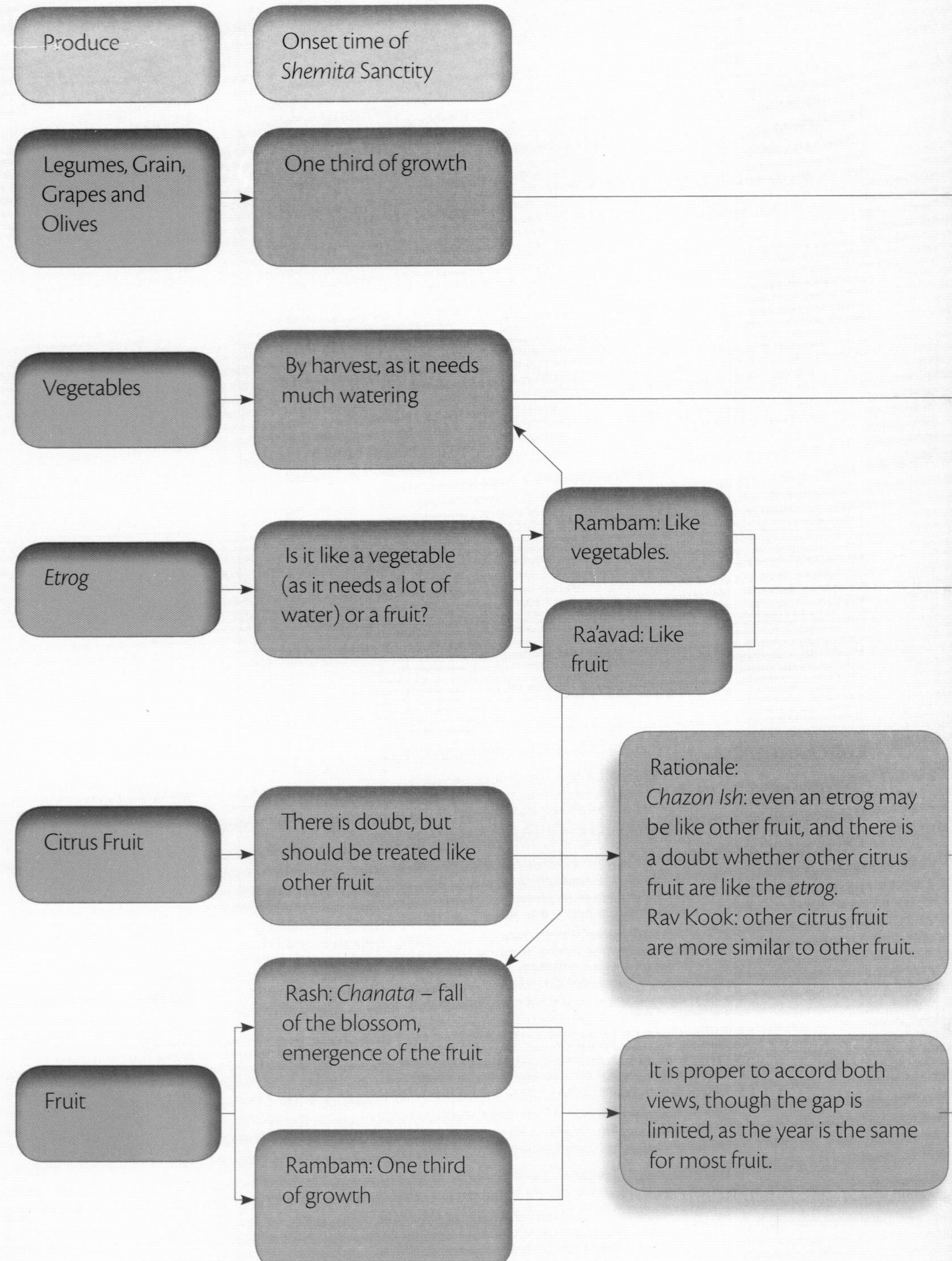
When does *Shemita* sanctity take effect?
Produce
Onset time of *Shemita* Sanctity
Legumes, Grain, Grapes and Olives
One third of growth
Vegetables
By harvest, as it needs much watering
Etrog
Is it like a vegetable (as it needs a lot of water) or a fruit?
Rambam: Like vegetables.
Ra'avad: Like fruit
Citrus Fruit
There is doubt, but should be treated like other fruit
Rationale: *Chazon Ish*: even an etrog may be like other fruit, and there is a doubt whether other citrus fruit are like the *etrog*. Rav Kook: other citrus fruit are more similar to other fruit.
Fruit
Rash: *Chanata* – fall of the blossom, emergence of the fruit
Rambam: One third of growth
It is proper to accord both views, though the gap is limited, as the year is the same for most fruit.

The time this produce is in the market

If it grew to one third between *Rosh Ha-shana* and 29 *Elul* (otherwise it lacks sanctity).

From the latter part of *Shemita* until the latter part of the eighth year

If it was harvested between *Rosh Ha-shana* and 29 *Elul*

From the beginning of *Shemita* until the first months of the eighth year

We try to accord both views, so an *etrog* that had *chanata* or was picked during *Shemita* has *Shemita* sanctity.

From the beginning of *Shemita* until Iyar of the eighth year

The law of citrus fruit is like other fruit. (some adopt stringency for the harvest year of lemons).

From the end of *Shemita* (or the beginning of the eighth year) until the beginning of the ninth year

Rabbenu Chananel: fruit that had *chanata* between *Tu bi-Shvat* of Shemita and *Tu bi-Shvat* of the eighth year.

From the latter months of *Shemita* (around *Iyar*) until the latter months of the eighth year

Implication of the Rambam: fruit that had *chanata* (one-third growth) from 1 *Tishrei* until 29 *Elul* of *Shemita*.

This is the halacha

SHEMITA SANCTITY FOR TREES THAT DO NOT BEAR FRUIT

All agree that produce can have *Shemita* sanctity even if it is only fit for animal consumption (Rambam, *Hilchot Shemita ve-Yovel 7:13*). What is the law regarding trees that do not bear any fruit at all?

As a rule, *Shemita* sanctity does not apply to trees that do not bear fruit. The Gemara in *Sukka* (*40a*; as well as *Bava Kama 101b-102a*) explains that *Shemita* sanctity applies to produce "that gives benefit at the same time as it is consumed," and therefore trees that do not serve as food but only as firewood, and provide benefit only after they have been consumed by the fire and turned into coals, have no *Shemita* sanctity:

> Wood does not have *Shemita* sanctity, as it was taught: "Leaves of reeds and leaves of the vine which were heaped up in the field, have *Shemita* sanctity if they were gathered for [animal] food. But if they were gathered for firewood, they do not have *Shemita* sanctity... since the Torah says: 'For you for food' (*Vayikra 25:6*) – thus comparing 'for you' to 'for food,' namely, that [produce is sanctified] when the benefit comes at the time of consumption; firewood is excluded since its benefit comes after its consumption."

Based on this logic, plants used as dyes do have *Shemita* sanctity, because the plants are consumed and the dyes are absorbed in the fabric at the same time. For the same reason, plants used for providing illumination also have *Shemita* sanctity, because the benefit occurs as the plant is consumed (Rashi, *Sukka 40a*).[30]

One might also suggest that wood which is meant for home construction or furniture making should have *Shemita* sanctity, for its benefit does not follow its consumption (as the wood is not destroyed in the construction). Nevertheless, the *Chazon Ish* claims

30. The *Tosafot* write (ad loc.) that if the wood is meant to be used for firewood, it does not have *Shemita* sanctity, even if it is also used for illumination.

that since this wood is not consumed but used while intact, it has no *Shemita* sanctity (*13, 8*).

Medicinal plants (where the plant is only used for treating the sick) do not have *Shemita* sanctity, because they provide benefit solely to sick people, and the Gemara in *Sukka* asserts that *Shemita* sanctity only attaches to produce that provides benefit to all people (following Rashi and *Tosafot, Sukka 40a; Minchat Yitzchak*, vol. VIII, no. *101; Kehilat Ya'akov, Zera'im 5, 2*).[31] Spices, on the other hand, do have *Shemita* sanctity (Rambam, *Hilchot Shemita ve-Yovel 5:22*).

31. For this reason, if such plants are meant to benefit healthy people as well, they do have *Shemita* sanctity. If the plants are **meant to provide food**, they have full *Shemita* sanctity and may not be used for medicinal uses (as explained later in this chapter).

FLOWERS

What are the rules for buying flowers during *Shemita*?

It seems to be explicitly stated in the Mishna (*Shevi'it 7:6*) that flowers have *Shemita* sanctity:

> *Shemita* sanctity applies to the rose, henna, balsam and the lotus trees and to the money used to purchase them.

The Mishna specifically mentions that a rose has *Shemita* sanctity. A rose is not food but rather a flower, so it seems clear that flowers have *Shemita* sanctity.

The **Yerushalmi** (*7:1*) questions whether **perfumes** have *Shemita* sanctity:

> Do perfumes have *Shemita* sanctity? Let us prove it from the following: "The *lavan* flower and the *orez* flower do not have *Shemita* sanctity..." Rabbi Shmuel said in the name of Rabbi Abahu: this is like the odorless flowers that grow in the area of Nesorta.[32]"

Fragrant spices are subject to sanctity.

The *Yerushalmi* questions whether perfumes have *Shemita* sanctity. It tries to find an answer from the case of the *lavan* flower

32. This translation is based on the explanation of Rash Sirilio.

which has no sanctity. Yet it rejects this proof, arguing that the *lavan* flower may be an **odorless** white flower, like the one that grows in Nesorta. But a flower that has an odor could have sanctity.

It is difficult to understand what leads to the *Yerushalmi*'s question, for we have seen that the **Mishna** clearly states that a rose – a scented flower – has *Shemita* sanctity.

The ***Chazon Ish*** (*Shevi'it 14:9,* s.v. *ve-ha di-tnan*) explains this as follows:

> That which is taught in the Mishna, "*Shemita* sanctity applies to the rose, henna, balsam and the lotus trees," which are fragrant spices, as explained by Rashi (*Nida 8a*), does not prove that there is *Shemita* sanctity to all fragrant spices, for these have taste as well as odor!

In other words, the **Mishna** speaks of a rose that is not only a spice but also a food – this is a rose that is put into a dish (perhaps to add flavor or odor to the food), and this is why it has *Shemita* sanctity, but regular spices lack *Shemita* sanctity.[33]

In light of this, **Rav Wosner** writes in the ***Responsa Shevet Ha-levi*** (*part II, 202*) :

> Regarding the question of *Shemita* sanctity in fragrant plants and flowers there are three categories. One category is of roses and similar flowers that are intended for both flavor and taste. A second is fragrant plants that have no function other than their

33. What is the underlying issue in the question of the *Yerushalmi*? Presumably the approach that there is *Shemita* sanctity in fragrant spices is difficult, as their **benefit precedes their consumption**, and we have seen that *Shemita* sanctity only applies to items similar to foods in that their **benefit and consumption are simultaneous** (for the fruit is consumed at the time of the benefit, the eating).
Rabbi Shlomo Sirilio (*Yerushalmi, Shevi'it 8:1*) explains that the Gemara might mean that *Shemita* sanctity does not apply to produce if the benefit is derived after the produce is consumed (as in the case of firewood, where the benefit derived from the coals comes only after the wood itself has been consumed). But if the benefit arrives before the produce is consumed, as in the case of flowers where the benefit provided by their scent arrives before the flowers are consumed (and the consumption is unrelated to the benefit), the Gemara agrees that *Shemita* sanctity applies to it. The Rash Sirilio's distinction may be understood as follows: when the benefit arrives after the produce is consumed, the person does not derive benefit from the produce itself, but from something new – that which is formed in the wake of the consumption of the produce. Therefore, the produce itself is not defined as standing for human use, and thus it has no *Shemita* sanctity. On the other hand, when the benefit and the consumption coincide, or alternatively when the benefit precedes the consumption, the person benefits from the *Shemita* produce itself and therefore *Shemita* sanctity applies to it. The *Ba'al ha-Ma'or* (on *Sukka 40a*) offers a similar distinction: "In the case of *lulav*, benefit is derived from it prior to its consumption, and this follows all the more so from the case of produce, the **benefit** from which comes **at the time** of its consumption." Rashi (ad loc.) implies, however, that only if the benefit and consumption coincide is there *Shemita* sanctity (see also *Chiddushei Rabbi Akiva Eiger, Bava Kama 101b*). (According to Rashi, we must say that a rose has *Shemita* sanctity because it can be eaten for its aroma and flavor and thus, like any other food, the benefit derived from it comes at the same time as its consumption.) The Rash Sirilio explains that this is precisely the doubt raised by the *Yerushalmi*: whether fragrant spices are considered to have concurrent benefit and consumption. The *Chazon Ish* explained that the *Yerushalmi*'s question is whether or not the enjoyment of the scent is a benefit shared by all people. The **Mishna** itself (according to the *Chazon Ish's* explanation) speaks of edible spices, from which benefit is derived as they are consumed.

scent. A third category is odorless, ornamental flowers that are purely decorative.

Rav Wosner continues to explain the law governing each type of flower:

> As for roses, [the Mishna] states that they have *Shemita* sanctity; as for flowers that have no scent, the *Yerushalmi* concludes that they have no *Shemita* sanctity; and as for flowers that have a scent, it is "a question that was not resolved," and owing to the uncertainty, it seems that in practice one should be stringent.

Based on these sources, it seems that fragrant plants that can be used as seasonings, like roses, have *Shemita* sanctity, and these are the flowers addressed in the Mishna. Odorless flowers have **no *Shemita* sanctity**, and therefore the *Yerushalmi* states that the *lavan* flower has no *Shemita* sanctity.[34] As for flowers that have a scent, the *Yerushalmi* does not decide the matter, and it stands to reason that one should be stringent.[35]

Decorative, scented flowers (not marketed for their scent)

The *Shevet ha-Levi*'s ruling regarding flowers that have a scent was accepted by other Acharonim as well (*Sefer ha-Shemita*, chap. 7, letter 4, no. 5; Rav Elyashiv, whose view is cited in *Mishpetei Aretz*, p. 118, no. 10), but not by all authorities. Rav Eliezer Waldenberg in his *Responsa Tzitz Eliezer* (vol. VI, no. 33), for example, rules leniently regarding the case questioned in the *Yerushalmi*, as neither the *Bavli* nor the Rambam mention it, ruling that even scented flowers have no *Shemita* sanctity. Rav Sh. Z. Auerbach (cited in *Mishpetei Aretz, Shevi'it*, 14, no. 10; see also *Ma'adanei Aretz, kovetz he'arot*, 8,

34. [It seems that the reason that *Shemita* sanctity does not attach to flowers that have no scent is that mere decorative use is not regarded as use (*Sefer ha-Shemita*, chap. 7, letter 4, no. 7; *Minchat Shlomo* 51, 10 at end and no. 23).]

35. Thus, the *Yerushalmi* does not contradict the Mishna. The Mishna discusses flowers that are used to season food, while the *Yerushalmi* deals with inedible flowers. Furthermore, the *Yerushalmi* may be dealing with flowers that are not widely used, thus their use is not universal and they lack sanctity on that count as well (see the ***Responsa*** *Tzitz Eli'ezer* ibid).

Odorless flowers: no sanctity.

11), agrees that scented flowers have *Shemita* sanctity, but he qualifies this ruling by saying that flowers that are primarily decorative have no *Shemita* sanctity even if they are scented:

Rav Sh. Z. Auerbach rules that ornamental flowers have no *Shemita* sanctity, for today their primary use is decoration.[36]

However, Rav Auerbach agrees that spices and perfumes have *Shemita* sanctity, as their main function is for scent.

36. Rav Sh. Z. Auerbach explains that the author of the *Sefer ha-Shemita* may have omitted this qualification, because in his day flowers served primarily for their scent.

SUMMARY

1. Flowers that also serve as seasonings have *Shemita* sanctity.
2. Odorless flowers do not have *Shemita* sanctity.
3. Scented flowers have *Shemita* sanctity according to the *Shevet ha-Levi* and Rav Elyashiv, whereas according to Rav Sh. Z. Auerbach, only have *Shemita* sanctity if they serve primarily as fragrance, and are not simply for ornamental purposes. According to Rav Eliezer Waldenberg, even flowers that serve primarily for fragrance have *Shemita* sanctity.

These laws have important ramifications when buying flowers during the *Shemita* year. We will deal with this issue below.

What is the **determining stage** for the *Shemita* sanctity of **scented flowers** (according to those who say they have it)? For a flower that grows on a perennial plant, the determining stage is the blossoming (*Be-tzet ha-shana* page *48*). For annuals, the determining stage is their picking (*Chazon Ish, 14:9,* s.v. *u-vi-tshuvat*).[37]

37. What is the determining date for branches that are used for scent or seasoning? The *Chazon Ish* (*7:16, 19:23*) wrote that it is difficult to ascertain the defining moment for these. Rav Mordechai Eliyahu maintains that it follows the sprouting of the branch, in which case branches that sprouted during the sixth year and were picked during *Shemita* would not have ***Shemita*** sanctity (see *Katif Shevi'it*, section 6, page 29).

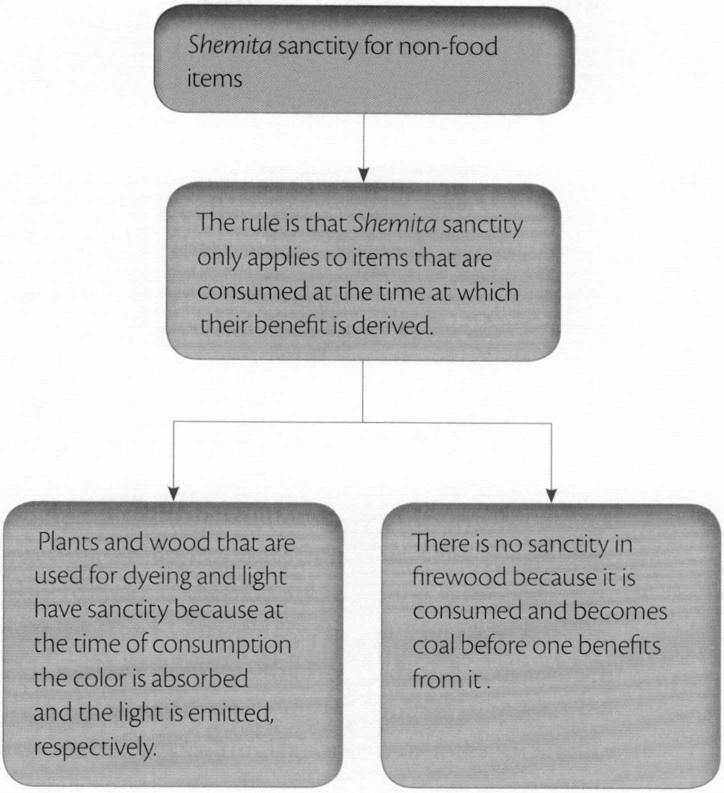

Shemita sanctity for non-food items

The rule is that *Shemita* sanctity only applies to items that are consumed at the time at which their benefit is derived.

Plants and wood that are used for dyeing and light have sanctity because at the time of consumption the color is absorbed and the light is emitted, respectively.

There is no sanctity in firewood because it is consumed and becomes coal before one benefits from it .

RAV WOSNER [*Shevet ha-Levi*]

Rav Wosner was born in Vienna in 1913. He was a student of Rav Meir Shapiro of Lublin. He moved to Israel before the Shoah where he became a student of the *Chazon Ish*. He wrote an important series of halachic works – Responsa *Shevet ha-Levi* (10 volumes) and is one of the leading *Posekim* of our generation. He established the Yeshiva "*Chachmei Lublin*" to commemorate the Yeshiva of his teacher.

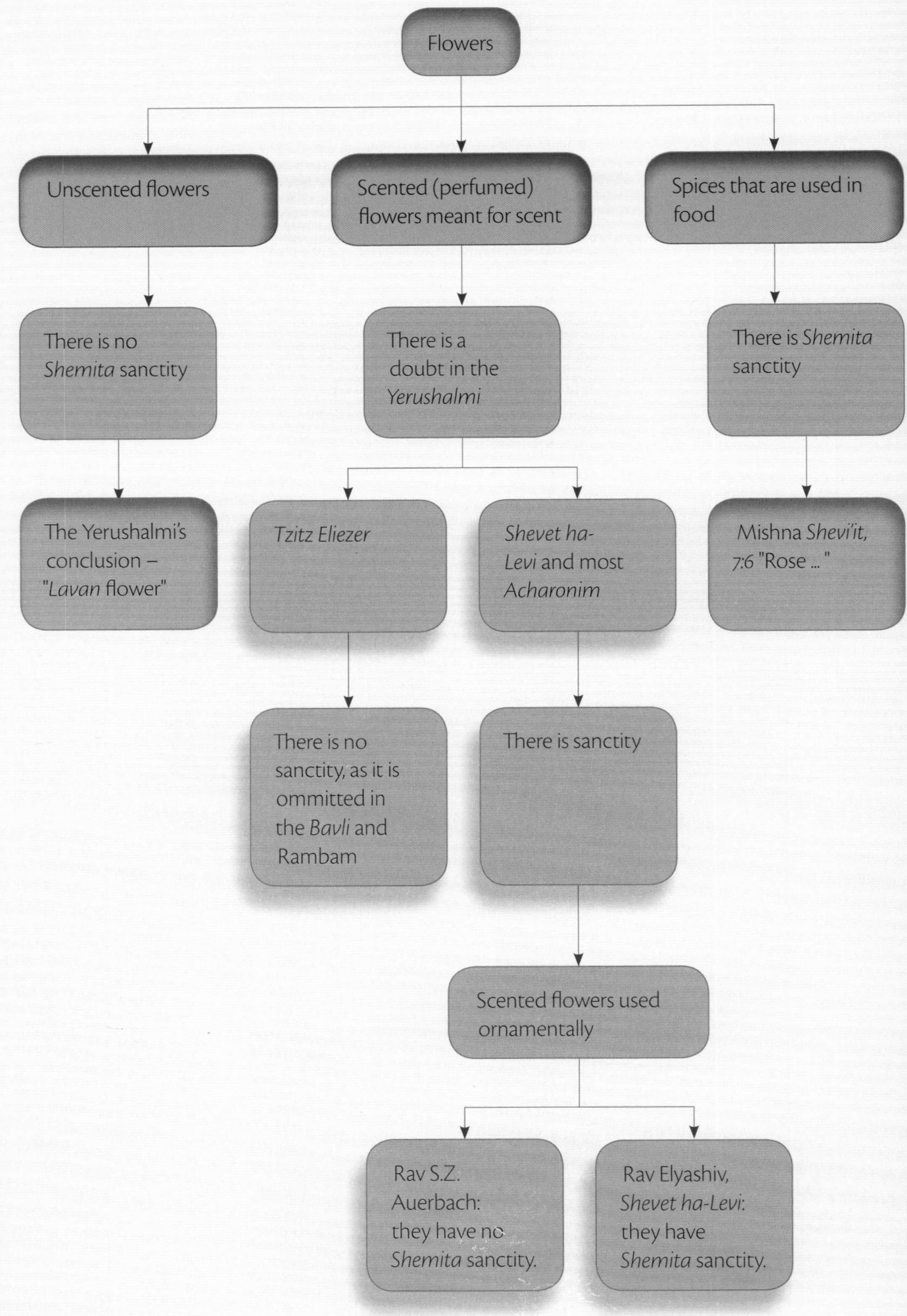
Flowers
Unscented flowers
Scented (perfumed) flowers meant for scent
Spices that are used in food
There is no *Shemita* sanctity
There is a doubt in the *Yerushalmi*
There is *Shemita* sanctity
The Yerushalmi's conclusion – "*Lavan* flower"
Tzitz Eliezer
Shevet ha-Levi and most *Acharonim*
Mishna *Shevi'it*, 7:6 "Rose ... "
There is no sanctity, as it is ommitted in the *Bavli* and Rambam
There is sanctity
Scented flowers used ornamentally
Rav S.Z. Auerbach: they have no *Shemita* sanctity.
Rav Elyashiv, *Shevet ha-Levi*: they have *Shemita* sanctity.

SHEMITA SANCTITY FOR VARIOUS TYPES OF PRODUCE

During the *Shemita* year various types of fruits and vegetables reach the markets: *Otzar Bet Din* produce, sixth-year produce, produce grown hydroponically, produce grown using the *heter mechira* and produce grown by gentiles. In the coming chapters we will provide complete explanations for each of these solutions; here we wish to examine which of these types of produce have *Shemita* sanctity.

1. *Otzar Bet Din* produce certainly has *Shemita* sanctity, as does produce grown in a person's own garden.
2. Produce grown hydroponically, in the manner that is common today, does not have *Shemita* sanctity.
3. Sixth-year produce does not have *Shemita* sanctity.
4. In the chapter dealing with the renunciation of ownership of *Shemita* produce we dealt with the disagreement between the *Bet Yosef* and the *Mabit* regarding whether or not *Shemita* sanctity applies to produce grown by non-Jews. The view of the *Bet Yosef*, that they lack sanctity, was accepted in Jerusalem and in most of the communities of Israel [in accordance with the ruling of Rav Kook (*Shabbat ha-Aretz,* introduction, chap. *11;* chap. *4,* hal. *29; Mishpat Kohen,* no. *70*), Rav Sh. Z. Auerbach (*Ma'adanei Aretz, 2,* s.v. *hine*), Rav T. P. Frank (*Har Tzvi, Zera'im,* vol. *II,* no. *39*) and Rav O. Yosef (*Responsa Yabi'a Omer,* vol. *III, Yoreh De'ah,* no. *19*)[38]]. Accordingly, we do not treat the produce of non-Jews as having *Shemita* sanctity. In contrast, in Bnei Brak, where the *Chazon Ish* lived, the ruling of the *Chazon Ish* (*20, 7; 9, 18*) in favor of the *Mabit,* that gentile produce has *Shemita* sanctity, has been widely accepted.
5. Produce grown in reliance on the *heter mechira* does not have *Shemita* sanctity [becaus the use of such produce is based on the assumption that non-Jewish ownership cancels the sanctity of the land, so that a Jew is permitted to work the land belonging to a non-Jew during the sabbatical year. By strict law, then, those who rely on the *heter mechira* are not required to treat such produce as having *Shemita* sanctity] (*Shabbat ha-Aretz 8, 8,* letter *5*). Nevertheless, Rav Kook writes that it is proper to be stringent and treat this produce

38. Rav Ovadya Yosef rules that one is forbidden to treat produce grown on land owned by gentiles as having *Shemita* sanctity, because the *Bet Yosef* proclaimed a ban on anyone who does not act in accordance with his ruling (*Respona Avkat Rochel*, end of no. 25. What is stated there, however, relates to the stringency that one must set aside *teruma* and *ma'asrot* from such produce; see also *Responsa Mishpat Kohen*, no. 70).

as if it had *Shemita* sanctity [because the *heter mechira* had originally been established only for times of great need, and therefore it should not be relied upon when not absolutely necessary (*Mishpat Kohen 67, 75, 76; Iggerot Ra'aya,* vol. *1, 310, 312, 318,* and elsewhere). We shall return to Rav Kook's position below.]

REGARDING *SHABBAT HA-ARETZ*

The work "*Shabbat ha-Aretz*" was written by Rav Kook zt"l. It was organized based upon the chapter of *Shemita* and *Yovel* of the Rambam. In this work Rav Kook surveys the different views, adding depth and sharpening the understanding of the respective viewpoints and provides a bottom line halachic ruling. Rav Zevin wrote the following about "*Shabat ha-Aretz*" (in his work "*Ishim ve-Shitot*", page 228): "In his work *Shabbat ha-Aretz,* Rav Kook delved into and expanded upon the principles and nuances of the matter, leaving neither anything great or small of the laws of *Shemita* without proper clarification."

This work makes clear that Rav Kook is not lenient in the laws of *Shemita.* On the contrary, he is very stringent on many matters of *Shemita* even beyond the *Chazon Ish* and other *Posekim.*

Shabbat ha-Aretz was reissued in 1993 in a new printing by the *Machon Ha-Torah ve-ha-Aretz,* which added comments and sources that enhance the study of the work.

In this work Rav Kook strengthened the *heter mechira,* which had been established earlier, as we will discuss below.

Rav Kook also included an important philosophic introduction to *Shabbat ha-Aretz,* in which he addressed the significance of *Shemita,* at the end of which he addressed the underlying understanding of the *heter mechira* as well.

While Rav Kook's philosophic writings are notoriously and uniquely difficult to comprehend, while writing his halachic writings he worked hard to assure clarity of language, as indicated by Rav Zevin (ibid):

> *Shabbat ha-Aretz is* a precious gem in halachic literature generally, and in the *Shemita* literature specifically.... There is no comparison between Rav Kook's style in *Shabbat ha-Aretz* ... and his style in his philosophic writing. In his philosophic works, Rav Kook utilizied a literary style that is beautiful, bold and difficult to comprehend. In halacha, on the other hand, his style is clear and cogent, and the style of presentation is straightforward and readily comprehensible.

THE LAWS OF PRODUCE WITH *SHEMITA* SANCTITY: NAVIGATING THE OPPORTUNITY

WHAT MUST BE DONE WITH TRIMMINGS AND LEFTOVERS?

ALLOWING *SHEMITA* PRODUCE TO BE LOST

The Gemara in *Pesachim* (*52b*) states:

> The Torah said: "The Sabbath produce of the land shall be food for you" (*Vayikra 25:6*) – for food, but not for destruction.

We see from here that one is permitted to eat *Shemita* produce, but not to destroy or waste it. It seems that this prohibition is due to the sanctity of the produce. Another explanation could also be suggested: as we have seen, one of the central, underlying principles of *Shemita* is the notion that **man is not the owner of the land; rather, God is.** When a person rents or borrows an object he has no right to destroy it, despite his permission to make use of it. Only the owner has the right to destroy objects that belong to him, not the renter or borrower. Thus, there is no greater sign of ownership than the permissibility to destroy an object. Given that during the *Shemita* year the produce is not the property of its human "owner," he has no right to destroy it.[39]

What then should be done with the trimmings and leftovers of *Shemita* produce? Of course one should try to eat as much of the *Shemita* produce as possible, and thus to minimize leftovers. We shall try to explain the laws pertaining to *Shemita* leftovers that will not be eaten in any event.

Generally speaking, one is permitted to discard leftovers that are unfit to be eaten by throwing them into an ordinary garbage can. The prohibition against destroying *Shemita* produce applies only to leftovers that are still fit for human or animal consumption.

What then should be done with leftovers that cannot be thrown into the garbage? The halachic solution for such leftovers is to set aside a special receptacle for saving produce that has Shemita sanctity. *Shemita* leftovers should be emptied into this receptacle and allowed to remain there until they rot,[40] and once they are no

39. I heard this explanation from my teacher and father-in-law, Rav Blumenzweig, shlita. This may also be the reason for the prohibition of "*bal tashchit*," which forbids destroying anything unnecessarily, for all property is ultimately God's (in most years the prohibition is only to destroy unnecessarily). The heightened sensitivity of *Shemita* should raise our awareness not to destroy food in subsequent years as well.

40. Allowing the leftovers to spoil is not regarded as destroying the produce, because they spoil on their own (*Mishpat Kohen* 95; *Chazon Ish* 14, 10. This solution is also brought in *Kuntrus Seder Shevi'it* (Rav. Z. Shapiro), letter 8; *Brit Olam* 5, 12; and *Chut ha-Shani, Shemita* 265).

longer fit for human consumption they may be thrown into an ordinary garbage can. It is advisable that this receptacle should be clearly marked as containing produce that has "*Shemita* sanctity," so as not to confuse it with an ordinary garbage can. So, too, the bag should be switched on a daily basis, so that one not throw today's leftovers which are still fit to be eaten into a bag filled with yesterday's leftovers which have already begun to rot, and thus actively contribute to the spoilage of today's leftovers.[41] When switching the bags, the previous day's bag should be set aside and when the food therein is thoroughly spoiled, it may be thrown into an ordinary garbage can.[42]

Various *Acharonim* bring the solution proposed above. For example, the *Mishpetei Aretz* (23, 2) writes as follows:

> The common practice is to designate a special receptacle for *Shemita* leftovers. Each day's leftovers are placed in a separate plastic bag, with all the bags kept in that receptacle until the leftovers have spoiled, at which time they may be thrown into the [ordinary] garbage.

Some people write on the receptacle set aside for *Shemita* leftovers "*pach Shemita,*" "*Shemita* garbage can." While it is true that the receptacle into which we throw our leftovers is generally referred to as a "garbage" can, in this context the term should be avoided. The leftovers under discussion are sacred produce of the *Shemita* year and

41. It stands to reason that one who throws *Shemita* produce into an ordinary garbage is regarded as actively destroying *Shemita* produce, and not merely as one who indirectly causes the destruction of such produce. See below regarding the indirect destruction of *Shemita* produce (see *Mishpetei Aretz* 5760, 21, note 5).

42. What is regarded as "spoiled"? According to Rav Kook (*Shabbat ha-Aretz* 7, 13), *Shemita* produce may not be destroyed even if the leftovers are only fit for animal consumption. Leftovers may only be discarded in an ordinary garbage once they are deemed unfit for animals. The *Chazon Ish* (14, 10, s.v. *ve-nir'e*), in contrast, writes that produce which most people do not use to feed animals loses its sanctity when it is not edible. In his opinion, produce that is not meant to be eaten by animals is considered to be spoiled as soon as it is no longer fit for human consumption (see also *Responsa Minchat Shlomo*, vol. III, 132, 10, who writes that if peels are not ordinarily fed to animals in a particular locality, leniency may be adopted). In practice, since, in any event, we place the leftovers in a separate bag, and technically such a bag can be thrown directly into the garbage (as will be explained below), one may be lenient. Accordingly, after several days have passed, and it is clear that the leftovers are no longer fit for human consumption, the bag may be thrown into an ordinary garbage can.

Suggestion: to emphasize the presence of sanctity, one should acquire a nice utensil (such as pottery) and write on it in a respectful way, "*kedushat shevi'it,*" "*Shemita* sanctity," and to place *Shemita* leftovers in a plastic bag in the utensil. In this way, we will not have two garbage cans (one for regular garbage and one for *Shemita* garbage), but rather an understanding that **we have been privileged to eat *Shemita*-sanctified produce**, such that we are even careful about the leftovers.

illustration on the pot: Ruth Greenberg

not ordinary garbage. The formulation we use has significance, and when the receptacle that we use is marked "*kedushat shevi'it,*" "*Shemita* sanctity," we will be constantly reminded that we are dealing with sacred produce.[43] For this reason, it seems that it would be most preferable to place the leftovers on a plate or in a bucket, and not into a container similar to a garbage can, so that it should be clear even to others that we are not dealing with ordinary refuse.

Another solution for leftovers is to put them into a bag, tie the bag shut,[44] and then throw it into the ordinary garbage.[45]

Even though this solution is commonly used even as a first choice for produce bearing the sanctity of *terumot* and *ma'asrot*, it might be problematic when applied to *Shemita* produce, for in this manner we hasten the destruction of the produce (when it is later thrown into the community garbage

43. I heard this suggestion from my revered teacher and father-in-law, Rav Blumenzweig, *shlita*.

44. Despite the fact that by sealing the bag, we accelerate the spoiling process, this is not a problem, for this falls into the category of *geram hefsed*, indirectly causing destruction (Rav Sh. Z. Auerbach, cited in *Hilchot Shemita*, at the end of *Kitzur Shulchan Aruch*, Blum; Rav Elyashiv, cited in *Peirot Shevi'it*, 19, note 9; *Responsa Az Nidberu*, vol. IV, no. 53). We shall deal with *geram hefsed* below.

45. See below, the testimony of Rav Chayim Kanievski, *shlita*, that this was the practice in the past. This is also the ruling that Rav Neuwirth issued to the students of the Kol Torah Yeshiva (*Halichot Sade*, 50, p. 17). Rav Wosner (cited in *Peirot Shevi'it*, 19, note 1) also writes that while preferably one should designate a special receptacle for *Shemita* produce, when necessary it is permissible even *lechatchila* to place the leftovers in a bag and throw the bag into the ordinary garbage.

bin, or the like), and thus we indirectly contribute to their spoilage.[46] Another problem with this solution is that it places a "stumbling block" before the sanitation workers, who compress the bags of garbage in their trucks, and thus they too indirectly contribute to the spoilage of the sacred produce.

Despite these problems, anyone who wishes to take advantage of this second solution may do so. There are several justifications for leniency on this issue:

1. While it is true that throwing the sacred leftovers into an ordinary garbage can hastens their spoiling, we are talking about *geram hefsed*, indirect destruction of the *Shemita* produce, and we will see later that the Posekim debate whether it is permissible to allow this. Rav Elyashiv (cited in *Mishpetei Aretz, 5760, 21*, note 25) maintains that the underlying rationale of those who forbid direct destruction is not the destruction itself, but rather because the produce will not be eaten:

   > It is reasonable to claim that *geram hefsed* (even according to those who prohibit it) is only forbidden if the produce could have been eaten. But there is no prohibition to cause food that was meant to go to waste to go to waste, because *geram hefsed* is not forbidden on account of the act itself, but only because it precludes the [attainment of the] objective for which the produce stands [consumption].

   Thus, according to Rav Elyashiv, produce that clearly will not be eaten is not subject to the prohibition of *geram hefsed*.[47] Thus there is no problem with indirectly causing the food to become spoiled when putting the bag immediately into the garbage, because in any event the leftovers will not be eaten.
2. Even according to the first solution - setting aside a special receptacle for leftover produce having *Shemita* sanctity - we usually have to rely on those authorities who are lenient about *geram hefsed* of *Shemita* produce. This is because even if we

46. *Terumot* and *ma'asrot* may be thrown into the garbage without problem, because by strict law they should be burned, and placing them in the garbage is regarded as burial (they must be wrapped so as to be treated in a respectful manner). In addition, regarding *terumot* and *ma'asrot* there is concern that if one leaves them to rot, one might come to eat them, and therefore it is preferable to eliminate them as quickly as possible (*Chazon Ish* 5, 10; and see also *Mishpetei Aretz, Shevi'it* 23, note 2).

47. This notion is also discussed by Rav Tzvi Pesach Frank (*Har Tzvi, Zera'im*, vol. II, 54).

switch the bags every day, it is likely that mixing all the various leftovers in the same receptacle will indirectly cause the spoilage of at least some of them. From this perspective, the second solution has a certain advantage, because each set of leftovers is discarded in a separate bag.

It is reported in the name of Rav C. Kanievski (*Peirot Shevi'it 19,* note *1*) that there was a time when people would wrap their *Shemita* leftovers and throw them into the garbage, in accordance with the second solution, but today "the generation has improved" and it has become customary to set aside a special receptacle:

> At first, people would treat *Shemita* produce in the same manner as they would treat *teruma* produce, wrapping it and throwing it into the garbage. The truth is that this suffices, but the generation has improved, and it is [now] customary to place it in a special receptacle.

As stated above, the first solution has the additional advantage that it does not create a "stumbling block" for **sanitation workers**. It should be noted that there are times that the first solution is also more convenient, because it involves only one bag per day, and there is no need to find a new bag for each set of leftovers.[48]

To summarize, strictly speaking, one may put sacred *Shemita* leftovers into a bag, tie it closed and place it in an ordinary garbage can. Those who wish to discard their leftovers in the most preferable manner, should set aside a special receptacle for leftovers having *Shemita* sanctity, line it with a bag that will receive all of the day's *Shemita* leftovers (aside from liquid materials which should be bagged separately), and the next day replace the old bag with a new bag for the new leftovers. The old bag should be thrown out several days later (after the produce has decayed).

Even one who wishes to be stringent and follow the first solution may, when necessary, follow the second solution, as it is in consonance with the basic law.

48. Even according to the second solution, it is possible to set aside a special receptacle into which a new bag is inserted every day, and at the end of the day to throw that bag into the regular garbage can.

INDIRECTLY CAUSING THE SPOILAGE OF *SHEMITA* PRODUCE

Thus far we have seen that it is forbidden to destroy *Shemita* produce. The question arises whether it is also forbidden to indirectly cause their destruction (*geram hefsed*). The *Maharit* (vol. *1*, no. *83*) maintains that *geram hefsed* of *Shemita* produce is permitted. He brings three proofs for his position, including a passage in the *Yerushalmi* (*Shevi'it 7:2*) which states that it is permitted to place *Shemita* vegetables on the roof, even though this will cause them to dry out and become ruined:

> [One is permitted to engage in a certain activity that will cause *Shemita* fruit to dry up and fall from the tree, because] this does not fall into the category of "for food, but not for destruction," since it is indirect destruction and one does not destroy the fruit directly. This can be proven from the *Yerushalmi*: "Vegetables may be brought up to the roof, where they will dry out by themselves."

The Ridbaz (*Bet Ridbaz, 5, 1*), also permits *geram hefsed* of *Shemita* produce, but the *Mishmeret ha-Bayit* commentary on the Ridbaz, and other *Acharonim,* forbid this. The *Chazon Ish* (*14, 1*) adds that the *Yerushalmi* should not be relied upon as grounds for leniency because the *Yerushalmi* deals with vegetables that are unfit for human

RABBI YOSEF TARANI (*The Maharit*)

Son of Rabbi Moshe Tarani (the *Mabit*). He was born in Tzfat in 1578 and served as *rosh yeshiva* there. When he was thirty he left for Kushta where he served as *rosh yeshiva*, and then as the Rabbi of Turkey.

The *Maharit* wrote several important works, the most famous of which is Responsa *Maharit*. This contains many important responsa on a variety of topics, including the *mitzva* of *Shemita* and other agricultural *mitzvot*.

He also wrote a commentary on the Talmud and published sermons.

consumption, and drying them out on the roof actually improves their taste and makes them fit for animal consumption.

In practice, there is no clear consensus among the *Acharonim*, though many do in fact allow *geram hefsed*[49] (see above, where the possibility is raised that in the case of leftovers that are to be eliminated anyway, all agree that *geram hefsed* is permitted).[50]

49. An allowance is found in *Sefer ha-Shemita* (7, 3), *Torat ha-Aretz* (8, 37-44) and *Kerem Tziyon* (*Shevi'it, Halachot Pesukot* 14, 1). On the other hand, the *Mikdash David* (no. 59) forbids this, and it seems that the *Chazon Ish* (14, 10), cited above forbids this as well.

50. **We can explore the following question from the perspective of the stringent view that does not allow for indirect destruction of *Shemita* produce.** This view can be understood in one of two ways: 1) Just as in *hilchot Shabbat* there is a Rabbinic prohibition against causing the performance of a *melacha* through *gerama*, there is a similar Rabbinic prohibition against causing the destruction of *Shemita* produce. 2) The problem with the destruction is not the **action** but the **result**. Even indirect destruction prevents the consumption of the produce. **The practical application** of this question would be in the case where the produce will not be consumed (e.g. table scraps). According to the first approach, the prohibition against causing their loss remains, while according to the second approach it would be permitted, for the produce is not being consumed anyway. We have seen (regarding table scraps) that *Rav Elyashiv* (cited in *Mishpetei Aretz 5760*, 21:25) follows the **second** approach to our question, that the problem lies in the **prevention of consumption**. Thus, Rav Elyashiv permitted indirect loss of produce that will be eliminated anyway. In light of this, one need not worry about placing a bag of leftovers directly into the garbage, since they will not be eaten anyway (though, as mentioned, there could be a problem with sanitation workers crushing the garbage).

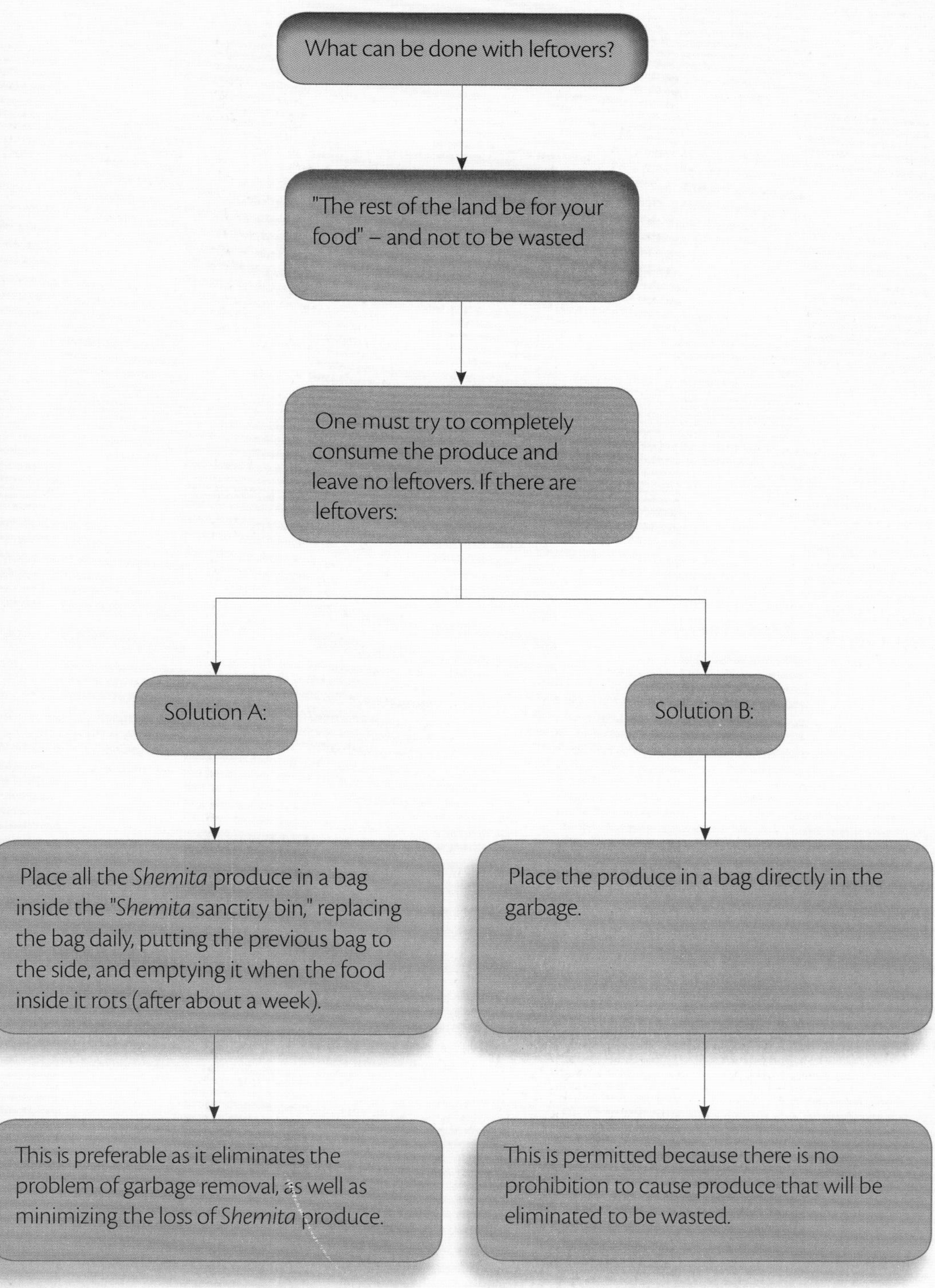
What can be done with leftovers?
"The rest of the land be for your food" – and not to be wasted
One must try to completely consume the produce and leave no leftovers. If there are leftovers:
Solution A:
Solution B:
Place all the *Shemita* produce in a bag inside the "*Shemita* sanctity bin," replacing the bag daily, putting the previous bag to the side, and emptying it when the food inside it rots (after about a week).
Place the produce in a bag directly in the garbage.
This is preferable as it eliminates the problem of garbage removal, as well as minimizing the loss of *Shemita* produce.
This is permitted because there is no prohibition to cause produce that will be eliminated to be wasted.

LEFTOVER SOUP

The Rambam rules (*Hilchot Shemita ve-Yovel 7:22*):

> In the case of *Shemita* carobs preserved in sixth-year or eighth-year wine, the wine is subject to the rules of *bi'ur* [explained below], since it is flavored with *Shemita* produce. This is the general rule: *Shemita* produce, however small its amount, mixed with other produce, if it is of the same species, imbues the mixture with *Shemita* status in any proportion; if it is not of the same species, it adds *Shemita* status to the mixture if it impacts the flavor of the mixture.

The Rambam implies that even mixtures containing only the **taste** of *Shemita* produce have *Shemita* sanctity. Accordingly, in the case of vegetable soup containing *Shemita* produce, as long as the *Shemita* produce is not nullified by sixty parts of non-*Shemita* produce, even the broth of the soup has *Shemita* sanctity.[51]

How, then, should leftover soup be discarded? The ideal solution, of course, is to put the leftovers in a separate bag and tie it. This, however, is often difficult with a liquid, and therefore an alternative solution may be necessary. The Rash (*8:2*), based on the *Yerushalmi*, writes that one is not obligated to eat food whose appearance has vanished (*she-avra tzurato*):

> [Quotation from the] *Yerushalmi*: "One is not required to eat bread that has become moldy, or a dish that has been ruined..." [A ruined dish is defined as one] that it has been left out overnight, as we have learned in the *Tosefta* (*6:2*) "whose appearance is gone" [and with the passing of a night, its appearance is gone]... This serves as proof regarding the case of a pot that has not been used since the preceding day ... Passing of the night impairs taste, even if twenty-four hours have not passed... and it is unfit for consumption after having been left out overnight.

According to the Rash, cooked food that had been left out

51. However, water in which *Shemita* potatoes were cooked does not have *Shemita* sanctity, because that water is ordinarily discarded and not considered food (Rav Elyashiv, cited in *Mishpetei Aretz, p. 178*, note 27). Moreover, the potatoes are regarded as imparting a "deteriorated taste" into the water, for the taste of the water itself is impaired by the potatoes.

(unrefrigerated, of course) overnight is regarded as foul. Based on this approach, if soup is left out overnight without refrigeration, it may be discarded in the morning in the usual manner, for it is no longer viewed as fit for human consumption. This is the ruling cited in the *Pe'at ha-Shulchan* (24:3; *Bet Yisra'el,* no. 6).

Some *Posekim* are skeptical about this solution. They insist that the soup be kept out until it is unquestionably spoiled,[52] as is explained in *Responsa Az Nidberu* (vol. IV, no. 56):

> The source of this law is in the *Tosefta* (*Shevi'it* 6): "One is not required [to consume] ... a dish whose appearance is gone (*nifsad tzurato*)"... Now since the Rambam wrote "A dish that was spoiled (*nifsad*)" (leaving out the word *tzurato*), implies that it must be really spoiled, and that being left out one night does not suffice.

His claim is that the Rambam worded his ruling differently from the language of the *tosefta,* because the Rambam believes that the overnight change is insufficient to justify eliminating the food, and he insists on its being **totally spoiled**. It should be noted that today it is much easier to dispose of leftover soup, because sealable plastic bags are readily available. However, one who chooses to follow the solution of leaving soup out overnight has adequate basis for this leniency.

52. The disagreement seems to be based on the question of what is considered unfit for consumption: Must the taste be impaired to the extent that people would not ordinarily eat such food, as argued by the Rash, or perhaps must it be totally unfit for consumption, as implied by *Responsa Az Nidbaru*? This debate connects to another fundamental discussion regarding *Shemita* sanctity: is the sanctity dependent on the status of the **food itself**, or on the **way people relate to the food**? (See the appendix regarding *Shemita* observance at the institutional level).

PITS AND PEELS

What is the status of left-overs that are fit, but not meant, for animals? Do they have *Shemita* sanctity?

In general, *Shemita* sanctity applies to food that is fit for animal consumption (Rambam *7:13*):

> The Sages have formulated an important general principle concerning *Shemita* produce: whatever is used as human food or as animal feed… has *Shemita* sanctity.

This being the case, it should be forbidden to discard most peels (to the exclusion of hard shells and the like), since they are fit for animal consumption. In order to clarify this point, however, we must define what is meant by food that is "unfit" for animal consumption. On the one hand, it might refer to food that animals are **unable**, or **unwilling**, to eat; on the other hand, it might refer to food that is not ordinarily fed to animals, even though they are capable of eating it.

An inedible pit with no *Shemita* sanctity

The *Chazon Ish* (*14, 10*) implies that the criterion is whether the food is ordinarily fed to animals (the second possibility):

> A peel that was removed still has *Shemita* sanctity, as there is food on it… One should put the peel into a receptacle until it becomes rotten and is no longer fit for human consumption, and then it may be discarded. If it is still fit for an animal, then it seems that if most people would still set it aside for an animal, it has *Shemita* sanctity, but if most people would not set it aside for an animal, it has lost its sanctity.

In contrast, Rav Kook (*Shabbat ha-Aretz 7, 13, 3*) writes that even produce that is not meant to be given to animals, but is fit to be eaten by them, has *Shemita* sanctity:

> It seems that with respect to "human food" or "animal feed" there is no need... that it be designated for that purpose. Rather, anything that is fit for human consumption, even if it would only be eaten in less than ideal circumstances, is regarded as human food. And the same applies to defining what is fit for animal consumption... with respect to the laws of *Shemita* sanctity.

A similar view emerges from *Responsa Shevet ha-Levi* (vol. *II*, no. *199;* brought also in *Mishnat Yosef*, vol. *III*, pg. *111*), who suggests an approach similar to Rav Kook's, but does not wish to dispute the conclusion of the *Chazon Ish*:

> In any case it has been demonstrated that whatever is fit [for animal consumption], but not regarded as animal feed, has *Shemita* sanctity... But how can I disagree with the *Chazon Ish*, even to be more stringent?

There is room for discussion as to how this dispute is to be resolved,[53] but this resolution may be unnecessary. It seems that even **Rav Kook would agree** that one is permitted to throw into the garbage *Shemita* produce that is **unfit for human consumption**, but that still can be eaten by animals. The reason is that even after these leftovers are thrown into the *garbage*, they are **still fit for animal consumption**. Throwing them into the garbage does not spoil them in any way!

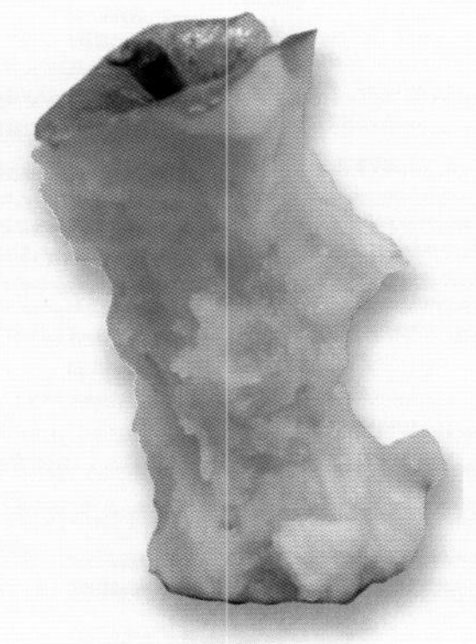

A pit with fruit left over.

Pits with the flesh of fruit: Thus far, we have related to pits that are unfit for human consumption, but what is the law regarding pits that still have bits of fruit on them? The

53. Rav Sh. Z. Auerbach (cited in *Mishnat Yosef*, vol. *I*, no. *30*) rules leniently on the matter, but he writes that the leniency may be limited to produce which was not meant, from the outset, for human or animal consumption. In his opinion,, produce that had once been fit for human consumption may not lose its *Shemita* sanctity as long as it is still fit for animal consumption (see also *Chazon Ish*, ad loc.).

Chazon Ish (*11, 11*) and the *Sefer ha-Shemita* (*p. 31, 1*) imply that in such a situation one must safeguard the Shemita sanctity of the flesh of the fruit:

> The base of a fig that has fruit on it, or the pits of fruit that have food in their crevices, such as plums and peaches, or if fruit juice remains on the pits, as with dates and olives – they must not be destroyed, for they are still fit to be eaten.

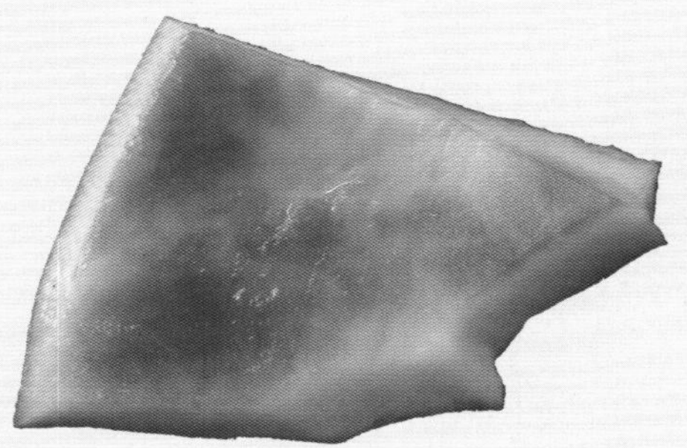

Rind totally eaten (with a bit leftover
Sefer Ha-Shemita: sanctity must be observed.
Rav Elyashiv: it can be discarded normally

Rav Elyashiv (cited in *Mishpetei Aretz,* p. *176,* no. *10*) maintains, however, that if a person removes all the fruit that he wishes to eat, he may discard the pit in the ordinary manner. Rav Elyashiv bases his ruling on the view of Rabbenu Tam cited in *Tosafot* (*Zevachim 86a,* s.v. *u-peliga*), that the pits of *teruma* that have fruit on them have sanctity and are forbidden to non-Kohanim, as long as a Kohen intends to eat the fruit, but the moment that the Kohen discards them, they lose their identity as food:

> In tractate *Terumot,* we say: "The pits of *teruma,* when in the possession of a Kohen, are forbidden [to others], but when he casts them away, they are permitted"… There [the Mishna] speaks of bones of sacrificial meat that are eaten… and there is meat on them. And it says that if [the Kohen] stores them he thereby attaches importance to them and they retain the status of sacrifices and are forbidden to others. But if he casts them away, they lose their status as food. The same goes for pits of *teruma* fruit that have food on them.

According to Tosafot, pits upon which remain small amounts of fruit may be discarded in the ordinary manner (and this also follows from Mahari Kurkus's understanding of the Rambam, *Hilchot Terumot 11:11,* on the assumption that a comparison may be drawn between *Shemita* produce and *teruma*).

In practice, though there are some who disagree with *Tosafot*, Rav Elyashiv rules leniently. In any event, one must clearly try to eat the pit clean of fruit before discarding it, and if a large amount of fruit remains on the pit, it should be cast into a *Shemita* container:

As long as a person has thoroughly removed the flesh of the fruit from the pits, and he has no intention of removing any more, no further efforts must be made and [the pits] may be thrown into the garbage as is.

Food residue may be washed off a plate as usual.

In light of what we have seen, if a person did not eat the pit clean, but rather left an amount of fruit that would normally be eaten, he must place what remains into a *Shemita* container. (At least during the *Shemita* year a person should habituate himself to eat fruit completely!) In the event that a person ate the fruit down to the core (in the manner that most people eat), even though a small amount of fruit remains on the pit, according to Rav Elyashiv one may cast what remains straight into the garbage. Nevertheless, it seems appropriate to be stringent and place such a pit into a *Shemita* container whenever possible.

Food sticking to a pot or to a plate: In light of the above discussion, leftovers remaining in a pot or on a plate should be treated like the flesh of fruit remaining on pits. Thus, there is no need to treat them with Shemita sanctity (*Mishpetei Aretz, p. 177*. See also Rav Chayim Berlin's comment in *Sefer ha-Shemita, p. 31,* note 5). Accordingly, one should first transfer those leftovers that are ordinarily removed before dish washing into a *Shemita* container, after which the pot or the plate may be washed in the ordinary manner.

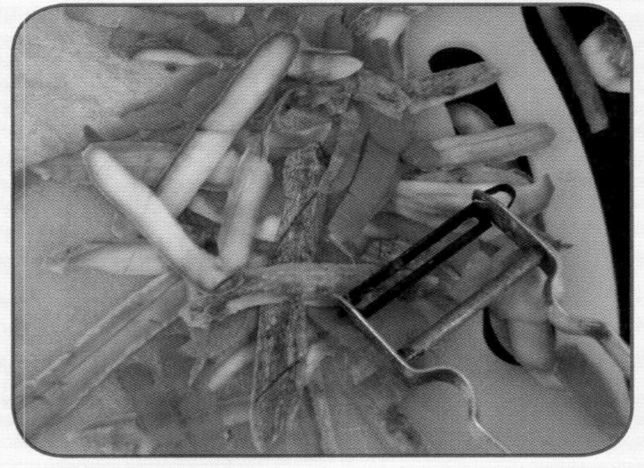

Edible leftovers

Peels: As was explained above, peels that are unfit for human or animal consumption may be discarded in the ordinary manner. Nevertheless, orange rinds that can be used to make candy would seem to have *Shemita* sanctity, even if currently they are unfit for human consumption (*Responsa Tzitz Eli'ezer,* vol. 11, 17). Nevertheless, the *Chazon Ish* (*Ma'asrot 1, 30*) rules that since most rinds are discarded they are not considered as human food.

May one use *Shemita* wine for *havdala*?

Wine: Rav Kook (*Shabbat ha-Aretz, Kuntres Acharon,* 22) rules that when *Shemita* wine is used for *havdala,* one should not fill the wine cup over the brim, because most people do not drink the wine on the plate and the spilled wine is regarded as ruined (there are, however, those who permit this; see *Mishpetei Aretz 21, 5*). If a person insists on filling the cup over the brim, he must afterwards drink the spilled wine.[54] Of course, one should not extinguish the *havdala* candle in *Shemita* wine, and at the *Pesach seder* one should not cast out drops when recounting the ten plagues (see Rav Kook, ibid.[55]).

54. It should be noted that Rav Kook had wanted to be stringent in general about *havdala* wine, because some women have the custom not to drink havdala wine, and so when *Shemita* wine is used for *havdala,* one reduces the potential for it to be drunk, unless he drinks the entire cup himself (*Shabbat ha-Aretz, Kuntres Acharon,* 22). Nevertheless, it follows from various *Acharonim* that it is only the reduction of the number of people who can eat *teruma* that is regarded as destruction, but the reduction of the number of people who can eat *Shemita* produce is not regarded as destruction (*Ridbaz* in *Bet Ridbaz,* 5, 6, s.v. *u-le-inyan she-pasak,* who reaches this conclusion in light of the difference in the Rambam's presentation of this law regarding *teruma,* and *Shemita*; see also *Minchat Shlomo,* vol. 1, 46, end). See the end of this volume, regarding observance of *Shemita* sanctity in institutions, where we discuss this issue at length.

55. There is room for leniency in this situation, because this is the normal way of using the wine, but in practice it is appropriate to follow the view of Rav Kook.

RAV YOSEF SHALOM ELYASHIV

was born in 1910. He was the grandson of Rav Shalom Elyashiv, author of the "*Leshem, Shevo ve-Achlama,*" and a great Kabbala scholar. He served for many years on the Rabbinical Courts of the Chief Rabbinate. He was considered **one of the leading *Posekim*** and became one of the leaders of the Lithuanian Charedi community. Rav Elyashiv did not publish his own works, but a collection of letters and short articles he wrote have been published, as have some of his novellae and halachic rulings, which have been written up and published by his students. Rav Elyashiv's rulings also appear in other contemporary halachic works, and one will rarely find a new halachihc work that does not cite him. Rav Elyashiv died in 2012.

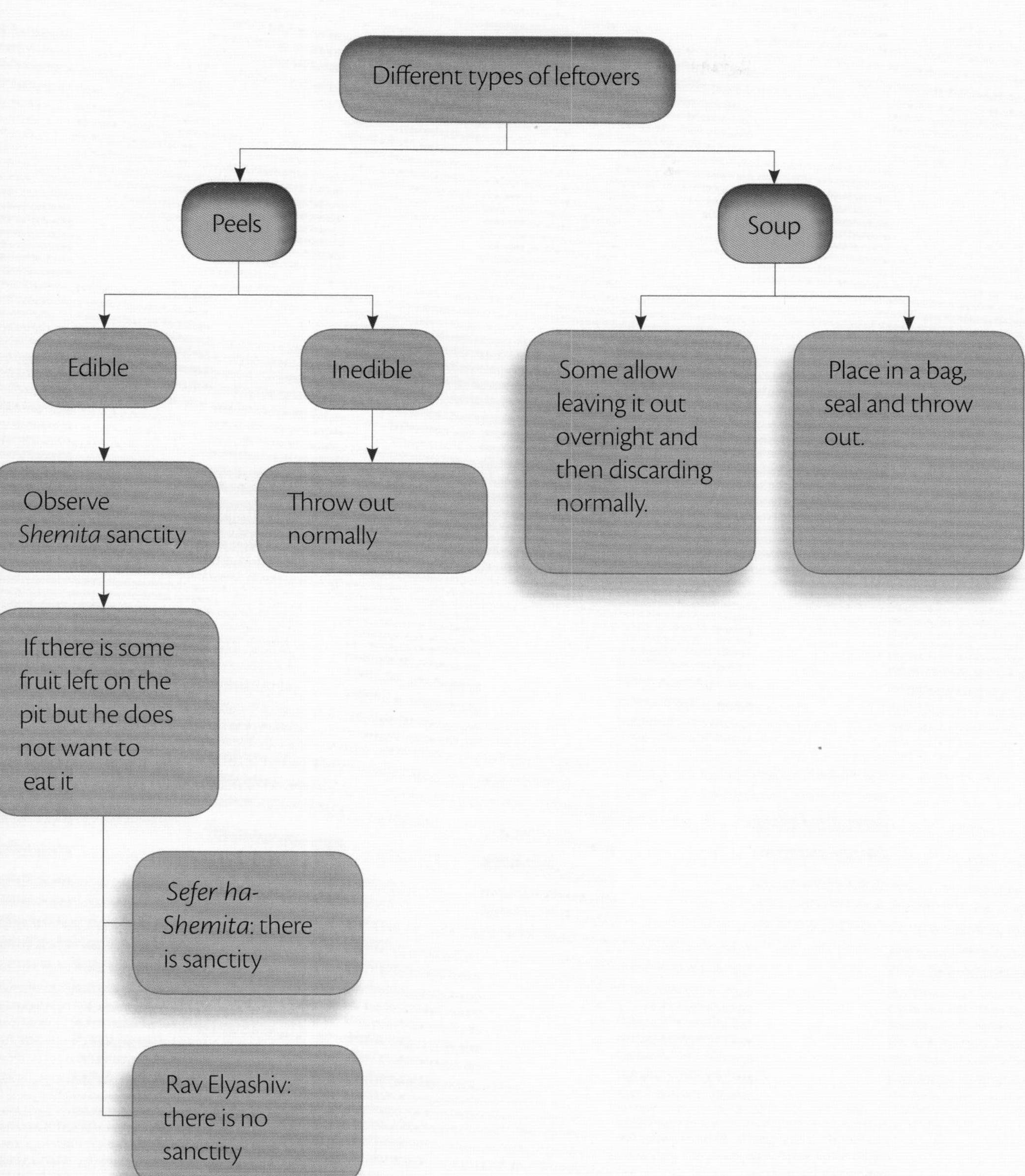
Different types of leftovers
Peels
Soup
Edible
Inedible
Some allow leaving it out overnight and then discarding normally.
Place in a bag, seal and throw out.
Observe *Shemita* sanctity
Throw out normally
If there is some fruit left on the pit but he does not want to eat it
Sefer ha-Shemita: there is sanctity
Rav Elyashiv: there is no sanctity

USING *SHEMITA* PRODUCE IN AN UNCOMMON WAY

The Mishna in *Terumot* (*11:3*) states that it is forbidden to divert *teruma* produce from its ordinary use, and therefore one may not make a beverage out of *teruma* produce that is ordinarily eaten as a food:

> One must not make dates into honey, apples into wine, winter-grapes into vinegar, or change any other kind of fruit that is *teruma* or *ma'aser sheni* from its natural state, with the sole exception of olives and grapes.

The Rambam (*Hilchot Shemita ve-Yovel 5:3*) rules that the Mishna's statement concerning *teruma* applies equally to *Shemita* produce:

> One may not divert [*Shemita*] produce from its natural use just as one may not divert *teruma* or *ma'aser sheni*. And similarly, one may not eat Shemita produce which is customarily made into a beverage as is the rule for *teruma* and *ma'aser sheni*.

The Rambam's ruling has several practical ramifications for the **proper use of *Shemita* produce**:

1. It is forbidden to make juice from fruit that is ordinarily eaten whole, or to eat whole fruit that is ordinarily squeezed for its juice.
2. The *Talmud Yerushalmi* (*8:2*) adds to the Mishna's statement as follows: "And similarly, if someone wishes to eat beets raw or to chew wheat kernels, we do not listen to him." That is to say, it is forbidden to cook produce that is ordinarily eaten raw (such as avocado, radish, or banana) or to eat raw produce that is ordinarily cooked (such as potato).[56]
3. It is forbidden to eat fruit that has not fully ripened (unripe figs or the like), as is stated explicitly in the Mishna in *Shevi'it* (*4:7*):

56. Cooking wine does not appear to present a problem, for it is normal to cook wine. Rav Kook (*Mishpat Kohen*, section 85), however, rules on the basis of the Rambam (*Hilchot Terumot 11:4*) that *Shemita* wine should not be cooked because cooking diminishes the quantity of wine. We find, however, that various *Acharonim* were lenient regarding the cooking of wine: 1) Rav Sh. Z. Auerbach (*Minchat Shlomo*, end of section 25) says that wine may be pasteurized in a sealed bottle. 2) *Mishpetei Aretz* allows one to add wine to a cake or to other dishes because that is an accepted use of wine (22, 7). He adds, however, that one must make sure that wine comprises at least one-sixtieth of the ingredients, so that the wine not be nullified in the cake. (This qualification is necessary only according to the view of the *Pe'at ha-Shulchan* [27:45] and the *Chazon Ish* [13:8], who maintain that one is forbidden to mix *Shemita* produce into a dish if the *Shemita* produce will be nullified by the mixture. The *Kerem Tziyon* [chap. 13] and the *Minchat Shlomo* [no. 46] permit the cancellation of *Shemita* sanctity by way of the law of nullification in a mixture.) **Practically**: for small scale home use, it is better to use non–*Shemita* wine for cooking, and to use the *Shemita* wine for other purposes. However, if there are large quantities at stake, .

From when may one begin to eat of the fruit of the trees in the seventh year? With unripe figs: as soon as they assume a rosy appearance one may eat thereof in the field with his bread. Once they have ripened, he may also take them home. And similarly, in the other years of the sabbatical cycle [when the latter stage has been reached] they are subject to tithes.

it would appear better to cook with the *Shemita* wine rather than reduce one's consumption of *Shemita* produce

That is to say, when the figs begin to ripen (*hizrichu* – apparently, when they begun to turn gold in the sun), one may pick a small amount of them in the field, but one may not pick a large quantity and bring them into the house. Only after the figs have ripened (*bichalu*) or at least have reached their full size, is it permitted to bring them into the house.

Rav Kook (*Mishpat Kohen,* beginning of no. 85) offers a general definition that we will relate to in detail below, regarding the forbidden diversion from ordinary use of *Shemita* produce:

> As for the foundation of the law regarding diversion from natural use, by Torah law there are four cases, each one teaching laws that apply to the others: teruma, ma'aser sheni, shevi'it and blessings. [Laws may] generally be inferred by analogy from any of these to the others, except in cases where there is clear proof that this analogy is invalid or problematic.

Fig before *chanata*

Unripe fig

Fig with a rosy appearance – one may eat a little of this in the field.

Ripe fig – one may bring this inside to eat.

WHY IS IT FORBIDDEN TO DIVERT SACRED PRODUCE FROM ITS NATURAL USE?

Why is it forbidden to use sacred produce in an abnormal manner? The *Rishonim* suggest two reasons for the prohibition to eat unripe sacred produce, and these reasons may extend to the issue of unusual consumption as well:

1 The Rash (*Shevi'it 4:4;* Rashi, *Yoma 86b*) writes that the problem with picking unripe fruit is that it leads to *hefsed* – destroying the produce:

> Because we learn: "For food," but not for destruction… if one eats [the produce] before it is ripe, that is destruction.

In light of the Rash's approach, one can claim that eating the produce in an unusual manner falls into the category of destroying the produce. Rav Kook adopts a similar approach (*Mishpat Kohen,* section 85).

2. The Rambam (commentary to the Mishna *4:7*) writes that one must not pick fruit before it is ripe, based on the verse (*Vayikra 25:12*): "You shall eat its [*Shemita year's*] produce out of the field:"

> "From when may one begin to eat of the fruit of the *Shemita* year?" … God said regarding the seventh year: "You shall eat its produce out of the field." And [the Sages] said (*Sifra*): It may not be eaten until it is "produce," namely, that one is forbidden to eat it unless it is fit for consumption.

The Rambam implies that there is a specific Torah prohibition that forbids the diversion of the produce from the ordinary manner in which it is eaten. Other authorities follow a similar approach, but write that the verse from which this prohibition is derived is *Vayikra* 25:6, "Food for you" – meaning only in the conventional manner of eating (Rash Sirilio *5:2,* s.v. *ein shome'in lo*).

There is a practical difference between these two approaches. What is the status of produce that had been improperly squeezed for its juice or cooked? Is the produce now forbidden? According to the Rambam, who maintains that the prohibition to divert the produce from its common use is derived from a special verse, it is possible that part of what is learned from the verse is that the food itself is forbidden when not eaten in the normal manner (perhaps the Rambam would explain that *Shemita* produce may only be consumed in its accepted form – "In your regular manner of eating"). However, according to the Rash, acording to whom the prohibition of diverting produce from its natural use is out of concern for its destruction, it may be that if the food has already been cooked, it is preferable to use it in that form rather than throw it out and destroy it completely. Accordingly, Rav Kook (*Mishpat Kohen,* section 85, s.v. *u-ma she-katav Kevod Torato*), who follows the Rash, rules that if the change was already made, the food is permitted, and it is even preferable that the food be eaten:[57]

> What my esteemed colleague has said to the effect that food is never prohibited after unusual use, even if this unusual use was improper, is correct and obvious. For the reason that something that is usually eaten raw should not be cooked is because in this way it is slightly ruined. But how can we say that because he slightly ruined it he should waste it altogether and not eat it? Rather, without a doubt, if it is fit to be eaten, he should eat it. Furthermore, it would appear that he is obligated to eat it, because it is only regarding moldy bread or vegetable trimmings or anything else that is not fit to be eaten that they said in the *Yerushalmi* that one is not obligated to eat it. But that which is fit to be eaten, why should we allow him to waste it entirely because he transgressed and wasted it partially? "If someone ate garlic [and thus emits a foul odor], should he then eat more garlic [to rid himself of it]?" (from *Berachot* 51a)

57. A similar ruling is found in the *Pe'at ha-Shulchan* (24, 4) and the *Chazon Ish* (19, 27).

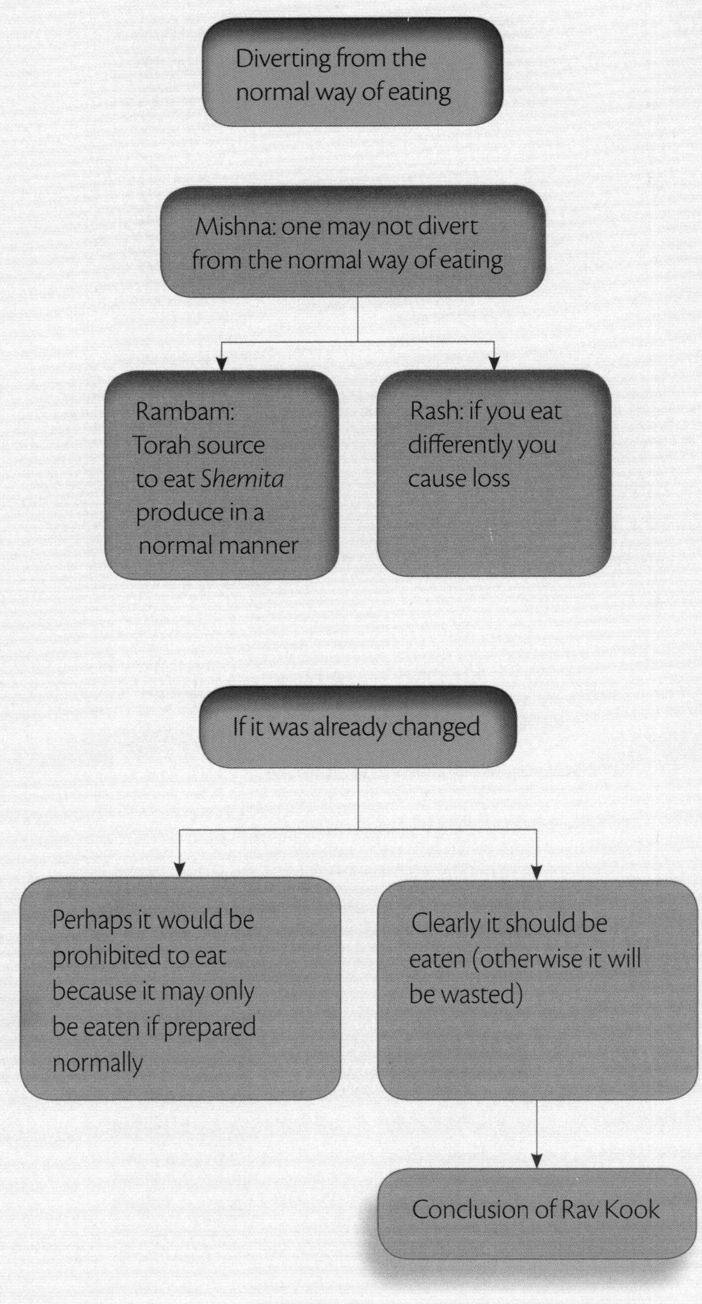
Diverting from the normal way of eating
Mishna: one may not divert from the normal way of eating
Rambam: Torah source to eat *Shemita* produce in a normal manner
Rash: if you eat differently you cause loss
If it was already changed
Perhaps it would be prohibited to eat because it may only be eaten if prepared normally
Clearly it should be eaten (otherwise it will be wasted)
Conclusion of Rav Kook

SQUEEZING FRUIT FOR ITS JUICE

We saw above that because of the prohibition to divert *Shemita* produce from its common use, squeezing *Shemita* fruit for its oil or juice is forbidden. The only exceptions are olives and grapes because extracting their oil and juice is viewed as the ordinary manner of consumption. Today, there are many types of fruit that are ordinarily squeezed for their juice in addition to olives and grapes. Is it still forbidden today to squeeze apples or oranges bearing *Shemita* sanctity in order to create juice?

The *Rishonim* disagree about the blessing to be recited over the juice of fruits that are commonly squeezed. The *Tosafot* and the Rosh (*Tosafot, Chullin 112b,* s.v. *ve-tuvan; Berachot 39a,* s.v. *maya;* Rosh, ad loc.) maintain that the juice is "mere moisture," and therefore the blessing recited over it is *she-ha-kol,* whereas the Rashba (*Berachot 38a*) writes that the juice of fruit that is commonly made into juice is treated like the fruit itself, and therefore the blessing recited over it is the blessing over fruit, *borei peri ha-etz.* Rav Kook (as we saw above) draws a general comparison between the laws of blessings and the laws of *Shemita,* and thus it would seem that, according to the *Tosafot* and the Rosh, juicing fruit is forbidden, whereas according to the Rashba, it would be permitted.

The *Chazon Ish* also compares the laws of blessings and the laws of *Shemita.* He concludes in accordance with the Rashba,[58] that since, with respect to blessings, juice is regarded like the fruit itself, and that its blessing is *bore peri ha-etz,*[59] so too with respect to *Shemita,* squeezing fruit that is ordinarily squeezed for its juice is not regarded as ruining the fruit:

> Regarding [juice] squeezed from oranges and the like… it is possible… that if one recites over [the juice] *bore peri ha-etz,* and it is treated like the fruit itself [like the Rashba, then it should be permitted to squeeze them even during the *Shemita* year]… But according to the view of the *Tosafot* and the Rosh, the implication is that even if most of that type of fruit is made into juice, [the juice] is nonetheless regarded as mere moisture [and it is not treated like the fruit itself,

58. According to the *Mishna Berura* (202, 47; 205, 14), however, the blessing recited over fruit juice is *she-ha-kol,* in accordance with the Rosh.

59. It should be noted that, owing to the uncertainty the customary practice is to recite the *she-ha-kol* blessing over fruit juice, as this is the "default" blessing in cases of doubt.

and its blessing is *she-ha-kol*], and therefore it is forbidden to squeeze *Shemita* fruits...

We can also learn regarding the common manner of squeezing oranges, where the entire fruit is poured into the cup, and nothing is left but waste, that this does not have the status of squeezing, but rather of mashing [and is permitted]... The Rema (ad loc.) maintains that essentially its blessing is *bore peri ha-etz* [and it is only owing to uncertainty that we are accustomed to recite *she-ha-kol*]... Regarding the practical application [of this law], further study is necessary.

While the *Chazon Ish* concluded by saying that the matter "requires further study," in various other places he explicitly writes that one is permitted to squeeze fruit that is ordinarily squeezed for its juice (*Kuntres Seder ha-Shevi'it, 9,* end of *Derech Emuna*):

And similarly one is permitted to squeeze the juice out of fruits that are ordinarily squeezed for juice, namely: olives, grapes, oranges, grapefruits and lemons.

The *Chazon Ish* adds that if, following the squeezing of the *Shemita* juice, all the pulp is mixed into the juice (such as is common with unfiltered citrus juices), the mixture might be permitted even according to the Rosh.[60]

Unlike the *Chazon Ish*, Rav Tykoczinski (*Sefer ha-Shemita,* p. *30,* chap. *7,* end of sec. *2,* and there in note *3*) forbids squeezing fruit for juice. It seems from his words that he understands that there is a specific Torah prohibtion that only olives and grapes may be pressed for their oil and wine. But he too notes at the end: "All this notwithstanding, I do not fix any hard and set rules on the matter."

Rav Sh. Z. Auerbach (*Minchat Shlomo,* vol. *46*) also discusses the issue of squeezing *Shemita* fruit for juice. Unlike the other *Posekim*, he distinguishes between squeezing *teruma* produce and squeezing *Shemita* produce. In his opinion, in addition to the prohibition against wasting *teruma* produce, there is also a prohibition against removing it from its sanctity, and therefore squeezing is forbidden, whereas regarding *Shemita* produce, there is only a prohibition to

60. When preparing juice at home, people do not generally recombine the pulp with the juice, but beverage companies thoroughly squeeze the fruit and extract all the juice from the pulp as well. This may be similar to recombining the pulp with the juice; though the matter requires further study. It should also be added that in the case of beverage companies, the fruit used for the production of juice is generally grown for that purpose, and in such a case there is even more reason to say that queezing the fruit for its juice is not regarded as destruction.

waste the produce, and squeezing fruit that is ordinarily used for juice is not considered wasting it:[61]

> According to this, we must say that while with respect to *teruma*, there are two reasons to forbid squeezing - one, because one destroys the fruit, and two, because one removes them from their sanctified state – and therefore it is forbidden even with respect to those kinds of fruits that are normally squeezed; nevertheless, with respect to *Shemita* produce it is forbidden only because of the first reason.... According to this, it is permissible to squeeze *Shemita* oranges, lemons and grapefruits in order to enjoy the juice extracted from them, but one must take care not to actively destroy what remains of the fruit.

In practice, most *Acharonim* are inclined to permit squeezing *Shemita* fruits that are normally squeezed for their juice (*Kerem Tziyon,* ad loc.; *Aruch ha-Shulchan ha-Atid 24:9*), and not to be concerned about wasting the small amount of fruit that is left on the skin. Accordingly, one may be lenient about squeezing oranges, grapefruit and the like, which are normally squeezed for their juice, but an effort should be made to squeeze the fruit in a most thorough manner.[62]

61. At the end of his comment, Rav Sh. Z. Auerbach raises the concern that if bits of fruit remain on the skin, which would have been consumed had the fruit been eaten in the normal manner, perhaps this should be regarded as wasting part of the fruit. In such a case, therefore, perhaps the squeezing is forbidden: "... Perhaps squeezing should be forbidden because that which remains of the fruit is too repulsive to eat for most people" (*Responsa Minchat Shlomo*, volume 1 no. 46, also cited in *Kerem Tziyon, Hilchot Shevi'it, Halachot Pesukot*, chap. 13, par. 8, notes 1 and 2).

62. Which fruits are considered "commonly squeezed"? The *Chayei Adam* (51, *Nishmat Adam*, note 1) writes with respect to blessings, that if many people squeeze the fruit for its juice, squeezing the fruit is regarded as a normal manner of consumption, even if most people do not squeeze it. On the other hand, the *Mishna Berura* expresses himself variously on the matter (in sec. 205 no.3; 202, no. 62), he writes that the normal method of consumption is determined by what most people do, whereas in sec. 202 no. 61 he writes that if "many people eat it in that manner" it is considered a normal manner of consumption. The phrase that he uses implies most people behave in that manner. The *Mishpetei Aretz* (22, note 6) writes, that even if the *Mishna Berura* requires a majority of people, it is possible that this applies only to the laws of blessings, but with respect to *Shemita*, he would agree that a large number of people who squeeze the fruit suffices to make squeezing a normal manner of consumption.

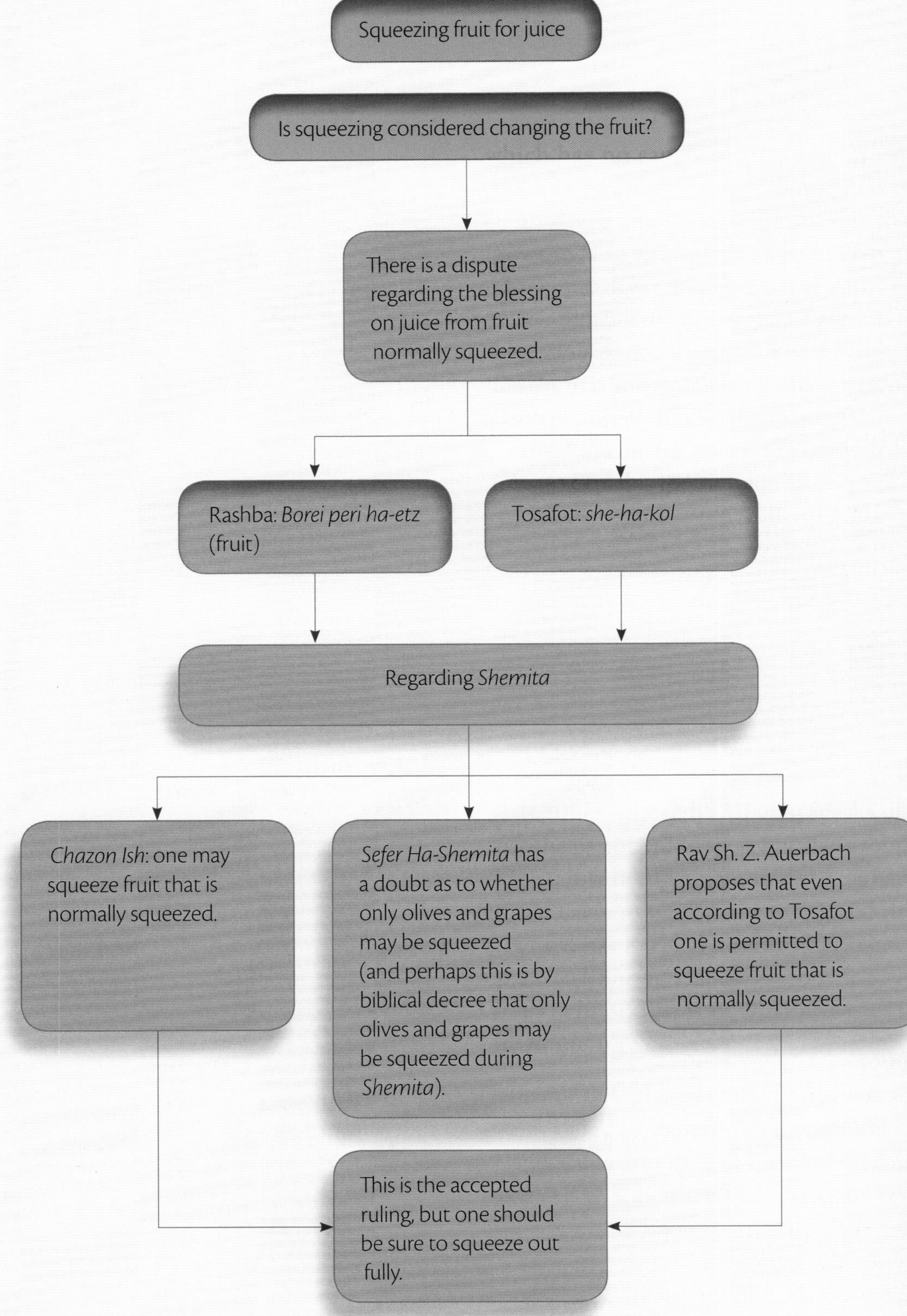
Squeezing fruit for juice
Is squeezing considered changing the fruit?
There is a dispute regarding the blessing on juice from fruit normally squeezed.
Rashba: *Borei peri ha-etz* (fruit)
Tosafot: *she-ha-kol*
Regarding *Shemita*
Chazon Ish: one may squeeze fruit that is normally squeezed.
Sefer Ha-Shemita has a doubt as to whether only olives and grapes may be squeezed (and perhaps this is by biblical decree that only olives and grapes may be squeezed during *Shemita*).
Rav Sh. Z. Auerbach proposes that even according to Tosafot one is permitted to squeeze fruit that is normally squeezed.
This is the accepted ruling, but one should be sure to squeeze out fully.

MASHING

According to the Gemara (*Berachot 38a*) as codified by the Rambam (*Hilchot Teruma 11:2*), it is permissible to mash *teruma* dates in order to make them into an edible paste. Presumably this would be true with respect to *Shemita* produce (*Pe'at ha-Shulchan 24:4*).

What type of mashing is meant? The Gemara explains that one recites *bore peri ha-etz* over mashed dates because the dates themselves are still intact even after they are mashed. Rashi (ad loc.) explains that the Gemara is not dealing with dates that are thoroughly mashed, based on which the *Terumat ha-Deshen* (no. 29) concludes:

Date spread (mashed but not liquefied) – The Rambam and *Terumat Ha-deshen* debate the law in this case

> This implies that if they are thoroughly mashed, one recites *she-ha-kol* over them.

One does not recite *bore peri ha-etz* over a fruit that is thoroughly mashed, because such a fruit has entirely lost its form and therefore also its identity.

The Rambam (*Hilchot Berachot 8:4*) disagrees:

> If one eats dates which have been mashed by hand and their pits have been removed such that they are dough-like, one recites *bore peri ha-etz*.

The Rambam appears to understand that the essential identity of the fruit still exists even after it has been thoroughly mashed, and so the blessing over the paste is still *bore peri ha-etz*.

The *Shulchan Aruch* (202:7) rules in accordance with the Rambam, whereas the Rema cites, in the name of "those who say," the position of the *Terumat ha-Deshen*. Even the Rema agrees that, fundamentally, one should recite *bore peri ha-etz*, but, owing to the convention that in cases of doubt regarding blessings, we incline

Liquefied spread

toward leniency, he prefers that one recite *she-ha-kol*. Since, according to the Rema, *she-ha-kol* is recited only on account of uncertainty, if a person erred and recited *bore peri ha-etz* over a fruit that was thoroughly mashed, he has fulfilled his obligation:

Whole date

There is no change in the blessing regarding dates which were mashed by hand and made into a dough and their pits removed, and one recites *bore peri ha-etz* before eating them and *beracha me-ein shalosh* (the blessing over foods from the "seven species" of the land of Israel) afterwards. Rema: And some say that one should recite *she-ha-kol* before eating them (*Terumat ha-Deshen* ...), and it is preferable to recite *she-ha-kol*, but if one recited *bore peri ha-etz*, one has fulfilled one's obligation, because that appears to be the correct position.

Crushed dates – recognizable as the fruit. The blessing is "*borei peri ha-eitz*" – fruit may be crushed in this way even if it is not normally crushed.

Therefore, both according to the *Shulchan Aruch* and according to the Rema, partial mashing does not constitute a significant change in the fruit or vegetable, and, fundamentally, *bore peri ha-etz* or *bore peri ha-adama* is still recited (see *Chazon Ish*, 25, 32, s.v. *omnam* and s.v. *min ha-amur*). For the same reason, it is permitted to mash or grate *Shemita* produce with a fork or grater, and this is not regarded as destruction of the produce.

Since, fundamentally, even the Rema rules like the Rambam, even thorough mashing by way of a blender or the like is permitted. It is possible, however, that even according to the Rambam, liquefying the fruit is forbidden.[63]

It should be noted that the previous discussion relates to fruits that are not normally mashed. As for fruits that are ordinarily mashed, mashing clearly does not constitute destruction, parallel to the *Chazon Ish*'s ruling regarding fruit juice.

63. As for the blessing to be recited in such a case, see *Aruch ha-Shulchan* (202:24).

To summarize, mashing by hand is permitted with respect to all fruit, whereas using a blender should preferably be restricted to fruit that is normally mashed. It should be noted that it is permitted to mash food for an infant, even if that food is not ordinarily mashed for an adult, and this is not considered destruction of the fruit (Rav Elyashiv, *Mishpetei Aretz,* p. 172, note 35).

In general, food preparation using *Shemita* produce should not be problematic, as long as the food is prepared in the normal manner. "Normal manner" refers to the manner in which a considerable number of people prepare their food, even if they do not constitute a majority (see above note 24).

RABBI YISRAEL BEN PETACHYA ISERLEIN

(*Terumat ha-Deshen*)

R. Iserlein was born in 1390 and died in 1460, and was one of the leading Rabbis of Ashkenazi Jewry. He was the Rabbi of Vienna, and fielded questions from numerous communities throughout the Jewish world. He authored the **Responsa *Terumat ha-Deshen*.** The **Shach** (in *Yoreh De'ah 156*) writes that the *Terumat ha-Deshen* is different from other responsa. While generally the author prints the questions he was asked and his answers to them, the *Terumat ha-Deshen* **composed these questions himself.** This is significant because it means that one can derive halachot from the **formulation of the question** itself, as the author composed it. (The second part of the *Terumat ha-Deshen* is based on questions he was asked by others.) The title page of the book has the following written on it: "We know by tradition from the righteous son of the author of *Ba'al Efrayim* that the author of the *Terumat ha-Deshen*… in a time of trouble for the Jewish people, miraculously saved the people with his wisdom."

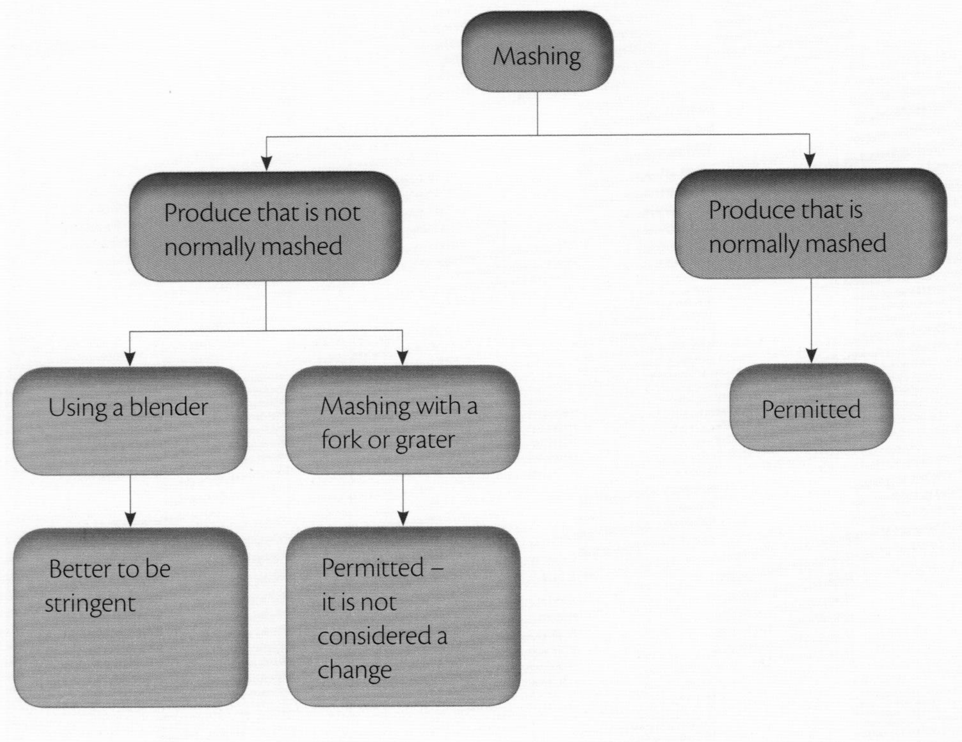

USING *SHEMITA* PRODUCE FOR PURPOSES OTHER THAN EATING

As we have seen earlier, *Shemita* sanctity does not ordinarily apply to trees that do not bear fruit. The Gemara in *Sukka* (*40a;* and similarly *Bava Kama 101b-102a*) states that *Shemita* sanctity only applies to plants that have a human use and the benefit from which comes at the same as their consumption, such as plants that serve for illumination or dyeing. On the other hand, trees that are used in a manner that the benefit derived from them does not come at the same time as their consumption, such as trees to be used as firewood (from which a person derives benefit only after they have been consumed by the fire and turned into coals), are not subject to *Shemita* sanctity.

From this it follows that deriving benefit from *Shemita* produce in ways other than eating is also only permitted when the consumption of the produce and the benefit derived from it come at the same time.

The Gemara in *Sukka* (*40a*) adds that it is forbidden to use *Shemita* produce for medical purposes: "'For food' – and not for a remedy." Therefore, it is permitted to prepare medicines and ointments only from plants that do not have *Shemita* sanctity. The creation of medicinal products that are commonly enjoyed even by healthy people, such as a drink that is imbibed by both sick people and those who are healthy, is permitted. Moreover, medicines that were prepared from *Shemita* produce in an improper manner are nonetheless permitted to be used (see above, *Aruch ha-Shulchan 81:7*).

Anointing: One is permitted to rub *Shemita* oil on one's body, because anointing is considered identical to drinking (Rambam, *Hilchot Shemita ve-Yovel 5:1, 6*). Oiling other objects with *Shemita* oil is, however, forbidden (ibid. 7).

Laundry: The Gemara in *Sukka* (*40a*) states that *Shemita* produce may not be used for laundering: "'For food' – and not for laundry." Accordingly, one may not use a lemon that has *Shemita* sanctity to remove stains from fabrics.[64] One is, however, permitted to use a powder containing *Shemita* lemons, because the lemons are no longer edible.

In summary, we shall cite what the Rambam (*Hilchot Shemita ve-Yovel 5*) says on the topic:

> *Shemita* produce may be used for food, drink, anointing, kindling a lamp, and dyeing...
>
> What are the rules for food and drink? One may eat that which is customarily eaten, and drink that which

64. Some people use lemon to clear the sink or to remove stains from their hands, and we shall examine these uses below:
The Gemara in *Bava Kamma* (*102b*) states, "'And the Sabbath of the land shall be for you to eat' – 'for you' – for all your needs." The Gemara in *Pesachim* (*52a*) also learns from this verse that "that which is generally eaten – shall be eaten. That which is generally used for laundry – shall be used for laundry. That which is generally used for dyeing – shall be used for dyeing." There is an apparent contradiction between this source and the Gemara in *Sukka*, cited above in the body of the work, which derives, "for eating and not for laundry." The Gemara resolves this contradiction by explaining that laundry is permitted only with *Shemita* produce that is not edible for people. The Gemara proceeds to explain that doing laundry with *Shemita* produce is prohibited because the benefit and the consumption are not simultaneous.
Rashi explains this to mean that the fruit is ruined immediately whereas the cleansing only takes places subsequently. On the other hand, the Rashba (as well as Rashi on *Sukka 40a*) maintains that the benefit derived from laundry is not the washing but the subsequent wearing of the clean garment. Laundering is prohibited because it takes place subsequent to washing.
The presumed practical difference between these two approaches would be the question with which we began: when one uses a lemon to clean a sink or one's hands, the benefit comes in the cleanliness of the sink or hands. Thus, according to the Rashba, this would presumably be permitted, for the benefit comes from the cleanliness itself rather than some subsequent result. (In fact, when the sink is used later, its cleanliness is already less significant.) On the other hand, according to Rashi, this would be prohibited, for the destruction of the lemon precedes the cleanliness. In practice, this is at most a doubtful prohibition, and thus it seems that there is room for leniency with regard to utilizing a lemon for these purposes.

is usually drunk, similar to the rule for *teruma* and *ma'aser sheni*...

What are the rules for anointing? One may anoint with that which is customarily used for anointing. One may not anoint with wine or vinegar, but one may do so with oil...

What are the rules for dyeing? One may dye for human use with substances regularly used for dyeing, even if they are also used for human food....

The Sages have established the following important principle concerning *Shemita* produce: anything used primarily for human food, such as wheat, figs, grapes, and the like, may not be used as a medicine or bandage, even for a person, as it is said: "For food for you," implying that whatever is usable for you must be used for consumption and not for medicinal purposes. Anything not used primarily for human food, such as tender thorns and thistles, may be used to make medicine for people.

SUMMARY:

We are greatly privileged to be able to eat the sacred produce of the *Shemita* year, and we might even fulfill a *mitzva* when we do so. It is, therefore, preferable to purchase produce having *Shemita* sanctity through an *Otzar Bet Din*, even if that will involve extra efforts on our part to safeguard that sanctity.

Fundamentally, there is no obligation to eat all the leftovers of *Shemita* produce. Nevertheless, it is proper to cook *Shemita* produce in appropriate quantities or to serve the leftovers at another meal, in order to reduce the quantity of uneaten portions of *Shemita* produce to a minimum.

In the event that *Shemita* produce is left over, it should not be disposed of in the ordinary manner, by throwing it directly into an ordinary garbage can. There are two ways of dealing with *Shemita* leftovers, with preference given to the first solution:

1. A special receptacle should be set aside for leftover *Shemita* produce, and it is proper to mark the container "*Shemita*

sanctity" (and not "*Shemita* garbage"). The bag that lines the receptacle should be replaced each day, and the old bag should be set aside or stored at the bottom of the receptacle (for a few days) until the food has decayed (to save the sanitation workers from destroying it directly), at which point it may be disposed of in the ordinary manner with the rest of one's garbage. Liquids should not be thrown into the container, because they will ruin the other leftovers. Liquid leftovers should be placed in a separate bag, sealed, and then put in the special *Shemita* container (or into the regular garbage can).

2. One should place the *Shemita* leftovers in a bag, tie the bag, and place the bag in the regular garbage can. One may be lenient and use this solution in one's private home, and institutions may certainly rely on this leniency even *lechatchila* (additional guidelines for institutions may be found in the appendix at the end the book).

Leftover Soup: In the case of soup containing *Shemita* vegetables, *Shemita* sanctity applies to the entire soup, including the broth. (The water in which potatoes are cooked is not subject to *Shemita* sanctity, because the potato flavor does not improve the taste of the water.) Some authorities are lenient and allow for the soup to be left out unrefrigerated overnight, at which point the taste of the soup is regarded as "deteriorated," so that the soup can then be disposed of in the ordinary manner. Others insist that the soup cannot be thrown out until it is actually spoiled. The preferable alternative is to put the soup into a sealed (e.g. Ziploc) bag, and then throw it into a regular garbage can. Nowadays it is very easy to find sealable plastic bags, and so this last solution appears to be the most appropriate. Those who rely on the first solutions, however, have sufficient halachic support for their practice.

Peels: Peels that are not fit to be eaten may be disposed of in the ordinary manner.

Pits that have bits of the flesh of fruit on them: If a person eats all portions of the fruit that he is interested in eating, Rav Elyashiv rules that he may be lenient and dispose of the pit in the ordinary manner, even if remnants of the fruit remain on the pit. It is preferable, however, to eat as much of the fruit as possible, and if a considerable amount of fruit remains uneaten, to put the pit into the special *Shemita* container.

Washing dishes used for *Shemita* produce: Pots and dishes with remnants of *Shemita* produce may be washed in the ordinary manner.

In addition to the special handling required for sacred leftovers, it is forbidden to divert *Shemita* produce from its ordinary use. Therefore:

Squeezing fruit: It is forbidden to squeeze fruit that is not normally squeezed for its juice. In any event, it is desirable to squeeze the fruit as thoroughly as possible in order to avoid wasting the fruit.

Mashing: There is no problem with mashing *Shemita* produce with a fork, grater or the like. Pulverizing the produce in a blender or creating a very liquidy paste should be restricted to foods that are normally mashed in this manner. In any event, it is permitted to mash food for an infant, even if that food is not ordinarily mashed for an adult.

In general, one should be careful not to use *Shemita* produce in a way that is not considered normal use. Therefore:

Medications: It is forbidden to prepare medicines from *Shemita* produce; nonetheless, medicines prepared from *Shemita* produce may be used. *Shemita* produce may be used to prepare something that could be used either as a medicine for a sick person or as food for a healthy person.

Laundry: *Shemita* produce may not be used for laundering. Therefore, one should not use a lemon that has *Shemita* sanctity as a stain remover.

***Havdala* wine:** When using *Shemita* wine, it is preferable not to fill the cup to the brim, so as not to waste the wine that spills over. It is only permitted if one will drink the wine that spills onto the plate. In any event, one should not extinguish the *havdala* candle with the wine, and at the *Pesach seder* one should not remove drops of wine when recounting the ten plagues.

The rule of thumb is that one who uses *Shemita* produce in the normal manner, and handles the leftovers with the proper care, fulfills the law of safeguarding *Shemita* sanctity. While this requires care and awareness, the effort is worthwhile and not as difficult as often imagined. In any event, it seems to be the very minimum that we can do for the great privilege of eating *Shemita* produce, strengthening agriculture in Eretz Yisrael, and observing the *Shemita* in the best possible manner.

THE RAIN OF *SHEMITA*

During the previous *Shemita* year, in the month of Cheshvan (5768), it began to rain in Alon Shevut. I was headed home from synagogue after the *Mincha* service, when suddenly a frightened little boy approached me and said, "Rabbi, it is raining." I looked at the child and said, "Isn't it wonderful? Finally it is raining."

The boy looked back at me and said, "But Rabbi, what will we do?" "What is the problem?" I asked. The boy explained, "But Rabbi, it is the *Shemita* year, and the rain is watering our gardens."

Of course, the sweet little boy's question has a simple answer: the prohibitions of *Shemita* apply to man, and not to nature. But the boy's question demonstrated to me how deeply sensitive he had become to the whole issue of *Shemita.* He does not live in an agricultural community, and he encounters *Shemita* primarily in the special care with which *Shemita* produce must be handled, and perhaps also in certain restrictions that apply in the garden. But when it suddenly began to rain, the boy's reaction was: "The land's rest has been violated." The boy became upset because the land's rest had been interrupted.

It is possible to discern and experience the sanctity of the *Shemita* year even if one is not a farmer. *Shemita* sanctity is all around us: in the fields, in the produce that we bring into our homes, in every place in Eretz Yisrael. A special sanctity rests in every corner of the land. It is our job to listen to the amazing occurrence that is taking place this year in Eretz Yisrael, to seek it out, and to draw from its sanctity.

If we listen carefully, we will be able to hear that the land is resting. If we continue to listen, we will learn that while we are resting, God is tending the garden. Listening to the rain, we will rejoice in God's special partnership with us in working the land. And if we keep on listening, we will come to a more profound understanding of the sanctity of the land, and to an appreciation of the immense sanctity that we merit to enjoy during the *Shemita* year.

BUYING FRUITS AND VEGETABLES DURING *SHEMITA*

CHALLENGES AND POTENTIAL PROBLEMS WITH BUYING PRODUCE DURING *SHEMITA*

BUYING FRUITS AND VEGETABLES DURING THE *SHEMITA* YEAR

THE CHALLENGES

What challenges may arise when purchasing fruits and vegetables during the *Shemita* year?
What is the prohibition of *sefichim*?
What are the concerns about paying for *Shemita* produce?

The main challenges that the consumer faces over the course of the *Shemita* year with respect to the purchase of *Shemita* produce are challenges regarding **the fruits and vegetables themselves** and challenges with **the process of purchasing them**.

CHALLENGES REGARDING THE PRODUCE ITSELF

1. *Shamur* ("guarded") and *ne'evad* ("worked") – *Shemita* produce that was not declared ownerless, but rather "guarded" by its owner is called *shamur*. The fruit that grew on trees that were cultivated in contravention of the law is called *ne'evad*. We saw earlier (p. 154–157) that the *Acharonim* tend to be lenient regarding such produce and permit its use.
2. The prohibition of *sefichim* ("aftergrowth").

CHALLENGES REGARDING THE PURCHASE PROCESS

1. Handing over *Shemita* money to an *am ha-aretz* (an ignorant person who is not scrupulous in his observance of the commandments).
2. Trading in *Shemita* produce.
3. Measuring *Shemita* produce.

THE PROHIBITION OF *SEFICHIM*

Why did the Sages institute the prohibition of sefichim? How can the problem of *sefichim* be circumvented? What are the special leniencies proposed by the *Chazon Ish* regarding the prohibition of *sefichim*? How does one buy flowers during the *Shemita* year?

The term *sefichim* refers to produce that grew during the *Shemita* year without having been purposely planted, as an aftergrowth of what had been planted during the previous year, such as grain that grew on its own from seeds that fell during the previous harvest or were brought there by the wind (*sefichim* – appended (*nispach*) to produce of the previous year).[1]

We saw in previous chapters (p. 132–138) that harvesting during the *Shemita* year is only forbidden when carried out in the manner in which it is normally done. One is therefore permitted to pick *Shemita* fruit for several days of household consumption, provided that the work is not performed in a commercial manner. One might have thought that this should also apply to vegetables that grew on their own. If this were so, however, it would be difficult to understand the Torah's meaning when it says: "And if you shall say: What shall we eat in the seventh year? Behold, we may not plant, **nor gather in our produce**" (*Vayikra 25:20*) – after all, one is allowed to gather produce that grew on its own!

Owing to this difficulty, Rabbi Akiva learned from this verse (*Torat Kohanim, Behar 4*) that harvesting *sefichim* is forbidden by Torah law. In other words: The Torah permits the picking of fruit during the *Shemita* year when not carried out in the normal manner, but it forbids the eating of **vegetables that fall into the category of *sefichim*** (annuals that were planted during the *Shemita* year), even if the seeds accidentally fell to the ground during the sixth year and grew on their own in the seventh year. The Sages, however, disagreed with Rabbi Akiva, arguing that *sefichim* are only forbidden by Rabbinic law. According to them, the Torah speaks of the people's concern that since it is forbidden to store away *Shemita* produce, as

1. For the term *sefi'ach*, in the sense of something attached and joined, see I *Shemu'el 2:36*: "And it shall come to pass, that everyone who is left in your house shall come and crouch to him for a piece of silver and a loaf of bread, and shall say, 'Join me (*sefacheni*), I pray you, to one of the Kohanim's offices, that I may eat a piece of bread.'" See Radak and *Metzudat David* (ad loc.) who explain this verse as follows: "Gather me up and attach me to one of the groups of Kohanim that I may eat a piece of bread." See also *Yeshayahu 14:1*: "For the Lord will have mercy on Ya'akov, and will yet again choose Israel, and set them in their own land; and the stranger shall join them, and they shall cleave (*ve-nispechu*) to the house of Ya'akov."

it has to be removed from the house at the time of *bi'ur*, there will be nothing to eat after the time of *bi'ur* has arrived:

> "And if you shall say" – You indeed will say: "What shall we eat in the seventh year? Behold, we may not plant, nor gather in our produce." If we do not plant, what shall we gather in? Rabbi Akiva said: From here the Sages brought support[2] for the fact that *sefichim* are forbidden during the seventh year. But the Sages said: *Sefichim* are not forbidden by Torah law, but by Rabbinic decree. If so, why does it say: "Behold, we may not plant, nor gather in our produce"? You said to us, "You may not plant," and that which we gather in, may we store it up? You said to us, "Remove it." What then should we eat from after the time of *bi'ur*?

2. When Rabbi Akiva says that "from here the Sages brought support," he means that the Sages understood the prohibition of *sefichim* as a Torah law, and not that the law is Rabbinic in origin. This is clearly evident from the Sages who disagree with Rabbi Akiva and say: "*Sefichim* are not forbidden by Torah law, but by Rabbinic decree."

The **Rambam** ruled in accordance with the Sages (*Hilchot Shemita ve-Yovel* 4:1-2), as did most of the other *Rishonim* (other than the *Semag* [negative commandment 168] and the *Yere'im* [158], who ruled in accordance with Rabbi Akiva).

VEGETABLES THAT WERE PLANTED DURING *SHEMITA*

There are three main positions regarding the relationship between the prohibition of planting during *Shemita* and the prohibition of *sefichim* that grew on their own during the seventh year:

1. The Rambam (*Hilchot Shemita ve-Yovel* 4:15) writes:

> If one transgressed and planted during the seventh year and the produce grew into the eighth year… it is forbidden during the eighth year like other *sefichim.*

The Rambam implies that just as the prohibition of *sefichim* applies to produce that grew on its own, so too it applies to that which was purposely planted during the seventh year. The Rambam's wording suggests that the Rabbinic prohibition of *sefichim* that grew on their own, which was implemented to prevent and remove incentive for planting during the *Shemita* year, is more severe than the prohibition of produce that was purposely planted, which is only forbidden "like other *sefichim!*"

Rav Sh. Z. Auerbach (cited in *Responsa Yeshu'ot Moshe,* I, 9, 4) accounts for this strange phenomenon as follows: The Sages were not trying to combat those who brazenly plant in the open during the *Shemita* year; their intention was to prevent and discourage people from covert planting. Therefore, they only prohibited *sefichim* that grew on their own, lest people come to plant as usual, and then say that the produce grew on its own. However, in order to prevent the absurd legal result of vegetation purposely planted having a less severe status than vegetation that grew on its own, the Sages also forbade produce planted intentionally.

2. **The *Chazon Ish*** (10, 6, s.v. *ve-im avar*) maintains that the original decree of *sefichim* applied only to that which was purposely planted during the *Shemita* year, and it was only later expanded to include that which grew on its own:

> The decree against *sefichim* is a prohibition applying to produce that has been inappropriately planted. To this they also added a prohibition upon that which grew on its own.

3. Some *Rishonim* imply that produce that was improperly planted during the *Shemita* year is forbidden by Torah law, and that it is only the ban on vegetables that grew on their own that is by Rabbinic decree.[3]

In practice, according to all views, vegetables that grew during the *Shemita* year are forbidden, whether they had been purposely planted or they grew on their own.

VEGETABLES THAT WERE PLANTED DURING THE SIXTH YEAR

We have seen that the Sages forbade *sefichim* that grew during the seventh year. Several *mishnayot*, however, refer to eating vegetables during the *Shemita* year. For example (*Shevi'it 8:4*):[4]

3. See above, p. 155, that there are those [such as the *Sema (Choshen Mishpat* 141)] who maintain that vegetables that were improperly planted during the *Shemita* year are indeed forbidden by Torah law.

4. Other examples include *Shevi'it* 9:1 (cited on *Sukka 39b*); 8:4 (cited on *Avoda Zara 62a*); and 7:3.

If one says to a laborer: "Take this *issar* and gather vegetables for me today," his payment is permitted.

The Rash (*Shevi'it* 9:1) explains that the prohibition of *sefichim* does not apply to vegetables that began to grow already in the sixth year (this suggestion is also made by the Ramban[5] in his commentary to the Torah, *Vayikra* 25:5):

5. This suggestion is also made by *Tosafot* (*Pesachim* 51b, s.v. *kol ha-sefichim be-sofo*, in the name of Ri); Maharam Chalawa (*Pesachim* 51b); Rosh (*Shevi'it* 9:1) and others. For further clarification of this position, see below.

> It may be asked: according to Rabbi Akiva, *sefichim* of the seventh year are forbidden by Torah law, and even the Sages agree that they are forbidden by Rabbinic decree... [This is difficult, for] we find in various *mishnayot* that they may be eaten!... It may be suggested those are all [dealing with vegetables that started growing] during the sixth year... and regarding vegetables we follow the time of picking [to determine the year of growth, thus these vegetables have *Shemita* sanctity]... But regarding the prohibition of *sefichim*... a vegetable that started to grow during the sixth year, and continued to grow during the seventh year is considered "*sefichim* of the sixth year" and not "*sefichim* of the seventh year."

On the other hand, the Rambam (*Hilchot Shemita ve-Yovel* 4:12) rules that all vegetables picked during the seventh year are governed by the prohibition of *sefichim*, even if they began to grow already in the sixth year:

> The rule [of *sefichim*] affecting vegetables depends upon the time of their gathering.

How does the Rambam explain the Mishna? The *Chazon Ish* (*9, 3; 9, 17*) explains that even the Rambam agrees that a vegetable that grew to its full size during the sixth year, but was picked only in the seventh year, is not included in the decree concerning *sefichim*, and this is the case discussed in the Mishna:

> It seems that regarding *sefichim* the Rambam agrees that the prohibition of *sefichim* applies only to that which grew during the seventh year, whether a little or a lot. But that which

did not grow at all during the seventh year is not governed by the prohibition of *sefichim* whatsoever.

As for the halacha, the *Pe'at ha-Shulchan* ruled (22:3, in a note) in accordance with the Rash and most *Rishonim*[6] that vegetables that began to grow in the sixth year are not included in the prohibition of *sefichim*. This is also the ruling of the *Chazon Ish* (9:17, s.v. *she-nigmar*; 10:17, s.v. *yerek*; 22:2, s.v. *nir'e de-yerek*; 26, *seder ha-shevi'it* 6, s.v. *yerakot*), *Sefer ha-Shemita* (16:1) and Rav Ovadya Yosef (*Yalkut Yosef, Shevi'it*, 23:14, *p.* 507).[7] The *Chazon Ish* explains this position as follows:

> A vegetable that began to grow in the sixth year, but reached its full size during the seventh year is forbidden according to the Rambam because of the prohibition of *sefichim*, whereas according to the Rash it is permitted. And this is also the view of the Ramban (*Vayikra* 25:5). Since it is [only] a Rabbinic prohibition, one can rely on the latter view.

We must now clarify the criteria for determining that a vegetable "began to grow during the sixth year."

The **Rosh** writes: "*Sefichim* that emerged during the sixth year, even if their entire growth was during the seventh year, are permitted." The implication is that it suffices that the vegetable merely "emerge" during the sixth year to permit its picking and eating during the seventh year. What is meant here by "emerging"? It is reported in the name of the *Chazon Ish* that minimal sprouting above ground suffices (see *Ma'adanei Eretz, p.* 131, note 16, and *Minchat Shlomo*, section 50).[8] At times the *Chazon Ish* was lenient even when only part of the vegetable crop had already sprouted above ground, as Rav Nissim Karelitz reports in his name (*Chut ha-Shani, Shemita*, 4, 3, letter 9, *p.* 162):

> There is a question as to the measure of what constitutes the beginning of growth [during the sixth year] so that there is no prohibition of *sefichim* according to the Rash... Our master the *Chazon Ish* instructed those from kibbutz Chafetz

6. Even though the Rambam's position is of prime importance in halachic decision-making (and there were periods when his rulings were accepted as law), when a majority of the *Posekim* disagree with the Rambam, we follow the majority position even in the case of a Torah law. In the case of a balanced doubt regarding a Rabbinic law, we follow the lenient position (even against the Rambam), in accordance with the rule, "we follow the lenient approach in ruling on a doubt about the application of a Rabbinic law." The *Chazon Ish* applied this rule with respect to *mitzvot* that depend on the land of Israel (*Shevi'it* 23, 5). See also *Yalkut Yosef* (*Shevi'it* 23, sub-section 14, *pp.* 507–508).

7. The *Mabit* (III, 45), however, rules in accordance with the Rambam, and Rav Ben Zion Abba Shaul writes (*Or le-Tziyon, Shevi'it, p.66*) that Sefaradim should be stringent on the matter. But even Rav Abba Shaul notes that when there is no alternative, "he who is lenient has what to rely upon."

8. In contrast, Rav Sh. Z. Auerbach writes that one may only pick a vegetable during the seventh year if it reached *chanata* or a third of its growth during the sixth year (*Ma'adanei Eretz*, responsa at the end of the book; *Minchat Shlomo* 49, 50). In practice, however, he rules leniently in accordance with the *Chazon Ish*.

Chazon Ish in an event in Netiva

Chayim who had consulted with him to plant prior to *Rosh ha-Shana* of the seventh year such that a bit of the stalk will sprout above the ground [during the sixth year]. It once happened in his day that on *Tzom Gedalya* [the 3rd of Tishrei] there were fields in which the stalks had not yet emerged from the ground. The *Chazon Ish* instructed them to examine the fields and see whether in at least three places the seeds had sent our roots, and to assess whether those roots[9] had already been sent out before *Rosh ha-Shana.* In such a case, it would be possible to permit the entire field with respect to the prohibition of *sefichim.*

This ruling was confirmed by people who were present when it was issued in Moshav Netiva (today's Yad Binyamin).[10] (A picture of the *Chazon Ish* that was taken on this occasion has also survived.)

Sprouting (the commonly-accepted ruling)

Full-grown vegetables (tomatoes)

9. Here the *Chazon Ish* ruled leniently even though there was no sprouting above ground, but merely the beginning of the sprouting of roots below ground. Rav Karelitz notes that the *Chazon Ish* may have issued this ruling only because it was a situation of great need, and this is how the *Chazon Ish's* position on this matter is cited in the *Achot Rabbenu* (Part II, page 334). According to some authorities, however, this is completely permitted (see *Responsa Shevet ha-Levi*, II, 200).

10. The source of this story is *Responsa Mishnat Yosef, Shevi'it* 9, 1, who writes that he was with the *Chazon Ish* in Moshav Netiva when the incident occurred. He writes that in several places there was no sprouting at all, but in one place the *Chazon Ish* discerned sprouting, "and based on the fact that there was sprouting in most of the field, he permitted the entire field," even where there was no sprouting. The *Chazon Ish* explained that "apparently the earth had not been properly worked at the edge of the field, and did not receive sufficient water." This incident is amazing testimony to the *Chazon Ish's* creative capacity for leniency.

As opposed to vegetables, grains and legumes may be harvested during the seventh year only if they reached a third of their size during the sixth year (*Rash, Shevi'it 9:1*).[11]

The pamphlet that accompanies this book includes a *sefichim* calendar, which spells out when the prohibition of *sefichim* begins to apply with respect to each different kind of vegetable. It should be noted that even when there is no prohibition of *sefichim*, any vegetable picked during the seventh year has *Shemita* sanctity. It is therefore possible that such a vegetable might fall into the category of *shamur* or *ne'evad* (even though the common practice is to be lenient with respect to these problems, as we saw in previous chapters). So too one must be careful to avoid the other prohibitions that apply to *Shemita* produce, as will be explained below.

The Rambam (*Hilchot Shemita ve-Yovel 4:5–6*) rules that the prohibition of *sefichim* applies even to vegetables that grew during the seventh year, but were picked during the eighth year. Two approaches have been suggested to understand this prohibition:

1. There is a concern that perhaps these vegetables were picked during the seventh year (*Chazon Ish 9:13; 15*).
2. This ruling stems from a concern that a person will plant during the *Shemita* year for the sake of the eighth year (*Ri Kurkus 4:5–7*).

Once the date is reached that vegetables of a given type planted in the eighth year could already be fully grown and ready to eat, the prohibition of *sefichim* no longer applies to that entire crop, which was picked in the eighth year, even to particular plants that grew during the seventh year. (This date is also indicated in the *sefichim* calendar that accompanies this book.)

Strictly speaking, *Shemita* sanctity should not apply to *sefichim* growing into the eighth year, because they are picked after *Shemita*. In practice, however, we are stringent, and treat them as if they have *Shemita* sanctity, out of concern for the possibility that they were picked in the seventh year, even when it is known with certainty that they were picked in the eighth year (*Chazon Ish 9, 16; 17*).[12]

11. The Rash issues this ruling based on the *Yerushalmi* (*Shevi'it 5:2*): "If it grew less than a third before the seventh year, and it went into the seventh year, it is forbidden on account of *sefichim*." As for grain, the Rambam agrees that if it became a third grown during the sixth year, it is not governed by the prohibition of *sefichim* (*Hilchot Shemita ve-Yovel 4:10*).

12. In contrast, the *Penei Moshe* (5:5) maintains that *sefichim* that are known to have been picked during the eighth year have no *Shemita* sanctity.

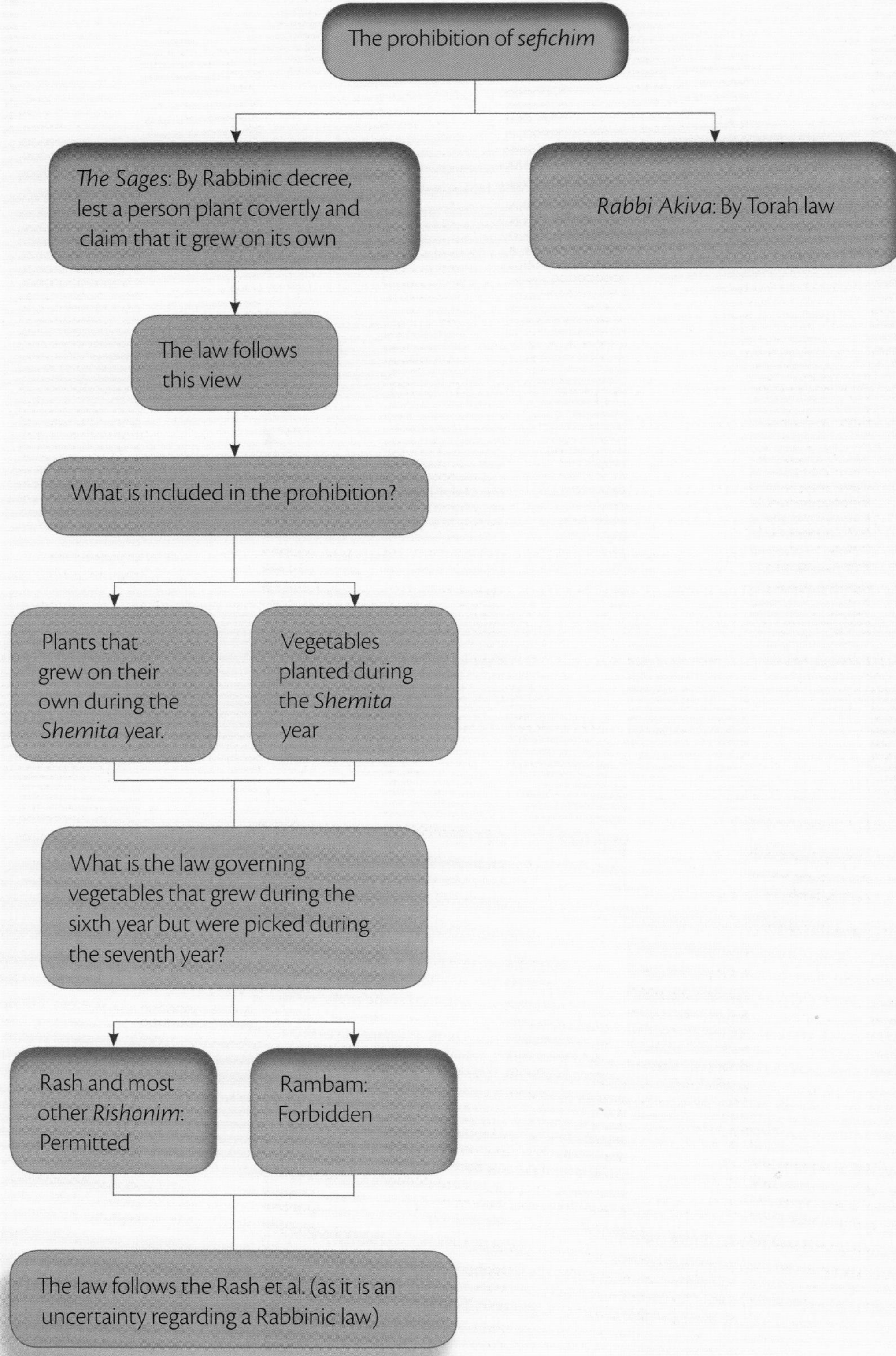

The prohibition of *sefichim*
The Sages: By Rabbinic decree, lest a person plant covertly and claim that it grew on its own
Rabbi Akiva: By Torah law
The law follows this view
What is included in the prohibition?
Plants that grew on their own during the *Shemita* year.
Vegetables planted during the *Shemita* year
What is the law governing vegetables that grew during the sixth year but were picked during the seventh year?
Rash and most other *Rishonim*: Permitted
Rambam: Forbidden
The law follows the Rash et al. (as it is an uncertainty regarding a Rabbinic law)

PRODUCE THAT IS NOT SUBJECT TO THE PROHIBITION OF *SEFICHIM*

1. **Fruit:** The prohibition of *sefichim* does not apply to fruit, because even if one plants a seedling during the seventh year, one cannot derive any benefit from it during that year. Therefore, the decree "lest a person come to plant during the seventh year itself" does not pertain to fruit.

   Perennials: The law applying to perennials is unclear.[13] In practice, **if the sprouting begins only after *Rosh ha-Shana*,** one should be stringent. But if the plant had already sprouted the previous year, even if vegetables grow again from the roots during the *Shemita* year one may be lenient, as is the case for mint, eggplants, and bananas.[14]

   Purchasing perennial vegetables: It stands to reason that unless one knows that they are forbidden *sefichim*, one need not be concerned that they might be such, for it is likely that they are not. Moreover, a person can plant such vegetables prior to the seventh year[15] (and thus they differ from ordinary *sefichim*, which in order to produce food during the *Shemita* year, must also be planted during that year).

2. **The produce of a gentile grown on his own land:** The Rambam (*Hilchot Shemita ve-Yovel 4:29*) rules that since a gentile is not governed by the prohibition of planting during the *Shemita* year, the entire decree of *sefichim* does not pertain to his produce:

   > If a gentile buys land in the Land of Israel and plants it in the sabbatical year, its produce is permitted, for the prohibition of *sefichim* is aimed at Jewish transgressors, and gentiles, not being subject to the sabbatical year, do not come under the prohibition.

3. **Produce growing in a field sold under the *heter mechira*:** Rav Kook writes (introduction to *Shabbat ha-Aretz, 11*) that the prohibition of *sefichim* does not apply to vegetables grown on fields subject to the *heter mechira*. Even though Rav Kook himself maintains that a Jew should not sow in such a field (see below, p. *411*), since there are *Rishonim* who disagree

13. See the sources below, which imply that the prohibition applies if the plant began to sprout in the *Shemita* year, and that the allowance applies only if there is a stalk or the like. See also Rimbatz, *Shevi'it* 5:5 and 7:1.

14. Rav Karelitz, *Chut ha-Shani*, p. 162, and *Derech Emuna, Shemita ve-Yovel, 4, no. 85*. See also Rash Sirillo (5:3, s.v. *be-ale luf*) and Rav Frank in *Kerem Tziyon*, XI, *Ga'on Tzvi, no.* 2, and *Yalkut Yosef, Shevi'it, p. 498*. As stated, the *Posekim* are also lenient about bananas (ibid., and also *Mishnat Yosef*, I, *no.* 20). As for banana plants, it should be noted that while they generally produce fruit during their first year, the bananas will ripen only in the eighth year.

15. Rav Mordechai Eliyahu, cited in *Katif Shevi'it*, chap. 16, note 7.

and allow a Jew to sow in such a field (such as the author of the *Teruma* and others – see p. 411 fotnote 74) – *sefichim* that grew from seeds that were planted by a Jew in a field subject to the *heter mechira* are not forbidden.[16] It should be noted that those who do not rely on the *heter mechira* would presumably forbid the produce of such a field as *sefichim*. However, they could conceivably agree that such produce is permitted, because the planting was carried out on the basis of a halachic allowance, even if they themselves do not rely on that allowance (see below, p.438–439).

16. This is the ruling of both Rav Ovadya Yosef (*Ha-Shevi'it ve-Halichoteha, "Be-Din Heter ha-Mechira"*; *Yalkut Yosef, Shemita, p. 34*) and Rav Yisraeli (*Chavat Binyamin, I, 9, 12*), especially today when the entire observance of *Shemita* is only by Rabbinic law.

4. In general, every few years a field is allowed to lie fallow for a year so that it may replenish its strength. During such years, the field falls into the category of *sedeh bur*, "a fallow field." The *Chazon Ish* (*22, 2; Madrich Shemita le-Chakla'im 16, 8*; based on the Rambam, *Hilchot Shemita ve-Yovel 4:4*) proposed that if one alters the planting cycle, and cultivates a field during the *Shemita* year, despite the fact that, according to schedule, it should have lied fallow – the produce of that field does not fall into the category of forbidden *sefichim*. He argues that a *sedeh bur* is considered a field that is unfit for agricultural use, and thus there is no concern that by permitting *sefichim* a person will come to plant in the field during the *Shemita* year. Hence, the prohibition of *sefichim* does not apply.

   Some farmers alternate their planting as follows: one year the field is planted with a winter crop, and the next year it is planted with a summer crop, so that each season of cultivation is followed by a season of lying fallow. The *Chazon Ish* adds that during the season that the field is supposed to lie fallow, it is treated as a *sedeh bur*. Therefore, if according to schedule, a field had not been designated for a winter crop during the *Shemita* year, produce growing in that field during the winter is not subject to the prohibition of *sefichim*.

   The *Chazon Ish* refers, of course, to a case where the field was planted during the sixth year, as planting during the *Shemita* year is forbidden under all circumstances:

> A field that is planted one year with grain that grows during the winter, and the next year it is left fallow during the winter and planted with legumes during the summer, the *sefichim* of grain that grow during the winter are not subject to the prohibition of *sefichim*... **According to this, even if a person planted [his field] before *Rosh ha-Shana* of the seventh year, because he did not want to leave it fallow, and thus allow Arabs to take control of it, the grain that grows there is not subject to the prohibition of *sefichim*...**

This method of planting in advance can help to solve the problem of vegetables during the *Shemita* year. Today, it is possible to plant during the sixth year such that the seeds will sprout only later, with the result that vegetables can grow over the course of the seventh year having been planted during the sixth year. The application of the *Chazon Ish's* proposal (by changing the cycle of planting) allows for planting without the vegetables becoming subject to the prohibition of *sefichim*.

Rav Sh. Z. Auerbach was doubtful about the ***Chazon Ish's*** solution, arguing that there is still room for concern about deception, namely, that a person will sow a *sedeh bur* during the seventh year and claim that the produce growing there grew on its own. Rav Auerbach proposed a different solution, suggesting that the prohibition of *sefichim* may not apply in a large and well-ordered field, where covert planting is impossible:[17]

> I was at first astonished by our master, the *Chazon Ish, zt"l,* who went to great lengths to find an allowance for the kibbutzim which observe *Shemita,* and suggested an exceedingly novel position... that if, according to the schedule followed by those farmers, that field should have been planted during the seventh year in the summer and not in the winter – if they plant it before *Rosh ha-Shana* of the seventh year so that

17. *Responsa Minchat Shlomo,* I, *no.* 50. See also *Shemita Mamlachtit,* 5760, *chap.* 8. There he adds that it is possible that since a person can sow his field in a permitted manner, we are not concerned that he will sow it in a forbidden manner.

> it should produce in the winter, this is treated like a *sedeh bur*, so that whatever grows there is not governed by the prohibition of *sefichim*. In my humble opinion, this requires careful examination, for surely the reason for the decree applies here. Since in the seventh year he cannot plant in the summer, he will go and plant covertly in the winter and later say that it grew by itself, for this year it is worth his while to change the regular order and plant in the winter…
>
> I said that it is better to rely on the argument that we have put forward that in very large areas, where everything is planted in an orderly manner, such that it is absolutely impossible to say that it grew on its own – that in such a case there is no prohibition of *sefichim*…
>
> Since, however, the Sages did not count this allowance among the "four fields," this proves that they did not distinguish between a large field… and since there is no mention anywhere that this is permitted, it stands to reason that it should not be permitted.

In practice, Rav Sh. Z. Auerbach did not issue an allowance in this case, suggesting that the sages did not differentiate between a large and a small field.

5. **Areas of Eretz Yisrael conquered when Israel left Egypt**: Areas that were part of the Israelite conquest following the exodus from Egypt, but did not return to Israel's possession after the return from the Babylonian exile, are not governed by the prohibition of *sefichim*, despite the fact that, by Rabbinic law, the *Shemita* prohibitions apply there as well (Rambam, *Hilchot Shemita ve-Yovel 4:26; 28*):

> All parts of the Land of Israel occupied by those who came up from Babylonia, as far as Keziv, may not be cultivated in the sabbatical year, and all aftergrowths

therein that sprout spontaneously (*sefichim*) are forbidden for consumption.

As for the parts of the Land occupied only by those who came up from Egypt, which are from Keziv to the River of Egypt and Amana, although it is forbidden to cultivate them in the sabbatical year, the aftergrowths that sprout in them are permitted for consumption.

For this reason, the prohibition of *sefichim* does not apply to the southern Arava (*Sefer Eretz Yisra'el, pp. 82-84*; *Responsa Shevet ha-Levi, v, no. 173*, is even more lenient), Gush Katif and Azza (see *Techumin, II, p. 364*).[18] Moreover, the prohibition of *sefichim* does not apply on the east bank of the Jordan, even though that territory was indeed conquered following the return from the Babylonian exile (Rambam, ibid.).

It should be noted that even if the prohibition of *sefichim* does not apply in these areas, this does not mean that they are not part of Eretz Yisrael! This discussion is strictly limited to the application of the prohibition of *sefichim* in these areas (*Kaftor va-Ferach, chap. 10*; *Responsa Yeshu'ot Molcho, Yore De'a, no. 67*; Rav Ariel, *Techumin, II, p. 377*. Regarding this principle, see also the introduction to *Shabbat ha-Aretz, 15*).

6. **Produce that grew indoors:** The prohibition of *sefichim* does not apply to produce that grew indoors. We already saw above that opinions differ as to whether or not planting indoors is forbidden during the *Shemita* year. In any event, there is certainly no reason to be stringent about the prohibition of *sefichim*, it being only a Rabbinic decree, as explained by Rav Chaim Berlin[19] (cited in *Sefer ha-Shemita, p. 28, note 2*):

> Since in the *Yerushalmi*... [there is uncertainty] regarding a tree that was planted indoors... whether the laws of *Shemita* apply to it at all... This being the case, one may be lenient with respect to produce that grew indoors regarding the prohibition of *sefichim* which is

18. The Gemara in the beginning of *Gittin* states that those who returned from the Babylonian exile did not reoccupy the portion of Eretz Yisrael from Rekem on. "Rekem" is generally identified with Petra. Thus, from Petra and southward, meaning the southern Arava, there is no prohibition of *sefichim*. There are other regions whose status is in doubt: the Bet Shean valley, the Jordan valley, the northern Golan, and others (see *Techumin II, p. 364*; *Techumin XIII, p. 30*; *Encyclopedia Talmudit*, appendix to *Eretz Yisrael*; Rav Tykoczinski, *Sefer Eretz Yisrael, pp. 34, 37, 82*; *Responsa Shevet ha-Levi, v, no. 173*; *Responsa Mishnat Yosef, I, nos. 44-45*, and *II, no. 47*.)

19. See *Mishpetei Aretz* (*17, note 36*) which cites this approach as the position of Rav Elyashiv.

only by Rabbinic decree, especially in our time [when *Shemita* itself may be only Rabbinic in nature].

7. **Produce that does not have *Shemita* sanctity**: Is produce that lacks *Shemita* sanctity governed by the prohibition of *sefichim*? Responsa *Az Nidbaru* (IV, *nos.* 3–5) maintains that there is no connection between these two laws. According to him, even produce that does not have *Shemita* sanctity might be subject to the prohibition of *sefichim*, for the decree is based on the concern that one may come to engage in covert planting, and this concern is valid even with respect to produce that does not have *Shemita* sanctity.

Annual flowers

Perennial flowers

In contrast, Rav Sh. Z. Auerbach disagrees and says that the prohibition of *sefichim* does not apply to produce that lacks *Shemita* sanctity (*Ma'adanei Eretz, note 11*; *Minchat Shlomo, 51, 11*). This is also the opinion of many other *Acharonim* (*Chazon Ish,*[20] *Shemita ke-Hilchatah, 2, 12*; *Yalkut Yosef, 23, note 9, p. 500*), and this has been accepted

20. The *Chazon Ish* in *Shevi'it* 9, 4 (s.v. *ha de-katvinan*) writes that the prohibition of *sefichim* applies even when there is no *Shemita* sanctity, but in 10, 12 (s.v. *Yerushalmi Shevi'it*) and in 9, 17 (and elsewhere), he writes differently. And so too we find in *Derech Emuna* (*Shemita ve-Yovel* 4, *no.* 28) in the name of the *Chazon Ish*.

as halacha. This ruling has a number of halachic ramifications, one of which relates to the treatment of flowers during the *Shemita* year.

Unscented flowers: As we saw in earlier chapters (p. 255), unscented flowers do not have *Shemita* sanctity. Thus, we rule that they are also not subject to the prohibition of *sefichim*. Strictly speaking, then, it is permitted to plant scentless flowers until *Rosh ha-Shana* of the seventh year, and there is no problem even if they did not sprout before the beginning of *Shemita*.[21]

Scented flowers: We saw above (p. 257) that the *Posekim* disagree whether or not flowers that only have a scent (but are not eaten) have *Shemita* sanctity. Therefore, if the prohibition of *sefichim* applies only to produce that has *Shemita* sanctity, that same disagreement would apply to the prohibition of *sefichim*. Due to the uncertainty, one should try and plant them such that they will sprout before *Rosh ha-Shana*.

Most flowers have a scent, and so they are subject to uncertain *Shemita* sanctity and thus an uncertain prohibition of *sefichim*. During the *Shemita* year, then, one should only buy perennial flowers, such as roses or lilies, to which the *sefichim* prohibition does not apply. Such flowers might still be subject to the problems of *shamur* and *ne'evad* (because they may have been grown in violation of the law), but we are generally lenient with regard to these problems.[22] Rav Sh. Z. Auerbach maintains that flowers that merely have a scent, but are not used primarily as fragrance, do not have *Shemita* sanctity, and thus they are not subject to the prohibitions of *sefichim*, *shamur* (because there is no requirement to make them ownerless), or picking (because the prohibition of picking applies exclusively to that which has *Shemita* sanctity).

Strictly speaking, then, **it is permitted to buy perennial flowers during the *Shemita* year, without any special *kashrut* certification**. It is best to avoid all uncertainty and purchase flowers that were grown hydroponically or at least flowers from land that was sold in the *heter mechira*.

21. Even though they are not subject to the prohibition of *sefichim*, and so it should be permissible to plant them until *Rosh ha-Shana*, some authorities are stringent and require that they be planted by the 26th of *Elul*. They maintain that there is a positive commandment that the land should rest, and so if the plant begins to grow during the *Shemita* year, the "rest of the land" is impaired. This follows from the words of Rav Kook (*Shabbat ha-Aretz* 3, 11, 2), though the *Chazon Ish* (22, 5) seems to be lenient – see the chapter on *tosefet shevi'it*. In any event, all agree that planting a plant together with its root stock and soil is permitted until *Rosh ha-Shana*.

22. Even though it may be that the leniency with respect to *shamur* and *ne'evad* is limited to produce that is eaten, and not to produce that is merely decorative (but, taken together with additional factors, this leniency is well based, as will be explained below).

Annual flowers: The *Shemita* status of annual flowers is more complex. Regarding such flowers, the concern exists that they were planted during the *Shemita* year itself, and therefore, according to some opinions, they are subject to the prohibition of *sefichim*, and in addition, buying such flowers supports those violating the law. Therefore, one should only buy annual flowers that were grown hydroponically. As we shall see below, those who buy annual flowers from land sold in the *heter mechira* have adequate basis to support this practice. It should be noted that if we know that the flowers started to grow during the sixth year, they are permitted even if they were picked in the seventh year (*Chazon Ish, 14, 9,* s.v. *u-vi-teshuvat*).

Summary: Perennial flowers (grown hydroponically or at least from *heter mechira*) may be purchased during the *Shemita* year even without *kashrut* certification, though it is preferable to buy such flowers that are certified as kosher. **Annual flowers** (grown hydroponically, though there is adequate basis to buy from *heter mechira*) require *kashrut* certification.[23] The tables that accompany this book list the time after which there is concern about each species of flower when special *kashrut* certification is required.

23. While in general the Israeli Rabbinate does not employ the *heter mechira* for flowers, very often commercial enterprises do. It is also possible that there is no prohibition of *sefichim* even with respect to annuals (for according to Rav Sh. Z. Auerbach they do not have *Shemita* sanctity). In addition, the prohibition of *sefichim* may apply only to eating and not to other forms of pleasure (see Rambam, *Hilchot Shemita ve-Yovel* 4:2: "All *sefichim* are forbidden to be eaten"; this is the way the Rambam was understood by *Mikdash David, Zera'im* 59, 3, s.v. *sefichim*). The *Chazon Ish* (*Shevi'it* 13, 16) writes that if the plant is not normally eaten, it is forbidden to derive benefit from it in the way that benefit is normally derived from it. Thus, the *Chazon Ish* applies the prohibition of *sefichim* to flowers (*Shevi'it* 14, 9, s.v. *u-vi-teshuvato*). See also Responsa *Minchat Shlomo* (*I*, 51, 11; and see also *Peirot Shevi'it*, 1, note 53).

RAV CHAYIM BERLIN

Rav Chayim Berlin was the son of the Rav Naftali Tzvi Berlin (the Netziv) of Volozhin and the brother of Rav Meir Bar Ilan (a leading figure in Religious Zionism). Rav Chayim Berlin was one of the most prominent authorities in the Charedi community in Eretz Yisrael, and, alongside Rav Shemuel Salant, one of the most important Rabbis in Jerusalem. He fiercely opposed secular studies, and even reported in the name of his father that it was in response to a government demand for secular studies that the Volozhin Yeshiva was closed down. His position on the matter gave rise to much controversy.

Rav Chayim Berlin also had a major influence on issues related to *Shemita* observance. Rav Berlin corresponded with Rav Kook on *Shemita* issues, and wrote in one of his letters that their views were in fact quite similar (Ha-Chavatzelet, 5670 (1910).

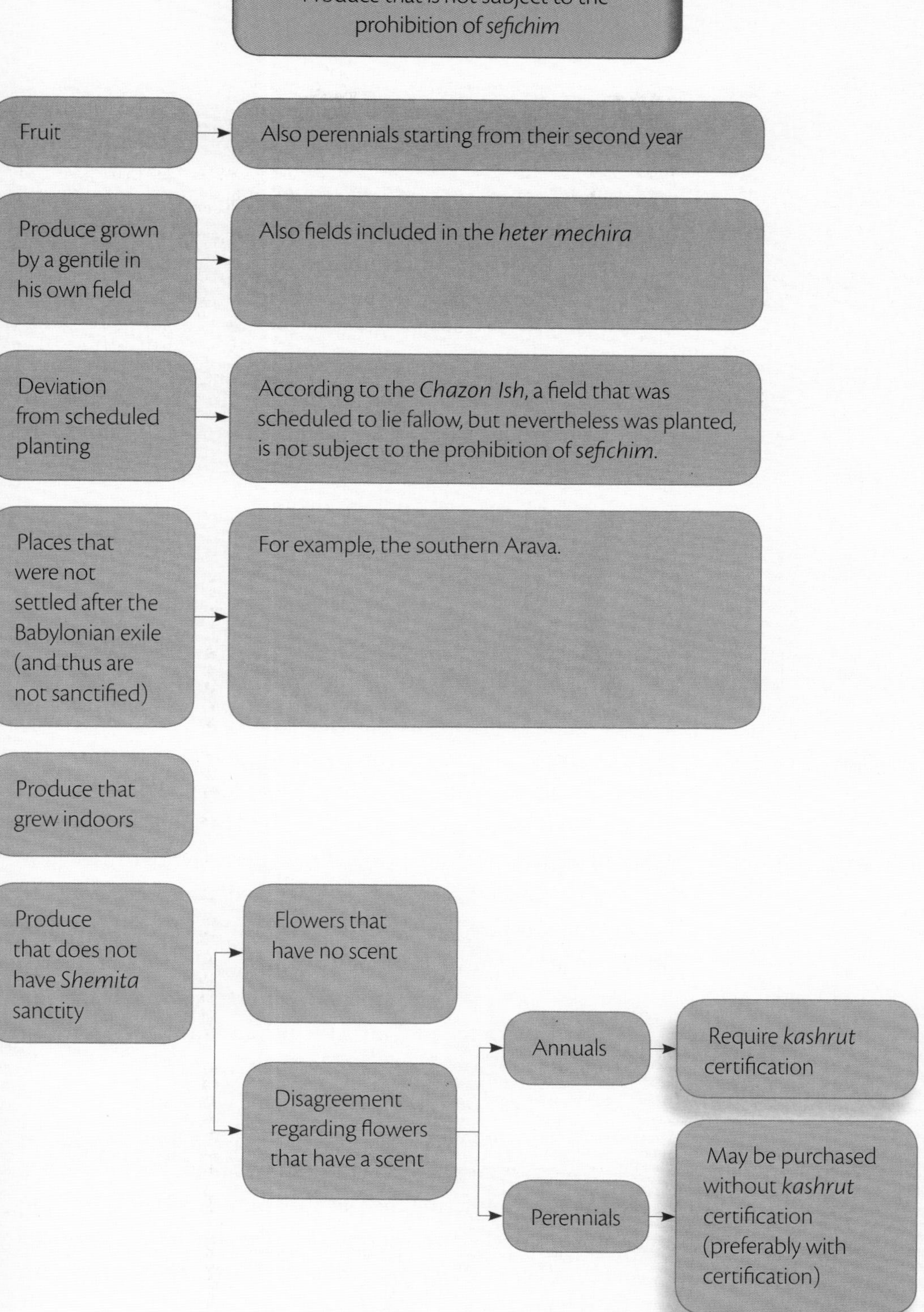
Produce that is not subject to the prohibition of *sefichim*
Fruit
Also perennials starting from their second year
Produce grown by a gentile in his own field
Also fields included in the *heter mechira*
Deviation from scheduled planting
According to the *Chazon Ish*, a field that was scheduled to lie fallow, but nevertheless was planted, is not subject to the prohibition of *sefichim*.
Places that were not settled after the Babylonian exile (and thus are not sanctified)
For example, the southern Arava.
Produce that grew indoors
Produce that does not have *Shemita* sanctity
Flowers that have no scent
Disagreement regarding flowers that have a scent
Annuals
Require *kashrut* certification
Perennials
May be purchased without *kashrut* certification (preferably with certification)

SHEMITA SANCTITY IN MONEY, MEAT AND FISH

Even when there is no problem of *sefichim, shamur* or *ne'evad,* the process of purchasing fruits and vegetables during the *Shemita* year can lead to a variety of problematic scenarios: handing over *Shemita* money to an *am ha-aretz* (an ignorant person who is not scrupulous in his observance of the commandments); doing commerce with *Shemita* produce and measuring *Shemita* produce. Before we begin to discuss these prohibitions, let us explain the idea of *Shemita* sanctity that applies to articles other than fruits and vegetables.

The Gemara in *Sukka (40b)* brings the following Baraita:

> A baraita supports the view of Rabbi Elazar: *Shemita* sanctity is transferred to money used to purchase the produce, as the verse states, "For it is the jubilee, it shall be holy to you" – just as for *hekdesh,* sanctity is transferred from that which is holy to the money used to redeem it, and it becomes prohibited for ordinary use, so too, *Shemita* produce transfers its sanctity to money that purchases it, and it becomes prohibited for ordinary use, while the produce itself remains holy. But in case you would say that just as with holy objects the money for which it is redeemed assumes its sanctity and the holy object itself loses its sanctity, so too with the produce of the seventh year the money for which it is redeemed assumes its sanctity, and the produce itself loses its sanctity, the Torah explicitly states: "it shall be" – it remains in its original consecrated state. How so? If one purchased meat with the produce of the seventh year, both the meat and the produce must be removed at the end of the seventh year. If one purchased fish with the meat, the meat loses its sanctity, and the fish assumes it. If one purchased wine with the fish, the fish loses its sanctity, and the wine assumes it. If one purchased oil with the wine, the wine loses its sanctity, and the oil assumes it. What principle is at work here? The last object [redeemed in exchange for the produce] assumes the sanctity of the seventh year, but the produce itself retains its sanctity.

The *Baraita* asserts that *Shemita* sanctity applies to the money for which *Shemita* produce is exchanged. We have already noted in earlier chapters (see p. 230), that in contrast to the redemption of *ma'aser sheni* and *hekdesh,* where the sanctity is transferred from the produce and consecrated property to the money, in the case of *Shemita* produce, the sanctity applies to the money but also remains in the produce. We explained this difference by suggesting that *Shemita* produce has inherent sanctity, as opposed to *ma'aser sheni* and *hekdesh,* the sanctity of which results from human action. We added that the goal of the sabbatical year is to demonstrate that the land belongs to God, and therefore, even the person who grew the produce is not treated as its owner, and cannot remove its sanctity.

Even if a person exchanges *Shemita* produce for meat or some other food, the sanctity is not removed from the produce, but rather both the produce and the meat are endowed with *Shemita* sanctity. But if he exchanges the meat (or the money) for fish, the sanctity is transferred from the meat to the fish, and the meat is no longer sanctified with *Shemita* sanctity. This is because the *Shemita* sanctity in the meat is not inherent sanctity, but merely sanctity that the person transferred to the meat by exchanging it for *Shemita* produce. Therefore, when the meat is exchanged for the fish, the sanctity is removed from the meat and passed over to the fish, just as other types of sanctity created by man can be transferred from one object to another by way of redemption.

We can summarize what we have seen thus far by saying that *Shemita* produce always retains its sanctity, even if it is sold many times over. If *Shemita* produce is exchanged for another article, and that article for another, and so on, *Shemita* sanctity applies to the last article in that series. All foods to which *Shemita* sanctity is applied must be treated in the same manner as *Shemita* produce itself.

This notion that *Shemita* sanctity applies to the food for which *Shemita* produce is exchanged applies only if the exchange is made **in a commercial manner** (sale of the sanctified produce in exchange for money, meat or other objects). The continuation of the Gemara in *Sukka* (*40b*) records a disagreement regarding the third link in a series of exchanges involving *Shemita* produce – food exchanged for the food that was exchanged for the *Shemita* produce. Does sanctity apply to the third food only by way of a sale, or perhaps it applies to it even by way of replacement, such as by stating that the sanctity should pass over to another object. The Rambam (*Hilchot Shemita ve-Yovel 6:8*) rules that from the second food and on the sanctity is transferred even by way of replacement:

> *Shemita* sanctity may be transferred only by way of purchase. To what does this apply? To the first produce [exchanged directly for the *Shemita* produce]. As for the second produce [the produce exchanged for the first exchanged produce], it may be transferred either by way of purchase or by way of designation.

What is the rationale behind this difference between the original produce and the produce for which it is exchanged?

As we explained above, the sanctity of the original produce is inherent, and therefore it cannot be redeemed and transferred to another object. In such a case, even though one cannot remove the sanctity from the produce, if a person executed a legal sale of the consecrated produce, since he sold an object of sanctity, the money that was involved in the legal transaction also acquires sanctity. Such an acquisition can only be done by way of the recognized transaction of sale. In contrast, the sanctity of the second produce is not inherent, and therefore it can be redeemed. For the same reason, the transfer of sanctity can be performed not only by way of a sale, but even by way of a decision that the sanctity should pass over to another object. Thus, it suffices to say, "May the sanctity in the meat be redeemed on the fish," or even "The fish in place of the meat," in order for the sanctity to pass to the third product.

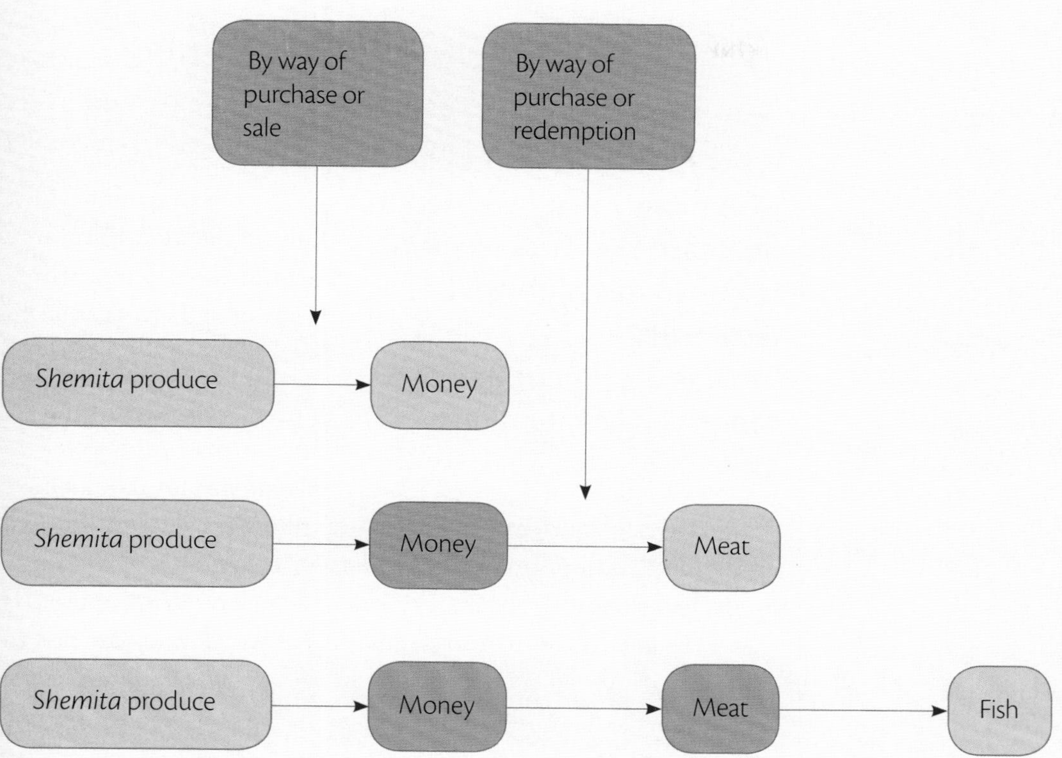

In sky blue = *Shemita* sanctity

TRANSFERRING *SHEMITA* MONEY TO AN *AM HA-ARETZ*

What is the unique problem with money that was used to purchase *Shemita* produce?
How can this problem be resolved?
What is the practical significance of "*Shemita* money" today?

The Gemara in *Sukka* (*39a–39b*) records a Baraita which prohibits handing over more *Shemita* money than three meals' worth to an *am ha-aretz*:

> It has been taught: One must not hand over *Shemita* money to an *am ha-aretz* more than is sufficient for three meals, but if he handed [him more], he should say: "This money shall be exchanged for [the ordinary] fruit which I have in my house," and he goes and eats the fruit as though it has *Shemita* sanctity.

One may not hand over *Shemita* money to an *am ha-aretz*, because *Shemita* money must be handled in a manner that reflects its sanctity, and an *am ha-aretz* is suspected of not doing so. According to the Gemara, if a person gave *Shemita* money to an *am ha-aretz* in violation of the law, he must redeem the money against produce that he has in his house, and then treat that produce as having *Shemita* sanctity. The Gemara continues by stating that one must not purchase produce grown during the *Shemita* year against the law, even less than three meals' worth, so as to not to support transgressors.

THE CONCERN ABOUT HANDING OVER SANCTIFIED MONEY TO AN *AM HA-ARETZ*

According to Rashi, it is permitted to hand over *Shemita* money to an *am ha-aretz* in an amount that suffices to buy food for three meals because the Sages wished to allow the seller to earn a minimal income on which to live. The Meiri adds another reason: the allowance was also issued for the buyer's benefit, so that he should be able to buy himself three meals worth of food.

Why is it forbidden to hand over a quantity of *Shemita* money sufficient to buy more than three meals to an *am ha-aretz*? Rashi and *Tosafot* (ad loc.) disagree on this point. According to Rashi, we are concerned that the *am ha-aretz* will keep the money for himself even after the time of *bi'ur*:

> The Torah said [that *Shemita* produce is meant] "for eating" and not for trade. This also means that all *Shemita* produce, and the money for which it is exchanged, must be removed [from the house] during the seventh year, and one must not trade in it, storing it until after the seventh year and as a result earning a large profit. An *am ha-aretz* is suspected of doing this. Therefore, one must not hand over *Shemita* money to him, for that is a violation of [the prohibition,] "You shall not put a stumbling block before the blind."

In contrast, the *Tosafot* (s.v. *she-ein*) understand the enactment differently:

> Rather, the reason [for the prohibition] is because there are many prohibitions [that can result from misuse of *Shemita* money]. **An *am ha-aretz* may not avoid** buying an unclean animal, slaves, land, a cloak, a shawl, or shoes with it [the *Shemita* money]. The rule is that it must not be given in payment to a well-master,[24] a bathhouse attendant, a sailor or a barber, for *Shemita* produce is meant for eating, drinking and anointing, and not for other purposes. And it is forbidden to pay back a debt with it. And there are countless laws and prohibitions that govern the produce of the seventh year which must be treated with *Shemita* sanctity.

According to the *Tosafot*, the concern is that the *am ha-aretz* will not treat the money in the manner dictated by its sanctity, there being so many prohibitions that apply to this money.

According to both views, the prohibition to hand over the money to an *am ha-aretz* is based on the prohibition not to put a stumbling block before the blind. At first glance, this presents a difficulty, as the

24. The Hebrew word used there is *bayar*, which is one who digs wells or supplies water from wells.

usual case of handing over *Shemita* money to an *am ha-aretz* involves the purchase of *Shemita* produce from him. Hence, even prior to the purchase, he was in possession of produce having *Shemita* sanctity! Why is it worse to give the *am ha-aretz* sanctified money, than to leave in his possession sanctified produce?

According to Rashi, the answer is clear. There is greater concern about the money because it is precisely money that the *am ha-aretz* might keep until after the time of *bi'ur* (because it does not spoil). According to the *Tosafot*, on the other hand, we are forced to say that there is greater concern about the money, because it is forbidden to repay a debt with *Shemita* money, or to pay for services with it, or the like. That is to say, there are many more prohibited uses of the money than of the produce, for the produce is generally eaten in any event. This also fits with *Tosafot's* emphasis that there are many laws regarding *Shemita* sanctity, as this is especially true with regard to *Shemita* money.

This law has an important ramification for anybody in possession of money that has *Shemita* sanctity. Such a person must be careful not to buy anything else with it but food[25] (Ramban, *Sukka 41*) and to maintain the sanctity of the food bought with it. For example, he must not pay wages with *Shemita* money,[26] as *Shemita* money may only be used for the purchase of food and drink (Rambam, *Hilchot Shemita ve-Yovel 6:11*, based on Mishna, *Shevi'it 8:5*; and see his commentary to the Mishna, ad loc.; *Bet Ridbaz 67:11*). It is particularly important to be careful about the sanctity of foods other than fruits and vegetables, because people are not accustomed to maintain the sanctity of meat, cookies or the like. Therefore, any food other than fresh produce that has *Shemita* sanctity should be marked as such.

If one purchases food with *Shemita* money, it should be used only for eating, as is stated in the Mishna (*Shevi'it 8:8*):

> Slaves, property, or unclean cattle may not be bought with money realized by sale of seventh year products.

The Ramban (*Avoda Zara 62a*) explains that *Shemita* money should be used only for the purchase of food to enable the

25. The Ritva implies that products that will endure for a long time may not be purchased with *Shemita* money, but anything that can be removed from the house at the time of *bi'ur* may be purchased. The accepted ruling is that it is forbidden to buy anything that is not food with *Shemita* money (see *Sefer ha-Shemita, chap. 8, note 8*; *Kehilot Ya'akov, Shevi'it 6, 4-5*).

26. See Responsa *Mishnat Yosef* (*1, no. 27*), who writes that one should not give *Shemita* produce as *mishlo'ach manot* on Purim. It is therefore preferable that the first set of *mishlo'ach manot* that one sends be comprised of two food items that do not have *Shemita* sanctity, as this is the minimum required for the *mitzva*.

maintenance of *Shemita* sanctity, namely, to eat the food in a manner dictated by *Shemita* sanctity. According to the Ramban, if *Shemita* money is used for the purchase of non-food items, the *Shemita* sanctity is removed:

> The Torah said that *Shemita* produce is meant for eating and not for anything else. Therefore it is forbidden by Torah law to purchase anything that cannot be eaten with *Shemita* produce, as the Mishna in *Shevi'it* (*8:8*) states: Slaves, property, or non-kosher animals may not be bought with money used to purchase seventh year products… And the same applies to a cloak or a shawl or anything else that is not fit to be eaten… But anything that is fit to be eaten can certainly be bought with the *Shemita* produce, or with the money exchanged for it… And the reason that something that is fit to be eaten is permitted is because it obtains *Shemita* sanctity and can be treated with *Shemita* sanctity. But that which cannot be treated with *Shemita* sanctity, such as a cloak, is forbidden, for he removes the sanctity, and we cannot apply "for food" to it.

Similarly, it is forbidden to exchange food that is fit for human consumption for food that is fit only for animals, for this reduces the level of sanctity (*Tosefta* 5:12; Rambam, *Hilchot Shemita ve-Yovel* 5:12).

Receiving change at the checkout counter: Anyone might come into possession of *Shemita* money, even if he never sells *Shemita* produce, when he receives change at the checkout counter. For example, if a person buys laundry detergent or any other product, and in the cash register there is money that has *Shemita* sanctity, and he pays for his purchase and receives change from that money, he now has money in his hand that has *Shemita* sanctity!

The *Chazon Ish* (*10, 17*, s.v. *ve-hu de-amar*) writes that unless we know that particular money is *Shemita* money, we need not assume that it is, because most money does not have *Shemita* sanctity. Responsa *Minchat Yitzchak* (*VI, no. 129*) agrees that if a person does not know that there is money in the cash register that has *Shemita* sanctity he may be lenient in accordance with the *Chazon Ish*. But if he knows that there is *Shemita* money in the register there is no room for leniency.

Shemita money is not nullified by the majority of non-*Shemita* money, since it is regarded as "something whose prohibition can or will lapse at some future time" (*davar she-yesh lo matirin*) which is not nullified when mixed with something of the same type (in our case, money mixed with money). The *Shemita* money in the cash register falls into this category because it can be exchanged for produce, and that produce can be eaten in a manner consistent with its sanctity:[27]

> One may be lenient about money in the marketplace, that unless one knows that *Shemita* money is circulating there, we follow the majority [that is not *Shemita* money]... But in banks or stores where we know with certainty that there is *Shemita* money mixed in – it is stated explicitly in the Mishna that it is not nullified (and so rules the Rambam, *Hilchot Shemita ve-Yovel,* end of chap. 7). And Radbaz writes there that the reason is that it is a *davar she-yesh lo matirin,* for he can exchange it for food.

What can be done then with the change? Rav Sh. Z. Auerbach (*Minchat Shlomo* 45) suggests that one can say to the seller that the sanctity in the change should be transferred to the purchase money, and thus it is only the seller's money that will have sanctity:

> And I believe that it is permitted to say to someone who is suspect regarding *Shemita* produce: Give me your *shekel* that is *Shemita* money, and I will give you a different *shekel* that will become sanctified in its place. This is because the exchange does not give rise to any new stumbling blocks, that there should be room to forbid [the exchange] on the grounds that one may not hand over *Shemita* money to an *am ha-aretz.* And all the more so in our case, where the *Shemita* money was obtained from the sale of produce from fields that were sold under the *heter mechira.* According to the seller, he acted in a permitted manner and because of this,

27. This explanation is based on Rashi's understanding of the law of *"davar she-yesh lo matirin."* The Ran's understanding of this law is worthy of a separate discussion, which is beyond our scope. *Responsa Minchat Shlomo* (*no.* 45) writes that the money is not nullified because of its significance.

as we already explained elsewhere, the prohibition of putting a stumbling block before the blind does not apply, and nor does the prohibition of handing over *Shemita* money to an *am ha-aretz.*

According to Rav Sh. Z. Auerbach, a buyer does not violate the prohibition of putting a stumbling block before the blind when he leaves sanctified money in the hands of the seller, even if there is reason to believe that the seller will not maintain its sanctity. This is because the *Shemita* money had already been in the seller's possession prior to the purchase. Thus, the buyer is merely replacing sanctified money with other sanctified money (even if not always the same amount), and no new stumbling block is placed before the seller![28]

28. In the case of produce subject to the *heter mechira*, there is even less concern, because sanctity is observed on this produce only out of stringency. See below.

This solution, however, is not always practical, and therefore another solution has been proposed. *Responsa Minchat Yitzchak* (*VI, no. 139*) suggests that one should purchase some food item in that same store, and declare: "All of the sanctified money in my possession should be redeemed on this food item." The sanctity of the money is thereby transferred to the food, and the food can now be eaten in accordance with its sanctity:

The best thing to do is to buy a food item – a piece of fruit, or the like, that is worth a *peruta* – and after cleaning the food from all dirt and waste, so that the food is fit to be eaten, without anything being left over… he should say: All *Shemita* money or anything exchanged for *Shemita* produce that is found in my possession should be redeemed on this food. And he should eat it in accordance with *Shemita* sanctity.

Fundamentally, the money can be redeemed even on produce that is found in one's house, and there is no obligation to redeem the money on produce purchased at the same time. It is a good idea, however, to redeem the money as soon as possible, so that one not inadvertently spend the *Shemita* money on other things.

Here, however, the question arises whether one can redeem a large sum of *Shemita* money on a piece of fruit that is worth a *peruta*.

In other words, can one redeem a sanctified object worth a *maneh* (*100 dinar*) on another object that is worth only a *peruta* (less than one percent of a *dinar*), as is done in the case of *ma'aser sheni*? Rash Sirillo (*Shevi'it 8:7*) writes that one can, but the *Chazon Ish* (*25, 5*) disagrees. According to the *Chazon Ish,* it is only *ma'aser sheni* that can be redeemed on a *peruta,* because today *ma'aser sheni* cannot be eaten. But money that is sanctified with *Shemita* sanctity, which can be redeemed on food of the same value, and that food can then be eaten in accordance with its sanctity, must be redeemed on produce of the same value!

However, even the *Chazon Ish* is lenient in the following two cases:

1. *Bedi'eved,* if a person redeemed a large sum of *Shemita* money on a *peruta,* the sanctity is transferred to the *peruta.*
2. It is permitted to redeem that which is worth a *maneh* on that which is worth a *peruta* in order to save another person from violating a prohibition.

It seems that in the case under discussion, since a doubt exists whether or not the change received from the cashier is sanctified money, one may be lenient and redeem the money *lechatchila* even on a single cookie. One must, of course, remember not to waste the cookie, and to treat it with *Shemita* sanctity.

WHERE DO WE ENCOUNTER MONEY THAT HAS *SHEMITA* SANCTITY?

Today, we do not regularly come across money that has *Shemita* sanctity: Money used in the purchase of produce from *Otzar Bet Din* has no sanctity (see below, p. 350[29]); money used in the purchase of produce that was grown hydroponically is generally viewed as not having *Shemita* sanctity (see below, p. 367); in most sections of the county (except for Bnei Brak, where the position of the *Chazon Ish* is followed), money used in the purchase of produce from gentiles is viewed as not having *Shemita* sanctity; and similarly money used in the purchase of produce from fields that were sold in the *heter mechira,* technically speaking, has no *Shemita* sanctity. It is, however,

29. Money that is paid is for the workers' service and not for the produce.

fitting to be stringent about produce bought on the basis of the *heter mechira*, and treat the purchase money as if it were sanctified with *Shemita* sanctity.

Accordingly, we only encounter *Shemita* money when produce is purchased from fields that were sold in the *heter mechira* (as a stringency) or when produce is purchased from gentiles (only for the residents of Bnei Brak who follow the rulings of the *Chazon Ish*). Only such money need be handled in accordance with the laws of *Shemita* sanctity. Therefore, when buying in a store that also sells produce from fields that were sold in the *heter mechira*, and certainly when buying from a store that sells *Shemita* produce that has no *kashrut* certification whatsoever, one must be concerned that the change that one receives may have *Shemita* sanctity. That money should be redeemed on a food item, and that food item must then be eaten in accordance with the laws of *Shemita* sanctity.[30]

RABBI MOSHE BEN NACHMAN (*Ramban*)

Rabbi Moshe ben Nachman was born in 4954 (1194) in Gerona, Spain. In his later years, despite great obstacles, he moved to Eretz Yisrael, where he wrote about the reality that he found there. The Ramban authored works in all areas of Torah study and is one of the great *Rishonim* of the Spanish school. He is most widely known for his commentary on the Torah, in which he combines the plain sense of the text with Rabbinic interpretations in addition to philosophical and kabbalistic insights. His novellae on the Talmud are of great importance, and reflect a major breakthrough in talmudic studies. The Ramban was a master in all fields – halacha, scripture, philosophy and kabbala.

30. The *Va'ad ha-Shemita* of the Chief Rabbinate redeems all the *Shemita* money in the country on a daily basis, because *bedi'eved* redemption of *Shemita* sanctity on a *peruta* is valid, and thus they save people from violating prohibitions. Of course, one should not rely on this solution *lechatchila*, and this procedure is performed only in order to save those who are not aware of the need to treat sanctified money in a manner that is dictated by *Shemita* sanctity.

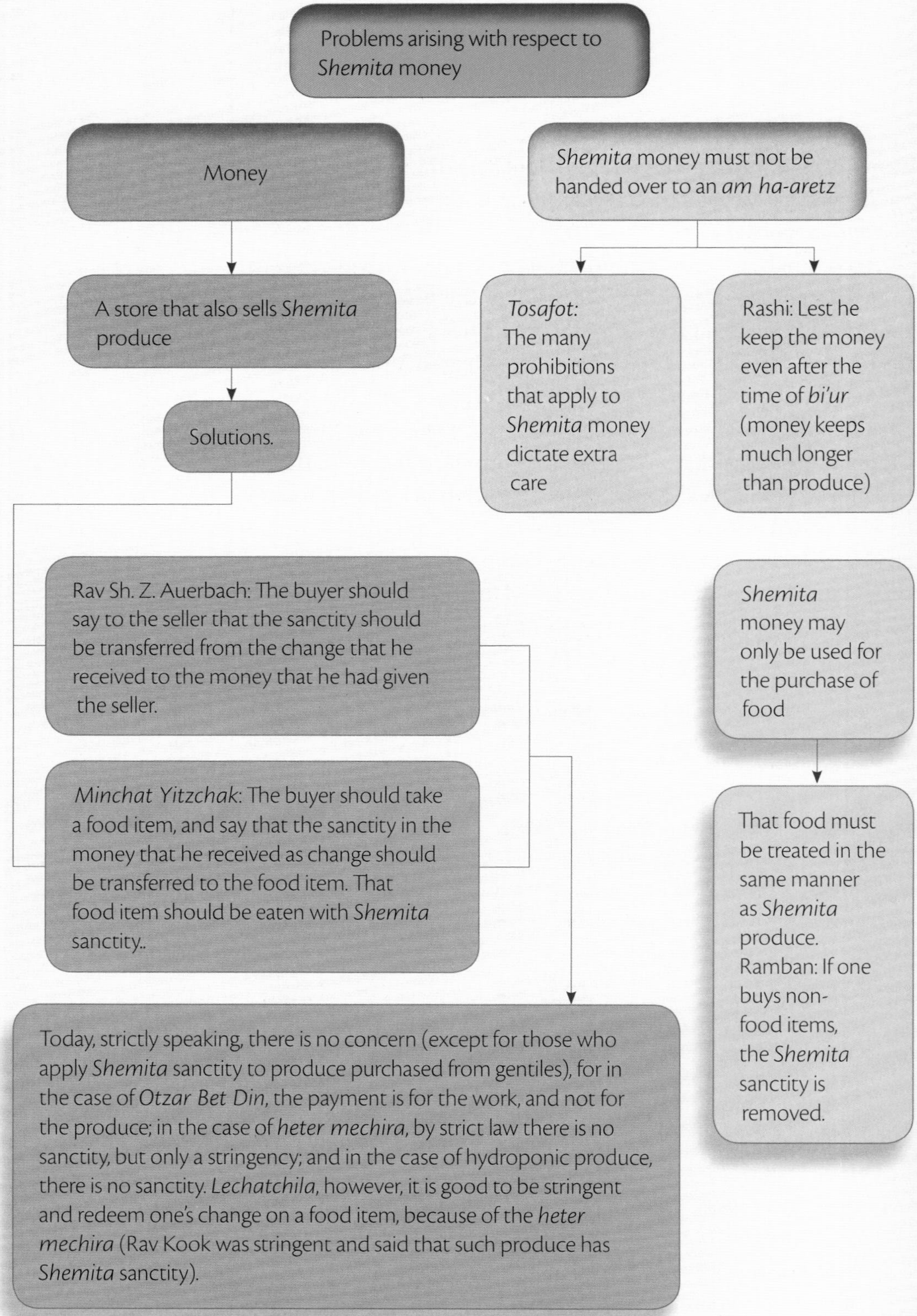

Problems arising with respect to *Shemita* money

Money

A store that also sells *Shemita* produce

Solutions.

Rav Sh. Z. Auerbach: The buyer should say to the seller that the sanctity should be transferred from the change that he received to the money that he had given the seller.

Minchat Yitzchak: The buyer should take a food item, and say that the sanctity in the money that he received as change should be transferred to the food item. That food item should be eaten with *Shemita* sanctity..

Today, strictly speaking, there is no concern (except for those who apply *Shemita* sanctity to produce purchased from gentiles), for in the case of *Otzar Bet Din*, the payment is for the work, and not for the produce; in the case of *heter mechira*, by strict law there is no sanctity, but only a stringency; and in the case of hydroponic produce, there is no sanctity. *Lechatchila*, however, it is good to be stringent and redeem one's change on a food item, because of the *heter mechira* (Rav Kook was stringent and said that such produce has *Shemita* sanctity).

Shemita money must not be handed over to an *am ha-aretz*

Tosafot: The many prohibitions that apply to *Shemita* money dictate extra care

Rashi: Lest he keep the money even after the time of *bi'ur* (money keeps much longer than produce)

Shemita money may only be used for the purchase of food

That food must be treated in the same manner as *Shemita* produce. Ramban: If one buys non-food items, the *Shemita* sanctity is removed.

WHEN DOES *SHEMITA* SANCTITY NOT APPLY TO MONEY?

There are various ways to prevent *Shemita* sanctity from applying to money even if the money is used for the purchase of *Shemita* produce:

1. **Credit:** The Gemara (*Avoda Zara 62b*) relates that the scholars of the school of Rabbi Yannai purchased produce during the seventh year on credit, and paid off the debt during the eighth year, and in that way *Shemita* sanctity did not apply to the produce:

> The scholars in the school of Rabbi Yannai used to borrow fruits of the sabbatical year from the poor and repay them in the eighth year. When this was reported to Rabbi Yochanan,[31] he said to them: "They act properly."

Why doesn't *Shemita* sanctity apply to the money in such a case? Rashi (s.v. *ya'ot*), the Ramban (s.v. *ya'ot*), the *Tosafot* (s.v. *ya'ot*) in their first explanation, the Ran (on the Rif, *30b*), and the Meiri (s.v. *hayu*) explain that when the buyer repays his debt, the produce is no longer extant, and thus there is nothing to cause *Shemita* sanctity to apply to the money. *Tosafot* bring an alternate explanation in the name of Rabbenu Yitzchak, who says that *Shemita* sanctity does not apply to the money even if the produce is still extant at the time of payment, because the money is not regarded as payment for the produce, but as repayment of a debt.[32]

There is an important practical difference between the two explanations: According to Rabbenu Yitzchak, as long as the purchase of *Shemita* produce is made on credit, *Shemita* sanctity does not apply to the money. According to most *Rishonim*, on the other hand, in order for *Shemita* sanctity not to apply to the money, the debt must be paid back only after the produce has already been consumed.

Rav Kook (*Shabbat ha-Aretz 8, 20*) rules stringently in accordance with the first position, and therefore only if the produce is no longer extant when the buyer pays for it does *Shemita* sanctity not apply to the money:

31. What objection was raised against the scholars of the school of Rabbi Yannai such that Rabbi Yochanan needed to defend them? Rashi explains the claim as follows: It was assumed that when payment was made for the produce, *Shemita* sanctity attached to the money. But when the payment was made in the eighth year, the time of *bi'ur* had already passed (because there was no longer produce in the field, and any remaining produce had to be removed from the house). Thus, it should have been forbidden to use the money, because it had the *Shemita* sanctity of produce that was already subject to *bi'ur*. Paying for seventh-year produce during the eighth year (when that produce is no longer found in the field) would, therefore, be inappropriate, because at that time the money can no longer be used.

32. The *Tosafot* bring another explanation in the name of Rabbi Elchanan, who agrees that *Shemita* sanctity does not attach to the money, even if the produce is extant, but adds that this is only true if the produce had been transferred to a third party. (So rules *Bet Ridbaz* [9, 10, in a note to *Pe'at ha-Shulchan*]). We cite here the words of *Tosafot* which include: (1) the view accepted by Rav Kook; (2) the view accepted by the Ridbaz; (3) the most lenient position that was accepted by the *Chazon Ish*: "'They act properly' – (1) Since [the produce] is no

longer extant at the time [of payment], it is not an exchange, and *Shemita* sanctity does not attach to [the money]. According to this, they could have made payment already during the seventh year, if the *Shemita* produce had already been consumed… (2) Rav Elchanan ruled that if a Jew has wine that is forbidden because of idolatry, or other forbidden items, and he sells them to a gentile on credit, and the gentile sells them to a third party before making payment to the Jew, the money [paid to the Jew] is permitted *bedi'eved*, even if the prohibited items are still extant. (3) Rabbenu Yitzchak added that [the money is permitted] even if the gentile did not sell [the prohibited items], provided that he drew them into his possession before making payment."

> Regarding the allowance to borrow produce from the poor during the seventh year and return [produce] to them during the eighth year… and *Shemita* sanctity does not apply to the eighth year produce – this is [only] if all the seventh year produce has been consumed… But if the seventh year produce has not been consumed, and it is extant, *Shemita* sanctity applies to the eighth year produce.

A similar ruling is found in the *Aruch ha-Shulchan he-Atid* (29:24) and in *Sefer ha-Shemita* (*p.* 42).

The *Chazon Ish*, on the other hand, rules that since *Shemita* is observed today only by Rabbinic law, we can rely on the second position (*10, 13,* s.v. *ve-hacha bi-shevi'it* and s.v. *be-hikfahu*; and *26, 6*; and so too in *Kerem Tziyon 16, 7*):

> If he bought [*Shemita* produce] on credit, and afterwards paid the seller, [the money] is permitted, as the *Tosafot* write in the name of Rabbenu Yitzchak…
>
> As for what we wrote that [when buying] on credit, the money does not attain [*Shemita* sanctity] – the Ramban is inclined to say that if the produce is still extant at the time of payment, the money attains [*Shemita* sanctity]… It seems that in the case of buying on credit, one can be lenient like the *Tosafot*, since *Shemita* today is [only] by Rabbinic law, and when a doubt exists regarding the application of a Rabbinic law, one follows the lenient position.

As for actual practice, by strict law we should follow the ruling of Rav Kook and most *Rishonim*. However, since we only encounter *Shemita* money in the case of money used to purchase produce based on the *heter mechira*, and even there, strictly speaking, there is no sanctity, we can follow the lenient position of the *Chazon Ish.*[33]

Paying by check: The *Acharonim* understand that according to the *Chazon Ish,* payment by check is regarded as a purchase on credit, and therefore if the produce is paid for by check, *Shemita* sanctity does not apply to the money (see *Chazon Ish 10, 13; 14, 5,* s.v. *ve-ha; Responsa Az Nidbaru,* x, no. 44; IV, no. 64; *Mishpetei Aretz, p. 111,* note 15). If possible, it is preferable to give a post-dated check (even for the next day), or to mark the check as "non-negotiable," for in such cases it is much easier to treat the check as credit.

It stands to reason that also in the case of payment by credit card, *Shemita* sanctity does not apply to any money, because there is no tangible money to which the sanctity could apply. This might work even according to Rav Kook, who is more stringent on the matter than the *Chazon Ish.*

2. **Gift:** As we saw above, a transaction involving *Shemita* produce only applies *Shemita* sanctity to the money if the transaction is defined as a sale. The Mishna in *Sukka* (3:11) relies on this principle to allow the transfer of ownership of *Shemita* produce without applying *Shemita* sanctity to the article for which it was exchanged:

> If a man purchases a *lulav* from his fellow in the Sabbatical year, the latter should give him the *etrog* as a gift.

The *Yerushalmi* (*Shevi'it* 7:3) also relates that Rabbi Yochanan would take wine from a storekeeper and give him money as a present, and in that way *Shemita* sanctity would not apply to the money.

3. ***Havla'a*** (indirect payment for an item by paying more for something else): The Gemara in *Sukka* (39a) discusses the process of selling a *lulav* and *etrog* during the seventh year. It asks about a case where the seller does not want to give the buyer the *etrog* as a present:

33. One who treats produce purchased from a gentile as though the produce has *Shemita* sanctity – if he does so only as a stringency, he too may practice leniency. If, on the other hand, he maintains that the produce of a gentile has *Shemita* sanctity strictly speaking, he should take Rav Kook's position into account and practice leniency only if the produce is no longer extant at the time of payment. In practice, however, since the custom in Jerusalem and most parts of the country is to be lenient with respect to the produce of a gentile, it can be treated as a double uncertainty (*sfek safeka*) regarding a Rabbinic prohibition. Even those who are stringent on the matter can, therefore, be lenient.

> What is the law if the other is unwilling to give it [the *etrog*] to him as a gift? Rav Huna said: He should include the price of the *etrog* in that of the *lulav.*

That is to say, the buyer can purchase several articles, and tell the seller that all the money exchanged between them is payment for the article that does not have *Shemita* sanctity.

Summary: When a person buys merchandise in a store that also sells produce that has *Shemita* sanctity (or if he sells *Shemita* produce in violation of halacha, or if he sells produce from fields that were sold in the *heter mechira*), he must be concerned that the change that he receives might have *Shemita* sanctity (for in such a case, we know that some of the money in the cash register has *Shemita* sanctity). Therefore, the money must be redeemed on a food item, which must then be eaten. Other ways to solve the problem include buying on credit, or paying by check or credit card (or giving the money to the seller as a gift or as payment for some other article that he buys from him). In such cases, *Shemita* sanctity does not apply to the money.

RAV YITZCHAK YA'AKOV WEISS

(*Responsa Minchat Yitzchak*)

Rav Yitzchak Ya'akov Weiss was born in 5662 (1902) in Poland. He later moved to Eretz Yisrael and served as Rabbi of the Charedi community in Jerusalem. Rav Weiss was one of the major *Posekim* of our generation. He authored ten volumes of *Responsa Minchat Yitzchak*. He died in 5749 (1989).

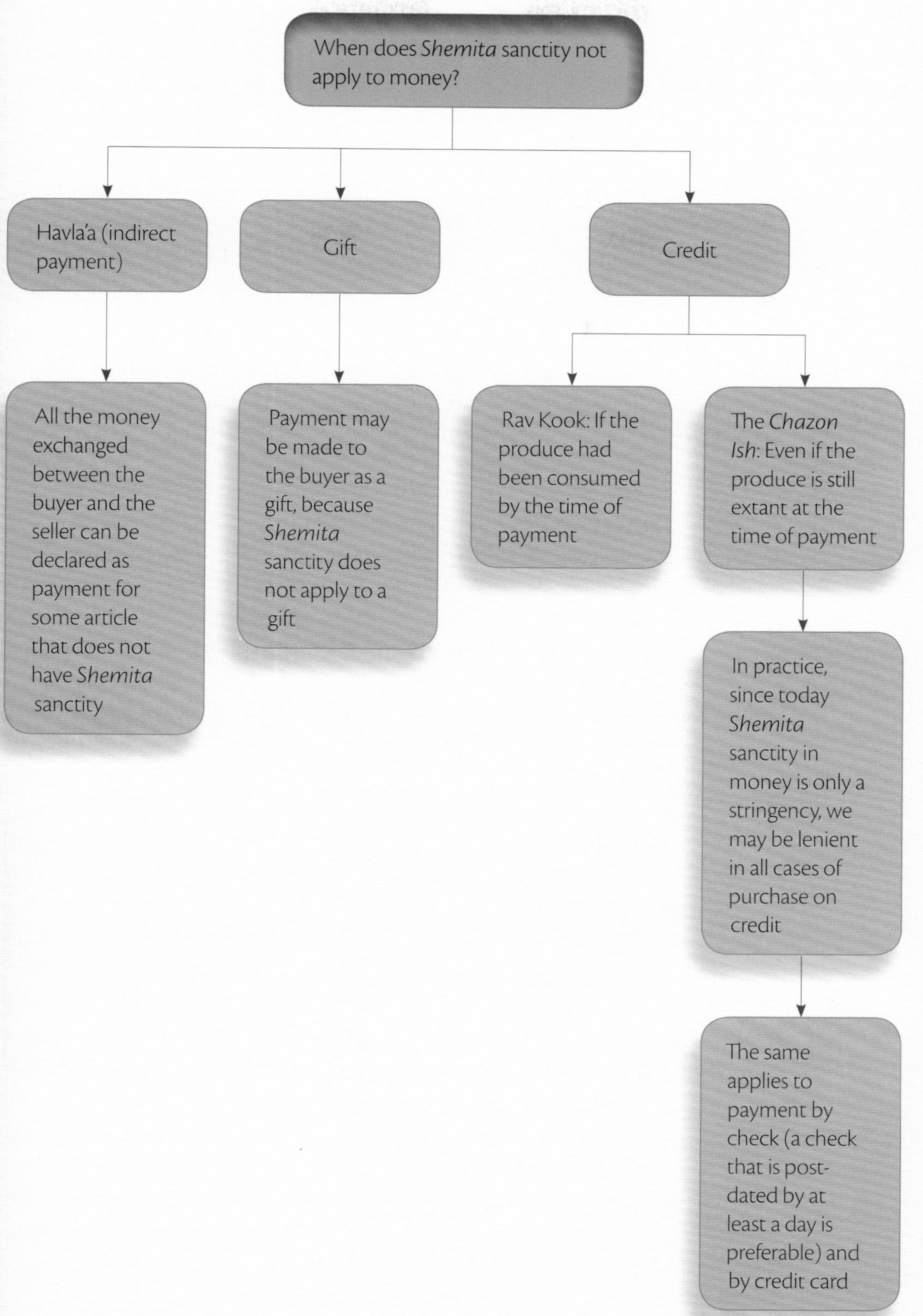
When does *Shemita* sanctity not apply to money?
Havla'a (indirect payment)
Gift
Credit
All the money exchanged between the buyer and the seller can be declared as payment for some article that does not have *Shemita* sanctity
Payment may be made to the buyer as a gift, because *Shemita* sanctity does not apply to a gift
Rav Kook: If the produce had been consumed by the time of payment
The *Chazon Ish*: Even if the produce is still extant at the time of payment
In practice, since today *Shemita* sanctity in money is only a stringency, we may be lenient in all cases of purchase on credit
The same applies to payment by check (a check that is post-dated by at least a day is preferable) and by credit card

THE PROHIBITION TO TRADE IN *SHEMITA* PRODUCE

Is there a way to sell *Shemita* produce?

The Mishna in *Shevi'it* (7:3) states that it is forbidden to trade in *Shemita* produce:

> One should not gather wild vegetables and sell them in the market; rather he gathers them [for personal use] and his son [may] sell them for him. If he gathered them for his own use, and something remains over, he may sell them.

According to the Gemara, there are permissible ways to sell such produce. We shall try to explain what these circumstances are.

The Gemara in *Avoda Zara* (62a) derives the prohibition to trade in *Shemita* produce from the verse, "And the Sabbath produce of the land shall be food for you" – to eat and not for trade (Rashi and *Tosafot, Kiddushin* 20a; and see Ramban, Addendum to Rambam's *Sefer ha-Mitzvot,* positive commandment 3).

The *Rishonim* disagree as to why selling *Shemita* produce is forbidden. According to Rashi (*Sukka* 39a, s.v. *ein*), *Shemita* produce must undergo *bi'ur* at the end of the year, and selling such produce will lead to a situation in which *Shemita* money, which is endowed with *Shemita* sanctity, will remain even after the time of *bi'ur*. According to the Ran (*Avoda Zara* 62a), the Torah wants *Shemita* produce to be eaten, and not used for any other purpose.

The *Rishonim* also disagree about the nature of the forbidden trade. We shall mention here only two of the many positions on the matter: According to the *Tosafot,* it is biblically prohibited to harvest *Shemita* produce in order to sell it wholesale in the market, but it is permitted to harvest a small amount of produce and sell it in the field. The Rambam (*Hilchot Shemita ve-Yovel* 6:2, according to the *Chazon Ish's* understanding, 13, 17), on the other hand, understands that it is permitted to harvest a small amount of produce even to sell it in the market; what is forbidden by Torah law is **to buy *Shemita* produce in order to sell it.** The Rambam apparently understood that "trading" *Shemita* produce refers to buying such produce only in order to resell it, rather than to eat it.[34]

34. The Gemara in *Kiddushin* (20a) speaks of the severity of trading in *Shemita* produce: "Come and see how severe the 'dust [indirect prohibition] of *Shemita*' is: A person buys and sells (*nose ve-noten*) *Shemita* produce, and ends up selling his possessions." It may be asked whether the prohibition of selling *Shemita* produce (*sechora*) is the same as the prohibition of buying and selling (*masa u-matan*) such produce. Rashi and *Tosafot* (both s.v. *avkah shel shevi'it*) imply that the prohibition of *masa u-matan* is by Torah law, whereas from the *Aruch* (s.v. *avak*) it seems that we are dealing with a Rabbinic prohibition. This seems to follow also from the term "dust of *Shemita*" appearing in the Gemara. This is also the way the *Aruch* was understood by Maharitz Chayes (*Rosh ha-Shana* 22a): "I found an exceedingly novel position in the *Aruch*… From the fact that he compares it to the 'dust of usury,' he implies that the entire prohibition of trafficking in *Shemita* produce is only Rabbinic, whereas all the *Posekim* maintain that it is by Torah law."

The *Chazon Ish* (*Masechet Shevi'it,* section 6) rules in accordance with the Rambam, and therefore writes that it is permitted to harvest produce in order to sell it. He adds that if the owner of the field has no buyers for his produce, he can give the produce to a storekeeper to sell it as his agent, and the storekeeper can receive payment as a worker (but not for the merchandise). Of course, even according to the Rambam, it is only permitted to harvest produce in the permitted measure, that is, the amount that a person ordinarily harvests for several days of domestic uses. After all of the produce has been sold from the first harvest, one can harvest and sell the same amount a second time (*Chazon Ish, Masechet Shevi'it,* section 6):

> It is permitted to harvest the permitted amount, even if his intention is not to eat it, but to sell it to others…
>
> If the picker has no buyers, he can give the produce over to a storekeeper to sell it as his agent. He may pay him as a worker, but he may not sell the produce to the storekeeper in order for the storekeeper to sell it.[35]

Selling by way of *havla'a*: If a person buys merchandise that has no *Shemita* sanctity together with *Shemita* produce, he can stipulate that his payment is exclusively for the non-sanctified merchandise (a sum that is greater than its actual worth), and thus avoid the prohibition of trading in *Shemita* produce, for no payment is made for the *Shemita* produce (*Rash* [7:3]; *Shabbat ha-Aretz* [8, 11, and elsewhere]; *Kerem Tziyon* [17, *Ga'on Tzvi,* no. 1]; Ridbaz [5, 18]). It is, however, reported in the name of the *Chazon Ish* [*Mishpetei Aretz* 12, note 20] that he was stringent about the matter and did not allow it. According to him, *havla'a* does not remove the prohibition of trading in *Shemita* produce; it only resolves the problem of *Shemita* money, as explained above.

35. The *Chazon Ish* continues: "When the picker himself sells the produce or gives it to a storekeeper to sell, he may not sell it in the market where he sells every year or in the store where he sells every year, but rather he must sell it in his house or in an alleyway or courtyard." In other words, the *Chazon Ish* adds that the sale of *Shemita* produce must be executed in a place that is not usually used for the sale of such merchandise, such as an alleyway or a person's house. This distinction does not appear in the Rambam, but it has a source in the *Tosafot* in *Sukka* (*39a,* s.v. *ve-leitiv*) and the Rash (*Shevi'it* 7:3).

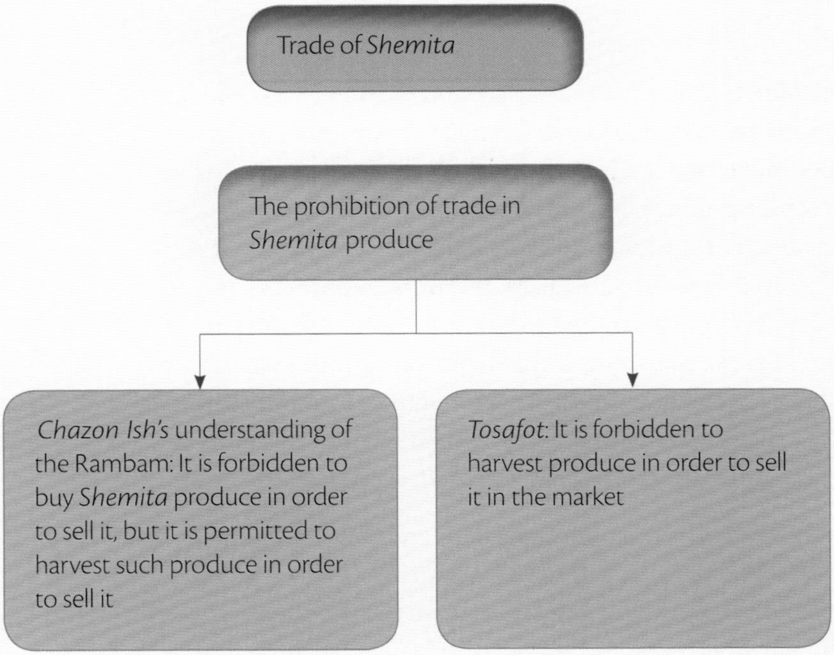

Trade of *Shemita*

The prohibition of trade in *Shemita* produce

Chazon Ish's understanding of the Rambam: It is forbidden to buy *Shemita* produce in order to sell it, but it is permitted to harvest such produce in order to sell it

Tosafot: It is forbidden to harvest produce in order to sell it in the market

THE PROHIBITION TO SELL *SHEMITA* PRODUCE BY THE MEASURE

May one weigh *Shemita* produce to bake a cake? Why was measuring *Shemita* produce prohibited?

The Mishna (*Shevi'it* 8:3; Rambam, *Hilchot Shevi'it* 6:3) states that it is forbidden to sell *Shemita* produce by measure, weight or number.

> Produce of the seventh year may not be sold by measure, weight or number.

As for the reason for this prohibition, the *Yerushalmi* writes (*Shevi'it* 8:3):

> Why? So that people will sell it cheaply. Let them weigh it and sell it cheaply! If you say that, we are concerned that the seller will not handle it in the manner dictated by its sanctity.

Rash Sirillo (ad loc.) explains that the *Yerushalmi* first understands that *Shemita* produce must not be sold by measure, so that people will sell it generously ("so that people will sell it cheaply"), and thus the price of the produce will go down. The *Yerushalmi,* however, raises an objection to this understanding: If the intention is to keep the produce prices down, it should be possible to sell the produce in precise amounts, but instruct the sellers to lower their prices ("let them weigh it and sell it cheaply"). The *Yerushalmi* answers: If the produce is sold in the regular manner, sellers will not remember that they are dealing with *Shemita* produce, and they will forget to handle the money in a manner dictated by its sanctity ("if you say that, he will not handle it in the manner dictated by its sanctity").

According to this explanation, there are two reasons to forbid the sale of *Shemita* produce by measure:

1. So that the produce will be sold cheaply.
2. So that the sellers will remember that the money that they receive through the sale has *Shemita* sanctity.

The Rambam (*Hilchot Shemita ve-Yovel*), on the other hand, writes that measuring *Shemita* produce is forbidden so that the transaction should not appear like trading in *Shemita* produce, and so that it will be emphasized that the produce is ownerless:

> When one sells *Shemita* produce, he should not sell it by measure, by weight, or by number, so that it should not appear as if he were trading *Shemita* produce. He should rather sell the little that he sells by approximation, to let it be known that it is ownerless, and that he is taking the money in order to buy other food.

The Vilna Gaon proposes another reason (Shnot Eliayahu mishna sheviit *8,3*):

> The reason regarding all of them [measure, weight, number] is [to avoid] disgrace.

That is to say, measuring, weighing and counting are regarded as disgraceful forms of treatment of the *Shemita* produce.

A practical difference between these reasons arises in a situation where a person wishes to measure *Shemita* produce in his home, not for commercial purposes. According to the plain sense of the *Yerushalmi* and the Rambam, it stands to reason that this is permitted, for they understand that the prohibition of measuring is closely connected to the prohibition of selling.[36] According to the Vilna Gaon, on the other hand, even measurement of this sort should be regarded as disgraceful treatment, and therefore forbidden.

As for the halachic ruling, Responsa *Az Nidbaru* (*x*, section *45*) writes that measurement that is not for the sake of selling is permitted. Accordingly, when preparing food using *Shemita* produce, it is permitted to weigh and measure. The *Derech Emuna* rules similarly (on the Rambam, *Bei'ur Halacha*, s.v. *ke-she-mocherin*). This appears to be the law in practice, for it follows from almost all the explanations of the prohibition to measure *Shemita* produce.

36. This follows from the Ra'avad's objection to the words of the Rambam: "The wording of the Mishna: 'And Bet Hillel says: That which is ordinarily tied up for household purposes may be tied up for the market.' This means: Since it is ordinarily bound up even when it is to be eaten in the house ... he may bind it up even when it is to be sold in the market, **for the binding is not done for commercial purposes.**"

THE GAON, RABBENU ELIYAHU

(*The Gra*)

Rabbenu Eliyahu of Vilna (the Gaon of Vilna) was born in 5480 (1720) in Brisk, and later lived in Vilna. The Gra was a genius in all areas – his encyclopedic knowledge, his grasp of the plain meaning of the texts, and his understanding of their deeper profundities. His commentary on all four sections of the *Shulchan Aruch* is extremely concise, but is filled with very novel ideas. Owing to the difficulty of his commentary, Rav Kook wrote a super-commentary explaining it (*Be'er Eliyahu*; Rav B. Rakover wrote a continuation – *Birkat Eliyahu*). The Gaon authored a commentary to the Mishna, *Shenot Eliyahu,* and commentaries to various Scriptural books. He wrote books on Kabbala and even on mathematics. A book recording his practices was published under the name *Ma'aseh Rav*.

The Gra is famous for his opposition to Chassidism. The Gra had a major impact on the way that the Chassidic movement developed, because in light of his opposition, the movement carefully examined itself and refined its beliefs and practices. The Gaon wanted to move to Eretz Yisrael, but he was unsuccessful in his journey and was forced to return home. He later encouraged his disciples to move to Eretz Yisrael, and indeed several groups of his disciples settled there.

The Gra wrote suggested emendations to the texts of the Mishna and the two Talmuds. Many of his emendations accord with readings discovered later in manuscripts (some of which the Gra may have seen in the course of his wanderings). The Gaon of Vilna died on 19 Tishrei 5558 (1797) in Vilna.

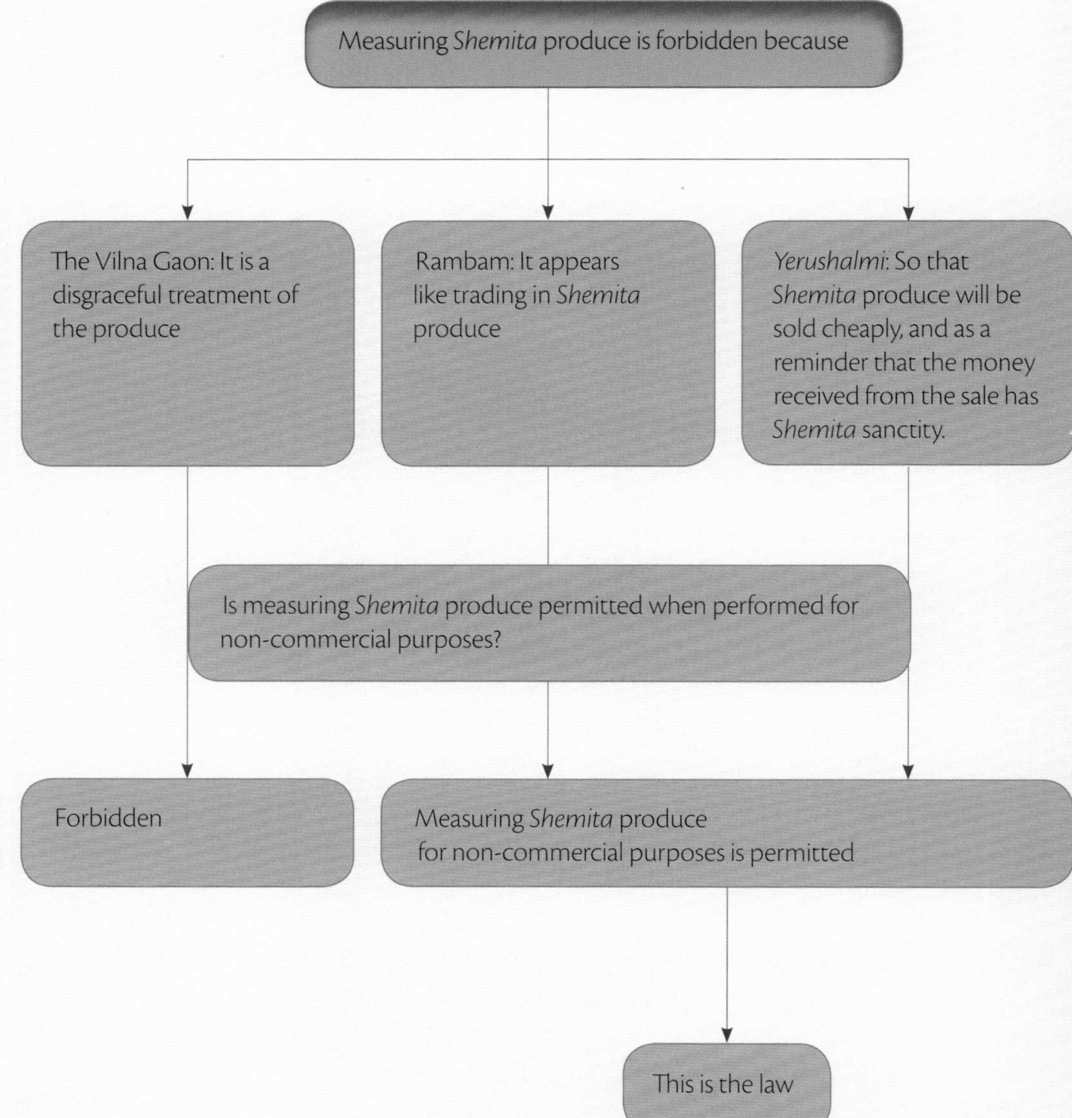
Measuring *Shemita* produce is forbidden because
The Vilna Gaon: It is a disgraceful treatment of the produce
Rambam: It appears like trading in *Shemita* produce
Yerushalmi: So that *Shemita* produce will be sold cheaply, and as a reminder that the money received from the sale has *Shemita* sanctity.
Is measuring *Shemita* produce permitted when performed for non-commercial purposes?
Forbidden
Measuring *Shemita* produce for non-commercial purposes is permitted
This is the law

THE VARIOUS SOLUTIONS

THE VARIOUS SOLUTIONS

OTZAR BET DIN

Is there a way to permit harvesting an entire crop of *Shemita* produce?
Is there a way to observe the mitzva of *Shemita* meticulously, and yet purchase only Jewish produce?

The earliest source to mention *Otzar Bet Din* as a means of dealing with produce during the sabbatical year is the ***Tosefta*** in *Shevi'it* (*8:1–2*, cited below). According to the *Tosefta*, the court would send out agents during the *Shemita* year to fields that it owned in order to harvest the produce and tend to the fields as needed. The court would later distribute the produce to all of the city's inhabitants, to each person according to his needs.

> Originally agents of the *bet din* would sit at the city gates, and upon seeing anyone with *Shemita* produce in his hand, they would take it from him and provide him with enough food for three meals, and they would put the rest into a storehouse in the city.
>
> When the time for harvesting figs arrived, the court's agents would hire workers to pick them, make them into cakes of pressed figs, put them into barrels, and put them into the storehouse [*otzar*] in the city. When the time for harvesting grapes arrived, the court's agents would hire workers to gather them, press them in a winepress, put [the wine] in barrels, and put them into the storehouse [*otzar*] in the city. When the time for harvesting olives arrived, the court's agents would hire workers to harvest them, press them in an olive-press, put the oil into barrels, and put them into the storehouse [*otzar*] in the city. And on Fridays, they would distribute the food from the storehouses to each and every person according to the needs of his family.

At first glance, this description is puzzling, for some of the labors mentioned here are explicitly forbidden during the *Shemita* year. For example, the ***Mishna* in *Shevi'it*** (*8:6*) states:

> Figs of the seventh year may not be cut with a fig-knife, but one may cut them with a sword. One may not press grapes in a wine-press, but he may press them in a kneading trough. Nor may one press olives in an olive-press or with a weighted beam, but he may crush the olives and put them in a small press.

In other words, *Shemita* produce may not be harvested or processed in the ordinary manner![1] How then does the Tosefta permit these labors during the sabbatical year when performed through a court? Even more strikingly, the Tosefta implies that the figs, grapes and olives would be picked and harvested in the ordinary manner. But surely Torah law forbids reaping and gathering of fruit in this way! How then could the workers hired by the court engage in these labors?

Indeed, the **Rash Sirilio** (*Yerushalmi, Shevi'it 9:6,* s.v. *ve-ani omer,* and s.v. *aval ha-emet; and similarly 9:4* [end], s.v. *chazor u-zechei bei*) raised these objections against the *Tosefta*:

> Is it permissible to make cakes of dried figs with *Shemita* produce? ... Is it permissible to pick *Shemita* grapes or to press them in a winepress? ... You cannot say that since they are agents of the court we permit them to treat *Shemita* produce like ordinary produce, for *Torat Kohanim* derives from verses ... you must not pick in the ordinary manner ...
>
> But the truth is ... that the latter part [of the *Tosefta*] refers to produce of the sixth year ... Homeowners would open the storehouses in their homes, and afterwards they would open the storehouses in the city that had been filled by the court.

Rash Sirillo had such great difficulty with the Tosefta that he interpreted it as dealing with the way to handle sixth-year produce during the *Shemita* year. This interpretation, however, is very difficult, for the first part of the *Tosefta,* which restricts the amount

1. One must not use a *muktzeh*, a tool specially intended for cutting figs, but rather a tool that is not designated for that purpose (Bartenura; see above chapter on harvesting for a full explanation of this *mishna*); one must not press grapes in a winepress, but rather in a trough (a utensil used for kneading dough); and one must not press olives in an ordinary olive-press, but rather in a small press, called a *bodida*. Elsewhere, the *Tosefta* (*Shevi'it 6:20*) states that one must not make cakes of pressed figs out of *Shemita* produce.

of produce that may be gathered to the amount needed for three meals, refers explicitly to *Shemita* produce. Rash Sirillo explained, therefore, that while the first part of the *Tosefta* refers to *Shemita* produce, the second part deals with produce that the court had stored away during the sixth year for the collective benefit, and therefore it was permissible to process that produce during the *Shemita* year in the ordinary manner.

The **Ramban** (*Vayikra 25:7*), on the other hand, understands the *Tosefta* differently:

> And in the Tosefta it is stated: "Originally agents of the court" ... And the Rabbis made various ordinances. Originally the court used to make a storehouse [*otzar*] in every city. As soon as the fruits ripened, they would take them from those who brought them [from their fields] and put them into the storehouse. When the time of harvest for the whole of that crop would arrive, such as when the time had come for reaping the grain or gathering the grapes, the agents of the court would hire workers to gather the grapes, pick the olives and harvest the whole of that species, and then they would press the grapes in a winepress and the olives in an olive-press as one does during any other year, and put them into their storehouse. This produce which was gathered into the storehouse of the court [*otzar bet din*] required no other act of "removal," since they were already removed from the homes [of their owners], and both poor and rich were permitted to come and receive them from the court after the time of the removal and eat them. The court went through the trouble of arranging this procedure to prevent people from holding on to it [the *Shemita* produce] or doing business with it.

The Ramban seems to take for granted that the court performed agricultural labors during the *Shemita* year in the regular way. Thus, the difficulty returns – these labors are not allowed to be performed on *Shemita* produce! The ***Chazon Ish*** (*Shevi'it 12:6*) cites the Ramban and explains the matter as follows:

From that which is taught in the *Tosefta* – that when there is an *otzar bet din*, one may press grapes in a winepress and olives in an olive-press – we learn that that which we learned [in the *Mishna*] that one must not press grapes in a winepress, refers specifically to the **owner**. But those who took possession of produce that had been declared ownerless are permitted to do all these things. And regarding the verse [which is understood to mean], "'You shall not pick' in the ordinary manner" – **the Torah refers to the owner.** The *Tosefta* implies that [the produce] may be picked all at once, and not [necessarily] little by little. And there is proof from here that even according to the Rambam, **the prohibition relates only to the owner.**

Solution to the mystery: Why may all the produce be harvested with an *otzar bet din*?

According to the ***Chazon Ish***, the prohibition of picking *Shemita* produce in the ordinary manner applies only to the produce's owner, and therefore this activity is permitted when performed by agents of the court. What is the reason for the distinction? It seems that an explanation can be offered based on a principle mentioned in previous chapters.

The fundamental idea that is expressed during the *Shemita* year is that "the land is Mine." That is to say, God is the true owner of the land, and not man. As opposed to planting and pruning, which are prohibited during the *Shemita* year because of their very essence, reaping and gathering fruit are forbidden only because of the results they cause. In other words: **there is no prohibition to reap and gather fruit during the *Shemita* year – it is the demonstration of ownership of the land through these labors that is prohibited.** Since it is forbidden to demonstrate ownership over land during the *Shemita* year, it is forbidden to reap or gather the produce of an entire field.[2]

If, however, the court performs the harvest, then these labors do not express ownership. When the court gathers in the crop

2. In light of this, the *Chazon Ish* (*Shevi'it* 12, 5, s.v. *da'at ha-Ramban*, and even more explicitly in sub-section 6) proposes the novel view that the prohibition of reaping during the *Shemita* year is restricted to a person's own field. But if he reaps in another person's field that had been declared ownerless, he does not violate the prohibition. Rav Sh. Z. Auerbach (*Ma'adanei Aretz*, 7, 4, s.v. *hineh*), however, disagrees with the *Chazon Ish*, and maintains that reaping and gathering fruit is forbidden in another person's field as well. See the lengthy discussion of this issue and the halachic foundations of *Otzar Bet Din* in Rav Ehud Achituv's article (*Ha-Torah ve-ha-Aretz, Shevi'it 6, pp.* 389-422). Is the court permitted to guard produce and prevent others from picking it? See the chapter on declaring produce ownerless and the laws governing produce that is guarded (*shamur*) or worked (*ne'evad*) (see also *Shemita Mamlachtit, chap.* 15, and *Ha-Torah ve-ha-Aretz, Shevi'it 6, pp.* 410-411).

from the field, no individual demonstrates his ownership, for the very essence of the court lies in the fact that it is not a private entity but rather a body that represents all of Israel. Since there is no demonstration of ownership when the court reaps or gathers the fruit, reaping and gathering of this sort was never forbidden.[3]

Another reason may be suggested that explains why reaping and gathering are permitted during the *Shemita* year when performed by the court. As we saw in previous chapters, it is only permitted for a private individual to reap or gather the produce of his field in the amount that will suffice for the next couple of days. Since the court represents all of Israel, when it gathers in the produce, it may gather in produce that will suffice for several meals for each and every member of Israel.[4]

Based on this explanation, *Otzar Bet Din* will allow *bet din* to harvest produce in the ordinary manner. The prohibition of trade also does not apply to *Otzar Bet Din* produce, and it may be distributed in the ordinary manner. The produce may be sold because the money that changes hands is wages for the workers who were hired by the court rather than payment for the *Shemita* produce. The produce is not actually **sold,** but rather it is **distributed**, and the money paid is for the labor. Therefore, *Shemita* sanctity does not apply to the money. It must be emphasized, however, that the produce itself has *Shemita* sanctity.[5]

What is the halacha in this case? Does

3. This seems to follow from the principle that we saw in the *Chazon Ish*, and it also follows from the words of Rav Yisraeli, *Chavat Binyamin, vol.* I, *no. 9, p. 68; vol.* III, *p. 622.*

4. This explanation is implicit in *Teshuvot ha-Rashbash* (*no. 298*) who writes, regarding *Otzar Bet Din* produce, that the court is regarded as the "'hand of the poor.'"

5. Since *Otzar Bet Din* produce has *Shemita* sanctity, it would seem that it should not be sold by the measure, but rather by approximation (see *Responsa Mishnat Yosef, vol.* I, *no. 23, 3; Halichot Sadeh 50, p. 35*). According to *Responsa Az Nidberu* (*vol.* X, *no. 45*), however, since we are dealing with the distribution of produce and not its sale, weighing the produce is permitted. This depends on whether the measurement of *Shemita* produce is forbidden in and of itself, or if it is only forbidden as part of the sale (see above, p.341). If the problem of measurement stems from the sale process, it stands to reason that the prohibition does not apply to *Otzar Bet Din* produce. As we saw, this is the primary understanding of the prohibition of measuring. It is possible, however, that even though there is no sale here, one should not weigh the produce in order to demonstrate that we are dealing with *Shemita* produce – see the aforementioned chapter, the section on measuring *Shemita* produce. It should be noted that even according to those who are stringent about weighing the produce, it is permissible to buy from a storekeeper who weighs it, because the seller has a halachic basis for his conduct (see below, p. 438, in the name of Rav Sh. Z. Auerbach).

the law follow the *Tosefta,* and if so, is it to be understood in accordance with the Ramban or in accordance with the Rash Sirilio? At first glance, it seems difficult to establish the law in accordance with the *Tosefta,* for the **Rambam** omitted it, implying that he maintains that it was not accepted as law.[6]

Nevertheless, various explanations may be suggested as to why Rambam omitted the *Tosefta.* The **Radbaz** (*Hilchot Shemita ve-Yovel 7:3*) proposed that Rambam did not quote the *Tosefta* because the language of the *Tosefta* states that it was only '"originally"' that the court assumed responsibility for worrying about the produce growing in the fields. We do not find any post-Mishnaic court that involved itself with this issue:

> He omitted the *Tosefta* about "the court agents who would go out, etc." because it was not accepted as law. Alternatively, it was only "originally" that the court would store up produce and distribute it.

Another possibility is that since the *Tosefta* does not state a law, but merely offers advice about how to deal with the prohibitions of agricultural labor during the *Shemita* year, the Rambam did not find it necessary to codify it. This argument is reinforced by what the Radbaz says, that throughout the years of Israel's exile this advice was never actualized.[7]

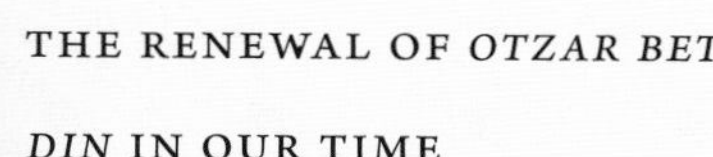

THE RENEWAL OF *OTZAR BET DIN* IN OUR TIME

In 5670 (1909), in the course of the controversy regarding the *heter mechira,* **Rav Kook** proposed that, along with the *heter mechira,* an *Otzar Bet Din* be established (see *Iggerot ha-Ra'aya,* vol. *I, 311, 313*). Rav Kook suggested that the farmers should transfer their fields to a

6. This is what follows from the Radbaz's first answer cited below, and this is also the view of Rav Ben Zion Abba Shaul (*Ha-Torah ve-ha-Aretz, vol. III, p. 180*) and Rav Mordechai Eliyahu (ibid.). These posekim feel that, owing to the Rambam's omission, one should only rely on *Otzar Bet Din* in a case of special need. Rav Ovadya Yosef (cited in *Or Torah, 319, 5754*) was originally of the opinion that it is better to rely on the *heter mechira* than on *Otzar Bet Din,* but later he himself established an *Otzar bet Din,* arguing that when it is run properly, making sure that the money that changes hands is solely to cover labor costs, and not for the produce, there is a *mitzva* to use *Otzar Bet Din* produce.

7. On the significance of the term '"originally"' in the *Tosefta,* see the appendix at the end of this chapter.

court, and the court would then appoint them as its agents to harvest the produce and tend to it. The people who buy the produce would pay for the expenses, and they would be asked to pay a relatively high price for the farmers' labors, so that in the end the farmers would receive payment for the produce in excess of their expenses[8] (brought in *Chavatzelet* 46 [5670]; and in *Iggerot ha-Ra'aya*, vol. 1, 313) :

№ 46
שנת הארבעים
חבצלת
מבשרת ציון
HABAZELETH
מכתב עתי להרשות, לספרות ולמדע ולכל דבר הרצוי לאיש יהודי, יו"ל
מאת
ישראל דוב פרומקין
מחיר הגליון הזה
שתי עשריות
JERUSALEM, 1 Juli 1910
ירושלים, יום הששי כ"ד סיון התר"ע

To the honorable and revered … Rav Chayim Berlin, *shlita*, peace and blessings.

I find myself bound to inform you that from the outset, when I saw the necessity of using the *heter mechira* for the general good of the settlement of the Holy Land, I decided, nonetheless, to do whatever is possible to satisfy all opinions. I therefore marked the produce with a symbol indicating that the price charged during the seventh year is exclusively for the supervisors and the labor, in order that *Shemita* sanctity not apply to the money, with no payment being made for the *Shemita* produce itself … And they [the owners] must transfer their authority to the court, and the court authorizes the aforementioned owners to care for their field as is necessary for the sale of the produce in a permitted manner, meaning, to charge a fee for their efforts and for the supervisors. From the outset I agreed that since we have the basis of the *heter mechira*, which has always been relied upon in itself, it is not necessary to be precise about how much is charged for the supervisors and the labor, since it is explicitly stated that the money is not being paid for the produce itself. And it is not right to oppress the people of the *moshavot* who are laden with the burden of their situation, May God raise them to greatness …

May this message bring peace and blessings of friendship to my dear friend, with great honor,

Avraham Yitzchak Hakohen Kook.

And, indeed, **Rav Chayim Berlin** was pleased with Rav Kook's suggestion[9] (*his letter is cited in Chavatzelet 50 (5670), p. 328*) :

8. Rav Kook added the fact that he was dealing with produce subject to the *heter mechira* as grounds for allowing payment of a higher price.

9. It should be noted that the Ridbaz objected to this proposal.

> Your letter gladdened my heart, because finally the Rabbis are making peace with each other ... From the day that I stood on my own, I have been a friend to all Torah scholars who increase peace in the world. Regarding the matter at hand, no matter how successful Satan was, owing to our many sins, in sowing arguments between Torah scholars, it did not involve any essential change, "And your people are all righteous" (*Yeshayahu* 60:21) with the help of blessed God, and all of their intentions were for the sake of heaven ...
>
> Your colleague, seeking your peace, looking ahead to the redemption,
>
> Chayim Berlin

In the end, an *Otzar Bet Din* was established in 5670 by the rabbis of Jerusalem and Rav Berlin, as a result of Rav Kook's proposal.[10] However, the extent to which this system was used at the time to permit agricultural work during the *Shemita* year is not known.[11] Rav Kook, who had proposed this solution, relied on it only in combination with the *heter mechira*, even though it seems that he would have relied on the institution of *Otzar Bet Din*, even without the *heter mechira*.[12]

10. This is what follows from a letter of Rav Charlop to Rav Kook from 8 Sivan, 5670: "'[It was decided] over a month ago at a member's meeting in the house of Rav Chayim Berlin, *shlita*, that in order to take all concerns into consideration, it [the *Otzar Beit Din*] should be done in the manner suggested last year by his honorable excellence, *shlita* [Rav Kook].'"

11. See, for example, the *Otzar Bet Din* agreement sent by the Badatz of Jerusalem to one of the farmers (cited in *Kerem Tziyon* 13, *Gidulei Tziyon, no.* 13, and in *Mara de-Ar'a de-Yisrael, p.* 188), which states explicitly: "'The harvesting must be done by gentile workers and with some kind of *shinui* [change from the usual manner].'" Rav Kook also speaks only of processing the harvested fruit, and it is not at all clear what he thinks about the harvest itself. The *Chazon Ish* (cited above), however, clearly writes that *Otzar Bet Din* permits reaping and gathering fruit in the ordinary manner, following the plain sense of the *Tosefta*.

12. Why did Rav Kook permit *Otzar Bet Din* only in combination with the *heter mechira*? It seems that this did not follow from any misgivings about *Otzar Bet Din*, but rather that Rav Kook was of the opinion that *Otzar Bet Din* by itself does not solve the problem. Rav Kook was very stringent about the laws of *Shemita;* among other things, he maintained that even labors that are only forbidden by rabbinic decree may not be performed during the *Shemita* year if the purpose is to preserve the fruit. This stringency does not allow for any reasonable work to be performed on trees even if the orchard is part of *Otzar Bet Din*. The *Chazon Ish*, on the other hand, permits labors forbidden by rabbinic decree when performed in order to preserve the fruit, and therefore, even without *heter mechira*, it is possible to perform certain vital labors (on trees, where the prohibition of *sefichim* does not apply). According to him, the main problem lies in harvesting and marketing the produce, and this problem can be overcome through *Otzar Bet Din*. Thus, according to the *Chazon Ish*, *Otzar Bet Din* is effective even without the *heter mechira*. See the appendix at the end of this volume regarding the disagreement between Rav Kook and the *Chazon Ish* with respect to *Shemita*.
It is possible, however, that through the mechanism of *Otzar Bet Din*, even Rav Kook would permit rabbinic labors when performed for the purpose of preserving the fruit. Rav Kook forbade labors for the purpose of preservation of fruit because the fruit is ownerless and thus there is no allowance to tend to them. However, with respect to the court agents who represent the community, the fruit is not ownerless, as the fruit belongs to the people of Israel as a whole. The court, therefore, as representative of the Jewish people, might be permitted to perform labors that will prevent damage to the collective (as opposed to the individual for whom there is no financial loss, and regarding whom the labors were never permitted. See the words of Rav Yisraeli cited above).
It is also possible that Rav Kook combined the *heter mechira* with *Otzar Bet Din* in order to enable raising the price. See more on this later.

Even though *Otzar Bet Din* was hardly used after the *Shemita* of 5670 (1909–10), the ***Chazon Ish*** revived the system for the *Shemita* of 5705 (1944–45) (and especially for the *Shemita* of 5712 [1951–52] and on) (see *Responsa Mishnat Yosef, vol. III, nos. 38–40, and Halichot Sadeh 50, pp. 35–37*). As we have seen, the *Chazon Ish* (*Shevi'it, 11, section 7,* s.v. *u-ma she-perash Maharashas*) understands that even Rambam maintained that the *Tosefta* is accepted as law,[13] and therefore he permitted harvesting, gathering, and processing the produce in the usual manner:

> We have nothing but the words of the *Rishonim,* of blessed memory, that it refers to *Shemita* produce, and that when it is in the hands of the court, it is permissible to press the grapes in a winepress, and they are exempt from *bi'ur.*

13. It should be noted that this *Tosefta* is mentioned by other *Rishonim* as well: **Rosh** (*Shevi'it 9:8*); ***Rabbenu David*** (*Pesachim 52b*); *Tosafot Rid (Pesachim 51b)*; Rashba (*Pesachim 53a*); *Tosafot Rabbenu Yehuda (Avoda Zara 62b)*; and others. In addition, we may add as grounds for leniency the view of the Rash, referred to in the discussion regarding reaping and gathering produce (p. 132–135), that produce growing in an ownerless field may be harvested in the usual manner.

PAYMENT FOR *OTZAR BET DIN* PRODUCE

The ***Tosefta*** speaks of "hiring workers," implying that these workers would be paid. The ***Chazon Ish*** concludes from this (*Shevi'it 12, 6*) that it is permitted for the court to collect payment from the people among whom it distributes the produce to cover **the costs of the harvest and other related costs.**

The *Chazon Ish* (*Iggerot Chazon Ish, vol. II, 73*) argued, however, that the farmers should not receive the full value of their produce. According to him, it must be evident that *Otzar Bet Din* produce is cheaper, so that the buyers will know that their payment is for the labor, and not for the produce:

Must the community pay for *Otzar Bet Din* produce?

> That which I wrote – that [the price] should be calculated according to the labor – is, of course, not in order to save money. Rather, it is our duty that our actions should proclaim our observance of the Torah and make known our observance of its commandments. If a person calculates the price as he does every year, he will forget about the idea of the *mitzva* of *Shemita.*

It makes no difference whether the labor is great or little, as long as this is evident.

We must examine, however, whether the price charged for *Otzar Bet Din* produce can exceed the cost of the wages paid to the workers in the field. It would seem that the underlying principle of *Otzar Bet Din* is that the price charged for the produce must be determined by the cost of the labor, unrelated to how the produce is marketed. Thus, there should be no problem to decide that the workers are to receive a high wage – as long as the wage does not fluctuate in accordance with the crop's success. It seems that even the *Chazon Ish* would agree with this principle, only that he maintained that people must know that the produce they are buying is from *Otzar Bet Din*, and therefore he insisted that the price charged for the produce must be lower than the regular price.[14]

Putting *Otzar Bet Din* into practice is a very complicated task, inasmuch as the court does not have money with which to pay the workers. It will only obtain money when the produce is sold. But what will it do if the produce doesn't sell well? What will it do if it promised the farmers a certain wage based on estimated sales, but there was a serious decline in demand?

In the *Shemita* observed in 5761 (2000–2001), for example, Tenuva established an *Otzar Bet Din*, which suffered losses of 10 million shekels, because people were hesitant about buying produce with *Shemita* sanctity!

Such a situation is clearly unreasonable. In order to make it possible for an *Otzar Bet Din* to be established, and for *Shemita* to be observed in the best possible manner, the community must be a partner in the efforts. In addition, *Otzar Bet Din* has special expenses, generated by the way that the trees must be cared for and by the way that the produce must be marketed, as we are dealing with land subject to the prohibitions of *Shemita*, on which agricultural work cannot proceed as usual. Only certain types of work may be performed, and this work can only be done in certain circumstances (as was explained in the chapters dealing with the types of labor forbidden during the *Shemita* year). Furthermore, the quality of *Otzar Bet Din* produce will not always be as high as that

14. See the lengthy discussion about the possibility of paying the farmers a high price in *Shemita Mamlachtit bi-Medinat Yisrael*, especially in the 5760 edition.

of regular produce, because it does not receive the usual care. The community must therefore make a special effort to buy *Otzar Bet Din* produce, even if the prices are not any lower than usual, and even if the produce is less attractive.

Otzar Bet Din is a halachic solution that has the fundamental approval of both **Rav Kook** and the ***Chazon Ish***. The **advantage** of *Otzar Bet Din* over the *heter mechira* lies in that it does not cancel the *Shemita* sanctity of the produce. All agree that the *heter mechira* is a temporary solution, for it is clearly not our desire to abolish the *mitzva* of *Shemita*. *Otzar Bet Din*, on the other hand, allows for the observance of the *mitzva* of *Shemita* and for eating produce that has *Shemita* sanctity.[15] The *mitzva* of *Shemita* remains in full force; *Otzar Bet Din* merely solves the problem of harvesting and distributing the *Shemita* produce, because this is done by the farmers acting as agents of the court. This solution may be adopted as a first choice,[16] and those who do so observe the *mitzva* of *Shemita* in a most meticulous manner. If the community demonstrates willingness to buy *Otzar Bet Din* produce, it will be possible to expand the system to include other farmers, and thereby widening the circle of those observing the *mitzva* of *Shemita* in the best possible manner.

It should be noted that *Otzar Bet Din* only solves the problems of harvesting and selling, but it does not permit planting during the *Shemita* year. Therefore, the solution of *Otzar Bet Din* only works with respect to fruit. Regarding vegetables, it works only in the first few months of *Shemita* (when there are still vegetables that were planted during the sixth year, but picked in the seventh). Later in the year, however, *Otzar Bet Din* does not help. We must, therefore, find another solution that will permit growing vegetables during the *Shemita* year, as we shall see below.

SUMMARY:

Otzar Bet Din means that the court acts as the owner of the field. The court appoints agents to harvest the crop. They are permitted to harvest the entire crop at the same time and in the usual manner,

15. For an expanded discussion of the importance of eating produce that has *Shemita* sanctity, see the chapter on *Shemita* sanctity (p. 228–233, 236–239).

16. Even though this too is not accepted by all authorities, as explained above, it has the basic approval of both Rav Kook and the *Chazon Ish*, and it provides a more ideal way of observing *Shemita*, allowing for meticulous observance of *Shemita* on the one hand and the survival of Jewish agriculture in Israel on the other.

because they are agents of the court and as such their actions do not involve a display of ownership.

The court **distributes the produce to the community as a gift,** but it may collect **money for the labor performed by the workers.** Sometimes the price charged for *Otzar Bet Din* produce will be similar to the regular market price (because harvesting a field with *Shemita* sanctity is more labor intensive, as explained above), but the payment will always be for **the cost of the labor, irrespective of the success of bringing the produce to market.**

APPENDIX TO CHAPTER DEALING WITH *OTZAR BET DIN*:

WHAT DOES THE *TOSEFTA* MEAN WHEN IT SAYS "ORIGINALLY"?

Why does the *Tosefta* open with the word "originally"? What does it mean to say?

According to the **Radbaz** (in his second explanation, cited above), this means that at one point the court dealt with this problem but later it stopped that pracice.

One possible way to understand this is that the payments made to the workers were taken from the half-shekel fund in the Temple treasury. The half-shekels collected from every member of Israel were used, among other things, for community needs in Jerusalem (*Shekalim 4:2*).[17] It is possible, then, that only "originally," when there was such a fund, was an "*Otzar Bet Din*" established, but later when there was no longer any money from which to pay the workers, the *Otzar Bet Din* ceased to exist.

The author of the ***Chasdei David*** (on the *Tosefta*, ad loc.) suggests another possible understanding: "Originally," when *Shemita* was by Torah law, the court would make sure to establish an "*Otzar Bet Din*," to prevent the situation in which people would refrain from declaring their fields ownerless and thus trade in *Shemita* produce. Later, however, when *Shemita* was only by rabbinic law, even though it was still obligatory to declare fields ownerless, the court did not exert itself in the same way to establish an "*Otzar Bet Din*", as, in any event, the danger and the concern were only by rabbinic decree.

Another possibility is that the *Tosefta* is speaking about **two different stages: Halacha 1** (the first paragraph) describes the earlier situation, when the people would bring their produce to the court on their own.[18] **Halacha 2** (the second paragraph) describes a later stage, when the system had become more advanced and the court agents themselves would harvest the crops.

17. The Mishna states "And the goat that was sent away and the crimson-colored strap come from the money stored in the Temple treasury. And the ramp for the red heifer, and the ramp for the goat that was sent away, and the strap between its horns, and the sewer [in the Temple courtyard], and the city wall and its towers, and all the city's needs came from the money remaining in the Temple treasury."

18. And they would pick the fruit in an unusual manner (according to the Bartenura), or else they would pick only a small quantity of fruit that would last a few days (according to the Rambam), but the court would leave them with food that would last for only three meals, and the rest would be stored away in storehouses.

HOTHOUSES AND *MATZA MENUTAK* (DETACHED FROM THE GROUND)

Matza menutak refers to produce grown on a bed that is detached from the ground, such as a container resting on plastic sheeting (usually polyethylene), either inside a hothouse or under a roof.[19]

We have already discussed the halachic foundations of the laws governing *matza menutak* when we dealt with indoor plant containers (see p. *104–114*). It was noted there that, according to the ***Chazon Ish,*** there is adequate basis to justify planting indoors in an *atzitz she-eino nakuv,* a container without a hole in the bottom, during the *Shemita* year. The allowance is based on the fact that according to the ***Yerushalmi,*** it might be permissible to plant indoors during the *Shemita* year, and it is not at all clear that during the *Shemita* year it is forbidden to plant outside in a container that is detached from the ground (and certainly, even if this is forbidden, it is at worst forbidden only by rabbinic decree).

In light of this, it should be permissible to plant during the *Shemita* year in containers inside hothouses, as hothouses are covered both by a roof and by screens.[20] This solution would make it possible to plant vegetables during the *Shemita* year. This method was tested in a limited way in Kibbutz Chafetz Chayim under the supervision of the *Chazon Ish.*

Several decades later, the farmers of Gush Katif who wished to observe *Shemita* in the best possible manner, revived the idea of hothouses and *matza menutak.* Several contemporary authorities considered this question, as is evident from the words of the ***Shevet ha-Levi*** (vol. *VIII*, no. *246*):

> I have come today to answer that which you have asked, with respect to the problem presented of the upcoming *Shemita,* when it will be close to impossible to make use of Arab fields in any way, because of the real danger to the lives of the supervisors. There is the option of buying vegetables from Jewish farmers in that region of the country called Gush Katif, past the city of Gaza. They plan to raise vegetables

19. For practical specifications, see *Be-Tzet ha-Shana; Ha-Torah ve-ha-Aretz* (vol. I); *Halichot Sadeh* (48); *Katif Shevi'it.*

20. The *Acharonim* dispute whether a permanent structure is needed in order to permit planting inside: The *Chazon Ish* (*22, 1*) is stringent, whereas Rav Frank (*Zera'im*, vol. II, section 34) is lenient. Practically speaking, this issue does not present a problem, because hothouses are permanent structures. Moreover, we have pictures of the hothouses that the *Chazon Ish* permitted in Kibbutz Chafetz Chayim, and today's hothouses are much more permanent than the ones he permitted.

> inside hothouses that are closed at the top and on all sides with thick plastic sheeting, using *atzitzim she-einam nakuvim* that are also of plastic which will be filled with soil and fertilizer, and there they plant. This is the essence of the question, and the rest of the reasons for leniency in this case will be brought later in our discussion. And I, as I am accustomed to do, without expanding at length … will try to establish this law on its foundation as is possible from here. May God be with us.

The *Shevet ha-Levi* inclines toward leniency in dealing with produce grown in hothouses in *atzitzim she-einam nakuvim*:

> We have before us a combination of several reasons for leniency: 1. planting indoors; 2. *Shemita* in our time is only rabbinic in nature; 3. an *atzitz she-eino nakuv*; 4. the uncertainty regarding whether this region is included in the second sanctification of Eretz Yisrael; 5. your proposal that the forbidden labors will be performed by gentiles.

Towards the end of the responsum, however, it becomes apparent that he was not pleased with allowing this. Moreover, he writes in the next responsum that he had heard that **Rav Sh. Z. Auerbach** permits hothouses and *matza menutak*, and therefore he suggests that those who plant in this manner should rely solely on Rav Sh. Z. Auerbach:

> I received your precious letter about issuing a practical ruling regarding produce grown in hothouses in *atzitzim she-einam nakuvim*, and you also sent me a letter from my colleague, Rav Sh. Z. Auerbach, *shlita*, where he inclines toward leniency. Thank God, you do not need me, and it is fitting to rely on him alone.

In a later responsum, the *Shevet ha-Levi* (vol. IX, no. 237) clearly rules that *matza menutak* is forbidden:

> Regarding hothouses that you asked me about as if I retracted what I had written earlier … I was afraid to permit this for

> all of Eretz Yisrael, for the reason that I wrote in another responsum, that I doubt that it was *Chazal's* intention to allow planting and harvesting during the *Shemita* year throughout Eretz Yisrael.

In other words, even if technically speaking planting on detached bedding in hothouses is permitted, *Chazal* would not have wanted this solution to be used in a wholesale manner, thus causing the cancellation of the *mitzva* of *Shemita.*

The ***Minchat Yitzchak*** (vol. *x,* no. *116*) also writes that we should not plant in hothouses because today this is a regular way of planting, and as such hothouses are subject to the law of a "field":

> Hothouses are different, because they are designed for large scale planting and it is common practice to erect them in vast areas and to plant in them, and therefore they have the law of a "field." It is not the same as the question in the *Yerushalmi* about planting indoors.

This argument, however, requires examination, for we do not generally change a law based on a reason suggested to explain a *mitzva*. How then do we know that the definition of a "field" is determined by common agricultural practices? Perhaps there is a scriptural decree that the laws of *Shemita* are restricted to open areas and do not apply in areas that are closed.

Moreover, since hothouses are very hot, they are often not very good environments for the produce growing there, and it is only because of special cooling systems that they can be used. If we define the halacha of a "house" as a hostile environment for plants, hothouses would fundamentally fall into that definition, only that by way of certain compensations we manage to grow crops there.[21] This argument is even stronger in the case of hothouses used to raise insect-free vegetables. The farmer knows that the hothouse is detrimental to his crop, but nevertheless he uses it so that his produce will be free of insects.

As the *Shevet ha-Levi* mentioned, one important halachic

21. This is the explanation of some experts. For example, Prof. Yiftach Ben Asher, head of the Agrobiological Center at Ben Gurion University in Be'er-Sheva (cited in *Ha-Torah ve-ha-Aretz, Shevi'it 6*), says: "As a scientist who has studied agricultural methods throughout the world, I have not found another place [other than Gush Katif] where leafy vegetables are grown in hothouses. It is important to note that the natural habitat of leafy vegetables is the open field. In order to separate between the leafy vegetables and insects, they must be grown in hothouses ... Owing to these requirements, the heat inside the hothouses often reaches a very high temperature (48° Celsius, 118° Fahrenheit, and higher), causing substantial damage to the plants ... Were these plants growing in an open field, which is their natural habitat, they would not be damaged."

authority who permitted planting in detached bedding in hothouses was **Rav Sh. Z. Auerbach** (*Responsa Minchat Shlomo,* vol. *III,* section *158, 7*):

> To my colleague ... Rav Kalman Kahana, *shlita* ... I received your precious letter and I also reviewed the other material that you sent to me, and here is my response in brief: Were we to rule that *Shemita* in our time is by Torah law, I would be a little concerned about the desirability of issuing a ruling on behalf of the entire community that it is permitted to plant in today's hothouses as a preferred option, even though this is an ordinary manner of planting ... Since, however, we rely in practice on those who rule that *Shemita* in our time is only by rabbinic decree, I therefore think that it is very proper to establish the matter in practice, as you have written ... together with the fact that the planting is done in an *atzitz she-eino nakuv,* even with respect to the four labors [forbidden by Torah law] and the sanctity of the produce.
>
> ... Sh. Z. Auerbach

In practice, Rav Sh. Z. Auerbach permits planting in hothouses on *matza menutak,* even if this is the regular way of planting in normal years. Among his considerations, he notes the fact that the whole observance of *Shemita* in our time is only by rabbinic decree.[22]

22. *Responsa Yeshu'at Moshe* (Rav Aharonsohn, vol. IV, section 12)

Rav Y. S. Elyashiv, on the other hand, raised doubts about the validity of this solution. He concludes that in the case of an ordinary hothouse, one should be stringent, but in the case of a hothouse that is detrimental to the crop, yet is nonetheless utilized for other reasons – such as in order to grow insect-free vegetables – there might be room for leniency (cited in *Mishpetei Aretz, Shevi'it, 248*):

1. Since in our time growing crops in hothouses is a regular method of farming, one should not practice leniency and plant in a hothouse. Even if we say that a hothouse is excluded from the category of "field," it does involve work in the field and in the vineyard that is forbidden by rabbinic decree. It is, therefore, forbidden to plant even in

an *atzitz she-eino nakuv* in a hothouse, and even in Gush Katif.

2. There is room to be lenient and plant in a hothouse those crops for which a hothouse is not beneficial ... and the farmer leaves the roof in place only because of the *Shemita* year. Crops for which the roof provides no agricultural benefit but for some other reason, the roof is left in place, such as for insect-free vegetables ... there is room for doubt.

Rav Elyashiv considers leniency only when the following four conditions are met:

> It is permissible to sell the *atzitzim she-einam nakuvim* in the hothouse to a gentile, and have gentile do the planting, and then a Jew is permitted to perform labors that are forbidden [only] by rabbinic law on these containers. The harvesting should be done by a gentile and these crops do not have *Shemita* sanctity. The fact that the hothouse is located in Gush Katif is irrelevant.

In other words, there is room to permit planting in a hothouse provided that four conditions are met:

1. Hothouses
2. Detached bed
3. The containers are sold to a gentile
4. Only rabbinic labors are performed by a Jew, but all Torah labors are performed by a gentile

As we saw above, **Rav Wosner** (in the *Shevet HaLevi*) concluded that it was not *Chazal's* desire to issue a wholesale allowance of this sort, but he also permits *matza menutak* when the conditions set by Rav Elyashiv are met (his view is cited in *Mishpetei Aretz*, p. 249):

> The ruling that was issued by Rav Y. S. Elyashiv, *shlita* stands to reason, given that there is a hothouse and [they are] also [planted in] *atzitzim she-einam nakuvim*, and it is truly sold to a gentile.[23]

23. Another disagreement regarding hothouses arose in light of the *Mishna* in *Shevi'it* – see the appendix at the end of this chapter (p. 370).

HOW TO CREATE A *MATZA MENUTAK*

It would seem that in order to create a *matza menutak*, it should suffice to lay down plastic sheeting on the ground inside the hothouse, cover it with soil, and plant in it. When this is done, the sheeting (*matza*) separates (*menatek*) between the soil in which the crops are grown and the ground. In practice, however, the matter is not so simple. We cannot expand upon the various problems that are involved in detail, but we will note them briefly.

The **Rosh** (*Responsa ha-Rosh, kelal 2,* section *4*) writes that a plant growing on a rock is treated like a plant growing in the ground.[24] This leads the Rosh to the conclusion that a grapevine planted on a roof is subject to the prohibition of *orla* (the prohibition to consume fruit from a tree in its first three years) and the grapes that grow on it are subject to *terumot* and *ma'asrot* (the tithings that must be separated in years other than *Shemita*). The Rosh's position was codified as law in the ***Shulchan Aruch*** (*Yoreh De'a 294:27*). The **Gra**, however, disagrees with the Rosh, but his ruling is not followed in practice as it is difficult to permit agricultural work during the *Shemita* year based on a solution that goes against a ruling of the *Shulchan Aruch*. Thus, it is possible that laying plastic sheeting on the ground does not suffice for the produce growing there to be regarded as detached from the ground.[25]

In order to overcome this difficulty, the planting should be done in movable

24. The question may be asked whether the plant is regarded as "'attached'" to the ground because of the rock's physical connection to the ground or rather because the plant draws its nourishment from the ground. This seems to be a dispute among the *Acharonim*. The *Chazon Ish* maintains that the plant is regarded as attached because it draws nourishment from the ground, and therefore when no nourishment is drawn, it is permitted, even according to the Rosh. Rav Sh. Z. Auerbach disagrees, maintaining that the connection due to which the plant senses "'the smell of the ground,'" leads to the conclusion that the plant growing on a detached platform forms a single unit with the ground.

25. There are, however, those who maintain that a plant that rests on plastic sheeting is indeed treated as if in an *atzitz she-eino nakuv*, as opposed to a plant resting on a rock. According to them, the Rosh is dealing with a plant that rests on a rock, but derives its nourishment from the ground. He would agree that a plant resting on plastic sheeting that was specially made to detach its contents from the ground below is not regarded as attached to the ground (see the views of Rav Eliyahu and Rav Shapira cited in *Betzet ha-Shana*, p. 87, 2, 3; as well as the view of Rav Yisraeli, cited in *Katif Shevi'it*, p. 110, note. 23, who permit this. In the end, however, Rav Eliyahu requires detached containers, which follows from what he says in *Sefer Zikaron la-Rav Daum*, vol. 1, and from the position cited in his name in *Katif Shevi'it*, ibid.).

containers which rest on the plastic sheeting. In this way, it is clear that the produce is detached from the ground.

Doing this in a serious and professional manner[26] requires a significant investment of resources. Every acre of hothouses and detached bedding costs thousands of shekels. Therefore, if we are to observe *Shemita* in the best possible manner, consumers must share the costs. This can be done by purchasing vegetables grown during the *Shemita* year on detached bedding in hothouses, even if the prices are higher than regular vegetables.

26. In advanced hothouses, the crops are grown on movable metal tracks that are inclined so as to allow water to flow out.

During the *Shemita* of 5761 (2000–2001), lettuce was grown in Gush Katif in about a million containers, one head of lettuce in each container. The crop was very successful, but unfortunately the hothouses have been destroyed (as a result of the Israeli evacuation of Gush Katif during the withdrawal from Gaza in 2005). There are farmers today, former residents of Gush Katif and others, who are trying to raise crops using this method, but, as explained above, this is a very costly enterprise. It seems that the proper thing to do is to establish a *Shemita* fund (as had been proposed already by Rav Kook, and which exists in certain places, but not on a widespread scale), that would make it possible to grow as many different kinds of vegetables as is possible in hothouses and on detached bedding. With the help of such a fund, it would be possible to establish an *Otzar Bet Din* of the highest caliber.

It should be added that the establishment of such a fund would allow Jews living in the Diaspora to play an active role in the *mitzva* of *Shemita* and help put into operation a system that allows Jewish farmers to earn their livelihood while meticulously observing the laws of *Shemita.*

To summarize, these are the conditions that permit growing crops in hothouses on detached bedding during the *Shemita* year:[27]

1. The hothouse must be constructed of netting with a density greater than 50 percent.[28] It is preferable that the netting be even denser, and that it be as close to solid as possible.[29]
2. The ground must be covered with a material that

27. For full, professional instructions, see *Katif Shevi'it* (chaps. 17, 18 and 39).

28. Rav Eliyahu, *Katif Shevi'it*, 17, p. 103.

29. Ibid. in the name of Rav Yisraeli.

is impermeable, preferably polyethylene sheeting (Palrig, a permeable cover, does not suffice).[30]

3. The plants should grow in containers.[31] It is best that the containers themselves be *atzitzim she-einam nakuvim* (or *atzitzim nakuvim* but resting on metal strips that are detached from the ground, as can be seen in the picture). Strictly speaking, however, there is room for leniency even if the containers are perforated, provided that the containers and the growth that extends beyond the containers are above the plastic sheeting.[32]
4. According to **Rav Elyashiv's** stringency, the containers should be sold to a gentile (this certainly does not involve the prohibition of *lo techanem* – not selling land in Israel to gentiles – and there is full agreement to the sale on the part of the seller).
5. Also according to Rav Elyashiv's stringency, only rabbinic labors should be performed by a Jew whereas Torah labors should be performed by a gentile.[33]

Buying vegetables grown in hothouses is an important solution for those who prefer not to rely on the *heter mechira* nor purchase gentile produce. Special efforts should therefore be made to purchase such

30. Care should be taken to prevent the formation of a layer of soil on top of the plastic sheeting (*Dapei Halacha la-Chakla'im*, p. 9).

31. The containers should be of a size that allows them to be moved, because a utensil that cannot be moved might be regarded as attached to the ground (according to *Eglei Tal, Kotzer*, 3, 10; *Aruch ha-Shulchan, Orach Chayyim* 336:31; Rav Mordecai Eliyahu, *Katif Shevi'it*, p. 110, note 21). Rav Yisraeli (ibid.) rules that one may be lenient about a large container, as long as it holds less than 40 *se'a* (300 liters), because a container that is larger than this is treated like a building (based on the *Shulchan Aruch, Orach Chayyim* 314:1).

32. As we have seen, there is a problem with using plastic sheeting alone. It would seem, therefore, that the containers used in the hothouses should be *atzitzim she-einam nakuvim* (*Chiddushim u-Bei'urim la-Rav Greineman, Shevi'it* 11; *Ha-Torah ve-ha-Aretz, Shevi'it* 6, p. 319). As we said above, however, it might be possible to be lenient and use *atzitzim nakuvim* on the plastic sheeting. The rationale for this allowance is that the plant derives no nourishment through the sheeting, and therefore the hole in the container is not a problem. In addition, since the container is a separate utensil, it is regarded as detached from the ground, even if it is an *atzitz nakuv* (see *Ha-Torah ve-ha-Aretz*, 6, p. 326). In practice one can be lenient about a *atzitz nakuv*, but in such a case it is preferable that the planting be performed at a special planting station (over metal that totally detaches it from the ground) and only afterwards should gentile workers move the *atzitzim nakuvim* onto the plastic sheeting. Today there is much more room for leniency because in most hothouses both Torah labors and rabbinic labors are performed exclusively by gentiles. There is also another factor allowing for leniency if the container is raised up from the ground more than 80 cm. (31.5 inches, 10 handbreadths) [see *Katif Shevi'it*, p. 111, note 24].

33. In most hothouses today, foreign workers perform the labors that are forbidden by Torah law as well as the labors that are forbidden by rabbinic decree, even during ordinary years.

vegetables even if they are more expensive because of the added costs that growing vegetables in this manner incurs. One of the major marketers of hothouse vegetables grown on detached bedding is "*Otzar ha-Aretz*" – which markets Jewish produce grown during the *Shemita* year according to the most meticulous standards.

SHEMITA SANCTITY OF PRODUCE GROWN ON DETACHED BEDDING

Planting indoors: As we saw in the chapter on *Shemita* sanctity (p. *104–105*), the *Yerushalmi* raises a doubt about the permissibility of planting indoors (in the ground or in a perforated container) during the *Shemita* year, because that which grows indoors does not grow in "your field," but does grow in "the land." As was explained there, according to the opinion that planting indoors is permitted, it stands to reason that the produce does not have *Shemita* sanctity. On the other hand, we saw that even if produce grown indoors is permitted, because it does not grow in "your field," it might have *Shemita* sanctity. This is because *Shemita* sanctity is derived from the verse, "And the Sabbath produce of the land shall be food for you," implying that it applies to anything grown in the "land," and not only that which grows in the "field" (*Kerem Tziyon,* chap. *3*, *Gidulei Tziyon,* no. *6*).

According to **Rav Kook** (*Kuntres Acharon, 3*) and **Rav Frank** (*Har Zvi, Zera'im,* vol. *II,* section *35*), the scope of the law of *Shemita* sanctity is the same as that of planting, and the doubt that the *Yerushalmi* raises about the permissibility of planting indoors carries over to a doubt about whether produce grown indoors is subject to *Shemita* sanctity. Therefore, just as we are stringent about labors forbidden by Torah law even indoors (in a perforated container), so too we are stringent about the *Shemita* sanctity of produce grown indoors, for its *Shemita* sanctity is also by Torah law.

Planting indoors in an *atzitz she-eino nakuv*: If the allowance to plant indoors in an ***atzitz she-eino nakuv*** is based on a double uncertainty leading away from prohibition (*sfek safeka*) as we previously suggested (see p. *108*), then it is possible that even if we permit planting, we will still be stringent about *Shemita* sanctity. According to the ***Kerem Tziyon***, indoor planting is subject to the laws governing the "land," including *Shemita* sanctity. Therefore in the case of a container, there is only one uncertainty, whether or not container planting is also subject to the laws governing the "land."

If, on the other hand, planting indoors in an *atzitz she-eino nakuv* is permitted for reasons of principle, because a container is not regarded as "land" and a house is not regarded as a "land" (as we wrote in the name of my teacher **Rav Lichtenstein**, *shlita*; see above, p. *109*), there is room to be lenient about *Shemita* sanctity as well.

In practice, there is room for leniency with respect to *Shemita* sanctity regarding hothouse vegetables grown on a detached bed,[34] especially if we add in other factors, such as the containers being sold to a gentile. This is the ruling of **Rav Elyashiv** (cited in *Mishpetei Aretz*, p. 234).

Summary: Growing vegetables in hothouses in containers that are detached from the ground is an excellent solution for the *Shemita* year. This method enjoys the approval of leading authorities (**Rav Sh. Z. Auerbach** and **Rav Elyashiv**), and there is evidence that the ***Chazon Ish*** approved of this as well.[35] This solution allows for the growing of vegetables during the *Shemita* year with meticulous observance of the *Shemita* laws, without having to resort to gentile produce grown in Israel or abroad. According to what we have said, such produce does not have *Shemita* sanctity and may be treated as regular produce.

34. Another reason for leniency is the fact that the entire observance of *Shemita* in our day is only by rabbinic decree, and therefore if there is a connection between the prohibition of planting and the sanctity of the produce, all the uncertainties relate to rabbinic prohibitions.

35. In Kibbutz Chafetz Chayyim. Pictures of these hothouses have been preserved.

Hothouses and detached bedding

Atzitz she-eino nakuv – detached bed – doubt regarding a rabbinic prohibition

"House" (roofed structure) – doubt in the *Yerushalmi*

Container and House (detached bedding and hothouse)

Chazon Ish: One who is lenient has a basis for his practice

Rav Sh. Z. Auerbach and Rav Y. Sh. Elyashiv accept the view of the *Chazon Ish*

Minchat Yitzchak: One should be stringent about hothouse produce, because that is the normal way of growing such produce

The law is that one may be lenient as a preferred solution

Conditions for planting in a hothouse

Torah labors should be performed by a gentile; rabbinic labors may be performed by a Jew (Rav Elyashiv's stringency)

Selling the containers to a gentile (Rav Elyashiv's stringency)

Planting in containers

Plastic sheeting on the ground

Hothouse

Such produce does not have *Shemita* sanctity (Rav Elyashiv)

APPENDIX – PRODUCE GROWN INDOORS – DOES THE *YERUSHALMI* CONTRADICT THE MISHNA?

The *Yerushalmi* is in doubt about whether planting indoors is permitted during the *Shemita* year (as we saw at length in the chapter about potted plants in the house). The ***Mishna*** in ***Shevi'it*** (2:4), however, seems to imply that **the prohibitions of *shevi'it* apply indoors as well.**

A sapling surrounded by a stone wall

The ***Mishna*** states that it is permissible to build "shelters" for saplings only until Rosh ha-Shana, implying that **during the *Shemita* year this is forbidden**, despite the fact that with a covering, the planting is indoors. Thus, it would appear that planting indoors is forbidden. The ***Chazon Ish*** explains (*Shevi'it 20, 6;* and *Ma'asrot 7, 5*):

> That which is stated in the *Mishna* (*Shevi'it 2:4*), "One may make shelters for them," refers not to planting indoors, for there ... the shelter enhances the growth. But when one plants indoors – the plants are in an unfavorable and undesirable climate, for they are denied the benefit of the rain, dew, fresh air and sunlight, and the house is detrimental to them.

A covered sapling

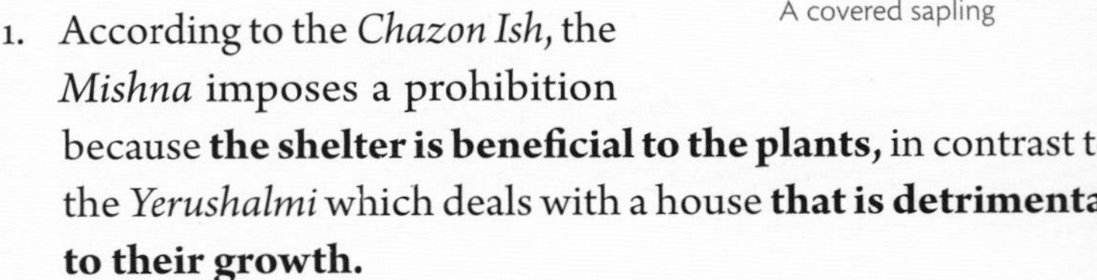

1. According to the *Chazon Ish*, the *Mishna* imposes a prohibition because **the shelter is beneficial to the plants,** in contrast to the *Yerushalmi* which deals with a house **that is detrimental to their growth.**

2. There are other ways to distinguish between the *Mishna* and the *Yerushalmi*. The ***Mishna* might be dealing with a temporary covering placed over the sapling**, which is not regarded as a house, but would be considered as providing **care** for the sapling which is forbidden during the *Shemita* year. On the other hand, **hothouses, which are strong and permanent structures**, are regarded as houses, and therefore permitted. In a different context (*Shevi'it 22:1*, not in relation to the Mishna in *Shevi'it*), the ***Chazon Ish*** himself proposes this resolution, namely that a temporary covering does not turn the area into a house:

   > All the more so if he erects a temporary covering in order to plant underneath it. This is not considered to be a significant separation, for a temporary covering does not cancel the status of a field.

3. Another distinction might be suggested. The ***Mishna*** in ***Shevi'it*** refers to a person who **plants in a field in the usual manner, and then spreads a cover over the planted area.** This does not cancel the status of "field," because the planting had been done in a field. When, however, the planting is done from the outset inside a hothouse, this might indeed have the status of a house, and so whatever grows there never becomes subject to the prohibitions of *Shemita*. This distinction was proposed by **Rav Kook** (*Shabbat ha-Aretz, Kuntres Acharon 3*[36]).
4. Yet another distinction is possible. Almost all the commentators to the Mishna (Rash, Rosh, Bartenura; Rashi, *Avoda Zara 50b*) understand that "making a shelter" means **building a cubit-high fence around the tree**. According to this, since **there is no covering**, it is not a house, and therefore caring for the saplings is forbidden. According to this, there is no connection between this *Mishna* and the *Yerushalmi* which speaks of a "house" as a covered structure (as defined by the *Chazon Ish* with respect to the *Yerushalmi*; the essential characteristic of a house is its roof) [see *Har Zvi*, section *14*, p. *91*; vol. *II*, section 35].

36. See *Torat ha-Aretz*, VI, p. 338, and editor's note.

Matza Menutak

GENTILE PRODUCE

SHEMITA SANCTITY WITH RESPECT TO PRODUCE PURCHASED FROM A GENTILE

In the chapter dealing with renouncing ownership of *Shemita* produce, we dealt with the disagreement between the ***Bet Yosef*** and the ***Mabit*** on the question of whether the produce of a gentile has *Shemita* sanctity (p. 144). As we have seen, the common practice in Jerusalem and most of Israel follows the view of the *Bet Yosef*, which was accepted by the ***Pe'at ha-Shulchan*** (23:12), **Rav Kook** (*Shabbat ha-Aretz*, introduction, chap. 11; chap. 4, 29; *Mishpat Kohen*, no. 70), **Rav Sh. Z. Auerbach** (*Ma'adanei Aretz* 2, s.v. *hinei*), **Rav Frank** (*Har Zvi, Zera'im*, vol. II, section 39) and **Rav Ovadya Yosef** (*Responsa Yabi'a Omer*, vol. III, *Yoreh De'a*, section 19).[37] It is therefore common practice in most places not to treat gentile produce as having *Shemita* sanctity. In Bnei Brak, however, which was the home of the ***Chazon Ish***, the practice follows his ruling (20, 7; 9, 18).

The disagreement between the *Bet Yosef* and the *Mabit* has great ramifications with respect to using gentile produce during the *Shemita* year. According to the custom of Jerusalem, such produce has no *Shemita* sanctity, and therefore it may be marketed during the *Shemita* year in the usual manner. According to the custom of Bnei Brak, trading in such produce during the *Shemita* year is forbidden because it has *Shemita* sanctity.[38] Moreover, according to this custom, the money paid for the produce has *Shemita* sanctity and may not be handed over to an *am ha-aretz* (an ignorant person who is not scrupulous in his observance of the commandments).

In light of this, the *Chazon Ish* established special "*va'adot Shemita*" (*Shemita* committees) charged with solving these problems. In a normal year, vegetable dealers purchase produce from gentile suppliers and then sell it to Jewish customers. During *Shemita*, these committees arrange for a dealer who acts as a mediator between the gentile produce suppliers and the consumers. Instead of receiving payment from consumers for the produce, this mediator receives a mediation fee. In this way, the consumers purchase the produce

37. Rav Ovadya Yosef is very strict in his ruling that it is forbidden to treat produce grown in the fields of gentiles as having *Shemita* sanctity, because the *Bet Yosef* imposed a ban on anyone who does not follow his ruling (*Responsa Avkat Rochel*, end of no. 25; there, however, the *Bet Yosef's* ruling is a stringency, because he maintains that the produce of a gentile is subject to *terumot* and *ma'asrot*; for a similar ruling see *Responsa Mishpat Kohen*, no. 70).

38. The *Mabit* himself writes (*Responsa ha-Mabit*, vol. I, section 36) that even though gentile produce has *Shemita* sanctity, it is not subject to the prohibition of trade. According to him, the prohibition to trade in *Shemita* produce stems from the obligation to declare the produce ownerless, and since the gentile is not obligated to declare his produce ownerless, the Jew who buys the produce from him is also exempt from declaring it ownerless, and thus there is no prohibition to trade in such produce. The *Chazon Ish* (26, *Seder ha-Shevi'it*, 3) ruled in accordance with the *Mabit*, while Rav Kook (*Kuntres Acharon*, section 1; *Mishpat Kohen*, section 64, 66) argued that if gentile produce has **Shemita** sanctity, it is also subject to the prohibition of trade.

directly from the gentile through the mediation of the produce dealer. This is not a problem, because a gentile is not bound by the prohibition to trade in produce having *Shemita* sanctity.[39]

At first glance, however, these *va'adot* do not solve all the problems. If gentile produce has *Shemita* sanctity, then the purchase money handed over to the gentile acquires *Shemita* sanctity. How is it possible to hand over money that has *Shemita* sanctity to a gentile, when such money may not even be handed over to an *am ha-aretz,* lest he come to treat it in an improper manner? In order to gain a deeper understanding of the matter, let us examine the *Shemita* status of money used in transactions with gentiles:

The ***Tosefta*** (chap. *6*) states:

> One may neither sell nor purchase *Shemita* produce from a gentile or from a Cuthean.

The **Ridbaz** (*9:10; 4:13*) explains that the concern here is that the gentile might hand the money over to a Jew who does not know that the money has *Shemita* sanctity. The Ridbaz clearly understands that the money received by the gentile in exchange for the produce acquires *Shemita* sanctity.

In contrast, the ***Chazon Ish*** (*10, 17*) maintains that the money handed over to the gentile does not acquire *Shemita* sanctity. According to him, the *Tosefta* is dealing with a case where the produce in the gentile's hands might actually belong to a Jew. In this case, the gentile is merely helping the Jew sell the produce, and thus the money must be treated as if it has *Shemita* sanctity. According to him, were it clear that the produce belongs to the gentile, the money used for their purchase would not acquire *Shemita* sanctity.

It should be added that even if the money received by the gentile in exchange for the *Shemita* produce acquires *Shemita* sanctity, as argued by the Ridbaz, it might not be forbidden to purchase the produce from him. Indeed, the ***Maharit*** maintains that *Shemita* sanctity applies to the money that is handed over to the gentile in exchange for his produce, but since the gentile is not subject to the laws of *Shemita* sanctity, there is no prohibition to buy the produce from him.

39. The prohibition of selling produce that has *Shemita* sanctity by measure, weight or number, when this system is used, needs to be addressed.

To summarize, the *Acharonim* permit the purchase of gentile produce and are not concerned about the *Shemita* sanctity of the money for two reasons: *Shemita* sanctity might not apply to the money, and even if it does, the gentile is not bound by the obligation to preserve that sanctity.

FRUITS AND VEGETABLES PURCHASED FROM A GENTILE – IN PRACTICE

Despite all the above discussion, buying gentile produce is still not a simple matter. Sometimes, and especially during the *Shemita* year, Jewish farmers sell their produce to Arabs in order to market it. Due to security concerns, even careful supervision cannot always trace the course of the produce, and it is often difficult to determine if it was really grown by a gentile or sold to him by a Jewish farmer.[40] Moreover, significant areas of land in Eretz Yisrael do not actually belong to the gentiles working them, but rather the lands have been illegally taken over by these gentiles from Jews. In such cases, the land is not regarded as the land of a gentile, and the vegetables growing there are subject to the prohibition of *sefichim* (*Responsa Maharam ben Baruch*, no. 536; *Torat ha-Aretz*, vol. II, section 3).

The most serious problem with buying gentile produce, however, lies in the fact that it strengthens the gentile hold on the land in Eretz Yisrael. Even if from a strict halachic perspective this does not fall under the prohibition of *lo techonem*, not granting gentiles a portion in the land (an assumption which is not at all clear), the fundamental problem underlying this prohibition certainly exists. In previous *Shemita* years, the increased demand on the part of religious Jews who wished to observe *Shemita* without relying on the *heter mechira* resulted in significantly increased Arab production. Owing to the increase in production, the allocation of water to Arab farmers was also increased, allowing them to seize control of additional areas of land which they continued to hold even after the *Shemita* year. Without a doubt, buying produce from gentiles undermines the idea behind the prohibition of *lo techonem*.[41]

And indeed, we find already in the ***Gemara*** that it is no simple

40. Before the previous Shemita year,, a rabbi related to this author that he had tried to convince a Jewish farmer to convert his production to detached bedding so that he would be able to continue farming during the *Shemita year*. The farmer told him that he had already promised his entire crop to an Arab who needed it in order to satisfy the great demand of religious Jews for gentile produce.

41. See *Peri Etz Hadar*, which reproduces letters written by great Torah authorities on the importance of buying specifically from a Jew. See also *Iggerot Ra'aya* (316, 318), and the appendix at the end of this volume (p. 499).

matter to purchase produce from a gentile during the *Shemita* year. The ***Mishna*** in ***Shevi'it*** (*4:3*) states that "one may strengthen the hands of gentiles during the seventh year, but not the hands of a Jew." There is a disagreement in the ***Yerushalmi*** (*Shevi'it 3:4*) whether it is permissible to say to a gentile during the *Shemita* year that he should plow his field well so that we may later buy his produce, or whether it is merely permissible to wish him good luck. The **Rosh** understands that there is no fundamental disagreement between these two positions and that all agree that an arrangement may be reached with the gentile that we will purchase the produce that he grows. Yet, according to the **Ri Kurkus** (on the Rambam, *Hilchot Shemita ve-Yovel 8:8;* and this seems to be the simple understanding of the Rambam), the two opinions disagree, and the law follows the view that one may only say to the gentile "good luck." According to this approach, it is forbidden to tell a gentile to plow an area especially for Jews. It is thus by no means clear then that it is permissible to tell a gentile that he should work the land during the *Shemita* year in order that we should be able to purchase the produce from him.

In practice, vegetables grown by gentiles that are purchased during ordinary years may be purchased during the *Shemita* year as well. One should not, however, go out specially to buy produce grown by gentiles in Israel during the *Shemita* year.[42]

It should be noted that importing produce grown by gentiles outside of Israel can also be exceedingly problematic.[43] Produce that is imported every year may be imported during the *Shemita* year as well. However, importing produce especially for the *Shemita* year (and in recent *Shemita* years, such imports have grown substantially and special areas of land have come under cultivation in Jordan for this purpose) can cause a serious blow to Israeli agriculture, which in the best of times must deal with serious competition.

Every effort should therefore be made to purchase Jewish produce. Those who wish to buy produce grown according to the most meticulous halachic standards may buy *Otzar Bet Din* produce, hothouse vegetables grown in containers, sixth year produce, or

42. This limitation should be respected, other than in exceptional circumstances and in restricted quantities, with the result being that the total consumption of vegetables grown by gentiles during the *Shemita* year should be the same as in ordinary years, as will be explained in the order of priorities laid down at the end of this chapter. It goes without saying that at all times we should try to purchase as much Jewish merchandise as possible (see appendix at the end of this volume p. 499).

43. Importing produce is sometimes even more problematic than buying domestic Arab produce, because the locally grown gentile produce does not always grow in volume, but is merely distributed differently, whereas importing produce hurts Israeli agriculture. Yet, this author's research has revealed that the profits of Arab farmers in Israel grows by more than 30 percent during *Shemita*. It should also be noted that in the past there were many vegetables that always came from Arabs (such as cucumbers), but that the Arab production of these vegetables has dropped to less than 50 percent of the Israeli market, and we need to be careful that the *Shemita* year does not cause us to increase our consumption of Arab produce.

produce grown in the Southern Arava. As we shall see later, produce acquired by way of the *heter mechira* is generally to be preferred over gentile produce.

Let us conclude with the frightening words of **Rav Kook**, (*Iggerot ha-Ra'aya,* vol. *1, 316*), which he wrote after having successfully reached an agreement with members of the old *yishuv* that during the *Shemita* year they would buy grapes from the *moshavot,* and then suddenly discovering that certain people had arrived and had begun to convince the members of the old *yishuv* to buy from gentiles. It is possible to feel in Rav Kook's words his sense of responsibility and feelings of love for the pioneering Jewish farmers:

The pen in my hand quivers in the wake of the despicable act that has just been committed against our brothers, the farmers in the *moshavot*. For after it had been finally established not to give a seal of *kashrut* to gentiles so as not to press the oppressed and weary who depend on the sale of grapes for their livelihood, and after an agreement had been reached with respect to the *Shemita* controversy, the essence of which was to benefit our brothers living in the *moshavot*, underminers have appeared, secretly counseling to buy specifically from gentiles and raise the banner of our enemies who "mock our rest" (based on Eicha 1:7). How we ourselves persecute our brothers, members of the covenant, O heaven …

Immeasurable is the disgrace, the desecration of God's name, and the enormity of the wickedness in this. The blood in my heart boils like a pot and my pain reaches heaven from this dreadful situation, from the fall of Torah and fear of heaven evident in this situation …

I wish to inform you that with respect to the vineyards of the gentiles, there is great concern about *orla* (the forbidden fruit from the first three years of the growth of a vine or tree) and *kil'ei ha-kerem* (prohibited mixtures between the grapevine and other plants) in these years … We are known for the very close supervision over our brothers' vineyards. How can we turn the tables and buy from gentiles that have no supervision, only in order to persecute our brothers, our own flesh?

… Avraham Yitzchak Hakohen Kook

HETER MECHIRA

The solution of *heter mechira* involves the sale of agricultural land to a gentile for the duration of the *Shemita* year. Following the sale, some of the labors that are forbidden during the *Shemita* year may be performed by gentiles, while others may be performed by Jews.

Before we discuss the *heter mechira* itself, it must be understood that it is based on several assumptions. We shall relate to the three most important among them and examine each one separately.

ASSUMPTION I:

THE OBSERVANCE OF *SHEMITA* IN OUR TIME IS BY RABBINIC DECREE

The **Gemara** in ***Mo'ed Katan*** *2b* (a similar discussion appears in *Gittin 36a*) records a Tannaitic dispute whether the observance of *Shemita* in our time is by Torah law or only by rabbinic decree. According to the Sages, *Shemita* observance in our time is by Torah law, whereas Rabbi Yehuda HaNasi argues that it is only by rabbinic decree:

> Mishna: An irrigated field may be watered during the festival [week] and in the seventh year …
>
> Gemara: … Abaye said: Our Mishna is speaking of the *Shemita* year in the present time and it follows the view of Rabbi [Yehuda HaNasi]. For it is taught: "And this is the manner of *Shemita,* release, *shamot,* release [by every creditor that which he has lent to his neighbor]" (*Devarim 15:2*) – the Torah speaks here of two forms of "release," the release of the soil from work, and the release of money, [the juxtaposition of] which tells us that as long as you must release the soil from work, you must release the money [debt], but when you do not release the soil, you need not release the money.

Rava said: You may even say that [the Mishna] follows the view of the Sages, but it is only the principal categories of labor [*avot*] that the Torah forbids, and not the derivative categories of labor [*toladot*].

As we see, the Mishna teaches that during the *Shemita* year it is permitted to irrigate a *bet ha-shelachin* (a field that depends on irrigation). The Gemara cites two possible explanations for this allowance:

1. According to Rabbi Yehuda HaNasi, whenever *yovel* is not in effect, *Shemita* is also not in effect. Since *yovel* is not in effect today, *Shemita* too is not in effect today by Torah law.[44] According to him, the Sages instituted *Shemita* in our time merely as a reminder of the *Shemita* that used to be observed by Torah law.
2. According to the Sages, even in our time the observance of *Shemita* is mandated by Torah law, but irrigation is not forbidden by Torah law.[45]

We see then that Rabbi Yehuda HaNasi connects the observance of *yovel* with the observance of *Shemita*, so that when the former is not in effect, the latter is also not in effect by Torah law. Why is *yovel* not in effect in our time? This is explained by the Gemara in ***Arachin*** (*32b*):

> For it was taught: When the tribe of Reuven, the tribe of Gad, and half the tribe of Menasheh went into exile, the *yovel* was abolished. For it is said: "And you shall proclaim liberty throughout the land unto **all** the inhabitants thereof" (*Vayikra 25:10*) – [only] at the time when all the inhabitants thereof shall dwell upon it, but not at the time when some of them are exiled.

In other words, *yovel* is only in effect when "all of the land's inhabitants dwell therein," and this condition is not fulfilled in our time.[46]

44. This is based on *Tosafot's* (*Gittin 36a*, s.v. *bi-zeman*; see also Rashi, ad loc.) explanation of Rabbi Yehuda HaNasi's view. They interpret his words as follows: When ***yovel*** is not in effect, ***Shemita*** is also not in effect. Therefore, since ***yovel*** is not in effect today, *Shemita* is also not in effect by Torah law, and it was the Sages who instituted *Shemita* in our time, as "a remembrance of *Shemita*."

45. Irrigation is a derivative category of labor (*tolada*), and according to the Sages, only principle categories of labor (*avot*) are forbidden during the *Shemita year*.

46. Even though Rambam also (*Hilchot Shemita ve-Yovel 10:8*) writes that ***yovel*** is in effect only "when **all** of its inhabitants dwell therein," it would seem that the word "all" is imprecise, and what is necessary is a majority of the land's inhabitants. This, indeed, is what follows from the words of the Ramban (*Gittin 36a*). It would appear from the *Tosafot* (ad loc. s.v. *bi-zeman*) that even a minority of the land's inhabitants suffices, provided that every tribe is represented (for a more extreme application, see *Piskei ha-Tosafot, Arachin*, letter 77).

The **Ramban** (*Sefer ha-Zechut, Gittin 36a*) and the **Rosh**[47] ruled in accordance with the view of the Sages. But **Rashi** (*Gittin 36b; Sanhedrin 26a*), the ***Tosafot*** (*Arachin 32b,* s.v. *manu*), the **Rashba** (*Gittin 36b; Responsa ha-Rashba,* vol. *III,* no. *32*), the **Ritva** (*Gittin 36b*), the **Ran** (ibid.); the ***Yad Rema*** (*Sanhedrin 26a*), the ***Tur*** (*Yoreh De'a 331:2*) and most other *Rishonim* (including the Ramban himself at the beginning of *Makkot*) ruled in accordance with Rabbi Yehuda HaNasi that the observance of *Shemita* in our time is only by rabbinic decree. This is also the simple understanding of the **Rambam's** ruling (*Hilchot Shemita ve-Yovel 10:9*):

> Whenever the *yovel* is in effect, the law of the Hebrew slave, the special regulations for [sale and redemption of] houses in walled cities ... the *Shemita* year is operative in the Land of Israel; and the cancellation of cash debts is effective in all places – all this by Torah law.
>
> Whenever the *yovel* is not in effect, none of these are in effect except for the *Shemita* year in the Land of Israel and the cancellation of cash debts in all places, [both of which are] by rabbinic law as we have explained.

The ***Kesef Mishneh*** (*4:25; 9:2; 10:9*), however, understands that when the Rambam speaks here of *Shemita* being mandated by rabbinic law, he refers only to the cancellation of cash debts. But *Shemita* with respect to the land, according to the Rambam, is by Torah law even in our time. That is to say, according to the *Kesef Mishneh,* the Rambam should be read as follows: "Whenever the *yovel* is not in effect, none of these are in effect, excepting the *Shemita* year in the Land of Israel. And the cancellation of cash debts in all places is mandated by rabbinic law, as we have explained":[48]

> And from the words of our master [the Rambam] it seems that he maintains that even when there is no Temple, *Shemita* with respect to the land is in effect by Torah law … And when he says, "by rabbinic law," it refers only to the cancellation of cash debts which immediately precedes that term, but the *Shemita* of land is in effect by Torah law at all times … .

47. *Tosafot Rosh, Mo'ed Katan 4a*; Rosh, *Yoma*, chap. 8, no. 14. This is also the view of the **Ritzva**, cited by the ***Or Zaru'a*** (vol. 4, no. 332, end), and others. The **Ra'avad** seems to contradict himself on this matter (in *Hilchot Shemita ve-Yovel 1:11*, he writes that *Shemita* in our time is by Torah law; but in *10:6*, he implies that *Shemita* in our time is only by rabbinic decree; see *Chazon Ish, 3, 8*).

48. According to the *Kesef Mishneh's* understanding of the Rambam, the Gemara in *Mo'ed Katan* (*2b*, cited above) must be understood as follows: "As long as you must release the soil – as long as the *yovel* is in effect – you must release the money – cancellation of cash debts at the *Shemita* year – but when you do not release the soil, you need not release the money [but you must still release the soil during the *Shemita* year by Torah law]."

The *Kesef Mishneh's* understanding is difficult for several reasons. First of all, according to the reading found in the Frankel edition of the *Mishneh Torah, Shemita* in our time is unquestionably by rabbinic law:

> The *Shemita* year is in effect in the Land of Israel **by rabbinic law**, and the cancellation of cash debts is similarly in effect in all places by rabbinic law, as we have explained.

In addition, the Rambam's words later in the *Mishneh Torah* prove that he maintains that even the *Shemita* of land is only by rabbinic decree in our time.

In *Hilchot Bet ha-Bechira* (6:16), the Rambam writes as follows:

> By contrast, the obligations arising out of the Land regarding the *Shemita* year and the tithes derive from the conquest of the land by the people of Israel as a nation ... and the laws of the *Shemita* year and the tithes apply to these lands in the manner we have described in *Hilchot Terumot.*

And in *Hilchot Terumot* (1:26), he writes:

> In our time, *teruma* is obligatory not by the authority of the Torah but by rabbinic law ... For the *teruma* demanded by the Torah applies only in the Land of Israel, and only at a time when all the children of Israel are there, as it is said: "When you shall come," implying when all of you shall come.

In other words, according to the Rambam, the Torah obligation of *teruma* requires *bi'at kulchem*, "when all of you [the Jewish people] shall come," and the same applies to *Shemita.*[49] Accordingly, in the absence of *bi'at kulchem, Shemita* does not apply by Torah law.

There are then two main reasons that *Shemita* observance is only by rabbinic decree in our time[50]:

1. *Shemita* only applies when the *yovel* does, and *yovel* is not in effect **in our time** because "the majority of the land's inhabitants" [a majority of the Jewish people] do not dwell there.
2. In order for *Shemita* to be in effect by Torah law, the condition of "*bi'at kulchem,*" arrival of the entire Jewish people, must be

49. There is a certain difficulty with the Rambam's words, for the verse, "When you shall come," does not refer to *teruma*; on the contrary, it refers to *Shemita* (see *Vayikra* 25:2)! Rav Chayim Soloveitchik (*Hilchot Shemita ve-Yovel* 2:16) explains that *teruma* is indeed learned from *Shemita*, but since *teruma* depends on the sabbatical cycle, the Rambam relates to the verse as if it were written with respect to *teruma* as well.

50. We find an even more radical position limiting the extent of *Shemita* application in our day. According to the Ra'avad (on the Rif to *Gittin* 36a), the *Ba'al ha-Ma'or* (cited in *Sefer ha-Terumot* 45, 4), and the *Meiri* (*Gittin*), *Shemita* observance in our time is merely a matter of pious custom.

fulfilled, and in the **days of Ezra**, when the "Second Sanctity" that exists to this day took effect, not all of Israel returned from Babylonia (as explained by the Rambam in the beginning of *Hilchot Terumot*).

RAV CHAYIM HALEVI SOLOVEITCHIK OF BRISK

Based on the previous explanation, the question arises: what would be the law if the majority of the Jewish people were living in Eretz Yisrael? **Rav Chayim Soloveitchik** (*Hilchot Shemita ve-Yovel 12:16*) explains that according to the first reason, if the majority of the Jewish people were living in Israel, *Shemita* observance would apply by Torah law. According to the second reason, however, since at the time of the *aliyah* of Ezra not all of Israel returned with him, there was a deficiency in the very conquest.[51] Therefore, even if the majority of the Jewish people were living today in Eretz Yisrael, the obligation of *Shemita* would still not be by Torah law:

> The law of "all its inhabitants" does not depend on the time of the sanctification of the land, whether or not at that time all of its inhabitants dwelled therein ... In the future, then, once all of its inhabitants have settled therein, *yovel* will once again be in effect ...
>
> The Rambam rules: "For the *teruma* demanded by the Torah applies only in the Land of Israel, and only at a time when all the children of Israel are there, as it is said: "When you shall come" – implying, when all of you shall have come." Now, the truth of the matter is that regarding *teruma* the Torah never says: "when you shall come." It is learned by analogy from "when you shall come," stated with respect to *Shemita* and *yovel*, and because *terumot* and *ma'asrot* depend on the sabbatical cycle ... Accordingly, it would certainly appear that *Shemita* and *yovel* also require *"bi'at kulchem,"* according to the Rambam, just like *teruma* and *ma'aser* ...
>
> Now, this law of "*bi'at kulchem*" is not the same as the law of "all its inhabitants dwelling therein," for it is explicit in the

51. This assumption, however, has not been accepted by all. Rav Isser Zalman Meltzer argues that were the entire Jewish people to come to Israel, the obligations of *teruma* and *ma'aser* would be by Torah law, even in fulfillment of the condition of "*bi'at kulchem*" (see Rav Neriah, "*Be-vo'achem – Bi'at Kulchem*," *Devar ha-Shemita*, p. 57). This point is of great practical importance, because in another few years, the majority of the Jewish people will be living in Eretz Yisrael.

חדושי
רבנו חיים הלוי

חדושים וביאורים על הרמב"ם

מאת

רבנו הגדול הגאון החסיד רבן ומאורן של כל בני ישראל
מרן רבנו חיים הלוי זצוקללה"ה סאלאווייציק
מלפנים ר"מ בהישיבה הגדולה דוואלאזין ואח"כ אב"ד ור"ם בעיר בריסק.

RAV CHAYIM HALEVI SOLOVEITCHIK OF BRISK

Rav Chayim was born in 1853. His father, Rav Yosef Ber Soloveitchik, was *rosh yeshiva* at the Volozhin yeshiva, and later Rav Chayim served as deputy *rosh yeshiva* under the *Netziv*.

Rav Chayim developed a unique method of study that strongly influenced Torah study in the yeshiva world. One of the central features of Rav Chayim's method was to resolve difficulties arising in the words of the *Rishonim* by proposing that there are two different principles at play, each with a different set of ramifications. Rav Chayim wrote novellae on the Rambam, and recently his novellae to various talmudic tractates (as they were handed down to his son, Rav Moshe, and from him to his grandson, Rav Yosef Dov Soloveitchik) were published. His students also published novellae on the Talmud based on his lectures. Rav Chayyim died in 1918.

passage in *Arachin* 32, cited earlier, that this depends solely on the *yovel* year at its time, whether or not "all its inhabitants" dwell there or not. But this is not the case with the law of "*bi'at kulchem*" – it refers to the [initial] time of coming and inheriting, for it is then that *"bi'at kulchem"* is necessary ... This is also proven by the language of the Rambam, *Hilchot Terumot*, chap. 1, where he writes: "As it is said: 'when you will have come,' implying, when all of you shall have come, as they did in the first settlement [in the time of Yehoshua], and as they are to do again at the third settlement [in the future], not as they did at the second settlement in the days of Ezra, when only some of them returned, and thus the Torah did not obligate them."

There is a third reason that *Shemita* in our time is only by rabbinic decree, according to those authorities who maintain that the second sanctification of Eretz Yisrael by Ezra after the return from the Babylonian exile was only temporary, and therefore lapsed when the land was conquered by Israel's enemies. All the *mitzvot* that depend upon the land of Israel are connected to the sanctity of the land. According to these authorities, then, the *mitzvot* that depend upon the land are not in effect by Torah law in our time. (This is the opinion of Rashi in *Gittin 36b* and others, as opposed to the Rambam in *Hilchot Terumot 1:5* and others, who maintain that the second sanctification never lapsed).

In practice, **Rav Kook** (introduction to *Shabbat ha-Aretz, 1–8; 4, 25*, letter 2) ruled that the observance of *Shemita* in our time is only by rabbinic decree.[52] This was also the position of the ***Chazon Ish*** (*3, 8*) and ***Pe'at ha-Shulchan*** (23:23).

52. While there are certain *Acharonim* who maintain that the observance of *Shemita* in our time is by Torah law (*Bet ha-Levi*, vol. III, no. 1; *Responsa Meshiv Davar*, vol. II, *Yoreh De'a*, no. 56), the dominant opinion among the *Acharonim* is that *Shemita* observance in our time is only by rabbinic decree (*Bach, Choshen Mishphat*, 67, 3; *Sema*, ibid. no. 2; *Avnei Nezer, Yoreh De'a*, vol. II, no. 458; *Responsa Achi'ezer, Yoreh De'a* 39; Responsa *Tzitz Eliezer* vol. 6, no. 39; *Responsa Yabi'a Omer*, vol. III, *Yoreh De'a*, no. 19; vol. VI, no. 24, and at the end of "*Ha-Shemita va-Halichoteha*"; *Responsa Minchat Yitzchak*, vol. VI, no. 128; and many others).

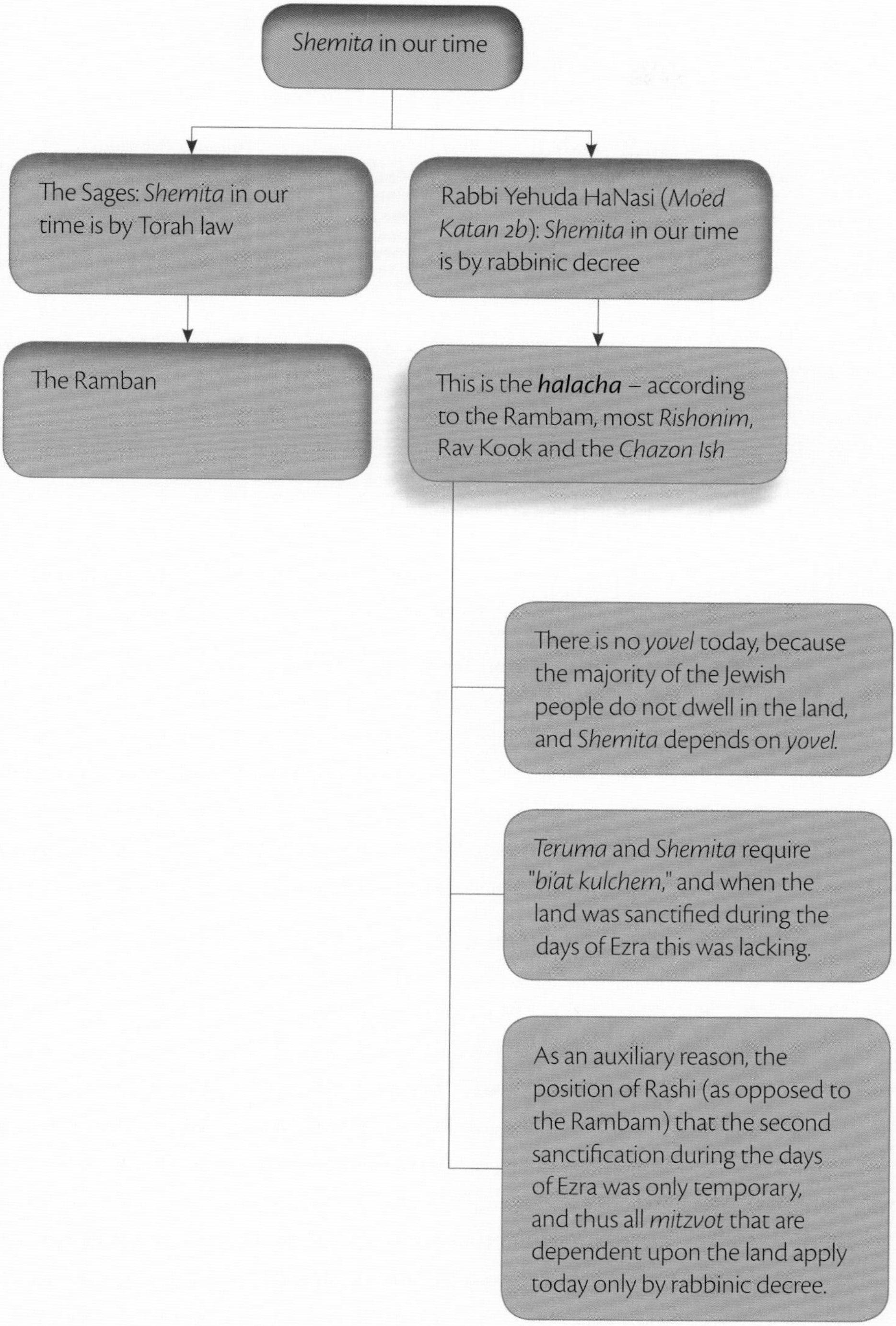

Shemita in our time

The Sages: *Shemita* in our time is by Torah law

Rabbi Yehuda HaNasi (*Mo'ed Katan 2b*): *Shemita* in our time is by rabbinic decree

The Ramban

This is the ***halacha*** – according to the Rambam, most *Rishonim*, Rav Kook and the *Chazon Ish*

There is no *yovel* today, because the majority of the Jewish people do not dwell in the land, and *Shemita* depends on *yovel.*

Teruma and *Shemita* require "*bi'at kulchem*," and when the land was sanctified during the days of Ezra this was lacking.

As an auxiliary reason, the position of Rashi (as opposed to the Rambam) that the second sanctification during the days of Ezra was only temporary, and thus all *mitzvot* that are dependent upon the land apply today only by rabbinic decree.

53. Both views fundamentally agree with the assertion that "the land is Mine," and therefore a gentile cannot acquire possession in Eretz Yisrael, because Eretz Yisrael belongs to God. According to **Rabba**, a gentile has no impact on the sanctity of the produce of Eretz Yisrael, but he can acquire **proprietary rights** there, and therefore he can dig pits there. **Rav Elazar** agrees that that a gentile cannot cancel the sanctity of Eretz Yisrael. He maintains that a gentile cannot even acquire **proprietary rights** there (and therefore he cannot dig pits), but with respect to the produce growing on the land, the gentile can cancel the sanctity. Let us try to explain this dispute, based on the words of Rav Chayim Soloveitchik. Rabbi Elazar maintains that **the transfer of sanctity from Eretz Yisrael to the produce** stems from **the unique sanctity of the people of Israel.** The sanctification of the land with respect to the *mitzvot* is achieved through the settlement of the land. This is not a one-time event, but rather it continues as long as **the people of Israel are on their land.** When a gentile possesses property in Eretz Yisrael, that piece of land remains sanctified but does not transmit its **sanctity to the produce.** This is significant with respect to the *mitzvot* that depend on the land. (See Rav Kook's introduction to *Shabbat ha-Aretz* [15], that a gentile's possession of property in

ASSUMPTION II:

DOES GENTILE OWNERSHIP CANCEL THE SANCTITY OF ERETZ YISRAEL?

The **Gemara** in ***Gittin*** (*47a,* and in a similar passage in the *Yerushalmi, Demai 5:8*) records a dispute regarding whether or not gentile ownership of property in Eretz Yisrael releases it from its various *mitzva* obligations:

> Rabba said: Although a gentile cannot own property in Eretz Yisrael so fully as to release it from the obligation of *ma'aser*, tithe, since the Torah says: "for the land is Mine" – [meaning] the sanctity of the land is Mine, yet a gentile can own land in Eretz Yisrael so fully as to have the right of digging pits, ditches and caves in it, as the verse states: "The heavens are the heavens of the Lord, but the earth He gave to the sons of man." Rav Elazar said: Although a gentile can own land so fully in Eretz Yisrael as to release it from the obligation of *ma'aser*, since it says: "[The *ma'aser* of] your grain" – and not the grain of the gentile, a gentile cannot own land in Eretz Yisrael so fully as to have the right of digging in it pits, ditches and caves, since it says: "The earth is the Lord's."

According to Rabba, a gentile's ownership of land in Eretz Yisrael does not release it from the obligation of *ma'aser*, and therefore even if the land is sold to a gentile, the laws of *ma'asrot* continue to apply to it. According to Rav Elazar, on the other hand, gentile ownership of property in Eretz Yisrael releases the produce that grows there from the obligation of *ma'aser.*[53] The **Rambam** (*Hilchot Terumot 1:10; 11*) and the ***Shulchan Aruch*** (*Yoreh De'a 331:3*) rule in accordance with the position of Rabba.

According to this approach, seventh-year produce growing on land belonging to a gentile is regarded as *Shemita* produce for all purposes, and it has *Shemita* sanctity. Whereas in ordinary years, such produce is subject to the laws of *terumot* and *ma'asrot,* during

the *Shemita* year, it is exempt from *terumot* and *ma'asrot*, like all other *Shemita* produce. This is the ruling of the ***Mabit*** (*vol. 1, nos. 11, 21, 217, 336*):

> I was asked about my position regarding produce growing during the *Shemita* year on land belonging to a gentile ... is it obligated in *ma'asrot* as in ordinary years ... My answer was that there is no obligation of *ma'asrot* in Eretz Yisrael during the *Shemita* year even with respect to [produce] purchased from a gentile prior to *miru'ach* (smoothing of the pile, the completion of the process of harvest and ingathering, the defining moment for *ma'aser*) ... because a gentile's

Eretz Yisrael does not effect its sanctity but only cancels the obligations with respect to *mitzvot* that depend on the land.)

ספר

בית אלהים

להרב הגאון המפורסם, החכם השלם והכולל, נר ישראל, סיני ועוקר הרים, כמהר"ר משה בכהר"ר יוסף נ"ע מטראני.

מחבר ס' קרית ספר על הרמב"ם, ושלשה חלקי תשובות נודעים בשם שו"ת מבי"ט:

נחלק לשלשה שערים

שער התפלה, שער התשובה, ושער היסודות (העקרים).

ועוד לו פרק מיוחד בביאור פרק שירה לחז"ל.

יוצא לאור מחדש

RABBI MOSHE BEN YOSEF TRANI (*the Mabit*)

The *Mabit* was born in Saloniki in 5260 (1500), and he grew up and studied Torah in Turkey. He moved to Tzefat and was among those who received *semicha* from Rav Ya'akov Berav (along with Rav Yosef Karo, author of the Bet Yosef and the *Shulchan Aruch*). Following the death of Rav Ya'akov Berav, the *Mabit* headed the Jewish community in Tzefat. Great controversy arose in Tzefat around the *Shemita* issue, leading to sharp debate between the *Bet Yosef* and the *Mabit*, harsh correspondence between the two sides, and even a ban that was pronounced at one point on those who act in accordance with the view of the *Mabit* regarding the produce of a gentile during the *Shemita* year. This disagreement regarding *Shemita* sanctity in produce belonging to a gentile continues to this very day. The *Mabit's* important works include: *Responsa ha-Mabit*; *Kiryat Sefer*; *Bet Elokim*. He was father to the *Maharit* – Rav Yosef Trani. The Mabit died in 5340 (1580).

> ownership [of land] in Eretz Yisrael does not release it of its sanctity with respect to *Shemita* produce.

The ***Bet Yosef*** (*Responsa Avkat Rochel,* no. 24; *Kesef Mishneh 4:29*), however, disagrees with the *Mabit,* and says that as long as the property is owned by a gentile it is not subject to the special *mitzvot* of Eretz Yisrael. His explanation is based on the concept known as "conquest of an individual," which is land that has been incorporated into Eretz Yisrael by a group of Jews (as opposed to the Jewish people on the whole), which is inadequate to impart the sanctity of the land to the produce (see Rambam *Hilchot Terumot 1:2*). The *Bet Yosef* claims that, according to the Rambam, although the produce lacks sanctity while owned by the gentile, if a Jews buys the property back from the gentile, it attains sanctity. The reason the produce is able to gain sanctity is due to the fact that the property never loses its sanctity altogether, because the gentile does not own the property so fully as to release it from its sanctity. Therefore, when the Jew buys the property, it will once again be subject to the various *mitzvot,* and it will not be considered "conquest of an individual." But even the Rambam agrees that as long as the gentile owns the property, the produce that grows there has no *Shemita* sanctity (*Hilchot Shemita ve-Yovel 4:29*):

> That which they said that a gentile does not own property in Eretz Yisrael so fully as to release it from *mitzvot,* that is to say that if a Jew goes ahead and buys the property back from him it is not regarded like the "conquest of an individual," but rather it is as if it had never been sold to the gentile. But as long as it is in the hands of the gentile, it is released [from the *mitzvot*]. And the produce of a gentile is only subject to *ma'asrot* when the *miru'ach* was performed by a Jew.

According to the *Bet Yosef,* the produce of a gentile has no *Shemita* sanctity. As for *terumot* and *ma'asrot,* if the *miru'ach* was performed by the gentile, the produce is not subject to *terumot* and *ma'asrot*. But if the *miru'ach* was performed by a Jew, it is subject to these obligations. (This stands in contrast to the view of the *Mabit,*

RAV YOSEF KARO (*the Bet Yosef*)

Rav Yosef Karo was born in Spain in 5248 (1488). At the age of four, when the Jews of Spain were expelled from the country, he moved to Turkey and later moved to Tzefat. He received *semicha* from Rav Yaakov Berav (who tried to renew the ancient *semicha*). His most important work is the *Shulchan Aruch*, the legal code that was accepted as authoritative by all Jewish communities. In his code, Rav Karo relies primarily on "the three pillars" of halachic decision-making: the Rambam, the Rif and the Rosh. Surprisingly, **the *Shulchan Aruch* omits the laws of *Shemita*,** despite the fact that he codifies many issues relating to the mitzvot that depend on the Land of Israel. Nevertheless, his positions on matters relating to *Shemita* are evident from his rulings elsewhere in the *Shulchan Aruch* and from his other works.

Rav Yosef Karo's other works include: the *Bet Yosef* (on the *Tur*); the *Kesef Mishneh* (on the Rambam); *Responsa Avkat Rochel*; *Maggid Mesharim* – a kabbalistic work based on teachings received from his "*maggid*." Rav Karo died in 5335 (1575).

who maintains that in any case there is no obligation of *terumot* and *ma'asrot* during the *Shemita* year, because even the produce of a gentile is *Shemita* produce).

The *Bet Yosef* adds that also the sages of Tzefat agree with his ruling.[54] Since the *Mabit* wanted to act in accordance with his own ruling, against the ruling of the Tzefat authorities, they decided to pronounce a ban on anyone who does not follow their ruling:

> Said Yosef Karo: After the sage, Rav Moshe Trani, wrote this second letter, he wanted to act in accordance with his own view during the previous *Shemita*, but [the other authorities] objected. During this *Shemita* of the year 5334 (1573-74), he

54. The Rema (*Yoreh De'a* 331:19) rules that *Shemita* produce that grew in a field belonging to a gentile is subject to *terumot* and *ma'asrot*. It would seem to follow from this that according to him *Shemita* sanctity does not apply to gentile produce. The *Chazon Ish* (20, 7), however, argues that it is possible that even the Rema agrees that gentile produce has *Shemita* sanctity, only that he maintains that *Shemita* produce's exemption from *terumot* and *ma'asrot* does not stem from their sanctity, but rather from the fact that they are ownerless. According to this understanding, gentile produce does in fact have *Shemita* sanctity, but it is not ownerless, and therefore the produce must be tithed (see also *Ma'adanei Eretz, Shevi'it* 7, 6, s.v. *le-aniyut da'ati*).

"hardened his spirit and strengthened his heart" to stand firmly and brazenly act in accordance with his own view. And all the sages examined both his earlier and his more recent words, and found them unconvincing. And they proclaimed in the synagogues, **under the threat of excommunication,** that everyone must set aside *terumot* and *ma'asrot* from the produce of a gentile on which a Jew performed *miru'ach* during the *Shemita* year as in other years.

Signed the Young Yosef Karo

In light of this responsum, some authorities write that it is forbidden to treat gentile produce as if it had *Shemita* sanctity. Others, however, maintain that the *Bet Yosef* later retracted his earlier position and adopted the view that gentile produce has *Shemita* sanctity (see *Chida, Birkei Yosef, Yoreh De'a 331,* no. *11; Pe'at ha-Shulchan 23:29; Responsa Mishnat Yosef,* vol. *III,* no. *1; Rav Ovadya Yosef, Responsa Yabi'a Omer, Yoreh De'a, vol. III, 19, 6,* and elsewhere; and other authorities as well).

The common practice follows the view of the *Bet* Yosef that gentile produce does not have *Shemita* sanctity. This is the ruling of many authorities, including the ***Pe'at ha-Shulchan*** (*23:29*):[55]

And I, from the time that God gave me the privilege to come here in the year 5570 (1810), set my heart to examine this law regarding the Holy Land ... And following my examination, it seems clear that the law is in accordance with our master, the *Bet Yosef* ... And this is the common practice now as well in all of Eretz Yisrael ... And so was the common practice in Jerusalem in the time of the Ralnach ... And the law is in accordance with those who conclude that [the produce of] a gentile is exempt from [the laws of] *Shemita*.

Rav Tykoczinski testifies that this indeed is the practice in Jerusalem and throughout Eretz Yisrael[56] (*Sefer ha-Shemita, 10, 2, 2*). The ***Chazon Ish*** (*20, 7,* at great length, and elsewhere), however, ruled in accordance with the *Mabit*:

55. *Responsa ha-Radbaz* (vol. V, no. 2221); *Derisha* (*Yoreh De'a* 331, no. 1); *Levush* (*Yoreh De'a* 331, 19); *Birkei Yosef* (*Yoreh De'a* 331, 10); *Shabbat ha-Aretz* (chap. 4, 29, 6 "*u-kvar*" – "there is a consensus that the law is that gentile produce is not treated in any way as having *Shemita* sanctity, and it is subject to *terumot* and *ma'asrot* when the processing is completed by a Jew"); *Responsa Minchat Yitzchak* (vol. VI, nos. 128-129); *Or le-Tziyon* (*Shevi'it*, 2, 14); *Responsa Tzitz Eli'ezer* (vol. XI, no. 15); and others.

56. The *Chazon Ish* (20, 7) writes, however, that "the *Pe'at ha-Shulchan* established the custom to practice leniency against the earlier custom to practice stringency." According to him, the original custom had been to practice stringency, and it was only since the time of the *Pe'at ha-Shulchan* that people began to practice leniency. The *Chazon Ish* was himself very stringent on this matter (see *Derech Emuna* 4, 29).

> We maintain as law that one may not work in a field belonging to a gentile during the *Shemita* year … . And we treat their produce as having *Shemita* sanctity, and we tithe it without [reciting] a benediction.

Therefore, in Bnei Brak – the *Chazon Ish's* city – there is a widespread custom to treat gentile produce as having *Shemita* sanctity.[57]

It should be noted once again that even according to those who maintain that a gentile who possesses property in Eretz Yisrael releases that property from the *mitzvot* that depend on the land, the gentile only cancels the obligation with respect to these *mitzvot*, while the sanctity of the land remains intact. The sanctity of Eretz Yisrael does not stem from the fact that Jews are in possession of the land, but rather it is inherent to the land itself and is not subject to cancellation (see the words of Rav Chayim Brisker, *Hilchot Terumot 1:10; Shabbat ha-Aretz,* Introduction, letter 15; *Iggerot Ra'aya,* no. 555 and others).

The *heter mechira* is based on the assumption that since *Shemita* sanctity does not apply to produce that grew on land belonging to a gentile, there is also no prohibition to work the land of a gentile.[58] It should be noted, however, that the ***Chazon Ish*** (*20, 7* [end], s.v. *ve-ha de-nechleku*) disagreed with this assumption as well, arguing that even according to those who say that the produce that grew on the land of a gentile is void of sanctity, performing forbidden labor on such land is prohibited:

> The Sages of Tzefat only disagreed about the sanctity of the produce, but as for plowing, planting, and the other labors, all agree that there is no difference between working land owned by a Jew and working land owned by a gentile, whether one performs a labor forbidden by Torah law or a labor forbidden by rabbinic decree, because all agree that the sanctity of the land is not cancelled.

57. Others who rules like the *Mabit* include the Ri Kurkus (*Hilchot Shemita ve-Yovel 7:3*), *Kaftor va-Ferach* (4), Rash Sirillo on the *Yerushalmi* (*Shevi'it* 6:1, s.v. *ve-achshav*), *Kehilot Ya'akov* (*Shevi'it* 1, 13);.See also *Derech Emuna* (4, 29).

58. Even if there is such a prohibition, it is only by rabbinic decree, not Torah law, even when *Shemita* observance is by Torah law. Thus we find in *Responsa Maharitatz* (no. 47), that working land belonging to a gentile is forbidden by rabbinic decree, because onlookers might mistakenly think that the work is being carried out on land belonging to a Jew. **Rav Kook** (Introduction to *Shabbat ha-Aretz,* 11) was also of the opinion that working the land of a gentile is forbidden by rabbinic decree (and according to the *Sefer ha-Teruma*, which will be cited below, in our time when *Shemita* is only by rabbinic decree, there is no prohibition whatsoever, and therefore there is room for leniency, because "their disagreement creates uncertainty regarding a matter that is forbidden by rabbinic decree" [end of letter 11 in Introduction]. That is to say, since even those who say that it is forbidden forbid it only by rabbinic decree, we can rule in accordance with those who permit it altogether, because regarding a doubt concerning a rabbinic decree one may practice leniency).

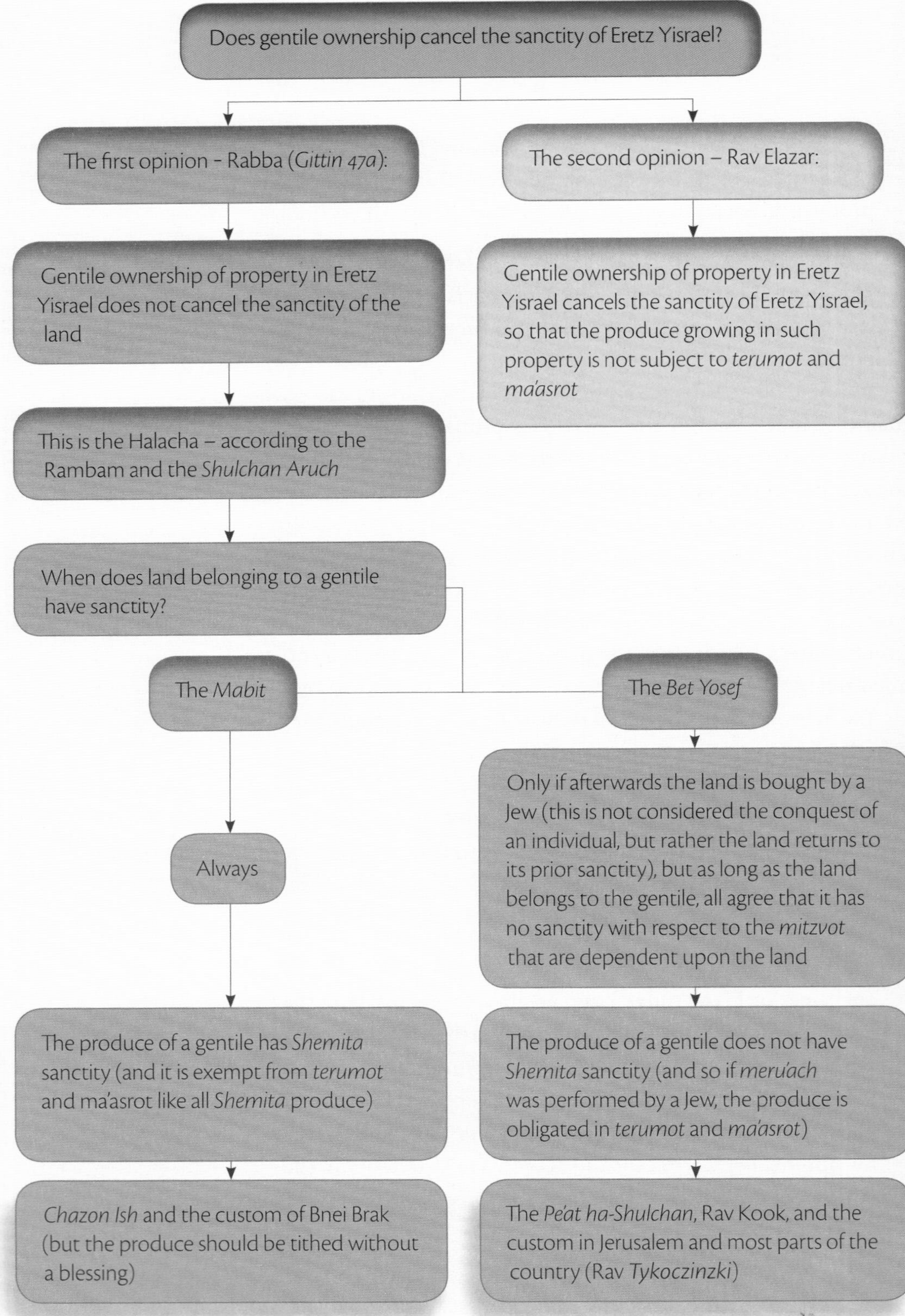
Does gentile ownership cancel the sanctity of Eretz Yisrael?
The first opinion - Rabba (Gittin 47a):
The second opinion – Rav Elazar:
Gentile ownership of property in Eretz Yisrael does not cancel the sanctity of the land
Gentile ownership of property in Eretz Yisrael cancels the sanctity of Eretz Yisrael, so that the produce growing in such property is not subject to terumot and ma'asrot
This is the Halacha – according to the Rambam and the Shulchan Aruch
When does land belonging to a gentile have sanctity?
The Mabit
The Bet Yosef
Always
Only if afterwards the land is bought by a Jew (this is not considered the conquest of an individual, but rather the land returns to its prior sanctity), but as long as the land belongs to the gentile, all agree that it has no sanctity with respect to the mitzvot that are dependent upon the land
The produce of a gentile has Shemita sanctity (and it is exempt from terumot and ma'asrot like all Shemita produce)
The produce of a gentile does not have Shemita sanctity (and so if meru'ach was performed by a Jew, the produce is obligated in terumot and ma'asrot)
Chazon Ish and the custom of Bnei Brak (but the produce should be tithed without a blessing)
The Pe'at ha-Shulchan, Rav Kook, and the custom in Jerusalem and most parts of the country (Rav Tykoczinzki)

ASSUMPTION III:

GENTILE OWNERSHIP CANCELS THE SANCTITY OF ERETZ YISRAEL WHEN *SHEMITA* IS ONLY BY RABBINIC DECREE

The **Rambam** (*Hilchot Terumot 1:10*) writes that in "Syria," where the sanctity of Eretz Yisrael is only by rabbinic decree, gentile ownership of the land cancels that sanctity:

> A gentile who purchases land in the Land of Israel does not thereby render it exempt from the commandments; rather it retains its status of holiness. Therefore, if a Jew repurchases it from him, it is not considered the same as an individual conquest, rather the Jew must set aside *terumot* and *ma'asrot* and must offer *bikkurim*. All these rules are applicable by Torah law, as if the field had never been sold to a gentile. In "Syria," however, the gentile's purchase of land is effective in exempting it from tithes and from *Shemita*, as will be explained.

The author of the ***Sefer Ha-Teruma*** (*Hilchot Eretz Yisrael, p. 63*[59]) infers from this that since *Shemita* in our time is only by rabbinic decree, gentile ownership of the land cancels the sanctity of Eretz Yisrael even according to those who maintain that generally speaking gentile ownership does not cancel that sanctity:

> We can explain that during the *Shemita* year [in our day, when it is only by rabbinic decree], it is permitted to plow and plant in land belonging to a gentile, even by rabbinic law.

This argument is brought in the *Teruma's* name by the **Vilna Gaon** (*Bei'ur ha-Gra, Yoreh De'a 331, 6*):

> He also wrote that in our time gentile ownership cancels [the sanctity of] Eretz Yisrael, since it [the sanctity] is by rabbinic decree ... and the same applies regarding *Shemita* in our time.

The **Gemara** in ***Sanhedrin*** (*26a*) states:

59. This might also be the view of Rabbenu Chananel and Rashi in *Sanhedrin* (*26a,* s.v. *agiston*); see also *Pe'at ha-Shulchan* (*16, 40*).

As Rabbi Yannai proclaimed: "Go and plant your field [even] in the *Shemita* year, because of the *arnona*."

According to the simple understanding, "*arnona*" refers to a certain tax that was collected by the king (Rashi, ad loc.). The ***Tosafot*** (ad loc., s.v. *mi-she-rabu ha-anasin*) ask: How could Rav Yannai have permitted sowing during the *Shemita* year, violation of a Torah prohibition, merely because of a tax?[60]

You might ask: Because of a tax, they permitted plowing and planting, which are forbidden by Torah law? We can answer: We are dealing with *Shemita* in our time which is by rabbinic decree.[61]

According to the *Tosafot*, Rav Yannai permitted planting to pay the *arnona* tax since *Shemita* observance in our time is only by rabbinic decree.[62]

RABBENU BARUCH BEN YITZCHAK

(Author of *Sefer Ha-Teruma*)

Rabbenu Baruch was born in France and died in 4971 (1211). He was among the authors of Tosafot (he is mentioned in *Tosafot's* commentary as the Sefer Ha-Teruma or as *Rabbenu Baruch*.)

He moved to Israel where he wrote his work, *Sefer Ha-Teruma*. He named his book the *Sefer Ha-Teruma* because all his teachings are from the "gifts" (*teruma*) of his teachers, and he did not suggest them on his own.

60. In his commentary to the Mishna (*Sanhedrin 3:3*), the Rambam offers a novel and surprising explanation of this passage. The Rambam writes that when the gentile authorities began to force Jews to provide them with food, "people gathered seed during the *Shemita* year." He seems to be saying that the issue was not planting but rather harvesting. This is significant, for it is much easier to permit harvesting than to permit planting, for harvesting is permitted when performed in an unusual manner, and according to the Rambam, harvesting in small amounts is permitted even when done in the usual manner. It is possible then that the allowance was to harvest the entire field, and this was permitted because if the harvest is not for one's own benefit but rather to pay a tax, the harvest does not demonstrates possession or ownership.

61. The *Tosafot* provide an additional explanation: "Alternatively, it may be argued that this was a matter of *piku'ach nefesh* (saving a life, for which purpose nearly all *mitzvot* can be overridden), for if the king would demand a tax and they would have nothing with which to pay, they would die in prison. This explanation is also found in the *Yerushalmi*: [That this was permitted] because of [danger to] life." This approach is cited also by the Ran, ad loc., and in the name of Rabbenu Tam by the *Tosafot* in *Gittin* (62a, s.v. *ein oderin*).

62. This explanation implies that when faced with financial loss, it is permitted to violate a rabbinic prohibition. This, however, is difficult, for it is generally assumed that one may not violate a rabbinic prohibition in order to avoid financial loss (see, for example, *Responsa Chavat Ya'ir*, no. 183; see also *Peri Megadim, Orach Chayyim*, 656, *Eshel Avraham*, no. 8, end, who is in doubt about the manner). The *Minchat Chinuch* (329, 12) suggests that owing to the exceptional circumstances, *Chazal* explicitly permitted the prohibition because of financial loss. The *Bikurei Ya'akov* (656, no. 14) adds that the Sages permitted irrigation during the *Shemita* year in a case of financial loss, despite the fact that irrigation is forbidden by rabbinic decree. We still must define what is considered financial loss. The *Maharit* (vol. II, no. 52, s.v. *ve-ho'il u-shevi'it*, and again later in the responsum) concludes that financial loss refers to loss of capital, and not merely loss of profit. On the other hand, the Ra'avad (*Hilchot Shemita ve-Yovel* 1:11) implies that the allowance only applies when there is concern about loss of the field, namely, that the field will be confiscated if the tax is not paid. The various positions are brought in *Shabbat ha-Aretz* 1, 11 (see also *Sefer ha-Shemita*, p. 72b). Rav Mordechai Elisberg, in a letter printed in *Ha-Melitz*, argued that in light of Rav Yannai's allowance, there is room to permit agricultural work even without the *heter mechira* (his view was not accepted).

ספר התרומה

אשר הורם ואשר הונף תרומת ה' מחד מגאוני קמאי, מרנא ורבנא רבינו
ברוך מגרמיזא בעל התוס' אשר הי' בזמן תתק"צ לאלף החמישי,
תלמידו של הר"י הזקן בעל התוס' זצללה"ה, והפליא עצה והגדיל תושיה
לברר שמעתתא אליבא דהלכתא בדיני א"ה וכמה הלכתא גברוותא
במצות וחקי חיים ובהלכות אישות, והנה כל הראשונים שתו בצמא דבריו,
הלא המה הרא"ש והרשב"א והטור.

הספר הקדוש הלז נדפס שני פעמים וזה יותר ממאה שנים שלא בא לבית
הדפוס וספר הזה ואין אחד בעיר ושנים במשפחה, לכן נתעוררתי לדפוס בע"ת
שמשון בהרב המאה"ג מהרי"ל זצללה"ה מליפנא

ווארשא

בדפוס מו"ה יעקב זאב ברי' אונטערהענדלער נ"י

שנת וזאת התרומה אשר תקחו לפ"ק

נדפס בארץ-ישראל
תשל"א

The title page of *Sefer Ha-Teruma*

This passage is easily understood if we accept the *Teruma's* principle, that since *Shemita* observance in our time is only by rabbinic decree, working land belonging to a gentile is permitted. According to this, it can be argued that when produce from a field is used to pay taxes to the king, that property is treated as if it belongs to the king, and therefore it is permissible to plant there.

This understanding is stated explicitly in ***Sefer Hilchot Eretz Yisrael*** (attributed to the ***Tur***,[63] *Kedushat ha-Aretz, 2*):

> *Shemita* is not in effect with respect to the prohibitions of planting and plowing in Eretz Yisrael by Torah law, but rather by rabbinic decree ... These are forbidden only in a field belonging to a Jew, not in a field belonging to a gentile. If the field belongs to a Jew, and part of [the yield] of each field must be given to the king, planting it is permitted. As Rava [Rav Yannai] proclaimed: "Go and plant your fields [even] in the *Shemita* year, because of the *arnona*."[64]

In any event, according to the *Teruma* and *Sefer Hilchot Eretz Yisrael*, when *Shemita* is only by rabbinic decree (as it is in our time), a Jew is permitted to perform labors that are forbidden by Torah law on land belonging to a gentile.

The **Chazon Ish** (*20, 7*) cites *Rishonim* who did not accept the *Teruma's* position:

> The *Sefer ha-Teruma* raised the possibility that our time is treated like "Syria" ... This, however, is not the view of the Rif, the Rosh, or the Rambam.

The ***Bet ha-Levi*** (vol. *III*, no. *1*, section *6*) also disagrees with the *Teruma*. He argues that it is only in "Syria," where there is no inherent sanctity, that gentile ownership cancels the sanctity of Eretz Yisrael.

63. Rav Kook raised doubt about the attribution of this work to the *Tur*.

64. As stated, the *Sefer ha-Teruma* permits planting in a field belonging to a gentile when *Shemita* is only by rabbinic decree. He does not understand the *arnona* allowance to be based on viewing the field as owned by the king, but rather on the financial burden of paying the *arnona*: "We can explain that during the *Shemita* year [in our day, when it is only by rabbinic decree], it is permitted to plow and sow in land belonging to a gentile, even by rabbinic law ... And that which Rabbi Ami proclaimed: 'Go and plant your fields [even] in the *Shemita* year, because of the *arnona*,' in order to pay the king the obligatory grain – that is even in land belonging to a Jew, since the prohibition is only by rabbinic decree. Therefore, owing to the *arnona*, it is totally permitted." In any event, the aforementioned *Sefer Hilchot Eretz Yisrael* understands that owing to the royal tax, the field is regarded as belonging to the king, and thus planting is permitted there in our time when *Shemita* is only by rabbinic decree. This understanding is found also in *Responsa Shemen ha-Mor* (no. 4). Rav Kook cites the position of *Sefer Hilchot Eretz Yisrael* in his introduction to *Shabbat ha-Aretz* (11) and in *Responsa Mishpat Kohen* (no. 63). For an alternative explanation, see *Otzerot Yosef*, vol. *I*, 19, s.v. *ve-hineh ma-she-katav*.

In Eretz Yisrael itself, however, the sanctity is part of the essence of the land, and therefore it cannot be cancelled. According to him, it is only for incidental reasons that the observance of *Shemita* in our time is only by rabbinic decree (Rav Kook responded to this argument in *Shabbat ha-Aretz,* Introduction, chap. *11*).

As we saw earlier, however, other *Rishonim* appear to agree with the *Teruma.* This is also the opinion of the **Vilna Gaon** (*Yoreh De'a 331,* no. *28 and* no. *6*), and the ruling of the ***Avnei Nezer*** (*Yoreh De'a,* vol. *II,* no. *458*) and **Rav Kook** (Introduction to *Shabbat ha-Aretz, 11*):

> The *heter mechira* is based primarily on the majority of early and later authorities who maintain that *Shemita* in our time is by rabbinic decree. This is the basis of Rashi's view that it is permitted to plow and perform all [types of] labor on land belonging to a gentile. This is also the view of Rabbenu Chananel in his commentary there ... And this is also the view of the *Teruma* and the *Aruch.*

In addition to the justifications outlined above, proponents of the *heter mechira* cite the following factors to support the allowance:

1. Disagreement exists about how to count the *Shemita* cycles (see Rambam, *Hilchot Shemita ve-Yovel 10:2–6,* who did not determine the *Shemita* year according to his own calculations, but according to Geonic tradition – see the appendix at the end of this volume), and thus we may be lenient as perhaps this is not the *Shemita* year.[65]
2. According to some authorities, the observance of *Shemita* in our time is merely a matter of pious custom (*midat chasidut*) (Rav Zerachya ha-Levi in his *Ba'al Ha-Ma'or*).[66]

65. Rav Kook (Introduction to *Shabbat ha-Aretz, 6-7*); *Otzerot Yosef* (p. 46); Rav Kasher (*No'am 1; No'am 9;* and *No'am 16*).

66. Brought in *Sefer ha-Terumot 45, 4; Nimukei Yosef, Gittin 37b; Meiri, Gittin 36b.* In connection with the *heter mechira,* see Introduction to *Shabbat ha-Aretz, 6-7; Sefer ha-Shemita, p. 72-73,* and elsewhere. He explains this position in two ways:
1. *Shemita* is fully dependent on *yovel,* so that when there is no *yovel,* there is also no *Shemita.*
2. The *Shemita* year requires sanctification by the court, and thus when there is no sanctification of the court, there is no *Shemita* (see Rav Neriah, "*Kiddush Shenat ha-Shemita,*" in *Devar ha-Shemita, p. 85*).

Does gentile ownership cancel the sanctity of Eretz Yisrael in our time when *Shemita* is only by Rabbinic

Rambam: Gentile ownership of property in "Syria" cancels the land's sanctity with respect to *terumot* and *ma'asrot*, because in "Syria" these obligations are only by rabbinic decree.

The *Ba'al Ha-Teruma*

Since *Shemita* observance in our time is only by rabbinic decree, gentile ownership cancels the sanctity of the land even in Eretz Yisrael. It was for this reason that Rav Yannai permitted planting during the *Shemita* year.

The Vilna Gaon's understanding of the Rema, the *Avnei Nezer*

This combination of views provide support for the *heter mechira*.

The *Bet ha-Levi* and the *Chazon Ish* based on an inference in other *Rishonim*

Even though *Shemita* in our time is only by rabbinic decree, gentile ownership of property in Eretz Yisrael does not cancel its sanctity. Only in "Syria," where there is no inherent sanctity, does gentile ownership cancel the sanctity with respect to *terumot* and *ma'asrot*.

THE ARGUMENTS OF THOSE WHO OPPOSE THE *HETER MECHIRA*

The opponents of the *heter mechira* disagree with its proponents on several issues. We have already seen some of these issues; we shall examine others below. Before analyzing each issue separately, let us list all the arguments put forward by those who oppose the *heter mechira*:

1. Some authorities maintain that the observance of *Shemita* is by Torah law even in our time (these authorities were cited above). It should be noted, however, that this is not the main issue in dispute, because the leading authorities, including both **Rav Kook** and the ***Chazon Ish*** agree that *Shemita* in our time is in effect only by rabbinic decree.
2. According to the ***Mabit,*** seventh-year produce that grew on land belonging to a gentile has *Shemita* sanctity, as opposed to the ***Bet Yosef***, who maintains that such produce does not have *Shemita* sanctity, and is therefore subject to the laws of *terumot* and *ma'asrot*. According to the ***Chazon Ish*** (*20, 7,* cited above), the law is in accordance with the *Mabit*.
3. Even according to the ***Bet Yosef***, who maintains that the produce of a gentile has no *Shemita* sanctity, **working the land of a gentile** during the *Shemita* year might nevertheless be **forbidden** (see *Chazon Ish 20, 7,* cited above; *Ma'adanei Aretz, 9-10;* and see also *Eretz Chemda, 1, 5, 8*).
4. The proponents of the *heter mechira* strengthened their position with the view of the ***Teruma*** and other *Rishonim*, that in our time, when *Shemita* is only by rabbinic decree, gentile ownership of land cancels its sanctity, even with respect to working the land. Those who oppose the allowance argue that the law does not follow this position of the *Teruma* (see *Chazon Ish 20, 7,* cited above).
5. Even if we do not accept any of these arguments, the *heter mechira* gives rise to **a new halachic problem, the prohibition of "*lo techonem*."** Owing to its great significance, we shall discuss this issue later in a more expanded manner.
6. **Legal force** – the sale of the land, as it is ordinarily executed,

has no legal force (see below on this point, where it will be clarified that today it **has** legal force).

7. ***Gemirut da'at*** ("firm intention") – those who sign on the sale do not really mean to sell their property to the gentile, and thus the transaction is invalid (see below).

LO TECHONEM

The **Gemara** in ***Avoda Zara*** (*20a*) derives from a verse that it is forbidden to sell land to a gentile in Eretz Yisrael: "'*Lo techonem*' (Devarim 7:2) – you shall not allow them to settle on the soil." Therefore, even if the sale of land to a gentile cancels its sanctity, it would seem that such a transaction involves a Torah prohibition (*Chazon Ish 24, 4*)!

The ***Netziv*** (*Responsa Meshiv Davar,* vol. *II,* no. *56*) was bothered by the fact that those who rely on the *heter mechira* do so in order to overcome the difficulties of *Shemita,* which in our time, according to most authorities, is only by rabbinic decree, but in doing so, they become entangled in the Torah prohibition of *lo techonem.* According to him, proponents of the *heter* "run away from a wolf into the arms of a lion":

> They run away from a wolf into the arms of a lion – for they wish to escape the prohibition of *Shemita* in our time which, according to most authorities, is [only] by rabbinic decree, and run into the prohibition of selling land to a gentile in Eretz Yisrael, which, according to everybody, is forbidden by Torah law!

RAV NAFTALI ZVI YEHUDA BERLIN
(The Netziv of Volozhin)

שו"ת
משיב דבר
חלק ראשון. וחלק שני.

Rosh Yeshiva of Volozhin, Lithuania (along with Rav Yosef Ber Soloveitchik, the *Beit HaLevi*), foremost among Yeshivot. The Netziv was born in Russia in 5577 (1817) and died in Poland in 5653 (1893). The Netziv studied the *Midrashim* of the *Tannaim* and the teachings of the *Geonim* extensively. He wrote a work on the *Mechilta* (*Birkat HaNetziv*) and on the *She'iltot* (*Ha'amek Davar*) as well as a commentary on the Talmud (*Meromei Sadeh*). The Netziv advocated analyzing the simple meaning of the text and made inferences based on that. He also wrote halachic responsa (*Responsa Meshiv Davar*).

The Netziv was a member of the *Chibat* Tziyon moverment, and placed great importance in resettlement of the land of Israel.

The proponents of the *heter mechira*, on the other hand, maintain that it is precisely in light of the prohibition of *lo techonem* that the allowance is so critical. They argue that the basis of the prohibition lies not in the technical sale of land in Eretz Yisrael to a gentile, but rather in enabling gentiles to settle in Eretz Yisrael. Therefore, when the goal of the sale is to strengthen Jewish settlement in Eretz Yisrael, there is no prohibition.

In this context, let us cite a short but clear passage from ***Responsa Yeshu'ot Malko*** (the Gaon of Kutna, *Yoreh De'a,* no. 55)[67]:

> I have said that it is obviously better to permit selling [the land] to a gentile, even though it is forbidden to give away or sell land in Eretz Yisrael. Inasmuch as this is done for the benefit of [Jewish] settlement [in Eretz Yisrael], there is obviously no prohibition of *lo techonem*!

Were it not for the *heter mechira*, Jewish agriculture would collapse, and in its place gentile agriculture would flourish. The *heter mechira* is necessary precisely to prevent the strengthening of gentile settlement in Eretz Yisrael.

The *heter mechira's* proponents provide additional reasons that the allowance does not involve the prohibition of *lo techonem* (see *Sefer ha-Shemita,* p. 106 and on):

1. A sale that is for a limited time only is not subject to the prohibition (Rav Kook, *Mishpat Kohen,* nos. 60 and 63; and many other proponents of the allowance: *Rav Frank, Har Zvi, Zera'im,* vol. II, no. 48, and others).
2. The prohibition of *lo techonem* might only apply to idolaters (Rav Yitzchak Elchanan Spector, cited in *Nitzanei Aretz, 6, 11–16,* and in *Mishpat Kohen,* nos. 9, 63).
3. The prohibition of *lo techonem* might only apply to a gentile who does not already have land in Eretz Yisrael (Rav Zalman Shach, Introduction to *Shabbat ha-Aretz, 12;* and see *Responsa Shemen ha-Mor,* no. 4, *s.v. asher ayin ro'eh,* who mentions a similar argument; and see *Sefer ha-Shemita,* p. 108).[68]

In addition, if the problem with the *heter mechira* stems from the prohibition of *lo techonem*, the problem pertains only to the farmer,

67. A similar approach can be found in the following sources: *Responsa Shemen ha-Mor* (*Yoreh De'a*, no. 4): "This enactment will strengthen Israel's settlement of the land, causing them to purchase vineyards in Eretz Yisrael; in such a case, it is a *mitzva*"; *Responsa Avnei Nezer* (vol. III, *Yoreh De'a*, no. 458); *Shabbat ha-Aretz* (Introduction, chap. 12); *Responsa Har Zvi* (*Zera'im*, vol. II, no. 47); *Le-Or ha-Halacha* (pp. 123-124); see also Ran (*Gittin*, 20b in Alfasi, s.v. *kol*).

68. Another solution was later suggested by Rav Naftali Hertz, the first rabbi of Yafo. He proposed that the trees be sold for cutting, and that the land be sold only as deep down as what provides the crops with nourishment. He argued that such a sale does not involve the prohibition of *lo techonem*. See below, "Attitude toward the *Heter Mechira*" (p. 418). The rabbinical authorities of Jerusalem agreed to this formulation for the *Shemita* of 5656 (1895–96) (See also *Sefer ha-Shemita*, p. 75).

but not to the consumer, because even if the farmer violates a prohibition, the produce that he grows does not become forbidden.

At first the ***Chazon Ish*** agreed that if the sale involves a prohibition, it is only the farmer who transgresses (*Chazon Ish 10, 6*). Later, however, he retracted this position and wrote that the produce is forbidden as well. He argued that since the sale of land to the gentile is executed through an agent, if the sale is subject to the prohibition of *lo techonem,* we invoke the rule that "there is no agency for the commission of a transgression," and so the sale is invalid from the outset (*Chazon Ish 10, 6*).

Rav Kook (*Mishpat Kohen,* no. *60*) and **Rav Frank** (*Har Zvi, Zera'im,* vol. *II,* no. *49*) both write, however, that even according to those who say that the sale involves a prohibition, the sale takes effect and there is no problem of "agency for the commission of a transgression." (This topic is worthy of a lengthy discussion, in light of *Tosafot Bava Metzia* 10b, but it is beyond the scope of this work). It should be noted that today (the *Shemita* of 5775 (2014–2015)), the sale is being executed directly and not by way of an agent (the farmers return their land to the Israel Lands Administration, and that office sells the land to a gentile), and therefore this issue is no longer a factor.

RAV YISRAEL YEHOSHUA OF KUTNA
(The Gaon of Kutna)

Rav Yehoshua was born in Poland in 5581 (1821) and served as a *rav* in various communities, until arriving at Kutna, where he served until his death. Rav Yehoshua earned the title "the Gaon of Kutna" because of the genius that was expressed in his writings, including *Yeshu'ot Yisrael* which is a commentary on the first part of *Shluchan Aruch Choshen Mishpat,* and *Yeshu'ot Malko,* which is *responsa* to other leading rabbis. Rav Yehoshua died in 5653 (1893).

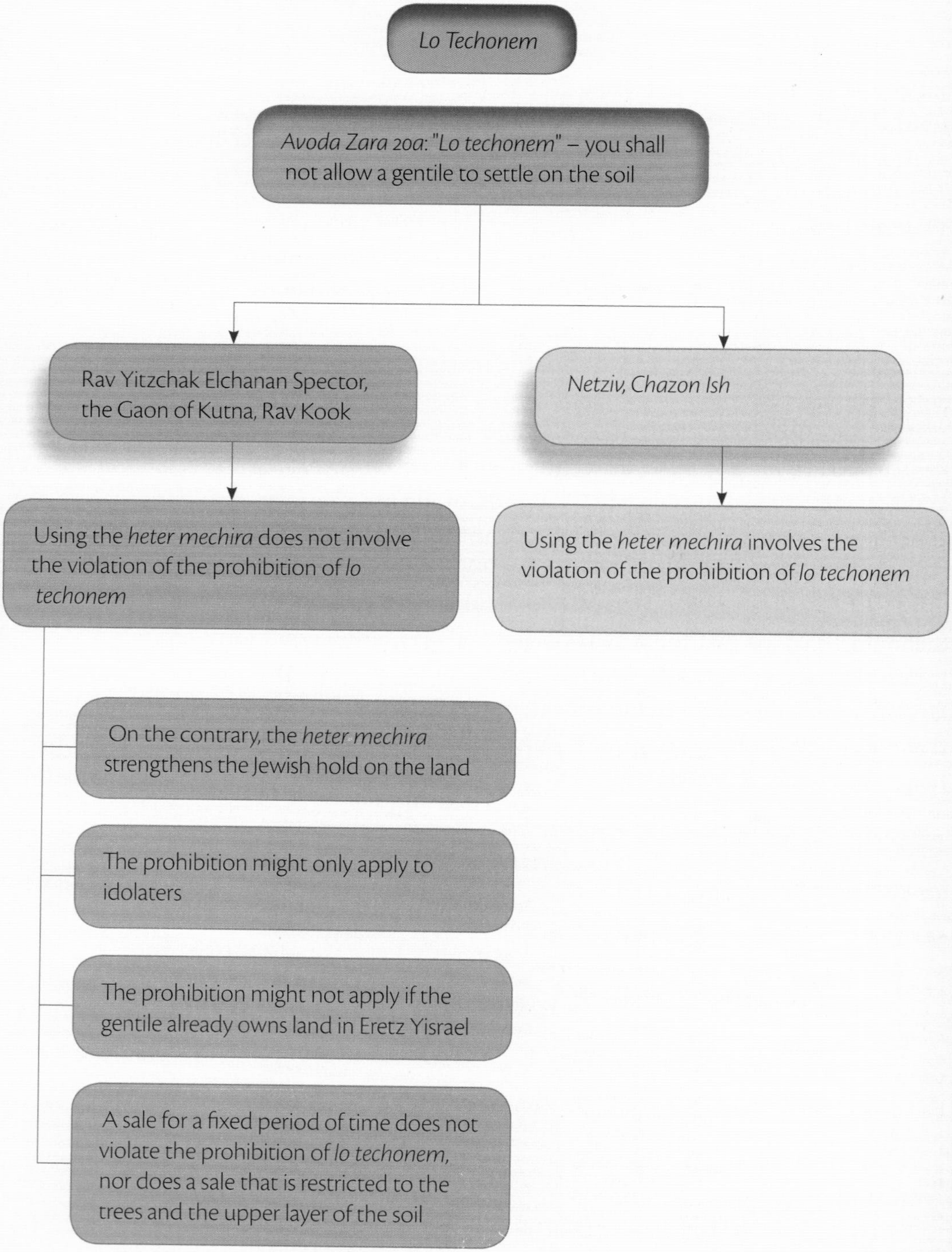

Lo Techonem

Avoda Zara 20a: "*Lo techonem*" – you shall not allow a gentile to settle on the soil

Rav Yitzchak Elchanan Spector, the Gaon of Kutna, Rav Kook

Using the *heter mechira* does not involve the violation of the prohibition of *lo techonem*

- On the contrary, the *heter mechira* strengthens the Jewish hold on the land
- The prohibition might only apply to idolaters
- The prohibition might not apply if the gentile already owns land in Eretz Yisrael
- A sale for a fixed period of time does not violate the prohibition of *lo techonem*, nor does a sale that is restricted to the trees and the upper layer of the soil

Netziv, Chazon Ish

Using the *heter mechira* involves the violation of the prohibition of *lo techonem*

LEGAL FORCE

In order for the sale of the land to be regarded as a serious transaction, it must have legal force. We must therefore examine the validity of the *heter mechira* when the sale of the land is not registered in the Israel Land Registry ("Tabu"), and therefore not recognized by the state as a legal sale (Land Law 5729–1969, sec. 7).[69] At first the ***Chazon Ish*** thought that registry in Tabu was not necessary for the sale to be valid, but later he changed his mind (*Bava Kama 10, 9*), and wrote that unless the sale is registered in Tabu, the land is still regarded as belonging to the Jew:

> Now ... I have retracted, and it seems to me ... regarding *terumot, ma'asrot,* and *Shemita,* as long as [the sale] is not registered in Tabu, it still belongs to the Jew in accordance with their laws (the sale is not valid).

This, however, is not so simple. Many authorities disagree with the *Chazon Ish,* saying that legal validity is not a requirement for halachic validity. For example, we find in ***Responsa Divrei Chayyim*** (*Orach Chayyim,* vol. *II,* no. 37), that even if the deed used for the sale of *chametz* was drawn up in Hebrew and lacks an official seal, so that it is invalid in a secular court of law, the *chametz* is regarded as sold, because by Torah law the deed is a valid deed of sale:

> Question: Regarding a deed used for the sale of *chametz* to a gentile that

69. I thank Dr. Michael Wygoda for referring me to this source. For an expanded discussion of this issue, see the article of Rav Daichovsky, member of the Supreme Rabbinical Court in Jerusalem (*Torah Shebe'al Peh* 28, pp. 104–114, and also Dr. Wygoda's own book). Rav Daichovsky suggests a solution to this problem. The Israel Lands Administration owns almost all of the agricultural land in the country. It might suffice if the state itself sells the land to a gentile (without obtaining the signatures of the Jewish farmers), in order for the land to be regarded as land belonging to a gentile that is leased to a Jew. If this solution works legally, then it is possible that land leased to a Jew would be regarded as the property of its gentile owner with respect to *Shemita*. Indeed, the Gemara in *Avoda Zara* (15*a*) concludes that rental does not constitute acquisition, and therefore land leased to a Jew should still be regarded as belonging to the gentile! This matter, however, is not so simple. The *Hagahot Oshri* (cited by the *Magen Avraham*, 246, no. 8) writes that rental is regarded as acquisition in all cases of stringency so we cannot rely on the fact that land leased to a Jew does not belong to him. However, later in the passage in *Avoda Zara* the Gemara states that a non-*kohen* who rents a cow from a *kohen* may feed it *teruma* vegetables. The *Magen Avraham* raises this as an objection to the *Hagahot Oshri*, for it implies that rental does not constitute acquisition even in a case of stringency, since we regard the rented cow as the *kohen's* property. The *acharonim* resolve this difficulty by suggesting that since vegetables are subject to *teruma* only by rabbinic decree, we don't apply the principle that rental constitutes acquisition in order to be stringent. In other words, rental constitutes acquisition in the case of Torah laws in order to be stringent, but in the case of rabbinic decrees it does not constitute acquisition whatsoever. Since *Shemita* in our time is only by rabbinic decree, it is therefore possible that land leased to a Jew is still regarded as the gentile's property, and once again we can use the solution proposed by Rav Daichovsky.

was written in Hebrew, is it valid inasmuch as the law of the land is that a deed written in Hebrew is invalid, and only [a deed written] in German [is valid] …

Answer … The truth is, we maintain that we follow our laws whether for leniency or for stringency … Indeed we must [say] this, because no deed in the world like this one is valid according to the laws [of the gentiles], for they have the

ספר
דברי חיים
חלק ראשון
על התורה
מונקאטש
דוב בער
תרל״ז
MUNKÁCS,
Gedruckt bei PINKAS BLAYER 1877.

RAV CHAIM HALBERSTAM OF SANS (*Divrei Chaim*)

Rav Chaim, the first *rebbe* of the dynasty of Sans, was born in Poland in 5553 [1793] and was very successful in his learning from childhood. He was ordained at a young age, and by the age of 37 became a rav and a *rebbe* in the city of Sans. Many rebbeim and *rabbanim* far and wide heard of his greatness. Rav Chaim died in 5636 [1876], and left behind an impressive line of *chasidim* and Torah scholars. His books are called "*Divrei Chaim*," and they include responsa, halachic works, and chasidic expositions.

An amazing story took place at the time of Rav Chaim's passing that is preserved by my family. My mother's grandmother had difficulty becoming pregnant, and went to ask for a bracha from Rav Chaim of Sans, who blessed her. A few months later, when the blessing had not yet been fulfilled, she returned to Rav Chaim who told her, "You are pregnant, and, please God, you will have a son." She asked him, "What shall the son be named?" Rav Chaim answered, "When he is born, you will know what to name him." As time went by, she was still unsure what to name the boy. When the time came the boy was born but no word came from Rav Chaim what to name him. On the day of the *brit* Rav Chaim passed away and the woman understood Rav Chaim's intent, and named her son Chaim (Wolkan).

law that a sale performed in order to cancel a prohibition is not a sale. Therefore there is no need for an [official] stamp, and no court will uphold this sale ... Without a doubt, we have nothing but the law as established by the Torah, and therefore it makes no difference whatsoever whether [the deed] is written in German or in Hebrew.

A similar argument is raised by the **Chatam Sofer** (vol. *I, Orach Chayyim, 113,* regarding a deed without a seal).[70]

It should be noted, however, that today this problem no longer exists. The Land Transactions Law (*Observance of Shemita, 5739-1979, 6*) states:

> A transaction involving land for the purpose of fulfilling the *mitzva* of *Shemita* that was performed with the approval of the Chief Rabbinate Council or with the approval of whomever was authorized by that council for this purpose, will be valid ... even if it is for a fixed time, and will be regarded as finalized even without registration.

According to present-day law, the sale of land as it is executed for the purpose of the *heter mechira,* has legal force even without registration in Tabu.[71]

GEMIRUT DA'AT (FIRM INTENTION)

In order for a transaction to be binding, the parties must fully intend that the relevant rights be transferred from one to the other. It stands to reason that when Jewish farmers sell their land to a gentile in order to circumvent the *Shemita* prohibitions, they do not always seriously intend to sell the land, even if they were to receive the full value of the land in exchange. This is not the only case where a sale is used to resolve a halachic problem. When we sell *chametz* or when we sell an animal's organ in order to redefine the animal as a blemished firstborn (for no labor may be done, nor may it be

70. See Rav Yitzchak Elchanan Spector (*Nitzanei Aretz, 6, p. 14*); *Responsa Har Zvi* (*Zera'im*, vol. *II*, no. 49); *Shabbat ha-Aretz* (Introduction, 14; *Mishpat Kohen*, no. 58; *Iggerot ha-Ra'aya*, vol. *I*, 312); *Ma'adanei Aretz* (nos. 18–19).

71. Some have raised an objection against the *heter mechira* based on the fact that the sale is for a limited time, and such a sale is not recognized by Israeli law. However, besides the fact that according to some authorities, legal force is unnecessary (see above), the law itself states that when land is sold in order to overcome the problem of *Shemita*, even a sale for a limited period of time is valid. It should be noted that in anticipation of the current *Shemita* year, the *Shemita* committee established by the Chief Rabbinite, headed by Rav Zev Witman, tried to institute that instead of a sale for a fixed period of time, the *heter mechira* should be based on a sale to which a stipulation that the property will be returned is attached– a sale which is recognized by Israeli law even without this special law.

eaten unless it develops a blemish), we rely on the sale despite the fact that the seller's intention is questionable.

Rav Kook (Introduction to *Shabbat ha-Aretz, 14; Mishpat Kohen,* no. *58; Iggerot ha-Ra'aya,* vol. *1, 312*) explains that the sale is valid even in the absence of full intention. It suffices if the seller is willing to execute the transaction in order to avoid violating a prohibition or for some other reason, even if he does not actually intend to transfer his property to the gentile. (Rav Shlomo Zalman Auerbach also agrees to this principle (cited in his book *Ma'adanei Aretz,* end of section *1*). Moreover, since the contract that he signs constitutes legal proof that he sold the property even if in his heart he is not interested in selling, his intention does not invalidate the sale. A person cannot sign a contract and then later claim that he didn't really mean it (see also *Ma'adanei Aretz, Shevi'it, Kuntres Mili de-Abba,* p. *283*).[72]

Today, however, the absence of full intention to sell poses less of a problem, even according to those who oppose the *heter mechira*. First of all, we are dealing with a sale for a fixed period of time. If in the end, the Jew receives the money agreed to in the contract, he might agree to the sale (as we say with respect to the sale of *chametz,* which addresses the *Chazon Ish*'s objection in 27:7, s.v. *ha-nilkatim*). Furthermore, today the sale is executed by way of a legal contract. The farmers examine it, show it to their lawyers, and there are even those who refuse to

72. Some argue that the absence of firm intention is particularly problematic in the case of the *heter mechira*, more so than in the case of the sale of *chametz*. According to them, the sale of the land should be invalid because it is going against thoughts that are "in the seller's heart and in the heart of all people." This is due to the fact that the Jew might otherwise agree to sell the ***chametz*** to the gentile, but he will never agree to sell his land to the gentile! As we saw, however, fundamentally we avoid this problem because the seller signed a legal contract. Moreover, the way the sale is formulated may also eliminate any problem. The sale is for a limited time, and only the upper portion of the land that is sold. If the gentile would be willing to pay the agreed-upon sum and receive the upper portion of the land for a year or two, it stands to reason that the farmer would agree, since he will profit more from the sale to the gentile than from the crop that he would grow during that period. Furthermore, at the end of the fixed period, the land will return to him. It should also be noted that there are other legal permits , including those that involve Torah prohibitions, where the level of firm intention is even lower, yet they are widely relied upon. For example, the *heter iska* arrangement that converts bank loans to investments in order to avoid the problem of charging interest to a fellow Jew. One could claim that when a customer invests in a savings account, there is a business transaction taking place between the customer and the bank, with the bank investing the money, and a distribution of the profits [unevenly ...]. However, when the customer has a deficit in his account, the deal is off. Hence there is a problem with going into a state of overdraft. We are lenient in this regard, despite the fact that charging interest to a fellow Jew is a Torah prohibition.

sign it due to conditions they find unacceptable. Thus, the seller's consent regarding the transaction might suffice even according to the most stringent opinions. (In this sense, the *heter mechira* is better than the *heter iska,* which most Jews rely on to circumvent problems of charging interest and the like, despite the fact that they involve potential Torah prohibitions). In addition, as stated above, some authorities were never troubled by the problem of the seller's intention.

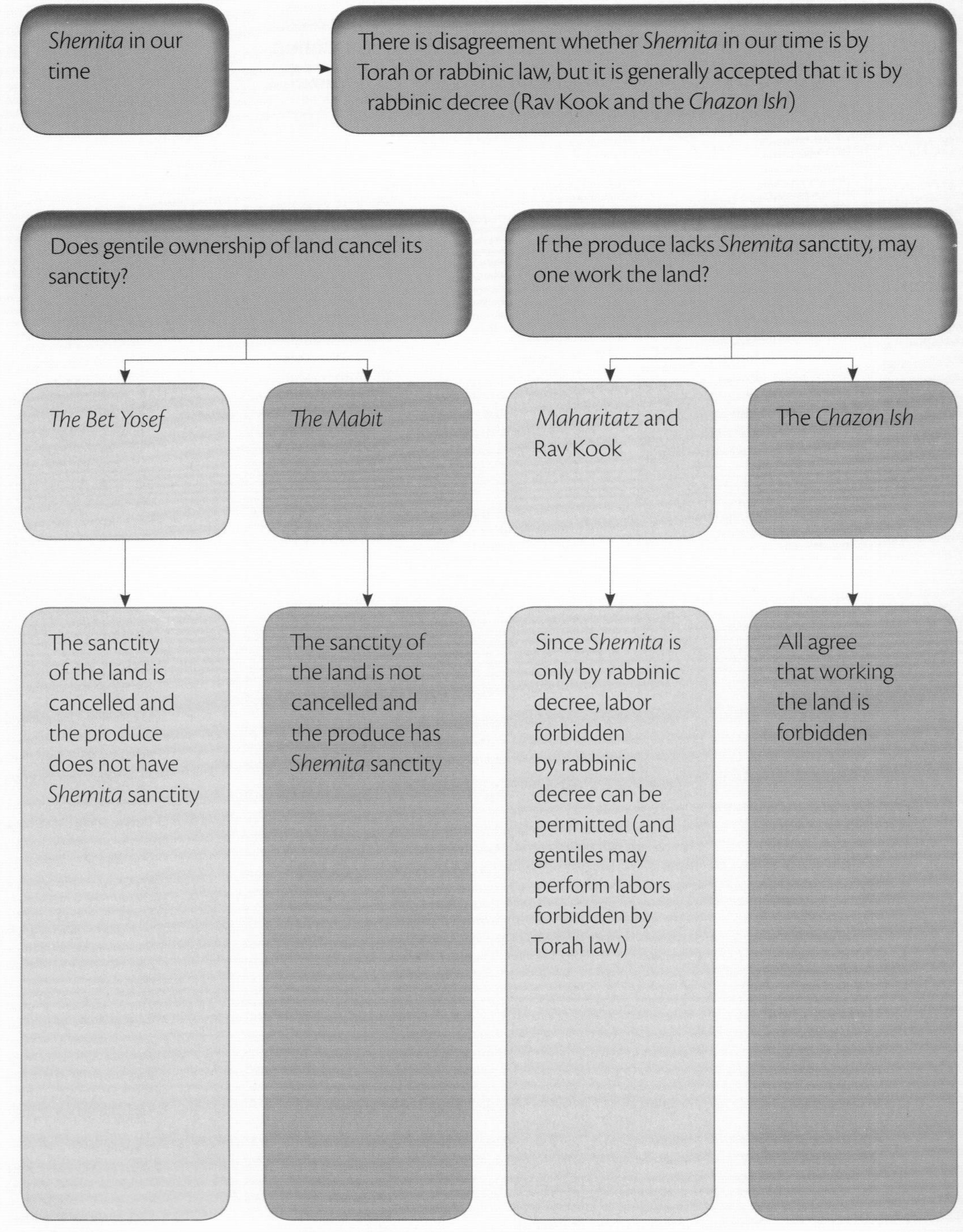
Overall summary of the ***heter mechira***
Shemita in our time
There is disagreement whether *Shemita* in our time is by Torah or rabbinic law, but it is generally accepted that it is by rabbinic decree (Rav Kook and the *Chazon Ish*)
Does gentile ownership of land cancel its sanctity?
If the produce lacks *Shemita* sanctity, may one work the land?
The Bet Yosef
The Mabit
Maharitatz and Rav Kook
The *Chazon Ish*
The sanctity of the land is cancelled and the produce does not have *Shemita* sanctity
The sanctity of the land is not cancelled and the produce has *Shemita* sanctity
Since *Shemita* is only by rabbinic decree, labor forbidden by rabbinic decree can be permitted (and gentiles may perform labors forbidden by Torah law)
All agree that working the land is forbidden

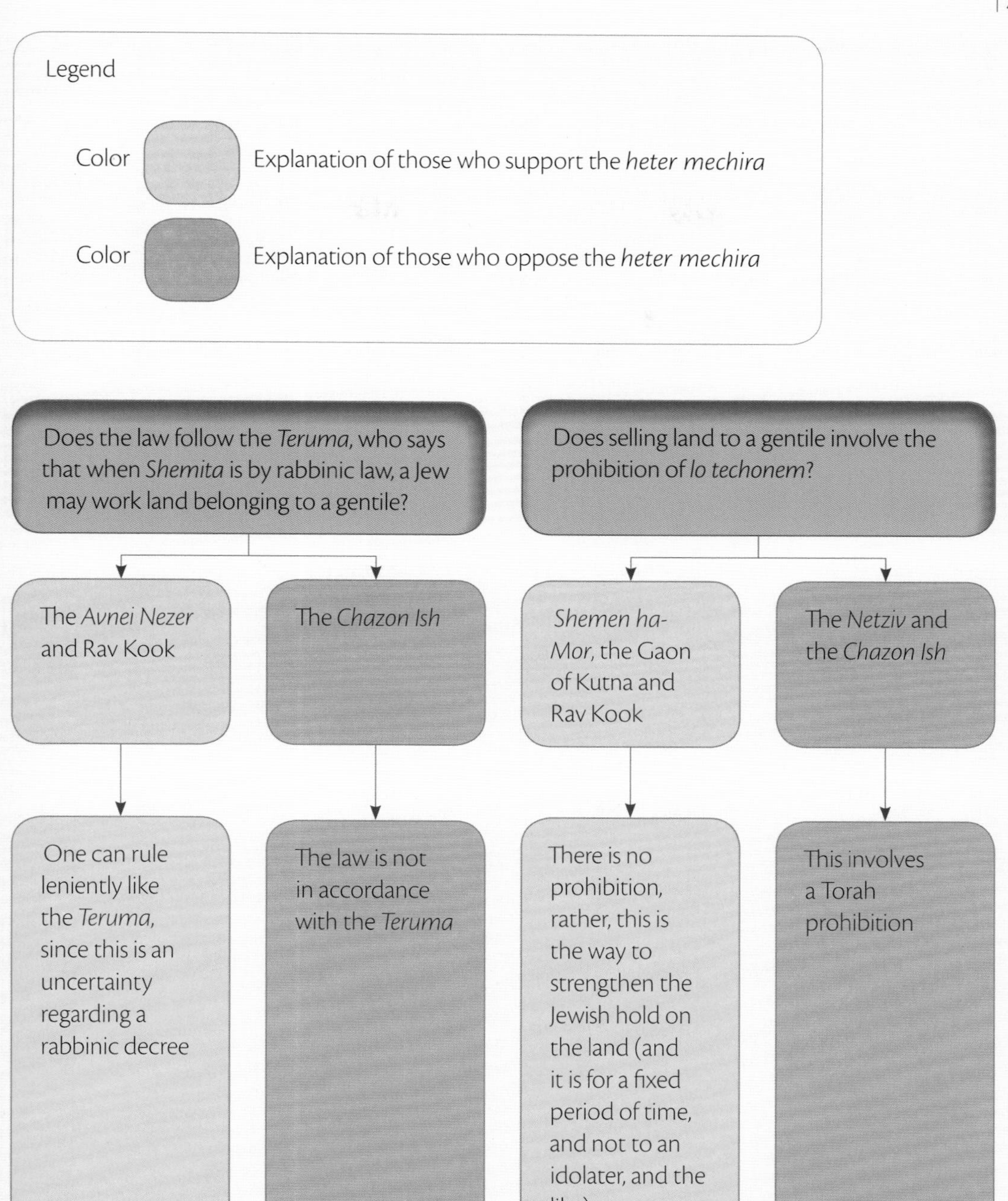
Legend
Color
Explanation of those who support the *heter mechira*
Color
Explanation of those who oppose the *heter mechira*
Does the law follow the *Teruma*, who says that when *Shemita* is by rabbinic law, a Jew may work land belonging to a gentile?
Does selling land to a gentile involve the prohibition of *lo techonem*?
The *Avnei Nezer* and Rav Kook
The *Chazon Ish*
Shemen ha-Mor, the Gaon of Kutna and Rav Kook
The *Netziv* and the *Chazon Ish*
One can rule leniently like the *Teruma*, since this is an uncertainty regarding a rabbinic decree
The law is not in accordance with the *Teruma*
There is no prohibition, rather, this is the way to strengthen the Jewish hold on the land (and it is for a fixed period of time, and not to an idolater, and the like)
This involves a Torah prohibition

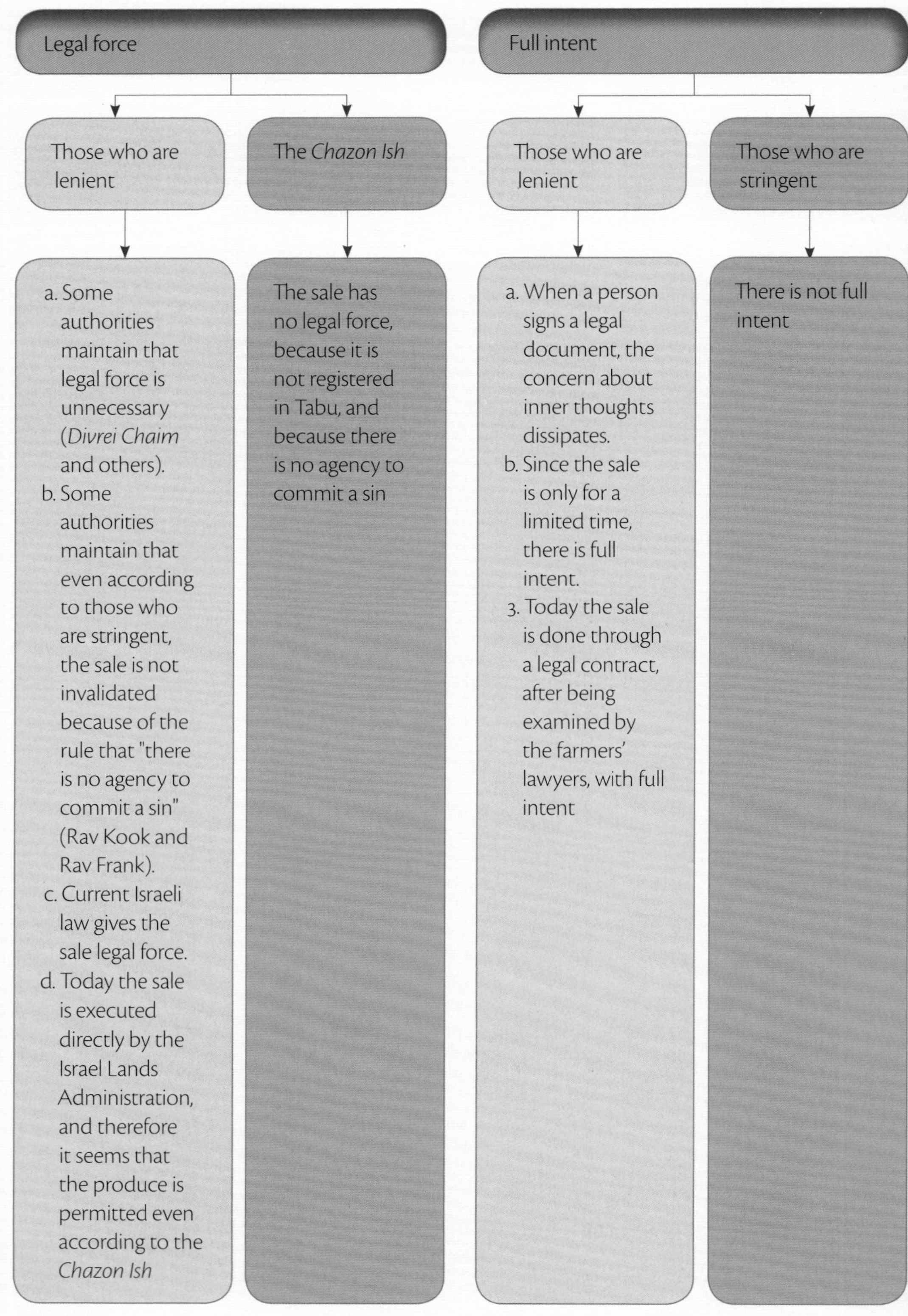
Legal force
Those who are lenient
a. Some authorities maintain that legal force is unnecessary (Divrei Chaim and others).
b. Some authorities maintain that even according to those who are stringent, the sale is not invalidated because of the rule that "there is no agency to commit a sin" (Rav Kook and Rav Frank).
c. Current Israeli law gives the sale legal force.
d. Today the sale is executed directly by the Israel Lands Administration, and therefore it seems that the produce is permitted even according to the Chazon Ish
The Chazon Ish
The sale has no legal force, because it is not registered in Tabu, and because there is no agency to commit a sin
Full intent
Those who are lenient
a. When a person signs a legal document, the concern about inner thoughts dissipates.
b. Since the sale is only for a limited time, there is full intent.
3. Today the sale is done through a legal contract, after being examined by the farmers' lawyers, with full intent
Those who are stringent
There is not full intent

DOES THE *HETER MECHIRA* PERMIT LABORS THAT ARE FORBIDDEN BY TORAH LAW?

Rav Kook (*Mishpat Kohen,* no. *71, 2–3; Shabbat ha-Aretz, 8, 8,* letter *5; Iggerot ha-Ra'aya,* vol. *1, 198, 232*) did not permit labors forbidden by Torah law in fields sold through the *heter mechira*:[73]

> We stipulated that following the sale one must not engage in any labor that is clearly forbidden by Torah law.

In light of this limitation, labors forbidden by Torah law, such as planting, may not be performed in fields sold through the *heter mechira*. To overcome this problem, these labors must be performed by a gentile, which according to most opinions is forbidden only by rabbinic decree. Another possibility is to perform the labor in an indirect manner (*gerama*) (see instructions issued by the Chief Rabbinate, *Shemita* of 5712 (1951–52); see chapter on planting, where this issue is discussed).

Unfortunately, however, farmers often ignored these instructions and sowed their fields during the *Shemita* year in the usual manner.[74] It should be noted that **there is a great difference between the *Shemita* years of our day (the current *Shemita* and the previous *Shemita* (5768 and 5775)) and *Shemita* years before that.** In previous *Shemita* years, many fields were planted by Jews. In recent years, however, the number of foreign workers in Israel has greatly increased, particularly in the agricultural sector, to the point that most farm-workers

73. Rav Yitzchak Elchanan Spector issued a similar ruling (*Nitzanei Aretz, 6, p. 16*). Rav Sh. Z. Auerbach (*Ma'adanei Aretz,* no. *2; Ha-Torah ve-ha-Medina,* vol. *IV,* p. *161*), however, argued that it is permissible **to harvest produce in the usual manner** in fields sold through the *heter mechira*. He argues that the prohibitions of harvesting fruit depend on the owner, and since the field is owned by a gentile, even if the Jew reaps the entire field, he does not do so in a manner that demonstrates ownership, and therefore it is permitted (for a discussion of Rav Sh. Z. Auerbach's novel approach, see *Sefer ha-Shemita*, pp. 103-104 and p. 125). Though it would seem that in terms of the law itself Rav Kook agreed with this position (*Mishpat Kohen*, no. 16), this is a very novel idea, and therefore it is preferable that the harvesting be performed by gentiles, especially today when there are so many foreign workers available.

74. Does the prohibition of *sefichim* apply in such a situation? According to the *Kesef Mishneh*, the prohibition of *sefichim* applies anytime a Jew plants; according to the Ri Kurkus, however, there is no prohibition of *sefichim* even if a Jew plants in this situation (see above, "The Prohibition of *Sefichim*," and *Shabbat ha-Aretz, 4, 29,* letter 2; *Ma'adanei Aretz, 9, 11; Chavot Binyamin,* vol. *1, 9, 9*). In practice one should only buy produce that was planted by a gentile, to support those farmers who follow Rav Kook's ruling, especially today, when there are so many foreign workers involved in agricultural work.

today are gentiles (on land that is owned by Jews during the other six years).[75] This reality has favorable ramifications regarding the *heter mechira,* because in most places the labors that are forbidden by Torah law are in any event performed by gentile laborers (in most places, even the labors forbidden by rabbinic decree are performed by gentiles).

SHEMITA SANCTITY IN *HETER MECHIRA* PRODUCE

Strictly speaking, *heter mechira* produce lacks *Shemita* sanctity, as the whole allowance is based on the fact that gentile ownership cancels the sanctity of Eretz Yisrael (*Shabbat ha-Aretz 8, 8,* letter *5*).

Nevertheless, **Rav Kook** wrote that it is proper to treat *heter mechira* produce as having *Shemita* sanctity. His reasoning was that the purpose of the allowance is only to save Jewish agriculture, but one should try to be stringent whenever appropriate (*Mishpat Kohen,* no. *67, 75, 76, 86, 87; Iggerot Ra'aya,* vol. *I,* nos. *310, 312, 318;* vol. *II,* no. *400*).[76]
To summarize, it is not necessary to treat *heter mechira* produce with *Shemita* sanctity, but there are those who are stringent and do in fact treat such produce with *Shemita* sanctity.

75. This phenomenon is constantly growing, with serious consequences. First of all, children born in Israel to these foreign workers have legal standing as citizens. Second, the fact that foreign workers have come to dominate agriculture has given rise to serious problems of unemployment. Third, the foreign workers work in shameful conditions, as much as seventeen hours a day for exceedingly low wages. Attempts must be made, therefore, to change this situation. A good example of change has already taken place in the construction industry. A few years ago there were 20,000 foreign workers employed in construction. In order to change this situation, the state demanded that these workers' terms of employment be improved. Owing to this demand, it became less worthwhile to hire foreign workers in the construction industry, and today there are only 6,000 such workers (this information was supplied by Tomer Moskowitz, former legal advisor to the Ministry of Commerce and Industry, and resident of Alon Shevut). In the field of agriculture there are currently more than 23,000 foreign workers.

76. According to the *Chazon Ish* (20,7) even if *Shemita* sanctity does not apply to produce growing in a field owned by a gentile, it is still forbidden to work the land.
It seems, however, that one can make the opposite argument: even if *Shemita* sanctity applies to produce growing in a field owned by a gentile, it may be permitted to work the land. The reason is that, as opposed to the sanctity of the produce which depends on the sanctity of the land, the prohibition to work the land might depend on the owner of the field. Therefore, if the field is owned by a gentile, it would not be subject to prohibitions of work. This seems to follow from *Responsa Avnei Nezer* (*Yoreh De'a,* no. 458) who rules leniently regarding the *heter mechira,* but nevertheless writes that the produce should be treated as having *Shemita* sanctity. This argument was also proposed by Rav Neriah ("*Torat Shevi'it be-Admat Hefker,*" *Devar ha-Shemita,* especially p. 105; see there regarding the disagreement about whether *Shemita* sanctity of the produce depends on the prohibition of working the land).

ATTITUDES TOWARD THE *HETER MECHIRA*

For a very long time, the observance of *Shemita* did not pose a challenge for the Jewish people, since there was no significant Jewish agriculture in Eretz Yisrael. The idea of circumventing the prohibitions of *Shemita* by way of selling the land to a gentile did, however, arise in places enjoying significant Jewish settlement. The basis of the allowance already appears in the words of the ***Mabit*** (vol. II, no. 64; vol. III, no. 48. The *Mabit* speaks of leasing the land to a gentile).[77] It also appears in the writings of his son, the ***Maharit*** (vol. II, no. 52; he speaks of leasing the land to a gentile with indirect payment). During that same period, Rav Moshe Galanti (*Responsa Maharam Galanti,* no. 57) also permitted working the land during the *Shemita* year by way of selling the land to a gentile.[78] All of these authorities, however, resorted to the leasing or sale of land in order to get around the prohibitions of *Shemita* in a temporary manner and as a localized issue. A long and impressive responsum on the matter was written by the rabbi of Chevron, Rav Mordechai Robbio (*Responsa Shemen ha-Mor, Yoreh De'a,* no. 4) over two hundred and fifty years ago:[79]

> [If] a Jew owns a vineyard in Chevron, and he leases it to a gentile to work the vineyard and tend to it ... what course and device should he choose to follow during the *Shemita* year? ...
>
> Through this solution [the *heter mechira*], he will cause Jews to have greater settlement in the land, for they will buy vineyards in Eretz Yisrael. In such a case, it is a *mitzva* ... This is what he should do in such a case ... to sell his vineyard to the gentile in an absolute manner, the land itself, by way of an explicit contract, for two years ...
>
> May God on high save us from error, and show us marvels from His Torah, so that we may understand and issue true rulings ...

The issue surfaced again one hundred thirty three years ago, in 5642 (1881–1882). Dr. Pinsker, a leader of the Hovivei Zion movement, turned to the ***Netziv*** (Rav Naftali Zvi Berlin) to arrange a *heter mechira*. The *Netziv*, however, opposed the idea (*Responsa*

77. The *Mabit* discusses a case where a person was compelled to work his field during the *Shemita* year. He first considers permitting forbidden labors based on the allowance of *arnona*, the need to pay tax on the land, but later he suggests that the field be leased to a gentile for two years (so that the lease during the *Shemita* year be part of a larger lease), so that working it will be permitted. "A Jew who leases his own field to a gentile or leases a field from a gentile and then leases it to a gentile prior to the *Shemita* year for several years – this is permitted." For historical precedents for the *heter mechira*, see Rav Neriah's article, "*Le-Toledot Kiyyum Mitzvat ha-Shemita*" (printed in many places, recently in *Devar ha-Shemita*, p. 107).

78. However, he permits working the land only in places which were not conquered in the second conquest of Eretz Yisrael, as opposed to the *Mabit*, the *Maharit*, and the *Shemen ha-Mor* (see below), who granted an allowance in all of Eretz Yisrael.

79. The entire responsum is also brought in *Kerem Tziyon* (*Shevi'it* pp. 20–32).

Meshiv Davar, vol. *II,* no. 56), arguing that meticulous observance of *Shemita* would strengthen Jewish settlement in Eretz Yisrael:[80]

> The principle that we must understand and take to heart is that the Jewish people exist under the arms of the world, and their existence does not follow natural human reason as to the way of the world. For as it would appear that there would be nothing better for Israel to do than to assimilate among the nations and try to become as close to them as possible, we see the opposite. The more we wish to draw close to the deeds of the nations of the world and draw closer than is necessary for the sake of livelihood, they hate us more, and when we lose the image of Israel, we are in their eyes like a monkey before man ... – so Eretz Yisrael is different than all countries, for its fundamental existence is not according to the natural ways of all the countries of the nations, and depends on nothing but God's providence according to His *mitzvot,* namely the setting aside of *terumot* and *ma'asrot,* as Malachi said (3:10), "[Bring all your *ma'aser* to the storehouses ...] and test Me with this ... [I shall open up the heavens and bring you boundless blessing]," and the same goes for the observance of the *mitzva* of *Shemita,* as is explicit in the Torah.[81]

80. Even the *Netziv* thought that an allowance had to be found that would permit working the land during the *Shemita* year, though he was not troubled by the financial losses that the farmers would suffer without such an allowance, as the Torah promises economic security to those who observe the laws of *Shemita*. The *Netziv* was bothered by a different problem – the problem of idleness and boredom among the farmers: "More than I am concerned about the destruction of the *yishuv*, of more concern is the people living in the *moshavot* that they not be idle for an entire year and come, God forbid, to idleness that leads to boredom and sin." Unfortunately, in the framework of this author's involvement in the organization, "Jobkatif," which was established in order to find jobs for the former residents of Gush Katif, he has seen first-hand that unemployment is not only a financial problem, but that the accompanying problems are often far more serious than the financial problems.

81. **While the Torah promises blessing to those who observe the laws of *Shemita*, it is not at all clear that this promise is still valid when Shemita is only by rabbinic decree**. According to the *Sema* (*Choshen Mishpat* 67, no. 2) and the *Chatam Sofer* (novellae to *Gittin 36b*, s.v. *ve-avru*), the promise is not in effect when *Shemita* is only by rabbinic decree. According to *Chidushei ha-Rim* (*Gittin 36b*) and the *Chazon Ish* (*Shevi'it*, 18, 4), the blessing applies today as well (see *Meshiv Davar*, vol. *II*, no. 56). They argue that if an earthly court established that *Shemita* must be observed, this influences the heavenly court as well. Moreover, inasmuch as there is a *mitzva* to obey the Sages, even when *Shemita* is only by rabbinic decree, God will certainly reward those who observe it. In addition, were it not for the fact that even those who observe *Shemita* by rabbinic decree will be blessed, the Sages would not have issued their decree (see *Shemitat Karka'ot*, 1, 8).

In preparation for the next *Shemita* year, in 5648 (1888), agents of Baron de Rothschild approached **Rav Yitzchak Elchanan Spektor**, the rabbi of Kovno, with the question of the *heter mechira*. Rav Spektor sent an agent to Berlin to obtain a copy of *Responsa Shemen ha-Mor*, which provided the earliest precedent for the allowance. In the meantime, *Hovevei Zion* also turned to other Torah authorities: **Rav Shmuel Mohliver, Rav Yisrael Yehoshua (Trunk) of Kutna** and **Rav Shmuel Klapfisch of Warsaw.** In light of the difficult situation of Jewish agriculture in Eretz Yisrael, these rabbis agreed to arrange a *heter mechira*.

ספר

שו"ת שמן המר

הרב המופלא

חברון מרדכי

רוביו שמן

המ"ר

אברהם רוביו

נדפס

פה ליוורנו

בשנת רחם ארחמנו

בדפוס המשובח של השותפים

יעקב נונים ואיס

רפאל מילדולה

Con Approvazione

RAV MORDECHAI ROBBIYO (Responsa *Shemen ha-Mor*)

Rav Mordechai was the rabbi of Chevron after the Chida and *rosh yeshiva* of Yeshivat Chesed le-Avraham. Before that he spent two years in Turkey and other Arab lands collecting on behalf of the Jewish communities in Israel. Rav Mordechai passed away in 5543 (1783), and after his death his responsa were collected in a volume called *Shemen ha-Mor*. This responsa was quite rare, and when Rav Yitzchak Elchanan Spector, rav of Kovno, wrote his responsum regarding the *heter mechira*, he sent a messenger to Berlin to bring him a copy of the Responsa *Shemen ha-Mor*.

THE LETTER OF THE FIRST PROPONENTS OF THE *HETER MECHIRA*

Inasmuch as we are drawing near to the *Shemita* year according to the Rambam's calculation and common custom, namely, 5649 (1888–1889), may it come to us for blessing; and with God's help we have been privileged that several villages, called colonies, have been established by Jews who support themselves by working the land, both from grain crops and vineyards; and if we forbid them to work the land and tend to the vineyards, the land will become desolate and this will, God forbid, lead to the destruction of the colonies, and hundreds of people will, God forbid, fade away in hunger – therefore, in order to save lives and [Jewish] settlement of the land, lives as well as property, we have found an allowance for this year, 5649, to sell the fields and vineyards and everything connected to working the land to gentiles, [that sale to take effect] this summer, may it come upon us for blessing, with the stipulation that when we return their down payment following the *Shemita* year, they will be obligated to return our fields and vineyards and everything connected to them.

The text of the aforementioned contract will be formulated by the Jerusalem rabbinical court and with their consent. Following the aforementioned sale based on such a contract, it will be permitted to work the land as necessary, both the fields and the vineyards. It is understood that colonists who have the means and can afford to hire gentile workers must not themselves do work that is forbidden during the *Shemita* year. The poor, however, who lack the means to hire gentile workers, may do the work themselves, but only in accordance with the guidelines provided to them by the

Jerusalem rabbinical court, who will instruct them in which labors are permitted and which are forbidden. All this applies only to [the *Shemita* of] 5649, but not to future years of *Shemita*, when a new allowance will have to be issued. Perhaps God, in His great mercy, will help deliver His people and bring them success, so that they not need the allowance, and they will be able to observe *Shemita* in accordance with Torah law.

We agree to the aforementioned allowance in its entirety, it being based on the law of our holy Torah, as we have explained at length in separate booklets. All this was done on condition that it will be approved by the brilliant leader of our generation, the honorable Rav Yitzchak Elchanan [Spektor], *Av Bet Din* of Kovno.

May God speedily bring our redemption, so that we will be able to fulfill, in the most meticulous manner, all the *mitzvot* that depend upon the Land of Israel.

We attach our signatures on Friday, 28 Shevat 5648, here in Warsaw:

Yisrael Yehoshua (Trunk), Kutna
Shmuel ... (Mohliver), Bialystok
Shmuel ... (Klapfisch), Warsaw

These rabbis did, however, attach certain stipulations to the sale:

> All this was done on condition that it will be approved by the brilliant leader of our generation, the honorable Rav Yitzchak Elchanan [Spektor], *Av Bet Din* of Kovno.

They also stipulated that labors forbidden by Torah law be performed by gentiles and Jews only perform labors that are forbidden by rabbinic decree.

As is evident, **Rav Yitzchak Elchanan Spektor** was deemed the most important halachic authority of his generation, and as such his assent was of critical importance. The letter was delivered to Rav Yitzchak Elchanan by special messenger, and in the end Rav Yitzchak Elchanan agreed to the *heter mechira.* He too, however, attached a stipulation:

> The text of the deed of sale will be drawn up by the rabbinical court of Jerusalem and with its consent.

The Sefardi rabbis of Jerusalem agreed to the *heter mechira* (*Ha-Zvi, 16*), but the Ashkenazi rabbis, **Rav Yehoshua Leib Diskin** and **Rav Shmuel Salant** opposed it (*Ha-Chavatzelet, 6, 5649*). In practice, during the *Shemita* of 5649 (*1888–1889*) the *heter* was accepted in most of Eretz Yisrael, with the exception of Petach Tikva, Ekron and Gedera (in the middle of the year, agricultural work resumed in Gedera owing to the pressure applied by Hovevei Zion).

By the next *Shemita* year (*5656, 1895–1896*), Jewish settlement in Eretz Yisrael had grown, and it became exceedingly difficult to manage without a *heter mechira.* That year Rav Yehoshua Leib Diskin and Rav Shmuel Salant gave their support to the *heter mechira*, according to the formula drawn up by **Rav Naftali Hertz,**[82] the first rabbi of Yafo. They made it clear, however, that their agreement was not to be taken as a ruling for future generations. The *heter mechira* continued in similar fashion in the next *Shemita* as well (*5663, 1902–1903*).

In the following *Shemita* (5670, 1909–1910), the rabbis of

82. According to Rav Hertz's formulation of the sale, the trees are sold only for cutting, and the land is sold only as deep down as what provides the crops with nourishment (in order to solve the problem of "*lo techonem*"). It should be noted that Rav Yitzchak Elchanan did not approve of this formulation (*Hora'at Sha'a*, p. 125), and preferred his own text.

שו״ת

מהר״ש מוהליבר

שאלות ותשובות וחקרי הלכה

מוסד הרב קוק · ירושלים

RAV SHMUEL MOHLIVER

Rav Mohliver was born in 5584 (1824) in Vilna and taught in the famous Yeshivat Volozhin. He was one of the early leaders of Religious Zionism and one of the founders of the Hovevei Tzion movement. He encouraged *aliyah* for Jews from all over the world. Rav Mohliver helped found the moshavot of Ekron (Mazkeret Batya) and Rechovot. He wrote several books that were lost in pogroms. A volume of his responsa was published and still exists. Rav Mohliver died in 5658 (1898).

Jerusalem, **Rav Salant** and **Rav Chayim Berlin**, tried to uphold the *mitzva* of *Shemita* without resorting to the *heter mechira*, because they thought that the improved situation made this possible. **Rav Shmuel Mohliver**, on the other hand, argued that owing to the large numbers of Jews who would lose their livelihood if the land is worked by gentiles, there was room to permit labors forbidden by Torah law in fields subject to the *heter mechira* even when performed by Jews:

Letter from Rav Mohilever – *Ha-Yehudi*, 5670, 26:

Then too (in 5649) other great authorities permitted all labors, [even] when performed by Jews. And I too was of the opinion then to permit all labors, even those that are forbidden by Torah law, [even] when performed by Jews, as I explained at length in my booklet. But I deferred to the Gaon of Kutna, *z"l*, who said that he was inclined to say that in any event some reminder of *Shemita* must be maintained, that a Jew should not do the work himself, at least not **labors that are forbidden by Torah law.** He too, however, added to what he wrote in his letter from 10 Sivan 5648: "I defer to the Sefardi rabbis in Eretz Yisrael." Now, therefore, when there are many Jewish workers in our country, whose entire livelihood is the wages for their work in their brothers' fields and vineyards – if we forbid them to work, we will cut off food from their mouths and they will die of starvation, God forbid. There are also labors that the Arabs are incapable of doing …

I, therefore, stand behind my opinion, as explained in my booklet, **to permit all labors, [even] when performed by a Jew …** And they must not do anything without consulting the Sefardi rabbinical court, and they must act in accordance with it rulings, whether lenient or stringent.

This too I say with respect to the wealthy colonists who have the means to hire workers – I am inclined to forbid them to do the work. Rather they should hire Jewish workers, their poor brothers (see *Orach Chayyim* 542:2). "May God command His blessing in their storehouses," (based on Vayikra 25:11) and may they not be dependent upon the gifts and loans of men, and may they be able to observe the *Shemita* years, may they come to us for blessing, in the most meticulous manner.

RAV KOOK AND THE *HETER MECHIRA*

The **Ridbaz**, who lived in Tzefat, challenged the very basis for the allowance (see his book on the *Pe'at ha-Shulchan*). At the same time, **Rav Kook**, who was then serving as the rabbi of Yafo, published his "*Shabbat ha-Aretz*," where he offered a detailed explanation of the halachic foundations of the *heter mechira*. Several letters were sent back and forth between Rav Kook and the Ridbaz regarding the validity of the *heter mechira* (the most famous of them include *Iggerot ha-Ra'aya*, vol. *II, no.* 555, and vol. *II, no.* 522, and others), which allow us to see the various approaches to the *Shemita* issue.

Rav Kook expresses his confidence in the *heter*, writing that "with respect to the *heter* itself, I see no grounds whatsoever for doubt" (*Mishpat Kohen, 71*, p. *126*). It was clear to him, however, that the allowance is merely a temporary ruling, and therefore it should be used in the most limited manner possible:

> Since the entire allowance is truly only because of the great need and it is issued as a temporary ruling, we have therefore instituted that one not plant any new saplings at all, for our entire objective was to preserve the settlement that has already been built, so that it not be destroyed ... to observe whatever is possible, and to guard in any event against that which is essentially a Torah prohibition.

Some of the proponents of the *heter mechira* went as far as to allow Jews to perform labors that are forbidden by Torah law (such as Rav Shmuel Mohliver in 5670 [1910]), but Rav Kook once again restricted the allowance to labors forbidden by rabbinic decree performed by a Jew and labors forbidden by Torah law performed by a gentile.[83] Rav Kook also wrote that we must continue to search for a way to observe the *mitzva* of *Shemita* without resorting to the *heter mechira*, and that every farmer who succeeds in fulfilling the *mitzva* of *Shemita* should be encouraged and celebrated:

> This does not prevent or exempt us from seeking out any counsel that God will send our way that will enable our brethren, the people of Israel living in the Holy Land, to properly

83. This stands in contrast to what is incorrectly stated in the pamphlet *Am Mekadeshei Shevi'i* (p. 29) that "Rav Kook ... decided to expand the *heter mechira* ... In what way was the *heter mechira* expanded? ... Rav Kook established that labors forbidden by rabbinic decree can be performed by a Jew, whereas the four labors forbidden by Torah law are forbidden to a Jew, and a gentile must perform them." This is incorrect, for the earliest advocates of the *heter mechira* allowed for labors forbidden by rabbinic decree to be performed by a Jew and labors forbidden by Torah law to be performed by a gentile, and it was only Rav Mohliver who expanded the allowance and permitted a Jew to perform labors forbidden by Torah law. Rav Kook once again restricted the allowance to what had been permitted at the beginning.

> observe the *mitzva* without cancellation [of ownership] and resorting to an allowance. And over every part, however small, of the Holy Land in the hands of Jews in which the *mitzva* of *Shemita* will be properly observed, we must rejoice "like one who finds great spoil" (Tehillim 119:162).

Rav Kook's approach drew sharp criticism from both sides. On the one hand, the members of the old *yishuv* were incensed that Rav Kook renewed the allowance, as is evident from the words of the Ridbaz (in the introduction to his *Bet Ridbaz*):

> By nature I have always been a great zealot, and when I saw that the pillars of Judaism were weakening and a chilling wind was blowing in the tents of Israel, I was unable to restrain myself and I zealously set out with all my strength ... Even with all of this I did not restrain myself, for in no way am I able to restrain my wrath.

Rav Kook (in *Iggerot Ha-Raya* 555) refers to the fact that the Ridbaz was upset by what was in his view an uprooting of the *mitzva* of *Shemita*.

The members of the *moshavot*, on the other hand, claimed that Rav Kook was overly stringent in his insistence that labors forbidden by Torah law be performed by gentiles (*Azkara, Toledot ha-Rav,* p. *123; Devar ha-Shemita, p. 128*):

> The *yishuv* is the life of my soul ... And it has not escaped me that there are those who have issued a more radical allowance. But I am not inclined to this direction, for just as we need the land [of Israel], so do we need religion, and we must deeply implant [the matter], lest the law of *Shemita* be forgotten in Israel.

This matter is expressed nicely by my grandfather, the poet **Rav Yosef Zvi Rimon**, *zt"l,* who was exceedingly close to Rav Kook, *zt"l,* and a frequent visitor in his home in Yafo and Jerusalem (*Rabbi Avraham Yitzchak ha-Kohen Kook ve-Ra'ayon ha-Techiya,* p. *10*):

Any person with understanding knows and understands based on those who have written about this period in Eretz Yisrael, that were it not for the fact that Rav Kook lived in the country at the time, the *yishuv* might have collapsed owing to the radicalism of both the old generation and the new generation, there being nothing in the center and no elevated and important influence upon them and upon life in general. Rav Kook did all this, arousing great anger from both sides and sometimes insult to his honor.

THE POET RAV YOSEF ZVI RIMON, ZT"L

Rav Yosef Zvi Rimon was born in 1889. He studied in Rav Reines's yeshiva in Lida, and moved to Eretz Yisrael at the age of 20. Rav Rimon's poetry is unique, giving powerful expression to his deepest feelings, his inner truth, and his uninterrupted connection to God. He writes about God, about Eretz Yisrael and about faith-based struggle with difficulties and questions.

Rav Rimon was a frequent visitor in the home of Rav Kook, who held him in high esteem. Rav Kook saw him as a unique poet, writing about him: "The time has come to awaken, to give due respect to the unique poet of our time, whose entire spirit and the strength of his poems flow from the living spring of the Light of Israel ... And he specifically could develop a new holy brand of poetry here in Israel, after it had been absent for centuries ... Be strong, man of spirit, our beloved poet, Rav Yosef Zvi Rimon ... ."

R. Binyamin, an Israeli author, wrote that many times the poems of Rav Yosef Zvi Rimon serve as commentary on words of Rav Kook.

His poetry was accepted and held in high regard both in religious and secular circles (Brener, Bialik, Tchernichovsky, Agnon, Asher Brosh and others.) [Avraham Kariv said "the amazing" is a description he reserved for Rav Rimon alone among all contemporary poets.]

His poetry draws on the past, but it took a new form, considered modern even today. Avraham Kariv describes it as follows: "A new soul sings here a new song ... his poetry draws from our sources, but it is itself a spring and a source." He passed away in 5718 (1958).

WAS RAV KOOK SUCCESSFUL?

As my grandfather, *zt"l*, wrote, Rav Kook succeeded in paving a middle course between the two extreme groups, which made it possible for them to live together despite all the difficulties. Indeed, each side expressed its esteem for Rav Kook, despite serious disagreement with his positions. Even the Ridbaz, who was very upset with Rav Kook about his support for the *heter mechira,* held him in high regard, as is evident from the following story.

A certain rabbi arrived in Yafo accompanied by a group of his followers and declared himself rabbi of the city. At the time, Rav Kook was the rabbi of Yafo. The rabbinical court of Jerusalem came out in Rav Kook's defense, publicly denouncing his challenger who had designated himself rabbi of Yafo when that office was already filled by "a famous and brilliant rabbi": "And especially to challenge a great rabbi whose name is known, the famous and brilliant rabbi, our master, Rav Avraham Yitzchak Hakohen Kook, *Av Bet Din* of the Holy City of Yafo and the *moshavot."* The Ridbaz is included among the signatories.

In addition, the Ridbaz penned a letter of his own, in which he relates how he had once visited Rav Kook in Yafo and spoke to him about his rabbinic challenger, and how Rav Kook had tried to change the subject. The Ridbaz writes as follows (the letter is cited in *Chayyei Ra'aya,* pp. 292–293):

> Who would have imagined that a wingless fly would fight against the great eagle, the great Gaon, whose name has gone forth throughout the world, and who is sought by all to illuminate them with his Torah, his righteousness and his wisdom. But when I passed through the holy camp and heard that it really happened, I spoke to the rabbi, the illustrious head of the rabbinic court [Rav Kook] on the matter, and he diverted me to other topics, not wishing to speak of the matter. I understood that this was because he felt uncomfortable about dealing with the issue.

The esteem in which Rav Kook was held by the members of

the *moshavot* is evidenced by the fact that on the day that he died, newspapers across the country carried a front-page announcement, proclaiming a day of national mourning (and a special assembly of the Zionist Congress).

In the end, Rav Kook's strength enabled the connection to be maintained between old and new – between the need to observe Torah and *mitzvot* on the one hand, and the new *yishuv* that was developing across the country and trying to run away from such observance on the other. He succeeded in imbuing the deep connection between the holy and the mundane, as well as a deepening of the foundations of faith in the reality of the redemption that was unfolding. [In addition, Rav Kook was successful in that he made it possible for people to maintain a nationalist outlook and at the same time hold fast to Torah and *mitzvot*. In Rav Kook's day this combination was restricted to a small set of individuals, but had it not been for his decisive influence, the entire national-Zionist community may well have distanced itself from Torah and *mitzvot*.]

In his letters Rav Kook teaches us **the correct way** to establish a connection with the non-religious community. There are those who try to imitate that community in the way they talk and conduct themselves. Rav Kook teaches us, however, that we don't have to change the things that we believe in order to create connections. We can and we must remain at a pure and elevated spiritual intensity, and draw close to non-religious people **out of true love for them** (letter 555):

> That which you criticize me … believe me: Most of the non-religious who are fond of me know and recognize that I am not, God forbid, one of them. And that, as the distance between east and west, so is the distance between my thoughts and ways and their thoughts and ways … but of necessity they are forced to admit … that I am blessed, thank God, that my entire being is filled with love of Israel.

Rav Kook explains to the Ridbaz that he is very far from the world of the non-religious, but the great love that he has for the members of that world makes it possible for them to feel that they are connected to him.

Rav Kook's love of the Jewish people was unique. He knew how to see the pure and beautiful elements in each individual, based on the understanding that there is good in each person. Nevertheless, he did not ignore their problems and failings, and in fact protested against them. His great love, however, allowed for true closeness, and reproach, when necessary, was out of integrity and fear of heaven:

> The great love that we have for our people does not blind our eyes and it does not prevent us from seeing all of its defects. But even after the freest inspection, we find its essence clean of all defects. (*Olat Ra'aya*, vol. *II*, p. 7)

The situation today is not simple, but we too must strive to judge the Jewish people in **a pure and positive light. We need to recognize, contemplate and seek out the good in others and in ourselves, and when seeing that good, thank God for all the goodness that He has bestowed upon us**. At the same time, we must remember that the good that is in us and in all of Israel gives us the strength to deal with the difficulties and repair our failures and inadequacies.

To illustrate Rav Kook's unique personality, I wish to cite the words of one of his outstanding disciples, **Rav Moshe Zvi Neriah** (*Devar ha-Shemita*, p. 159 and on):

> He fulfills the verse "Who teaches like Him" (*Iyov 36:22*). He is a halachic decisor who issues clear rulings on difficult matters that were forgotten during the years of exile from our land ...
>
> In his responsa, his great strength in Torah is evident; his rulings are clear and based on strong foundations, starting from the talmudic sources, both the Babylonian and Jerusalem Talmud, through the positions of the *Rishonim*, and ending with the responsa of the *Acharonim* ...

> The promptness of his responsa is amazing – "your letter has just arrived" – and he immediately answers at length ...
>
> Through the upheaval over the *Shemita* of 5670 (1910), Rav Kook, *zt"l*, emerges in his full stature, as a giant in Halacha, a giant in his outlook and thought, and a giant in communal leadership. And over all of these there hovers a spirit of humility, purity of character, respect for heaven and respect for man ...
>
> In a conversation with me years ago, Rav Sh. Z. Auerbach, *z"l*, expanded at length about his high regard for Rav Kook's manner of ruling in his responsa, and he mentioned also *Shabbat ha-Aretz* ... Years later, he [Rav Sh. Z. Auerbach] said: "There are those who are great in their scholarship, great in their righteousness, great in their character, great in a particular branch of the Torah, great in the exoteric [parts of the Torah] and great in the esoteric [parts]. Rav [Kook] was great in all of these. A true Torah renaissance man, from whatever perspective that I would look at him, I would see his greatness, his uniqueness. A genius who mastered all the treasures of the Torah, the exoteric and the esoteric, a righteous man in all his ways and all his deeds, in the particulars of *mitzvot* and in personal attributes, in diligence of study and in acts of lovingkindness.

Let us try to emulate Rav Kook's love for all of God's world, and especially for the people of Israel:

> Great is my love for all creatures, for the entire world ... In my whole being I feel my great love for all creatures, and especially for human beings, and most of all for the people of Israel ... I do not wish to diminish the dignity of any human being. It is my wish that all should rise, that all should be treated with dignity ... . (*Shemoneh Kevatzim, kovetz 8, 116*)

RAV MOSHE ZVI NERIAH (MANEKIN)

Rav Moshe Zvi Neriah was born in Lodz, Poland in 5673 (1913). His father was Rav Petachya Manekin. On the eve of World War I, his family moved to Russia, and from there he moved to Eretz Yisrael, after having secured an immigration certificate through the yeshiva in which he was to study – Ha-Yeshiva ha-Merkazit ha-Olamit (later Yeshivat Merkaz ha-Rav), headed by Rav Kook. He became one of the leaders of the Bnei Akiva movement, and even composed its anthem. Rav Neriah played a leading role in molding the religious-Zionist community in Israel. He was a driving force behind the establishment of yeshivot and the strengthening of intensive Torah study. Rav Neriah raised the spirits of the religious youth, replacing embarrassment from the *kippot* on their heads with a sense of religious pride. He served as Rosh Yeshiva of the first Yeshiva High School to combine religious and secular studies, in Kfar ha-Ro'eh. Rav Neriah was a great Torah scholar and authored many articles in the realm of Halacha (which were later collected in *Tzenif Melucha* and *Invei Petachya*).

Rav Binyamin Tabory, one of the Ramim in Yeshivat Har Etzion, related to me that during a visit to the United States, Rav Neriah sat in on a *shiur* given by Rav Yosef Soloveitchik. The *shiur* was delivered in English, but Rav Neriah sat and listened. Rav Soloveitchik raised a very difficult question to which he had no answer. At the end of the *shiur*, Rav Soloveitchik announced that Rav Neriah was visiting from Israel, and asked him to share a few words. Rav Neriah opened by saying that the *Acharonim* offer three answers to Rav Soloveitchik's question, and he proceeded to explain the three answers. Rav Tabory noted that even though Rav Neriah had not known beforehand the topic of Rav Soloveitchik's *shiur*, and even though the *shiur* was delivered in English, Rav Neriah's presentation of the three answers was exceedingly impressive.

Rav Neriah wrote extensively about Rav Kook. He died in 5755 (1995). His last words were: "I seek sanctity. Give me the sanctity of Eretz Yisrael. Give me the sanctity of the love of Israel."

DOES THE *HETER MECHIRA* INVOLVE DECEPTION?

At first glance, the *heter mechira,* as well as the other allowances described above, fail to conform to the basic standards of halachic integrity. It seems that these solutions circumvent Halacha, avoiding proper fulfillment of the words of the Torah. We shall now attempt to examine whether or not such feelings are indeed justified.[84]

Let us remember that one of the assumptions underlying the *heter mechira* is that gentile ownership of land in Eretz Yisrael cancels the land's sanctity with respect to *mitzvot.* Therefore, the produce growing there has no *Shemita* sanctity, and there are various ways to permit working the land. We saw above that **Rav Kook** argued (*Mishpat Kohen,* no. 75) that labors forbidden by rabbinic decree may be performed on such land, but nevertheless the produce that grew there should be treated as having *Shemita* sanctity[85]:

> I see no contradiction that raises doubts about the allowance in all its aspects, [but nevertheless it is necessary] that we practice stringency wherever possible provided that it does not lead to the destruction of the *yishuv* as a whole ... For it is only because of the great need that we rely on the allowance, and it is [only] as a temporary ruling. I, therefore, advise that the vintners should accept the proposal to treat their produce with *Shemita* sanctity wherever that is possible, and may a blessing come upon them.

There is a certain difficulty understanding why on the one hand, Rav Kook insists that there are no grounds for raising doubts about the allowance, while on the other hand he maintains that is preferable to practice stringency wherever possible. Does Rav Kook not trust the validity of the *heter mechira*?

One of the most discomforting aspects of the *heter mechira* is that it reminds us of a loophole that allows a criminal to walk free. The truth, however, is that the *heter* is far from a legal trick. In a normal legal system, as soon as a loophole is discovered, the law is emended in order to "seal" the hole that had gone unnoticed when

84. This discussion is also relevant to other halachic solutions that at first glance seem to be based on deception: *heter iska* (recasting bank loans as investments to avoid problems of charging interest to a fellow Jew), *pruzbol* (a document turning debts over to the court to avoid their cancellation at the conclusion of the *Shemita* year), the sale of *chametz,* and the like.

85. See above, in the notes to the section dealing with *Shemita* sanctity in *heter mechira* produce, that there is room to argue that fundamentally the produce has *Shemita* sanctity, but working the land is nevertheless permitted. This, however, was not Rav Kook's position, as is evident from the aforementioned responsa. According to him the two issues are interdependent, the *heter* being based on the assumption that the produce does not have *Shemita* sanctity.

the law was first legislated. All human legal codes include many amendments that are meant to seal such loopholes. In civil law, had the legislature foreseen that a certain loophole would be exploited, it would have sealed the hole from the outset, rather than leave a breach that invites the criminal to commit his offense. God, however, is prescient and all-knowing. If a breach is found in the Torah, it cannot be that God was not aware of it from the very beginning. **A loophole in the Torah must have been intentionally included so that it might be used at the appropriate time.**

This is implied by the **Ritva** (*Eruvin 13b*):

> The French rabbis [Tosafot] asked: How is possible that "both this and that are the words of the living God," when this one forbids and that one permits? They answer that when Moshe went on high to receive the Torah, he was shown on each and every matter forty-nine reasons to forbid, and forty-nine reasons to permit. He asked the Holy One, blessed be He, about this, and He said that it would be **handed over to [the discretion of] the Sages of Israel in each and every generation, and that the decision would be in their hands.** This is correct on the midrashic level, and on the level of truth, there is a secret reason to the matter.

One question still remains: if the Torah wants us to use the *heter mechira,* then why does it not mention this solution explicitly? It seems that the Torah is teaching us that in ordinary circumstances we are obligated to fulfill the *mitzva* according to its plain sense. The Torah knew, however, that the day would come when it would be necessary to make use of the *heter mechira, pruzbol,* the sale of *chametz,* and *heter iska,* and therefore it left various loopholes in place that would allow for these solutions. Using these halachic solutions does not constitute deceitful circumvention, for were this not what the Torah wanted, it would have sealed these breaches from the very beginning.

When a person exploits these loopholes with no justification, he is "a scoundrel acting within the Torah's rules." According to the

Ritva, use of such loopholes is "handed over to [the discretion of] the Sages of Israel in each and every generation, and the decision is left in their hands." Therefore, with respect to the *heter mechira,* the allowance's proponents understand that present circumstances make it necessary to exploit the loophole that permits the *heter mechira,* and therefore there are no grounds whatsoever for raising doubts about the allowance. But since we are dealing with a loophole, and the Torah clearly wants us to fulfill its commandments according to their plain sense, it is befitting to practice stringency wherever possible.

THE *HETER MECHIRA* IN OUR DAY

As we have seen, **Rav Kook** permitted reliance on the *heter mechira* at a time that Jewish agriculture in Eretz Yisrael could not have survived without the allowance. This being the case, current circumstances must be examined regularly to see whether the need for the *heter mechira* still exists. It stands to reason that were Israeli society more observant it would often be possible to find a better solution than *heter mechira*, at least for much of the agricultural industry. In any case the matter would by no means be simple, especially in the present situation, where in the absence of the *heter mechira* some farmers would work their lands against Halacha, while others would be forced out of agriculture.

Clearly observant Jews must make an effort to observe the *mitzva* of *Shemita* without resorting to the *heter mechira*. However, the Chief Rabbinate of the State of Israel arranges the *heter mechira* for those farmers who would otherwise work their land in violation of the *Shemita* prohibitions and those who cannot manage without the *heter mechira*. The *heter mechira* was established out of concern for the people of Israel as a whole, and not out of a desire to break Halacha (see Rav Kook's words in letter no. 555 and no. 522).

Moreover, on the national level, it might be impossible for Jewish agriculture in Israel to survive without the *heter mechira*. For example, a farmer who exports his produce cannot tell his customers that this year he will not be supplying them with fruits or vegetables. Multi-year contracts are signed, and they cannot be put on hold for a year. Supplying produce during *Shemita* is a problem in terms of growing the vegetables and in terms of their export, which is prohibited.[86] For this reason as well, we are forced to use the *heter mechira* until a better solution can be found.[87] This is one of the differences between relating to the *Shemita* issue on a personal level (a particular individual can manage without the *heter mechira*) and relating to it on the national level.

It should be further noted that even were we to provide subsidies for farmers that would allow them to let their land lie totally fallow,

86. As for the prohibition to export *Shemita* produce, a question arises whether the prohibition applies to vegetables that were grown especially for that purpose, and are not needed for domestic consumption. See the appendix at the end of this volume, p. 523).

87. It should be noted that giving up altogether on agriculture in Eretz Yisrael is unimaginable. First of all, the Torah clearly wants there to be agriculture in Eretz Yisrael, so that we may eat of the fruit of the land, satiate ourselves with its bounty, and fulfill the *mitzvot* that depend on the land (see *Iggerot ha-Ra'aya*, vol. I, no. 311; vol. II, no. 334). Second, a country needs to develop its own agriculture in order to survive. Even countries like the United States invest huge amounts of resources on domestic agriculture. This is essential because in exceptional situations, such as a global boycott, a country that has not developed its own agriculture is doomed. Therefore, even were it economically possible to give up entirely on agriculture in Israel, this would be an untenable situation. Moreover, agriculture is used today to gain control over undeveloped land.

this will not solve the problem. We would also need to find money for the workers and all the supporting services. Modern agriculture is based on packaging plants, trucking services, markets and the like. The total abolition of the *heter mechira* would require financial support not only for agriculture but for all the related industries.

Despite the difficulty involved, many religious farmers try to find preferable solutions (such as the *matza menutak* that was started on a large scale in Gush Katif and is now done primarily by *Otzar ha-aretz*, or the *Otzar Bet Din*), in order to limit the *heter mechira* as much as possible, without leading to the collapse of the agricultural industry. We have already pointed out that purchasing from gentiles is not a viable solution, and doing so is not recommended.

THE DIFFERENCE BETWEEN THE FARMER AND THE CONSUMER

Many of the problems connected to the *heter mechira* arise with respect to the farmer, including the problem of *lo techonem* and the prohibition of planting, discussed in earlier chapters. In contrast, the problems facing the consumer are much less serious. If one has reservations about the allowance and questions the propriety of the solution, one must indeed be careful to buy fruits and vegetables that were grown by way of the other solutions. But if one thinks that the sale is valid, only that it would be preferable not to use the *heter* unless absolutely necessary, then once the produce has already grown, it is permitted to purchase it.

The **Chazon Ish** objected to the *heter mechira* (24, 4), but he explicitly ruled that the sale is valid and that *heter mechira* produce is permitted after it was grown (on condition that the sale was executed directly and not through an agent, as explained above):

> Those who sell [their land] themselves, even though they transgress thereby the prohibition of *lo techonem*, nevertheless the sale is valid, and according to the *Sefer ha-Teruma*, [the produce growing there] has no *Shemita* sanctity. And while it is difficult to rely on this, as we wrote above, **nevertheless**

they have on what to rely, and therefore their produce is not forbidden after the fact.

Certain improvements were made (by the *Shemita* Commission of the Chief Rabbinate, headed by Rav Zeev Weitman in the *Shemita* of 5768) in the sale executed in preparation for the previous *Shemita* of 5768 (2007–2008):

1. We saw that the *Chazon Ish* argued that there is a problem if the sale is not registered in Tabu, but in the previous *Shemita* the sale was recognized as valid by Israeli law (as was explained above).
2. The *Chazon Ish* argued that if the sale is executed through an agent, it is invalid, because there is no agent for the commission of a sin. In the previous *Shemita,* however, the sale was executed directly by the Israel Lands Administration. Therefore, after the fact, even the *Chazon Ish* would agree that the produce was not forbidden.
3. Labors that are forbidden by Torah law are performed today by gentiles (as they are in non-*Shemita* years).
4. The *heter mechira* was drawn up as a legal contract, such that many farmers were initially unwilling to sign it, until they showed it to their lawyers or convened a meeting of their kibbutz. In the end, about 95% of the vegetable growers signed, but only after careful study and with full intent.

All this notwithstanding, as we saw in the words of Rav Kook, we must continue searching for solutions that are better than the *heter mechira.* This is particularly important today, for it is altogether possible that the observance of *Shemita* will soon be by Torah law, and the proponents of the *heter mechira* based their allowance on the fact that *Shemita* in our time is by rabbinic decree.

The proper thing to do would be to set up a major *Shemita* fund (as had been proposed already by Rav Kook). This mission should be undertaken already now, so that the entire Jewish people, in Israel and across the world, will be able to finance hothouses and container farming in as many places as possible, and thus allow for the growing of vegetables according to the strictest halachic standards.

(The main problem with the *heter mechira* involves vegetables, because with respect to fruit most of the normal procedures are in any event permitted, at least according to the *Chazon Ish*, and certainly when they are done by gentiles.) This fund can also be used to set up an ***Otzar Bet Din*** according to the strictest standards. This will allow for meticulous observance of *Shemita* and provide Jewish farmers with a living, in keeping with the wishes of **Rav Kook**, as well as **the actions and rulings of the *Chazon Ish*.**

PRACTICAL GUIDE TO PURCHASING FRUITS AND VEGETABLES

<table>
<tr><td rowspan="12">5775 (seventh year)</td><td>Tishrei</td><td rowspan="6">Fruit I</td><td rowspan="4">Vegetables II</td></tr>
<tr><td>Cheshvan</td></tr>
<tr><td>Kislev</td></tr>
<tr><td>Tevet</td></tr>
<tr><td>Shevat</td><td rowspan="9">Vegetables III</td></tr>
<tr><td>Adar I & II</td></tr>
<tr><td>Nisan</td><td rowspan="12">Fruit II</td></tr>
<tr><td>Iyar</td></tr>
<tr><td>Sivan</td></tr>
<tr><td>Tamuz</td></tr>
<tr><td>Av</td></tr>
<tr><td>Elul</td></tr>
<tr><td rowspan="7">5776 (eighth year)</td><td>Tishrei</td></tr>
<tr><td>Cheshvan</td><td rowspan="6"></td></tr>
<tr><td>Kislev</td></tr>
<tr><td>Tevet</td></tr>
<tr><td>Shevat</td></tr>
<tr><td>Adar</td></tr>
<tr><td>Nisan</td><td></td></tr>
</table>

1. **FRUIT I** – FRUIT DURING THE FIRST MONTHS OF THE SEVENTH YEAR.

The fruit that is available at the beginning of the seventh year does not have *Shemita* sanctity (because the fruit began to take form during the sixth year). The fruit may therefore be purchased in the usual manner. It may also be picked in the usual manner, even though it is forbidden to work the land throughout the *Shemita* year, regardless of the type of fruit growing on the trees.

2. **VEGETABLES II** – VEGETABLES DURING THE FIRST FEW WEEKS OF THE SEVENTH YEAR, BASED ON THE *SEFICHIM* TABLE. **FRUIT II** – ALL *SHEMITA* FRUIT.

It is best to purchase *Otzar Bet Din* fruits and vegetables. First of all, this strengthens the observance of *Shemita* without resorting to allowances (and as Rav Kook said, we must rejoice over every farmer who observes *Shemita* like one who finds great treasure). Second, this produce has *Shemita* sanctity according to all opinions, and since it is a great privilege to eat *Shemita* produce (see above, pp. 228–233, 236–239), one should certainly strive to purchase such produce. Obviously, one can also buy sixth-year produce (and much of this produce is put into cold storage), but as we shall see, strictly speaking one can buy such produce from *heter mechira* (even if one does not rely on the *heter mechira*). Let us explain.

***Heter mechira* fruits and vegetables (of type II)** are not subject to the prohibition of *sefichim*, but there is a problem of *shamur* (guarded) and *ne'evad* (worked), for one who does not rely on the *heter mechira*. As we have seen, however, various *Acharonim* write that it is common custom to practice leniency with respect to *shamur* and *ne'evad* (based on the *Aruch ha-Shulchan*, the *Chazon Ish* and Rav Sh. Z. Auerbach). Since *Shemita* observance in our time is only by rabbinic decree and because in cases of uncertainty regarding a rabbinic law we follow the lenient view, there is even more reason to be lenient. In addition, it stands to reason that even those who are stringent about *shamur* and *ne'evad* would be lenient with respect to *heter mechira* produce, as we saw in the words of various *Acharonim* (*Responsa Iggerot Moshe, Orach Chayyim,* no. *186; Kerem Tziyon, 19, 3; Hilchot Shevi'it 9*).

As for the problems arising from trading *Shemita* produce (handing over *Shemita* money to an *am ha-aretz,* measuring *Shemita* produce and the like), strictly speaking there is no problem for those who rely on the *heter mechira* to trade in *heter mechira* produce (*Mishpat Kohen,* no. *76; Ma'adanei Aretz,* nos. *9–10*).[88] It would seem that someone who does not rely on the *heter mechira* has a problem, because he assists the seller in violating the prohibitions of trading and measuring *Shemita* produce, and he hands over *Shemita* money to an *am ha-aretz.* **Rav Sh. Z. Auerbach**, however, is lenient on this issue (*Ma'adanei Aretz,* notes, no. *7;* notes, no. *8, 23*):

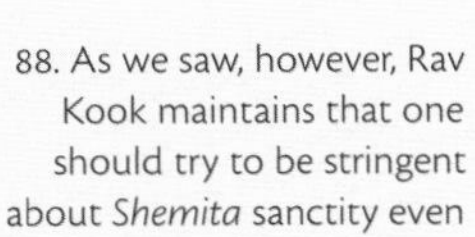

88. As we saw, however, Rav Kook maintains that one should try to be stringent about *Shemita* sanctity even with *heter mechira* produce.

> In my humble opinion, it seems that even those who wish to be stringent and not rely at all on the *heter mechira,* nevertheless, according to the customary practice in keeping with the ruling of the *Acharonim* to be lenient in our time about the prohibitions of *shamur* and *ne'evad,* (even the *Chazon Ish* writes that the produce is not forbidden after the fact, and it is permitted to others), it seems that is permissible even for those who are stringent to purchase *Shemita* fruits and those vegetables that are not subject to the prohibition of *sefichim* from storekeepers who rely on the *heter,* and weigh and measure and trade in *Shemita* produce; and the buyer need not be concerned about the prohibition of *lifnei iver* (setting up a stumbling block) ... and this does not involve *lifnei iver* or assisting transgressors, because even though the other person knows that there are those who forbid the practice, he acts in accordance with those who permit it ... even in a case where the giver thinks that it is certainly forbidden, and that anyone who permits the practice is in error, even so it is permitted ... And even though, owing to the spread of the *heter,* there are many storekeepers who unfortunately know nothing of the laws of *Shemita,* nevertheless if it is clear that if they would know they would certainly follow those who

permit the *heter mechira,* there is no need to be concerned about setting a stumbling block [before the ignorant].

According to Rav Sh. Z. Auerbach, even someone who does not rely on the *heter mechira* may buy fruit (or vegetables at the beginning of the year, before there is a problem of *sefichim*) from a storekeeper who relies on the *heter mechira.* He offers two justifications: first of all, it is permissible to eat such produce, because according to common practice we are lenient about *shamur* and *ne'evad*; second, the purchase itself does not involve handing over *Shemita* money to an *am ha-aretz,* and the like, because the seller himself conducts himself according to the *heter mechira,* and therefore the prohibition of *lifnei iver* does not apply, even if the buyer does not rely on that allowance.[89] Therefore, Rav Sh. Z. Auerbach concludes that even if the seller is unaware of the *heter mechira,* buying from him does not involve setting a stumbling block before him.

Should preference be given to *heter mechira* produce or to produce grown by gentiles? The answer is clear: Preference should be given to *heter mechira* produce, which, according to many authorities, may be eaten even by one who does not rely on the allowance. The alternative strengthens gentile agriculture while weakening Jewish agriculture. Buying produce from a gentile does not require reliance on the *heter mechira,* but it involves *lo techonem* in its most basic sense: strengthening the gentile hold on Eretz Yisrael precisely during the *Shemita* year.

Preference should be given to *heter* mechira produce over imported produce as well, because imports also strike a blow at Jewish agriculture in Israel, and sometimes cause even more damage than does locally grown Arab produce.

3) VEGETABLES III – VEGETABLES SEVERAL WEEKS INTO THE *SHEMITA* YEAR, WHEN THERE IS ALREADY A PROBLEM OF *SEFICHIM*.

Such vegetables (when grown without one of the solutions) are subject to the serious problem of the **prohibition of *sefichim*** (they

89. Rav Sh. Z. Auerbach's ruling assumes that the prohibition of trading in *Shemita* produce pertains only to the seller, and that the buyer is only guilty of *lifnei iver*. This is the view of several other *Acharonim: Kappot Temarim* (*Sukka* 39a, on *Tosafot,* s.v. *ve-letiv*), *Responsa Yeshu'at Moshe* (*Zera'im* 9, 1–2), and others. The *Sefer Ha-makneh* (*Kiddushin* 52a, s.v. *ha-mekadesh*), however, maintains that the prohibition of trade applies to the buyer as well, and according to him, buying *heter mechira* produce remains problematic for someone who does not accept the allowance. Regarding the prohibition of measuring *Shemita* produce as well, Rav Sh. Z. Auerbach's leniency assumes that the prohibition applies only to the seller. See *Mishnat Yosef* (vol. III, p. 126), who writes that this issue depends on the various understandings of the prohibition of measuring *Shemita* produce.

are prohibited out of a concern that perhaps they were planted during the *Shemita* year), and therefore forbidden. The solution of gentile produce is a poor solution, as was explained above, (in addition, Jews who do not succeed in marketing their produce occasionally sell their produce to Arabs so that they should market it). On the other hand, the solution of *heter mechira* is also an inferior solution if the vegetables were planted during the *Shemita* year by Jews (Rav Kook only permitted planting by gentiles). Moreover, if the *heter* is invalid, the vegetables might be subject to the prohibition of *sefichim* (as opposed to Vegetables II, which even without the *heter mechira* are at worst *shamur* and *ne'evad* but not forbidden to eat).[90] In practice, since both solutions are problematic, one should try very hard to buy hothouse vegetables grown in containers. One should purchase such vegetables even if it involves extra effort and additional expense, and even if it involves making do with vegetables of lesser quality and doing without certain types of vegetables. The effort to observe *Shemita* in a meticulous manner must be made not only by farmers but by consumers as well. If hothouse vegetables grown in containers are not available, one should purchase vegetables grown in the Southern Arava (with the *heter mechira*) which are not subject to the prohibition of *sefichim.*

The reality of the current *Shemita* year (5775, 2014-2015), however, is that all planting (and other labors forbidden by Torah law) of *heter mechira* produce is done by gentiles (as will be explained below). Thus, the produce is clearly permitted even during the period of the prohibition of *sefichim*, and so it is clearly preferable to eat such produce rather than gentile produce.

In any event, Arab produce should not be purchased, unless such produce is bought from Arabs during ordinary years as well.[91]

As for imported produce, if the alternative is *heter mechira* produce planted by a Jew, preference should be given to the imported produce, because Rav Kook (and most proponents of the *heter*) insisted that the planting of fields subject to the *heter mechira* must be done by gentiles.[92] If the *heter mechira* produce was planted by a gentile (which is generally the case today), preference should be

90. It should be noted that regarding the prohibition of *sefichim*, *Chazal* created what appears to be an absurd situation: The Torah prohibition of working the land during the *Shemita* year is more lenient than the rabbinic decree regarding *sefichim*, and therefore a fruit that was planted in violation of the law during the *Shemita* year itself is preferable to a vegetable that grew on its own during that year.

91 The guiding rule is that a person must take care during the *Shemita* year not to increase the total amount of vegetables that are purchased from gentiles. **Practically speaking: During the previous *Shemita* year of 5761, most of the cucumbers, zucchini, and certain other vegetables were gentile produce.** In recent years, Arab production has declined, and the majority of vegetable production is now in Jewish hands. Nevertheless, almost half of the cucumbers, zucchini and certain other vegetables are Arab grown (even in ordinary years), and this can effect our purchases during the *Shemita* year as well.

92. See above, the disagreement whether or not the prohibition of *sefichim* applies to produce planted by a Jew in a field belonging to a gentile.

given to *heter mechira* produce over imported produce, except for those vegetables that are generally imported during regular years.[93]

Preference should generally be given to *heter mechira* produce because **there are various factors that join together in favor of leniency**: Even according to those who oppose the *heter mechira*, the sale is effective once it has been done; the prohibition of *sefichim* is by rabbinic decree; the observance of *Shemita* in our time is by rabbinic decree; and as stated, agricultural work is generally performed today

93. The Consumer's Guide to *Shemita* published by Machon ha-Torah ve-ha-Aretz suggests that one buy vegetables that were planted in containers (in addition to *heter mechira*). That is to say, the seeds were not planted in the ground, but in soil-filled containers. Such vegetables are not subject to the prohibition of *sefichim*. It should be noted that certain vegetables are planted in this manner in ordinary years as well: tomatoes, celery, peppers, watermelon, eggplant and others.

RAV SH. Z. AUERBACH

ספר

מעדני ארץ

כולל באורים חדושים וחקרי הלכות בעניני שביעית

ונלוה אליו קונטרס לאפרושי מאיסורא
בענין הפרשת תרומות ומעשרות

חובר בס"ד מאת
שלמה זלמן אויערבאך
בהרב הגאון המפורסם מוהר"ר חיים יהודא ליב זצ"ל

יצא לאור על ידי ישיבת מדרש בני ציון
ירושלם — תשי"ד — ערב שנת השמיטה

נדפס מחדש על ידי
בית מדרש הלכה
מוריה
ירושלים, תשנ"ב

Rav Shlomo Zalman Auerbach was born in 5670 (1910) in Jerusalem. His father was a leading Kabbalist. Rav Sh. Z. Auerbach was one of the leading *poskim* of our generation. At age 22 he published his first work on the laws of electricity on Shabbat – *Me'orei Esh*. In this work, as in all his works, he displays tremendous Torah knowledge, as well as an impressive understanding of science and technology. Rav Sh. Z. Auerbach was not only a genius in Torah but also a giant in character and humility. He was never associated with any political groups and was accepted by all.

One can sense his tremendous human sensitivity along with his analytic power and vast knowledge from reading his *responsa*. For example, he rules that one may give a worker a drink in one's house, even if he will not recite a blessing (despite a ruling of the Rema to the contrary), so as to avoid causing the worker to commit the graver sin of hating religion and fellow Jews.

His rulings have been published in Responsa *Minchat Shlomo*, in his works titled *Ma'adanei Aretz*, in his comments on *Shemirat Shabbat Ke-hilchatah*, in many articles he wrote and in numerous quotes on his words in contemporary halachic works. He passed away in 5755 (1995).

by gentiles, and therefore produce that is certified as *heter mechira* can be eaten. In light of this, while it may be preferable to buy *Otzar Bet Din* produce or hothouse produce grown in containers, it is permitted to eat *heter mechira* produce (even vegetables), and this is clearly preferable to buying gentile produce, which negatively impacts Jewish agriculture in Israel.[94]

Of course one who chooses to buy *heter mechira* produce, especially vegetables, must make sure that the store is certified as selling *heter mechira* produce.[95]

If a person prefers not to eat *heter mechira* vegetables, but also decides that buying gentile produce is not an acceptable solution, one can limit produce consumption during the *Shemita* year to Jewish vegetables grown in meticulous observance of the *Shemita* laws. Even if a person is generally accustomed to a wide variety of vegetables, for a limited period of time it is possible to make do with the available *Otzar Bet Din* or hothouse vegetables, and not buy other vegetables.

Our Sages (*Eicha Rabba, petichta 17*) tell of the terrible difficulties that the Jewish people had during the *Shemita* year, and how they ate no vegetables, but only thorns:

> Rabbi Abahu opened [his sermon on Eicha]: "They who sit in the gate talk of me" (*Tehilim 69:13*) – this refers to the nations of the world who sit in theaters and circuses ... Since they sit and eat and drink and get drunk, they sit and talk of me and mock me ... they bring a camel on stage with its covers on, and they say to each other: Why is this one grieving? And they say: **Those Jews observe the sabbatical year, and they have no vegetables, and they ate his thorns,** and he grieves over them.

This is not suggesting that during the *Shemita* year one restrict one's intake to thorns. Our eating habits, however, are very different from those of the past, and we are accustomed today to a wide variety of vegetables. It is, therefore, possible to eat a generous amount of a particular vegetable during a certain period of time, and

94. See *Ma'adanei Aretz* (*Shevi'it*, notes no. 7), who writes that if a person asked a rabbi about a question of rabbinic law and the rabbi issued a stringent ruling, and then that person consulted with a second rabbi who issued a more lenient ruling – then if that person goes back to the first rabbi, and reports to him about what happened, the first rabbi must tell the person that he may practice leniency. The reason for this is that the second rabbi issued a lenient ruling, and the rule is that in cases of uncertainty regarding a rabbinic law, we follow leniency. As noted above, however, efforts should be made not to rely on the ***heter** mechira* with respect to vegetables that are subject to the prohibition of *sefichim*.

95. Technological advances have made it easier to observe *Shemita*. For example, even before the prior *Shemita* year, tomato plants have been developed that can survive for a year and a half. This advance makes it unnecessary to plant tomatoes during the *Shemita* year, and makes it possible for certain *Otzar Bet Din* vegetables to be available the entire year.

eat less of other kinds, in accordance with the availability of Jewish produce grown according to the most meticulous standards. One who conducts himself in this manner and during the *Shemita* year buys primarily Jewish vegetables, can buy a small amount of gentile vegetables, such that he buys at least as much, if not more, Jewish produce during the *Shemita* year as he buys during ordinary years.

We must, of course, try to ensure that there is an ample supply of a wide variety of vegetables grown by Jews according to meticulous halachic standards. As stated earlier, this is more possible today than in the past, but in order to realize this goal, the assistance of world Jewry is necessary (the organization of such a project must begin several years before *Shemita*, and it would be a good idea to start already now in preparation for the next *Shemita*).

SUMMARY – BUYING FRUITS AND VEGETABLES DURING THE *SHEMITA* YEAR

Vegetables: During the first few months of the *Shemita* year (when the problem of *sefichim* does not yet apply), one may purchase *heter mechira* produce, and those who are more stringent should purchase *Otzar Bet Din* produce and the like. After the first few months (when there is already concern about *sefichim*), efforts should be made to use one of the preferred solutions, such as hothouse vegetables grown in containers. If such a solution does not exist, preference should be given to *heter mechira* produce (even vegetables) over gentile produce.

Fruit: At the beginning of the year, fruit may be purchased and then treated in the usual manner. After several months, one may purchase *heter mechira* produce, though it is preferable to purchase *Otzar Bet Din* produce.

FLOWERS DURING *SHEMITA*

It is preferable that all flowers purchased during the *Shemita* year have *kashrut* certification.

Annuals: Annuals, from the time that there is concern that they may have been planted during the *Shemita* year (check the timetables), should be purchased with *kashrut* certification[96] (preferably, one should purchase flowers raised in hothouses, and when those are unavailable, flowers from fields sold through the *heter mechira*).

Perennials: Perennials may be purchased in the usual manner (because there is no concern that they were planted during the *Shemita* year, and thus they are not subject to the prohibition of *sefichim*). It is, however, preferable, that they be purchased with *kashrut* certification (hothouse flowers, or *heter mechira*).

We practice leniency regarding perennial flowers because since there is no risk that these flowers were planted during the *Shemita* year, the only problems are *shamur* and *ne'evad*, and as we have seen above, there is considerable room for leniency regarding *shamur* and *ne'evad* in fields that were sold. In addition, as we saw above (p. 144), the law of *shamur* derives from *Shemita* sanctity, and therefore, flowers that do not have *Shemita* sanctity may be harvested in the usual manner and there is no need to declare them ownerless.

Flowers that lack a scent do not have *Shemita* sanctity. According to **Rav Sh. Z. Auerbach**, the same applies to flowers that have a scent but are grown for ornamental purposes (see p. 258) rather than for their scent.

For more information about flowers, see p. 255 and p. 316.

96. There might be room for leniency even with respect to annuals since according to some authorities flowers are not subject to the prohibition of *sefichim*. Furthermore, even among those who maintain such a prohibition, some say that the prohibition relates only to eating but not to other forms of benefit.

SUMMARY[97]

97. A convenient summary is also found in the abridged laws of *Shemita* appearing at the beginning of this volume, as well as on the *Shemita* magnet that comes with this book.

FRUIT: At the beginning of the year, fruits may be purchased and handled in the usual manner (based on the timetables for each fruit). Beginning in the second half of the year, fruits require special *kashrut* certification with respect to *Shemita*. Strictly speaking, one may buy *heter mechira* produce, but preference should be given to *Otzar Bet Din* produce or sixth-year produce (and when that is no longer available, produce from the Southern Arava).

VEGETABLES: At the beginning of the year (as long as there is no problem of *sefichim*, based on the tables which list the date for each type of vegetable), the order of priority is the same as that regarding fruit (*Otzar Bet Din*, frozen vegetables or vegetables in cold storage, container vegetables, Southern Arava and *heter mechira*).

Later in the year (when there is a problem of *sefichim*), efforts should be made to purchase *Otzar Bet Din*, frozen, cold storage, container, or Southern Arava vegetables (farms raising vegetables in the Southern Arava vegetables should also make use of the *heter mechira*). If none of these solutions are possible (as stated above, it is desirable to invest effort and money in order to make use of these solutions), *heter mechira* vegetables (where the planting was done by a gentile, which is the presumed situation regarding *heter mechira* produce during the current *Shemita* of 5775) are preferable to imported vegetables or locally-grown gentile produce.

Alternatively, one can make slight changes in one's eating habits, and restrict one's consumption of vegetables to the available Jewish vegetables grown in accordance with the more meticulous standards. In such a case, one may be lenient and purchase a small amount of gentile produce, such that one will eat at least as much Jewish produce as he does in ordinary years.

FLOWERS: Annuals: It is preferable to buy flowers grown in detached containers, or the like, but when they are unavailable, one may buy *heter mechira* flowers.

Perennials (or annuals until the date listed in the tables) may be purchased in the usual manner, but it is preferable that they be purchased with special *kashrut* certification (at least *heter mechira*).

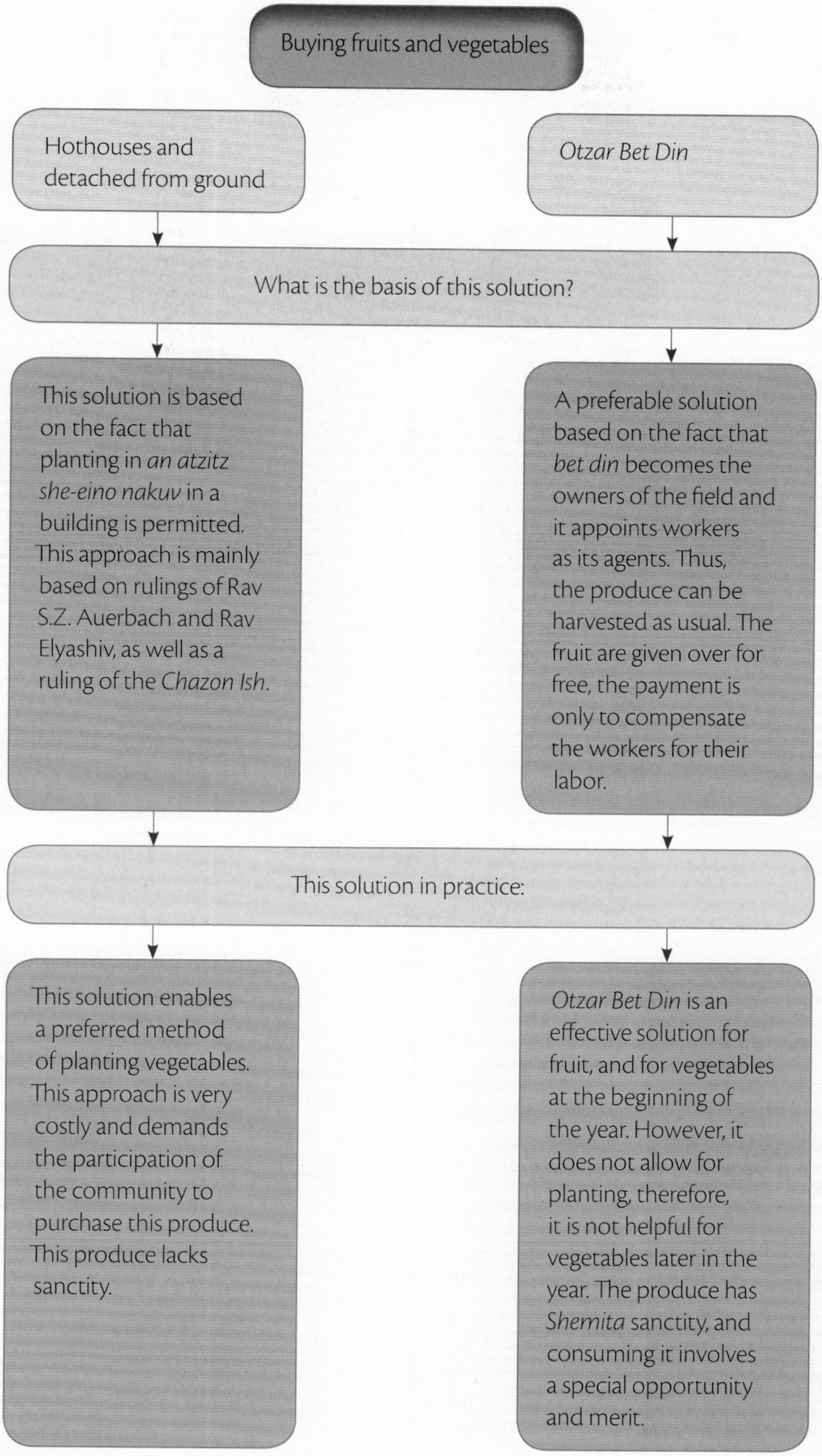

Buying fruits and vegetables

Hothouses and detached from ground

Otzar Bet Din

What is the basis of this solution?

Hothouses and detached from ground: This solution is based on the fact that planting in *an atzitz she-eino nakuv* in a building is permitted. This approach is mainly based on rulings of Rav S.Z. Auerbach and Rav Elyashiv, as well as a ruling of the *Chazon Ish*.

***Otzar Bet Din*:** A preferable solution based on the fact that *bet din* becomes the owners of the field and it appoints workers as its agents. Thus, the produce can be harvested as usual. The fruit are given over for free, the payment is only to compensate the workers for their labor.

This solution in practice:

Hothouses and detached from ground: This solution enables a preferred method of planting vegetables. This approach is very costly and demands the participation of the community to purchase this produce. This produce lacks sanctity.

***Otzar Bet Din*:** *Otzar Bet Din* is an effective solution for fruit, and for vegetables at the beginning of the year. However, it does not allow for planting, therefore, it is not helpful for vegetables later in the year. The produce has *Shemita* sanctity, and consuming it involves a special opportunity and merit.

Heter Mechira

What is the basis of this solution?

This approach is based on the (temporary) sale of the land to a gentile, which allows for the performance of rabbinic labors by Jews and Torah labors by gentiles.

This solution in practice:

This approach is a matter of debate, and even those who permit it point out that one should seek out other, preferable approaches. Thus, *otzar bet din* and hothouse produce are preferable. However, when those are not available, one may purchase fruit from the *heter mechira* (even for those who do not rely on the *heter*, as there is no prohibition involved in the planting; the same goes for vegetables at the beginning of the year). Regarding vegetables later in the year: if the vegetables were planted by a gentile (as Rav Kook requires), it seems that if there is no preferable alternative, this should be preferred to imported produce (unless this is produce that generally comes from gentile fields in all years).

Other Alternatives

Sixth year produce: there is no *Shemita* sanctity and this should be a first choice.
Southern Arava (with *heter mechira*): the prohibition of *sefichim* does not apply to this region, thus one may purchase this produce as a first choice.
Imported vegetables: if they are imported in all years, one may purchase them during *Shemita* as well, but produce imported especially for *Shemita* harms the agriculture here in Israel. It is therefore preferable to buy from *otzar bet din*, hothouses, and *heter mechira* planted by gentiles (based on Rav Kook), before buying imported vegetables.
Gentile produce from Israel: This produce should not be purchased specially during *Shemita* (if this produce is purchased during all years, it may be purchased during *Shemita* as well).

SHEMITAT KESAFIM – RELEASE OF DEBTS

SHEMITAT KESAFIM – RELEASE OF DEBTS

In *Parashat Re'eh* (*Devarim* 15), the Torah commands that debts must be released during the seventh year. The verses speak of three different elements to this *mitzva*:

1. At the end of every seven years you shall make a release (*shemita*).
2. And this is the manner of the *shemita*: every creditor that lends anything to his neighbor shall release it; he shall not demand it of his neighbor, or of his brother; because he has proclaimed a *shemita* to the Lord.
3. You may demand it from a gentile: but that which is yours, and now with your brother your hand shall release ...
9. Beware lest there be an unworthy thought in you heart, saying, the seventh year, the year of *shemita* is at hand; and your eye become evil against your poor brother, and you give him nothing; and he will cry to the Lord against you; and it shall be reckoned to you as sin.
10. You shall surely give him, and your heart shall not be grieved when you give to him: because on account of this the Lord your God shall bless you in all your works, and in all that to which you put your hand.

Mitzva 1: A **positive *mitzva*,** to release all debts: "Every creditor that lends anything to his neighbor shall release it."

Mitzva 2: A **negative *mitzva*,** not to demand the repayment of debts: "He shall not demand it of his neighbor, or of his brother."

Mitzva 3: A **negative *mitzva*,** not to refrain from lending money before the *shemita* year, for fear that the debt will be released: "Beware lest there be an unworthy thought ...."

THE FORCE OF THE OBLIGATION TODAY

The Gemara in ***Gittin* 36a** records the view of the Sages who maintain that even today the *mitzva* of *shemitat kesafim* is in force by Torah law. Later in the passage, the Gemara cites the position of **Rabbi Yehuda HaNasi**:

> Rabbi [Yehuda HaNasi] says: It is written: "And this is the manner of the *shemita*; every creditor shall release (*shamot*)." The text indicates here two kinds of *shemita* or release, one the release of land (*shemita* of the land) and the other the release of money (*shemitat kesafim*). When the release of land is in effect, the release of money is to be operative, and when the release of land is not in effect, the release of money is not to be operative.

Rashi understands this to mean that when the *shemita* of land is in force the *shemita* of money is similarly in force, and therefore, in our time, when the *shemita* of land is only by rabbinic decree, the *shemita* of money is also only by rabbinic decree. The ***Tosafot***, on the other hand, understand Rabbi Yehuda HaNasi's position differently: When the *yovel* year is in force ("when the release of land is in effect"),[1] then *shemita* is also in force with respect to both the land and money. However, when the *yovel* year is not in force, *shemita* is not in force, neither with respect to the land nor with respect to money.

The **Ra'avad** (objections to Rif, ad loc.) understands the gemara like the ***Tosafot***. He therefore concludes that since *yovel* is not in force today, even by rabbinic decree, the same is true regarding *shemita* – with respect to both land and money. Though the gemara mentions Amoraim who observed *shemitat kesafim*, the **Ra'avad** understands that they did so merely as an act of piety. This is also the opinion of **Rav Zerachya Halevi,** author of the ***Ba'al Ha-ma'or*** (cited by the *Terumot, sha'ar 45*) and the **Meiri** (*Magen Avot*, no. 15). The ***Ittur*** (part *1*, s.v. *pruzbol*), on the other hand, understands that *shemitat kesafim* in our time is in effect by **Torah law**, and this is also the position of the **Ramban**[2] (*Sefer ha-Zechut, Gittin 37*).

Most *Rishonim* maintain that *shemitat kesafim* is in force today only by rabbinic decree (implication of Rashi, *Gittin* 36a; Rabbenu

1. Because the *yovel* year demands a release of land but not of money.

2. According to his view, *shemita* of the land is also by Torah law even in our time (see the discussion of the issue of *shemita* in our time in the chapter that discusses the *heter mechira*). In his novellae to *Makkot* 3b, however, **Ramban** writes that *shemitat kesafim* in our time is only by rabbinic decree.

Tam cited by the Rosh, *Gittin 4:13*; Rashba, Ritva, and *Nimukei Yosef*, *Gittin* 36b; the Rambam, *Hilchot Shemita ve-Yovel* 9:2).

Outside Eretz Yisrael: It is generally accepted that the *mitzva* of *shemitat kesafim* applies even outside of Eretz Yisrael, inasmuch as it is a personal obligation that is not dependent on the land (see ***Kiddushin* 38b**; *Shulchan Aruch, Choshen Mishpat 67:1*).

HUMAN RELEASE OR "ROYAL DISPENSATION"

If the borrower wishes to repay a debt after the *shemita* year, the lender should say to him: "I remit it," or "I allow *shemita* to cancel it" (***Shevi'it*** *10:8-9*; **Rambam**, *Hilchot Shemita ve-Yovel 9:28*). If the borrower then says: "Please accept it anyway" – the lender may accept the money. Moreover, ***Chazal*** say (*Shevi'it 10:8–9*) that the Sages are pleased with one who repays a debt that had been released by the *shemita* year:

> If a man repays money that he owes in the *shemita* year, the other should say to him: "I remit it." If the debtor then says: "All the same take it", he may take it from him...
>
> Regarding one who repays a debt in the seventh year, the Sages are pleased with him...

What is the law if the lender fails to say: "I remit it"? The ***Minchat Chinuch*** (*mitzva 477*) discusses the issue and argues that the answer to this question is subject to a dispute between the ***Yere'im*** and the ***Or Zaru'a***. The ***Yere'im*** (*mitzva 164* [*278*]) maintains that if the lender does not say, "I remit it," the debt is not released.[3] In such a case, the lender violates a negative *mitzva* and the court may take measures to force him to release the debt:

> After the *shemita* year, a debtor may only withhold repayment of his debt with the agreement of his creditor, for as long as the creditor does not release the debt, the debtor is obligated to repay it. But the debtor can take the creditor to court, demanding that he release his debt... As we have learned at the end of *Shevi'it* (*10:8*), as is brought in *Gittin*

3. According to the *Yere'im*, the debt still exists after *shemita*, though there is a *mitzva* to release it. This approach sheds light on an otherwise difficult passage in the ***Yerushalmi*** (*Shevi'it 10:3*) which rules that the creditor must say, "I have released the debt," but at the same time he may stretch out his hand and thus allude that he would like to receive payment: "One who repays a debt during the *shemita* year, and he says to him, 'I have released it,' the Sages are pleased with him. Rav Huna says: With lax lips and his right hand outstretched to receive." The logic underlying this position is that fundamentally the debt exists, and that if the debtor has money, he truly must repay what he owes, only that the creditor has no right to demand it, because in fact everything belongs to God.
This idea is also found in the *Bavli*, in *Gittin 37b*. There Rabba says that even after the creditor says, "I remit it," he can still apply pressure to the debtor until he says "All the same, take it" (see Rashi, s.v. *ve-tali leh*). Similarly, the continuation of that Gemara rules that the creditor may pressure the debtor until the latter agrees to give the former the money as a present. This again implies that the debt still exists, but that the creditor has no right to demand it. However, according to the understanding that we shall suggest below, every loan has an element of a grant.

37b: "If a man repays money which he owes in the *shemita* year, the latter should say to the former, 'I remit it.' ... But if the creditor does not want to say, 'I remit it,' the court coerces him... [for] regarding refusal to fulfill] a positive *mitzva*... the rule is that he may be whipped 'until his soul departs.'"

The ***Minchat Chinuch*** notes, however, that most *Rishonim* maintain that the debt is released even if the creditor fails to say, 'I remit it.' Thus, for example, the ***Or Zaru'a*** (*Avoda Zara*, no. *108*) quotes, and then rejects, the view of the *Yere'im*:[4]

> I do not accept what the Yere'im writes to the effect that a debtor may only withhold repayment of his debt if the creditor says "I remit it." Rather, even if the creditor sues him in court to pay, and insists, "I do not remit it," the debtor need not be concerned with what he says, for the Torah released the debt...
>
> When must the creditor say, "I remit it?" Only when the debtor brings him the money, in which case the creditor must fulfill the *mitzva* and say, "I remit it..."

Accordingly, since the debt is automatically released even against the creditor's will, if the creditor takes the money from the debtor without telling him that the debt is canceled, he violates the prohibition of theft.[5]

Another practical ramification to this question: If the creditor refuses to release the debt and seizes assets belonging to the debtor, and then dies – according to most *Rishonim*, the debtor may collect from the heirs, as in the case of theft. According to the ***Yere'im***, he cannot collect from them, because the money is theirs by right, and their father's *mitzva* to remit the debt does not apply to them (it would, of course, be appropriate for them to return the money).[6]

It turns out then that according to the ***Yere'im***, the Torah commands **a person to release any money that is owed him**, whereas according to **most *Rishonim*, debts are automatically released**.

On the one hand, there is a certain logic in requiring the person himself to remit the debt (as argued by the ***Yere'im***). The Torah

4. ***Responsa ha-Rashba*** (*I*, no. *775*) also writes that the release of debts is a "royal dispensation" (further study, however, is required to determine the precise meaning of his words).

5. Though the Mishna states that the creditor must say, "I remit the debt," the *Or Zaru'a* explains that this does not mean that the creditor must say that he remits the debt in order for it to be released. The creditor's words do not bring about a change in the halachic status of the debt, but are, rather, a reflection of that status. That is to say, **if the debtor wishes to repay the money,** the creditor should not accept it, but rather he should say that the debt is canceled.

6. Yet another practical difference: What is the law in a case of uncertainty regarding *shemitat kesafim*, and especially today when *shemita* observance is only by rabbinic decree. It would appear that according to most *Rishonim*, **the money should remain in the hands of the debtor**, in keeping with the rule that **the burden of proof falls upon the plaintiff**. According to the ***Yere'im***, however, the money should be returned to the creditor, as the **creditor has presumed possession, inasmuch as the money certainly belongs to him**; the uncertainty relates merely to the **observance of the *mitzva***, and in a case of uncertainty regarding a

rabbinic law we practice leniency. (This is raised by the *Sha'ar ha-Mishpat*, 67, no. 1. The other *Rishonim* might accept his conclusion, because we rule leniently regarding the uncertainties raised in the Gemara, such as a ten-year loan, because *shemita* in our time is only by rabbinic decree, and it is possible that since the whole law of *shemitat kesafim* is by rabbinic decree, it does not apply in cases of uncertainty.)

teaches individuals that they should come **on their own** and release their debts. Most *Rishonim*, however, appear to have understood that **the foundation of *shemita* is not that a person should forego money that is owed him.** The underlying principle of *shemita* is that **the money does not belong to the creditor!** There is no need for the creditor to cancel the debt. Everything belongs to God, and therefore the debt is automatically cancelled!

WHEN IS THE DEBT RELEASED?

The Torah states (*Devarim* 15:1): "**At the end** of every seven years you shall make a release." A similar verse relates to the *mitzva* of ***hakhel***: "At the end of every seven years, in the time of the year of release, during the holiday of *Sukkot*" (*Devarim 31:10*). Given that *hakhel* is held following the conclusion of the *shemita* year, the **Gemara** in ***Arachin* 28b** infers from this similar expression that the debts are cancelled at the end of the *shemita* year. This is the understanding of **Rashi** (ad loc.) and the **Rambam** (*Hilchot Shemita ve-Yovel 9:4*).

The **Rosh** (*Gittin 4:18, 20*) cites the **Tosefta** (*Shevi'it 8*) which implies that the *shemita* year cancels debts at the **beginning** of the year: "When is the *pruzbol* written? On the eve of *Rosh ha-Shana* of the *shemita* year." The **Rosh** writes that while the debts are only cancelled at the end of the year, the negative *mitzva* of "he shall not exact it" takes effect already at the beginning of the year. In other words, from the very beginning of the year, it is forbidden to demand payment of money, but if the debtor offers to repay his debt, the creditor is not required to say, "I remit it."

Other *Rishonim* disagree with the **Rosh** and explain the Gemara according to its plain sense.[7] In practice, the ***Shulchan Aruch*** (*Choshen Mishpat 67:30*) rules that the *shemita* year cancels debts at the end of the year. It is, therefore, permissible to collect debts during the *shemita* year, even for loans that were given during the *shemita* year, but it is forbidden to collect debts after the *shemita* year, whether the money was lent during the *shemita* year or beforehand. There are those who take the **Rosh's** position into consideration, and draw up a *pruzbol* not only at the end of the *shemita* year, but

7. According to the Responsa attributed to the Ramban (no. 98), the reading in the *Tosefta* is "the day before *Rosh ha-Shana* of the eighth year." In his commentary to the Torah, the Ibn Ezra explains, similarly to the *Rosh*, that the verse is referring to the beginning of the seventh year.

before the *shemita* year as well (***Shulchan Aruch ha-Rav, Choshen Mishpat, Halva'a* 36**).[8]

Even those who draw up a *pruzbol* before the beginning of the *shemita* year must draw up another *pruzbol* prior to the end of the *shemita* year to cover the debts that were created during the *shemita* year itself after the writing of the first *pruzbol*. In light of this, the *pruzbol* should be drawn up **at the end of the month of Elul of the *shemita* year** (and those who want to take the Rosh's view into account should also draw up a *pruzbol* at the end of Elul of the sixth year).

8. My revered teacher, HaRav Aharon Lichtenstein, also adopts this stringency. See, however, ***Responsa Chatam Sofer*** (*Choshen Mishpat*, no. 50), who writes that one of his disciples wished to practice stringency, and the *Chatam Sofer* told him that this was not the custom of his teacher Rav Nathan Adler.

THE DEBTS THAT ARE RELEASED

A ten-year loan:

The Gemara in ***Makkot* 3b** records a disagreement as to whether *shemita* cancels a **ten-year loan.**

The **Rosh** cites the **Riva** who rules that *shemita* does indeed release a debt of this kind. ***Tosafot*** (ad loc.), however, cite **Rabbenu Tam** who rules that a ten-year loan is not cancelled by the *shemita* year. This latter position is also the ruling of the **Rambam** (*Hilchot Shemita ve-Yovel 9:9*), the **Ramban**, the **Ritva** (*Makkot 3b*) and the ***Shulchan Aruch*** (*Choshen Mishpat 67:10*):

> If someone lends money to another person and sets the time of repayment at ten years, (or a bit more or less than ten years), the *shemita* year that falls out during that period does not cancel the debt, because "he shall not exact it" does not apply at the time of *shemita*.

The rationale for this ruling, cited above, is explained by the Gemara. The Torah says, "He shall not exact it," that is to say, at the end of the *shemita* year (the 29th of Elul) it is forbidden **to demand repayment of the money owed to him.** A debt that can only be collected at the end of ten years is, in any case, not subject to collection on the 29th of Elul, as collection can never be demanded before the completion of the term of the loan. Since the prohibition of "He shall not exact it" does not apply, the positive *mitzva* of *shemitat kesafim* also does not apply.

From here we learn an important rule: Any debt **that is not subject to collection at the end of the *shemita* year is not cancelled by the *shemita* year.** Accordingly, if someone lends money to another person, and stipulates with the borrower that he will repay the debt **on a particular date after the *shemita* year**, the debt is not cancelled and the borrower is obligated to repay the money that he owes.

Bank accounts: We shall discuss the various aspects of bank accounts below. Here let us point out one ramification of the rule presented above. Term deposits that will reach maturity in a year or two years or even in a few months, their due date arriving only **after** the end of the *shemita* year, are treated like a ten-year loan, since they are not subject to collection at the end of the *shemita* year.

While it may be possible to withdraw the money prematurely, if a person comes to withdraw his money at the end of the *shemita* year, it will still take several days before he can collect the money. Thus, he cannot collect the money at the end of the *shemita* year, and so the debt is not cancelled (unless he informs the bank of his desire to withdraw his funds several days earlier).

Another argument to support this claim: On the day before *Rosh ha-Shana*, **banks are closed** in Israel, and so a person is unable to collect the money that is owed him. This argument, however, appears to be insufficient, because the inability to collect is an external **technical** matter – merely because the bank is closed – and not an essential aspect of the debt.

Shop debts:
The **Mishna** in ***Shevi'it*** (*10:1*) states:

> Shop debt is not subject to the law of *shemita*, but if he turned it into a loan, it is subject to the law of release.

Why is shop debt (debt for purchased merchandise) not subject to the law of release during the *shemita* year? The plain sense of the

Mishna suggests that **only a loan is subject to *shemitat kesafim*, but other types of debt are not.** Accordingly, "if he turned it into a loan," that is to say, if the shopkeeper fixed a time for payment of the debt (**Rosh**, *Gittin* chap. 4; **Rema**, *Choshen Mishpat 67:14*), the debt is regarded as a loan and subject to the law of *shemita*. According to the **Mordechai** (cited by the Rema, ibid.), even if the shopkeeper merely summed up the debt, the debt is considered to be a loan and is subject to the law of *shemita*.

This principle regarding shop debt is explained in the ***Sifrei*** (*Devarim, 112*):

> "Every creditor that lends anything to his neighbor shall release it" – You might say that the law of *shemita* even applies to stolen property or to a deposit. Therefore the verse states: "Every **creditor** that lends anything"... You might say that the law of *shemita* even applies to a workman's wages and shop debt. Therefore the verse states: "that **lends** anything to his neighbor"...

We see that only a debt stemming **from a loan** is subject to the law of *shemita*. Other debts are not subject to the law of *shemita*, unless the debtor turned them into loans. This is also the implication of the **Rambam** in his commentary to the (aforementioned) Mishna. This approach is also suggested by the ***Bach*** (*Choshen Mishpat 67, 19*), the ***Levush*** (*67, 14*), the ***Tumim*** (*67, 15*), and the ***Pe'at ha-Shulchan*** (*29:30*). According to these authorities, this is also the position of the *Shulchan Aruch* (*Choshen Mishpat 67:4*).[9]

The ***Kesef Mishneh*** (*Hilchot Shemita ve-Yovel* 9:11; *Bet Yosef, Choshen Mishpat* 67, 19) writes, however, that all debts are subject to the law of *shemita*, whether they originated from a loan or from a purchase. Why, then, is shop debt not subject to the law of *shemita*? The ***Bet Yosef*** explains that the shop debt that the Mishna refers to is a debt that is ordinarily paid only after a year or two; since the debt will not become due during the *shemita* year, it is not subject to the laws of *shemita*.[10] The ***Sema*** (67, no. 26) and ***Shulchan Aruch ha-Rav*** (*Halva'a*, 39) agree with the ***Bet Yosef*** (this is also the position of the ***Tosafot Yom Tov***, *Shevi'it* 10:2).

9. The ***Shulchan Aruch*** writes that *shemita* only releases loans. He might, however, have meant to say that *shemita* does not release a deposit, but that any debt, even if not generated by a loan, is released. We will see below that, according to the ***Bet Yosef***, *shemita* does, in fact, release all debts, which supports the alternative understanding of the position of the *Shulchan Aruch* and not the reading of the *Pe'at ha-Shulchan*.

10. In fact, even if the payment generally takes place in a shorter timeframe, as long as there is an extended period for payment it is as if the shopkeeper set a time after the *shemita* year, and the debt is not canceled. However, in places where the time for payment is short and defined, the debt is indeed subject to the laws of *shemita*.

What is the rationale underlying the position that only a loan is subject to the laws of *shemita*, while other types of debt are not?

Before answering this question, let us first raise two additional questions regarding loans, to help arrive at a fuller understanding of the difference between loans and other types of debt:

1. Why does the prohibition of charging interest apply only to a loan?[11]
2. The Gemara discusses the question of whether one is obligated to repay a loan, or whether doing so is merely a positive commandment – "Repaying one's debtor is a *mitzva*." In all other cases of debt, a person is clearly obligated to pay whatever he owes. Why is it only in the case of a loan that the law is different?

11. In a case of purchases as well, if interest is charged for deferring payment after the due date has arrived, the debt is regarded as a loan. On the other hand, it is permitted to sell an article at an inflated price and set the date of payment some time after the date of purchase.

These two questions lead us to one principle. The Torah ordains that a loan is, essentially, a grant. On the one hand, the Torah allows a person to earn money in accordance with his abilities, but on the other hand, it establishes that **one must lend money to another person when that other person is in need**. The Torah teaches that **this loan should be treated as a grant, because the money does not really belong to the lender in the first place, rather it belongs to God.**

This idea is expressed in the Gemara's statement that "a loan is given to be spent." When a person extends a loan, the lender can no longer use the money to betroth a woman because the money was given to the borrower "to spend," as a grant, and it no longer belongs to the lender. Accordingly, the lender has no rights **at this time** to the money, because it is the property of the borrower. Therefore, if the lender charges interest, he is guilty of theft.[12]

12. I heard this from my revered father-in-law, Rav E. Blumenzweig.

We can now understand why the *shemita* year only releases loans (according to those who maintain this position, as explained above). When a person owes money because of a purchase, there is no reason that such a debt should be canceled. In the case of a loan, however, the borrower received a grant. The Torah does command the borrower to return the grant, but not when the *shemita* year falls out in the meantime.[13]

13. Indeed, without the Torah's restrictions on the lender, the natural relationship between borrower and lender is characterized by the verse, "the borrower is servant to the lender" (*Mishlei* 22:7). The lender would become the borrower's master. The Torah comes, however, and reverses the relationship: not only is the lender not the master, **but he is legally and morally obligated to grant the loan**.

This principle is stated explicitly by the ***Or ha-Chayim*** (*Shemot 22:24*):

> "If you lend money" – if you have more money than you need, to the point that you can even lend to others, know that the portion of "the poor is with you" – you are holding the portion of the poor person.

According to the common understanding, the default is that a person's property belongs to him, though there may be certain reasons why he might be obligated to hand some of it over to another person. According to what we have suggested here, the reverse is true. A person's property does not really belong to him – "You are holding the portion of the poor person." The excess money in a person's possession is actually a deposit in his hands, and he must give it to one who needs it more than he does.

This idea might be reflected in the word *tzedaka*, usually translated as "charity." We generally associate the word *tzedaka* with the idea of "a donation to the needy" (Even Shoshan Hebrew Dictionary, explanation no. 4). But the fact is that the word *tzedaka* is related etymologically to the word *tzedek*, "justice" (Even Shoshan, explanation no. 1). That is to say, one who gives *tzedaka* is not giving a donation, but rather executing justice, by doing that which is just and right. The laws governing loans are also part of this system of justice.

In practice, however, there are those who take into consideration the view of the ***Bet Yosef*** that all forms of debt are released during the *Shemita* year. Accordingly, a *pruzbol* should also be made for debts generated through purchases.

Wages:

The **Mishna** in ***Shevi'it*** (*10:1*) states that wages are not subject to the law of release during the *Shemita* year:

> A worker's wages are not subject to the law of *Shemita* – release, but if he turned them into a loan, they are subject to the law of *Shemita*.

Here, too, the halachic authorities disagree why wages are not subject to the law of *shemita*. Is it a matter of principle, namely, that wages are a debt but not a loan, or is it for a side reason, namely, that the wages do not come due at the end of the *shemita* year?

Today, wages are generally paid in Israel once a month. Therefore, wages that should have been paid before the end of the *shemita* year are, according to the ***Bet Yosef*** and the ***Sema***, subject to the law of *shemita*, whereas according to the ***Bach*** and the ***Tumim***, they are not subject to the law of *shemita*. Hence, a *pruzbol* should be made for such debts as well.

Charity:

The **Rashba** (*Bava Kama 36a*) writes that charity funds are not subject to the law of *shemita* (because the court is responsible for such funds, and it is as if the debts had been transferred to the court). Both the ***Shulchan Aruch*** (*Choshen Mishpat 67:28*) and ***Yechaveh Da'at*** (*IV*, no. *64*) rule in accordance with this position.

As for the rationale underlying this law, it stands to reason that an individual's debts are released in order to show that the money does not really belong to him. In the case of charity funds, however, there is no private ownership, and so the debts are not released.

Savings accounts:

It would seem that the *heter iska* that permits a person to receive interest on the money deposited in a bank (by recasting the deposit as an investment rather than a loan) should be effective with regard to *shemitat kesafim* as well. It is possible, however, that the *heter iska* does not help with respect to *shemita*. *Heter iska* generally creates a transaction that is half a loan and half a deposit. The transaction is conducted in this manner, so that if the money should become lost through circumstances beyond human control, in which case a guardian is generally exempt from responsibility, the borrower will still be obligated to return the money based on the law governing loans.

The **_Shulchan Aruch_** (*Choshen Mishpat 67:3*) rules that *shemita* cancels the portion of an investment that is cast as a loan:

> If someone has an investment, the part that is a loan is released by *shemita*.

The **Radbaz** (*Responsa, IV*, no. *214*), however, is lenient about this matter. According to him, we are not dealing with a real loan, but rather with a loan that is really an investment, and therefore it is not released by *shemita*:

> It stands to reason that *shemita* does not release an investment at all, for in truth, it is not a loan, but rather the Rabbis treated it as half loan and half deposit, which is good for both of them, but not so that *shemita* should cancel it.

It would seem that the need for a *pruzbol* for savings accounts depends on this disagreement – according to the **_Shulchan Aruch_**, a *pruzbol* is necessary, whereas according to the **Radbaz**, it is unnecessary.[14]

There may be another reason that *shemita* does not cancel bank debts. The managers of a bank are not personally responsible for the money owed to the bank by its customers, and there is no **individual** who is commanded to release those debts. Similarly, a person who has deposited money in a bank is not obligated to release the bank's debt – "that which is yours with **your brother** your hand shall release," but not that which is with a **corporation**, such as a bank. The **Rogachover** seems to have adopted this approach (*Tzofnat Pa'ane'ach*, no. *184*):

> As for a bank, the institution is an abstract corporation lacking an individual "address," for even those who own a bank are not personally indebted…

Rav Elyashiv is also inclined to this direction, (cited in *Shemitat Kesafim ke-Hilchatah* 10, note 1) regarding a bank's obligations to its customers (that these obligations are not cancelled by *shemita*).

Responsa Iggerot Moshe (*Choshen Mishpat, II*, no. *15*) also implies

14. For an expanded discussion of this issue, see Rav Yuval Cherlow's article in *Mishnat ha-Shemita, II*, p. 624.

that **if the borrower is not indebted** to the lender, the transaction is not a loan. Since the owners of a bank are not personally indebted to the bank's customers (a bank is a corporation with limited liability), the bank's debts are not cancelled.

As stated above, the same rule may also apply in the opposite direction, so that debts owed to a bank are also not released during the *shemita* year.

Many authorities maintain, however, that a bank is treated as a **partnership,** which can have debts like an individual (***Yechaveh Da'at***, *IV*, no. *64*; ***Minchat Yitzchak,*** *III*, no. *1*).

In practice, it is proper to write a *pruzbol* for savings accounts.[15]

Checks:

If a person received a check before the end of the *shemita* year but did not yet cash it, is the check released by *shemita* at the end of the year?

1. If the check was **postdated**, it stands to reason that the debt is not released, as the creditor cannot cash the check at the end of the *shemita* year (see also ***Iggerot Moshe***, *Choshen Mishpat*, *II*, no. *15*, s.v. *ve-hinei im*).
2. If the check could have been cashed before the end of the *shemita* year, but was not, it would appear that the debt is released. It is possible, however, that with the handing over of a check **the debt is regarded as having been paid**, and thus it is not released (in general, when a person pays with a check, the parties regard the transaction as having been completed). In practice, there are those who incline to stringency (see ***Minchat Yitzchak,*** *II*, no. *119*), while others incline to leniency (**Rav Sh. Z. Auerbach**, cited in *Shemitat Kesafim ke-Hilchatah, Shevivei Esh*, no. *13*, and similarly **Rav Wosner**, ibid. *Shevivei Esh*, no. *9*; see also ***Responsa Shevet ha-Levi***, *VI*, no. *222*; the aforementioned *Iggerot Moshe* implies likewise; see also *Dinei Shemita u-Pruzbol*).

15. We already suggested another reason that bank accounts should not be subject to the laws of *shemita*. Term deposits that cannot be withdrawn at the end of the *shemita* year should not be subject to the laws of release, because they are treated like a ten-year loan. It might be argued that such deposits should be subject to the laws of *shemita*, because it is possible to pay a certain penalty and withdraw the money early. We proposed above that there is room for leniency on the matter, because banks are closed on the day before *Rosh ha-Shana*, and so a person cannot collect the money that is owed him. We noted that this argument is by no means simple. See *Shevivei Esh* (in *Shemitat Kesafim ke-Hilchatah*), no. 32, who is inclined to be lenient, ruling that such deposits are not subject to the laws of *shemita*.

PRUZBOL

WHAT IS A *PRUZBOL*?

The **Mishna** in ***Shevi'it*** (*10:3*) states that when Hillel saw that many people refused to lend money in the time leading up to the *shemita* year because they were afraid that they would not get their money back, he instituted the *pruzbol* which allows for loans to be collected after the *shemita* year (*proz* = enactment; *bul* = rich – an enactment for the rich so that they would lend to the poor).

The Gemara in ***Gittin* 36a** asks, how could Hillel have uprooted a Torah law? The Gemara cites two answers: According to **Rava**, he could uproot a Torah law because of the rule that the Rabbis have the authority to expropriate property (*hefker bet din hefker*). According to **Abaye**, he could do this because *shemita* in our time is only in effect by rabbinic decree:

> But is it possible that, while according to the Torah the seventh year releases, Hillel should ordain that it should not release? Abaye said: It is due to fact that *shemita* in our time is rabbinic… Rava said: The Rabbis have power to expropriate for the benefit of the public…

The practical difference between these two explanations will be whether a *pruzbol* can be utilized when *shemitat kesafim* is in effect by Torah law.

The general rule is that, apart from six known exceptions, the law follows **Rava** when he disagrees with **Abaye**, but nevertheless the **Rambam** (*Hilchot Shemita ve-Yovel 5:16*) rules that the enactment of *pruzbol* is only in effect when the observance of *shemita* is by rabbinic decree. The **Ra'avad** (ad loc.) disagrees with the Rambam and says that the enactment of *pruzbol* is in effect even when *shemita* observance is by Torah law. This view also follows from **Rashi's** comment in *Gittin*, and it is also the views of both the **Rashba** and the **Ran**.

How are we to understand the Rambam's position? The ***Kesef Mishneh*** explains (like the ***Tosafot*** in ***Gittin***) that Rava's explanation builds off of Abaye's explanation, that is to say, only because the remission of debts is a rabbinic law did the Rabbis invoke their authority to expropriate property.

This disagreement might stem from a difference of opinions regarding the Rabbis' authority to expropriate property. Are the Rabbis only authorized to **divest** a person of his proprietary rights, or are they also authorized to **transfer** such rights to a new owner? This question, however, is beyond the scope of the present discussion.[16]

How does *pruzbol* work?

The **Mishna** in ***Shevi'it*** (*10:2*) states:

> One who hands over his bonds to a court – his debts are not remitted.

The rationale underlying this ruling is given in the ***Sifrei*** (*Re'eh 113*) and in the ***Yerushalmi*** (*10:1*): "That which is yours with **your brother** your hand shall release," but not that which is with the court. Accordingly, the laws of *shemita* do not apply to a court.

This is understandable if we assume that the essence of *shemitat kesafim* stems from the prohibition to demonstrate ownership of the money. Therefore, *shemitat kesafim* would not apply to that which belongs to the court (the judges are not owners of the property, but merely the community's representatives). See the similar explanation suggested above for *Otzar Bet Din*.

Similarly, the **Mishna** (ibid. 3-4) describes Hillel's enacting of the *pruzbol*:

> A *pruzbol* prevents the remission of debts in the *shemita* year. This is one of the regulations made by Hillel the Elder. For he saw that people were unwilling to lend money to one another, disregarding the warning laid down in the Torah, "Beware lest there be an unworthy thought in your heart saying, etc." He therefore decided to institute the *pruzbol*.
>
> The text of the *pruzbol* is as follows: "I hand over to you, so-and-so, the judges in such-and-such a place, my bonds, so

16. It is possible that the distinction between divesting a person of his proprietary rights and transferring them to another person stems from the **source** of the law of *hefker bet din hefker*. Various talmudic passages imply that the Sages did in fact **transfer** proprietary rights from the original owner to another person. It seems, therefore, that all agree that the Sages have the authority to transfer such rights, but they did not always **wish to exercise this authority** (see *Minchat Asher, Gittin*, nos. 60–61). See also *Responsa Devar Avraham*, I, no. 1).

> that I may be able to recover any money owed to me from so-and-so at any time I shall desire;" and the *pruzbol* was to be signed by the judges or witnesses.

In other words, the creditor **hands over** the debts that are owed him to a **court. Rashi** (*Makkot 3b,* s.v. *moser shetarotav*) explains:

> He hands over his bonds to the court – This is the *pruzbol* enacted by Hillel in which it is written: "I hand over to you, so-and-so, the judges in such-and-such a place, my bonds, so that I may be able to recover any money owed to me from so-and-so at any time I shall desire."

According to **Rashi,** a *pruzbol* is **handing over bonds to a court** (Rashi writes the same in *Ketubot 89a,* s.v. *pruzbol; Gittin 32b,* s.v. *moserani*). It follows that handing over bonds to a court prevents the remission of debts because of Hillel's enactment**.** The ***Tosafot*** (*Makkot 3b*), however, disagree with Rashi:

> Thus it seems that they are two different things, and that when one hands over bonds to a court, it is by Torah law that there is no remission of the debts.

According to the ***Tosafot,*** handing over bonds to a court prevents the remission of debts **by Torah law.** *Pruzbol* is an **enactment** introduced by Hillel, and does not parallel handing over bonds to a court (the author of *Sefer ha-Terumot,* letter 11, writes the same; and this also seems to be the position of the Rambam and the *Shulchan Aruch* who record the two as separate laws). How are we to understand the position of **Rashi**?

1. The ***Tosafot*** (*Gittin* 36a) and the **Ramban** (in his novellae) explain that according to **Rashi**, the derivation in the ***Sifrei*** and the ***Yerushalmi*** is merely an *asmachta,* an allusion to the law, rather than its actual source.
2. It might be possible to understand **Rashi** in light of a suggestion proposed by ***Tosafot*** in ***Gittin*** (*36a*). Handing bonds over to the court is indeed effective by Torah law, but this was not the accepted practice, because the courts did not want to

receive the bonds (they preferred that the debts be remitted in keeping with the Torah's desire). **Hillel enacted that this procedure become the accepted practice,** so that people would hand over their bonds to the court, rather than refrain from lending in anticipation of the *shemita* year. This explanation could fit with Rashi's approach as well.

According to the *Tosafot* in *Makkot* and most *Rishonim*, who maintain that *pruzbol* is not the same thing as handing over bonds to a court, we must clarify the novelty in Hillel's enactment, and explain why it was necessary, when handing over bonds to a court is effective by Torah law!

1. The author of the ***Terumot*** (*sha'ar* 45, no. 11, cited in the *Bet Yosef, Choshen Mishpat,* no. 47) explains that when using the *pruzbol,* one need not actually hand over the bonds themselves to the court, but rather a declaration that he is handing over the bonds to the court suffices. **Rabbenu Crescas, Ran** (on the Rif) and **Meiri** (in his first explanation) agree.[17]
2. **Rambam**, in his commentary to the Mishna (Shevi'it *10:4*) offers a novel understanding of *pruzbol,* whereby *pruzbol* does not involve a declaration regarding handing over of bonds, but rather it is a declaration that the creditor wishes to collect his debts.

What is the rationale underlying the enactment of *pruzbol*? We saw earlier that only a debt owed to an individual is subject to remission. It is difficult, however, to use this rule to explain *pruzbol.* Even when a *pruzbol* is used, the money is not owed to the court, and the court does not collect the debt. This is especially true according to the approach that *pruzbol* is merely a declaration regarding the debt.

The ***Ritva*** in *Makkot* (*3b,* and Rashi explains similarly in *Bava Batra 27a*) explains:

> Rather, without a doubt anyone who actually hands over his bonds to a court – by Torah law there is no remission of debts, because they are regarded as having already been collected.

17. This might also be what Rashi meant to say, namely, that *pruzbol* works in the manner of handing over bonds to a court, though there is no need to actually hand them over.

> And Hillel enacted that it is not necessary to actually hand over the bonds to the court.

The **Ritva** argues that when the bonds have been handed over to the court, the debts are not released, because they are regarded as having already been collected. Hillel's enactment was that it is not necessary for the bonds to be handed over to the court. Even if a person merely declares that he is handing over the bonds (and a similar explanation could be given according to those who maintain that the creditor declares his intention to collect the debts), we see that as **the beginning of the process of collecting the debts** (or perhaps we even see the debts as having been collected, and the money is now a deposit in the hands of the debtors). Accordingly there is no remission of debt when there is a *pruzbol,* because the actual collection of the debt does not involve a violation of the prohibition of "he shall not exact it."

To summarize, there are three ways to understand *pruzbol*:

1. handing over bonds to a court (Rashi)
2. a declaration regarding the handing over of bonds to a court, without actually handing them over
3. a declaration of the creditor's desire to collect his debts.

In practice, we do not actually hand over bonds to the court, but merely **make a declaration** (and this may be understood within either of the two latter approaches). It is not necessary to specify the debts, and it suffices to write **one *pruzbol*,** in which a person declares that he is handing over all of his debts to the court.

As for the philosophical question surrounding the **deception involved in a *pruzbol*,** see our explanation in the section dealing with the *heter mechira* (above, p. 429).

THE TIME TO WRITE A *PRUZBOL*

We saw earlier that the *pruzbol* is drawn up in **Elul of the *shemita* year** (it cannot be written after *Rosh ha-Shana,* because by then the debt is already remitted). It would seem that the *pruzbol* should be drawn up on the last day of Elul, or else it would not prevent the remission of debts that came into being after the writing of the *pruzbol*. Many *Acharonim*, however, are lenient and allow the *pruzbol* to be drawn up already at the beginning of Elul, because any debt with an unspecified due date only becomes due after thirty days,[18] and therefore loans granted during the month of Elul are not subject to remission (because on *Rosh ha-Shana*, they are not yet subject to collection, like a ten-year loan discussed above).

THE COURT

The type of court:
The **Gemara** in ***Gittin* 36b** states:

> Come and hear, for Shmuel has said: We do not make out a *pruzbol* in any court other than the court of Sura and the court of Nehardea.

This statement implies that the writing of a *pruzbol* requires a court comprised of leading Torah authorities. This led **Rabbenu Tam** (cited by the Rosh, ad loc., no. *13*) to the conclusion that a *pruzbol* cannot be written in our time, because today's Torah authorities are not of the same caliber as those in the time of the Gemara (in light of this, the **Meiri** writes that it is preferable not to make a *pruzbol*, but rather to stipulate that the debtor will repay the debt).[19]
Ramban (*Sefer ha-Zechut, 18b* in the Rif pagination), **Rashba** (*Gittin 37b*) and **Rosh** (no. *13*) maintain, however, that a *pruzbol* may be written in any court. According to them, the law is not in accordance with **Shmuel,** as the continuation of the talmudic passage implies that Shmuel said what he said because his goal was to **abolish the enactment of *pruzbol*** – "If I am ever in a position, I will abolish it." The other Amoraim, however, said just the opposite: "If I am ever in a position, I will confirm it." The full passage also goes on to teach that writing a *pruzbol* is not a difficult matter (and for this reason a person is believed when he says that he had a *pruzbol*, but lost it; since it is easy to write a *pruzbol*, a person would not forgo doing so and collect his debt in violation of a Torah prohibition

18. According to the ***Bach*** (*Choshen Mishpat 67, 13*), even though a loan that comes due after the *shemita* year is not subject to the laws of release, this only applies to a loan whose due date was explicitly set for after the *shemita* year. But if a loan was granted without specifying when it will come due, it is subject to the laws of release (even if the loan was granted during the month of Elul; this is also the position of the ***Tumim***). The ***Minchat Chinuch*** (*mitzva 477*) and the **Rashash** (*Makkot 3b*) disagree and say that even such a loan is not subject to the laws of release. ***Devar Avraham*** (*I*, no. *32*) discusses the issue, and writes that the **Ran** (*Shabbat 148b*) states explicitly that even such a loan is not subject to the laws of release. ***Yechaveh Da'at***, *IV*, no. *62* (end), also follows this approach and brings additional sources in support of leniency.

19. Such a stipulation is valid, because as long as the creditor stipulates that he will pay back the loan rather than stipulate that *shemita* should not release the debt, it is not regarded as a stipulation that runs contrary to Torah law (*Makkot 3b*; Rambam, *Hilchot Shemita ve-Yovel 9:10*).

when the permitted alternative is simple), from which it may be inferred that a *pruzbol* may be written in any court.

Rabbenu Tam himself moderated his position and said that what is needed is the leading court of the generation, or the leading court in the area. In his *Sefer ha-Yashar,* **Rabbenu Tam** writes that what is essential is that it not be a court of laymen:

> Rabbenu Tam, *z"l,* writes in *Sefer ha-Yashar* that *shemita* is in force in our time… and that a *pruzbol* should not be written in our time, because we are not experts like Rav Ami and Rav Asi. Rabbenu Tam later retracted this position, and he himself wrote a *pruzbol,* because he would say that what we need is the leading court in the generation…

Rambam (*Hilchot Shemita ve-Yovel 9:17*) rules in accordance with Shmuel, and therefore requires a leading court:

> A *pruzbol* may only be written by a court comprised of the greatest Sages, like the court of Rabbi Ami and Rabbi Asi, who were authorized to divest a person of his property, but other courts may not write a *pruzbol.*

The ***Shulchan Aruch*** (*Choshen Mishpat 67:18*) rules that a *pruzbol* may only be written in an important court, which is fluent in the laws of *shemita,* whom the majority has recognized as an authority over them (he is stringent in that he requires an important court, but he is more flexible in his definition of such a court). The **Rema**, however, writes that a *pruzbol* may be written in any court, especially in our time when the remission of debts during the *shemita* year is only by rabbinic decree. (Elsewhere, he also takes into consideration the position that the remission of debts in our time is only an act of piety):

> A *pruzbol* prevents the remission of debts during the *shemita* year. It may only be written in an important court, namely, three people who are experts in the law and in the matter of *pruzbol,* know the laws of *shemita,* and whom the majority has recognized as an authority over them in that city.

> Rema: Some authorities say that a *pruzbol* may be written in any court (*Tur* and *Bet Yosef* in the name of the *posekim*), and it seems to me that one may be lenient in our time.

The actual presence of the court:
The **Mishna** in ***Shevi'it*** (*10:3*) concludes its description of the procedure of *pruzbol* as follows: "And the judges or the witnesses sign at the bottom." On this the ***Yerushalmi*** states (*10:2*): "It was taught: Even if they are in Rome."

The *Rishonim* disagree about the meaning of this *Yerushalmi*: The **Mordechai** (*Gittin*, no. 380) explains that the *pruzbol* does not have to be written before the court. Even if the **judges** are in Rome, the *pruzbol* may be written in the presence of the witnesses (this is also the understanding of the *Penei Moshe*, ad loc.):

> Even if they are in Rome – this means, the judges. That is, he can say, "I hand over to you, so-and-so, the judges in such-and-such a place," even if they are very far away from him...

The **Ran** (*Gittin 36b*), on the other hand, explains that "even if they are in Rome" refers to the creditor's **bonds**: even if they are in a different country and not currently in his hands, he can still make a *pruzbol* for them (as we saw that this is the novelty of a *pruzbol* as opposed to actual handing over the bonds):

> Even if they are in Rome – namely, the bonds.

According to the **Ran**, the *pruzbol* must always be drawn up in the presence of judges. This is also the position of the **Rashba** (*Responsa, II*, no. *333*) and others.

The **Ran** and the **Rashba** might not disagree with the Mordechai's halachic conclusion, but only with his interpretation of the Mishna. That is to say, they understand that the bonds are in Rome, and that this is the novelty of *pruzbol* as opposed to the actual handing over of the bonds to a court. But they might agree that the actual presence of the judges in not necessary (this is the understanding of **Mahari Kurkus**, *Hilchot Shemita ve-Yovel* 9:17, and also of the ***Bach***).

In practice, the ***Shulchan Aruch*** (*Choshen Mishpat* 67:21) rules in accordance with the **Mordechai** that a *pruzbol* does not have to be written in the presence of the judges, and the **Rema** agrees with this ruling (ibid., 20).

What is preferable – a court of expert judges, but a *pruzbol* signed not in their presence, or a regular court, but a *pruzbol* signed in their presence? According to the ***Shulchan Aruch***, preference should be given to the court of expert judges, for he rules that expert judges are required, but it is not necessary that the *pruzbol* be signed in the judges' presence. According to the **Rema**, it is not clear which option is to be preferred.

My revered teacher, Rav Aharon Lichtenstein, *shlita*, does both. That is to say, he recommends making a *pruzbol* that records the names of expert judges. But rather than there be only **two witnesses, three witnesses** sign the *pruzbol*, and the *pruzbol* includes a stipulation that if it is only effective when drawn up in the presence of the judges, then the bonds are handed over to the three signatories (a regular court).[20]

Relatives:

The *posekim* are lenient in that they allow the judges to be related to each other (***Responsa Yabi'a Omer***, III, *Choshen Mishpat*, no. 6; ***Responsa Minchat Yitzchak***, X, no. 141; **Rav Wosner**, cited in *Shevivei Esh*, no. 22). Some authorities insist that the judges not

20. This is also the position of Rav Elyashiv (cited in *Shemitat Kesafim ke-Hilchatah, Shevivei Esh*, no. 18, p. 241). There is room to question whether it is possible to use such a text, perhaps when the language includes two possible courts, then no court whatsoever is receiving the bonds (as noted by Rav Daichovski, on the first edition of my book, *Shi'urei Shevi'it*)! If we understand, as Rambam *did*, that when a person makes a *pruzbol*, he merely informs the court that he will be collecting his debts, there should be no problem with informing two courts of this intention. But if we understand that pruzbol entails the actual handing over of bonds (especially according to Rashi, but perhaps even according to the other *Rishonim*, the bonds are handed over by way of the person's declaration), there is room to consider the matter. In any event, Rav Lichtenstein and Rav Elyashiv agree that it is possible to arrange a *pruzbol* in this manner. It would seem that the *pruzbol* is valid because there is no practical barrier to collecting the debt, for the two courts can approach the debtor together and collect the debt, or one can authorize the other to collect the debt. I suggested this rationale to Rav Lichtenstein and he accepted it, and was happy to hear that this was also the position of Rav Elyashiv. At first I thought to add an authorization of the part of the three judges to the Supreme Rabbinical Court, but my revered father-in-law, Rav Blumenzweig, argued that this is unnecessary, because the *pruzbol* already states that if the court fails to collect the debts, the creditor will collect them himself. (He also added that the condition that we have attached to the *pruzbol* is much stronger than conditions that we ordinarily rely upon, such as conditions related to the performance of *mitzvot*).

be related to the creditor. However, a *pruzbol* drawn up by Rav Sh. Z. Auerbach (brought at the end of *Dinei Shevi'it*) in Rav Auerbach's own handwriting, included related parties (Rav Auerbach wrote a *pruzbol* for his grandson, and the court included Rav Auerbach and his son-in-law).

There are those who have the custom to lend out a small amount of money after writing the *pruzbol*, so that it will be possible to fulfill the *mitzva* of remitting debts during the *shemita* year (***Ben Ish Chai***, *Ki-Tavo*).

LAND

The Gemara in *Gittin* 37a states that a *pruzbol* is not written unless the debtor has land. The *Shulchan Aruch* (*Choshen Mishpat 67:22*) records this ruling. What is the rationale underlying this law? The *Tosafot* write that it is unusual for a borrower not to have land, and the enactment of *pruzbol* does not apply to unusual cases. The Ran (in the name of the Rash) explains that in order to circumvent the prohibition of exacting a debt, the debt must be regarded as having already been collected, and when the borrower has land, the debt may be seen as having been collected.[21] This approach accords with the Ritva's understanding of *pruzbol* cited above.

The land need not belong to the debtor; it suffices if it is borrowed[22] or rented (*Gittin 37a*; *Shulchan Aruch 67:3*). Every person has four cubits of land, whether they be borrowed or rented,[23] and therefore everyone can make a *pruzbol*. Nevertheless, there are those who write in the *pruzbol* that if the debtor has no land, then the creditor presents him with land as a gift.[24]

My revered teacher, **Rav Aharon Lichtenstein**, composed one *pruzbol* text for a creditor who owns land, which allows him to present the debtor with land (when this text is used, the judges should give the creditor some article to lift up and perform thereby *kinyan sudar*, a symbolic form of barter), and a second text for a creditor who does not own land. If the creditor does not own land,

21. This disagreement might depend on how we understand the lien that a loan establishes on the debtor's land, whether the land is regarded as having been acquired by the creditor, so that the debt is regarded as having already been collected, or whether there is no acquisition, but mere potential for collection.

22. In the case of yeshiva students who live in a dormitory, the dormitory is regarded as borrowed land (**Rav Sh. Z. Auerbach**, *Dinei Shevi'it ha-Shalem, 31, 8*). For additional details regarding the law of borrowed land, see *Shemitat Kesafim ke-Hilchatah*, chap. 20.

23. But the four cubits that every Jew owns in Eretz Yisrael does not suffice (*Derisha 67*, no. 24).

24. According to **Rabbenu Tam's** version of the *pruzbol* (*Sefer ha-Yashar*, no. 138), the creditor writes that he presents the debtor with land. This is also found in other versions of the text. In most places, however, it is not customary to add this (***Chochmat Adam***, *Sha'arei Tzedek*, chap. 21; see also ***Responsa ha-Mabit***, 1, no. 301).

but only rents or borrows it, there is no reason (and perhaps no possibility[25]) of presenting that land to the debtor since the debtor has borrowed land.

It should be noted that a *pruzbol* may be written even if the creditor does not own any land. It is only the debtor who might be required to own land. But if the creditor has land, and the debtor does not, it is recommended that the creditor present the debtor with land, in consideration of those who maintain that the debtor must have land.

WOMEN

Women are obligated in the *mitzva* of releasing debts during the *shemita* year, and thus they too are included in the enactment of *pruzbol*. They are certainly bound by the prohibition to demand repayment of debts. One might have thought that they are exempt from the positive *mitzva* to release debts, inasmuch as it is a time-bound positive *mitzva*, from which women are generally exempt. In practice, however, they are obligated in the *mitzva* for a variety of reasons, the main one being that **women are indeed obligated in time-bound positive *mitzvot*, the fulfillment of which is achieved by refraining from action** (*Respona Rabbi Akiva Eiger, III*, no. *80*; *Responsa Sho'el u-Meishiv, I*, no. *61*; and third series, *I*, no. *464*).

If a woman has a joint bank account with her husband, her husband's *pruzbol* is valid for her as well (the Steipler, *Orchot Rabbenu, II*, p. *386*). If she has her own account, she must make her own *pruzbol* (Rav Auerbach, cited in *Shemitat Kesafim ke-Hilchatah, 21*, p. *11*; see addenda at the end of the volume, *Mishneh Kesef*, to p. *182*). She can appoint her husband as her agent[26] (in which case he writes in his *pruzbol* that he is handing over his loans and the loans granted by his wife). According to Rav Sh. Z. Auerbach (ibid.), the husband can include his wife in his *pruzbol* even if she does not explicitly appoint him to do so.

25. According to *Responsa of the Rashba* (*I*, no. *1145*), a borrower can lend out land without informing the owner, for it works with respect to *pruzbol*, and *pruzbol* requires land from which the debt may be collected. See also *Machaneh Efrayim, Sechirut*, no. *12*. There is, however, room to discuss whether this is possible. In any event, even if it is possible, there is no reason to do so when the debtor already has borrowed land.

26. Owing to the rule that "words cannot be transferred to an agent," it is questionable whether or not an agent can be appointed for this task. In practice, however, there is room for leniency, because the agent performs the action (the *pruzbol*) by himself, rather than transfering the "words" to another agent. This is the ruling of Rav Ovadya Yosef (*Yalkut Yosef*, p. *581*).

THE *PRUZBOL* TEXT

According to the Mishna (*Shevi'it 10:4*), the essential text of the *pruzbol* is as follows: "I hand over to you, so-and-so, the judges in such-and-such a place, [my bonds], so that I may be able to recover any money owing to me from so-and-so at any time I shall desire." The *pruzbol* was to be signed by the judges or witnesses (one version reads "witnesses," that is to say, they attest that the bonds were handed over to the court; and another version reads "judges," that is to say, the judges themselves declare that they received the bonds).

The text varies in accordance with the type of court – see above our discussion of the court, and Rav Lichtenstein's proposal in that regard – and in accordance with whether or not the creditor has land – see above our discussion regarding land.

There is no need to spell out the names of the debtors; it suffices to write that the creditor has handed over all of the debts that are due him.

Practical guidance for writing a *pruzbol*:

A *pruzbol* that does not include presentation of land. This is the most common *pruzbol*, which may be used even by one who owns land; the *pruzbol* formula for one who owns land is merely an added enhancement to the *mitzva*: The creditor recites the text (marked by quotation marks in the formula brought below), and the court signs the document and fills in the name, date and place (according to Rav Lichtenstein, there is no need for *kinyan sudar*).

A *pruzbol* that includes presentation of land: The creditor recites the first section, "Acquire from me," lifts up some article (received from the judges) in order to perform a *kinyan sudar,* and then recites the second section and the judges sign, as above.

The following *pruzbol* text was based on the formula proposed by Rav Lichtenstein. It was used in the previous Shemita of 5768, with the names of the judges who served on the Rabbinic court at the time.

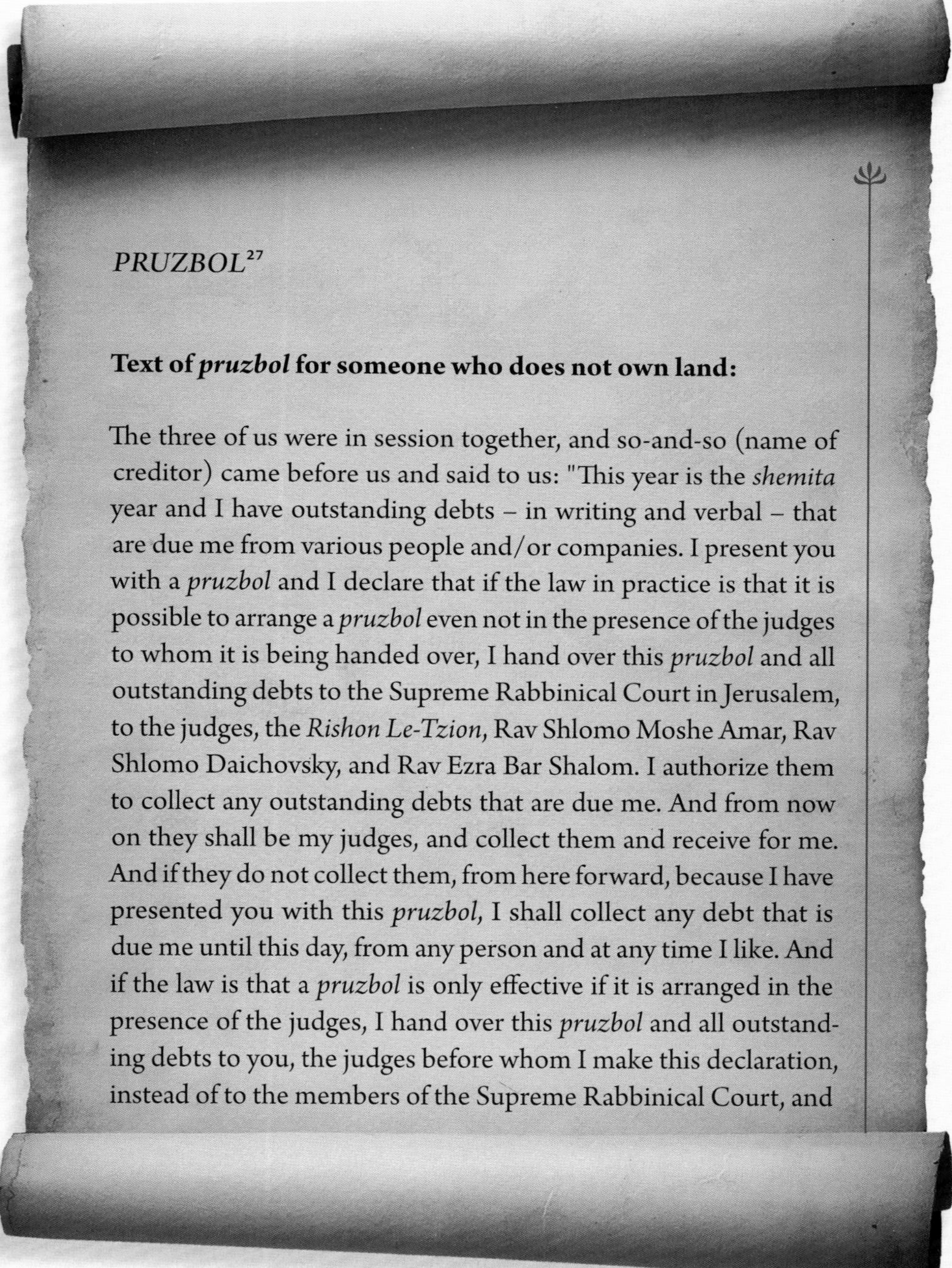

PRUZBOL[27]

Text of *pruzbol* for someone who does not own land:

The three of us were in session together, and so-and-so (name of creditor) came before us and said to us: "This year is the *shemita* year and I have outstanding debts – in writing and verbal – that are due me from various people and/or companies. I present you with a *pruzbol* and I declare that if the law in practice is that it is possible to arrange a *pruzbol* even not in the presence of the judges to whom it is being handed over, I hand over this *pruzbol* and all outstanding debts to the Supreme Rabbinical Court in Jerusalem, to the judges, the *Rishon Le-Tzion*, Rav Shlomo Moshe Amar, Rav Shlomo Daichovsky, and Rav Ezra Bar Shalom. I authorize them to collect any outstanding debts that are due me. And from now on they shall be my judges, and collect them and receive for me. And if they do not collect them, from here forward, because I have presented you with this *pruzbol*, I shall collect any debt that is due me until this day, from any person and at any time I like. And if the law is that a *pruzbol* is only effective if it is arranged in the presence of the judges, I hand over this *pruzbol* and all outstanding debts to you, the judges before whom I make this declaration, instead of to the members of the Supreme Rabbinical Court, and

27. This is the ordinary version of the *pruzbol*. With this version, the creditor does not present the debtor with land, because the creditor only has rented or borrowed land – see above. Anyone can use this version, but a person who actually owns land can use the preferred text found on the next page, by way of which he presents four cubits of land to each of his debtors.

this *pruzbol* shall be valid, all as explained above, with respect to you and through you."

And we the court, the members of which have signed below, since we have seen his words to be correct, and since he has arranged the *pruzbol* before us in accordance with the enactment of Hillel and the Sages, we have established that the *shemita* year not release his debts, and that he be able to collect all of his debts at any time that he likes.

Signed on the ______ day of the month of ______, in the year ______, here in the city of ______.

Signed __________
Signed __________
Signed __________

Text of *pruzbol* for someone who owns land:

The three of us were in session together, and so-and-so (name of creditor) came before us and said to us: "Perform a fully valid act of acquisition with an article that is fit for such an act of acquisition, so that through you I may give a gift of land that I own to each of the debtors who owe me money and don't own land." And we performed a fully valid act of acquisition with an article that is fit for such an act of acquisition.

And the aforementioned person also said to us: "This year is the *shemita* year and I have outstanding debts – in writing and verbal – that are due me from various people and/or companies. I present you with a *pruzbol* and I declare that if the law in practice is that it is possible to arrange a *pruzbol* even not in the presence of the judges to whom it is being handed over, I hand over this *pruzbol* and all outstanding debts to the Supreme Rabbinical Court in Jerusalem, to the judges, the *Rishon Le-Tzion*, Rav Shlomo Moshe Amar, Rav Shlomo Daichovsky, and Rav Ezra Bar Shalom. Through you I give them as a gift for a day four cubits of soil from the land I own, and as an adjunct I authorize them to collect any outstanding debts that are due me. And from now on they shall be my judges, and collect them and receive for me. And if they do not collect them, from here forward, because I have presented you with this *pruzbol*, I shall collect any debt that is due me until this day, from any person and at any time I like. And if the law is that a *pruzbol* is only effective if it is arranged in the presence of the judges, I hand over this *pruzbol* and all outstanding debts, as an adjunct of a gift

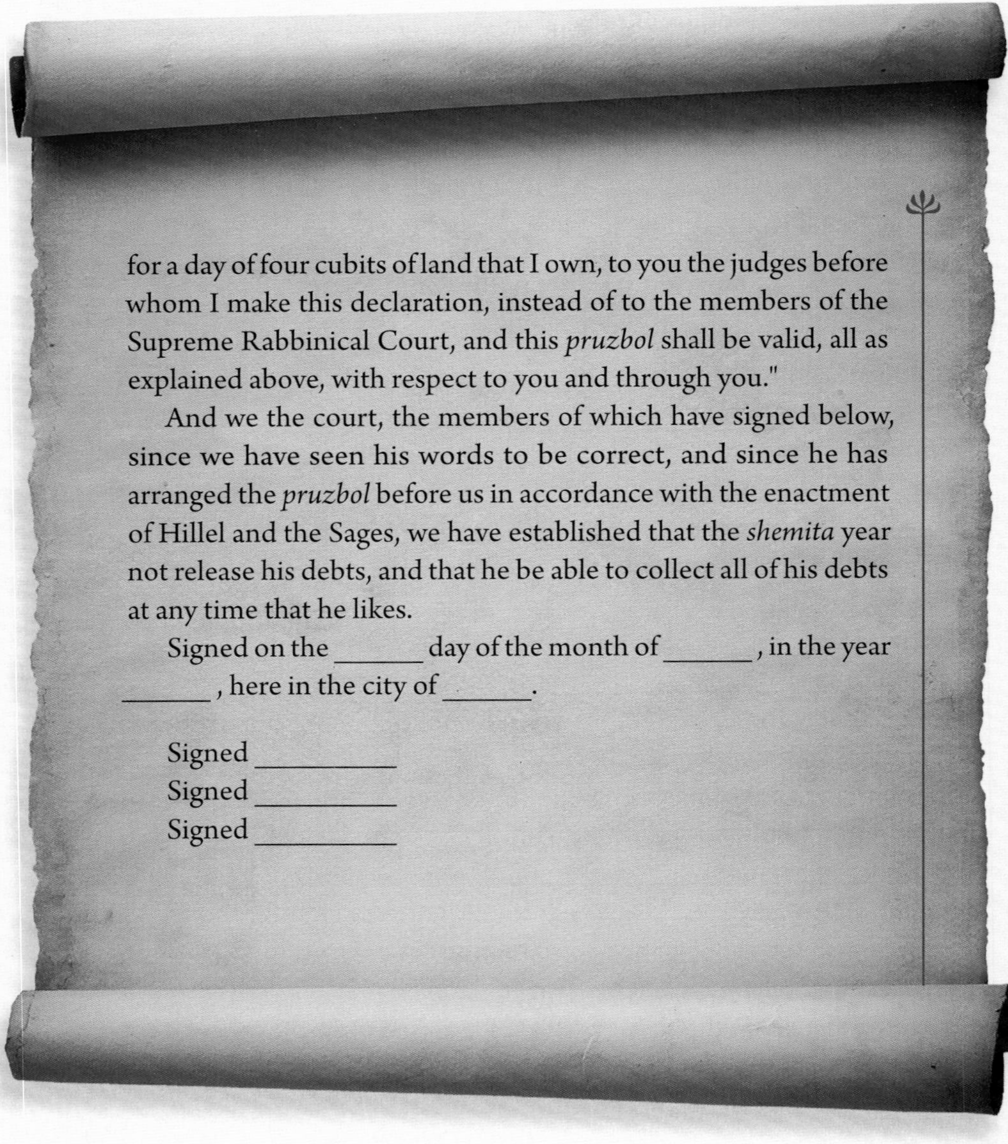

for a day of four cubits of land that I own, to you the judges before whom I make this declaration, instead of to the members of the Supreme Rabbinical Court, and this *pruzbol* shall be valid, all as explained above, with respect to you and through you."

And we the court, the members of which have signed below, since we have seen his words to be correct, and since he has arranged the *pruzbol* before us in accordance with the enactment of Hillel and the Sages, we have established that the *shemita* year not release his debts, and that he be able to collect all of his debts at any time that he likes.

Signed on the ______ day of the month of ______, in the year ______, here in the city of ______.

Signed __________
Signed __________
Signed __________

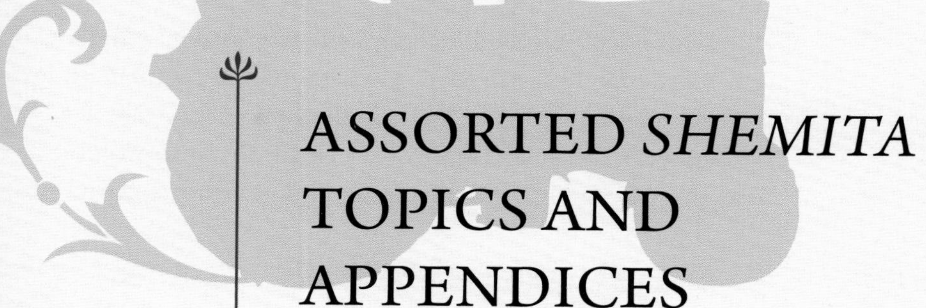

ASSORTED *SHEMITA* TOPICS AND APPENDICES

SHEMITA REMNANTS AND THE PROHIBITION OF SELECTING (*BORER*) ON *SHABBAT*

Question: Is it permissible to separate out *Shemita* remnants that are mixed together with other food, in order to set them aside in a special receptacle so as to preserve their sanctity?

Answer: This seems to involve a violation of the prohibition of selecting on *Shabbat*, but the matter requires further clarification.

The **Mishna** in ***Shabbat* 139b** states that an egg may be passed through a mustard strainer on *Shabbat* in order to separate the yolk from the white. The **Gemara** (*140a*) explains:

Because it is only done for coloring.

At first glance, this explanation is puzzling. What difference does it make whether we are interested in separating the yolk from the white for coloring or for some other purpose? The very fact that we are interested exclusively in the yolk for some purpose should turn the act into one of forbidden selection (*borer*).

Rashi (ad loc.) explains:

> Because it is only done for coloring – for appearances, because the yolk is better for color than is the white. Therefore, both are regarded as food, and there is no selection of food from refuse.

That is to say, since the egg is being strained so that the yolk can be used for coloring, there is no problem of *borer*. Rashi, however, adds that therefore both the yolk and the white are regarded as foods, and so the act does not involve selecting food from refuse.

Rashi's words are difficult. Rashi maintains that the prohibition of *borer* does not apply to a mixture of two kinds of foods (*Shabbat* 74b), and therefore it should have sufficed for him to write here: "Both are regarded as food." Why then do both the Gemara and Rashi add the argument: "Because it is only done for coloring"?

The ***Acharonim*** disagree about how to understand **Rashi**:

The **Bach** (*Orach Chayim, 319*) explains that when food is separated from refuse, one violates the prohibition of *borer* whether one does so for the sake of eating or for some other purpose. But when food is separated from food, one only violates the prohibition when one does so for the sake of eating. The allowance here is based, therefore, on two factors:

1. Both the yolk and the white are foods.
2. The yoke is being separated not for the sake of eating, but for coloring (this is also the implication of the *Tur*).[1]

The ***Peri Megadim*** (*Orach Chayim 319, Mishbetzot Zahav*, nos. 2 and 12, following his understanding of the *Taz, no. 12*) understands that the Gemara means to say that there is no prohibition of **sorting** in the case of two foods. If one is food and the other is refuse, the moment that a person separates between the two, he separates food from refuse. But in the case of two foods, if the sorter is not interested in using either of them at the present time, but only later (this is the definition of sorting), we cannot say that one is refuse and the other is food.

In our case, **Rashi** emphasizes that we are dealing with two types of food – "both are regarded as food." If a person wishes to eat the yolk now (and it is for this reason that he passes it through the strainer), this would be prohibited, because the white of the egg would then be regarded as refuse. But in the case at hand the person has no intention of eating the yolk at the present time. Now it is being used solely **for coloring**. At a later point he will eat both – the yolk and the white. Separating the yolk from the white is, therefore, permitted, because sorting in this manner is permitted.

The ***Magen Avraham*** (*no. 16*) explains that the yolk and the white are regarded as one type of food, and therefore one is permitted to separate the one from the other. Why then does the Gemara say: "Because it is only done for coloring"? The ***Magen Avraham*** explains (see *Machatzit ha-Shekel*) that this sentence is not explaining the reason for the allowance, but rather it comes to prove that both the yolk and the white are regarded as food. One might have thought that the separated elements are not both regarded as food, and now

1. The *Bach's* distinction is logically puzzling: What is the basis of this distinction? Why are two foods worse than two kinds of garments, regarding which we say that the prohibition of *borer* applies, even though a person is interested in wearing them, and not in eating them. It seems that the prohibition only applies when a person is interested in the object's essential use.

the yolk, when it becomes mixed with the mustard, turns into a food (according to this understanding, the separation would be forbidden, because in such a case the white would be regarded as refuse). The gemara, therefore, explains that the entire reason for putting the yolk into the mustard is for coloring, and not to turn it into food.

The ***Be'ur Halacha*** (*319, 3,* s.v. *hayu lefanav*) disagrees with the ***Peri Megadim.*** He explains:

> There neither of them ever stand to be eaten, for the white became mixed in with the refuse of the mustard and he does not want to eat it, and the yolk went down through the strainer for coloring, and not for eating. Therefore, it does not fall into the category of *borer,* because the selection never prepares it to be eaten. When, however, he separates out two types of food in order to eat each food separately later, he prepares each of them for eating by way of his separation, and this is full-fledged *borer.*

The implication is that since the yolk and the white are not meant to be eaten, but rather they are both refuse, separating one from the other does not constitute a significant improvement, and therefore such selection is permitted. This stands in contrast to sorting, where the person is interested in each type of food separately, and therefore separating the one from the other is regarded as an improvement, which is forbidden.

The ***Be'ur Halacha*** implies that it is permitted to select one type of food from the other, if they are both refuse, because such separation is considered insignificant.

The ***Chazon Ish*** (*Orach Chayim 53,* s.v. *u-le-inyan*) also implies that it is permitted to select something that will be going to waste immediately with the selection. He learns this from the law governing the squeezing of fruit: if a person squeezes fruit in such a way that the juice will go to waste there is no culpability for squeezing (there are those who maintain that even this is forbidden by rabbinic decree). He implies that *borer* is only forbidden when it involves improving something so that it may be eaten or used in some other way. If, however, the food will not be used, but rather it will go entirely to waste (or if the selected portion will go to waste, and the remaining portion has no significance), there is no violation of the prohibition of *borer.*

This explains the leniency practiced with respect to pouring things into a sink that has a strainer, an act that one might have thought involves a violation of the prohibition of *borer.* According to what was said above, however, there is no problem, because both that which is caught by the strainer and that which passes through will go to waste, thus there is no problem of *borer.*

Indeed, the leading authorities of our generation have permitted the use of a strainer in the sink: ***Iggerot Moshe*** (vol. *IV,* no. 74), ***Tzitz Eliezer*** (vol. *VII,* no. 12), **Rav Elyashiv** and **Rav Zilber** (cited in *Ayil Meshulash,* 7, note 111), and ***Shemirat Shabbat ke-Hilchatah*** (12, 16).

We now come to the issue of *Shemita* remnants mixed with non-*Shemita* remnants. At first glance it would seem to be forbidden to select the *Shemita* produce, even if we regard this as separating food from refuse, because it is not being separated for immediate use. In light of what was said above, however, there is room for allowance, because neither the *Shemita* remnants nor the non-*Shemita* remnants are going to be eaten; we merely wish to place them in separate receptacles. This, however, is not a simple argument, because we are not dealing with two sets of "garbage" divided between two receptacles. There is "garbage" mixed together with produce containing *Shemita* sanctity, the one being fundamentally different from the other.

IMMEDIATE USE

Even if we adopt a stringent position regarding the previous consideration, there might be room for leniency if we regard the *Shemita* remnants as **food,** so that when they are being separated out, we are removing **food from refuse.** This, however, does not solve the problem, because it does not appear to fall into the category of selection for immediate use. It might, however, be possible to categorize this as selection for immediate use, because the "use" of *Shemita* remnants is for them to be placed in a receptacle that preserves their *Shemita* sanctity. Putting it into such a receptacle is therefore its use, and since this is done immediately following the selection, it is considered immediate use.

"REFUSE" OWING TO HALACHIC RESTRICTIONS

It is also possible that there is no violation of the prohibition of *borer* in such a case, because the difference between the products is a byproduct of the halachic restrictions that govern them, not their respective usages. The halachic authorities disagree on the following issue: **Does the prohibition of *borer* apply to water that is potable, but is subject to a halachic prohibition that forbids drinking it?** The ***Chayei Adam*** (*Hilchot Shabbat 16, 8*) discusses the matter. He addresses the case of water containing forbidden insects, which, barring the prohibition to eat insects, would be fit for drinking. He adduces proof (in *Nishmat Adam,* no. 5) from a ruling by the ***Kolbo*** that water may be filtered to remove *yavchushin* (a type of gnat). According to the ***Chayei Adam,*** since non-Jews, who are not bound by the prohibition, drink the water, there is room to permit this separation. In practice, however, the *Chayei Adam* leaves this as an open question.

The ***Tehila le-David*** (*319, 16*) rejects the *Chayei Adam's* proof, arguing that water containing *yavchushin* is permitted to be drunk even by Jews. ***Minchat Yitzchak*** (vol. *VII,* no. 23), however, adds to the uncertainty raised by the *Chayei Adam,* writing that it is unclear whether the ***Kolbo*** permitted such filtering even when the water is subject to a clear-cut prohibition, or whether he only permitted it when, strictly speaking, it is permissible to drink the water, and "it is only on account of special caution that sin-fearing people filter the water."

The ***Eglei Tal*** discusses this point in the context of a mixture of meat and *gid ha-nasheh,* the forbidden sinew, or a mixture of meat and forbidden fat. He writes (*borer 20, 4*) that even though it is forbidden to eat the *gid ha-nasheh* and the fat, since they are considered edible, and we refrain from eating them only because of a Divine command, the mixtures are regarded as consisting of uniform kinds, and therefore not subject to the prohibition of *borer.*

The ***Minchat Chinuch*** (*Mosach ha-Shabbat, borer*) also addresses the question of whether a mixture of a forbidden food and a permitted food of the same physical kind is considered as one with respect to the prohibition of *borer,* or perhaps, because one is forbidden and the other is permitted, they are regarded as two kinds. He cites the **Ran** (*Shabbat,* chap. *Chavit*) who discusses whether it is permitted to milk a goat straight into a dish of food on *Shabbat,* as is permitted on *Yom Tov.* This is permitted on *Yom Tov* because both the milk and the goat are regarded as food, as one may slaughter the goat for food. On *Shabbat,* however, slaughtering the goat is forbidden. Is the goat nonetheless regarded as food even on *Shabbat*? The **Ran** records a disagreement on this issue. This seems to parallel our question: The goat is fit to be eaten (and therefore it is regarded as food), but in practice it cannot be eaten on *Shabbat* owing to the prohibition of slaughtering.[2]

In practice, contemporary authorities disagree on the matter. **Rav Wosner** (*Kovetz mi-Bet Levi, 5,* no. *163*) and **Rav Elyashiv** (*Ayil Meshulash, 9,* note *78*) are stringent, whereas **Rav Nissim Karelitz** (*Kovetz mi-Bet Levi,* ibid.) is lenient.

2. There is much to add on this issue. See: *Be-Tzel ha-Chochma,* vol. *VI,* no. *98*; *Maharshag,* vol. *I, Orach Chayim,* no. *47*; *Yalkut Yosef, Shabbat* vol. *3,* p. *294*; *Shemirat Shabbat ke-Hilchatah,* chap. *3,* note *100.*

IN PRACTICE

Ideally, it is preferable not to separate *Shemita* remnants from non-*Shemita* produce on *Shabbat,* due to the prohibition of *borer.* A distinction may be made, however, between various cases. In the case of a vegetable salad, it is unnecessary to sort out the different components, and everything can be placed in the receptacle set aside for *Shemita* leftovers, since the remnants do not cause immediate spoilage (see the appendix dealing with *Shemita* sanctity in institutions).

Regarding leftovers on one's plate, if the *Shemita* vegetables rest apart on the side of the plate, there is no mixture and those vegetables may be removed and placed in the receptacle set aside for *Shemita* leftovers. If the *Shemita* remnants are mixed together with the rest of the food on the plate, such as with *cholent*, it is best not to separate the *Shemita* remnants from the rest of the food, out of concern for the prohibition of *borer*. In such a case, the entire contents of the plate cannot be placed in the receptacle set aside for *Shemita* sanctity, because the leftover *cholent* will cause the immediate spoilage of the *Shemita* produce in the receptacle. It is, therefore, best to place all the intermingled leftovers on the plate (the *cholent* together with the salad) into a plastic bag[3] (for nothing is changed in the process) and then throw the bag in the garbage.[4]

3. Care must be taken to tie the bag in a manner that is permitted on *Shabbat*, such as a single knot formed by holding the bag by its two sides.

4. Alternatively, one may remove the *Shemita* remnants with a small amount of the other food, so that, on the one hand, there is no violation of the prohibition of *borer* (at least according to the *Mishna Berura*, based on the *Taz*, that one is permitted to remove refuse along with a small amount of food), while, on the other hand, the small amount of other food (*cholent* or the like) will not cause the immediate spoilage of the *Shemita* remnants.

OBSERVANCE OF *SHEMITA* IN INSTITUTIONS

I was asked about observing the laws of *Shemita* sanctity in institutional kitchens, as to whether it might be preferable to purchase produce that does not have *Shemita* sanctity, owing to the difficulty of handling *Shemita* produce in the proper manner in such frameworks.

Observing the laws of *Shemita* sanctity on the institutional level is undoubtedly much more complicated than doing so in one's home. In institutions, *Shemita* leftovers cannot be deposited into special receptacles and allowed to remain there until they decay.

When the diners are religiously observant, the difficulty can be overcome relatively easily. The diners can be asked to separate out their *Shemita* leftovers and place them in a special receptacle. At the end of the meal, the bag should be tied shut, after which it can be thrown into a regular garbage can (this follows from what we wrote in the chapter dealing with *Shemita* sanctity; and Rav Neuwirth writes to the same effect in *Halichot Sadeh*, 50, p. 17).

Problems arise in certain institutions, especially those that cater to a non-observant clientele who cannot be relied upon to separate out their *Shemita* leftovers.

In such situations, the diners should be instructed to place all of their leftover vegetables and fruits (those that have *Shemita* sanctity together with those that do not have *Shemita* sanctity) into a single receptacle, on the assumption that such action will not cause immediate spoilage of the *Shemita* produce (this is certainly true when the various foods are already mixed together, but this allowance can be used even when they are still separate).

The rationale underlying this allowance is that mixing the *Shemita* leftovers with the other fruits and vegetables does not cause the immediate ruin of the *Shemita* produce, and it is only later that the produce will deteriorate to the point that it can no longer be eaten. This falls into the category of indirect spoiling of *Shemita* produce which is permitted.

It is possible that even mixing the *Shemita* fruits and vegetables with other foods – to the exclusion of soup and the like that cause immediate spoilage – should be regarded as indirect spoiling of the *Shemita* produce, which is permitted.

The validity of this solution depends upon whether the prohibition to destroy *Shemita* produce is limited to the actual destruction of the produce itself, or whether it applies to any action that causes people to refrain from eating the produce. In our case, there is no immediate ruining of the *Shemita* produce itself, but people will no longer eat the *Shemita* fruits and vegetables because they were mixed together with other foodstuffs.

Regarding ***ma'aser sheni,*** the Mishna states (*Ma'aser Sheni* 3:2):

> One may not purchase *teruma* with *ma'aser sheni* money, because he limits its consumption.

Teruma is forbidden to a *tevul yom* (one who was ritually impure, immersed himself in a *mikveh,* and is now waiting for nightfall) and to a non-*kohen*. *Ma'aser sheni,* however, is permitted to such people. If a person takes *ma'aser sheni* money and purchases *teruma* with it, he diminishes the possibility of its consumption, because fewer people can now eat it, and therefore this is forbidden. The ***Pe'at ha-Shulchan*** (5:6) rules that the same applies to *Shemita* produce: It is forbidden to do anything to the produce that will diminish the number of people who are able to eat it.

Rav Kook (*Mishpat Kohen,* no. 85 [end]) raised the following question:

> As for throwing away peels, if they are fit to be cleaned and eaten and have not become so repulsive, it might be argued that this is not destruction. But it might also be argued that if a person who saw them when they were repulsive would no longer eat them because of their repulsiveness, this is regarded as destruction.

That is to say, is the prohibition against destroying *Shemita* produce limited to situations where **the produce itself is ruined**, or does it apply also to situations in which the produce is not ruined, but **people recoil from eating it**? Put differently, is the destruction of *Shemita* produce determined by the objective status of the food or by the subjective opinion of a person choosing whether or not to eat it?

Rav Kook ruled stringently that if a person does something to make *Shemita* produce loathsome to other people, he is guilty of destroying *Shemita* produce. According to him, this follows from what *Tosafot* say in *Ketubot* 30b about a case of damages.

Tosafot refer to a case where someone puts food belonging to another person into his mouth but does not eat it. If the owner saw him put the food into his mouth, the owner would no longer eat it, and he is therefore entitled to damages. But if the owner did not see him put it into his mouth, the owner would still eat it, and so there is no liability. We see that the very fact that people are now unwilling to eat a certain food constitutes ruin.

It is possible, however, that this is only true with respect to **damages.** Regarding damages, an article's value is measured by how it is viewed by people. If people would no longer use a certain article, it is regarded as damaged. But as for *Shemita,* it is possible that ruin is limited to the actual destruction of the produce.

In fact, this *Tosafot* can be used as a basis for leniency. *Tosafot* argue that **for someone who saw** the food in the other person's mouth the food is ruined, but for someone who did not see the food in the other person's mouth it is not ruined. Returning to our case, most people do not see the leftover *Shemita* produce mixed together with the other foodstuffs. Theoretically, a person could take the leftovers and rinse them off, and the food would be in no worse state than before it had been mixed with other food. (The food could certainly be ground up and prepared in such a manner that a person who was unaware of what took place would have no difficulty eating the food). But there might still be reason for stringency, because practically speaking, nobody is going to take leftovers out of a garbage.

Rav Kook was stringent for a similar reason regarding the use of *Shemita* wine for *havdala,* because when wine is used for *havdala* the number of people who can drink it is diminished, inasmuch as women have the custom not to drink *havdala* wine (*Shabbat ha-Aretz, Kuntres Acharon, 22*).

Some *Acharonim*, however, imply that it is only with respect to ***teruma*** that reducing the number of people who will eat it is viewed as destruction, but regarding ***Shemita* produce** reducing the number of people who will eat it is not considered destruction.

This is the position of the **Ridbaz** (*Bet Ridbaz 5, 6*, s.v. *u-le-inyan she-pasak*), who reaches this conclusion based on comparing the Rambam's ruling regarding *teruma* to his ruling about *Shemita* produce (see also *Minchat Shelomo, 1*, no. *46* [end]).[1] These *Acharonim*, however, deal with a case where there are now fewer people who will eat the *Shemita* produce. Our case is worse, because almost no one would eat *Shemita* leftovers once they have been discarded.

This issue might depend on whether or not there is a *mitzva* to eat *Shemita* produce. Eating *teruma* is a *mitzva*, and therefore it stands to reason that reducing the number of people who will eat it is considered a form of destruction. If we accept the position that there is no *mitzva* to eat *Shemita* produce, there should be nothing problematic in reducing the number of people who will eat it, and the problem of ruining *Shemita* produce would be limited to the actual destruction of the produce itself (see *Bet Ridbaz*, ibid.).[2]

Put differently, if there is a *mitzva* to eat *Shemita* produce, it is possible that we do not consider the objective state of the produce, but rather the relationship between the produce and the person who is commanded to eat it. Accordingly, produce that nobody would eat is regarded as having been ruined. If there is no *mitzva* to eat *Shemita* produce, it is possible that we consider the objective state of the produce, and, accordingly, only produce that has actually gone bad is treated as ruined.

This discussion is also relevant to the common practice of placing *Shemita* leftovers into a separate receptacle. Most people would not eat any leftovers cast into such a receptacle. (People are willing to eat the leftovers on their own plate, but they are not prepared to eat them after they have been mixed together with other people's

1. In the course of a discussion about squeezing fruit, after which the fruit is no longer edible, but only drinkable, Rav Sh. Z. Auerbach writes as follows: "According to this, we must say that in the case of *teruma* there are two reasons to forbid squeezing, first, because one ruins the fruit, and second, because he removes it from its sanctity, and therefore it is forbidden even in the case of fruit that is meant to be squeezed. However, in the case of *Shemita* produce, squeezing is only forbidden for the first reason. Accordingly, we must say that the Rambam did not totally equate *Shemita* produce and *teruma*. All he meant to say is that the prohibition in both cases is the same when it involves ruining the fruit. Accordingly, it is permitted to squeeze *Shemita* oranges, lemons and grapefruits in order to derive benefit from their juice."

2. Of course, if we say that the fact that people recoil from eating the produce, even though the produce itself has not gone bad, is considered destruction of the produce, the very act of throwing the different fruits and vegetables into the same container would be considered direct, rather than indirect destruction of the produce.

leftovers). It is, therefore, possible that while adding other foodstuffs will make the *Shemita* leftovers even more repulsive, the principle is the same: in both cases there is no damage to the *Shemita* produce itself; there is only a change in people's attitude toward it. It stands to reason that this allowance does not apply if soup or other liquids are added, because this involves direct and active destruction of the *Shemita* produce (despite the fact that it might still be theoretically possible to wash the fruits and vegetables, and reprocess them in such a way that the product would be fit for consumption for someone who did not see that the food had been cast into the garbage, so that it should not be considered direct and active destruction).

There may be additional grounds to permit throwing all the leftovers into the same bag. Inasmuch as the decision has already been made to throw away the *Shemita* leftovers, they might not be subject to the prohibition of destruction. Furthermore, leftovers that had been prepared in an institutional kitchen are regarded by the general public as unfit for further consumption[3] and are generally not served a second time, but rather discarded (they are also generally subject to health guidelines, which forbid them to be reused).

It might be possible to derive this principle from the **Tosefta** (*Shevi'it 6:11*). The Tosefta states that a person who is suspected of ignoring the laws of *Shemita* may be given perishable *Shemita* produce. This implies that there is no concern that he will destroy the produce,[4] because presumably he will use the produce in the normal manner. But why is there no concern that he will throw out the leftovers? Perhaps we can infer from here that throwing away *Shemita* leftovers in an ordinary manner is not forbidden, because something slated to be thrown away is not subject to the prohibition of destruction.

It may also be possible to derive this principle from Tosefta *Shevi'it* (*6:1*), accepted as halacha by the **Rambam** (*Hilchot Shemita ve-Yovel 5:2*), which states that no obligation exists to eat moldy *Shemita* bread. There are several ways to understand this law. One possibility is that something that is ordinarily not eaten is not subject to the prohibition of destruction. The Torah said: "The Sabbath

3. This argument by itself is not conclusive. The Tosefta (*Shevi'it 6:1*) and the Rambam (*Hilchot Shemita ve-Yovel 5:2*) state that a person is not obligated to eat moldy bread. One might have understood from this that the very fact that people do not ordinarily eat such bread suffices to allow the bread to be thrown out. Many *Acharonim*, however, maintain that even such bread has *Shemita* sanctity, and that it is for other reasons that one is not obligated to eat it (such as the fact that it is regarded as eating in an unusual manner – *Chazon Ish*; see above). In any event, this Tosefta cannot serve as proof regarding the matter under discussion, as the Tosefta deals with bread that is objectively problematic (it is moldy), and not with bread that merely is slated to be thrown out. See also below.

4. Even though there the discussion focuses on the fact that there is no prohibition of trade, and not on the prohibition of destruction, nevertheless, if destruction were an issue, this should have been mentioned as well.

produce of the land shall be food for you" (*Vayikra* 25:6), from which *Chazal* learned: "For food, but not for destruction." Only that which is generally eaten as food[5] is subject to the prohibition of destruction (see also *Har Tzvi*, II, no. 54, regarding the difference between *Shemita* produce and *teruma*).[6]

The **Mishna** in ***Terumot*** (*11:5–8*), ***Tosafot*** (*Zevachim 86a*, s.v. *u-peliga*), and what is reported in the name of Rav Elyashiv regarding throwing away the flesh of a fruit found on a pit, also seem to indicate that leftovers that are slated to be thrown away are not subject to the prohibition of destruction. This conclusion, however, does not necessarily follow from these sources, because they deal with small amounts of *Shemita* produce (it is possible, however, that in an institutional framework, even a larger amount should be governed by the same law, though this requires further clarification). Moreover, the plain sense of the *Tosefta* (*Shevi'it 7:2*) seems to prove that leftovers that stand to be thrown away do indeed have *Shemita* sanctity: "A stringency regarding *Shemita* produce that does not apply to *ma'aser sheni* – the refuse of food is treated like food." This source, however, is subject to various interpretations (see *Mikdash David* 59, 4, s.v. *katav ha-Rambam*; see also *Devar ha-Shemita 8:2*, s.v. *ve-ha*, who understands that this refers to *bi'ur*, and not to the prohibition of destruction).

In practice, one should not adopt this lenient approach, but rather one should be

5. See the article of Rav Y. Amichai, *Ha-Torah ve-ha-Aretz*, VI, p. 235, and p. 247, that this is what he understood from *Devar ha-Shemita* 8:2. This, however, is not a necessary conclusion. In the case of moldy bread, the food itself went bad, and therefore people do not eat it. It might prove nothing about food that is still objectively good, but nonetheless people do not eat. The *Chazon Ish* (*Seder Shevi'it*, printed at the end of *Shenat ha-Sheva*) understood that the *tosefta* is dealing with bread that is unfit for human consumption, and therefore required that *Shemita* leftovers be treated as having *Shemita* sanctity. Rav Mordechai Immanuel wrote to me that it stands to reason that we are not dealing with entirely moldy bread, but rather with bread that has a spot of mold on it which will cause people to refrain from eating that bread (even though it is still edible). According to this, all the leftovers in institutions, which for hygienic and sanitary reasons are not saved, should fall into this category, and may be thrown out in the ordinary manner (even he agrees that preferably one should also take into consideration the position of the *Chazon Ish*). See also the notes above.

6. What the *Har Tzvi* says cannot serve as proof for the matter under discussion, because he is dealing with something that from the very outset was not meant to be eaten (the rind of an *etrog*), and it is possible that only in a similar case is there no *Shemita* sanctity. But one may infer from his words that there is a connection between the fact that a certain food is slated to be eaten and the prohibition against destroying it. See also *Ha-Torah ve-ha-Aretz*, VI, pp. 228–248, on these issues, and also regarding composting during the *Shemita* year.

careful about the prohibition of destroying *Shemita* produce, even with respect to leftovers that will be discarded. However, one can rely on the lenient views, so that if people do throw away their leftovers in the usual manner, those who provide them with the food are not guilty of *lifnei iver* (placing a stumbling block before the blind). This is especially true when discarding the leftovers does not cause the immediate ruin of the *Shemita* produce, as explained above.

This principle may be inferred from the words of **Rav Sh. Z. Auerbach**, who writes about buying *heter mechira* produce for one who does not rely on the *heter mechira*:

> This does not involve *lifnei iver* or assisting transgressors, because even the other person knows that there are those who forbid the practice, but he acts in accordance with those who permit it... even in a case where the giver thinks that it is certainly forbidden, and that anyone who permits the practice is in error, even so it is permitted... And even though owing to the spread of the *heter* there are many storekeepers who unfortunately know nothing of the laws of *Shemita*, nevertheless if it is clear that would they know they would certainly follow those who permit the practice, there is no need to be concerned about setting a stumbling block before the ignorant. (*Ma'adanei Eretz*, notes, no. 7; notes, no. 8, 23)

We see then that where there are grounds for leniency, even when they are weak, the prohibition of *lifnei iver* does not apply.

In addition, the prohibition of *lifnei iver* may not apply when people can obtain *Shemita* produce from other sources.[7] This is similar to the allowance to sell food to people whom we know will not recite a blessing before they eat.[8]

An explicit Mishna seems to forbid handing over *Shemita* produce to a person who will not handle it in accordance with the rules of *Shemita* sanctity. The Mishna in *Ma'asrot* (5:3) states:

> A person must not sell his produce once it has reached the time of tithes to one who is not trusted regarding tithes, and

7. If we are dealing with "one side of the river," as in, for example, *Tosafot Shabbat 3a*, s.v. *bava*, *Pitche Teshuva, Yoreh Deah 160:1*.

8. See at length, my article, "*Lifnei Iver*," *Alon Shevut*, 153.

> he must not sell his produce during the *Shemita* year to one who is suspected of ignoring the laws of *Shemita.*

That is to say, *Shemita* produce should not be sold to one who is suspected of ignoring the laws of *Shemita*. Similarly, we find in the Tosefta (*Shevi'it 4:3*):

> One must not sell *Shemita* produce to one who is suspected of ignoring the laws of *Shemita*, neither seeds that are eaten nor seeds that are not eaten.

The prohibition in both sources seems to follow from concern about *bi'ur* and proper handling of produce that has *Shemita* sanctity (and concern that the other person will plant the seeds).

Another Tosefta (*Shevi'it* 6:11), however, explicitly permits giving *Shemita* produce to one who is suspected of ignoring the laws of *Shemita*:

> One must only sell *Shemita* produce to someone who is suspected of ignoring the laws of *Shemita* in the amount that suffices for three meals. When does this apply? In the case of non-perishable food. But perishables may be sold even in the amount that suffices for a hundred meals.

The Tosefta explicitly states that the problem of handing over *Shemita* produce to one who is suspected of ignoring the laws of *Shemita* applies only to non-perishable food, and even then only in large quantities. This clearly indicates that the concern is about one of two things:

1. a concern that the person will hold on to the produce even after the time of *bi'ur* has arrived (as explained by the *Chasdei David*, ad loc.)
2. a concern that he will use the produce for trade or for some purpose other than eating (*Minchat Bikkurim*, ad loc.; *Rivag*, ad loc.; see also the Rambam's commentary to the Mishna; *Shevi'it 9:1*). This accounts for the allowance to give such a person perishable *Shemita* produce or small amounts of non-

perishable produce, because such produce will not be stored away until after the time of *bi'ur* or used for trade.

In light of this, it is reasonable that both the Tosefta in chapter 4 and the Mishna in *Ma'asrot* are dealing with the same case, namely, non-perishable produce or produce that could be used for trade, so that these sources do not contradict the Tosefta in chapter 6. Thus it is clear why neither the Rambam nor any other authority rules that one must not give *Shemita* produce to one who is suspected of ignoring the laws of *Shemita*. The only problem is with money attained from *Shemita* produce, because it is not consumed, and there is concern that it will be spent on non-food items[9] or kept after the time of *bi'ur*.

This also follows from the words of *Tosafot*. *Tosafot* (*Sukka 39a*) say: "*Shemita* produce must not be given as payment to a well-master, or a bath-house keeper, or a barber, because *Shemita* produce is for eating, drinking and anointing, and not for other purposes." The *Tosafot* forbid a person to give *Shemita* produce to people suspected of using *Shemita* money in an improper manner, not to buy food. But they are not concerned about giving the money to people who will use it to buy food which will have *Shemita* santity, even if they will throw out the leftovers.

The *Chazon Ish* (*Shevi'it 12, 17,* s.v. *tanya*) rules that the prohibition of handing *Shemita* produce over to an ignorant person only applies to non-perishable foods, owing to the concern that he will put the produce in storage (and keep it after the time of *bi'ur*). However, there is no concern about giving perishable *Shemita* produce or *Shemita* produce in the amount that suffices for only three meals, because it is unlikely that the recipient will destroy the *Shemita* produce or use it in an unusual manner, since people by and large eat in a normal manner and do not destroy the produce in their possession:

> It may be asked, why is it permitted to give perishable produce to an ignorant person? This implies that we are not concerned that he will not be careful about destroying it, or about changing the manner in which he eats it, or the like, for that is uncommon, and we assume that he will use it in

9. See, however, Rav Tykoczinzki's *Sefer ha-Shemita*, 8, note. 11, as he was inclined towards stringency, as was *Minchat Yitzchak*, VI, no. 130, letter 4. Nevertheless, regarding a person who is suspected of ignoring the laws of *Shemita*, there is more room for concern about giving him *Shemita* produce that he will take home with him than about serving him *Shemita* produce in a public cafeteria, as mentioned above.

> the permitted manner, which is more common... Rather the primary concern is about storing away *Shemita* produce, for that is common, because produce is likely to rise in price during the *Shemita* year... Therefore, regarding perishable produce, the Sages did not impose a prohibition, and regarding food that suffices for three meals, they permitted even non-perishables.

There are several reasons then that public institutions may purchase fruits and vegetables from *Otzar Bet Din*:

1. Even if all the leftover fruits and vegetables (even those that do not have *Shemita* sanctity) are cast into the same bag, generally speaking the *Shemita* produce does not suffer immediate deterioration.
2. Even if other refuse is put in the same bag, it might not be considered immediate destruction of the *Shemita* produce (if we assume that only actual destruction of the produce itself is regarded as destruction), but rather indirect destruction.
3. Some authorities maintain that leftovers that are slated to be thrown away are not subject to the prohibition of destruction, and while we generally do not rely upon this leniency, it suffices to remove the prohibition of *lifnei iver.*
4. According to the plain sense of the *Tosefta,* it is permitted to give *Shemita* produce to a person who is suspected of ignoring the laws of *Shemita,* and there is no concern that the person will handle it in a manner inappropriate for produce having *Shemita* sanctity, provided that the produce is for immediate consumption.

In any event, the institution should make sure that the garbage cans are lined with bags. At the end of each meal, the bags should be tied up and cast into a larger garbage bin, in order to avoid the situation in which the *Shemita* leftovers are cast directly into the larger bin, which will certainly lead to immediate destruction of the *Shemita* produce.

In addition, it should be noted that all of these uncertainties are uncertainties about rabbinic laws, as *Shemita* observance in our time is by rabbinic decree (Rav Kook, introduction to *Shabbat ha-Aretz,*

1–8; 4, 25; Chazon Ish, 3, 8; Pe'at ha-Shulchan 23, 23).[10] On the other side of the scale stands the livelihood of those farmers who are making tremendous efforts to observe the laws of *Shemita* in the best possible manner, and regarding whom the Torah says, "that your brother shall live with you."[11]

When we approach the issue from a wider perspective, there is another factor that must be taken into consideration. On the national level, it is clearly desirable that there be a great supply of produce having *Shemita* sanctity (all fruit-bearing trees). This is what the Torah means when it states: "And the Sabbath produce of the land shall be food for you." This is especially true in light of our aspiration that *Shemita* should be observed in the best possible manner (reducing as much as possible reliance on the *heter mechira*).[12] If this produce is not purchased, both by individuals and by institutions, it will end up being destroyed (this, unfortunately, is what happened during the *Shemita* year prior to the last *Shemita* year), and people will eat imported produce in its place.[13] Is it the Torah's intention that *Shemita* produce not be eaten and end up being destroyed? While it is clearly preferable that the produce be eaten and that the *Shemita* sanctity of the leftovers be fully respected, even the situation where the produce is eaten and the leftovers are discarded is undoubtedly preferable to the alternative that the *Shemita* produce itself be shamefully destroyed and not serve as food whatsoever!

10. See, however, the *Chazon Ish* (22, 1; 26, 4) regarding this principle with respect to planting indoors.

11. See *Responsa ha-Rema*, no. 10; *Responsa ha-Tashbetz*, III, no. 151; the words of Rav Kalman Kahana cited in *Minchat Yitzchak*, III, no. 139.

12. It should be noted that regarding fruit, Rav Sh. Z. Auerbach (*Ma'adanei Aretz*, notes, no. 7, notes, no. 8, 23) writes that even those who do not rely on the *heter mechira* may purchase *heter mechira* produce (see above, p. 433), because we are lenient about *shamur* and *ne'evad*, and there is no problem of *lifnei iver*, as the grocer relies on those authorities who permit the sale. Thus, it is clearly preferable to purchase *heter mechira* produce rather than imported produce. (As for vegetables, the matter is more complicated, and it might depend on the manner in which the *heter* was arranged, and which labors were performed). However, if it is possible to buy *Otzar Bet Din* produce, then that is certainly preferable, even if it complicates matters, as was explained above, as that allows for *Shemita* to be observed in the best possible manner.

13. Of course, if produce that grew in Eretz Yisrael during the sixth year is available, there is no issue of "that your brother shall live with you." But imported produce is a problem, as the very importing of produce from abroad (when there is sufficient produce in Eretz Yisrael) leads to the destruction of *Shemita* produce grown in Eretz Yisrael.

To summarize: Even institutions should view buying *Otzar Bet Din* produce as a great privilege.[14] The institution should post clear instructions that the *Shemita* leftovers be placed in the special receptacles assigned for that purpose. This will also serve as a tool for increasing public awareness of *Shemita* and *Shemita* sanctity.

If this is not a realistic option, then instructions should be given that all fruits and vegetables (even those that do not have *Shemita* sanctity) should be placed in these receptacles. When it is unreasonable to expect people to meet even this standard, then a separate receptacle should at least be set aside for liquids, so that the *Shemita* leftovers will not be immediately ruined when they are thrown into the garbage.

The institution should make sure that the regular garbage cans are lined with bags, and that these bags are tied up at the end of each meal, so that even if *Shemita* leftovers are thrown into the garbage, they will not suffer immediate ruin.

When a person is at home, and even when he is in an institutional setting, he should place all his *Shemita* leftovers in a separate receptacle set aside for that purpose. In the case of institutions, however, the above measures suffice to avoid violation of the prohibition of *lifnei iver*, and to allow the institution to buy *Otzar Bet Din* produce.

These guidelines allow public institutions to serve *Shemita* produce and at the same time to maintain their sanctity.[15]

14. They can also make use of the other preferred solutions discussed earlier in this volume.

15. Another problem that arises in institutional kitchens relates to the use of institutional potato peelers. Some authorities forbid them (*Orchot Rabbenu*, II, p. 349), while other permit them (see *Ha-Torah ve-ha-Aretz*, VI, Rav. Y. Amichai, p. 242). In addition to what was written above regarding that which is slated to be thrown out, today's machines remove almost nothing but the outer peel, which is fit only for animals, and it is reasonable that since those peels are not meant to be given to animals, they are no longer subject to the prohibition of destruction (see *Responsa Minchat Shelomo*, I, no. 51, 8; *Chazon Ish, Shevi'it*, 13, 11; and *Perot Shevi'it*, 18, note 22). It would be preferable to find a way to collect the peels, but, strictly speaking, when the machine removes almost nothing but the peel, there is room for leniency. See the appendix in *Techumin* XXVII (5767).

THE PREFERENCE GIVEN TO JEWISH PRODUCE OVER IMPORTED PRODUCE

To what extent should one exert oneself to buy Jewish produce during the *Shemita* year?

Does buying Jewish produce justify lowering other halachic standards?

In previous years of *Shemita* the primary issue facing the Torah observant community in Israel was whether to prefer Jewish produce (*Otzar Bet Din*, hothouse and container produce, and *heter mechira*) or Arab produce. During the current year of *Shemita*, Arab produce has become much less of an issue. The question still remains, however, whether to give priority to Jewish produce or to imported produce.

Imported produce is likely to be cheaper, it relieves the consumer of having to deal with *Shemita* sanctity (in private homes and especially in institutions), and it spares us the need to find halachic solutions for the *Shemita* year.

On the other hand, giving preference to imported produce is liable to cause Israeli farmers heavy economic losses, bring about the collapse of many branches of agriculture, and lead to serious setbacks in the process of raising the standards of *Shemita* observance. The larger the community interested in purchasing *Shemita* produce, the easier it will be to employ the superior methods of dealing with the halachic difficulties posed by *Shemita*, such as *Otzar Bet Din* or hothouses and container produce, or to improve the *heter mechira* so that it will be executed in the most halachically preferred manner.

We will now examine the principles that underlie this issue.

PREFERENCE GIVEN TO JEWISH PRODUCE

The Midrash ***Torat Kohanim*** in *Parashat Behar* (beginning of *parasha* 3) states:

> From where do we know that when a person sells he must sell only to his neighbor? The verse states: "And if you sell

anything to your neighbor" (*Vayikra* 25:14). And from where do we know that when a person buys he must buy only from his neighbor? The verse states: "Or buy anything from your neighbor's hand (ibid.). This would only teach me about land. From where do I know to include movable property in this principle? The verse states: *"Mimkar"* ("matter of sale") – to include movables.

The *Torat Kohanim* derives from the verse "Or buy anything from your neighbor's hand" that preference must be given to making purchases from a Jew – "you must buy only from your neighbor's hand."

Several points in the *Torat Kohanim* must be examined:

1. What are the limits set on preferring Jewish merchandise: Is this only when the Jewish and the gentile merchandise are available at the same price, or perhaps even when the Jewish merchandise is more expensive? If even when the Jewish merchandise is more expensive, is there a limit to the price differential, or perhaps priority must always be given to Jewish merchandise? What is the law when buying from a Jew involves considerably greater effort?
2. Was this ruling accepted as law? It is not cited in either the Rambam or in the *Shulchan Aruch*. Does this prove that this ruling was never accepted as law?

THE POSITION OF THE *TOSAFOT*:

The Gemara in ***Avoda Zara*** *20a* records the verse in *Devarim* 14:21: "You shall not eat of any animal that dies of itself; you shall give it to the stranger who is in your gates, that he may eat it; or you may sell it to an alien." The Torah presents two possible ways of dealing with an animal that has died of itself:
1. giving it as a gift to a "stranger" (a *ger toshav*, a resident alien who has accepted some of the laws of Judaism and has certain rights, but is not regarded as a Jew); 2. selling it to an alien, namely, a gentile.

Is it preferable to give the carcass to a *ger toshav* rather than sell it to a gentile? The **Gemara** states that it is preferable to give the carcass to the *ger toshav*. According to **Rabbi Yehuda**, this is derived from the extraneous term, "or" ("*or* you may sell it to an alien"). According to **Rabbi Meir**, this follows from a logical argument: since we are commanded to sustain and provide assistance to a *ger toshav*, we clearly must show him preference over any other gentile.

It would seem then that we have here yet another source that we must give preference to buying from a Jew over buying from a gentile. If preference must be shown to a *ger toshav* over a gentile in commercial matters, then all the more so must preference be shown to a Jew. We also see from here that this applies even in a case of financial loss, because a person could have sold the carcass to a gentile and earned money, but instead he is required to give it as a gift to a *ger toshav*.

Tosafot (s.v. *ve-Rav Meir*), however, do not accept this argument:

> You might ask: If a person has an article to sell, must he give it to a *ger toshav* rather than sell it to a gentile? But surely he is not commanded to do so even with respect to a Jew! It can be answered that this is only in the case of a carcass which has little value to a Jew (for there were few gentiles among them) but to a *ger toshav* it has great value, like any other meat.

The ***Tosafot*** object that it cannot be that preference must be shown to giving to a *ger toshav* over selling to a gentile. Would we say in all cases that one must give an article to a *ger toshav* rather than sell it to a gentile? Why should the Jew have to suffer a loss and give the article as a gift to the *ger toshav*? In light of this objection, the *Tosafot* argue that it is only in this case of a carcass that the Torah commands that it be given as a gift to the *ger toshav,* because "it has little value to a Jew ... but to a *ger toshav* it has great value, like any other meat." That is to say, only when the Jew will suffer a small loss must he prefer the *ger toshav* to the gentile. But if he would suffer a great loss, he is clearly under no obligation to show preference even to a Jew over a gentile.[1]

The Gemara in ***Bava Kama*** (*114a*) states that if a Jew owns a parcel of land next to land belonging to another Jew (*bar metzra*),

1. *Tosafot's* formulation is that for the Jew the loss is small (*davar mu'at*), whereas for the ***ger*** it has great value (*shaveh harbeh*). We are left with the impression that we are dealing with a situation close to *middat Sedom*, "behavior characteristic of Sedom" [lack of kindness for little material gain]: the Jew hardly suffers any loss at all, whereas the *ger* has much to gain. What is the law when there is little loss to the one party, but also little gain for the other? This is unclear from the *Tosafot*, but there are other *Rishonim* who speak only of a small loss, without mentioning the great gain of the ***ger*** (see, for example, Rabbenu Peretz on *Pesachim 21b*).

he may not sell his property to a gentile. The ***Tosafot*** (s.v. *ad*) comment:

> Rabbenu Tam says: This only applies when the Jew is willing to pay him the same sum that he would receive from the gentile. But if the gentile is ready to give him more [the owner of the property,] does not have to suffer a loss.

In other words, only when the Jew has the opportunity to sell his property to another Jew for the same price is he forbidden to sell it to a gentile. But if the gentile is ready to pay him more money, the Jew may sell the property to him. The Gemara refers to the sale of land, but it would seem that the same law should apply to movable property (*Torat Kohanim* indeed refers to both). A logical *kal vachomer* argument can even be presented, for if regarding the sale of land, which is enduring, one may give precedence to a gentile over a Jew when this is economically worthwhile, one should certainly be permitted to do so in the case of movable goods. The *Shulchan Aruch* (*Choshen Mishpat 175:41*) rules in accordance with this view.

The *Tosafot's* fundamental approach is clear: there is no obligation to buy from a Jew over a gentile when doing so would cause a financial loss. According to the ***Tosafot*** in ***Bava Kama*** (*114a*), this applies to any loss, no matter how small, whereas according to the ***Tosafot*** in ***Avoda Zara*** (*20a*), it seems that in the case of a small loss, preference must indeed be given to buying from a Jew.

THE POSITION OF THE *TASHBETZ* AND THE REMA

The ***Tashbetz*** (vol. *III*, no. *151*) discusses selling to Jewish merchants as opposed to selling to gentiles:

> When the price is the same, the Torah did not even need to teach that one should give preference to a Jew over a gentile. Rather, the verse teaches that preference must be given to a Jew even when he will pay less and the gentile will pay more.

The ***Tashbetz*** writes that at the same price, it is obvious that one must buy from a Jew. For this, no special verse or derivation would be necessary. If the *Torat Kohanim* derives a law from an extraneous word, it must be the obligation to give precedence to a Jew over a gentile, even when this involves a financial loss. The *Tashbetz* does not, however, define the level of loss or the price differential between the Jew's offer and that of the gentile.

A heated controversy broke out in the Jewish world in the wake of a sixteenth century printing of the **Rambam's *Mishneh Torah*.** The Rambam's work was published at the same time by both the **Maharam Padua** and a gentile publisher, and the latter sold it at a slightly lower price. The **Rema** was asked to rule on the matter (*Responsa ha-Rema,* no. *10*):

> In the *midrash Torat Kohanim, Parashat Behar,* the Torah teaches that if you come to buy, buy from the hand of your neighbor, and the same applies to selling ... Do not say that this applies only when the gentile and the Jew are selling at the same price, while if the gentile's price is much cheaper, it is permitted to buy from him in order to profit on the purchase. These are words of nonsense, for we learned in *Eizehu Neshech* (*Bava Metzia* 71a): Rav Yosef taught: "If you lend money to My people" (*Shemot* 22:24) – "My people or a gentile – My people comes first. The poor or the wealthy – the poor comes first." And the Gemara asks: "My people or a gentile – My people comes first. This is obvious!" And it answers: "Rav Nachman said in the name of Rav Huna: It is only needed to teach us that it applies even if the loan to the gentile was for interest, and the loan to the Jew was not, as required." For it is stated: "To the gentile you shall charge interest" (*Devarim* 23:21). Even so, the positive precept of "If you lend money" sets aside this positive precept ...
>
> And you should not say that this is only where he doesn't suffer an actual loss, but merely doesn't earn a profit, but if he would suffer an actual loss, as in our case, he would not have to give preference to the Jew but he must prefer the Jew even at a loss ... And in *Pesachim*, chapter *Kol Sha'a* (*Pesachim*

21b) the following is stated: "It was taught in a *baraita*: 'You shall not eat of any animal that dies of itself; you shall give it to the stranger who is within your gates, that he may eat it; or you may sell it to a gentile' (*Devarim* 14:21)…." If so, then that which the Torah states, "from the hand of your neighbor,"[teaching that preference is to be given to your fellow Jew over the gentile], refers to a case where the gentile's price is cheaper, for if the Torah refers to a case where the price is the same, there would be no need for a verse, for it is obvious that it is one's neighbor [a Jew] whom one is obligated to sustain. Rather, infer from this as follows, that even if transacting with the gentile can be done at a profit, and from his friend at a loss, nevertheless his friend is given preference. Thus, this ruling – that one should purchase from the Jewish printing over the gentile one – should be applied without delay.

In a similar vein to the *Tashbetz,* the **Rema** maintains that there would be no need for the Torah to speak of the case where the Jew and the gentile offer their merchandise at the same price, as in such a case it is obvious that the Jew is to be given precedence. Thus, it follows that even if a person will suffer a loss if he buys from the Jew, he must still give preference to the Jew. The **Rema** does not discuss the level of loss, but it is clear from his words that his ruling applies even when there is a significant price differential between the Jew and the gentile. For he rejects the notion that when "the gentile is **much cheaper,**" one may buy from him, because even in such a case one must buy from the Jew. Here we are dealing with a significant differential: "much cheaper."

The ***Tashbetz*** does not say that this law applies even when there is a large price differential, but he also does not limit it to a small difference in price. He is silent on the question of the degree of difference. Thus, it stands to reason that the *Tashbetz* refers to a loss that is not insignificant, but he might still agree with the *Tosafot* that in the case of a great loss, one need not give preference to buying from a Jew.

To summarize, according to the Rema, preference must be given to the Jew even in the case of a substantial price differential. According to the *Tashbetz,* preference must be given to buying from a Jew even when there is a certain difference in price, but if that differential is substantial, he might agree that one is not obligated to buy from the Jew.[2]

According to the ***Tosafot,*** on the other hand, only when the Jew and the gentile offer their wares at the same price (*Tosafot, Bava Kama 114a*), or when buying from the Jew will lead only to a small loss (*Tosafot, Avoda Zara 20a*), must one give preference to buying from the Jew over buying from the gentile.

2. This understanding of the difference between the Rema and the *Tashbetz* is also found in *Minchat Yitzchak* (vol. III, no. 129, 3). On the other hand, see *Ahavat Chesed* (of the *Chafetz Chayyim,* 5, 5) who writes that *Teshuvot ha-Rema* implies that preference should be given to buying from a Jew when the price differential is small. The simple understanding of the Rema, however, is that preference should be given to Jewish merchandise even if the price differential is substantial, as he was understood by the aforementioned *Minchat Yitzchak.*

MERCHANTS

A talmudic passage in ***Bava Metzia*** *71a* is also relevant to our discussion:

> "If you lend money to My people" (*Shemot 22:24*) – My people or a gentile – My people comes first... It was stated above: "My people or a gentile – My people comes first." This is obvious! Rav Nachman said: Huna said to me: It is only needed to teach us that it applies even if the loan to the gentile was for interest, and the loan to the Jew was for free.

The Gemara asserts that one must give priority to lending to a Jew at no interest over lending to a gentile at interest. When a person lends money to his fellow Jew at no interest, he forfeits the interest that he could have charged the gentile. Nevertheless, preference must be given to the Jew. From here we see that even when the difference is substantial (the value of the interest), preference must be given to the Jew.

Rav Moshe Feinstein (*Responsa Iggerot Moshe, Yoreh De'a, vol. III,* no. 93) mentions a principle similar to that of the *Tosafot,* and thereby significantly restricts the applicability of the Gemara in *Bava Metzia* 71b:

> In my humble opinion it is obvious that what Rav Nachman said in the name of Rav Huna that My people comes

> first regarding a loan even when the loan to the gentile is at interest, and the loan to the Jew is for nothing (*Bava Metzia* 71a) – this does not apply to a large sum. For why should the profit from interest be different than other profits? And, after all, a person is permitted to do business with his money, even though there are people who are in need of a loan. This is certainly the case when this lending is necessary to make a living, but even in our time, regarding which the *Tosafot* write that it is customary practice to lend at interest even to become wealthy, for this livelihood is no different than other livelihoods.

In other words, that which the Gemara in *Bava Metzia* says that one must give priority to lending money to a Jew at no interest over lending to a gentile at interest, only applies when the sum involved is small. Profit earned from lending money at interest to a gentile is legitimate profit, and a person is permitted to earn a livelihood with his money.

A similar argument is made by the author of the ***Aguda*** (*Bava Metzia 5,* no. *99*), who writes that today "our entire livelihood comes from lending money to gentiles," and therefore priority may be given to lending money at interest to gentiles over lending money at no interest to Jews, for just as a person must be concerned about his neighbor's livelihood [in giving him a loan], so must he be concerned about his own livelihood, and "your life comes before the life of your neighbor."

It is possible, then, that in our time, when Jews regularly engage in business with gentiles, that a businessman whose livelihood depends on commercial transactions would not be obligated to buy from a Jew, if the same merchandise could be purchased from a gentile at a lower price, for he too must earn a living.

This also follows from ***Responsa Maharam Shick*** (*Choshen Mishpat,* no. *31*), which distinguishes between an ordinary person making a purchase and a businessman. A businessman is not required to buy from a Jew if the latter's merchandise is more expensive, for this is the businessman's livelihood. Of course, the goal should be to buy

from a Jew, certainly when the price is the same. Even when there is a price differential, if the difference is small, even a businessman should use the Jewish supplier. The Jewish supplier should also be offered the opportunity to match the price of his gentile competitor, in order that the deal should be concluded with him, for as stated, the goal should certainly be to conduct one's business with Jews to the extent possible.

THE HALACHA

The rule of giving preference to lending money to a Jew at no interest over lending money to a gentile at interest is brought by the Rif (*Bava Metzia,* ad loc.), the Rambam (*Hilchot Malveh ve-Loveh* 5:7), and the Rosh (*Bava Metzia,* ad loc.). The *Shulchan Aruch,* however, omits it (the Gemara's statement about giving priority to lending money to a Jew is recorded in *Choshen Mishpat* 97:1,, but without stating that this applies even if a loan could have been extended to a gentile at interest).

The *Torat Kohanim's* teaching regarding the preference to buy from a Jew is also not brought in the *Shulchan Aruch.* It is possible that the *Torat Kohanim's* position was not accepted as law.

The *Torat Kohanim's* teaching does not appear in the Gemara.[3] Moreover, in *Kiddushin* 26a and in *Bechorot* 13a the Gemara uses the very same verse, "or buy anything from his neighbor's hand," to derive other regulations relating to the law of *meshicha* (acquiring a movable object by pulling it into one's possession), namely, that *meshicha* is only valid when acquiring from a Jew. Does this mean that the Gemara does not accept this law? It is difficult to prove this definitively.[4]

This teaching also appears in the *Pesikta* (*Vayikra* 25, 14) in a different formulation:

> The Torah teaches you proper conduct (*derech eretz*) that one should only sell to one's neighbor and only buy from the hand of one's neighbor...

The *Pesikta* implies that we are dealing here not with a matter

3. *Torat Kohanim's* teaching is, however, cited by Rashi in his commentary to this verse, by *Sefer ha-Chinuch* (*mitzva* no. 337) by Rabbenu Bechaye (*Vayikra* 25:14), and others.

4. The *Rishonim* and the *Acharonim* disagree about the force of rabbinic expositions that do not appear in the Talmud. The Rambam (*Responsa Pe'er ha-Dor,* no. 27) writes to the sages of Lunel about a *midrash* that it is not accepted as law because it does not appear in either the Talmud or in the Tosefta. On the other hand, the *Kesef Mishneh* (*Hilchot Nedarim,* chap. 12) writes that unless we find that the Talmud disagrees, there is no reason to reject a *baraita* merely because "it is not mentioned in one of the Talmuds or in the *Tosefta*... and in several places our master [the Rambam] rules in accordance with a *baraita* in the *Sifrei,* even though it is not mentioned in the Gemara or in the *Tosefta.*" There is much to be said on this matter, but it is beyond the scope of this work. See also *Yad Mal'achi, kelalei shenei ha-talmudim,* no. 4; *Yabi'a Omer,* vol. III, *Orach Chayim,* no. 3, 5; ibid., vol. IV, *Even ha-Ezer,* 8, 1; *Ateret Paz,* vol. III, *Choshen Mishpat,* no. 10, 8.

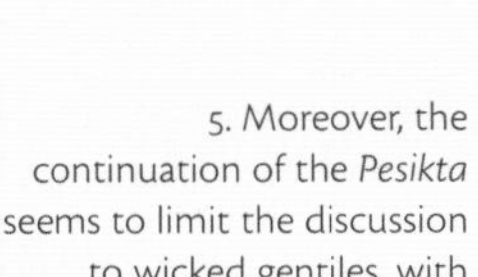

of law, but merely with proper conduct, meaning that this is the proper way that a person should conduct himself but not a legally binding statement.[5]

5. Moreover, the continuation of the *Pesikta* seems to limit the discussion to wicked gentiles, with whom it recommends that one not engage in commercial transactions.

Perhaps these are the reasons that led the *Shulchan Aruch* to omit this law. On the other hand, various talmudic passages imply the principle that preference should be given to buying from a Jew. Moreover, the Rema and the *Tashbetz* saw this as legally binding, and this was also the ruling of the *Chatam Sofer* (*Responsa Chatam Sofer, Choshen Mishpat,* no. 79).

THE PRICE DIFFERENTIAL

We have seen that according to the simple understanding of the **Rema,** preference should be given to buying from a Jew even when this involves a major financial loss. The later halachic authorities imply, however, that even if we assume that preference should be given to buying from a Jew, this does not apply in the case of a major loss. This follows from ***Minchat Yitzchak*** (vol. *III,* no. *129*), ***Iggerot* Moshe** (*Yoreh De'a,* vol. *III,* no. 93) and ***Ateret Paz*** (vol. *III,* no. *10*), who imply that preference must be given to a Jew only when the price differential is minor. This is also the position of ***Yaskil Avdi*** (vol. *IV,* no. *6*), who writes that giving preference to a Jew even in the case of a major loss, while commendable behavior, is not required by the law (see also *Chikrei Lev, Choshen Mishpat,* no. 139).[6]

What is considered a minor price differential? ***Minchat Yitzchak*** (*vol. III, no. 129*) discusses the matter and concludes that the differential is a sixth, that is to say, 16.6%. ***Piskei Uziel*** (*no. 48*) discusses the importance of buying from Jews, and writes that the added price that must be paid is not measured in percentages, but rather it varies "in accordance with the standard of living." According to this, there is room to reexamine from time to time the price differential in light of current and local circumstances.

As was noted earlier (according to the Maharam Shick), with respect to a businessman, even a minor differential can be significant enough to permit buying from a gentile. Clearly, however, if

6. Regarding these issues, see also Rav Y. Shaviv, *Betzir Aviezer*, p. 52; Rav Sh. Aviner, *Shana be-Shana*, 5747, p. 235.

the price differential is only minor (the price differential should not be measured per unit, but according to the transaction as a whole), one should try to buy from the Jew (or at least to offer him the opportunity to match the price charged by the gentile).

In addition to the law discussed above, there is an additional *mitzva* of "You shall support him" (*Vayikra 25:35*). In a famous passage (*Hilchot Matanot Aniyim 10:7*), the **Rambam** writes as follows:

> There are eight levels of charity, each greater than the next. The greatest level, above which there is no other, is to strengthen the hand of another Jew who has grown poor by giving him a present or a loan, or entering into a partnership with him, or finding him a job in order to strengthen his hand before he needs to beg from people. For it is said: "You shall strengthen him, though he be a stranger or a sojourner, that he may live with you" (*Vayikra 25:35*), that is to say, strengthen him before he falls and becomes needy.

Oftentimes when a person buys from a Jew, he enables him to earn a living. In such a case, in addition to giving priority to buying from a Jew, he fulfills the *mitzvot* of giving charity.

Therefore, when there exists a price differential between the Jewish and the gentile merchandise, and the Jewish seller is a man of means, there is no reason that the buyer should buy from him and suffer a loss, for the verse, "That your brother may live with you," applies to the buyer as well. If the Jewish seller is not wealthy, there is reason to show him preference even if his merchandise is slightly more expensive, based on the law of "or buy anything from your neighbor's hand." If the Jewish seller is in dire economic straits, then in addition to the obligation of conducting one's business with a Jew, there is also a *mitzva* "that your brother may live with you," and the buyer fulfills the highest level of giving charity. According to this, the buyer may deduct the price differential from his charity obligation, his *ma'aser kesafim*, provided that he buys from the Jew in order to support him (according to *Responsa Teshuvot ve-Hanhagot*, vol. *II*, no. *477*).

Even in the case where the seller himself is wealthy, if he offers his merchandise at the same price as the gentile, preference must be given to buying from the Jew. This follows from the aforementioned *Torat Kohanim,* and from *Avoda Zara* 20a, even according to *Tosafot* and other *Rishonim* who limit the application of the law. It also stands to reason that in general, preference should be given to benefitting a Jew over benefitting a gentile. (This is obvious to all the aforementioned authorities, such as the *Tashbetz,* and even to those who do not see it as an obligation by strict law, such as *Maharam Shick,* no. 31; *Yaskil Avdi,* vol. IV, *Choshen Mishpat,* nos. 6, 2, 8, and others.)

EXTRA EFFORT

Sometimes buying from a Jew does not involve paying more, but it requires extra effort, such as extra travel or the like. The **Rashba** (*Responsa ha-Rashba,* vol. *1, nos. 430* and *687,* cited by the *Bet Yosef, Yoreh De'a 109*) implies that the effort of having to go somewhere else is not regarded as trouble. ***Responsa ha-Maharsham*** (vol. *II,* no. *81*), however, cites the Rashba's ruling and adds that having to go a short distance is not regarded as a loss, but having to go a long distance is indeed treated like a loss. The ***Chochmat Adam*** (*53,* no. *23*) (with respect to a forbidden utensil that became intermingled with other utensils,) writes that major effort is regarded as a loss (and therefore we can invoke the law of *bittul* and not require that the utensils be *koshered*). Sometimes, and especially in the modern world, trouble and effort can be measured in monetary terms. In any event, it is clear that one should make minor efforts in order to buy from a Jew (see the aforementioned *Responsa Maharam Shik* and *Yaskil Avdi*).

SUMMARY:

When a person wishes to buy a certain article, and it can be purchased from a Jew or from a gentile –

1. If the price is the same and there is also no difference in the effort, preference must be given to buying from the Jew (in light of the passage in *Avoda Zara* 20a according to all understandings, *Torat Kohanim,* and natural feelings of Jewish solidarity).
2. If buying from the Jew requires only minor added effort, it is fitting that one buy from the Jew (based on the Rashba, who claims that such effort is not regarded as a loss).
3. If there is a substantial price differential, it is permitted to buy from the gentile (in order to maintain one's own financial well-being as well). If the Jewish seller is in dire financial straits, then based on the law of "that your brother may live with you" and in fulfillment of the *mitzva* of giving charity, it is meritorious to buy from the Jew when this is economically feasible for the buyer. In such a case, the price differential may be deducted from his charity obligation.
4. If there is only a minor price differential (some say 16.6%, while others write that it varies according to circumstances), it is fitting to buy from the Jew (according to the Rema and the *Tashbetz,* this is required by law, whereas according to Maharam Shick, *Yaskil Avdi* and *Teshuvot ve-Hanhagot,* it is commendable behavior but not required). If, however, the Jewish seller is wealthy, the Jewish buyer is under no obligation to pay more and thereby suffer a loss.
5. If the buyer is also a businessman, even a small price differential can be significant, since this is the buyer's livelihood, and therefore, it is permitted to buy from the gentile. Even in such a case, however, the goal must be to buy from Jews (both because of the *Torat Kohanim's* teaching regarding "or buy", and because of the importance of benefitting Jews and supporting Jewish commerce). The Jewish buyer should, therefore, carefully examine whether or not the price differential is really significant for him, and should also try to negotiate a lower price that will allow both parties to profit.

GIVING PREFERENCE TO JEWISH PRODUCE DURING *SHEMITA*

The aforementioned rules regarding buying from Jews apply in all realms of commerce and at all times. During the *Shemita* year another element must be considered. As we have seen, the cost of *Shemita* observance is very high. In the past, the financial consequences of *Shemita* were shared by all of Jewish society. Today, the agricultural sector constitutes less than 2% of the Israeli population, and the costs of *Shemita* observance fall almost exclusively on the shoulders of farmers.

Economically speaking, it might be cheaper to import produce, but this would land a severe blow upon Israeli farmers and destroy their livelihood. This is one reason to prefer buying Jewish produce, even at a higher price. As stated above, supporting Jewish farmers so that they not collapse constitutes a fulfillment of the *mitzvah,* "That your brother may live with you."

Supporting Jewish farmers involves supporting Jewish agriculture in Eretz Yisrael. One might have suggested that we do away with Jewish agriculture and rely solely on imported produce. But is this what the Torah really wants? Without a doubt, the Torah wishes that, with regard to the land of Israel, "we eat of its fruit and fill ourselves with its goodness." To meet this end, we must make sure that Israel's farmers are able to bear the burden, and that they will continue to work the land after the *Shemita* year as well.

In addition, buying Jewish produce means participating in the *mitzva* of *Shemita* which is meant to apply to the entire Jewish people. Most people continue to earn their usual livelihood during the *Shemita* year. It is only upon the agricultural sector (and those working in related industries) that *Shemita* observance has a significant economic impact. The rest of the population pays a relatively small price, while the major burden falls upon the farmers.

And furthermore, buying Jewish produce gives halachic support to the *Shemita* year. As we have seen, in order to observe the *Shemita* year, and certainly to do so in the halachically preferred manner, financial investment is necessary. There are farmers who rely on the *heter mechira,* but invest resources so that labors that are forbidden by Torah law will not be performed by Jews. Other farmers try to observe *Shemita* to a high standard and market their produce through "*Otzar Bet Din,*" which generally means a drop in income (and sometimes puts the court that collects the produce in financial jeopardy). Using *Otzar Bet Din* also forces farmers to employ different agricultural methods, which create more work and yield an inferior crop (manifest, among other things, in the produce's appearance), because of the labors that are forbidden during the *Shemita* year.

Some farmers try to observe *Shemita* to a high standard by raising crops in hothouses and on detached bedding – changes that are very costly. The more we buy produce that is grown in a halachically satisfactory manner or in a halachically preferred manner, the more we support stricter *Shemita* observance. Those who rely on the *heter mechira* will make sure that the crops are planted by gentiles. "Supply and demand" will impact the farmers' level of observance of the laws of *Shemita.*

When we buy *Shemita* produce, we allow more farmers to join the circle of stricter *Shemita* observance, and thus we strengthen the observance of *Shemita.* People outside the agricultural sector are given the opportunity to be partners in the observance of the *mitzva* of *Shemita* in the best possible manner. When we buy *Otzar Bet Din* produce, we also merit to eat produce sanctified with *Shemita* sanctity.

To summarize: It is a *mitzva* to buy *Shemita* produce marketed through *Otzar Bet Din* or produce grown on detached bedding, rather than to buy imported produce. One may also buy sixth year produce, produce planted in the sixth year, and produce grown in the Southern Arava.

When such produce is not available, one may buy *heter mechira* fruit (or *heter mechira* vegetables that were planted during the sixth year). When it is necessary to buy *heter mechira* vegetables that were planted during the seventh year: If the planting was done by gentiles in accordance with Rav Kook's stipulations (and this is the case with the *heter mechira* produce of the current *Shemita* year), preference should be given to such produce over imported or other gentile produce. *Heter mechira* fruits and vegetables are certainly permissible to be eaten, and while there are halachically preferred alternatives, they are limited to Jewish produce. Gentile produce cannot be regarded as halachically preferable. There is no such thing as "*Shemita le-mehadrin* – gentile produce." "*Shemita le-mehadrin*" can only apply to Jewish produce!

Even though preference should be given to Jewish produce, if, in ordinary years, certain produce is obtained from gentile sources, such produce may be purchased from gentiles in the *Shemita* year as well.[7] Similarly, if most of the vegetables that one buys were grown by Jews in a halachically preferred manner, one may also buy a small amount of other vegetables grown by gentiles, making sure that the sum total of Jewish produce bought during the *Shemita* year is no less than the Jewish produce bought in regular years.

Raising crops while observing *Shemita* in the best possible manner requires an investment of resources. Purchasing such produce sometimes demands greater efforts on the part of the consumer in order to reach the distribution centers. *Shemita* produce grown in accordance with the strictest standards is sometimes more expensive (farmers must also be careful not to raise their prices unnecessarily). And maintaining the sanctity of such produce sometimes demands more careful attention and greater efforts in the kitchen.

Despite all of these difficulties, we must make great efforts to buy *Shemita* produce grown by Jews, and not to buy imported produce when doing so will harm Jewish agriculture in Eretz Yisrael (with

7. Until several years ago, 90% of certain major crops of vegetables (such as cucumbers) were grown in Israel by gentiles. Today, these numbers have dropped significantly, and only 50%, or even less, of these crops are grown by gentiles.

the exception of commodities that are imported to Israel in ordinary years as well). The reasons are as follows:

1. According to the **Rema** and the ***Tashbetz***, based on ***Torat Kohanim***, one is obligated to buy from a Jew and not from a gentile. There is a disagreement whether this applies only when the price differential is minor or even when the difference is substantial, but in the case of a small differential and minor added effort, one is clearly obligated to show preference to the Jew (for details, see the summary above).
2. Failure to buy Jewish produce is liable to bring the Jewish farmers to economic ruin. Therefore, buying from Jews constitutes a fulfillment of the *mitzva* "That your brother may live with you." As Rav Kalman Kahana has warned, the positive commandment "that your brother may live with you" is oftentimes lest strictly observed than simple customs (see Dr. Moshe Sachs, "*Shemirat Shemita, Ha-Kesher bein Yetzur u-Tzericha,*" *Shana be-Shana,* 5761).
3. When we buy from Jews, we strengthen Jewish agriculture in Eretz Yisrael, helping to prevent it from collapsing so that we will continue to "eat of its fruit and satiate ourselves with its goodness," and not from imported produce.
4. Buying Jewish produce during the *Shemita* year is a way to participate in the observance of the *mitzva* of *Shemita*. The financial burden spreads out over all of Israel (as the Torah had in mind), and is not limited to 2% of the population.
5. Raising crops during the *Shemita* year is costly to the farmers and certainly involves much more work. This is especially true about produce grown on detached bedding, and often true about *Otzar Bet Din* produce as well (and even *heter mechira* produce when biblically-forbidden labors are performed by gentiles). Therefore, even if the prices are higher than usual, they reflect costs that we, as consumers, should be willing to absorb (the farmers must, of course, be careful to charge a fair price for their produce).
6. Buying produce that was grown in a halachically satisfactory

8. See at length this author's article in *Emunat Itecha* 70, 5767.

manner or in a halachically preferred manner strengthens the observance of *Shemita,* and brings farmers to stricter observance with each successive *Shemita.*

7. When we buy *Otzar Bet Din* produce, we enjoy the added privilege of eating *Shemita* produce and partaking of the unique sanctity of the produce of Eretz Yisrael during the *Shemita* year.[8]

May we all try to buy and eat during the *Shemita* year produce grown in the best possible manner by Jews in Eretz Yisrael, and thus be partners in the observance of the *mitzva* of *Shemita*.

THE FOUR SPECIES – *LULAV, ETROG, HADASIM* AND *ARAVOT* – DURING *SHEMITA*

Do any special problems arise with respect to the purchase of the four species of *Sukkot* – *lulav, etrog, hadasim* and *aravot* – during the *Shemita* year? Let us briefly examine the law regarding each of the four species.

Etrog*:** The *Shemita* sanctity of vegetables is determined by the date of **harvest.** This is why, from the very beginning of the *Shemita* year, one must be careful when purchasing vegetables, because if they were picked after *Rosh ha-Shana*, they have *Shemita* sanctity. Regarding fruit, on the other hand, the critical date is that of ***chanata (either when the fruit first begins to assume shape, or when it reaches a third of its growth). Therefore, the fruit that is brought to the market at the beginning of the *Shemita* year does not have *Shemita* sanctity, and it is only towards *Pesach* that fruit with *Shemita* sanctity becomes available.

How do we categorize the *etrog*? At first glance, it seems clear that an *etrog* is the fruit of a tree, and therefore *Shemita* sanctity should apply to it only in the eighth year (because any *etrog* that is available for *Sukkot* of the seventh year had reached *chanata* during the sixth year). This is the position of the **Ra'avad** (*Hilchot Ma'aser Sheni 1:5*) and most *Rishonim*, based on the *Mishna* in *Bikkurim* (*2:6*). The **Rambam** (ibid.), however, rules that an *etrog* is treated like a vegetable (because an *etrog* needs extensive watering just like a vegetable, as indicated by the *Gemara Kiddushin* 3a), and therefore the critical date regarding *Shemita* sanctity is the date on which the *etrog* is **picked** (see at length in the chapter dealing with *Shemita* sanctity).

According to most *Rishonim*, the *etrog* used on *Sukkot* (celebrated at the beginning of the *Shemita* year) does not have *Shemita* sanctity. However, according to the Rambam, it does have *Shemita* sanctity. In practice, despite the fact that strictly speaking an *etrog* is treated like a fruit, we try to be stringent and assign it *Shemita* sanctity according to the date of its **harvest**, as if it were a vegetable (see *Chazon Ish, Shevi'it 7, 10; Shevet ha-Levi, I*, no. 175).

Strictly speaking, **it is permitted to use a *Shemita etrog* to fulfill the *mitzva* of the four species**, only that the sale of such an *etrog* raises certain problems (it must be done through the *Otzar Bet Din)*. For this reason, *etrogim* are generally picked **before *Rosh ha-Shana* of the *Shemita* year** (as is done in ordinary years as well, in order to allow time for the *etrogim* to be sorted and brought to market), and thus they do not have *Shemita* sanctity. During **the eighth year** (in accordance with most *Rishonim), etrogim* do have *Shemita* sanctity, and therefore they must be sold through the ***Otzar Bet Din***. (After *Sukkot,* the *etrog* should not be thrown into the garbage, but rather it should be eaten, or else placed in a bag and later discarded in a respectful manner).

When an *etrog* is purchased with *kashrut* certification, the certification presumably relates to the *Shemita* sanctity as well.

***Lulav*:** The Gemara in *Sukka* 39b states that a *lulav* has *Shemita* sanctity. As Rashi explains, this is because a *lulav* can be used to sweep the house (and "its benefit comes at the time of its consumption"). The **Rambam**, however, omits this law (and in his commentary to the *Mishna* he writes explicitly that a *lulav* does not have *Shemita* sanctity). **Rabbenu Gershom** (*Bechorot 31b*) and others[1] also write that *Shemita* sanctity does not apply to a *lulav.*

What is the halachic ruling on this matter? **Rabbi Akiva Eiger** (on the Mishna, *Sukka 3:11*) rules that a *lulav* has *Shemita* sanctity, because there are places where it is still used to sweep the house. According to the **Bartenura** (*Sukka 3:11,* and *Tosafot, Bava Kama 102a,* s.v. *ve-ha-ikka,* and Rabbenu Chananel, ad loc. and others), a *lulav* does not have *Shemita* sanctity because it is regarded as a mere piece of wood.

According to Rav Auerbach (*Minchat Shlomo, I,* no. 51), *Shemita* sanctity does not apply to a *lulav*, because *lulavim* are no longer used to sweep the floor.[2]

Thus, in practice, ***Shemita* sanctity does not apply to *lulavim*, and they may be cut down as usual.** (Even those who wish to be more stringent may cut them, but not in a commercial manner. In

1. According to them, it would appear that *Shemita* sanctity only applies to that which is intended for human or animal consumption (Rashba, *Bava Kama 102a*, s.v. *hachi garas ha-Ra'avad*; Ritva, *Sukka 40a*). Alternatively, they maintain that since most wood is intended to be used for heating, *Shemita* sanctity does not apply even to *lulavim* (*Kappot Temarim, Sukka 40a*, s.v. *od katav Rashi*). There is also room to discuss whether sweeping the house is regarded as "consumption."

2. The *Chazon Ish's* position on this issue is unclear, though it stands to reason that he maintains that *Shemita* sanctity does not apply to *lulavim*, even though it is possible to sweep with them, because according to the *Chazon Ish*, the determining factor is the actual use (*Chazon Ish, Shevi'it*, 14). However, in *Chazon Ish* 13, 7, he writes that *Shemita* sanctity does apply to things from which brooms are made, and so too we find in *Responsa Az Nidberu* (IV, no. 57) and in *Orchot Rabbenu* (II, p. 326) that one should be stringent. It seems that the prevailing approach is to be lenient, in accordance with the *Chazon Ish's* fundamental position, that anything that does not actually serve a particular purpose has no *Shemita* sanctity, even if it theoretically could be used for a particular task. Rav Kook was stringent on this issue, yet there is room to discuss whether his stringency would also apply.

any event, all agree that regarding *Sukkot* of the seventh year, *Shemita* sanctity does not apply to the *lulavim*, because their main growth was during the sixth year).

***Hadasim*:** The *Yerushalmi* (7:1) questions whether or not aromatic plants have *Shemita* sanctity, and the *Acharonim* have generally ruled stringently (Rav Auerbach, Rav Wosner, Rav Elyashiv). Accordingly, *Shemita* sanctity should apply to *hadasim*. According to **Maharil Diskin** (*Sefer ha-Shemita*, chap. 7:4, 6, in his name) and **Rav Auerbach** (cited in *Responsa Mishnat Yosef*, I, no. 25), however, *Shemita* sanctity does not apply to the *hadasim* used for the *mitzva*, because they are not intended for their fragrance, but rather for the *mitzva*. Some write that the *Chazon Ish* was stringent on the matter (*Hilchot Shevi'it, Kuntres Dalet Minim*, 1, 8; *Orchot Rabbenu*, II, p. 326. In any event, all agree that regarding *Sukkot* during the seventh year, *Shemita* sanctity does not apply to the *hadasim*, because their main growth was during the sixth year).

In practice: One may be lenient with respect to *hadasim*. All agree that one may cut them and use them (the only question is about cutting them in a commercial manner and selling them). Even in ordinary years, it is customary to bag the *hadasim* after the holiday before discarding them, rather than throw them directly into the garbage. (On *Sukkot* during the seventh year, they clearly have no *Shemita* sanctity, because their main growth was during the sixth year).

***Aravot*:** All agree that *Shemita* sanctity does not apply to *aravot*, and therefore they may be cut and sold in the usual manner.

***Sechach* or branches overhanging a *sukka*:** These have no *Shemita* sanctity and may be cut as usual (even palm fronds). They should not, however, be cut in a special manner in order to stimulate additional growth.

SUMMARY:

***Etrog*:** According to most opinions, the *etrog* used on *Sukkot* of the eighth year has *Shemita* sanctity (even if it was picked in the eighth year). The *etrog* used on *Sukkot* of the seventh year, however, does

to a *lulav*, since it is possible that he would be lenient in light of the words of the Rambam and others. This is also the ruling of *Shevi'it ba-Halacha* (p. 198) and *Shevet ha-Levi* (I, no. 181).

not have *Shemita* sanctity (even if it was picked during the seventh year). In general, the *etrogim* used during the seventh year are picked already in the sixth year, and therefore all agree that there is no *Shemita* sanctity.

***Lulav*:** In practice, a *lulav* does not have *Shemita* sanctity, because it is no longer used for any other purpose (Rav Auerbach). Some authorities are stringent.

***Hadasim*:** In practice, *hadasim* do not have *Shemita* sanctity, because they are intended for the *mitzva,* and not for their fragrance (Rav Auerbach). Some authorities are stringent.

***Aravot*:** *Aravot* have no *Shemita* sanctity.

Even if and when *Shemita* sanctity applies to the four species, they may still be cut and used, but must be cut and sold in a manner that is appropriate for *Shemita* produce.

Sechach* and branches overhanging a *sukka: May be cut in the usual manner.

SHEMITA OIL AND *MISHLO'ACH MANOT* DURING THE *SHEMITA* YEAR

Is it permitted to light Shabbat candles with *Shemita* oil?

Is it permitted to send *mishlo'ach manot* on Purim consisting of *Shemita* produce?

***Shemita* oil**: **Lighting Shabbat candles:** It is permitted to light Shabbat candles with *Shemita* oil, because deriving benefit from the light produced by *Shemita* oil is the same as deriving benefit from eating *Shemita* produce (Mishna, *Shevi'it 8:2*; Rambam, *Hilchot Shemita ve-Yovel 5:1*).

Lighting Chanuka candles: According to the **Ridbaz** (*Bet Ridbaz, 5, 9*), it is forbidden to light Chanuka candles with *Shemita* oil, because it is forbidden to derive benefit from the light of Chanuka candles, and thus lighting Chanuka candles with *Shemita* oil involves destruction of *Shemita* produce (*Responsa Imrei Yosher*, no. 100 writes the same). This ruling is difficult to understand. First of all, why should it be forbidden to use *Shemita* produce for the fulfillment of a *mitzva*? Is it possible to say that using *Shemita* produce for the fulfillment of a *mitzva* constitutes destruction of the produce?! This argument is put forward by Rav Auerbach (*Responsa Minchat Shlomo, 1,* no. *42*): "How can one say that it is permitted to light *Shemita* oil for personal needs, but for the sake of a *mitzva* it is forbidden?" Indeed, there is a principle that "*mitzvot* were not given for the pleasure derived therefrom," but this does not mean that it is forbidden to derive pleasure from a *mitzva*, but only that such pleasure is not defined as pleasure and therefore a *mitzva* item is not technically considered an item from which deriving pleasure is forbidden. Moreover, it might be permitted to derive benefit from the light of Chanuka candles from a distance, at least for certain purposes (see *Mishna Berura 673*, no. *11*; *Sha'ar ha-Tziyun*, ad loc. no. *11*; *Sha'arei Teshuva*, ad loc.). The same argument is also put forth in ***Responsa Shevet ha-Levi*** (*1, 184*). Additionally, today we use an extra candle as the *shamash*, which might make it permissible to derive benefit from the light of all the candles together (see Rema

673:1 and *Taz,* ad loc. But see also *Mishna Berura* and *Bei'ur Halacha,* ad loc.) The rationale underlying this allowance is that when deriving benefit in such a manner, people will not say that the candles were lit for their light. The rationale for a prohibition, on the other hand, is that even in such a case, there is concern that people will say that the candles were lit for their light there may be an independent prohibition to derive benefit from the light of Chanuka candles, similar to the prohibition to derive benefit from the Temple. (See also *Ha-Torah ve-ha-Aretz,* pp. *81* and *211*).

In practice: The **Ridbaz** (ibid.) and the ***Imrei Yosher*** (ibid.) forbid lighting Chanuka candles with *Shemita* oil, whereas **Rav Auerbach** permits it. ***Responsa Shevet ha-Levi*** writes that it should be permitted, but since there are great authorities who are stringent, we should follow them, even though "their rationale is not very clear to us."

It would seem, therefore, that in the absence of some special need, it is preferable not to use *Shemita* oil for lighting Chanuka candles, and to save the oil for other purposes. When, however, there is some special need (including a financial one), one may be lenient and use the *Shemita* oil for the Chanuka candles, because the lenient position is extremely reasonable.

***Mishlo'ach Manot* consisting of *Shemita* produce**: Some authorities argue that one must not send *Shemita* produce as *mishlo'ach manot,* because that would involve paying a debt with *Shemita* produce (*Responsa Mishnat Yosef, I,* no. *27*; *III,* no. *41*; *Mishnat Ya'avetz, Shevi'it* p. *92*). Strictly speaking, however, one may be lenient, because *mishlo'ach manot* is not really payment of a debt and it is not similar to trading in *Shemita* produce, as it is given as a gift. This is the view of most halachic authorities (Rav Auerbach, *Dinei Shevi'it ha-Shalem, 17, 9*; Rav Ya'akov Yisra'el Kanievsky, *Orchot Rabbenu,* p. *334*; Rav Elyashiv, *Mevakshei Torah,* Adar *II, 5755,* p. *187*; *Minchat Yitzchak,* X, no. *57*; and see also *Ha-Torah ve-ha-Aretz 6,* p. *216*). One who wishes to be stringent should make sure that the first set of *mishlo'ach manot* that he sends includes two items that do not have *Shemita* sanctity.

REMOVING *SHEMITA* PRODUCE FROM ERETZ YISRAEL

Oil [of impure *teruma*] that must be burned and *Shemita* produce must not be removed from Eretz Yisrael.

The prohibition to remove *Shemita* produce from Eretz Yisrael is recorded in the **Mishna** (*Shevi'it 6:5,* and also *in Torat Kohanim, Behar, parasha 1, 9*).

This prohibition is codified by the **Rambam** (*Hilchot Shemita ve-Yovel 5:13*), and also by the *Acharonim* (*Pe'at ha-Shulchan 24:18; Shabbat ha-Aretz, 5, 13, 1–3*). The prohibition is restricted to produce that has *Shemita* sanctity. Hence, non-fragrant flowers may be exported, and according to Rav Auerbach, so may fragrant flowers that are grown for ornamental use.

The halachic authorities disagree whether taking *Shemita* produce out of Eretz Yisrael is prohibited by Torah law or by rabbinic decree. According to the ***Responsa Meshiv Davar*** (*II,* no. *56*) and the **Ridbaz** (*Bet Ridbaz, 5, 18*), it is a Torah prohibition. The Ridbaz adds, however, that according to the **Ra'avad**, the prohibition is only by rabbinic decree, and according to the ***Chazon Ish*** (*13, 3*) this is the *halacha*.[1]

WHY IS IT FORBIDDEN TO TAKE *SHEMITA* PRODUCE OUT OF ERETZ YISRAEL?

1. The **Rash** (*Shevi'it 6:5*), the **Rosh** (ibid.) and the **Bartenura** (ibid.) understand that the prohibition stems from the need to perform *bi'ur* (removal from the house) at the appropriate time, and *bi'ur* can only be performed in Eretz Yisrael.[2]
2. The **Rash** (on *Torat Kohanim, Behar, parasha 1, 9*) and the **Ra'avad** (ibid.) understand that *Shemita* produce must not be taken out of Eretz Yisrael for fear that it will not be handled in accordance with its *Shemita* sanctity, because it will become mixed together with produce that grew outside of Eretz Yisrael.

1. According to *Shabbat ha-Aretz* (*Kuntres Acharon, 23,* and similarly *Mishmeret ha-Bayit 21b*), the Rash rules that there is no difference between the prohibition to remove produce from Eretz Yisrael during the *Shemita* year and the prohibition to do so during ordinary years. While this position has not been accepted as *halacha*, it can be combined with other opinions in support of leniency.

2. This is their resolution to the Tannaitic dispute on *Pesachim 52a*.

Practical differences between these two understandings are whether or not the prohibition to remove *Shemita* produce from Eretz Yisrael applies to the following: to *Shemita* produce after the *mitzva* of *bi'ur* has already been fulfilled, to *Shemita* produce that is not subject to the obligation of *bi'ur*, and to a small quantity of *Shemita* produce that will certainly be consumed before the time of *bi'ur* arrives. The **Ridbaz** (*Bet Ridbaz, 5, 18,* in a note), indeed, permits the removal of *Shemita* produce from Eretz Yisrael in these scenarios, and the ***Aderet*** (*Shemen Ra'anan, 11, Kuntres Shabbat ha-Aretz*) is similarly lenient. In light of this, there is room to be lenient and permit the export of fresh *Shemita* produce from Israel, when it is known with certainty that the produce will be eaten prior to the time of *bi'ur.*

Some of the *posekim* suggest another possibility, namely, that *Shemita* produce must not be taken out of Eretz Yisrael because that produce is to be eaten specifically by those who live in Eretz Yisrael. This explanation sheds light on the ruling of **Rav Chayim Berlin** (cited in *Bet Ridbaz, 72b* in a note, where he writes that he does not know the source for the ruling) and the **Maharsham** (*Mishmeret Shalom,* in *Mishpat Shalom, Choshen Mishpat 231*), that if the produce was designated for export from the time of planting, there is no prohibition to remove it from Eretz Yisrael. In such a case, exporting the produce does not hurt the residents of Eretz Yisrael.

This explanation also allows us to understand the views brought in *Bet Ridbaz* (*Mishmeret ha-Bayit 22a,* cited also in *Responsa Mishnat Yosef,* no. *86,* p. *162*), that if there is more *Shemita* produce than can be eaten by the people living in Eretz Yisrael, the excess may be exported. It seems that there is greater room to apply this leniency to *Otzar Bet Din* produce, because the court can decide that the excess produce is not needed in Eretz Yisrael, and therefore can be exported.[3]

3. On this entire issue, see *Shemita Mamlachtit*, ch. 14.

This is clearly a complex issue, and the question of whether it is preferable to export produce during the *Shemita* year using the *heter mechira* or some other solution, such as *Otzar Bet Din,* must be carefully examined.

TERUMOT AND *MA'ASROT* DURING THE *SHEMITA* YEAR

Rashi (*Rosh ha-Shana 15a,* s.v. *amar leh Abaye*) notes in the name of the ***Mechilta*** that *Shemita* produce is exempt from *terumot* and *ma'asrot*:

> As it was taught in the *Mechilta*: "That the poor of your people may eat: and what they leave, the beasts of the field shall eat" (*Shemot 23:11*). Just as a beast eats and is exempt from tithes, so too a person is exempt.

Why is *Shemita* produce exempt from tithes?

Rashi (ad loc., s.v. *yad ha-kol*) explains that *Shemita* produce is exempt from *terumot* and *ma'asrot* because such produce is ownerless and "ownerless produce is exempt from tithes." A similar explanation is offered by the **Rambam** (*Hilchot Matenot Aniyim 6:5*).

Tosafot (ad loc. s.v. *yad ha-kol*) argue that it is unnecessary to introduce the element of ownerless produce. *Shemita* produce is exempt from *terumot* and *ma'asrot* because of its very sanctity. *Tosafot's* position is very reasonable, because if the exemption really stemmed from the fact that the produce is ownerless, there would be no need for a special verse teaching us that *Shemita* produce is exempt, since there is a general rule that ownerless produce is not subject to the laws of *terumot* and *ma'asrot* (see *Turei Even, Rosh ha-Shana,* ibid. s.v. *petura,* and *Responsa Minchat Yitzchak,* vol. *VI,* no. *129*).

The ***Bet Yosef*** (*Responsa Avkat Rochel,* no. *24,* s.v. *ve-ata ra'iti; Yoreh De'a 331*) follows the position of the **Rambam** that *Shemita* produce is exempt from *terumot* and *ma'asrot* because it is ownerless, and ownerless produce is exempt from tithes (*Hilchot Ma'asrot 1:1*). The **Mabit** (*Responsa,* vol. *I, no.* 11) seems to follow the position of ***Tosafot*** that it is the *Shemita* sanctity itself that exempts the produce from *terumot* and *ma'asrot*.

As opposed to the laws of *terumot* and *ma'asrot,* the laws of *orla* and *reva'i* (which prohibit all benefit from fruit from trees in their first three years, and require the consumption of the fruit in its fourth year in Jerusalem) do apply to *Shemita* produce (*Rambam, Hilchot Ma'aser Sheni ve-Neta Reva'i 9:6*). Produce that grew on detached bedding should be tithed without reciting the usual blessing.

THE PRODUCE OF A GENTILE

The general rule with regard to tithing is that there is no obligation to tithe produce until its harvesting and ingathering is completed (*gemar melacha*). If the *gemar melacha* takes place while the produce is in the hands of a gentile, the produce need not be tithed. The ***Bet Yosef*** and the **Mabit** disagree regarding a case where the *gemar melacha* takes place while the produce is in a Jew's possession (such as if a Jew purchases grapes from a gentile, and then presses them to make wine, as we explained in the chapter dealing with declaring *Shemita* produce ownerless and in the discussion about the *heter mechira*).

The ***Bet Yosef*** argues that during the *Shemita* year the produce of a gentile is subject to *terumot* and *ma'asrot* (if the *gemar melacha* takes place in the hands of the Jew). He bases his position on two assumptions (though either one would suffice to lead to his conclusion):

1. The produce of a gentile has no *Shemita* sanctity, and thus it is like the produce of other years and subject to *terumot* and *ma'asrot*.
2. Even if the produce of a gentile would have *Shemita* sanctity (as argued by the Mabit), it would still be necessary to tithe it, because that produce was never declared ownerless, and the exemption from *terumot* and *ma'asrot* during the *Shemita* year follows from the fact that the produce is ownerless.

The **Mabit** disagrees with both of these assumptions. As for the *Bet Yosef's* first argument, the Mabit maintains that the produce of a gentile has *Shemita* sanctity. As for the second argument, he disagrees on two points: First, he maintains that *Shemita* produce is independently exempt from *terumot* and *ma'asrot*, not because of the law governing ownerless produce. Second, even if we accept the Rambam's view that the exemption stems from the laws of ownerless produce, the Mabit maintains that *Shemita* produce is regarded as ownerless even if it was never declared as such, and even if it is grown by a non-Jew on land which he owns.

The *Bet Yosef* was so convinced about the correctness of his position that he declared a ban on anybody who refrains from tithing produce purchased from a gentile during the *Shemita* year (*Responsa Avkat Rochel,* no. 25). The Maharit notes (no. 43), however, that even the *Bet Yosef* himself established that such produce requires tithing only as an added stringency, and that later he retracted his view and agreed with the Mabit that the produce of a gentile need not be tithed. The Mabit himself maintains that the produce of a gentile should not be tithed, even as an added stringency, because it is a stringency that leads to leniency, namely, the destruction of the *Shemita* produce set aside as tithes (and this is also mentioned in the *Sefer Charedim*). On the other hand, the **Chida** (*Birket Yosef, Yoreh De'a 331, 10*) writes that the *Bet Yosef* never retracted his view, and the ***Pe'at ha-Shulchan*** also rules in accordance with the position of the *Bet Yosef* cited above (*23:19*).

According to the **Rema** (*Yoreh De'a 331:19*), gentile produce must be tithed, and the ***Chazon Ish*** ruled that this should be done without reciting a blessing (*20, 7; 9, 18*). It should be noted that *gemar melacha* – completion of the harvesting and ingathering – usually takes place in the hands of the gentile (at least in the case of the individual consumer), so that in any case the produce need not be tithed. If, however, a person buys grapes for wine or olives for oil, *terumot* and *ma'asrot* should be set aside without a blessing.

Which tithe should be set aside from such produce? We know that in the first, second, fourth and fifth years of the sabbatical cycle we set aside *ma'aser sheni* (second-tithe), and that in the third and sixth years we set aside *ma'aser ani* (tithe for the poor). However, it is not clear which tithe should be set aside during the seventh year in cases when *terumot* and *ma'asrot* must be set aside.

The Rema (ibid.) adds that in addition to *teruma gedola* (the initial separation of a minimal portion meant for the Kohen that has *teruma* sanctity and must be set aside), *terumat ma'aser* (an additional 1% meant for the Levi to separate out from his portion and give to the Kohen that also has *teruma* sanctity) and *ma'aser rishon* (10% meant for the Levi that nowadays is declared to be separated but not removed), one should also set aside *ma'aser ani*. Inasmuch as the matter is unclear, conditional *ma'aser sheni* should be set aside as well. **Rav Kook** writes that it is best to first set aside *ma'aser sheni* and redeem it without reciting a blessing, and then to say: "If *ma'aser ani* is required this year, then let what had [previously] been designated as *ma'aser sheni* be *ma'saer ani*" (*Responsa Da'at Kohen,* no. 239; *Minchat Shelomo,* no. 37).

HETER MECHIRA PRODUCE

In the case of *heter mechira* produce, if the *gemar melacha* is performed by a Jew (that is when the produce is harvested and packed by Jews) *terumot* and *ma'asrot* should be set aside without a blessing (*Minchat Shlomo,* nos. 38–39). On the one hand, the tithing in this case is much more significant than the tithing of produce that grew on land permanently owned by a gentile, as the *heter mechira* is based on the view of the *Bet Yosef,* according to which the produce is not regarded as *Shemita* produce, and thus it is subject to *terumot* and *ma'asrot*. On the other hand, if the *heter* is not valid, the produce is ordinary *Shemita* produce, which is tithed without a blessing and *ma'asrot*. If the *gemar melacha* was performed by a gentile, it is unnecessary to tithe the *heter mechira* produce.[1]

To summarize, *Shemita* produce (*Otzar Bet Din,* garden-grown produce) is not subject to *terumot* and *ma'asrot,* but it is subject to the laws of *orla* and *neta reva'i*. As for the produce of a gentile, *heter mechira* produce and produce that grew on detached bedding, *terumot* and *ma'asrot* should be set aside without a blessing.[2]

1. This matter is more complicated, as it depends on two further factors: does the gentile own the produce or does the Jew? Second, can the gentile legally represent the Jew to perform this act? See an extensive treatment of these questions in *Ha-Torah Ve-ha-aretz 6*, pp. 516–528.

2. Regarding separation of *terumot* and *ma'asrot* from detached bedding produce, this depends on a question of by the *Talmud Yerushalmi* cited earlier on p. 104 in the chapter on planting inside the house, and on the dispute between the Rambam and the Ra'avad (*Hilchot Ma'aser 1:6*), as well as that regarding ownership of plants and pots. See *Ha-Torah Ve-ha-aretz 6*, p. 529.

DETERMINING THE *SHEMITA* YEAR

A. The Gemara in ***Nedarim*** (*61a*) records a dispute between **the Sages and Rabbi Yehuda** whether or not the fiftieth year (the year of *yovel*) itself counts toward the next sabbatical and jubilee cycles. According to the **Sages,** the *yovel* year is not included in the next sabbatical and jubilee cycles. That is to say, following seven sabbatical cycles, there is a year of *yovel*, and the "fifty-first year" of the previous cycle is the first year of the next sabbatical and jubilee cycle. According to **Rabbi Yehuda,** the *yovel* year itself is included in the next sabbatical and jubilee cycles; in other words, the fiftieth year of the previous cycle is also the first year of the next sabbatical and jubilee cycle.

This disagreement has two practical ramifications. First, with respect to determining the year of *yovel* – does it fall out every fifty years or every forty-ninth year. And second, with respect to the year of *Shemita* – is every seventh year *Shemita* or perhaps after seven sabbatical cycles there is a one year break in the count of years. This issue has practical relevance in our time as well (assuming that we continue to count jubilee cycles even when the laws of *yovel* are no longer in effect) as far as establishing which year is *Shemita* and when one must set aside *ma'aser sheni* and *ma'aser ani.*

Most *Rishonim* ruled that the law is in accordance with the position of Rabbi Yehuda. The **Rambam** (*Hilchot Shemita ve-Yovel 10:6–7*) maintained that the law *should* be in accordance with the Sages, but owing to the Geonic tradition that the common practice is in accordance with the view of Rabbi Yehuda, he retracted his own position and ruled in accordance with Rabbi Yehuda (this is how the *Bet Yosef* and the Radbaz explain the Rambam):

> For tradition and practice are great pillars in halachic decision-making, and it is fitting that we should rely upon them.

According to this, the law is that every seventh year is *Shemita,* the *yovel* year playing no role in the calculation.[1]

B. In order to determine which year is *Shemita,* we must count seven-year cycles starting with a year that we know with certainty was a year of *Shemita.* The Gemara in *Ta'anit* (*19b*) states that the second

1. At least after the destruction of the Temple, when the laws of *yovel* are no longer in effect – see *Chiddushei ha-Grach al ha-Rambam*, ad loc.

Temple was destroyed in the year following *Shemita*. Based on this, it should be possible to determine all later *Shemita* years.

This, however, is not a simple matter, because the *Rishonim* disagree about the year during which the Temple was destroyed. All agree that the second Temple was built in 3410 to Creation (350 B.C.E).[2] And all agree that the second Temple stood for 420 years, as stated in the Gemara in *Arachin* (*12b*). Rashi and Rabbenu Tam disagree, however, whether the second Temple was destroyed in its 420th year (Rashi) or in its 421st year (Rabbenu Tam).

According to **Rashi,** the second Temple was destroyed in its 420th year in 3829 (69 C.E.). According to **Rabbenu Tam**, the second Temple was destroyed in its 421st year in 3830 (70 C.E.). The Gemara asserts that the year of the destruction was the year following *Shemita,* from which it follows that the previous year was a year of *Shemita*. According to Rashi, then, the year 3828 (68 C.E.) was *Shemita,* whereas according to Rabbenu Tam, *Shemita* fell out in 3829 (69 C.E.).

The **Rambam** (*Hilchot Shemita ve-Yovel 10:4–7*) agrees with Rashi that the destruction took place during the second Temple's 420th year (69 C.E.), but according to him, that year was a year of *Shemita,* and not the year following *Shemita*. In terms of counting for *Shemita,* then, the Rambam agrees with Rabbenu Tam.[3]

The ***Tur*** (*Choshen Mishpat, 67*) rules in accordance with **Rashi**, but the ***Shulchan Aruch*** and the **Rema** rule in accordance with **Rabbenu Tam**, and the common practice today follows their ruling. Therefore, since according to Rabbenu Tam the year 3829 (69 C.E.) was *Shemita,* and the current year is 5775 (2015), 1946 years have passed since the destruction (which took place during the first year of the sabbatical cycle). If we divide this figure by 7, we arrive at 278. According to this, there have been 277 *Shemita* years since the destruction, and we are currently in the *Shemita* year of the 278th cycle.

C. There is another, easier way to calculate the year of *Shemita*: If we divide the number of years that have passed since Creation by 7, the remainder will indicate the year within the present

2. Rashi in *Avoda Zara* (9b, s.v. *matnita*) and the Rambam (*Hilchot Shemita ve-Yovel 10:3*) write that the second Temple was built in 3409, but they are referring to what we call 3410. The discrepancy is explained by the fact that Rashi and the Rambam count the years from the *molad* (creation) of man (called *"molad 6-14"* – at 6 days, 14 hours to creation), whereas we count from the *molad* of *tohu* (the beginning of creation), which was on the 25th of Elul. Thus, it turns out that we begin the count from Creation a year earlier (our *molad* is called "*molad 2-5-204*" – 2 days, 5 hours and 204 parts of the hour). According to this, year 3409 according to Rashi and Rambam is year 3410 according to our count.

3. According to the Rambam, the destruction took place on the 9th of Av in the year 69 C.E. Since only a few months remained until the end of the year, the Sages related to the year as if it had already ended, and therefore when the Gemara speaks of the year after the *Shemita* year, it is referring to the year 70.

sabbatical cycle. (When there is no remainder, it is *Shemita*). For example, it is currently year 5775 to the Creation. If we divide this figure by 7, we arrive at 825 with no remainder. This means that we are now in the seventh year of the current *Shemita* cycle.

This calculation is rooted in the words of the ***Ba'al ha-Ma'or*** (*Avoda Zara 9a*). This, however, is merely a device for calculating the *Shemita* year, for at the time of Creation, there was no count of *Shemita* years. The count of *Shemita* years only began after Israel entered into the land, and only after 14 years of conquest and division of the land. As is stated in the *Sifra* (*Parashat Behar*) in connection with the verse: "You shall neither plant your field, nor prune your vineyard" (*Vayikra 25:4*): "'Your field' – when each and every person had determined his field; 'your vineyard' – when each and every person has determined his vineyard."

Moreover, during the second Temple period, the count of *Shemita* years began anew, and thus the previous years of *Shemita* have no relevance.

While this method of calculating the *Shemita* year (dividing the number of years since Creation by seven) is purely coincidental, it is easy and it works.

THE *SHEMITA* YEAR MAY NOT BE INTERCALATED

The **Gemara** in ***Sanhedrin*** (12b; and *Yerushalmi, Sanhedrin 1:2*) cites a Tosefta (*Sanhedrin 2:9*) which states that we may not intercalate the *Shemita* year, turning it into a leap year.

> We may not intercalate the *Shemita* year, nor the year following the *Shemita* year. Which year do we usually intercalate? The year before the *Shemita* year.

We shall not expand on this law, but merely cite the main views, and try to understand how it is possible that the current year of *Shemita* (5775) is a leap year.

Why must we not intercalate the *Shemita* year? **Rashi** (ad loc., this explanation also appears in *Yerushalmi, Shekalim 1:1*) explains that this rule was introduced in order not to add another month during which agricultural work is forbidden:

> "Not the *Shemita* year" – because we would be extending the prohibition on agricultural work.

If this is the case, how can this year, 5768 be a leap year? The answer seems to be that the Gemara's rule only applied when the court determines and proclaims the leap years. When the leap years are determined by a fixed calendar, however, we do not consider whether or not the year is *Shemita*. Thus, in our day it is possible for a *Shemita* year to be intercalated. The rule that we may not intercalate the *Shemita* year is apparently only by rabbinic decree and only a recommendation for preferred practice,[4] so as not to impose added hardship on those who observe *Shemita*, and therefore it was overlooked when the calendar was set.

The **Rambam** (*Hilchot Kiddush ha-Chodesh 4:15–16*) understands the matter differently. According to him, we may not intercalate the *Shemita* year, in order to insure that there will be sufficient wheat and barley (that grew on their own, and are thus permitted by Torah law), from which the *omer* (the barley offering brought on 16 Nisan) and the *shetei ha-lechem* (the wheat offering brought on *Shavuot*) offerings can be brought. If we are forced to wait another month, there may not remain sufficient grain for these purposes.

According to the **Rambam**, this law is only relevant when the Temple stands, and thus it is clear that today when the Temple is no longer standing, it is possible to intercalate the *Shemita* year.[5]

4. The Rambam's position on this matter will be cited below, but it should be noted that he explicitly states (*Hilchot Kiddush ha-Chodesh 4:16*) that the rule that we may not intercalate the *Shemita* year is only a recommendation for preferred practice, but if intercalation is necessary for other reasons, the *Shemita* year may be intercalated even when the Temple stands.

5. The *Yad Rema* (*Sanhedrin*, ad loc.) disagrees with the Rambam. See also the Gra (*Pe'a 5:1*, and *Shekalim*, beginning of chap. 1), and the article of Rav Y. Epstein, *Ha-Torah ve-ha-Aretz 6*, p. 494.

ZEMIRA – PRUNING – PROFESSIONAL AND SCIENTIFIC BACKGROUND

What is *zemira*? *Zemira* is a type of pruning. Pruning a vine or tree involves removing the outermost growth of its branches to encourage the growth of side branches from dormant buds. Since pruning stimulates the growth of an existing vine or tree, it is considered a derivative category of labor (*tolada*) under the principle category of labor (*av*) of *zeri'a*, planting.

The word *zemira* is related to the word *zemora*, the branch of a grapevine. All along the branch of a grapevine there are joints, and at each joint there is a bud.

Pruning a grapevine involves two steps. Most of the branches are entirely removed; those branches will produce no yield. A small number of branches are cut back leaving two buds (or sometimes more).

Pruning requires professional skill and judgment. First, the gardener must decide which branches to prune. Generally the stronger branches are allowed to remain, but this varies based on the positioning of the vine and other factors. How many buds are to remain? In which direction should the remaining branches be trained to grow? Due to the complication of the task and the expert judgment required, the ***Chazon Ish*** considered the possibility that non-professional pruning is permitted during the *Shemita* year.

In the case of a grapevine, whether it is cultivated for its grapes or for wine, pruning is a critical procedure that must be performed every year during the winter, when the vine is dormant.

What is the goal of pruning? In the case of a grapevine, pruning is understood today as a means of limiting the number of grape clusters that the vine will produce in the following season. If the vine is not pruned, new shoots will sprout all along the main branches and produce more grape clusters than the vine can successfully bear. Many of the grapes will not ripen properly and the fruit will have no value (they will be watery, deficient in sugar, and small).

Proper pruning leaves an appropriate number of buds and regulates the yield for the following year. For example, in the case of particularly productive strains of grapes, the branches are cut back leaving only two buds, whereas in the case of less productive strains, three or more buds are left.

It should be noted that while the purpose of pruning is to limit the number of grapes growing on the vine, it enhances the quality of the grapes that will grow from the buds that are allowed to remain.

In some cases, failure to prune will result in the vine producing no fruit at all. Today, however, most cultivated vines will produce fruit, even without having been pruned one year, and even in larger quantities than usual. The fruit is likely to be of reasonable quality (though, as stated above, they will have a lower sugar content). Failure to prune will, however, cause the vine extensive damage to the vine in future years. This is one of the greatest difficulties that farmers must contend with during the *Shemita* year. It has been suggested that when the Torah forbids *zemira*, it might not be referring to the procedure of cutting off all the branches (see, Rav Kook's comment).

Pruning other trees: For most other fruit trees, pruning (or at least annual pruning) is not as critical as it is for grapevines. This is true for deciduous trees such as apple, pear, plum and almond, and all evergreen trees (citrus, avocado, mango and olive). These trees do not share the enormous, wild growth of a grapevine, and so their pruning is less crucial. There are, however, certain trees, such as kiwi, that in this respect are similar to grapevines. This has led some halachic authorities (including the *Chazon Ish*) to suggest that pruning trees other than a grapevine is only forbidden by rabbinic decree.

Can pruning be performed in advance? From a halachic perspective, pruning in advance, before Rosh ha-Shana of the *Shemita* year, is an ideal solution. Practically, however, it is not that simple. Pruning that is performed too early is less effective. Moreover, pruning cannot be performed until all the fruit of the previous season has been harvested, and today many grapevines are still laden with fruit even after Rosh ha-Shana.

New solutions: A mechanized pruning method that prunes in an imprecise manner has been developed in Australia. In some places in Israel, attempts are being made to solve the problem by sawing off branches with a pruning saw in an imprecise manner (following the view of the *Chazon Ish*, that imprecise pruning is not forbidden). Even though the result is not perfect, and it leaves more buds than necessary (some of which can be broken off afterwards by hand), this procedure reduces the damage to the vine in future years.

Attempts are being made to grow certain varieties of grapes (hanging the branches in a special way) which will not require pruning, but these methods still require considerable development.

Professional pruning of a rosebush falls into the category of forbidden ***zemira***, because it stimulates the production of new flowers.

Cutting roses for use is permitted when performed in a non-professional manner.

THE DISAGREEMENTS BETWEEN RAV KOOK AND THE *CHAZON ISH* REGARDING *SHEMITA*

The two Torah giants **Rav Avraham Yitzchak Kook** and **Rav Avraham Yeshayahu Karelitz,** known as **the *Chazon Ish,*** were both exceedingly involved in the *Shemita* issue and other halachic matters relating to Eretz Yisrael. The very week that the *Chazon Ish* arrived in Eretz Yisrael, he sent a question to Rav Kook concerning *terumot* and *ma'asrot* (*Mishpat Kohen,* no. 53). From that time on, the *Chazon Ish* dealt extensively with the special *mitzvot* that are dependent upon Eretz Yisrael. The rulings of Rav Kook and the *Chazon Ish* on *Shemita*-related issues have many points in common. For example, both authorities agreed that the observance of ***Shemita* in our day is only by rabbinic decree** (introduction to *Shabbat ha-Aretz, 1–8; 4, 25,* letter 2; *Chazon Ish 3, 8*), and both agreed that **labors that are forbidden by Torah law are not to be permitted**, even in a case of **financial loss**, despite the fact that *Shemita* observance is only by rabbinic decree (*Shabbat ha-Aretz, Kuntres Acharon 2, 2; Chazon Ish 21, 17* – against the *Maharit, II,* no. 52, who ruled leniently on this matter).[1]

Another common theme in the writing of these two scholars was the importance of strengthening Jewish agriculture in Eretz Yisrael, and to find solutions that would enable Jewish agriculture to persevere through the *Shemita* year.

While they agreed on a common set of values, they debated details of practical halacha. **Rav Kook** was generally more stringent in his rulings about *Shemita* than the *Chazon Ish.*[2] See below for a partial list of the major disagreements between them.

Some of the disagreements between Rav Kook and the *Chazon Ish* are extremely significant. We will briefly explain some of the practical ramifications of these disagreements. Analyzing their respective positions, it becomes clear that these two great Torah authorities, each in his own way, strove to preserve the observance of the laws of *Shemita* and at the same time preserve Jewish agriculture in Eretz Yisrael.

Labors that are forbidden by rabbinic decree are permitted in a

1. Both Rav Kook and the *Chazon Ish* permitted labors forbidden by rabbinic decree when performed for the purpose of preservation (each according to his own position – for the preservation of the tree or for the preservation of the fruit), even when the labor is performed on the tree itself (*Chazon Ish 17, 19; Shabbat ha-Aretz 1, 5,* letter 8, and *Kuntres Acharon 10–11; Iggerot, II,* no. 555, p. 192; against the *Pe'at ha-Shulchan* (20:11) who forbids this.

2. There are certain cases in which Rav Kook issued a lenient ruling and the *Chazon Ish* was stringent, but relatively speaking these are exceptional instances, and usually on less significant issues, except, of course, for the *heter mechira.* On this point, see Rav Neria Gutal's article in *Ha-Tzofeh* 3 Sivan 5761, though he writes there that the leniencies and stringencies of Rav Kook and the *Chazon Ish* are balanced. In my opinion, while it is true that on certain issues Rav Kook was lenient and the *Chazon Ish* was stringent, generally speaking, Rav Kook was much more stringent than was the *Chazon Ish* on *Shemita*-related issues, and apparently this is part of what forced him to accept the *heter mechira.* In the table that follows I have presented the main disagreements between Rav

case of financial loss. It is therefore permitted to irrigate and fertilize when refraining from doing so would cause financial loss. In general, a relatively small amount of care suffices to prevent actual damage to a tree, but much more work is necessary in order to ensure that its fruit will grow properly. What is the law in the case where there is no threat of loss to the tree, but there is likely to be a loss regarding the fruit (i.e. the fruit will not grow properly)?

Rav Kook was stringent on the matter, whereas the *Chazon Ish* was lenient. It is reported in the name of the *Chazon Ish* that a loss of just over a sixth of the crop suffices to allow for leniency. Practically speaking, this is a very significant leniency. It is economically unnecessary to plant trees during the *Shemita* year, but already existing trees and the fruit growing on them require care. According to Rav Kook, only the most minimal work is permitted – work performed to ensure that the trees will not die. This limitation makes it impossible to maintain an orchard as a commercial enterprise, because the fruit will either not grow at all or grow in such a way that it cannot be marketed. According to the *Chazon Ish*, however, the orchard may be watered, fertilized, and weeded whenever necessary for the preservation of the fruit. Consistent with his position, the *Chazon Ish* even permitted the pruning of citrus trees, because he was concerned about a financial loss with respect to fruit, and he was of the opinion that pruning trees other than grapevines is forbidden only by rabbinic decree.

The *Chazon Ish* expanded and strengthened the institution of *Otzar Bet Din* and permitted the harvest of entire orchards by Jews, in a manner that had not been explicitly permitted in previous generations (indeed the rabbinical court in Jerusalem that had instituted an *Otzar Bet Din* on a one-time basis during the *Shemita* of 5670 [1909-1910], did not sanction the fruit being picked by Jews). The *Chazon Ish* was also lenient about planting vegetables in advance of *Shemita*, and permitted the vegetables as long as the seeds sprouted above ground, and perhaps even if they only sent out roots prior to the beginning of the *Shemita* year. In a certain case (in Moshav Netiva), seeds were planted prior to the *Shemita* year, but *Rosh ha-Shana* arrived and there was no evidence of any

Kook and the *Chazon Ish*. I have added certain novel positions of the *Chazon Ish*, about which Rav Kook did not express his opinion. In general the *Chazon Ish* bore those halachic novelties on his own shoulders, never having been suggested by previous authorities (of course, only halachic and Torah shoulders as broad as those of the *Chazon Ish* could have born these novel leniencies).
At the end of the table I have included certain **unique stringencies of Rav Kook**, regarding which we do not know the view of the *Chazon Ish*. Most authorities, however, are lenient on these matters, including the **Ridbaz**, who was one of the authorities who opposed the *heter mechira*.

sprouting. The *Chazon Ish* looked in one section of the field, and then in another, but did not find any sprouting. Finally, he located one section where the seeds had begun to sprout (actually to root, i.e. to sprout downwards), and based on this, permitted the entire field, arguing that the surrounding areas had apparently not been properly worked or sufficiently watered (*Mishnat Yosef, Shevi'it 9, 1*).

The *Chazon Ish's* work in this area was very impressive, as he successfully found halachic solutions according to which the produce would continue to have *Shemita* sanctity. Since the observance of *Shemita* in our time is only by rabbinic decree, there is room to accept most of the lenient rulings of the *Chazon Ish* in order to preserve Jewish agriculture in Eretz Yisrael. It may be stated in the clearest of terms that were it not for the *Chazon Ish's* profound occupation with the intricacies of the laws of *Shemita* and his novel ideas about them, we would be unable to find a way to deal with *Shemita* in our current circumstances.

The late rabbi of Kfar Pines, Rav Avraham Goldberg, describes the *Chazon's Ish's* efforts regarding *Shemita* matters as follows (*Mitzvot ha-Aretz ke-Hilchatan*, p. 322):

> As is well known, the *Gaon*, the *Chazon Ish, zt"l*, vigorously opposed the *heter mechira*... On the other hand, he toiled significantly to reach the depths of this great law [*Shemita*]; he clarified the matter and refined it, he proposed novel understandings and issued various allowances... these rulings of our master constitute the foundations for maintaining the farms of those who meticulously observe *Shemita.*

As stated above, Rav Kook was stringent on many of these issues, and instead adopted the *heter mechira*, which had been approved by some of the leading authorities of the previous generation. While Rav Kook was confident about the validity of the *heter mechira*, he saw it as a temporary measure, to be restricted to the greatest extent possible. In our present circumstances, it is possible to greatly expand alternative solutions (such as hothouses and detached containers) and the use of *Otzar Bet Din*, and this is the preferred path that should be followed.[3] What we must find, however, is

3. The *heter mechira*, however, should still be implemented as a temporary measure, because of the problem of exports, for certain field crops, and for people who are not prepared to accept the more preferable solutions (to save them from violating a prohibition). It should be understood that compensating idle farmers does not solve the problem, because many other workers are dependent upon agriculture, such as those who pack and process the produce, truckers and the like. The *heter mechira* should be implemented with the stipulations set by Rav Kook, namely, that labors that are forbidden by Torah law should be performed by gentiles (see the chapter on the *heter mechira* which clarifies these matters and emphasizes the importance of maintaining Jewish agriculture in *Eretz Yisrael*). As was noted earlier, the *heter mechira* is much less of a problem for the **consumer** than it is for the **farmer**. Both Rav Sh. Z. Auerbach and Rav M. Feinstein write that even if a person wishes to be stringent and not rely on the *heter mechira*, he may still eat *heter mechira* fruit (see the *heter mechira* section). Another reason for finding alternative solutions is that it is very possible that in the near future *Shemita* will once again be in force by Torah law, and the leading proponents of the *heter mechira* are only lenient when *Shemita* observance is by rabbinic decree.

not merely a solution for isolated groups, but **national solutions** that can answer the needs of the entire population. Such solutions are much more possible today than ever before, and with a little creative thinking and increased investment of resources on the part of the Jewish people in Israel and throughout the world, it would be possible to allow a majority of the country to observe *Shemita* in the best possible manner.

Both Rav Kook and the *Chazon Ish*, each in his own way, understood the need to support and preserve Jewish agriculture in Eretz Yisrael (as well as the need to make sure that a portion of the fields lie fallow during the *Shemita* year and not be worked at all). Prof. Meir Schwartz, who met with the *Chazon Ish* several times to discuss the rigorous *Shemita* observance in Kibbutz Chafetz Chayim, relates as follows:

> "My first discussion about hydroponics with our master... the *Chazon Ish* was when he visited the kibbutz. At that time hydroponics was carried out in barrels cut in half lengthwise... Our master saw this as an appropriate solution for *Shemita*. The issue of a 'roof' was also discussed on that occasion, and sheets of burlap were positioned over the plants..." I remember that the *Chazon Ish's* primary interest in developing this method was that we should not be dependent upon the Arabs for our supply of vegetables, but rather that we be independent (*Mi-Dor le-Dor*, p. 55).

The *Chazon Ish* himself writes (22, 2) with respect to his allowance involving a change in the planting cycle: "Because they did not want to let the field lie fallow, lest the Arabs take control of it."

Relying exclusively on Arab or imported produce during the *Shemita* year, and thereby destroying Jewish agriculture in Eretz Yisrael, **would constitute a halachic tragedy,** sanctioned neither by the approach of Rav Kook nor by that of the *Chazon Ish*. Our goal should be to fulfill the *mitzva* of *Shemita* in the finest possible manner, and to merit to fulfill what the Torah says about *Shemita*: "And the sabbath produce of the land shall be food for you" (*Vayikra* 25:6).

The Issue	Rav Kook	The *Chazon Ish*
Are labors that are forbidden by rabbinic decree permitted when performed **for the preservation of the produce?**	Labors forbidden by rabbinic decree may not be performed to save the fruit (*Shabbat ha-Aretz* 1, 5; and see *Chavot Binyamin*, III, p. 623).	Labors forbidden by rabbinic decree are permitted to save the fruit (*Chazon Ish* 21, 14).
Is it permissible to **prune trees other than grapevines** to prevent financial loss?	Rav Kook developed an argument for leniency, even for pruning a grapevine, when done in an unusual manner (*Shabbat ha-Aretz, Kuntres Acharon* 11), but it seems that he did not rely on this in practice (see *Iggerot ha-Ra'aya* 555).	Pruning trees other than grapevines is forbidden by rabbinic decree, and therefore permitted when performed for preservation (*Chazon Ish* 21, 15, 17).
Must the plant **take root prior to the *Shemita* year**, or may one plant just before *Shemita*, such that the plant will take root during the *Shemita* year?	The plant must take root before the *Shemita* year based on the verse, "but in the seventh year shall be a Sabbath year of solemn rest in the land for the Lord."	The *Chazon Ish* (22, 5) permits (one need not worry about the land resting before the *Shemita* year begins).
In the case of *Otzar Bet Din* produce, is it permissible for a Jew to **harvest the entire field**?	For the *Otzar Bet Din* of 5670, Rav Kook permitted the sale of produce, but it is unclear whether he allowed Jews to pick the fruit. Some write that the entire harvest was performed by gentiles (*Chavatzelet* 46, 5670; *Iggerot*, I, 313).	This is permitted because the fruit is not picked in a manner that displays ownership.

An action that does not stimulate growth, but rather **inhibits growth** or prevents damage (*Katif*, p. *46*).	This seems to be forbidden (unless it involves a financial loss) (*Shabbat ha-Aretz, Kuntres Acharon* 10; see also *Shabbat ha-Aretz 1:10, 3*).	It is permitted in principle (*Chazon Ish 17, 20*, s.v. *ve-nir'eh*; *27*, s.v. *ve-yesh* (end).
If someone buys *Shemita* produce **on credit**, and the produce is still extant at the time of payment, does *Shemita* sanctity apply to the money?	Rav Kook was stringent in accordance with the position of Rashi, the first opinion in *Tosafot*, Ramban, Ran, and Meiri (*Shabbat ha-Aretz 8, 20*).	The *Chazon Ish* was lenient in accordance with Rav Yitzchak in the *Tosafot* because *Shemita* in our time is only by rabbinic decree (*10, 13*).
Does *Shemita* sanctity apply to produce that is fit for animal consumption, but not intended for that purpose?	Such produce should be treated as having *Shemita* sanctity (*Shabbat ha-Aretz 7, 13*).	It does not have *Shemita* sanctity, and may be disposed of in the usual manner (*Chazon Ish 14, 10*).
Regarding *sefichim* – according to the Ramban – does the beginning of growth during the sixth year suffice to remove the prohibition?	The Ramban is lenient only in a case where most of the growth took place during the sixth year. Rav Kook (*Shabbat ha-Aretz 4, 3*) cites the view of the Rash who is lenient even if growth merely begins during the sixth year, but his ruling on the matter is unclear.	The *Chazon Ish* (*9, 16*) rules leniently that it suffices if the produce began to grow during the sixth year, based, among other things, on the assumption that the Ramban was lenient on the matter.

Regarding *sefichim* – from when are they permitted?	Rav Kook speaks of the beginning of growth, and this may have been his ruling (he may have required that the major growth have taken place during the sixth year). It does not appear that he was lenient if the seeds only took root during the sixth year (*Shabbat ha-Aretz* 4, 3).	In a case of great need, the *Chazon Ish* permitted an entire field based on the fact that some of the seeds had germinated below ground (*Chazon Ish*, according to *Chut ha-Shani*, 4, 3).
Regarding *sefichim* – altering the planting cycle	Rav Kook does not relate to the issue. The *Chazon Ish's* ruling seems to be unique to him and not cited by other authorities.	The *Chazon Ish* permits produce that grew in a field which according to the regular planting cycle should not have been planted that year, provided that it was planted **during the sixth year** (*Chazon Ish* 22, 2).
Is it permissible to juice *Shemita* produce (other than olives and grapes)?	Rav Kook's position is unclear. *Sefer ha-Shemita* inclines toward prohibition, with the exception of olives and grapes.	It is permissible to juice any fruit that is regularly juiced (*Kuntres Seder Shevi'it* 9).
Destroying *Shemita* produce – is it only a prohibition of destroying the produce itself, or is it even forbidden to make it undesirable?	One should be stringent and not make produce undesirable even if the produce is still usable (*Mishpat Kohen*, end of 85).	The Ridbaz (*Bet Ridbaz* 5, 6) is lenient about making produce undesirable as long as it is still edible.

Havdala over *Shemita* wine	It is best not to recite *havdala* over such wine because the number of drinkers is limited (women do not generally drink it) (*Shabbat ha-Aretz, Kuntres Acharon* 22).	The consensus of *Poskim,* including the Ridbaz (according to *Bet Ridbaz, 5, 6*) is lenient.
Washing hands before eating *Shemita* produce	It is proper to be stringent (*Shabbat ha-Aretz, Kuntres Acharon* 25).	This stringency is not mentioned by the *Chazon Ish* or most of the *Acharonim.*

MAKING COMPOST DURING *SHEMITA*

Is it permissible to make compost during the *Shemita* year?

What is compost? Unrelated to *Shemita* observance, many people collect their kitchen and garden waste and place it in a special container in which it slowly decomposes rather than throwing it away. Over time the organic refuse is converted into compost which can be used for fertilizing and conditioning soil.

Is it permissible to make compost during the *Shemita* year? The problem is that if the upper layer of the compost heap has already begun to decompose, and one adds remnants of *Shemita* produce to the pile, those remnants will suffer immediate ruin, which is a violation of their *Shemita* sanctity.

In the appendix dealing with observing *Shemita* sanctity in institutional kitchens, we expanded at length on the sanctity of *Shemita* remnants and leftovers. As we saw, the common practice is not to throw *Shemita* remnants into a regular garbage can (even if nobody will eat them), but rather to place them in a bag or receptacle specially designated for produce with *Shemita* sanctity.

We also saw that while it is forbidden to destroy *Shemita* fruits and vegetables, there is no prohibition when the destruction is caused indirectly (*gerama*).[1]

This being the case, if the upper level of the compost heap has not yet decomposed, one may add new remnants of *Shemita* fruits and vegetables to the pile. If, however, the upper level has already begun to decompose, the pile should be covered with a thin layer of sand, newspaper, or the like, and only then should the new *Shemita* remnants be added. Even though these remnants will begin to decompose within a few hours, since the decomposition does not take place immediately it is considered indirect destruction of the *Shemita* produce, and therefore permitted.

All this applies to home compost production. In the case of a compost heap in one's garden, care should be taken that it not appear as if he were preparing heaps of fertilizer in order to fertilize his garden. It is explicitly stated in the Mishna in *Shevi'it* (3:1) and

1. Some authorities maintain that indirect destruction of *Shemita* produce is forbidden. Even those who are stringent would seem to agree that there is no prohibition if the *Shemita* remnants will not be eaten in any case. This is also the opinion of Rav Elyashiv (see the aforementioned discussion of *Shemita* sanctity in institutions).

by the **Rambam** (*Hilchot Shemita ve-Yovel 2:1*): "A person must not carry out manure from his courtyard and deposit it in his field during the *Shemita* year, because it would appear as if he were fertilizing his field." Thus, it is preferable that a person make compost indoors, or if outside, in a composter resting on stones. When making compost in the garden, one should not deposit vegetable refuse directly on the ground, but rather in a special receptacle standing off to the side, so that it should be clear to all that one is merely making compost, and not preparing a heap in order to fertilize the garden.[2]

The compost that is formed may not be used during the *Shemita* year (apart from the case of a farmer who must fertilize his crops in order to prevent them from dying; a person with a home garden generally does not encounter such a situation).

To summarize: It is permissible to prepare compost during the *Shemita* year (and it is even desirable, as it allows one to make full use of his *Shemita* remnants), but one should not place a new layer of *Shemita* refuse directly on the previous layer (unless the previous layer has not yet begun to decompose), so as not to cause the immediate destruction of the new remnants. A thin layer of sand or newspaper should be placed on the upper layer, and the new *Shemita* remnants should be placed on top of that (so that their destruction will be indirect). The compost site should be set up in such a manner that it does not appear as if the person plans on spreading the compost across his field (but rather that he is merely making the compost). Compost should not be used during the *Shemita* year (except for farmers who must compost their fields in order to prevent their crops from dying).

2. See the **Rambam** (*Hilchot Shemita ve-Yovel 2:3*): "If he deposits the manure on a rock, or if he digs down three handbreadths and piles the manure there, or if he builds up three handbreadths and piles the manure there, the [previously mentioned] measures are unnecessary." See also Rav Y. Amichai's article in *Ha-Torah ve-ha-Aretz 6, p. 234*.

EATING IN ANOTHER PERSON'S HOME DURING *SHEMITA*

May a person who does not eat *heter mechira* produce eat in the home of one who does? May a person who does not buy gentile produce eat in the home of one who does?

The Mishna in *Yevamot* 13b relates the following about Bet Hillel and Bet Shammai:

> Even though there are marriage-related laws that the one group forbids and the other permits, the one group declares the child unfit and the other group declares the child fit, Bet Shammai did not abstain from marrying women from Bet Hillel, nor did Bet Hillel abstain from marrying women from Bet Shammai.

We see that the halachic differences between Bet Hillel and Bet Shammai on crucial laws related to marriage did not prevent members of the two groups from intermarrying. The Gemara (*ibid. 14a*) explains that each school would always be sure to inform the other in cases where the other maintained that there was a halachic problem.

We find a similar phenomenon in *Chullin* 111b. The Gemara relates that despite the many disagreements between Rav and Shmuel, Rav would come as a guest to the house of Shmuel, confident that Shmuel would never feed him something that was forbidden according to Rav's position: "I do not suspect that the son of Abba bar Abba [= Shmuel] would feed me something which I do not permit."

The **Rema** rules in this manner as well (*Yoreh De'a 119:7*):

> One who considers a given food to be forbidden, whether because he maintains that this is the law, or because he practices a certain stringency, is permitted to eat together with others who permit it, as they would certainly not feed him something that he considers to be forbidden (based on *Hagahot Mordechai*, first chapter of *Yevamot*; Responsa *Binyamin*

Ze'ev 312; Rabbenu Yerucham, end of *netiv* 3 in the name of Rema).

What is the law if a person is concerned that people will feed him food that is forbidden according to his custom?

The **Mordechai** writes that when a **guest** is present, a host who is ordinarily careful to eat only *pat Yisrael* (bread baked by a Jew) may recite the blessing over bread baked by a gentile, if it is a nicer loaf than the available Jewish bread. This ruling was codified by the ***Shulchan Aruch*** (*Yoreh De'a 112:13*):

> If someone who is not stringent about eating only *pat Yisrael* was dining at the table of one who is stringent on the matter, and on the table there is both *pat Yisrael* and bread baked by a gentile, the latter being a nicer loaf than the former, the host should break the nicer loaf, and throughout that meal he is permitted to eat the gentile-baked bread.

The ***Shach*** (*no. 21*) explains this allowance as based on the desire to avoid **enmity.** The ***Mishna Berura*** (*165,* no. *21;* and see *Bei'ur Halacha 168, 5*) understands this practice as **a show of respect toward the guest**, and therefore, when there is no guest, there is no such allowance.

The practice described above is rooted in **the blessing, which the host recites on behalf of all those present at the table.** But he is permitted to continue eating the gentile-baked bread throughout the meal (as is explicitly stated in the *Shulchan Aruch*), because it would be absurd to recite the blessing over that bread, but then refrain from eating the very bread over which he had recited the blessing, (*Torah Chatat 75, 9*).

One who eats with two others who eat gentile bread: The Rema (*Yoreh De'a 112:15*) writes that even in such a case, one who is stringent is permitted to eat gentile-baked bread with the two others (even though he does not recite a blessing on their behalf) **in order to avoid enmity**:

> Some authorities rule that if someone stringent about gentile bread is eating with others who are lenient, he may eat the

gentile-baked bread with them in order to avoid enmity and strife. Since there would be enmity were he not to eat their bread, which is the main part of the meal, the rabbis permitted him to eat this bread in order to avoid enmity. Nothing may be inferred from here about other prohibitions (based on *Bet Yosef* in the name of *Teshuvat Ashkenazit* which is *Teshuvat Maharil*, no. 35).

The **Rema** emphasizes that nothing may be inferred from this ruling to other prohibitions. The ***Shach*** (*no. 26*) explains that this ruling may not even be extended to the butter of a gentile, for it was only the bread of a gentile that they allowed, "**because man lives primarily on bread.**"

In a case where **only two people are eating together** (one who is stringent about gentile-baked bread and one who is lenient), the ***Shach*** (*no. 21*) rules that because there is no risk of enmity (there is no reason to prefer the practice of the lenient person over the practice of the stringent one and therefore no grounds for resentment), there is no allowance.

In any event, we see from here that one must not change his custom if there is no concern for enmity. Let us try to apply what we have seen to situations involving eating during *Shemita*.

The role of the host: If a person who regularly eats food that has standard *kashrut* certification hosts a guest who only eats food that is certified as *mehadrin* – the host must certainly try to raise the level of *kashrut* observed in his home during the period of his guest's stay, so that the guest can eat at his desired level of *kashrut*. Not complying with the guest's stricter *kashrut* standards would be like inviting a vegetarian for a meal and then serving him meat. A host must ensure that his guests will be comfortable with the food he serves them, with respect to both its taste and to its *kashrut*. Thus, there are times that he must raise his own standards of *kashrut* so that they satisfy everybody.

When, however, the discrepancy involved is merely a **stringency,** the guest can veer from him usual practice and eat freely at his host's table. As a result, people generally eat in one another's homes unquestioningly (provided that they are Torah-observant Jews), even though they might differ in their customs.

The same rule applies with respect to ***Shemita***. The *heter mechira* is less problematic than many of the *kashrut* issues about which there are differences in custom. We are dealing with an uncertainty regarding a prohibition that is only a rabbinic decree on two counts (the entire observance of *Shemita* in our time is only by rabbinic decree, and the entire prohibition of *sefichim* is only by rabbinic decree). While there are good reasons for a farmer to be stringent, it is difficult to say that the produce grown on the basis of the *heter mechira* is forbidden to the consumer. (The main contentious issue regarding the *heter mechira* is **whether the sale should be conducted**, but not **whether the sale is valid.** Even those who say that the sale should not be conducted agree that once performed the sale is valid).

The same applies to gentile produce. A substantial portion of the vegetables that we eat even in ordinary years is gentile produce. Clearly, then, it is not forbidden for a guest to eat at his host's table, even if the latter buys produce grown by gentiles.

In addition, the laws of *Shemita* create a unique situation in which it frequently happens that **what one person regards as leniency, another views as stringency.** Regarding the laws of *Shemita,* it is difficult to "raise the standards" to accommodate both sides. Each side advocates a different approach in defining that raised standard. Therefore, since in any event the product is kosher, and we are dealing merely with different priorities, and since it is impossible to find a raised standard common to all, it is reasonable that people may eat in each other's homes, despite their differences in practice.

Of course, it is always appropriate for the host to find a solution that is good for himself and also for his guests (for example, buying *Otzar Bet Din* produce or produce grown in detached containers), and to serve food at the highest halachic standard that is acceptable to all.

In any event, if the host knows that his own practice differs from that of his guest, he must inform the guest and not deceive him in any way, allowing the guest to decide for himself what to do. This is stated by ***Meiri*** (*Yevamot 14a*):

> Whenever two people disagree, one saying it is permitted, the other saying it is forbidden, he who says it is permitted must not conceal the facts from the one who says it is forbidden. Rather he must inform him that this is forbidden to him according to his position. As long as he has not told him otherwise, he can assume that there is nothing forbidden [being served to him].

Someone who deceives another person on such a matter might even violate the Torah prohibition of "*lifnei iver*," putting a stumbling block before the blind, interpreted by the rabbis to refer to misleading another on matters where he is "blind" to the facts.

All that has been said thus far applies to someone who disapproves of the *heter mechira*, and even regards it as a form of deception, but nevertheless maintains that the sale is valid. Someone who absolutely rejects the allowance and maintains that it is not at all a sale, may still eat *heter mechira* fruits (and *heter mechira* vegetables in the first few months of the *Shemita* year), but he may not eat *Shemita* vegetables once there is concern about the prohibition of *sefichim.*

It is important to note that even if someone maintains that the *heter mechira* is invalid, and that *heter mechira* produce is forbidden (though we disagree, as was explained earlier in this volume), the **utensils** in which the *heter mechira* produce was cooked are not forbidden to him. Such a person may, therefore, eat in the home of someone who relies on the *heter mechira*, if the food that he is served meets his standards. As the **Rema** writes (*Yoreh De'a 64:9*):

> *Shulchan Aruch*: Fat that adheres to the stomach that is under the *perisa* is forbidden.
>
> Rema: This is the custom in all places, except for in the Rheinland, where it is customary to allow part of it. We do not object to the practice, because a distinguished authority issued this ruling for them (*Hagahot Oshri*, Mordechai and most Ashkenazic authorities of the time). Wherever the custom is to forbid it, it is like other prohibited fats regarding nullification within sixty times its volume (*Issur ve-Heter*

he-Aroch). However, we do not forbid the utensils of the people of the Rheinland communities, since they legitimately regard it as permitted.

Thus, the common practice is to be lenient and allow a person who eats only *glatt* meat to eat in the home of a person who also eats non-*glatt* meat, if the host cooks *glatt* meat for him. This leniency is also based on the principle that utensils are presumed not to have been used in the last twenty-four hours (see *Darchei Teshuva, Yoreh De'a, 122,* no. *27*. See also Rav Elyashiv's ruling regarding vegetables after the time of *bi'ur,* where he permits cooking in pots that have not been used for twenty-four hours – *Kovetz Mevakshei Torah, 13,* Tevet *5755,* pp. *101–102; Responsa Yechaveh Da'at, IV,* no. *53*; introduction to *Kuntres Devar ha-Shemita,* p. *7*).

To summarize: It is permissible to eat in other people's homes during *Shemita,* as is the practice in ordinary years, even if the guest does not eat *heter mechira* produce, while the host does, and even if the guest is particular not to buy gentile produce, while the host buys only gentile produce. Both of these practices are far less serious than other halachic issues, regarding which it is common practice to change one's halachic standards in order to eat in another's home. If the guest maintains that eating *heter mechira* produce is truly forbidden (against our position), the host should prepare foods acceptable to both parties, and he should certainly be careful not to deceive his guest. Even in such a case, it is unnecessary to *kasher* the host's utensils. Following these rules should enable the observance of the laws of the *Shemita* year to promote and support friendship between Jews.

BI'UR (REMOVAL) OF *SHEMITA* PRODUCE

> "And for your cattle, and for the beast in your land, shall all its produce be food" (*Vayikra* 25:7) – cattle are compared to beasts – as long as the beast eats the produce in the field, the cattle eat the produce in the house; if it disappeared for the beast from the field, remove it from your cattle in your house. (*Torat Kohanim, Behar* 1, 1, 8)

As long as produce of a particular species remains in the field ("the beast eats from the produce in the field"), one may eat of that species in the house as well ("the cattle eat from the produce in the house"). However, as soon as that species is no longer found in the field, all produce of that species must also be removed from the house. A similar interpretation of the verse is found in the ***Yerushalmi*** (9:3):

> "You shall eat its produce out of the field" (*Vayikra* 25:12) – as long as you eat the produce] in the field, you may eat the produce] in the house; if it disappeared from the field, remove it from your house.

The obligation to remove *Shemita* produce from one's house seems to be connected to the feeling of lack of ownership over the land that is meant to characterize the *Shemita* year. In order to demonstrate that the so-called owner does not truly own "his" property, he may eat of its produce only as long as everyone has the opportunity to eat of it (see *Chazon Ish, Likkutim*, end of *Zera'im*, no. 10).

WHAT IS *BI'UR*?

The **Rambam** (*Hilchot Shemita ve-Yovel* 7:3) explains that *bi'ur* means burning the produce. ***Tosafot*** (*Pesachim* 52b, s.v. *mitba'arin*), the **Ramban** (*Vayikra* 25:7), and most *Rishonim* understand that *bi'ur* means renouncing ownership of the produce by declaring it ownerless. **Mahari Kurkus** (7:3), ***Chochmat Adam*** (*Sha'arei Tzedek*,

19, 4), **Rav Kook** (*Mishpat Kohen*, no. 83), and the ***Chazon Ish*** (11, 8) all rule that *bi'ur* involves declaring the produce ownerless. On the contrary, burning the produce is forbidden during the *Shemita* year, because it constitutes destruction of *Shemita* produce.

The Rambam's position requires clarification: What is the reason for burning the leftover *Shemita* produce? Even the Rambam might agree that the objective of *bi'ur* is to thwart a person's feeling of ownership over the produce. According to him, however, the Torah insisted that the produce be destroyed by way of burning, in order to encourage a person to share the stores of produce in his possession.[1] That is to say, burning is not the objective of the *bi'ur*, but rather a means to encourage a person to share his produce with others (food sufficient for three meals for each person), and thus to internalize the idea that he enjoys no more title to the produce than any other person does.[2]

WHAT IS SUBJECT TO *BI'UR*?

Only produce that has *Shemita* sanctity is subject to the laws of *bi'ur*. Accordingly, produce that grew on the land of a gentile clearly does not require *bi'ur* according to the ***Bet Yosef*** who says that it does not have *Shemita* sanctity. It should be noted that the ***Mabit*** agrees with the *Bet Yosef* in this case that there is no need to remove such produce, despite his view that it has *Shemita* sanctity. According to him, since the produce came from a gentile, and the gentile was not required to clear it out of his house and declare it ownerless – the Jew who now owns the produce is also not obligated to remove it from his house (*Responsa Mabit*, vol. 1, no. 336). In contrast, the ***Chazon Ish*** (25, 25) maintains that even the produce of a gentile is subject to *bi'ur* (as does Rash Sirillo 6:1).

Accordingly, it is unnecessary to apply the laws of *bi'ur* to produce farmed through the *heter mechira,* because such produce grew in a field owned by a gentile. There might, however, be room to be stringent and apply the laws of *bi'ur,* just as there is room to be stringent and relate to such produce as having *Shemita* sanctity

1. In line with the dominant position among the *Rishonim*, the common practice today is to declare the produce ownerless and then immediately return the produce to one's house. Thus, *bi'ur* has been reduced to a formal act that does not internalize the feeling of a lack of ownership. The Rambam's position, however, serves to undermine the feeling of ownership in a way that this other position does not. According to the Rambam, since a person will otherwise have to burn the produce remaining in his possession after the time of *bi'ur*, he will, in practice, distribute his produce to other people.

2. See Rav Yona Immanuel's *Birkat ha-Aretz*, p. 74.

(see above, p. 135), even though the law of *bi'ur* is more lenient than *Shemita* sanctity for this purpose.

Money which has attained *Shemita* sanctity is also subject to *bi'ur*. The time of *bi'ur* of the exchanged produce also determines the time of *bi'ur* for the money. (Rambam, *Hilchot Shemita ve-Yovel* 7:7).

Otzar Bet Din produce is not subject to the laws of *bi'ur* (see Ramban, *Vayikra* 25:7), as long as it is still in the control of the court. Produce that was in the control of the court at the time of *bi'ur* does not subsequently become subject to *bi'ur*, because it is regarded as having already undergone *bi'ur* (*Chazon Ish* 11, 7, s.v. *be-ma she-katav* and s.v. *u-ma*). On the other hand, *Otzar Bet Din* produce purchased prior to the time of *bi'ur* is subject to the laws of *bi'ur* at the appropriate time (*Responsa Minchat Shlomo* 51, 17).

WHEN DOES *BI'UR* TAKE PLACE?

Each species of produce has its own time of *bi'ur* – the time that such produce is no longer found in the field. The **Gemara** in ***Pesachim*** 53a writes that the time of *bi'ur* for figs is Chanuka; for dates, it is Purim; for grapes and wine, it is Pesach; and for olives and oil, it is Shavu'ot. These dates are provided for someone who does not know whether the particular species is already gone from the field, but someone who knows with certainty that it is no longer in the field must apply the laws of *bi'ur* in accordance with that information (*Pe'at ha-Shulchan* 7:11). As a practical guide, a table has been appended to this volume listing the estimated times of *bi'ur* for each species.

HOW IS *BI'UR* PERFORMED?

The **Tosefta** (8:4) explains:

Someone who has *Shemita* produce in his possession, when the time for *bi'ur* arrives may distribute it among his neighbors, relatives and acquaintances, and must take out the rest and set it down at the entrance to his house, saying: "My

> brothers, the entire house of Israel, whoever is in need should come and take!" He may then bring the produce back inside and continue eating it until it is consumed.

When the time of *bi'ur* arrives a person may keep food that suffices for three meals for each member of his household (Mishna, *Shevi'it* 9:8; Rambam, *Hilchot Shemita ve-Yovel* 7:3).

The ***Chazon Ish*** (*26, 1*) writes that the produce must be declared ownerless in the presence of three people, as in any other renunciation of ownership. The **Vilna Gaon** (on the *Yerushalmi 9:4*) explains, however, that if a person brings the produce to the marketplace, he need not declare it ownerless in the presence of three people, and if he declares it ownerless in the presence of three people, he need not bring the produce to the marketplace. In practice, one should declare the produce ownerless and not rely on bringing it to the marketplace. Ideally, a person should take the produce outside and declare it ownerless, but in a case of need he may take it out to the stairwell of his building (if he lives in an apartment building) and declare it ownerless there in the presence of three people (Rav Elyashiv, cited in *Mishpetei Aretz 31*, note *16*).[3] After he declares the produce ownerless, he may reacquire it, as stated in the Tosefta.

3. When this is not feasible, one may follow the Vilna Gaon's leniency.

The three people who observe this declaration may include friends who will not take the produce in any case (*Yerushalmi 9:2; Chazon Ish 26, Seder ha-Shevi'it 1*), but not people whom the owner financially supports. According to Rav Elyashiv (cited in *Mishpetei Aretz 31*, note *14*), it suffices if there are two adults and one minor, because all that is necessary is one person who can acquire the produce and two witnesses.

A person who is far away from his produce when the time of *bi'ur* arrives can declare the produce ownerless from his present location. As stated above, it is preferable that he instruct another person to remove the produce from his house at the time of renunciation of ownership.

As for produce whose time of *bi'ur* is unclear, the ***Chazon Ish*** (26, *Seder ha-Shevi'it* 5) writes that it should be declared ownerless every day until the time of *bi'ur* has certainly passed. **Rav Sh. Z Auerbach** disagrees (*Minchat Shlomo*, nos. 21, 18; *Ma'adanei Aretz, kovetz he'arot* 8, 18), and says that it is preferable to declare the produce ownerless only once, and then have in mind not to reacquire it. The common practice follows the view of Rav Auerbach, due to, among other reasons, its greater practicality. Therefore, if a person is in doubt as to the time of *bi'ur* of a particular species, he should declare that produce ownerless once, and announce that while he is moving the produce back into his house, he does not have in mind to reacquire it. Whenever he wishes to eat a particular fruit, he should reacquire it (*Sefer ha-Shemita* 9, 12; Rav Elyashiv, *Mishpetei Aretz* 31, notes 29 and 31).

If the time of *bi'ur* passed and a person did not remove the produce from his house, **Rashi** (*Yoma* 83a, s.v. *tevel*) and the **Ramban** (*Vayikra* 25:7) write that the produce may not be eaten. Some authorities maintain that if a person failed to remove his produce from his house for reasons beyond his control, he may perform *bi'ur* as soon as it becomes possible, and the produce is not forbidden (*Sefer Charedim, mitzvot ha-teluyot ba-aretz,* cited in *Sha'arei Tzedek* 19, 5). This ruling was accepted by *Sefer ha-Shemita* (9, 10).

Rav Sh. Z Auerbach (*Minchat Shlomo* 21, 17) writes that there is room for leniency and allowance of the produce in any case where the failure to perform *bi'ur* was unintentional.[4] According to him, since the prohibition to eat the produce is a rabbinic penalty, it is reasonable that the penalty was only imposed on a person who intentionally held on to the produce after the time of *bi'ur*, but not when the failure to perform *bi'ur* was unintentional or for reasons beyond his control:

> It seems to me that since the prohibition of the produce is only a rabbinic penalty, it is reasonable that the prohibition was only imposed when the failure to perform *bi'ur* was intentional. Unintentional failure, however, is considered beyond one's control. Therefore, when it is clear that a person did not have in mind to hold on to the produce after the time of *bi'ur*, and his failure to perform *bi'ur* was merely an unintended lapse resulting from his ignorance of the

4. The *Chazon Ish* (14, 13, s.v. *zevachim*), however, is stringent in a case of unintentional failure to perform *bi'ur* (i.e. *shogeg*), and he notes that even in the case of circumstances beyond one's control, the *halacha* might be strict.

fact that the time of *bi'ur* had already arrived, the produce is permitted.

If a person receives produce from another person after the time of *bi'ur*, and is in doubt whether *bi'ur* was performed, he may perform *bi'ur* when he receives the produce and it may then be eaten (*Shabbat ha-Aretz 7, 3; Chazon Ish 11, 6*). **Rav Sh. Z Auerbach** (*Minchat Shlomo,* no. *51, 17*) adds that even if he is certain that *bi'ur* was not performed, he may still perform *bi'ur* upon receiving the produce and then eat it, because it is reasonable that the Sages only penalized the owner of the produce, but not someone who receives the produce from him:

> It is reasonable that in such a case one may rely on the position of the *Mishna Rishona* (on *Shevi'it* 9:9), who allows a person to give the produce to another for free, who will then perform the *bi'ur*, as this was the position of Rash Sirillo, and the Ridbaz said that this ruling is correct.

According to Rav Auerbach, even one who was fully aware that the time of *bi'ur* had arrived, but nevertheless failed to perform *bi'ur*, can still give the produce to another person as a gift, and that other person can declare the produce ownerless and then eat it.

In practice, when the time of *bi'ur* of a particular species arrives (as explained in the *bi'ur* chart), a person must declare any produce of that species currently in his possession as ownerless in the presence of three people. It is preferable that the produce be taken out into the public domain, or at the very least to the entrance of his house. After declaring the produce as ownerless, he may then reacquire it. If the time of that species' *bi'ur* is in doubt, he should have in mind not to reacquire it, and whenever he desires to eat of that produce, he should reacquire the amount needed.

NEGLECTING THE GARDEN?

A pious Jew once said to me: "I don't touch my garden during the *Shemita* year. Everything grows wild, weeds shoot up all around, the lawn is destroyed, and I"– so he said – "am happy. My garden is resting during the *Shemita* year!"

Another good Jew said to me: "I try to avoid all gardening tasks during the *Shemita* year, even those that are permitted." Why so? He explained: "My neighbors are non-observant. If they see me working in my garden, they are liable to think that everything is permitted."

My response to both of them was the same: If Halacha permits certain gardening tasks during the *Shemita* year, nothing is gained by failing to perform them and allowing the garden to look run-down and abandoned. On the contrary, such an approach would suggest that Halacha is unable to deal with the real world; that observing Halacha leads to devastation and desolation. And nothing is further from the truth. The laws of *Shemita* are by no means simple. Certain things are indeed forbidden during the *Shemita* year. But Halacha does not prohibit labors that are performed for the purpose of maintaining that which already exists. Halacha does not demand that one allow their entire garden to be destroyed during the *Shemita* year.

The concern that one's neighbors might mistakenly think that it is permitted to perform forbidden labors is insignificant in comparison to the concern that people might come to think that Halacha is incompatible with the real world.

We must meticulously observe all the prohibitions of *Shemita*, both those imposed by Torah law and those that are in force by rabbinic decree. At the same time, however, we must demonstrate that the gardens of those who observe *Shemita* remain green; that even when "the land keeps a Sabbath for the Lord," the land continues to endure and go on. The land's Sabbath does not lead to desolation. On the contrary, it brings sanctity to the land. The land's Sabbath marks a year in which we refrain from further creation, but nevertheless we preserve that which already exists. We watch over the resting land and enjoy its flowering sanctity.